(9–1)

$$S^2_{\text{Pooled}} = \frac{df_1}{df_{\text{Total}}}(S^2_1) + \frac{df_2}{df_{\text{Total}}}(S^2_2)$$

The pooled estimate of the population variance is the degrees of freedom in the first sample divided by the total degrees of freedom (from both samples) times the population variance estimate based on the first sample, plus the degrees of freedom in the second sample divided by the total degrees of freedom times the population variance estimate based on the second sample.

(9–2)

$$S^2_{M_1} = \frac{S^2_{\text{Pooled}}}{N_1}$$

The variance of the distribution of means for the first population (based on an estimated population variance) is the pooled estimate of the population variance divided by the number of participants in the sample from the first population.

(9–4)

$$S^2_{\text{Difference}} = S^2_{M_1} + S^2_{M_2}$$

The variance of the distribution of differences between means is the variance of the distribution of means for the first population (based on an estimated population variance) plus the variance of the distribution of means for the second population (based on an estimated population variance).

(9–7)

$$t = \frac{M_1 - M_2}{S_{\text{Difference}}}$$

The t score in a t test for independent means is the difference between the two sample means divided by the standard deviation of the distribution of differences between means.

(10–1)

$$S^2_{\text{Within}} = \frac{S^2_1 + S^2_2 + \cdots + S^2_{\text{Last}}}{N_{\text{Groups}}}$$

The within-groups population variance estimate is the sum of the population variance estimates based on each sample, divided by the number of groups.

(10–2)

$$S^2_M = \frac{\Sigma(M - GM)^2}{df_{\text{Between}}}$$

The estimated variance of the distribution of means is the sum of each sample mean's squared deviation from the overall mean, divided by the degrees of freedom for the between-groups population variance estimate.

(10–4)

$$S^2_{\text{Between}} = (S^2_M)(n)$$

The between-groups population variance estimate is the estimated variance of the distribution of means multiplied by the number of scores in each group.

(10–5)

$$F = \frac{S^2_{\text{Between}}}{S^2_{\text{Within}}}$$

The F ratio is the between-groups population variance estimate divided by the within-groups population variance estimate.

(11–1)

$$\chi^2 = \Sigma\frac{(O - E)^2}{E}$$

Chi-square is the sum, over all the categories or cells, of the squared difference between observed and expected frequencies divided by the expected frequency.

(11–2)

$$E = \left(\frac{R}{N}\right)(C)$$

A cell's expected frequency is the number in its row divided by the total, multiplied by the number in its column.

STATISTICS FOR THE BEHAVIORAL AND SOCIAL SCIENCES

A Brief Course
Third Edition

Arthur Aron
Elaine N. Aron
State University of New York at Stony Brook

Elliot J. Coups
Memorial Sloan-Kettering Cancer Center

PEARSON
Prentice Hall

Upper Saddle River, New Jersey 07458

Library of Congress Cataloging-in-Publication Data

Aron, Arthur.
   Statistics for the behavioral and social sciences: a brief course / Arthur Aron,
      Elaine N. Aron, Elliot J. Coups. -- 3rd ed.
         p. cm.
Includes bibliographical references and index.
   ISBN 0-13-150508-4
   1. Social sciences—Statistical methods. 2. Social sciences--Data processing.
   I. Aron, Elaine.   II. Coups, Elliot J.   III. Title.
   HA29.A745 2005
      300' .1'5195--dc21

                                                    2004010158

VP/Editorial Director: Leah Jewell
Sponsoring Editor: Stephanie Johnson
Assistant Managing Editor: Maureen Richardson
Production Liaison: Fran Russello
Marketing Director: Beth Mejia
Production Editor: Bruce Hobart
Manufacturing Buyer: Tricia Kenny
Cover Design: Kiwi Design
Cover Image: Nigel Shuttleworth/Life File/ Getly Images, Inc.— Photodisc
Composition/Full-Service Project Management: Pine Tree Composition
Printer/Binder: Courier Companies Inc.
Cover Printer: The Lehigh Press, Inc.

Pearson Education Ltd., London
Pearson Education Singapore, Pte. Ltd
Pearson Education, Canada, Ltd
Pearson Education—Japan
Pearson Education Australia PTY, Limited
Pearson Education North Asia Ltd
Pearson Educación de Mexico, S.A. de C.V.
Pearson Education Malaysia, Pte. Ltd
Pearson Education, Upper Saddle River, New Jersey

10 9 8 7 6 5 4 3 2 1
0-13-150508-4

Brief Contents

Contents

Preface to the Instructor

The heart of this book was written over a summer in a small apartment near the Place Saint Ferdinand, having been outlined in nearby cafes and on walks in the Bois de Boulogne. It is based on our 40 years of experience teaching, researching, and writing. We believe that this book is as different from the conventional lot of statistics books as Paris is from Calcutta, yet still comfortable and stimulating to the long-suffering community of statistics instructors.

The approach embodied in this text has been developed during our combined 40 years of successful teaching—successful not only in the sense that students have consistently rated the course (a statistics course, remember) as a highlight of their undergraduate years, but also in the sense that students come back to us later saying, "I was light-years ahead of my fellow graduate students because of your course," or "Even though I don't do research, your course has really helped me understand statistics that I read about in my field."

In this third edition of this *Brief Course* we have tried to maintain those things about the book that have been especially appreciated, while reworking the text to take into account the feedback we have received, our own experiences, and advances and changes in the field. We have also added new pedagogical features to make the book even more accessible for students. However, before turning to the third edition, we want to reiterate some comments we made in the first edition about how this book from the beginning has been quite different from other statistics texts.

WHAT WE HAVE DONE DIFFERENTLY

We continue to do what the best of the newer books are already doing well: emphasizing the intuitive, deemphasizing the mathematical, and explaining everything in direct, simple language. But what we have done differs from these other books in 10 key respects.

1. *The definitional formulas are brought to center stage* because they provide a concise symbolic summary of the logic of each particular procedure. All our explanations, examples, practice problems, and test bank items are based on these definitional formulas. (The amount of data to be processed in our practice problems and test items are reduced appropriately to keep computations manageable.)

Why this approach? To date, statistics texts have failed to adjust to technologic reality. What is important is not that the students learn to calculate a correlation coefficient with a large data set—computers can do that for them. What is important is that students work problems in a way that they remain constantly aware of the underlying logic of what they are doing. Consider the population variance—the average of the squared deviations from the mean. This concept is immediately clear from the definitional formula (once the student is used to the symbols): Variance = $\Sigma(X - M)^2/N$. Repeatedly working problems using this formula ingrains the meaning in the student's mind. In contrast, the usual computational version of this formula only obscures this meaning: Variance = $[\Sigma X^2 - (\Sigma X)^2/N]/N$. Repeatedly working problems using this formula does nothing but teach the student the difference between ΣX^2 and $(\Sigma X)^2$!

Teaching computational formulas today is an anachronism. Researchers do their statistics on computers now. At the same time, the use of statistical software makes the understanding of the basic principles, as they are symbolically expressed in the definitional formula, more important than ever. Students still need to work lots of problems by hand to learn the material. But they need to work them using the definitional formulas that reinforce the concepts, not using the computational formulas that obscure them. Those formulas once made some sense as time-savers for researchers who had to work with large data sets by hand, but they were always poor teaching tools. (Because some instructors may feel naked without them, we still provide the computational formulas, usually in a brief footnote, at the point in the chapter where they would traditionally have been introduced.)

2. *Each procedure is taught both verbally and numerically—and usually visually as well.*

In fact, when we introduce *every* formula, it has attached to it a concise statement of the formula in words. Typically, each example lays out the procedures in worked-out formulas, in words (often with a list of steps), and illustrated with an easy-to-grasp figure. Practice exercises and test bank items, in turn, require the student to calculate results, write a short explanation in layperson's language of what they have done, and make a sketch (for example, of the distributions involved in a *t* test). The chapter material completely prepares the student for these kinds of practice problems and test questions.

It is our repeated experience that these different ways of expressing an idea are crucial for permanently establishing a concept in a student's mind. Many students in the social and behavioral sciences are more at ease with words than with numbers. In fact, some have a positive fear of all mathematics. Writing the formula in words and providing the lay-language explanation gives them an opportunity to do what they do best.

3. A main goal of any introductory statistics course in the social and behavioral sciences is to *prepare students to read research articles.* The way a procedure such as a *t* test or chi-square is described in a research article is often quite different from what the student expects from the standard textbook discussions. Therefore, as this book teaches a statistical method, it also gives examples of how that method is reported in journal articles. And we don't just leave it there. The practice problems and test bank items also include excerpts from journal articles for the student to explain.

4. The book is ***unusually up-to-date.*** For some reason, most introductory statistics textbooks read as if they were written in the 1950s. The basics are still the basics, but statisticians and researchers think far more subtly about those basics now. Today, the basics are undergirded by a new appreciation of issues like effect size, power, the accumulation of results through meta-analysis, the critical role of models, and a whole host of new orientations arising from the central role of the computer in statistical analyses. We are much engaged in the latest developments in statistical theory and application, and this book reflects that engagement. For example, we devote an entire early chapter to effect size and power and then return to these topics as we teach each technique. Furthermore, we discuss how to handle situations in which assumptions are violated, and we cover data transformations (this widely used approach is easily accessible to introductory students but is rarely mentioned in current introductory texts).

5. We ***capitalize on the students' motivations.*** We do this in two ways. First, our examples, while attempting to represent the diversity of social and behavioral science research, emphasize topics or populations that students seem to find most interesting. The very first example is from a real study in which 151 students in their first week of an introductory statistics class rate how much stress they feel they are under. Also, our examples continually emphasize the usefulness of statistical methods and ideas as tools in the research process, never allowing students to feel that what they are learning is theory for the sake of theory.

Second, we have worked to make the book extremely straightforward and systematic in its explanation of basic concepts so that students can have frequent "aha!" experiences. Such experiences bolster self-confidence and motivate further learning. It is quite inspiring to *us* to see even fairly modest students glow from having mastered some concept like negative correlation or the distinction between failing to reject the null hypothesis and supporting the null hypothesis. At the same time, we do not constantly remind them how greatly oversimplified we have made things, as some books do.

6. ***We emphasize statistical methods as a living, growing field of research.*** Each chapter includes one or more "boxes" about famous statisticians or interesting side-lights. The goal is for students to see statistical methods as human efforts to make sense out of the jumble of numbers generated by a research study; to see that statistics are not "given" by nature, not infallible, not perfect descriptions of the events they try to describe but rather constitute a language that is constantly improving through the careful thought of those who use it. We hope that this orientation will help them maintain a questioning, alert attitude as students and later as professionals.

7. ***The final chapter looks at advanced procedures*** without actually teaching them in detail. It explains in simple terms how to make sense out of these statistics when they are encountered in research articles. Most research articles today use methods such as analysis of covariance, multivariate analysis of variance, hierarchical multiple regression, factor analysis, or structural equation modeling. Students completing the ordinary introductory statistics course are ill-equipped to comprehend most of the articles they must read to prepare a paper or study a course topic in further depth. This chapter makes use of the basics that students have just learned (along with extensive excerpts from current research articles) to give a rudimentary understanding of these advanced procedures. This chapter also serves as a reference guide that students can keep and use in the future when reading such articles.

8. The accompanying ***Student's Study Guide and Computer Workbook*** focuses on mastering concepts and also includes instructions and examples for working problems using a computer. Most study guides focus on plugging numbers into formulas and memorizing rules (which is consistent with the emphasis of the textbooks they accompany). For each chapter, our *Student's Study Guide and Computer Workbook* provides learning objectives, a detailed chapter outline, the chapter's formulas (with all symbols defined), and summaries of steps of conducting each procedure covered in the chapter, plus a set of self-tests, including multiple-choice, fill-in, and problem/essay questions. In addition, for each procedure covered in the chapter, the study guide furnishes a thorough outline for writing an essay explaining the procedure to a person who has never had a course in statistics (a task they are frequently given in the practice problems and test bank items).

Also, our *Student's Study Guide and Computer Workbook* provides the needed support for teaching students to conduct statistical analyses on the computer. First, there is a special appendix on getting started with SPSS. Then, in each chapter corresponding to the text chapters, there is a section showing in detail how to carry out the chapter's procedures with SPSS. (These sections include step-by-step instructions, examples, and illustrations of how each menu and each output appears on the screen.) There are also special activities for using the computer to strengthen understanding. As far as we know, no other statistics textbook package provides this much depth of explanation.

9. We have written an ***Instructor's Manual that really helps teach the course.*** The manual begins with a chapter summarizing what we have gleaned from our own teaching experience and the research literature on effectiveness in college teaching. The next chapter discusses alternative organizations of the course, including tables of possible schedules and a sample syllabus. Then each chapter, corresponding to the text chapters, provides full lecture outlines and *additional worked-out examples not found in the text* (in a form suitable for copying onto transparencies or for student handouts). These worked-out examples are especially useful to new instructors or those using our book for the first time, since creating good examples is one of the most difficult parts of preparing statistics lectures.

10. Our ***Test Bank*** section of the ***Instructor's Manual*** **makes preparing good exams easy.** We supply approximately 40 multiple-choice, 25 fill-in, and 10 to 12 problem/essay questions for each chapter. Considering that the emphasis of the course is so conceptual, the multiple-choice questions will be particularly useful for those of you who do not have the resources to grade essays. This supplement also includes computational answers to each textbook chapter's practice problems that are not given in the text. (The textbook provides answers to selected practice problems, including at least one example answer to an essay-type question for each chapter.)

ABOUT THIS *BRIEF COURSE*

We were thrilled by the enthusiastic response of instructors and students to the first, second, and third editions of our *Statistics for Psychology* (Aron & Aron, 1994, 1999, 2003), as well as the positive comments of reviewers, including the most encouraging evaluation in *Contemporary Psychology* (Bourgeois, 1997).

This *Brief Course* was our answer to the many requests we received from instructors and students for a textbook using our approach that is (a) more general in its focus than psychology alone and (b) shorter, to accommodate less comprehensive courses. Of course, we tried to retain all the qualities that endeared the original to our readers. At the same time, the *Brief Course* was not a cosmetic revision. The broadening of focus meant using examples from the entire range of the social and behavioral sciences, from anthropology to political science. Most important, the broadening informed the relative emphasis (and inclusion) of different topics and the tenor of the discussion of these topics. The shortening was also dramatic: This *Brief Course* is substantially shorter than the original, making it quite feasible to do the whole book, even in a quarter-length course.

INFLUENCES ON THE THIRD EDITION

We did the revision for the third edition in New York. We hope that this has not re-sulted in a loss of whatever romance the first edition gained from being written in Paris. We have also added an author to the book: Drawing on his experience using earler editions of the book, Elliot Coups has joined us in developing this new edi-tion of the text. As you will see, we have made many exciting enhancements in this third edition.

This revision is enriched by what we learned teaching with the first and second editions and by what we learned from the many instructors who have written to us about their experiences using the book. This revision is also informed by our own use of statistical methods. The last several years have been quite productive for all of us in our own research programs. Our recent research endeavors have focused on diverse topics in personality, social, and health psychology, including the social neuroscience of romantic attraction, childhood roots of adult experience, and health behaviors among cancer survivors. Perhaps particularly useful has been that during much of the last few years, one of us (A. A.) served as an associate editor for the *Journal of Personality and Social Psychology*. This has kept us in touch with how the best researchers are using statistics (as well as how reviewers rate their col-leagues' use of statistics). In addition to reworking the book to keep it up to date in obvious and subtle ways, we have made a special effort in this edition to bring in to the text significant new pedagogical features.

SPECIFIC CHANGES IN THE THIRD EDITION

1. *New pedagogical features.* The most obvious changes to those familiar with the book will be the following additions we have made to ease the learning process.

- **Tripling the number of practice problems.** Each chapter now has up to 24 practice problems. This gives instructors greater flexibility in the kinds and numbers of problems to assign. Also, the practice problems are now divided into two sets: Set I offers answers in the Appendix, so students can check their work; Set II answers appear only in the Instructor's Manual and can be assigned by instructors as homework problems.
- **"How Are You Doing?" sections.** These are brief self-tests focusing on concepts, inserted at the end of each main section of each chapter. These give students a chance to check that they have learned what they have just read, help them identify the central material in what they have just read, re-inforce this material before going on to the next section, and divide the chapter into more accessible "chunks".
- **With each new formula there is a boxed concise statement of the formula in words.** This is important for helping students to see the under-lying principle embedded in the formula, and keeps this verbal understand-ing directly available to them as they become accustomed to working with the symbols. This feature will be particularly helpful for students who fear symbols and math.

- **"Tips for Success" in margins.** These brief tips point out common errors and provide hints to enhance understanding and learning of the material.
- **"Stat Links" in margins.** We have included internet addresses of relevant statistics websites in the margin. These websites provide links to resources for students to check, and extend, their understanding of the material in the text.
- **Example Worked-Out Problems.** These are included just before the practice problems at the end of each chapter. These give students the chance to check their knowledge before starting their assigned problems and provide a model to follow when working them out, thus easing anxiety and helping students do the problems correctly.

   2. *Writing.* In this revision, we have once again thoroughly reviewed every sentence, simplifying constructions and terminology wherever possible and sometimes rewriting from scratch entire paragraps or sections. It is hard enough to learn statistics without having to read complicated sentences.

   3. *Updating examples.* In the sections on how to understand and evaluate statistics in research articles we have replaced dozens of examples with new ones published in the last year or two.

   4. *There is now a unique Website for the text* available to instructors and students. We are particularly excited about the potential of the Web for aiding learning of statistics. Features of the website include: Powerpoint presentation materials, online student study guide, flash card exercises, all formulas in symbols and in words, a downloadable mini-chapter for students on the logic and language of research, and a downloadable mini-chapter for students on applying statistics in their own research projects.

   5. *Some changes we have not made.* The 10 points noted earlier in this Preface remain as the central, unique features of this book. Also, we have not changed each chapter's major teaching examples. Instructors using the second edition told us they have built their lectures around these examples and don't want to have to start from scratch with new ones.

KEEP IN TOUCH

Our goal is to do whatever we can to help you make your course a success. If you have any questions or suggestions, please write or e-mail (**Arthur.Aron@sunysb .edu** will do for all of us). Also, if you should find an error somewhere, for everyone's benefit, please let us know right away. When errors have come up in the past, we have usually been able to fix them in the very next printing.

ACKNOWLEDGMENTS

First and foremost, we are grateful to our students through the years, who have shaped our approach to teaching by rewarding us with their appreciation for what we have done well, as well as their various means of extinguishing what we have done not so well. We also much appreciate all those instructors who have sent us their ideas and encouragement.

   We remain grateful to all of those who helped us with the first and second editions of this book, as well as to those who helped with the first three editions of the larger book. For their very helpful input on the development of this third edition of the *Brief Course,* we want to thank Jwa K. Kim, Middle Tennessee State University; Ann Lynn, Ithaca College; Patrice M. Miller, Salem State College; Amy R. Pearce, Arkansas State University; and Virgil Sheets, Indiana State University. We are extremely grateful to Stephanie Johnson of Prentice Hall for her good ideas for improving the book and for superbly leading us through the long revision process.

We also particularly want to acknowledge Ayorkor Gaba for her assistance in locating many of the new examples for this edition, Marie Thomas for identifying many crucial final changes to the text, Susan Nolan for her thorough and thoughtful work on revising the *Students Study Guide and Computer Workbook,* and Ken Savitsky for his valuable work on the companion website for the text.

Arthur Aron

Elaine N. Aron

Elliot J. Coups

CREDITS

Data in tables 3–13, 3–14, 8–8, 8–9, 9–4, 9–5, 10–8, 10–9, 11–7, 11–8, and 11–9 are based on tables in Cohen, J. (1988). *Statistical power analysis for the behavioral sciences* (2nd ed.). Copyright © 1988 by Lawrence Erlbaum Associates, Inc. Reprinted by permission.

INTRODUCTION TO THE STUDENT

The goal of this book is to help you *understand* statistics. We emphasize meaning and concepts, not just symbols and numbers.

This emphasis plays to your strength. Most social and behavioral science students are not lovers of mathematics but are keenly attuned to ideas. And we want to underscore the following, based on our 40 years' experience in teaching: *We have never had a student who could do well in other college courses who could not also do well in this course.* (However, we will admit that doing well in this course may require more work than doing well in others.)

In this introduction, we discuss why you are taking this course and how you can gain the most from it.

WHY LEARN STATISTICS? (BESIDES FULFILLING A REQUIREMENT)

1. *Understanding statistics is crucial to being able to read research results.* In most of the social and behavioral sciences, nearly every course you take will emphasize the results of research studies, and these usually include statistics. If you do not understand the basic logic of statistics—if you cannot make sense of the jargon, the tables, and the graphs that are at the heart of any research report—your reading of research will be very superficial. (We also recommend that you take a course on how to design good research. In this book, we focus on the statistical methods for making sense of the data collected through research. However, we have included a downloadable mini-chapter on the website for the book that provides an overview of the logic and language of behavioral and social sciences research.)

2. *Understanding statistics is crucial to doing research yourself.* Many students eventually go on to graduate school. Graduate study in the social and behavioral sciences almost always involves *doing* research. In fact, learning to do research on your own is often the entire focus of graduate school, and doing research almost always involves statistics. This course gives you a solid foundation in the statistics you need for doing research. Further, by mastering the basic logic and ways of thinking about statistics, you will be unusually well prepared for the advanced courses, which focus on the nitty-gritty of analyzing research results.

Many universities also offer opportunities for undergraduates to do research. The main focus of this book is understanding statistics, not using statistics. Still, you will learn the basics you need to analyze the results of the kinds of research you are likely to do. (Also, the website that accompanies this book has a special mini-chapter to help you with practical issues in using what you learn in this book for analyzing results of your own research.)

3. *Understanding statistics develops your analytic and critical thinking.* Social and behavioral science students are often most interested in people and in improving things in the practical world. This does not mean that you avoid abstractions. In fact, the students we know are exhilarated most by the almost philosophical levels of abstraction where the secrets of human experience so often seem to hide. Yet even this kind of abstraction often is grasped only superficially at first, as slogans instead of useful knowledge. Of all the courses you are likely to take in the social and behavioral sciences, this course will probably do the most to help you learn to think precisely, to evaluate information, and to apply logical analysis at a very high level.

HOW TO GAIN THE MOST FROM THIS COURSE

There are five things we can advise:

1. *Keep your attention on the concepts.* Treat this course less like a math course and more like a course in logic. When you read a section of a chapter, your attention should be on grasping the principles. When working the exercises, think about why you are doing each step. If you simply try to memorize how to come up with the right numbers, you will have learned very little of use in your future studies—nor will you do very well on the tests in this course.

2. *Be sure you know each concept before you go on to the next.* Statistics is cumulative. Each new concept is built on the last one. There are short "How Are You Doing?" self-tests at the end of each main chapter section. Be sure you do them. And if you are having trouble answering a question—or even if you can answer it but aren't sure you really understand it—*stop*. Reread the section, rethink it, ask for help. Do whatever you need to do to grasp it. Don't go on to the next section until you are completely confident you have gotten this one. (If you are not sure, and you've already done the "How Are You Doing?" questions, take a look at the "Example Worked-Out Problems" towards the end of the chapter, or try working a practice problem on this material from the end of the chapter.)

Having to read the material in this book over and over does not mean that you are stupid. Most students have to read each chapter several times. And each reading in statistics is usually much slower than that in other textbooks. Statistics reading has to be pored over with clear, calm attention for it to sink in. Allow plenty of time for this kind of reading and rereading.

3. *Keep up.* Again, statistics is cumulative. If you fall behind in your reading or miss lectures, the lectures you then attend will be almost meaningless. It will get harder and harder to catch up.

4. *Study especially intensely in the first half of the course.* It is especially important to master the material thoroughly at the start of the course. Everything else you learn in statistics is built on what you learn at the start. Yet the beginning of the semester is often when students study least.

If you have mastered the first half of the course—not just learned the general idea, but really know it—the second half will be easier. If you have not mastered the first half, the second half will be close to impossible.

5. *Help each other.* There is no better way to solidify and deepen your understanding of statistics than to try to explain it to someone having a harder time. (Of course, this explaining has to be done with patience and respect.) For those of you who are having a harder time, there is no better way to work through the difficult parts than by learning from another student who has just mastered the material.

Thus, we strongly urge you to form study groups with one to three other students. It is best if your group includes some who expect this material to come easily and some who don't. Those who learn statistics easily will get the very most from helping others who have to struggle with it—the latter will tax the former's supposed understanding enormously. Those who fear trouble ahead, you need to work with those who do not—the blind leading the blind is no way to learn. Pick group members who live near you so that it is easy for you to get together. Also, meet often—between each class, if possible.

A FINAL NOTE

Believe it or not, we love teaching statistics. Time and again, we have had the wonderful experience of having beaming students come to us to say, "Professor, I got a 90% on this exam. I can't believe it! Me, a 90 on a statistics exam!" Or the student who tells us, "This is actually fun. Don't tell anyone, but I'm actually enjoying . . . statistics, of all things!" We hope you will have these kinds of experiences in this course.

Arthur Aron

Elaine N. Aron

Elliot J. Coups

C H A P T E R 1

Displaying the Order in a Group of Numbers

Welcome to *Statistics for the Behavioral and Social Sciences: A Brief Course.* We imagine you to be as unique as the other students we have known who have taken this course. Some of you are highly scientific sorts; others are more intuitive. Some of you are fond of math; others are less so, or even afraid of it. Whatever your style, we welcome you. We want to assure you that if you give this book some special attention (perhaps a little more than most other textbooks require), you *will* learn statistics. The approach used in this book has successfully taught all sorts of students before you, including people who had taken statistics previously and done poorly. With this book, and your instructor's help, you will learn statistics and learn it well.

Given that you *can* learn statistics, you still have to decide if you want to make the effort it will require. Why would you want to do that, except to meet a requirement of your major? (Not a very energizing motive.) First, you will be far better equipped to read research articles in your major. Second, you'll be on your way to being able to do your own research if you so choose. Third, you will improve both your reasoning and your intuition.

What is statistics, really? **Statistics** is a branch of mathematics that focuses on the organization, analysis, and interpretation of a group of numbers. Think of statistics as a tool that extends a basic thinking process that every human employs: You observe a thing; you wonder what it means or what caused it; you have an insight or make an intuitive guess; you observe again, but now in detail, or you try making

Web Link

http://www.scc.ms.unimelb.edu.au/ discday/dyk.html. Find out various practical applications of statistics.

Statistics

some little changes in the process to test your intuition. Then you face the eternal problem: Was your hunch confirmed or not? What are the chances that what you observed this second time will happen again and again so that you can announce your insight to the world as something probably true? Statistics is a method of pursuing truth. At the very least, statistics can tell you the likelihood that your hunch is true in this time and place, with these sorts of people. (The truths of statistics also depend on how carefully you have collected your information, but good research design is another topic altogether.) This pursuit of truth, or at least of future likelihood, is the essence of science. It is also the essence of human evolution and survival. Think of the first research questions: What will the mammoths do next spring? What will happen if I eat this root? It is easy to see how the accurate have survived. You are among them. Because your ancestors exercised brains as well as brawn, you are here. Do those who come after you the same favor: Think carefully about outcomes. Statistics is one good way to do that.

THE TWO BRANCHES OF STATISTICAL METHODS

There are two main branches of statistical methods:

descriptive statistics

1. **Descriptive statistics.** Social and behavioral scientists use descriptive statistics to summarize and make understandable—to describe—a group of numbers from a research study.

inferential statistics

2. **Inferential statistics.** Social and behavioral scientists use inferential statistics to draw conclusions and inferences that are based on the numbers from a research study, but go beyond these numbers.

In this chapter and the next two, we focus on descriptive statistics. This topic is important in its own right, but it also prepares you to understand inferential statistics. Inferential statistics are the focus of the remainder of the book.

In this chapter, we introduce you to some basic concepts, and then you learn to use tables and graphs to describe a group of numbers. The purpose of descriptive statistics is to make a group of numbers easy to understand. As you will see, tables and graphs help a great deal.

SOME BASIC CONCEPTS

VARIABLES, VALUES, AND SCORES

As part of a larger study (Aron, Paris, & Aron, 1995), researchers gave a questionnaire to 151 students in an introductory statistics class during the first week of class. One question asked was, "How stressed have you been in the last 2 1/2 weeks, on a scale of 0 to 10, with 0 being *not at all stressed* and 10 being *as stressed as possible*?" (How would *you* answer?)

variable

values

score

In this example, level of stress is a **variable,** which can have **values** from 0 to 10, and the value of any particular person's answer is the person's **score.** If you had answered 6, your score would be 6; it would have a value of 6 on the variable called level of stress.

More formally, a variable is a condition or characteristic that can have different values. In short, it can vary. In our stress example, the variable is level of stress. It can have values of 0 through 10. Height is a variable, social class is a variable, score on a creativity test is a variable, number of people absent from work on a given day is a variable, dosage of a medication is a variable, political party preference is a variable, and class size is a variable.

A value is just a number, such as 4, −81, or 367.12. A value can also be a category, such as male or female or the country you live in (Canada, the United States, Australia, and so forth).

Finally, on any variable, each person has a particular number or score that is that person's value on the variable. For example, your score on the stress variable might have a value of 6. Another student's score might have a value of 8. We often use the word *score* for a particular person's value on a variable. This is because much social and behavioral science research involves scores on some type of test.

Social and behavioral science research is about variables, values, and scores (see Table 1–1). We will be using these terms throughout the book. The formal definitions are a bit abstract. In practice, you will find that what we mean when we use these words is usually obvious.

KINDS OF VARIABLES

Most of the variables social and behavioral scientists use are like those in the stress ratings example. The scores are numbers that tell you how much there is of the thing being measured. In the stress ratings example, the higher the number, the more stress. We call this kind of variable a **numeric variable.** (Numeric variables also are called *quantitative variables.*)

numeric variable

Social and behavioral scientists use two main kinds of numeric variables. The kind of variable used most often is a variable in which the numbers stand for about equal amounts of what is being measured. This is called an **equal-interval variable.** Take grade point average (GPA). This is a roughly equal-interval variable. For example, the difference between a GPA of 2.5 and 2.8 means about as much of a difference as the difference between that of 3.0 and 3.3 (both are a difference of 0.3 of a GPA). Most social and behavioral scientists also consider scales like the 0 to 10 stress ratings as roughly equal interval. So, for example, a difference between stress ratings of 4 and 6 means about as much difference in degree of stress as a difference between 7 and 9.

equal-interval variable

The other kind of numeric variable social scientists often use is where the numbers only stand for relative rankings. This is called a **rank-order variable.** (Rank-order variables are also commonly referred to as *ordinal variables.*) An example is rank in one's graduating class. Notice that with a rank-order variable, the difference between one number and the next does not always mean the same amount of the underlying thing being measured. For example, the difference between being second and third in your graduating class could be a very unlike amount of difference in underlying GPA than the difference between being eighth and ninth. There is

rank-order variable

TABLE 1–1	Some Basic Terminolgy	
Term	Definition	Examples
Variable	Condition or characteristic that can have different values	Stress level, age gender, religion
Value	Number or category	0, 1, 2, 3, 4, 25, 85, female, Catholic
Score	A particular person's value on a variable	0, 1, 2, 3, 4, 25, 85, female, Catholic

nominal variable

somewhat less information in the rank-order variable. It is less precise. However, social and behavioral scientists often use rank-order variables because they are the only information available.

There is also a kind of variable that is not about numbers at all, but which refers just to categories. This is called a **nominal variable.** The term *nominal* comes from the idea that its values are names. (Nominal variables are also called *categorical variables* because their values are categories.) For example, for the nominal variable gender, the values are female and male. A person's "score" on the variable gender is one of these two values. Similarly, hair color has values, such as brown, black, and so forth. Sometimes frequency tables are used for nominal variables, so that the table gives the frequency for each value or category of the nominal variable.

In this book, we focus mostly on numeric equal-interval variables. However, rank-order and nominal variables also are fairly common in the social and behavioral sciences. We discuss some statistical procedures specifically designed for using rank-order and nominal variables in Chapter 11.

HOW ARE YOU DOING?

1. A father rates his daughter as a 2 on a 7-point scale (from 1 to 7) of crankiness. In this example, (a) what is the variable, (b) what is the particular score, and (c) what is the range of values?
2. What is the difference between a numeric and a nominal variable?
3. Name the kind of variable for each of the following variables: (a) a person's nationality (Mexican, American, Canadian, Australian, etc.), (b) a person's score on a standardized IQ test, (c) a person's place on a waiting list (first in line, second in line, etc.).

ANSWERS

1. (a) crankiness, (b) 2, (c) 1 to 7
2. A numeric variable has values that are numbers that tell you the degree or extent of what the variable measures; nominal variable has values that are different categories and have no particular numeric order.
3. (a) nominal, (b) equal-interval, (c) rank-order

FREQUENCY TABLES

AN EXAMPLE

Let's return to the stress rating example. Recall that in this study, students in an introductory statistics class during the first week of the course answered the question "How stressed have you been in the last 2½ weeks, on a scale of 0 to 10, with 0 being *not at all stressed* and 10 being *as stressed as possible*?" The 151 students' scores (their ratings on the scale) were as follows:

4, 7, 7, 7, 8, 8, 7, 8, 9, 4, 7, 3, 6, 9, 10, 5, 7, 10, 6, 8, 7, 8, 7, 8, 7, 4, 5, 10, 10, 0, 9, 8, 3, 7, 9, 7, 9, 5, 8, 5, 0, 4, 6, 6, 7, 5, 3, 2, 8, 5, 10, 9, 10, 6, 4, 8, 8, 8, 4, 8, 7, 3, 8, 8, 8, 8, 7, 9, 7, 5, 6, 3, 4, 8, 7, 5, 7, 3, 3, 6, 5, 7, 5, 7, 8, 8, 7, 10, 5, 4, 3, 7, 6, 3, 9, 7, 8, 5, 7, 9, 9, 3, 1, 8, 6, 6, 4, 8, 5, 10, 4, 8, 10, 5, 5, 4, 9, 4, 7, 7, 7, 6, 6, 4, 4, 4, 9, 7, 10, 4, 7, 5, 10, 7, 9, 2, 7, 5, 9, 10, 3, 7, 2, 5, 9, 8, 10, 10, 6, 8, 3

It takes a while just to look at all these ratings. Looking through them gives some sense of the overall tendencies, but this is hardly an accurate method. One solution is to make a table showing how many students used each of the 11 values the ratings can have (0, 1, 2, and so on, through 10). We have done this in Table 1–2. We also figured the percentage each value's frequency is of the total number of scores. Tables like this sometimes give only the raw-number frequencies and not the percentages, or only the percentages and not the raw-number frequencies.[1]

Table 1–2 is called a **frequency table** because it shows how frequently (how many times) each rating number was used. A frequency table makes the pattern of numbers easy to see. In this example, you can see that most of the students rated their stress around 7 or 8, with few rating it very low.

HOW TO MAKE A FREQUENCY TABLE

There are four steps for making a frequency table.

❶ **Make a list of each possible value down the left edge of a page, starting from the highest and ending with the lowest.** In the stress rating results, the list goes from 10, the highest possible rating, down through 0, the lowest possible rating. Note that even if one of the ratings between 10 and 0 had not been used, you would still include that value in the listing, showing it as having a frequency of 0. For example, if no one in the class had given a stress rating of 2, you would still include 2 as one of the values on the frequency table.

❷ **Go one by one through the scores, making a mark for each next to its value on your list.** This is shown in Figure 1–1.

frequency table

TABLE 1–2	Number of Students Rating Each Value of the Stress Scale	
Stress Rating	Frequency	Percent
10	14	9.3
9	15	9.9
8	26	17.2
7	31	20.5
6	13	8.6
5	18	11.9
4	16	10.6
3	12	7.9
2	3	2.0
1	1	0.7
0	2	1.3

Source: Data from Aron, Paris, & Aron (1995).

Tip for Success

When doing Step 2, you are less likely to make mistakes if you cross off each score as you mark it on the list.

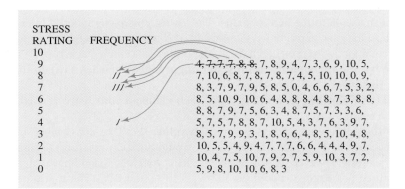

FIGURE 1–1   *Making a frequency table for the stress rating scores. (Data from Aron et al., 1995)*

[1]In addition, some frequency tables include, for each value, the total number of scores with that value and all values preceding it. These are called *cumulative frequencies* because they tell how many scores are accumulated up to this point on the table. If percentages are used, cumulative percentages also may be included. Cumulative percentages would give, for each value, the percentage of scores up to and including that value. The cumulative percentage for any given value (or for a score that has that value) also is called a *percentile*.

Tip for Success

You can cross-check your work by adding up these totals. This sum should equal the total number of scores you started with.

❸ **Make a table showing how many times each value on your list was used.** To do this, add up the number of marks beside each value.

❹ **Figure the percentage of scores for each value.** To do this, take the frequency for that value, divide it by the total number of scores, and multiply by 100. You usually will need to round off the percentage. As a rough guideline, with fewer than 10 values, round to the nearest whole percentage; with 10 to 20 values, round to one decimal place; with more than 20 values, round to two decimal places. Note that because of the rounding, your percentages will not usually add up to exactly 100% (but it should be close).

A SECOND EXAMPLE

McLaughlin-Volpe, Aron, and Reis (2001) had 94 first- and second-year university students keep a diary of their social interactions for a week during the regular semester. Each time a student had a social interaction lasting 10 minutes or longer, the student would fill out a card. The card included questions about who were the other people in the interaction, and about various aspects of the conversation. Excluding family and work situations, the number of social interactions of 10 minutes or longer over a week for these 94 students were as follows:

48, 15, 33, 3, 21, 19, 17, 16, 44, 25, 30, 3, 5, 9, 35, 32, 26, 13, 14, 14, 47, 47, 29, 18, 11, 5, 19, 24, 17, 6, 25, 8, 18, 29, 1, 18, 22, 3, 22, 29, 2, 6, 10, 29, 10, 21, 38, 41, 16, 17, 8, 40, 8, 10, 18, 7, 4, 4, 8, 11, 3, 23, 10, 19, 21, 13, 12, 10, 4, 17, 11, 21, 9, 8, 7, 5, 3, 22, 14, 25, 4, 11, 10, 18, 1, 28, 27, 19, 24, 35, 9, 30, 8, 26

Now, let's follow our four steps for making a frequency table.

❶ **Make a list of each possible value down the left edge of a page, starting from the highest and ending with the lowest.** In this study, the highest number of interactions could be any number. However, the highest actual number in this group was 48, so we can use 48 as the highest value. The lowest possible number of interactions is 0. Thus, the first step is to list these values down a page. (It might be good to use several columns so that you can have all the scores on a single page.)

❷ **Go one by one through the scores, making a mark for each next to its value on your list.** Figure 1–2 shows this.

❸ **Make a table showing how many times each value on your list was used.** Table 1–3 is the result.

❹ **Figure the percentage of scores for each value.** We have *not* done so in this example because with so many categories, it would not help much for seeing the pattern of scores. However, if you want to check your understanding of this step, the first three percentages would be 1.06%, 2.13%, and 0%. (These are the percentages for frequencies of 1, 2, and 0. We have rounded to two decimal places.)

48 - /	31 -	15 - /
47 - //	30 - //	14 - ///
46 -	29 - ////	13 - //
45 -	28 - /	12 - /
44 - /	27 - /	11 - ////
43 -	26 - //	10 - 7HL /
42 -	25 - ///	9 - ///
41 - /	24 - //	8 - 7HL /
40 - /	23 - /	7 - //
39 -	22 - ///	6 - //
38 - /	21 - ////	5 - ///
37 -	20 -	4 - ////
36 -	19 - ////	3 - 7HL
35 - //	18 - 7HL	2 - /
34 -	17 - ////	1 - //
33 - /	16 - //	0 -
32 - /		

FIGURE 1–2 *Making a frequency table of students' social interactions over a week. (Data from McLaughlin-Volpe et al., 2001)*

GROUPED FREQUENCY TABLES

Sometimes there are so many possible values that a frequency table is too awkward to give a simple picture of the scores. The last example was a bit like that, wasn't it? The solution is to make groupings of values that include all values within a certain range. For example, consider our stress example. Instead of having a separate frequency figure for the students who rated their stress as 8 and another for those who rated it as 9, you could have a combined category of 8 and 9. This combined cate-

TABLE 1–3 Frequency Table for Number of Social Interactions During a Week for 94 College Students

Score	Frequency	Score	Frequency	Score	Frequency
48	1	31	0	15	1
47	2	30	2	14	3
46	0	29	4	13	2
45	0	28	1	12	1
44	1	27	1	11	4
43	0	26	2	10	6
42	0	25	3	9	3
41	1	24	2	8	6
40	1	23	1	7	2
39	0	22	3	6	2
38	1	21	4	5	3
37	0	20	0	4	4
36	0	19	4	3	5
35	2	18	5	2	1
34	0	17	4	1	2
33	1	16	2	0	0
32	1				

Source: Data from McLaughlin-Volpe et al. (2001).

gory is a range of values that includes these two values. A combined category like this is called an **interval.** This particular interval of 8 and 9 has a frequency of 41 (the sum of the 26 scores with a value of 8 and the 15 scores with a value of 9).

A frequency table that uses intervals is called a **grouped frequency table.** Table 1–4 is a grouped frequency table for the stress ratings example. (However, in this example, the full frequency table has only 11 different values. Thus, a grouped frequency table was not really necessary.) Table 1–5 is a grouped frequency table for the 94 students' numbers of social interactions over a week.

Making a grouped frequency table involves combining the individual values into the intervals (groups of adjacent values). There are some rules about how this is done. Most important, there should be about 5 to 15 intervals. Also, all intervals should be of the same size (except that sometimes researchers use a different size for the highest or lowest interval). If you study the examples closely, you will see that we have followed some additional principles. The low end of each interval is always a multiple of the interval size. (For example, if the interval size is 3, then the low end of the intervals contains multiples of 3, such as 0, 3, 6, 9, and so on.) It also is standard to make the intervals a round number, such as 2, 3, 5, 10, or a multiple of 10. (Table 1–4 uses intervals of 2 each. Table 1–5 uses intervals of 5 each.)

The big question in actually designing a grouped frequency table is determining the interval size and the number of intervals. There are various guidelines to help researchers with this, but in practice it is done automatically by the researcher's computer. Thus, we will not focus on it in this book. However, should you have to make a grouped frequency table on your own, the key thing is to experiment with the interval size until you come up with an interval size that is a round

interval

grouped frequency table

TABLE 1–4 Grouped Frequency Table for Stress Ratings

Stress Rating Interval	Frequency	Percent
10–11	14	9
8–9	41	27
6–7	44	29
4–5	34	23
2–3	15	10
0–1	3	2

Source: Data from Aron, Paris, & Aron (1995).

TABLE 1–5 Grouped Frequency Table for Numbers of Social Interactions during a Week for 94 College Students

Interval	Frequency	Percent
45–49	3	3.2
40–44	3	3.2
35–39	3	3.2
30–34	4	4.3
25–29	11	11.7
20–24	10	10.6
15–19	16	17.0
10–14	16	17.0
5–9	16	17.0
0–4	12	12.8

Source: Data from McLaughlin-Volpe et al. (2001).

number and that creates about 5 to 15 intervals. Then when actually setting up the table, be sure you set the low end of each interval to a multiple of the interval size and the top end of each interval to the number that is just below the low end of the next interval.

HOW ARE YOU DOING?

1. What is a frequency table?
2. Why would a researcher want to make a frequency table?
3. Make a frequency table for the following scores: 5, 7, 4, 5, 6, 5, 4
4. What does a grouped frequency table group?

ANSWERS

1. A systematic listing of the number of scores (the frequency) of each value in the group studied.
2. It makes it easy to see the pattern in a large group of scores.
3.

Value	Frequency	Percent
7	1	14
6	1	14
5	3	43
4	2	29

4. It groups together the frequencies of adjacent values into intervals.

FREQUENCY GRAPHS

A graph is another good way to make a large group of scores easy to understand. "A picture is worth a thousand words"—and sometimes a thousand numbers. A straightforward approach is to make a graph of the frequency table. There are two main kinds of such graphs: histograms and frequency polygons.

HISTOGRAMS

histogram

One way to graph the information in a frequency table is to make a special kind of bar chart called a **histogram.** In a histogram, the height of each bar is the frequency of each value in the frequency table, and all the bars are put next to each other with no space in between.

A histogram looks a bit like a city skyline. Figure 1–3 shows two histograms based on the stress ratings example, one based on the ordinary frequency table and one based on the grouped frequency table. (When making a histogram for the frequencies of the different values of a nominal variable, the bars are usually separated, making the familiar bar graph.)

HOW TO MAKE A HISTOGRAM

There are four steps for making a histogram.

❶ **Make a frequency table.**

❷ **Put the values along the bottom of the page.** The numbers should go from left to right, from lowest to highest. For a grouped frequency table, the histogram is of the intervals. Mark only the midpoint of each interval, under the center of each bar. The midpoint is the middle of where the interval starts and the next interval be-

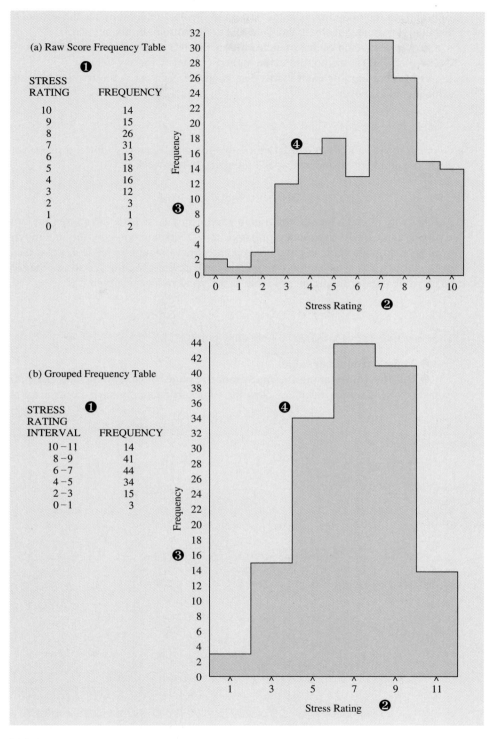

(a) Raw Score Frequency Table ❶

STRESS RATING	FREQUENCY
10	14
9	15
8	26
7	31
6	13
5	18
4	16
3	12
2	3
1	1
0	2

(b) Grouped Frequency Table

STRESS RATING INTERVAL	FREQUENCY
10–11	14
8–9	41
6–7	44
4–5	34
2–3	15
0–1	3

FIGURE 1–3   *Four steps in making a histogram based on (a) a frequency table and (b) a grouped frequency table for the stress ratings example (Data from Aron et al., 1995).* ❶ *Make a frequency table.* ❷ *Put the values along the bottom of the page.* ❸ *Make a scale of frequencies along the left edge of the page.* ❹ *Make a bar for each value.*

gins. (To get the midpoint, take the bottom of the next interval minus the bottom of this interval; divide this by 2; then add this to the bottom of this interval.)

❸ **Make a scale of frequencies along the left edge of the page.** The scale should go from 0 at the bottom to the highest frequency for any value.

❹ **Make a bar for each value.** The height of each bar is the frequency of the value it is placed over.

ADDITIONAL HISTOGRAM EXAMPLE

Figure 1–4 shows a histogram based on the grouped frequency table for the example of the numbers of students' social interactions in a week.

FREQUENCY POLYGONS

frequency polygon

Another way to graph the information in a frequency table is to make a special kind of line graph called a **frequency polygon.** In a frequency polygon, the line moves from point to point. The height of each point shows the number of scores that have that value. This creates a kind of mountain-peak skyline. Figure 1–5 shows the frequency polygon for the frequency table in the stress ratings example.

HOW TO MAKE A FREQUENCY POLYGON

There are five steps for making a frequency polygon.

❶ **Make a frequency table.**

❷ **Put the values along the bottom of the page.** Be sure to include one extra value above and one extra value below the values that actually have scores in them.

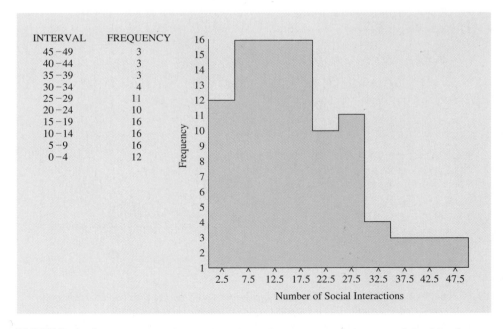

INTERVAL	FREQUENCY
45–49	3
40–44	3
35–39	3
30–34	4
25–29	11
20–24	10
15–19	16
10–14	16
5–9	16
0–4	12

FIGURE 1–4   *Histogram for number of social interactions during a week for 94 college students, based on grouped frequencies. (Data from McLaughlin-Volpe et al., 2001)*

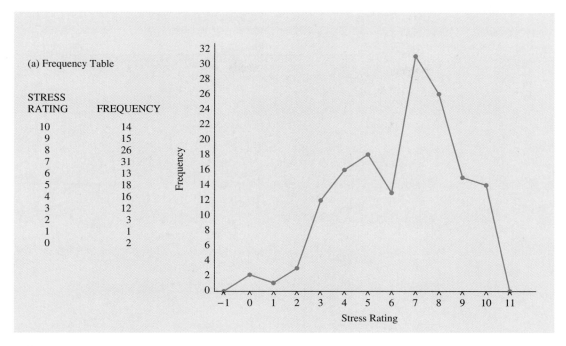

(a) Frequency Table

STRESS RATING	FREQUENCY
10	14
9	15
8	26
7	31
6	13
5	18
4	16
3	12
2	3
1	1
0	2

FIGURE 1–5   *Frequency polygon based on a frequency table for the stress ratings example (Data from Aron et al., 1995).*

You need the extra value so that the line starts and ends along the baseline of the graph, at zero frequency. This creates a closed or "polygon" figure.

❸ **Along the left of the page, make a scale of frequencies that goes from 0 at the bottom to the highest frequency for any value.**

❹ **Mark a point above each value with a height for the frequency of that value.**

❺ **Connect the points with lines.**

Figure 1–6 shows the five steps for making a frequency polygon based on the grouped frequency table for the students' social interactions example.

Tip for Success

Making a histogram or frequency polygon is easiest if you use graph paper.

HOW ARE YOU DOING?

1. Why do researchers make frequency graphs?
2. When making a histogram from a frequency table, (a) what goes along the bottom, (b) what goes along the left edge, and (c) what goes above each value?
3. Based on the frequency table below, make (a) a histogram and (b) a frequency polygon.

Value	Frequency
5	2
4	5
3	8
2	4
1	3

4. How are histograms and frequency polygons (a) similar and (b) different?
5. Why does a frequency polygon include an extra value at the start and end along the bottom?

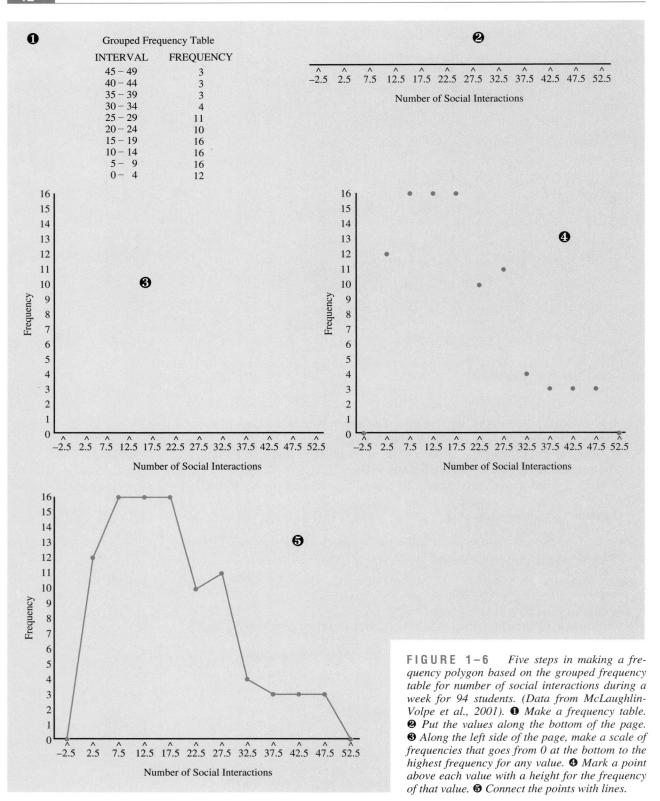

FIGURE 1–6   *Five steps in making a frequency polygon based on the grouped frequency table for number of social interactions during a week for 94 students. (Data from McLaughlin-Volpe et al., 2001).* ❶ *Make a frequency table.* ❷ *Put the values along the bottom of the page.* ❸ *Along the left side of the page, make a scale of frequencies that goes from 0 at the bottom to the highest frequency for any value.* ❹ *Mark a point above each value with a height for the frequency of that value.* ❺ *Connect the points with lines.*

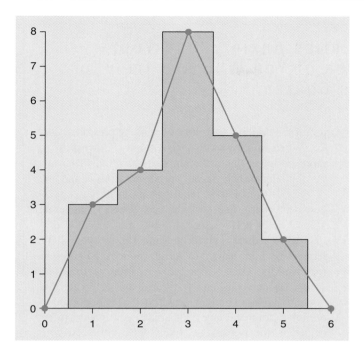

FIGURE 1–7   *Histogram and frequency polygon for "How Are You Doing?" question 3.*

ANSWERS:

1. To visually show the pattern in a frequency table.
2. (a) The values, from lowest to highest; (b) the frequencies from 0 at the bottom to the highest frequency of any value at the top; (c) a bar with a height of the frequency for that value.
3. See Figure 1–7.
4. (a) Both show the frequency table visually, with heights for each value for the frequency of that value. (b) A histogram uses bars; a frequency polygon is a line graph.
5. The extra values make the line start and end at zero frequency so that the line and the bottom of the graph together make a closed figure (a polygon).

SHAPES OF FREQUENCY DISTRIBUTIONS

A frequency table, histogram, or frequency polygon describes a **frequency distribution.** That is, these show the pattern or shape of how the frequencies are spread out, or "distributed." Social and behavioral scientists also describe this shape in words. Describing the shape of a distribution is important both for the descriptive statistics we focus on in this chapter and also for the inferential statistics you will learn in later chapters.

frequency distribution

UNIMODAL AND BIMODAL FREQUENCY DISTRIBUTIONS

One important aspect of a distribution's shape is whether it has only one main high point (one high "tower" in the histogram or one main "peak" in the frequency polygon). For example, in the stress ratings study, the most frequent score is a 7, giving

BOX 1–1   Math Anxiety, Statistics Anxiety, and You: A Message for Those of You Who Are Truly Worried About This Course

Let's face it: Many of you dread this course, even to the point of having a full-blown case of "statistics anxiety" (Zeidner, 1991). If you become tense the minute you see numbers, we need to talk about that right now.

First, this course is a chance for a fresh start with digits. Your past performance in (or avoidance of) geometry, trigonometry, calculus, or similar horrors need not influence in any way how well you comprehend statistics. This is largely a different subject.

Second, if your worry persists, you need to decide where it is coming from. Math or statistics anxiety, test anxiety, general anxiety, and general low self-confidence each seems to play its own role in students' difficulties with math courses (Cooper & Robinson, 1989; Dwinell & Higbee, 1991).

Is your problem mainly math/statistics anxiety? There are wonderful books and websites to help you. Do a search, or try *http://www.mathanxiety.net* or *http://www.mathpower.com.* We highly recommend Sheila Tobias's (1995) book, *Overcoming Math Anxiety.* Tobias, a former math avoider herself, suggests that your goal be "math mental health," which she defines as "the willingness to learn the math you need when you need it" (p. 12). (Could it be that this course in statistics is one of those times?)

Tobias explains that math mental health is usually lost in elementary school, when you are called to the blackboard, your mind goes blank, and you are unable to produce the one right answer to an arithmetic problem. What confidence remained probably faded during timed tests, which you did not realize were difficult for everyone except the most proficient few.

Tobias says that students who are good at math are not necessarily smarter than the rest of us, but they really know their strengths and weaknesses, their styles of thinking and feeling around a problem. They do not judge themselves harshly for mistakes. In particular, they do not expect to understand things instantly. Allowing yourself to be a "slow learner" does not mean that you are less intelligent. It shows that you are growing in math mental health.

Is your problem test anxiety? Then you need to learn to handle anxiety better. Test taking requires the use of the thinking part of our brain, the prefrontal cortex. When we are anxious, we naturally "downshift" to more basic, instinctual brain systems. And that ruins our thinking ability. Anxiety produces arousal, and one of the best understood relationships in psychology is between arousal and performance. Whereas moderate arousal helps performance, too much or too little dramatically reduces performance. Things you have learned become harder to recall. Your mind starts to race, and this creates more anxiety, more arousal, and so on. Because during a test you may be fearing that you are "no good and never will be," it is important to rethink beforehand any poor grades you may have received in the past—most likely these reflected your problems with tests more than your abilities.

There are many ways to reduce anxiety and arousal in general, such as learning to breathe properly and to take a quick break to relax deeply. Your counseling center should be able to help you or direct you to some good books on the subject. Again, there are also many websites about reducing anxiety.

Test anxiety specifically is first reduced by overpreparing for a few tests, so that you go in with the certainty that you cannot possibly fail, no matter how aroused you become. The best time to begin applying this tactic is the first test of this course: There will be no old material to review, success will not depend on having understood previous material, and it will help you do better throughout the course. (You also might enlist the sympathy of your instructor or teaching assistant. Bring in a list of what you have studied, state why you are being so exacting, and ask if you have missed anything.) Your preparation must be ridiculously thorough, but only for a few exams. After these successes, your test anxiety should decline.

Also, create a practice test situation as similar to a real test as possible, making a special effort to duplicate the aspects that bother you most. If feeling rushed is the troubling part, once you think you are well prepared, set yourself a time limit for solving some homework problems. Make yourself write out answers fully and legibly. This may be part of what makes you feel slow during a test. If the presence of others bothers you, the sound of their scurrying pencils while yours is frozen in midair, do your practice test with others in your course. Even make it an explicit contest to see who can finish first.

Is your problem a general lack of confidence? Is there something else in your life causing you to worry or feel bad about yourself? Then we suggest that it is time you tried your friendly college counseling center.

Lastly, could you be highly sensitive? A final word about anxiety and arousal. About 15 to 20 percent of humans (and all higher animals) seem to be born with a temperament trait that has been seen traditionally as shyness, hesitancy, or introversion (Eysenck, 1981; Kagan, 1994). But this shyness or hesitancy seems actually due to a preference to observe and an ability to notice subtle stimulation and process information deeply (Aron, 1996; Aron & Aron, 1997). This often causes highly sensitive persons (HSPs) to be very intuitive or even gifted. But it also means they are more easily overaroused by high levels of stimulation, like tests.

You might want to find out if you are an HSP (go to *http://www.hsperson.com*). If you are, appreciate the trait's assets and make some allowances for its one disadvantage, this tendency to become easily overaroused. It has to affect your performance on tests. What matters is what you actually know, which is probably quite a bit. This simple act of self-acceptance—that you are *not* less smart but *are* more sensitive—may in itself help ease your arousal when trying to express your statistical knowledge.

So good luck to all of you. We wish you the best while taking this course and in your lives.

---

a graph with only one very high area. This is called a **unimodal distribution.** If a distribution has two fairly equal high points, it is called a **bimodal distribution.** Any distribution with two or more high points is also called a **multimodal distribution.** Finally, if all the values have about the same frequency, it is called a **rectangular distribution.** These frequency distributions are shown in Figure 1–8.

The information we collect in social and behavioral science research is usually approximately unimodal. Bimodal and other multimodal distributions occasionally turn up. A bimodal example would be the distribution of the number of employees whose names have come to the attention of higher-level managers. If you made a frequency distribution for the quality of work of such employees, the large frequencies would be at the values for a quality of work was either very low or very high. An example of a rectangular distribution is the number of children at each grade level attending an elementary school. There would be about the same number in first grade, second grade, and so on. These examples are illustrated in Figure 1–9.

unimodal distribution

bimodal distribution

multimodal distribution

rectangular distribution

symmetrical distribution

skewed distribution

SYMMETRICAL AND SKEWED DISTRIBUTIONS

Look again at the frequency graphs of the stress rating example (Figures 1–3 and 1–5). The distribution is lopsided, with more scores near the high end. This is somewhat unusual. Most things we measure in the social and behavioral sciences have about equal numbers on both sides of the middle. That is, most of the time, the scores follow an approximately **symmetrical distribution** (if you fold the graph of a symmetrical distribution in half, the two halves look the same).

A distribution that clearly is not symmetrical is called a **skewed distribution.** The stress ratings distribution is an example of a skewed distribution. A skewed distribution has one side that is long and spread out, somewhat like a tail. The side with *fewer* scores (the side that looks more like a tail) describes the direction of the skew. Thus a distribution with fewer scores left of the peak, like our stress ratings example, is *skewed to the left.* The other example we have examined in this chapter, the distributions of students' numbers of interactions in a week, is *skewed to the*

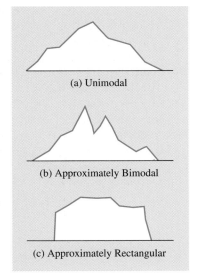

(a) Unimodal

(b) Approximately Bimodal

(c) Approximately Rectangular

FIGURE 1–8 *Examples of (a) unimodal, (b) approximately bimodal, and (c) approximately rectangular frequency polygons.*

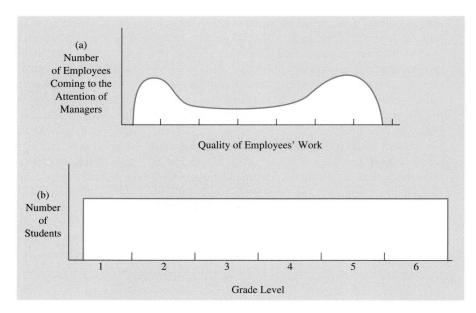

FIGURE 1–9   *Fictional examples of distributions that are not unimodal: (a) A bimodal distribution showing the possible frequencies for different levels of quality of work of employees who come to the attention of higher-level managers. (b) A rectangular distribution showing the possible frequencies of students at different grade levels in an elementary school.*

floor effect

ceiling effect

right. Figure 1–10 shows examples of approximately symmetrical and skewed distributions.

A distribution that is skewed to the right is also called *positively skewed.* A distribution skewed to the left is also called *negatively skewed.*

Strongly skewed distributions come up in the social and behavioral sciences mainly when what is being measured has some lower or upper limit. For example, the number of social interactions in a week cannot be fewer than zero interactions. This kind of situation in which many scores pile up at the low end because it is impossible to have a lower score is called a **floor effect.**

A skewed distribution caused by an upper limit is shown in Figure 1–11. This is a distribution of adults' scores on a multiplication table test. This distribution is strongly skewed to the left. Most of the scores pile up at the right, the high end (a perfect score). This is an example of a **ceiling effect.** The stress ratings example also shows a mild ceiling effect. This is because many students had high levels of

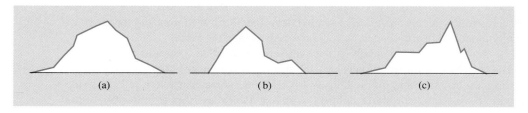

FIGURE 1–10   *Examples of frequency polygons of distributions that are (a) approximately symmetrical, (b) skewed to the right (positively skewed), and (c) skewed to the left (negatively skewed).*

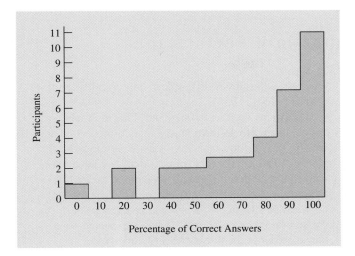

FIGURE 1–11 *A distribution skewed to the left due to a ceiling effect: fictional distribution of adults' scores on a multiplication table test.*

stress, the maximum rating was 10, and people often do not like to use ratings right at the maximum.

NORMAL, HEAVY-TAILED, AND LIGHT-TAILED DISTRIBUTIONS

Social and behavioral scientists also describe a distribution in terms of whether its tails are particularly "heavy" (thick, with many scores in them) or "light" (thin, with few scores in them). These are called **heavy-tailed distributions** and **light-tailed distributions.** (This aspect of the shape of a distribution is also called *kurtosis* [see DeCarlo, 1997].) The standard of comparison is a bell-shaped curve. In social and behavioral science research and in nature generally, distributions often are quite similar to this bell-shaped standard, called the **normal curve.** We discuss this curve in some detail in later chapters. For now, however, the important thing is that the normal curve is a unimodal, symmetrical curve with average tails—the sort of bell shape shown in Figure 1–12a. The stress ratings example in this chapter is very roughly like a normal curve, except that it is somewhat skewed to the left. In our

heavy-tailed distributions

light-tailed distributions

normal curve

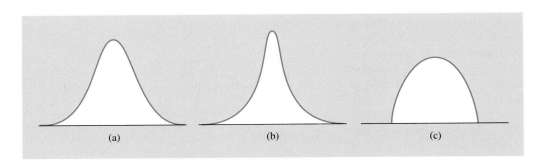

FIGURE 1–12 *Examples of (a) normal, (b) heavy-tailed, and (c) light-tailed distributions. (Adapted from DeCarlo, 1997.)*

BOX 1-2   Gender, Ethnicity, and Math Performance

From time to time, someone tries to argue that because some groups of people score better on math tests and make careers out of mathematics, this means that these groups have some genetic advantage in math (or statistics). Other groups are said or implied to be innately inferior at math. The issue comes up about gender and also racial and ethnic groups, and of course in arguments about overall intelligence as well as math. There's no evidence for such genetic differences that can't be refuted (a must-see article: Block, 1995). But the stereotypes persist.

The impact of these stereotypes has been well established in research by Steele and his colleagues (1997), who have done numerous studies on what they call "stereotype threat," which occurs when a negative stereotype about a group you belong to becomes relevant to you because of the situation you are in, like taking a math test, and provides an explanation for how you will behave. A typical experiment creating stereotype threat (Spencer, Steele, & Quinn, 1999) involved women taking a difficult math test. Half were told that men generally do better on the test and the other half that women generally do equally well. When told that women do worse, the women did indeed score substantially lower. In the other condition there was no difference. (In fact, in two separate studies, men performed a little worse when they were told there was no gender difference, as if they had lost some of their confidence.)

The same results occur when African Americans are given parts of the Graduate Record Exam—they do fine on the test when they are told no racial differences in the scores have been found, and do worse when they are told such differences have been found (Steele, 1997).

These results certainly argue against there being any inherent differences in ability in these groups. But that is nothing new. Many lines of research indicate that prejudices, not genetics, are the probable cause of differences in test scores between groups. For example, the same difference of 15 IQ points between a dominant and minority group has been found all over the world, even when there is no genetic difference between the groups, and in cases where opportunities for a group have changed, as

when they emigrate, differences have rapidly disappeared (Block, 1995).

If groups such as women and African Americans are not inherently inferior in any area of intellectual endeavor, but perform worse on tests, what might be the reasons? The usual explanation is that they have internalized the "superior" group's prejudices. Steele thinks the problem might not be so internal but may have to do with the situation. The stigmatized groups perform worse when they know that's what is expected—when they experience the threat of being stereotyped.

Of course, in Steele's studies, everyone tested had roughly the same initial educational background so that they knew the answers under the nonthreatening condition. Under the threatening condition, there is evidence that they try even harder. Too hard. And they become anxious. Just as often, however, members of groups expected to do poorly simply stop caring about how they do. They disidentify with the whole goal of doing well in math, for example. They avoid the subject or take easy classes and just shrug off any low grades.

WHAT CAN YOU DO FOR YOURSELF?

So, do you feel you belong to a group that is expected to do worse at math? (This includes white males who feel they are among the "math dumbbells.") What can you do to get out from under the shadow of "stereotype threat" as you take this course?

First, care about learning statistics. Don't discount it to save your self-esteem and separate yourself from the rest of the class. Fight for your right to know this subject. What a triumph for those who hold the prejudice if you give up. Consider these words from the former president of the Mathematics Association of America:

> The paradox of our times is that as mathematics becomes increasingly powerful, only the powerful seem to benefit from it. The ability to think mathematically—broadly interpreted—is absolutely crucial to advancement in virtually every career. Confidence in dealing with data, skepticism in analyzing arguments, persistence in penetrating complex problems, and literacy in communicating about technical matters are the enabling arts offered by the new mathematical sciences. (Steen, 1987, p. xviii)

Second, once you care about succeeding at statistics, realize you are going to be affected by stereotype threat. Think of it as a stereotype-induced form of test anxiety and work on it that way (see Box 1–1).

Third, in yourself, root out the effects of that stereotype as much as you can. It takes some effort. That's why we are spending time on it here. Research on stereotypes shows that they can be activated without our awareness (Fiske, 1998), even when we are otherwise low in prejudice or a member of the stereotyped group. To keep from being prejudiced about ourselves or others, we have to consciously resist stereotypes. So, to avoid unconsciously handicapping yourself in this course, as those in Steele's experiments probably did, you must make an active effort; you must consciously dismantle the stereotype and think about its falsehood.

SOME POINTS TO THINK ABOUT

- Women: Every bit of evidence for thinking that men are genetically better at math can and has been well disputed. For example, yes, the very top performers tend to be male, but the differences are slight, and the lowest performers are not more likely to be female, as would probably be the case if there were a genetic difference. Tobias (1982) cites numerous studies providing nongenetic explanations for why women might not make it to the very top in math. For example, in a study of students identified by a math talent search, it was found that few parents arranged for their daughters to be coached before the talent exams. Sons were almost invariably coached. In another study, parents of mathematically gifted girls were not even aware of their daughters' abilities, whereas parents of boys invariably were. In general, girls tend to avoid higher math classes, according to Tobias, because parents, peers, and even teachers often advise them against pursuing too much math. So even though women are earning more PhDs in math than ever before, it is not surprising that math is the field with the highest dropout rate for women.
- We checked the grades in our own introductory statistics classes and simply found no reliable difference for gender. More generally, Schram (1996) analyzed results of 13 independent studies of performance in college statistics and found an overall average difference of almost exactly zero (the slight direction of difference favored females). It has never even occurred to us to look for racial or ethnic differences, as they are so obviously not present.
- Persons of color: Keep in mind that only 7 percent of the genetic variation in humans is between races (Block, 1995). Mostly, we are all the same.
- Associate with people who have a positive attitude about you and your group. Watch for subtle signs of prejudice and reject it. For example, Steele found that the grades of African Americans in a large midwestern university rose substantially when they were enrolled in a transition-to-college program emphasizing that they were the cream of the crop and much was expected of them, while African American students at the same school who were enrolled in a "remedial program for minorities" received considerable attention, but their grades improved very little and many more of them dropped out of school. Steele argues that the very idea of a remedial program exposed those students to a subtle stereotype threat.
- Work hard during this course. If you are stuck, get help. If you work at it, you can do it. This is not about genetics. Think about a study cited by Tobias (1995) comparing students in Asia and the United States on an international mathematics test. The U.S. students were thoroughly outperformed, but more important was why: Interviews revealed that Asian students saw math as an ability fairly equally distributed among people and thought that differences in performance were due to hard work. Contrarily, U.S. students thought some people are just born better at math, so hard work matters little.

In short, our culture's belief that "math just comes naturally to some people" is false and harmful. It especially harms students who hear it early in their career with numbers and believe it explains their difficulties, when their real problem is due to gender or racial stereotypes or difficulty with English. But once you vow to undo the harm done to you, you can overcome effects of prejudice. Doing well in this course may even be more satisfying for you than for others. And it will certainly be a fine thing that you have modeled that achievement for others in your group.

experience, most distributions that result from social and behavioral science research are actually closer to the normal curve than this example.

Figures 1–12b and 1–12c show examples of heavy-tailed and light-tailed distributions. Distributions that have tails that are heavier (thicker) or lighter (thinner) than a normal curve also tend to have a different shape in the middle. Those with heavy tails are usually more peaked than the normal curve (see Figure 1–12b). It is as if the normal curve got pinched in the middle and some of it went up into a sharp peak and the rest spread out into thick tails. Those with light tails are usually flatter than the normal curve (see Figure 1–13c). It is as if the tails and the top of the curve both got sucked in to right near the middle on both sides. (An extreme case of a light-tailed distribution would be a rectangular distribution.)

HOW ARE YOU DOING?

1. Describe the difference between a unimodal and multimodal distribution in terms of (a) a frequency graph and (b) a frequency table.
2. What does it mean to say that a distribution is skewed to the left?
3. What kind of skew is created by (a) a floor effect and (b) a ceiling effect?
4. When a distribution is described as heavy-tailed or light-tailed, what is it being compared to?

ANSWERS:

1. (a) A unimodal distribution has one main high point; a multimodal distribution has more than one main high point. (b) A unimodal distribution has one value with a higher frequency than all the other frequencies; a multimodal distribution has more than one value with large frequencies compared to the values around it.
2. Fewer scores have low values than have high values.
3. (a) Skewed to the right; (b) skewed to the left.
4. The normal curve.

FREQUENCY TABLES, HISTOGRAMS, AND FREQUENCY POLYGONS IN RESEARCH ARTICLES

Frequency tables, histograms, and frequency polygons are used by researchers mainly as a step in more elaborate statistical procedures. They usually are not included in research articles. The most common of these in research articles are frequency tables. For example, in an article published in *The Journal of Special Education,* Hosp and Reschly (2003) reported how often students of different racial groups in the United States were referred for special education. They found 10 previous research studies that had been done on this and published as journal articles, dissertations, or technical reports. These 10 studies reported on a total of 44 separate groups (school districts or similar areas). They called each group a subsample. Table 1–6 (Hosp & Reschly's Table 2) shows the characteristics of these 44 subsamples. It gives the frequencies and percentages for six variables: type of publication in which the subsample was reported; the publication year; state; length of study of the subsample; school setting; and the predominant racial group of the subsample. For example, the table shows that most of the subsamples were in New York State and almost all of the groups were studied for 11 months.

TABLE 1–6 Characteristics of Included Subsamples		
Variable	*n*	%
Publication type		
Journal article	8	18
Dissertation	2	5
Technical report	34	77
Publication year		
1978	1	2
1983	3	7
1990	1	2
1994	32	73
1995	1	2
1996	1	2
1997	2	5
1998	1	2
1999	2	5
State conducted in		
New York	32	73
Other than New York	12	27
Length of study (in months)		
11	41	93
24	1	2
Setting		
Elementary school	6	14
Elementary & middle school	33	75
All levels	5	11
Predominant racial group		
Caucasian	16	36
African American	15	34
Hispanic	13	30

Note. Due to rounding, some percentages may not add to 100.
Source: Hosp, J. L., & Reschly, D. J. (2003). Referral rates for intervention or assessment: A meta-analysis of racial differences. *Journal of Special Education, 37,* 67–80. Copyright © 2003 by PRO-ED, Inc. Adapted with permission.

SUMMARY

1. Social and behavioral scientists use descriptive statistics to describe—to summarize and make understandable—a group of numbers from a research study.

2. A value is a number or category; a variable is a characteristic that can have different values; a score is a particular person's value on the variable.

3. Most variables in the social and behaviorial sciences are numeric with approximately equal intervals. However, some numeric variables are rank-order (where the values are ranks), and some variables are not numeric at all, but are nominal (where the values are categories).

4. A frequency table organizes the numbers into a table in which each of the possible values is listed from highest to lowest, along with its frequency (number of scores that have that value, and percentage).

5. When there are many different values, a grouped frequency table will be more useful. It is like an ordinary frequency table except that the frequencies are given for intervals that include a range of values.

6. The pattern of frequencies in a distribution can be shown visually with a histogram, a kind of bar graph in which the height of each bar is the frequency for a particular value and there are no spaces between the bars. An alternative is a frequency polygon, in which a line connects dots, the height of each of which is the frequency for a particular value.

7. The general shape of a histogram or frequency polygon can be unimodal (having a single peak), bimodal, multimodal (including bimodal), or rectangular (having no peak); it can be symmetrical or skewed (having a long tail) to the right or the left; and compared to the bell-shaped normal curve, it can be light-tailed or heavy-tailed.

8. Frequency tables rarely appear in research articles. When they do, they often involve frequencies (and percentages) for various categories of a nominal variable. Histograms and frequency polygons almost never appear in articles, though the shapes of distributions (normal, skewed, and so on) occasionally are described in words.

KEY TERMS

statistics (p. 1)
descriptive statistics (p. 2)
inferential statistics (p. 2)
variable (p. 2)
value (p. 2)
score (p. 2)
numeric variable (p. 3)
equal-interval variable (p. 3)
rank-order variable (p. 3)
nominal variable (p. 4)
frequency table (p. 5)
interval (p. 7)

grouped frequency table (p. 7)
histogram (p. 8)
frequency polygon (p. 10)
frequency distribution (p. 13)
unimodal distribution (p. 13)
bimodal distribution (p. 15)
multimodal distribution (p. 15)

rectangular distribution (p. 15)
symmetrical distribution (p. 15)
skewed distribution (p. 15)
floor effect (p. 16)
ceiling effect (p. 16)
heavy-tailed distribution (p. 17)
light-tailed distribution (p. 17)
normal curve (p. 17)

EXAMPLE WORKED-OUT PROBLEMS

Ten first-year students rated their interest in graduate school on a scale from 1 = no interest at all to 6 = high interest. Their scores were as follows: 2, 4, 5, 5, 1, 3, 6, 3, 6, 6.

MAKING A FREQUENCY TABLE

See Figure 1–13.

MAKING A HISTOGRAM

See Figure 1–14.

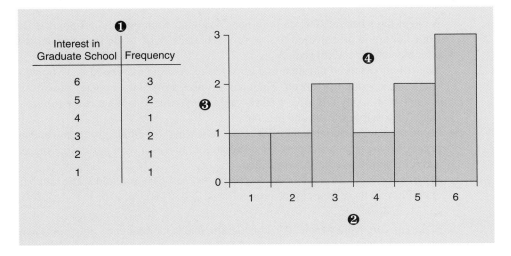

Interest in Graduate School ❸	Frequency	❹ Percent	❷
6	3	30	///
5	2	20	//
4	1	10	/
3	2	20	//
2	1	10	/
1	1	10	/

2,4,5,5,1,3,6,3,6,6

FIGURE 1–13 *Answer to Example Worked-Out Problem for making a frequency table.* ❶ *Make a list of each possible value down the left edge of a page, starting from the highest and ending with the lowest.* ❷ *Go one by one through the scores, making a mark for each next to its value on your list.* ❸ *Make a table showing how many times each value on your list is used.* ❹ *Figure the percentage of scores for each value.*

MAKING A FREQUENCY POLYGON

See Figure 1–15.

PRACTICE PROBLEMS

These problems involve tabulation and making graphs. Most real-life statistics problems are done on a computer with special statistical software. Even if you have such software, do these problems by hand to ingrain the method in your mind.

Interest in Graduate School ❶	Frequency
6	3
5	2
4	1
3	2
2	1
1	1

FIGURE 1–14 *Answer to Example Worked-Out Problem for making a histogram.* ❶ *Make a frequency table.* ❷ *Put the values along the bottom of the page (from left to right, from lowest to highest).* ❸ *Make a scale of frequencies along the left edge of the page (going from 0 at the bottom to the highest frequency for any value).* ❹ *Make a bar for each value (with a height for the frequency of that value).*

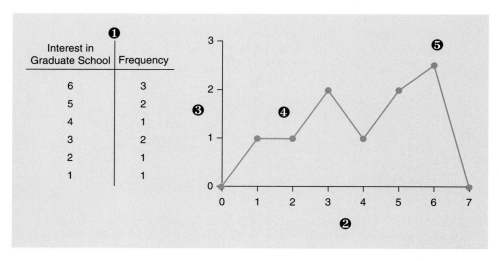

FIGURE 1-15 *Answer to Example Worked-Out Problem for making a frequency polygon. ❶ Make a frequency table. ❷ Put the values along the bottom of the page (from left to right, starting one value below the lowest value and ending one value above the highest value). ❸ Along the left edge of the page, make a scale of frequencies that goes from 0 at the bottom to the highest frequency for any value. ❹ Mark a point above each value with a height for the frequency of that value. ❺ Connect the points with lines.*

For practice in using a computer to solve statistics problems, refer to the computer section of each chapter of the *Student's Study Guide and Computer Workbook* that accompanies this text.

All data are fictional unless an actual citation is given.

For answers to Set I problems, see pp. 421–23.

SET I

1. A client rates her satisfaction with her vocational counselor on a 4-point scale from 1 = not at all satisfied to 4 = very satisfied. What is the (a) variable, (b) possible values, and (c) score?

2. You fill out a survey question that asks you to give the likelihood that you will vote in an upcoming election. The question uses a 5-point response scale from 1 = not at all likely to 5 = very likely and you answer "5". What is the (a) variable, (b) possible values, and (c) score?

3. Name the kind of variable for each of the following: (a) ethnic group to which a person belongs, (b) number of times an animal makes a wrong turn in a maze, and (c) position one finishes in a race.

4. A particular block in a suburban neighborhood has 20 households. The number of children in these households is as follows: 2, 4, 2, 1, 0, 3, 6, 0, 1, 1, 2, 3, 2, 0, 1, 2, 1, 0, 2, 2.

   Make (a) a frequency table, (b) a histogram, and (c) a frequency polygon. Then (d) describe the general shape of the distribution.

5. Fifty students were asked how many hours they had studied this weekend. Here are their answers:

   11, 2, 0, 13, 5, 7, 1, 8, 12, 11, 7, 8, 9, 10, 7, 4, 6, 10, 4, 7, 8, 6, 7, 10, 7, 3, 11, 18, 2, 9, 7, 3, 8, 7, 3, 13, 9, 8, 7, 7, 10, 4, 15, 3, 5, 6, 9, 7, 10, 6.

Make (a) a frequency table, (b) a histogram, and (c) a frequency polygon. Then, (d) describe the general shape of the distribution.

6. Following are the speeds of 40 cars clocked by radar on a particular road in a 35-mph zone on a particular afternoon:

30, 36, 42, 36, 30, 52, 36, 34, 36, 33, 30, 32, 35, 32, 37, 34, 36, 31, 35, 20, 24, 46, 23, 31, 32, 45, 34, 37, 28, 40, 34, 38, 40, 52, 31, 33, 15, 27, 36, 40.

Make (a) a frequency table, (b) a histogram, and (c) a frequency polygon. Then (d) describe the general shape of the distribution.

7. These are the scores on a measure of sensitivity to smell taken by 25 chefs attending a national conference:

96, 83, 59, 64, 73, 74, 80, 68, 87, 67, 64, 92, 76, 71, 68, 50, 85, 75, 81, 70, 76, 91, 69, 83, 75.

Make (a) a frequency table and (b) histogram. (c) Make a grouped frequency table using intervals of 50–59, 60–69, 70–79, 80–89, and 90–99. Based on the grouped frequency table, (d) make a histogram and (e) describe the general shape of the distribution.

8. Below are the number of minutes it took each of a group of 34 10-year-olds to do a series of abstract puzzles:

24, 83, 36, 22, 81, 39, 60, 62, 38, 66, 38, 36, 45, 20, 20, 67, 41, 87, 41, 82, 35, 82, 28, 80, 80, 68, 40, 27, 43, 80, 31, 89, 83, 24.

Make (a) a frequency table and (b) a frequency polygon. (c) Make a grouped frequency table using intervals of 20–29, 30–39, 40–49, 50–59, 60–69, 70–79, and 80–89. Based on the grouped frequency table, (d) make a histogram and (e) describe the general shape of the distribution.

9. Describe the shapes of the three distributions illustrated.

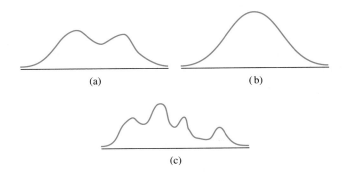

(a)   (b)

(c)

10. Explain to a person who has never had a course in statistics what is meant by (a) a symmetrical unimodal distribution and (b) a negatively skewed unimodal distribution. (Be sure to include in your first answer an explanation of what is meant by a distribution.)

11. What is a ceiling effect?

12. McKee and Ptacek (2001) asked 90 college students about a time they had "delivered bad news" to someone. Table 1–7 (their Table 1) shows the results for the type of bad news given. (a) Using this table as an example, explain the idea of a frequency table to a person who has never had a course in statistics. (b) Explain the general meaning of the pattern of results.

TABLE 1–7	Descriptive Statistics for the Type of News Given		
Category		**Frequency**	**Percentage**
1. Relationship with family		19	21.1
2. School		1	1.1
3. Job/work		6	6.7
4. Relationship with actual/potential girlfriend/boyfriend		17	18.9
5. Personal health		1	1.1
6. Finance		1	1.1
7. Relationship with friends		21	23.3
8. Health of family member/friend		23	25.6
9. Other		1	1.1

Source: McKee, T. L. E., & Ptacek, J. T. (2001). I'm afraid I have something bad to tell you: Breaking bad news from the perspective of the giver. *Journal of Applied Social Psychology, 31,* 246–273. Reprinted by permission.

SET II

13. A participant in a research study is given 50 words to remember and later asked to recall as many as he can of those 50 words. This participant recalls 17. What is the (a) variable, (b) possible values, and (c) score?

14. Explain and give an example for each of the following types of variables: (a) equal-interval, (b) rank-order, and (c) nominal.

15. Here are the number of children in each of 30 classrooms in a particular elementary school.

    24, 20, 35, 25, 25, 22, 26, 28, 38, 15, 25, 21, 24, 25, 25, 24, 25, 20, 32, 25, 22, 26, 26, 28, 24, 22, 26, 21, 25, 24

    Make (a) a frequency table, and (b) a histogram. Then (c) describe the general shape of the distribution.

16. Pick a book and page number of your choice (select a page with at least 30 lines; *do not pick a textbook or any book with tables or illustrations*). Make a list of the number of words on each line; use that list as your data set. Make (a) a frequency table, (b) a histogram, and (c) a frequency polygon. Then (d) describe the general shape of the distribution. (Be sure to give the name, author, publisher, and year of the book you used, along with the page number, with your answer.)

17. An organizational researcher asks 20 employees in a particular company to rate their job satisfaction on a 5-point scale from 1 = very unsatisfied to 5 = very satisfied. The ratings were as follows:

    3, 2, 3, 4, 1, 3, 3, 4, 5, 2, 3, 5, 2, 3, 3, 4, 1, 3, 2, 4.

    Make (a) a frequency table, (b) a histogram, and (c) a frequency polygon. Then (d) describe the general shape of the distribution.

18. A researcher asked 15 college students how many times they "fell in love" (or had a strong infatuation) before they were 11 years old. The numbers of times were as follows:

    2, 0, 6, 0, 3, 1, 0, 4, 9, 0, 5, 6, 1, 0, 2.

    Make (a) a frequency table, (b) a histogram, and (c) a frequency polygon. Then (d) describe the general shape of the distribution.

19. Here are the number of holiday gifts purchased by 25 families randomly inter-viewed at a local mall at the end of the holiday season:

    22, 18, 22, 26, 19, 14, 23, 27, 2, 18, 28, 28, 11, 16, 34, 28, 13, 21, 32, 17, 6, 29, 23, 22, 19.

    Make (a) a frequency table and (b) a frequency polygon. (c) Make a grouped frequency table using intervals of 0–4, 5–9, 10–14, 15–19, 20–24, 25–29, and 30–34. Based on the grouped frequency table, (d) make a histogram and (e) de-scribe the general shape of the distribution.

20. Explain to a person who has never taken a course in statistics the meaning of (a) a grouped frequency table and (b) a frequency polygon.

21. Nownes (2000) surveyed representatives of interest groups who were registered as lobbyists of three U.S. state legislatures. One of the issues he studied was whether interest groups are in competition with each other. Table 1–8 (Nownes's Table 1) shows the results for one such question. (a) Using this table as an exam-ple, explain the idea of a frequency table to a person who has never had a course in statistics. (b) Explain the general meaning of the pattern of results.

22. Mouradian (2001) surveyed college students selected from a screening session to include two groups: (a) "Perpetrators"—students who reported at least one violent act (hitting, shoving, etc.) against their partner in their current or most recent relationship—and (b) "Comparisons"—students who did not report any such uses of violence in any of their last three relationships. At the actual test-ing session, the students first read a description of an aggressive behavior such as "Throw something at his or her partner" or "Say something to upset his or her partner." They then were asked to write "as many examples of circum-stances of situations as [they could] in which a person might engage in behav-iors or acts of this sort with or toward their significant other." Table 1–9 (Mouradian's Table 3) shows the "Dominant Category of Explanation" (the category a participant used most) for females and males, broken down by com-parisons and perpetrators. (a) Using this table as an example, explain the idea of a frequency table to a person who has never had a course in statistics. (b) Ex-plain the general meaning of the pattern of results.

23. Draw an example of each of the following distributions: (a) symmetrical, (b) rectangular, and (c) skewed to the right.

TABLE 1–8 Competition for Members and Other Resources

| Answer | Question: How much competition does this group face from other groups with similar goals for members and other resources? | |
	Percentage	Number
No competition	20	118
Some competition	58	342
A lot of competition	22	131
Total	100	591

Note: There were no statistically significant differences between states. For full results of significance tests, contact the author.

Source: Nownes, A. J. (2001). Policy conflict and the structure of interest communities. *American Poli-tics Quarterly, Vol. 28,* No. 3, July 2000, p. 316. Copyright © 2000. Reprinted by permission of Sage Publications, Inc.

TABLE 1–9 Dominant Category of Explanation for Intimate Aggression by Gender and Perpetrator Status

	Group							
	Female				Male			
	Comparisons ($n = 36$)		Perpetrators ($n = 33$)		Comparisons ($n = 32$)		Perpetrators ($n = 25$)	
Category	f	%	f	%	f	%	f	%
Self-defense	2	6	3	9	3	9	1	4
Control motives	8	22	9	27	9	28	3	12
Expressive aggression	4	11	3	9	3	9	8	32
Face/self-esteem preservation	1	3	2	6	2	6	3	12
Exculpatory explanations	5	14	3	9	3	9	3	12
Rejection of perpetrator or act	12	33	6	18	10	31	7	28
Prosocial/acceptable explanations	0	0	0	0	0	0	0	0
Tied categories	4	11	7	21	2	6	0	0

Note: f = frequency. % = percentage of respondents in a given group who provided a particular category of explanation.
Source: Mouradian, V. E. (2001). Applying schema theory to intimate aggression: Individual and gender differences in representation of contexts and goals. *Journal of Applied Social Psychology, 31,* 376–408. Reprinted by permission of the publisher.

24. Give an example of something having these distribution shapes: (a) bimodal, (b) approximately rectangular, and (c) positively skewed. Do not use an example given in this book or in class.

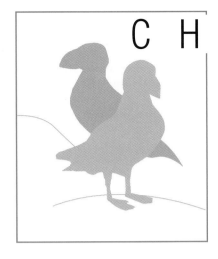

CHAPTER 2

The Mean, Variance, Standard Deviation, and *Z* Scores

As we noted in Chapter 1, the purpose of descriptive statistics is to make a group of scores understandable. We looked at some ways of getting that understanding through tables and graphs. In this chapter, we consider the main statistical techniques for describing a group of scores with numbers. The first way in which we describe a group of scores is in terms of a representative (or typical) value. Identifying such a value is a useful and efficient way to describe a group of scores (which may consist of hundreds or even thousands of numbers). The main representative value we focus on is the mean. Next, we focus on ways of describing how spread out the numbers are in a group of scores. In other words, we consider the amount of variation among the scores. The two measures of variation you will learn about are called the variance and standard deviation. Finally, we show you how to describe a particular score in terms of how much that score varies from the average. To do this, you will learn how to combine the mean and standard deviation to create a *Z* score.

In this chapter, for the first time in this book, you will come across statistical formulas. Such formulas are not designed to confuse you. Hopefully, you will come to see that they actually provide a very efficient way of describing statistical procedures.

Tip for Success

*Before beginning this chapter, you should be sure you are comfortable with the key terms of **variable, score**, and **value** that we considered in Chapter 1. It is also helpful to have developed a solid understanding from Chapter 1 of frequency tables, histograms, and frequency polygons.*

THE MEAN

mean (M)

Usually, the best single number for describing a group of scores is the ordinary average, the sum of all the scores divided by the number of scores. In statistics, this is called the **mean (M).** Suppose that a political scientist does a study on years of experience in elected office. As part of this research, the political scientist finds out the number of years served by mayors of the 10 largest cities in a particular region. The numbers of years served were as follows:

> 7, 8, 8, 7, 3, 1, 6, 9, 3, 8

The mean of these 10 scores is 6 (the sum of 60 years served divided by 10 mayors). That is, on average, these 10 mayors had served 6 years in office. The information for the 10 mayors is thus summarized by this single number, 6.

Many students find it helpful to think of the mean as a kind of balancing point for the distribution of scores. Try it by visualizing a board balanced over a log, like a rudimentary teeter-totter. On the board, imagine piles of blocks set along the board according to their values, one for each score in the distribution. (This is a little like a histogram made of blocks.) The mean would be the point on the board where the weight of the blocks on each side would balance exactly. Figure 2–1 shows this for our 10 mayors.

Some other examples are shown in Figure 2–2. Notice that there doesn't have to be a block right at the balance point. That is, the mean doesn't have to be a value actually in the distribution. The mean is the average of the values, the balance point. The mean can be a decimal number, even if all the scores in the distribution have to be whole numbers (a mean of 2.3 children, for example). (By the way, this analogy to blocks on a board, in reality, would work out precisely only if the board had no weight of its own.)

FORMULA FOR THE MEAN AND STATISTICAL SYMBOLS

The rule for figuring the mean is to add up all the scores and divide by the number of scores. This can be stated as the following formula:

Tip for Success

Think of each formula as a statistical recipe. The ingredients of each formula are written using statistical symbols. Before you use each formula, be sure you know what statistical term each symbol stands for. (For example, as you will learn later in this chapter, the symbol "N" means "number of scores".) Then, step by step, carefully follow the formula to come up with the end result. As with any recipe, it make take a couple of attempts to master this process; but after that, you should get perfect results every time. Also, don't forget to focus on understanding the logic behind each formula.

The mean is the sum of the scores divided by the number of scores.

$$M = \frac{\Sigma X}{N} \qquad\qquad (2\text{-}1)$$

M is a symbol for the mean. An alternative symbol, $\overline{X}$, sometimes called "X-bar," is also used. But M is most commonly used in research publications. In fact, you should know that there is not a general agreement for most of the symbols used in statistics. (In this book, we generally use the symbols most widely found in research publications.)

FIGURE 2–1 *Mean of the distribution of the numbers of years in office for 10 mayors, illustrated using blocks on a board balanced on a log.*

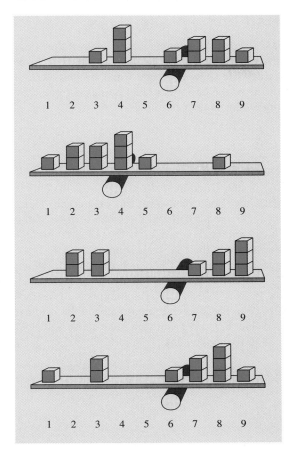

FIGURE 2-2 *Means of various distributions illustrated with blocks on a board balanced on a log.*

Σ, the capital Greek letter "sigma," is the symbol for "sum of." It means "add Σ
up all the numbers" for whatever follows. It is the most common special arithmetic symbol used in statistics.

X stands for the scores in the distribution of the variable *X*. We could have picked any letter. However, if there is only one variable, it is usually called *X*. In later chapters we use formulas with more than one variable. In those formulas, we use a second letter along with *X* (usually *Y*) or subscripts (such as X_1 and X_2.).

ΣX means "the sum of *X*." That is, this tells you to add up all the scores in the distribution of the variable *X*. Suppose *X* is the number of years in office in our example of 10 mayors: ΣX would be 60, the sum of $7 + 8 + 8 + 7 + 3 + 1 + 6 + 9 + 3 + 8$.

N stands for number—the number of scores in a distribution. In our example,   *N*
there are 10 scores. Thus, *N* equals 10.

Overall, the formula says to divide the sum of all the scores for the variable *X* by the total number of scores, *N*. In our example, this tells us that we divide 60 by 10. Put in terms of the formula,

$$M = \frac{\Sigma X}{N} = \frac{60}{10} = 6$$

ADDITIONAL EXAMPLES OF FIGURING THE MEAN

Consider the examples from Chapter 1. The first example was a study of the stress level of 151 students in their first week taking a statistics course (Aron, Paris, & Aron, 1995). The 151 stress level ratings are shown on page 4 and are laid out as a frequency table in Table 1–2. The mean of the 151 stress level ratings is figured by adding up all the ratings and dividing by the number of ratings.

$$M = \frac{\Sigma X}{N} = \frac{975}{151} = 6.46$$

This tells you that the average rating on the 10-point stress scale was 6.46. This is clearly higher than the middle of that scale. You can also see this on a graph. Think again of the histogram as a pile of blocks on a board and the mean of 6.46 as the point where the board balances on a fulcrum (see Figure 2–3). This single representative value much simplifies the information in the 151 stress scores.

Similarly, consider the other main example from Chapter 1, the study in which 94 college students, for a full week, recorded every social interaction of 10 minutes or longer (McLaughlin-Volpe, Aron, & Reis, 2001). The actual numbers of interactions for the students are listed on page 6. In Chapter 1, we organized the original scores into a frequency table (see Table 1–3). We can now take those same 94 scores, add them up, and divide by 94 to figure the mean:

$$M = \frac{\Sigma X}{N} = \frac{1,635}{94} = 17.39$$

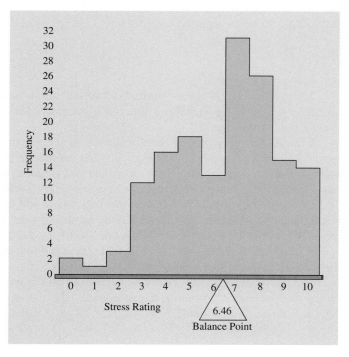

FIGURE 2–3   *Analogy of blocks on a board balanced on a fulcrum showing the mean for 151 statistics students' ratings of their stress level. (Data from Aron et al., 1995)*

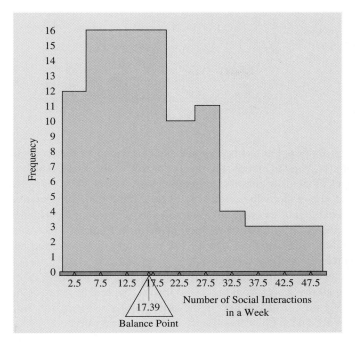

FIGURE 2-4   *Analogy of blocks on a board balanced on a fulcrum illustrating the mean for number of social interactions during a week for 94 college students. (Data from McLaughlin-Volpe et al., 2001)*

This is shown in Figure 2–4.

This tells us that during this week these students had an average of 17.39 social interactions.

STEPS FOR FIGURING THE MEAN

You figure the mean in two steps.

> ❶ **Add up all the scores.** That is, figure ΣX.
> ❷ **Divide this sum by the number of scores.** That is, divide ΣX by N.

OTHER MEASURES OF THE REPRESENTATIVE VALUE OF A GROUP OF SCORES

The mean is only one of several ways of describing the representative (or typical) value in a group of scores. A different measure is the **mode.** The mode is the most common single number in a distribution. In our mayors' example, the mode is 8 because there are three mayors with 8 years served in office and no other number of years served in office with as many mayors. Another way to think of the mode is that it is the value with the largest frequency in a frequency table, the high point or peak of a distribution's frequency polygon or histogram (as shown in Figure 2–5).

In a perfectly symmetrical unimodal distribution, the mode is the same as the mean. However, what happens when the mode and the mean are not the same? In that situation the mode is usually not a very good representative value for scores in the distribution. In fact, sometimes researchers compare the mode to the mean in order to show that the distribution is *not* perfectly symmetrical and unimodal. Also, the mode can be a particularly poor representative value because it does not reflect

mode

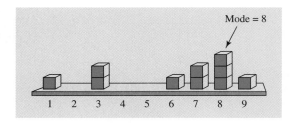

FIGURE 2–5 *The mode as the high point in a distribution's histogram, using the example of the number of years in office served by 10 mayors.*

many aspects of the distribution. For example, you can change some of the scores in a distribution without affecting the mode—but this is not true of the mean, which is affected by any changes in the distribution (see Figure 2–6).

On the other hand, the mode *is* the usual way of describing the representative value for a nominal variable. For example, if you know the religions of a particular group of people, the mode tells you which religion is the most frequent. However, when it comes to the numerical variables that we use most often in social and behavioral science research, the mode is rarely used.

Another different measure of the representative value of a group of scores is the **median.** If you line up all the scores from highest to lowest, the middle score is the median. As shown in Figure 2–7, if you line up the numbers of years in office from highest to lowest, the fifth and sixth scores (the two middle ones), are both 7s. Either way, the median is 7 years.

median

Tip for Success

One of the most common errors statistics students make when figuring the median is to forget to first line the scores up from highest to lowest.

FIGURE 2–6 *The effect on the mean and on the mode of changing some scores, using the example of the number of years in office served by 10 mayors.*

FIGURE 2–7 *The median is the middle score when scores are lined up from highest to lowest, using the example of the number of years in office served by 10 mayors.*

When you have an even number of scores, the median will be between two numbers. In that situation, the median is the average (the mean) of the two numbers.

Sometimes, the median is better than the mean as a representative value for a group of scores. This happens when there are a few extreme scores that would strongly affect the mean but would not affect the median. For example, suppose that among the 100 families on a banana plantation in Central America, 99 families have an annual income of $100 and 1 family (the owner's) has an annual income of $90,100. The mean family income on this plantation would be $1,000 (99 × 100 = 9,900; 9,900 + 90,100 = 100,000; 100,000/100 = 1,000). That is, no family has an income even close to $1,000, so this number is completely misleading. The median income in this example would be $100—an income much more representative of whomever you would meet if you walked up to someone randomly on the plantation.

As this example illustrates, social and behavioral scientists use the median as a descriptive statistic mainly in situations where there are a few extreme scores that would make the mean unrepresentative of most of the scores. An extreme score like this is called an **outlier.** There are also times when the median is used as part of more complex statistical methods. However, unless there are extreme scores, social and behavioral scientists almost always use the mean as the measure of the representative value of a group of scores. In fact, the mean is a fundamental building block for most other statistical techniques.

Web Link

http://www.phoenix5.org/articles/ GouldMessage.html. Read a brief, interesting article that presents a real-world example of the median and skewed distributions.

outlier

STEPS FOR FINDING THE MEDIAN

The procedure for finding the median can be summarized as three steps.

❶ **Line up all the scores from highest to lowest.**

❷ **Figure how many scores there are to the middle score, by adding 1 to the number of scores and dividing by 2.** For example, with 29 scores, adding 1 and dividing by 2 gives you 15. The 15th score is the middle score. If there are 50 scores, adding 1 and dividing by 2 gives you 25½. There are no half scores, so the 25th and 26th scores (the scores either side of 25½) are the middle scores.

❸ **Count up to the middle score or scores.** If you have one middle score, this is the median. If you have two middle scores, the median is the average (the mean) of these two scores.

HOW ARE YOU DOING?

1. Name and define three measures of the representative value of a group of scores.
2. Write the formula for the mean and define each of the symbols.
3. Figure the mean of the following scores: 2, 8, 3, 6, and 6.
4. For the following scores, find (a) the mode and (b) the median: 5, 4, 2, 8, 2.

ANSWERS:

1. The mean is the ordinary average—the sum of the scores divided by the number of scores. The mode is the most frequent score in a distribution. The median is the middle score— that is, if you line the scores up from highest to lowest, it is the score halfway along.
2. $M = \Sigma X/N$. M is the mean; Σ is the symbol for "sum of"—add up all the scores that follow; X is for the variable whose scores you are adding up; N is the number of scores.
3. $M = \Sigma X/N = (2 + 8 + 3 + 6 + 6)/5 = 5$.
4. (a) 2. (b) 4.

THE VARIANCE AND THE STANDARD DEVIATION

Researchers also want to know how spread out a distribution is. For example, suppose you were asked, "How old are the students in your statistics class?" At a city-based university with many returning and part-time students, the mean age might be 38. You could answer, "The average age of the students in my class is 38." However, this would not tell the whole story. You could, for example, have a mean of 38 because every student in the class was exactly 38 years old. If this is the case, the distribution is not spread out at all. In other words, there is no variation. Or, you could have a mean of 38 because exactly half the class was 18 and the other half was 58. In this situation, the distribution is much more spread out. There is considerable variation among the scores.

The general principle is that distributions with the same mean can have very different amounts of spread around the mean; also, distributions with different means can have the same amount of spread around the mean. To illustrate this, Figure 2–8a shows three different frequency distributions with the same mean but different amounts of spread around the mean and Figure 2–8b shows three different frequency distributions with different means but the same amount of spread.

THE VARIANCE

variance (SD^2)

The **variance (SD^2)** of a group of scores tells you how spread out the scores are around the mean.[1] To be precise, the variance is the average of each score's squared difference from the mean. Here are the four steps to figure the variance.

deviation score

❶ **Subtract the mean from each score.** This gives each score's **deviation score.** The deviation score is how far away the actual score is from the mean.

❷ **Square each of these deviation scores** (multiply each by itself). This gives each score's **squared deviation score.**

squared deviation score

❸ **Add up the squared deviation scores.** This total is called the **sum of squared deviations.**

sum of squared deviations

❹ **Divide the sum of squared deviations by the number of scores.** This gives the average of the squared deviations, called the variance.

This procedure may seem a bit awkward or hard to remember at first; but it works quite well. Suppose one distribution is more spread out than another. The

---

[1]This section focuses on the variance and standard deviation as measures of spread (or variation). There is also another way to describe the spread of a group of scores, the *range*—the highest score minus the lowest score. Suppose that for a particular class of students the highest score on a midterm is 98 and the lowest score on the midterm is 60; the range is 38 (that is, $98 - 60 = 38$). Researchers rarely use the range because it is a very crude way of describing the spread. It is crude because it considers only two scores from the group of scores and does not take into account how clumped together the scores are within the range.

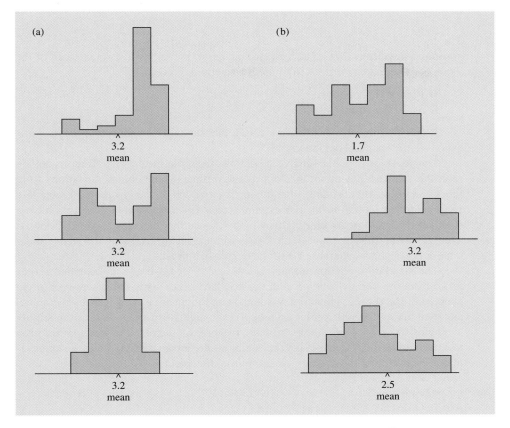

FIGURE 2–8   *Examples of distributions with (a) the same mean but different amounts of spread and (b) different means but the same amount of spread.*

more spread-out distribution has a larger variance because being spread makes the deviation scores bigger. If the deviation scores are bigger, the squared deviation scores also are bigger; thus the average of the squared deviation scores (the variance) is bigger.

In the example of the class in which everyone was exactly 38 years old, the variance would be exactly 0. That is, there would be no variance. (In terms of the numbers, each person's deviation score would be $38 - 38 = 0$; 0 squared is 0. The average of a bunch of zeros is 0.) By contrast, the class of half 18-year-olds and half 58-year-olds would have a rather large variance of 400. (The 18-year-olds would each have deviation scores of $18 - 38 = -20$. The 58-year-olds would have deviation scores of $58 - 38 = 20$. All the squared deviation scores, which are -20 squared or 20 squared, would come out to 400. The average of all 400s is 400.)

The variance is extremely important in many statistical procedures you will learn about later. However, the variance is rarely used as a descriptive statistic. This is because the variance is based on *squared* deviation scores, which do not give a very easy-to-understand sense of how spread out the actual, nonsquared scores are. For example, it is clear that a class with a variance of 400 has a more spread-out distribution than one whose variance is 10. However, the number 400 does not give an obvious insight into the actual variation among the ages, none of which are anywhere near 400.

THE STANDARD DEVIATION

standard deviation (SD)

The most widely used way of *describing* the spread of a group of scores is the **standard deviation (SD).** The standard deviation is the positive square root of the variance. There are two steps to figure the standard deviation.

❶ **Figure the variance.**
❷ **Take the square root.**

If the variance of a distribution is 400, the standard deviation is 20. If the variance is 9, the standard deviation is 3.

The variance is about squared deviations from the mean. Therefore, its square root, the standard deviation, is about direct, ordinary, not-squared deviations from the mean. *Roughly speaking, the standard deviation is the average amount that scores differ from the mean.* For example, consider a class where the ages have a standard deviation of 20 years. This would tell you that the ages are spread out, on average, about 20 years in each direction from the mean. Knowing the standard deviation gives you a general sense of the degree of spread.

The standard deviation usually is not *exactly* the average amount that scores differ from the mean. To be precise, the standard deviation is the square root of the average of the scores' squared deviations from the mean. This squaring, averaging, and then taking the square root usually gives a slightly different result from simply averaging the scores' deviations from the mean. Still, the result of this approach has technical advantages to outweigh this slight disadvantage of giving only an approximate description of the average variation from the mean.

FORMULAS FOR THE VARIANCE AND THE STANDARD DEVIATION

We have seen that the variance is the average squared deviation from the mean. Here is the formula for the variance

The variance is the sum of the squared deviations of the scores from the mean, divided by the number of scores.

$$SD^2 = \frac{\Sigma(X - M)^2}{N}$$

(2-2)

SD^2 is the symbol for the variance. (In Chapter 8 you learn another symbol, S^2. This other symbol is for a slightly different kind of variance.) SD is short for *standard deviation.* The symbol SD^2 emphasizes that the variance is the standard deviation squared.

The top part of the formula is the sum of squared deviations. X is for each score and M is the mean. Thus, $X - M$ is the score minus the mean, the deviation score. The exponent 2 tells you to square each deviation score. Finally, the sum sign (Σ) tells you to add together all these squared deviation scores. The bottom part of the formula tells you to divide the sum of squared deviation scores by N, the number of scores.

The standard deviation is the square root of the variance. So, if you already know the variance, the formula is

The standard deviation is the square root of the variance

$$SD = \sqrt{SD^2}$$

(2-3)

TABLE 2–1	Figuring of Variance and Standard Deviation in the Example of Number of Years Served by 10 Mayors			
Score (Number of Years Served)	−	Mean score (Mean Number of Years Served) =	Deviation score	Squared Deviation score
7		6	1	1
8		6	2	4
8		6	2	4
7		6	1	1
3		6	−3	9
1		6	−5	25
6		6	0	0
9		6	3	9
3		6	−3	9
8		6	2	4
			Σ: 0	66

$$\text{Variance} = SD^2 = \frac{\Sigma (X - M)^2}{N} = \frac{66}{10} = 6.6$$

$$\text{Standard deviation} = SD = \sqrt{SD^2} = \sqrt{6.6} = 2.57$$

EXAMPLE OF FIGURING THE VARIANCE AND THE STANDARD DEVIATION

Table 2–1 shows the figuring for the variance and standard deviation for our example of mayors. (The table assumes we already have figured out the mean to be 6 years in office.) Usually, it is easiest to do your figuring using a calculator, especially one with a square root key. The standard deviation of 2.57 tells you that roughly speaking, on average, the number of years the mayors were in office varied by about 2½ from the mean of 6.

ADDITIONAL EXAMPLE OF FIGURING THE VARIANCE AND THE STANDARD DEVIATION

Table 2–2 shows the figuring for the variance and standard deviation for the example of students' numbers of social interactions during a week. To save space, the table shows only the first few and last few scores.

Roughly speaking, this result indicates that a student's number of social interactions in a week varies from the mean by an average of 11.49 interactions. This can also be shown on a histogram (Figure 2–9).

COMPUTATIONAL AND DEFINITIONAL FORMULAS

In actual research situations, social and behavioral scientists must often figure the variance and the standard deviation for distributions with a great many scores, often involving decimals or large numbers. This can make the whole process quite time-consuming, even with a calculator. To deal with this problem, over the years researchers have developed a number of shortcut formulas to simplify the figuring. A shortcut formula of this type is called a **computational formula.** The computational formula for the variance is

computational formula

Tip for Success

When figuring the variance and standard deviation, lay your working out as shown in Tables 2–1 and 2–2. This will help to ensure that you follow all of the steps and end up with the correct answers.

Tip for Success

A common error when figuring the standard deviation is to jump straight from the sum of squared deviations to the standard deviation (by taking the square root of the sum of squared deviations). Remember, before finding the standard deviation, you first have to figure the variance (by dividing the sum of squared deviations by the number of scores, N). Then take the square root of the variance to find the standard deviation.)

TABLE 2–2 Figuring the Variance and Standard Deviation for Number of Social Interactions during a Week for 94 College Students

Number of Interactions	−	Mean Number of Interactions	=	Deviation Score	Squared Deviation Score
48		17.39		30.61	936.97
15		17.39		−2.39	5.71
33		17.39		15.61	243.67
3		17.39		−14.39	207.07
21		17.39		3.61	13.03
.		.		.	.
.		.		.	.
.		.		.	.
35		17.39		17.61	310.11
9		17.39		−8.39	70.39
30		17.39		12.61	159.01
8		17.39		−9.39	88.17
26		17.39		8.61	74.13
				Σ: 0.00	12,406.44

$$\text{Variance} = SD^2 = \frac{\Sigma(X - M)^2}{N} = \frac{12,406.44}{94} = 131.98$$

$$\text{Standard deviation} = \sqrt{SD^2} = \sqrt{131.98} = 11.49$$

Source: Data from McLaughlin-Volpe et al. (2001).

The variance is the sum of the squared scores minus the result of taking the sum of all the scores, squaring this sum and dividing by the number of scores, then taking this whole difference and dividing it by the number of scores.

$$SD^2 = \frac{\Sigma X^2 - ((\Sigma X)^2/N)}{N} \tag{2-4}$$

Note that ΣX^2 means that you square each score and then take the sum of these squared scores. However, $(\Sigma X)^2$ means that you add up all the scores first and then take the square of this sum. This formula is easier to use if you are figuring the variance for a lot of numbers by hand because you do not have to first find the deviation score for each score.

However, these days computational formulas are mainly of historical interest. They are used by researchers only when computers are not readily available to do the figuring. In fact, even many hand calculators are set up so that you need only enter the scores and press a button or two to get the variance and the standard deviation.

In this book, we give a few computational formulas (mainly in footnotes), just so you will have them if you someday do a research project with a lot of numbers and you don't have access to a computer with statistical software. However, we recommend *not* using the computational formulas when you are learning statistics. The problem is that the computational formulas tend to make it harder to understand the *meaning* of what you are figuring. It is much better to use the regular formulas we give when doing the practice problems. These are the formulas designed to help you

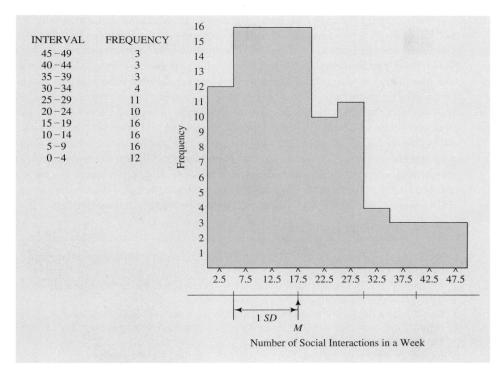

INTERVAL	FREQUENCY
45 – 49	3
40 – 44	3
35 – 39	3
30 – 34	4
25 – 29	11
20 – 24	10
15 – 19	16
10 – 14	16
5 – 9	16
0 – 4	12

FIGURE 2–9   *The standard deviation as the distance along the base of a histogram, using the example of number of social interactions in a week. (Data from McLaughlin-Volpe et al., 2001)*

strengthen your understanding of what the figuring *means*. These usual formulas we give are called **definitional formulas.**

definitional formula

The purpose of this book is to help you understand statistical procedures, not to turn you into a computer by having you memorize computational formulas you will rarely, if ever, use. To simplify the actual figuring, however, our practice problems generally use small groups of whole numbers. For students who have access to a computer and statistics software, the *Study Guide and Computer Workbook* accompanying this textbook includes material designed to give you experience doing statistics as social and behavioral scientists normally would, working with standard statistics programs on a computer.

THE VARIANCE AS THE SUM OF SQUARED DEVIATIONS DIVIDED BY N − 1

Researchers often use a slightly different kind of variance. We have defined the variance as the average of the squared deviation scores. Using that definition, you divide the sum of squared deviation scores by the number of scores. But you learn in Chapter 8 that for many purposes it is better to define the variance as the sum of squared deviation scores *divided by 1 less than the number of scores.* That is, for those purposes, the variance is the sum of squared deviations divided by $N − 1$. (As you learn in Chapter 8, you use this $N − 1$ approach when you have scores from a particular group of people and you want to estimate what the variance would be for the larger group of people these individuals represent.)

The variances and standard deviations given in research articles are usually figured using the $N - 1$ approach. Also, when calculators or computers give the variance or the standard deviation automatically, they may be figured in this way. (Note that you don't need special statistics software to figure the variance, standard deviation, and many other statistical procedures—most spreadsheet programs can also do the figuring automatically.) The approach you are learning in this chapter of dividing by N is entirely correct for our purpose here, which is describing the variation in a particular group of scores. It is also entirely correct for the material covered in the rest of this chapter (Z scores of the kind we are using), and for the material you learn in Chapters 3 through 7. We mention this $N - 1$ approach now only so you will not be confused when you read about variance or standard deviation in other places or if your calculator or a computer program gives a surprising result. To keep things simple, we wait to discuss the $N - 1$ approach until it is needed, starting in Chapter 8.

HOW ARE YOU DOING?

1. (a) Define the variance and (b) indicate what it tells you about a distribution and how this is different from what the mean tells you.
2. (a) Define the standard deviation, (b) describe its relation to the variance, and (c) explain what it tells you approximately about a group of scores.
3. Give the full formula for the variance and indicate what each of the symbols mean.
4. Figure the (a) variance and (b) standard deviation for the following scores: 2, 4, 3, and 7 ($M = 4$).
5. Explain the difference between a definitional and a computational formula.

ANSWERS:

1. (a) The variance is the average of each score's squared differences from the mean. (b) The variance tells you about how spread out the scores are, while the mean tells you the representative value of the distribution.
2. (a) The standard deviation is the square root of the average of the squared deviations from the mean. (b) The standard deviation is the square root of the variance. (c) The standard deviation tells you approximately the average amount that scores differ from the mean.
3. $SD^2 = \Sigma (X - M)^2/N$. SD^2 is the variance. Σ means the sum of what follows. X is for the scores for the variable being studied. M is the mean of the scores. N is the number of scores.
4. (a) $SD^2 = \Sigma (X - M)^2/N = [(2 - 4)^2 + (4 - 4)^2 + (3 - 4)^2 + (7 - 4)^2]/4 = 14/4 = 3.5$
   (b) $SD = \sqrt{SD^2} = \sqrt{3.5} = 1.87$.
5. A definitional formula is the standard formula that is in the straightforward form that shows the meaning of what the formula is figuring. A computational formula is a mathematically equivalent variation of the definitional formula that is easier to use if figuring by hand with a lot of scores, but it tends not to show the underlying meaning.

Z SCORES

So far in this chapter you have learned about describing a group of scores in terms of a representative score and variation. In this section, you learn how to describe a particular score in terms of where it fits into the overall group of scores. That is, you learn to describe a score in terms of whether it is above or below the average and how much it is above or below the average.

Suppose that you were told that a particular mayor, the Honorable Julia Hernandez, has served in this office in her town for 9 years. Now, suppose we did not know anything about the number of years served in office by other mayors in the re-

BOX 2–1 The Psychology of Statistics and the Tyranny of the Mean

Looking in the social and behavioral science research journals, you would think that statistical methods are their sole tool and language, but there have also been rebellions against the reign of statistics. We are most familiar with this issue in psychology, where one of the most unexpected oppositions came from the leader of behaviorism, the school of psychology most dedicated to keeping the field strictly scientific.

Behaviorism opposed the study of inner states because inner events are impossible to observe objectively. (Today most research psychologists claim to measure inner events indirectly but objectively.) Behaviorism's most famous advocate, B. F. Skinner, was quite opposed to statistics. Skinner even said, "I would much rather see a graduate student in psychology taking a course in physical chemistry than in statistics. And I would include [before statistics] other sciences, even poetry, music, and art" (Evans, 1976, p. 93).

Skinner was constantly pointing to the information lost by averaging the results of a number of cases. For instance, Skinner (1956) cited the example of three overeating mice—one naturally obese, one poisoned with gold, and one whose hypothalamus had been altered. Each had a different curve for learning to press a bar for food. If these learning curves had been summed or merged statistically, the result would have represented no actual eating habits of any real mouse at all. As Skinner said, "These three individual curves contain more information than could probably ever be generated with measures requiring statistical treatment, yet they will be viewed with suspicion by many psychologists because they are single cases" (p. 232).

A different voice of caution was raised by another school of psychology, humanistic psychology, which began in the 1950s as a "third force" in reaction to Freudian psychoanalysis and behaviorism. The point of humanistic psychology was that human consciousness should be studied intact, as a whole, as it is experienced by individuals. Although statistics can be usefully applied to ascertain the mathematical relationships between phenomena, including events in consciousness, human conscious experience can never be fully explained by reducing it to numbers (any more than it can be reduced to words). Each individual's experience is unique.

This viewpoint existed in psychology even before humanistic psychology. In clinical psychology and the study of personality, voices have always been raised in favor of the in-depth study of one person instead of or as well as the averaging of persons. The philosophical underpinnings of the in-depth study of individuals can be found in phenomenology, which began in Europe after World War I (Husserl, 1970). This viewpoint has been important throughout the social sciences, not just in psychology.

Today, the rebellion is led in psychology by qualitative research methodologies (e.g., McCracken, 1988), an approach that is much more prominent in other social and behavioral sciences. The qualitative research methods were developed mainly in anthropology and can involve long interviews or observations of a few individuals. The highly skilled researcher decides, as the event is taking place, what is important to remember, record, and pursue through more questions or observations. The mind of the researcher is the main tool because, according to this approach, only that mind can find the important relationships among the many categories of events arising in the respondent's speech.

Many who favor qualitative methods argue for a blend: First, discover the important categories through a qualitative approach. Then, determine their incidence in the larger population through quantitative methods. Too often, these advocates would argue, quantitative researchers jump to conclusions about a phenomenon without first exploring the human experience of it through free-response interviews or observations.

Finally, Carl Jung, founder of Jungian psychology, sometimes spoke of the "statistical mood" and its effect on a person's feeling of uniqueness. The Jungian analyst Marie Louise von Franz (1979) wrote about Jung's thoughts on this subject: When we walk down a street and observe the hundreds of blank faces and begin to feel diminished, or even so overwhelmed by overpopulation that we are glad that humans don't live forever, this is the statistical mood. We feel how much we are just part of the crowd, ordinary. Yet von Franz points out that if some catastrophe were to happen, each person would respond uniquely. There is at least as much irregularity to life as ordinariness. As she puts it,

(continued)

The fact that this table does not levitate, but remains where it is, is only because the billions and billions and billions of electrons which constitute the table tend statistically to behave like that. But each electron in itself could do something else. (pp. IV–17)

Likewise, when we are in love, we feel that the other person is unique and wonderful. Yet in a statistical mood, we realize that the other person is ordinary, like many others.

Jung did not cherish individual uniqueness just to be romantic about it, however. He held that the important contributions to culture tend to come from people thinking at least a little independently or creatively, and their independence is damaged by this statistical mood.

Furthermore, von Franz argues that a statistical mood is damaging to love and life. "An act of loyalty is required towards one's own feelings" (pp. IV–18). Feeling "makes your life and your relationships and deeds feel unique and gives them a definite value" (pp. IV–19). In particular, feeling the importance of our single action makes immoral acts—war and killing, for example—less possible. We cannot count the dead as numbers but must treat them as persons with emotions and purposes, like ourselves.

In short, there have been many who have questioned an exclusively statistical view of our subject matters, and their voices should be considered too as you proceed with your study of what has become the predominant, but not exclusive, means of doing behavioral and social science.

gion. In that case, it would be hard to tell whether this mayor had served a lot or a few years in relation to other mayors in her region. However, suppose we do know that for the 10 mayors in her region, the mean is 6 and the standard deviation is 2.57. With this knowledge, it is clear that Ms. Hernandez has served an above-average number of years. It is also clear that the amount she has served more than the average (3 years in office more than average) was a bit more than the amount mayors in her region typically vary from the average. This is all shown in Figure 2–10.

WHAT IS A Z SCORE?

Z score

A **Z score** is the number of standard deviations the actual score is above the mean (if it is positive) or below the mean (if it is negative). The standard deviation now becomes a kind of yardstick, a unit of measure in its own right. In our mayoral example, Ms. Hernandez, who has served 9 years in office, has a Z score of +1.17 be-

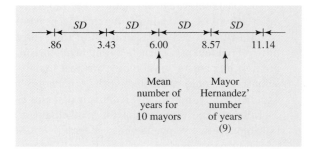

FIGURE 2–10   *Number of years in office served by a particular mayor (Ms. Hernandez) in relation to the overall distribution of number of years in office served by all mayors in a particular (fictional) region.*

FIGURE 2–11   *Scales of Z scores and raw scores in the mayoral example.*

cause her years in office are 1.17 standard deviations above the mean (a little more than 1 standard deviation of 2.57 years in office above the mean). Another mayor, the Honorable Samuel Phillips, has served 6 years in office. He has a *Z* score of 0 because his score is exactly the mean. That is, his number of years in office is 0 standard deviations above or below the mean. What about a mayor who had served only 1 year in office? That mayor has served 5 years less than average. This would be nearly 2 standard deviations below the mean (a *Z* score of −1.95). In terms of years in office, this mayor would be about twice as far below average as mayors in this region typically vary from the average.

Z scores have many practical uses. They also are part of many of the statistical procedures you learn later in this book. It is important that you become very familiar with them.

Z SCORES AS A SCALE

Figure 2–11 shows, for our mayoral example, a scale of *Z* scores lined up against a scale of raw scores. A **raw score** is an ordinary score, as opposed to a *Z* score. The two scales are something like a ruler with inches lined up on one side and centimeters on the other.

raw score

Suppose that a developmental specialist observed 3-year-old Peter in a standardized laboratory situation playing with other children of the same age. During the observation, the specialist counted the number of times Peter spoke to the other children. The result, over several observations, is that Peter spoke to other children about 8 times per hour of play. Without any standard of comparison, it would be hard to draw any conclusions from this. Let's assume, however, that it was known from previous research that under similar conditions the mean number of times children speak is 12, with a standard deviation of 4. Clearly, Peter spoke less often than other children in general, but not extremely less often. Peter would have a *Z* score of −1 (*M* = 12 and *SD* = 4, thus a score of 8 is 1 *SD* below *M*).

Suppose Ian was observed speaking to other children 20 times in an hour. Ian would clearly be unusually talkative, with a *Z* score of +2. Ian would speak not merely more than the average but more by twice as much as children tend to vary from the average! (See Figure 2–12.)

FIGURE 2–12   *Number of times each hour that two children spoke, expressed as raw scores and Z scores.*

Z SCORES AS PROVIDING A GENERALIZED STANDARD OF COMPARISON

Another advantage of Z scores is that scores on completely different variables can be made into Z scores and compared. With Z scores, the mean is always 0 and the standard deviation is always 1. Suppose the same children in our example were also measured on a test of language skill. In this situation, we could directly compare the Z scores on language skill to the Z scores on speaking to other children. Let's say Peter had a score of 100 on the language skill test. If the mean on that test was 82 and the standard deviation was 6, then Peter is much better than average at language skill, with a Z score of +3. Thus, it seems unlikely that Peter's less-than-usual amount of speaking to other children is due to poorer-than-usual language skill. (See Figure 2–13.)

Notice in this latest example that by using Z scores, we can directly compare the results of both the specialist's observation of the amount of talking and the language skill test. This is almost as wonderful as being able to compare apples and oranges! Converting a number to a Z score is a bit like converting the words for measurement in various obscure languages into one language that everyone can understand—inches, cubits, and zinqles (we made up that last one), for example, into centimeters. It is a very valuable tool.

FORMULA TO CHANGE A RAW SCORE TO A Z SCORE

As we have seen, a Z score is the number of standard deviations the raw score is above or below the mean. To figure a Z score, subtract the mean from the raw score, giving the deviation score. Then, divide the deviation score by the standard deviation. In symbols, the formula is

A Z score is the raw score minus the mean, divided by the standard deviation.

$$Z = \frac{X - M}{SD} \qquad (2\text{-}5)$$

For example, using the formula for the child who scored 100 on the language test,

$$Z = \frac{X - M}{SD} = \frac{100 - 82}{6} = \frac{18}{6} = 3$$

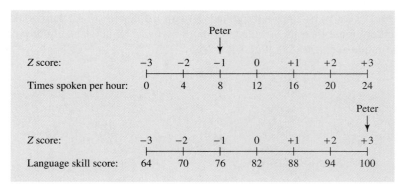

FIGURE 2–13 *Scales of Z scores and raw scores for number of times spoken per hour and language skill, showing the first child's score on each.*

STEPS TO CHANGE A RAW SCORE TO A Z SCORE

❶ **Figure the deviation score: Subtract the mean from the raw score.**
❷ **Figure the Z score: Divide the deviation score by the standard deviation.**

Using these steps for the child who scored 100 on the language test:

❶ **Figure the deviation score: Subtract the mean from the raw score.**
$100 - 82 = 18$
❷ **Figure the Z score: Divide the deviation score by the standard deviation.**
$18/6 = 3$

FORMULA TO CHANGE A Z SCORE TO A RAW SCORE

To change a Z score back to a raw score, the process is reversed: You multiply the Z score by the standard deviation and then add the mean. The formula is

(2-6)
$$X = (Z)(SD) + M$$

The raw score is the Z score times the standard deviation, plus the mean

(Remember that when two symbols, or two parentheses, are next to each other in a formula, you are supposed to multiply them. If we used "X" to mean multiply in a formula like this, it might be confused with the X meaning the score.)

Suppose a child has a Z score of -1.5 on the language ability test, then the child is 1.5 standard deviations below the mean. Because the standard deviation in this example is 6 raw score points, the child is 9 raw score points below the mean. The mean is 82. Thus, 9 points below this is 73. Using the formula,

$$X = (Z)(SD) + M = (21.5)(6) + 82 = 29 + 82 = 73$$

STEPS TO CHANGE A Z SCORE TO A RAW SCORE

❶ **Figure the deviation score: Multiply the Z score by the standard deviation.**
❷ **Figure the raw score: Add the mean to the deviation score.**

Using these steps for the child with a Z score of -1.5 on the language test:

❶ **Figure the deviation score: Multiply the Z score by the standard deviation.** $-1.5 \times 6 = -9$
❷ **Figure the raw score: Add the mean to the deviation score.** $-9 + 82 = 73$

FIGURE 2–14   *Raw score and Z score scales for 151 statistics students' ratings of their stress levels, showing the scores of two sample students. (Data from Aron et al., 1995)*

ADDITIONAL EXAMPLES OF CHANGING RAW SCORES TO Z SCORES AND VICE VERSA

Consider again the stress ratings example. The mean of the 151 students was 6.46, and the standard deviation was 2.30. Figure 2–14 shows the raw score and Z score scales. Suppose a student's stress raw score is 9. That student is well above the mean. Specifically, using the formula

$$Z = \frac{X - M}{SD} = \frac{9 - 6.46}{2.30} = \frac{2.54}{2.30} = 1.10$$

That is, the student's stress level is 1.10 standard deviations above the mean.

Another student has a Z score of −2.81, a stress level well below the mean. You can find the exact raw stress score for this student using the formula

$$X = (Z)\,(SD) + M = (-2.81)\,(2.30) + 6.46 = -6.46 + 6.46 = 0$$

Let's also consider some examples from the study of students' numbers of social interactions in a week (McLaughlin-Volpe et al., 2001). The mean is 17.39 and the standard deviation is 11.49. A student who had 17 interactions in a week had a deviation score of −.39 (that is, 17 − 17.39 = −.39). The Z score is then −.03 (that is, −.39/11.49 = −.03). This number of interactions is just below the mean. Similarly, a student who has 36 social interactions in a week has a deviation score of 18.61 (that is, 36 − 17.39 = 18.61). The Z score is 1.62 (that is, 18.61/11.49 = 1.62). This student is 1.62 standard deviations above the mean in terms of social interactions in a week.

To go the other way, suppose that you knew that a student's Z score was .57. This student's raw score would be the Z score times the standard deviation, plus the mean: (.57) (11.49) + 17.39 = 23.94 (rounded off, this person had 24 social interactions). This is all shown in Figure 2–15.

HOW ARE YOU DOING?

1. What is a Z score (that is, how is it related to a raw score)?
2. Write the formula for changing a raw score to a Z score, and define each of the symbols.
3. For a particular group of scores, M = 20 and SD = 5. Give the Z score for (a) 30, (b) 15, (c) 20, and (d) 22.5.

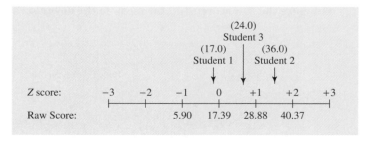

FIGURE 2–15 *Raw score and Z score scales for 94 students' number of social interactions in a week, showing scores of three sample students (Data from McLaughlin-Volpe et al., 2001)*

4. Write the formula for changing a *Z* score to a raw score, and define each of the symbols.
5. For a particular group of scores, $M = 10$ and $SD = 2$. Give the raw score for a *Z* score of (a) +2, (b) +.5, (c) 0, and (d) −3.
6. Suppose a person has a *Z* score for overall health of +2 and a *Z* score for overall sense of humor of +1. What does it mean to say that this person is healthier than she is funny?

ANSWERS

1. A *Z* score is the number of standard deviations a raw score is above or below the mean.
2. $Z = (X − M)/SD$. *Z* is the *Z* score; *X* is the raw score; *M* is the mean; *SD* is the standard deviation.
3. (a) $Z = (X − M)/SD = (30 − 20)/5 = 10/5 = 2$; (b) −1; (c) 0; (d) +.5
4. $X = (Z)(SD) + M$. *X* is the raw score; *Z* is the *Z* score; *SD* is the standard deviation; *M* is the mean.
5. (a) $X = (Z)(SD) + M = (2)(2) + 10 = 4 + 10 = 14$; (b) 11; (c) 10; (d) 4.
6. This person is more above the average in health (in terms of how much people typically vary from average in health) than this person is above the average in humor (in terms of how much people typically vary from the average in humor).

MEAN, VARIANCE, STANDARD DEVIATION, AND *Z* SCORES IN RESEARCH ARTICLES

The mean and the standard deviation (and occasionally, the variance) are commonly reported in research articles. The median and the mode are less often reported in research articles. *Z* scores are rarely reported in research articles. Sometimes the mean and standard deviation are included in the text of an article. For example, our fictional political scientist, in a research article about the mayors of this region, would write, "At the time of the study, the mean number of years in office for the 10 mayors in this region was 6.0 ($SD = 2.57$)."

More commonly, however, means and standard deviations are given in tables, especially if there are different groups studied, or several variables are involved. For example, as part of a study published in the *American Journal of Public Health,* Cohen and colleagues (2003) looked at the health of people living in 107 cities in the United States. (The 107 cities represent all U.S. cities with populations over 150,000.) They carried out the study using information obtained from the 1990 U.S. Census, the Centers for Disease Control and Prevention, and the National Center for Health Statistics. As part of their report, Cohen and her colleagues included a table (see Table 2–3, reproduced from Cohen and colleagues' Table 1) showing demographic information for the 107 cities. The demographic variables they looked at include the percentage of people married, the percentage of people unemployed, and the number of boarded-up housing units per 1,000 housing units. For each variable, they listed the mean, the standard deviation, the minimum, and the maximum. As you can see, the table provides a concise summary of the demographic variables for the 107 cities.

A particularly interesting example is shown in Table 2–4 (reproduced from Norcross, Hanych, & Terranova, 1996). The table shows the application and enrollment statistics for psychology doctoral programs, broken down by area of psychology and year (1973, 1979, and 1992). The table does not give standard deviations, but it does give both means and medians. For example, in 1992 the mean number of applicants to doctoral counseling psychology programs was 120.2, but the median was only 110. This suggests that there were some programs with very high numbers of applicants that skewed the distribution. In fact, you can see from the table that in almost every case, and for both applications and enrollments, the means are

TABLE 2–3 Demographic Data on 107 U.S. Cities

	Mean	SD	Minimum	Maximum
1990 population	493,476	812,742	143,485	7,322,564
Percentage Black	23.14	17.78	1.32	75.67
Percentage married	50.13	6.40	35.00	63.77
Percentage in poverty	17.56	5.69	4.25	32.41
Percentage with less than high school education	9.14	4.97	2.35	31.92
Percentage unemployed	7.45	2.52	2.80	19.67
Boarded up units per 1000	0.709	0.657	0.02	3.61
Percentage population change from 1980 to 1990	11.00	19.72	16.41	89.53
Percentage uninsured	14.33	5.64	5.00	29.70

Note: Data are from the 1990 U.S. Census.
Source: Cohen, D. D., Mason, K., Bedimo, A., Scribner, R., Bosolo, V., & Farley, T. A. (2003). Neighborhood physical conditions and health. *American Journal of Public Health, 93,* 467–471.

TABLE 2–4 Application and Enrollment Statistics by Area and Year: Doctoral Programs

	Applications									Enrollments	
	N of programs			M			Mdn			M	Mdn
Program	1973[a]	1979[a]	1992	1973[a]	1979[a]	1992	1973[a]	1979[a]	1992	1992	1992
Clinical	105	130	225	314.4	252.6	191.1	290	234	168	12.0	8
Cognitive			47			24.6			22	2.6	2
Community	4	2	5	90.5		24.4	60		23	3.2	2
Counseling	29	43	62	133.4	90.9	120.2	120	84	110	7.3	6
Developmental	56	72	97	54.1	38.9	27.6	41	30	24	2.8	2
Educational	23	28	30	67.8	39.7	20.0	34	26	12	6.0	4
Experimental and general	118	127	78	56.2	33.2	31.3	42	25	26	4.4	3
Health			7			40.7			30	4.4	5
Industrial/organizational	20	25	49	39.9	54.7	66.2	37	48	70	4.9	4
Personality	23	15	10	42.5	24.7	12.3	33	17	6	1.0	1
Perception/psychophysics			15			8.3			6	1.4	1
Physiological/biopsychology	40	43	76	33.2	29.3	20.0	29	24	20	3.9	2
School	30	39	56	78.5	54.0	31.3	53	34	32	5.4	5
Social	58	72	59	46.7	30.9	47.1	40	24	37	3.3	3
Other	47	37	273	61.6	74.1	26.6	27	25	15	3.3	2
Total	566	645	1,089	106.1	85.2	69.4			31	5.6	4

Note. The academic years correspond to the 1975–1976, 1981–1982, and 1994 editors of *Graduate Study in Psychology,* respectively.
[a]Data are from Stoup and Benjamin (1982).
Source: Norcross, J. C, Hanych, J. M, & Terranova, R. D. (1996). Graduate study in psychology: 1992–1993. *American Psychologist, 51,* 631–643. Copyright © 1996 by The American Psychological Association. Reprinted with permission of the authors and the American Psychological Association.

typically higher than the medians. (You may also be struck by just how competitive it is to get into doctoral programs in many areas of psychology. It is our experience that one of the factors that makes a lot of difference is doing well in statistics courses!)

SUMMARY

1. The mean is the most commonly used way of describing the representative value of a group of scores. The mean is the ordinary average—the sum of the scores divided by the number of scores. In symbols, $M = \Sigma X/N$.

2. Other, less frequently used ways of describing the representative value of a group of scores are the mode (the most common single value) and the median (the value of the middle score if all the scores were lined up from highest to lowest).

3. The variation among a group of scores can be described by the variance— the average of the squared deviation of each score from the mean. In symbols, $SD^2 = \Sigma(X - M)^2/N$.

4. The variation among a group of scores can also be described by the standard deviation. The standard deviation is the square root of the variance. In symbols, $SD = \sqrt{SD^2}$. It can be best understood as approximately the average amount that scores differ from the mean.

5. A Z score is the number of standard deviations a raw score is above or below the mean. Among other uses, with Z scores you can compare scores on variables that have different scales.

6. Means and standard deviations are often given in research articles in the text or in tables. Z scores rarely are reported in research articles.

KEY TERMS

mean (M) (p. 30)
Σ (sum of) (p. 31)
N (the number of scores) (p. 31)
mode (p. 33)
median (p. 34)
outlier (p. 35)
variance (SD^2) (p. 36)

deviation score (p. 36)
squared deviation score (p. 36)
sum of squared deviations (p. 36)
standard deviation (SD) (p. 38)

computational formula (p. 39)
definitional formula (p. 41)
Z score (p. 44)
raw score (p. 45)

EXAMPLE WORKED-OUT PROBLEMS

FIGURING THE MEAN

Find the mean for the following scores: 8, 6, 6, 9, 6, 5, 6, 2.

ANSWER

You can figure the mean using the formula or the steps.
    Using the formula: $M = \Sigma X/N = 48/8 = 6$.
    Using the steps:

❶ **Add up all the scores.** $8 + 6 + 6 + 9 + 6 + 5 + 6 + 2 = 48$
❷ **Divide this sum by the number of scores.** $48/8 = 6$

FINDING THE MEDIAN

Find the median for the following scores: 1, 7, 4, 2, 3, 6, 2, 9, 7.

ANSWER

❶ **Line up all the scores from highest to lowest.** 9, 7, 7, 6, 4, 3, 2, 2, 1.
❷ **Figure how many scores there are to the middle score by adding 1 to the number of scores and dividing by 2.** There are 9 scores, so the middle score is 9 plus 1, divided by 2, which comes out to 5. The middle score is the fifth score.
❸ **Count up to the middle score or scores.** The fifth score is a 4, so the median is 4.

FIGURING THE SUM OF SQUARED DEVIATIONS AND THE VARIANCE

Find the sum of squared deviations and the variance for the following scores: 8, 6, 6, 9, 6, 5, 6, 2. (These are the same scores used above for the mean. $M = 6$.)

ANSWER

You can figure the sum of squared deviations and the variance using the formulas or the steps.

Using the formulas:

Sum of squared deviations $= \Sigma(X - M)^2 = (8 - 6)^2 + (6 - 6)^2 + (6 - 6)^2 + (9 - 6)^2 + (6 - 6)^2 + (5 - 6)^2 + (6 - 6)^2 + (2 - 6)^2$
$= 2^2 + 0^2 + 0^2 + 3^2 + 0^2 + -1^2 + 0^2 + -4^2 = 4 + 0 + 0 + 9 + 0 + 1 + 0 + 16 = 30$
$SD^2 = \Sigma(X - M)^2/N = 30/8 = 3.75$

Table 2–5 shows the figuring, using the following steps:

❶ **Subtract the mean from each score.** This gives deviation scores of 2, 0, 0, 3, 0, −1, 0, −4.
❷ **Square each of these deviation scores.** This gives squared deviation scores of 4, 0, 0, 9, 0, 1, 0, 16.

TABLE 2–5 Figuring for Example Worked-Out Problem for the Sum of Squared Deviations and Variance Using Steps

Score	Mean	❶ Deviation	❷ Squared Deviation
8	6	2	4
6	6	0	0
6	6	0	0
9	6	3	9
6	6	0	0
5	6	−1	1
6	6	0	0
2	6	−4	16
			$\Sigma = 30$ ❸

❹ Variance = 30/8 = 3.75

❸ **Add up the squared deviation scores.** $4 + 0 + 0 + 9 + 0 + 1 + 0 + 16 = 30$. This is the sum of squared deviations.

❹ **Divide the sum of squared deviations by the number of scores.** The sum of squared deviations, 30, divided by the number of scores, 8, gives a variance of 3.75.

FIGURING THE STANDARD DEVIATION

Find the standard deviation for the following scores: 8, 6, 6, 9, 6, 5, 6, 2. (These are the same scores used above for the mean, sum of squared deviations, and variance. $SD^2 = 3.75$.)

ANSWER

You can figure the standard deviation using the formula or the steps.

Using the formula: $SD = \sqrt{SD^2} = \sqrt{3.75} = 1.94$.

Using the steps:

❶ **Figure the variance.** The variance (from above) is 3.75.

❷ **Take the square root.** The square root of 3.75 is 1.94.

CHANGING A RAW SCORE TO A Z SCORE

A distribution has a mean of 80 and a standard deviation of 20. Find the Z score for a raw score of 65.

ANSWER

You can change a raw score to a Z score using the formula or the steps.

Using the formula: $Z = (X - M)/SD = (65 - 80)/20 = -15/20 = -.75$

Using the steps:

❶ **Figure the deviation score: Subtract the mean from the raw score.** $65 - 80 = -15$

❷ **Figure the Z score: Divide the deviation score by the standard deviation.** $-15/20 = -.75$

CHANGING A Z SCORE TO A RAW SCORE

A distribution has a mean of 200 and a standard deviation of 50. A person has a Z score of 1.26. What is the person's raw score?

ANSWER

You can change a Z score to a raw score using the formula or the steps.

Using the formula: $X = (Z)(SD) + M = (1.26)(50) + 200 = 63 + 200 = 263$

Using the steps:

❶ **Figure the deviation score: Multiply the Z score by the standard deviation.** $1.26 \times 50 = 63$

❷ **Figure the raw score: Add the mean to the deviation score.** $63 + 200 = 263$

PRACTICE PROBLEMS

These problems involve figuring. Most real-life statistics problems are done on a computer with special statistical software. Even if you have such software, do these problems by hand (with the help of a calculator) to ingrain the method in your mind. Also, in all problems involving figuring, be sure to show your work.

For practice in using a computer to solve statistics problems, refer to the computer section of each chapter of the *Student's Study Guide and Computer Workbook* that accompanies this text.

All data are fictional unless an actual citation is given.

For answers to Set I problems, see pp. 423–24.

SET I

1. Find the (a) mean, (b) median, (c) sum of squared deviations, (d) variance, and (e) standard deviation for the following scores:

   32, 28, 24, 28, 28, 31, 35, 29, 26

2. Find the (a) mean, (b) median, (c) sum of squared deviations, (d) variance, and (e) standard deviation for the following scores:

   6, 1, 4, 2, 3, 4, 6, 6

3. Here are the noon temperatures (in degrees Celsius) in a particular Canadian city on December 26 for the 10 years from 1995 through 2004: -5, -4, -1, -1, 0, -8, -5, -9, -13, and -24. Describe the representative (typical) temperature and the amount of variation to a person who has never had a course in statistics. Give three ways of describing the representative temperature and two ways of describing its variation, explaining the differences and how you figured each. (You will learn more if you try to write your own answer first, before reading our answer at the back of the book.)

4. A researcher is studying the amygdala (a part of the brain involved in emotion). Six participants in a particular fMRI (brain scan) study are measured for the increase in activation of their amygdala while they are viewing pictures of violent scenes. The activation increases are .43, .32, .64, .21, .29, and .51. Figure the (a) mean and (b) standard deviation for these six activation increases. (c) Explain what you have done and what the results mean to a person who has never had a course in statistics.

5. On a measure of concern for the environment, the mean is 79 and the standard deviation is 12 (scores on the measure can vary from 0 to 150). What are the Z scores for each of the following raw scores? (a) 91, (b) 68, and (c) 103.

6. If the mean of a measure is -11.46 and the standard deviation is 2.28, what are the Z scores for each of the following raw scores? (a) -13.12, (b) -7.26, and (c) -11.23.

7. If the mean of a measure is 145 and the standard deviation is 19, what are the raw scores for each of the following Z scores? (a) 0, (b) 1.43, (c) -2.54.

8. Six months after a divorce, the former wife and husband each take a test that measures divorce adjustment. The wife's score is 63, and the husband's score is 59. Overall, the mean score for divorced women on this test is 60 ($SD = 6$); the mean score for divorced men is 55 ($SD = 4$). Which of the two has adjusted better to the divorce in relation to other divorced people of their own gender? Explain your answer to a person who has never had a course in statistics.

9. A researcher studied the number of nights students reported having too little sleep over a 4-week period. In an article describing the results of the study, the researcher reports: "The mean number of nights of too little sleep was 6.84 ($SD = 3.18$)." Explain these results to a person who has never had a course in statistics.

10. In a study by Gonzaga, Keltner, Londahl, and Smith (2001), romantic couples answered questions about how much they loved their partner and also were

TABLE 2–6 Mean Levels of Emotions and Cue Display in Study 1

Indicator	Women (n = 60)		Men (n = 60)	
	M	SD	M	SD
Emotion reports				
Self-reported love	5.02	2.16	5.11	2.08
Partner-estimated love	4.85	2.13	4.58	2.20
Affiliation-cue display				
Affirmative head nods	1.28	2.89	1.21	1.91
Duchenne smiles	4.45	5.24	5.78	5.59
Leaning toward partner	32.27	20.36	31.36	21.08
Gesticulation	0.13	0.40	0.25	0.77

Note: Emotions are rated on a scale of 0 (*none*) to 8 (*extreme*). Cue displays are shown as mean seconds displayed per 60 s.
Source: Gonzaga, G. C., Keltner, D., Londahl, E. A., & Smith, M. D. (2001). Love and the commitment problem in romantic relations and friendship. *Journal of Personality and Social Psychology, 81,* 247–262. Copyright © The American Psychological Association. Reprinted with permission of the authors and The American Psychological Association.

videotaped while revealing something about themselves to their partner. The videotapes were later rated by trained judges for various signs of affiliation. Table 2–6 (reproduced from their Table 2) shows some of the results. Explain to a person who has never had a course in statistics the results for self-reported love for the partner and for the number of seconds "leaning toward the partner."

SET II

11. (a) Describe and explain the difference between the mean, median, and mode. (b) Make up an example (not in the book or in your lectures) in which the median would be the preferred measure of central tendency.

12. (a) Describe the variance and standard deviation. (b) Explain why the standard deviation is more often used as a descriptive statistic.

13. For the following scores, find the (a) mean, (b) median, (c) sum of squared deviations, (d) variance, and (e) standard deviation.

    2, 2, 0, 5, 1, 4, 1, 3, 0, 0, 1, 4, 4, 0, 1, 4, 3, 4, 2, 1, 0

14. For the following scores, find the (a) mean, (b) median, (c) sum of squared deviations, (d) variance, and (e) standard deviation.

    1,112; 1,245; 1,361; 1,372; 1,472

15. For the following scores, find the (a) mean, (b) median, (c) sum of squared deviations, (d) variance, and (e) standard deviation.

    3.0, 3.4, 2.6, 3.3, 3.5, 3.2

16. For the following scores, find the (a) mean, (b) median, (c) sum of squared deviations, (d) variance, and (e) standard deviation.

    8, −5, 7, −10, 5

17. Make up three sets of scores: (a) one with the mean greater than the median, (b) one with the median and the mean the same, and (c) one with the mode greater than the median. (Each made-up set of scores should include at least 5 scores.)

18. A researcher interested in political behavior measured the square footage of the desks in the official office of four U.S. governors and of four chief executive

TABLE 2–7 Descriptive Statistics for News Coverage Variables Aggregated by Month, *New York Times Index*, January 1981–November 1992.

	Mean	Standard Deviation	Range	Total
Total Front-Page Articles	5.84	4.10	0–22	835
Positive Front-Page Articles	1.64	1.33	0–6	261
Negative Front-Page Articles	1.83	1.92	0–11	234

Source: New York Times Index.
From Goidel, R. K., & Langley, R. E. (1995). Media coverage of the economy and aggregate economic evaluations: Uncovering evidence of indirect media effects. *Political Research Quarterly, 48,* 313–328. Copyright © 1995 by the University of Utah. Reprinted by permission.

officers (CEOs) of major U.S. corporations. The figures for the governors were 44, 36, 52, and 40 square feet. The figures for the CEOs were 32, 60, 48, and 36 square feet. (a) Figure the mean and the standard deviation for the governors and for the CEOs. (b) Explain what you have done to a person who has never had a course in statistics. (c) Note the ways in which the means and standard deviations differ, and speculate on the possible meaning of these differences, presuming that they are representative of U.S. governors and large U.S. corporations' CEOs in general.

19. A developmental specialist studies the number of words seven infants have learned at a particular age. The numbers are 10, 12, 8, 0, 3, 40, and 18. Figure the (a) mean, (b) median, and (c) standard deviation for the number of words learned by these seven infants. (d) Explain what you have done and what the results mean to a person who has never had a course in statistics.

20. On a measure of artistic ability, the mean for college students in New Zealand is 150 and the standard deviation is 25. Give the Z scores for New Zealand college students who score (a) 100, (b) 120, (c) 140, and (d) 160. Give the raw scores for persons whose Z scores on this test are (e) -1, (f) $-.8$, (g) $-.2$, and (h) $+1.38$.

21. On a standard measure of peer influence among adolescents, the mean is 300 and the standard deviation is 20. Give the Z scores for adolescents who score (a) 340, (b) 310, and (c) 260. Give the raw scores for adolescents whose Z scores on this measure are (d) 2.4, (e) 1.5, (f) 0, and (g) -4.5.

22. A person scores 81 on a test of verbal ability and 6.4 on a test of math ability. For the verbal ability test, the mean for people in general is 50 and the standard deviation is 20. For the math ability test, the mean for people in general is 0 and the standard deviation is 5. Which is this person's stronger ability, verbal or math? Explain your answer to a person who has never had a course in statistics.

23. A study involves measuring the number of days absent from work for 216 employees of a large company during the preceding year. As part of the results, the researcher reports, "The number of days absent during the preceding year ($M = 9.21$; $SD = 7.34$) was . . ." Explain the material in parentheses to a person who has never had a course in statistics.

24. Goidel and Langley (1995) studied the positivity and negativity of newspaper accounts of economic events in the period just before the 1992 U.S. Presidential election. Table 2–7, reproduced from their report, describes the numbers of front-page articles on economic news in the *New York Times* for the 23 months preceding the election. Explain the results in the Mean and Standard Deviation columns to a person who has never had a course in statistics. (Be sure to explain some specific numbers as well as the general principle.)

C H A P T E R　3

Correlation and Prediction

Tip for Success

Before beginning this chapter, ensure you have mastered the material in Chapter 2 on mean, standard deviation, and Z scores.

So far, in Chapters 1 and 2, you have learned about descriptive statistics for a single variable. In Chapter 1, you learned how to use tables and graphs to describe a group of numbers. In Chapter 2, you learned some statistical techniques for describing a group of scores with numbers (such as the mean, variance, standard deviation, and Z scores). We now move on to look at some descriptive statistics for the relationship between two or more variables. To give you an idea of what we mean by that, let's look at an example.

One hundred thirteen married people in the small college town of Santa Cruz, California, responded to a questionnaire in the local newspaper about their marriage. (This was part of a larger study reported by Aron, Norman, Aron, McKenna, & Heyman, 2000.) As part of the questionnaire, they answered the question, "How exciting are the things you do together with your partner?" using a scale from 1 "Not exciting at all" to 5 "Extremely exciting." The questionnaire also contained a standard measure of marital satisfaction (that included items such as "In general, how often do you think that things between you and your partner are going well?").

The researchers were interested in finding out the relationship between doing exciting things with a marital partner and the level of marital satisfaction people reported. In other words, they wanted to compare two groups of scores: the group of scores for doing exciting things, and the group of scores for marital satisfaction. As shown in Figure 3–1, the relationship between these two groups of scores can be shown very clearly using a graph. The horizontal axis is for responses to the question, "How

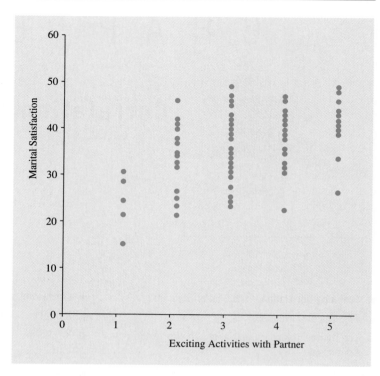

FIGURE 3-1 *Scatter diagram showing the correlation for 113 married individuals between doing exciting activities with their partner and their marital satisfaction. (Data from Aron et al., 2000)*

exciting are the things you do together with your partner?". The vertical axis is for scores on the measure of marital satisfaction. Each person's score is shown as a dot.

The overall pattern is that the dots go from the lower left to the upper right. That is, lower scores on the variable "doing exciting activities with your partner" more often go with lower scores on the variable "marital satisfaction," and higher with higher. So, in general, this graph shows that the more that people engaged in exciting activities with their partner, the more satisfied they reported being in their marriage. Even though the pattern is far from one to one, you can see a general trend. This general pattern of high scores on one variable going with high scores on the other variable, low scores going with low scores, and moderate with moderate, is an example of a **correlation.**

correlation

There are countless examples of correlations: Among students, there is a correlation between high school grades and college grades; in children, there is a correlation between age and coordination skills; among students, there is a correlation between amount of time studying and amount learned; in the marketplace, we often assume that a correlation exists between price and quality—that high prices go with high quality and low with low.

This chapter explores correlation, including how to describe it graphically, different types of correlations, how to figure the correlation coefficient (which describes the degree of correlation), issues about how to interpret a correlation coefficient, and how you can use correlation to predict the score on one variable from knowledge of a person's score on another correlated variable (such as predicting college grades from high school grades).

GRAPHING CORRELATIONS: THE SCATTER DIAGRAM

Figure 3–1, showing the correlation between exciting activities and marital satisfaction, is an example of a **scatter diagram** (also called a *scatterplot*). A scatter diagram shows you at a glance the degree and pattern of the relationship between two variables.

scatter diagram

HOW TO MAKE A SCATTER DIAGRAM

There are three steps to making a scatter diagram.

❶ **Draw the axes and decide which variable goes on which axis.** Often, it doesn't matter which variable goes on which axis. However, sometimes the logic of the study is that one variable is thought of as predicting or causing the other. In that situation, the variable that is doing the predicting goes on the horizontal axis and the variable that is being predicted goes on the vertical axis. In Figure 3–1, we put exciting activities on the horizontal axis and marital satisfaction on the vertical axis, because in the context of the study, we were working from a theory that exciting activities predict marital satisfaction. (We will have more to say about prediction later in the chapter.)

❷ **Determine the range of values to use for each variable and mark them on the axes.** Your numbers should go from low to high on each axis, starting from where the axes meet. Usually, your low value on each axis is 0. However, you can use a higher value to start each axis if the lowest value your measure can possibly have in the group you are studying is a lot higher than 0. For example, if a variable is age and you are studying college students, you might start that axis with 16 or 17, rather than 0.

The axis should continue to the highest value your measure can possibly have. When there is no obvious highest possible value, make the axis go to a value that is as high as people ordinarily score in the group of people of interest for your study.

In Figure 3–1, the horizontal axis is for the question about exciting activities, which participants answered on a scale of 1 to 5. We start the axis at 0, because this is standard, even though the lowest possible score on the scale is 1. We went up to 5, because that is the highest possible value on the scale. Similarly, the vertical axis goes from 0 to 60, since the highest possible score on the marital satisfaction measure is 60. (The measure had 10 items, each answered on a 1 to 6 scale.)

Note also that scatter diagrams are usually made roughly square, with the horizontal and vertical axes being about the same length (a 1:1 ratio).

❸ **Mark a dot for each person's pair of scores.** Find the place on the horizontal axis for the first person's score on the horizontal-axis variable. Next, move up to the height for that person's score on the vertical-axis variable. Then mark a clear dot. Continue this process for the remaining people. Sometimes there are two people with the same pair of scores. This means that the dots for these people would go in the same place. When this happens, you can put a second dot as near as possible to the first—touching, if possible—but making it clear that there are in fact two dots in the one place. Alternatively, you can put the number 2 in that place.

Tip for Success

When making a scatter diagram, it is easiest if you use graph paper.

AN EXAMPLE

Suppose a researcher is studying the relation of sleep to mood. As an initial test, the researcher asks 10 students in her morning seminar two questions:

1. How many hours did you sleep last night?
2. How happy do you feel right now on a scale from 0 "Not at all happy" to 8 "Extremely happy"?

TABLE 3–1	Hours Slept Last Night and Happy Mood Example (Fictional Data)

Hours Slept	Happy Mood
7	4
9	5
8	3
9	7
8	4
6	1
8	3
7	2
10	6
8	5

The (fictional) results are shown in Table 3–1. (In practice, a much larger group would be used in this kind of research. We are using an example with just 10 to keep things simple for learning. In fact, we have done a real version of this study. Results of the real study are similar to what we show here, except not as strong as the ones we made up to make the pattern clear for learning.)

❶ **Draw the axes and decide which variable goes on which axis.** Because sleep comes before mood, it makes most sense to think of sleep as the predictor. (However, it is certainly possible that people who are in general in a good mood are able to get more sleep.) Thus, we put hours slept on the horizontal axis and happy mood on the vertical axis. (See Figure 3–2a.)

❷ **Determine the range of values to use for each variable and mark them on the axes.** For the horizontal axis, we start at 0 as usual (and the minimum amount of sleep possible is 0 hours). We do not know the maximum possible, but let us assume that students rarely sleep more than 12 hours. The vertical axis goes from 0 to 8, the lowest and highest scores possible on the happiness question. (See Figure 3–2b.)

❸ **Mark a dot for each person's pair of scores.** For the first student, the number of hours slept last night was 7. Move across to 7 on the horizontal axis. Then, move up to the point across from the 4 (the happy mood rating for the first student) on the vertical axis. Place a dot at this point. (See Figure 3–2c.) Do the same for each of the other nine students. The result should look like Figure 3–2d.

HOW ARE YOU DOING?

1. What does a scatter diagram show, and what does it consist of?
2. (a) Which variable goes on the horizontal axis? (b) Which on the vertical axis?
3. Make a scatter diagram for the scores shown below for four people who were each tested on two variables, X and Y. X is the variable we are predicting from; it can have scores ranging from 0 to 6. Y is the variable being predicted; it can have scores from 0 to 7.

Person	X	Y
A	3	4
B	6	7
C	1	2
D	4	6

ANSWERS:

1. A scatter diagram is a graph that shows the relation between two variables. One axis is for one variable; the other axis, for the other variable. The graph has a dot for each person's pair of scores. The dot for each person is placed above that person's score on the horizontal axis variable and directly across from that person's score on the vertical axis variable.
2. (a) The variable that is doing the predicting. (b) The variable that is being predicted.
3. See Figure 3–3.

PATTERNS OF CORRELATION

LINEAR AND CURVILINEAR CORRELATIONS

linear correlation

In each example so far, the pattern in the scatter diagram very roughly approximates a straight line. Thus, each is an example of a **linear correlation.** In the scatter diagram for the study of exciting activities and marital satisfaction (Figure 3–1), you could draw a line showing the general trend of the dots, as we have done

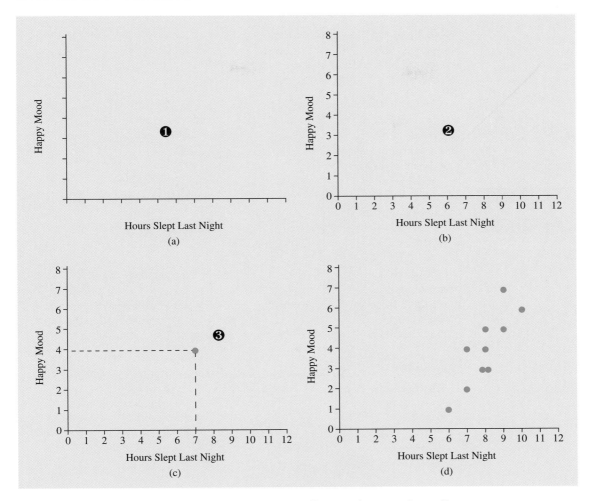

FIGURE 3–2 *Steps for making a scatter diagram. (a)* ❶ *Set up the axes—the predictor variable (Hours Slept Last Night) on the horizontal axis, the other (Happy Mood) on the other axis. (b)* ❷ *Determine the range of values and mark them on the axes. (c)* ❸ *Place a dot for the pair of scores for the first student. (d)* ❸ *continued: Place dots for the pairs of scores for all 10 students.*

in Figure 3–4. Similarly, you could draw such a line in the happy mood and sleep study example, as shown in Figure 3–5. Notice that the scores do not all fall right on the line, far from it in fact. Notice, however, that the line does describe the general tendency of the scores.

Sometimes, however, the general relationship between two variables does not follow a straight line at all, but instead follows the more complex pattern of a **curvilinear correlation.** For example, it is known that up to a point, more physiological arousal makes you do better on almost any kind of task (such as on a math test). Beyond that point, still greater physiological arousal makes you do worse. That is, going from being nearly asleep to a moderate level of arousal makes you more effective. Beyond that moderate level, further increases in arousal may make you too "keyed up" to do well. This particular curvilinear pattern is shown in Figure 3–6. Notice that the line you could draw to describe this pattern is *not* a straight

curvilinear correlation

FIGURE 3-3   *Scatter diagram for scores in "How Are You Doing?" question 3.*

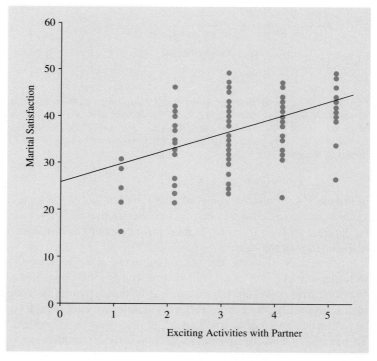

FIGURE 3-4   *The scatter diagram of Figure 3–1 with a line drawn in to show the general trend. (Data from Aron et al., 2000)*

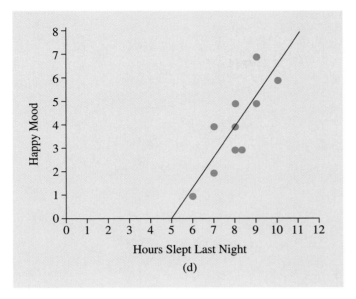

FIGURE 3–5 *The scatter diagram of Figure 3–2d with a line drawn in to show the general trend.*

line. There are many different kinds of curvilinear pattern. The curvilinear pattern in Figure 3–6 looks a little like the letter *n*. Other curvilinear patterns can look like the letter *u*, the letter *v*, the letter *c*, or in fact any systematic pattern that is not a straight line.

NO CORRELATION

It is also possible for two variables to be essentially unrelated to each other. For example, if you were to do a study of income and shoe size, your results might appear as shown in Figure 3–7. The dots are spread everywhere, and there is no line, straight or otherwise, that is any reasonable representation of a trend. There is simply **no correlation.**

no correlation

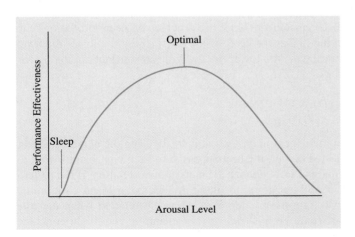

FIGURE 3–6 *Example of a curvilinear relationship: task performance and arousal.*

FIGURE 3–7 *Two variables with no association with each other: income and shoe size (fictional data).*

POSITIVE AND NEGATIVE LINEAR CORRELATIONS

positive correlation

In the examples so far of linear correlations, such as exciting activities and marital satisfaction, high scores go with high scores, lows with lows, and mediums with mediums. This situation is called a **positive correlation.** (One reason for the term "positive" is that in geometry, the slope of a line is positive when it goes up and to the right on a graph like this. Notice that in Figures 3–4 and 3–5 the lines go up and to the right.)

negative correlation

Sometimes, however, high scores go with low scores and lows with highs. This is called a **negative correlation.** For example, in the newspaper survey about marriage, the researchers also asked about boredom with the relationship and the partner. Not surprisingly, the more bored a person was, the *lower* was the person's marital satisfaction. That is, high scores on one variable went with low scores on the other. This is shown in Figure 3–8, where we also put in a line to emphasize the general trend. You can see that as it goes from left to right, it slopes slightly downward. (Compare this to the result for the relation of exciting activities and marital satisfaction shown in Figure 3–4, which slopes upward.)

Another study (Mirvis & Lawler, 1977) also illustrates a negative correlation. That study found that absenteeism from work had a negative linear correlation with job satisfaction. That is, the higher the level of job satisfaction, the lower the level of absenteeism. Put another way, the lower the level of job satisfaction, the higher the absenteeism.

IMPORTANCE OF IDENTIFYING THE PATTERN OF CORRELATION

The procedure you learn in the next main section is for figuring the degree of linear correlation. As we suggested earlier, the best approach to such a problem is *first* to make a scatter diagram and use it to identify the pattern of correlation. If the pattern is curvilinear, then you would not go on to figure the degree of linear correlation. This is important because figuring the degree of linear correlation when the true correlation is curvilinear would be misleading. (For example, you might conclude that there is little or no correlation when in fact it is large, just not linear.) You should assume that the correlation is linear, unless the scatter diagram shows a

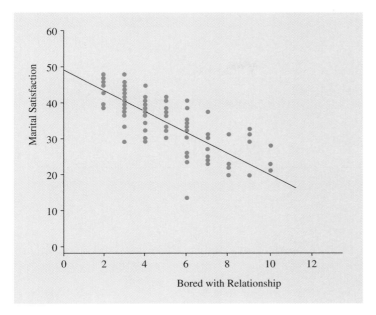

FIGURE 3–8 *Scatter diagram with the line drawn in to show the general trend for negative correlation between two variables: Greater boredom with the relationship goes with lower marital satisfaction. (Data from Aron et al., 2000)*

curvilinear correlation. We say this because when the linear correlation is small, the dots will fall far from a straight line. In such situations, it can sometimes be hard to imagine a straight line that roughly shows the pattern of dots.

If the correlation appears to be linear, it is also important to "eyeball" the scatter diagram a bit more. The idea is to note the direction (positive or negative) of the linear correlation and also to make a rough guess as to the degree of correlation. There is a "small" (or "weak") correlation when you can barely tell there is a correlation at all—the dots fall far from a straight line. There is a "large" (or "strong") correlation if the dots fall very close to a straight line. The correlation is "moderate" if the pattern of dots is somewhere between a small and a large correlation. Some examples of scatter diagrams with different degrees of correlation are shown in Figure 3–9. Noting the direction and making a rough guess as to the degree of correlation is important because it lets you check to see whether you have made a major mistake when you then do the figuring you learn in the next section.

HOW ARE YOU DOING?

1. What is the difference between a linear and curvilinear correlation in terms of how they appear in a scatter diagram?
2. What does it mean to say that two variables have no correlation?
3. What is the difference between a positive and negative linear correlation? Answer this question in terms of (a) the patterns in a scatter diagram and (b) what those patterns tell you about the relationship between the two variables.
4. For each of the scatter diagrams shown in Figure 3–10, say whether the pattern is roughly linear, curvilinear, or no correlation. If the pattern is roughly linear, also say if it is positive or negative.
5. Give two reasons why it is important to identify the pattern of correlation in a scatter diagram before proceeding to figure the degree of correlation.

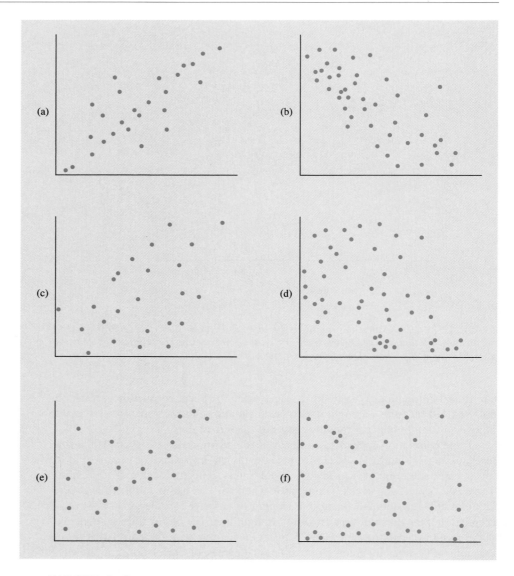

FIGURE 3-9   *Examples of scatter diagrams with different degrees of correlation.*

ANSWERS:

1. In a linear correlation, the pattern of dots roughly follow a straight line; in a curvilinear correlation, there is a clear (systematic) pattern to the dots, but it is not a straight line.
2. There is no pattern of relationship between the two variables.
3. (a) In a scatter diagram for a positive linear correlation, the line that roughly describes the pattern of dots goes up and to the right; in a negative linear correlation, the line goes down and to the right. (b) In a positive linear correlation, the basic pattern is that high scores on one variable go with high scores on the other, mediums go with mediums, and lows go with lows; in a negative linear correlation, high scores on one variable go with low scores on the other, mediums go with mediums, and lows go with highs.
4. (a) linear, negative. (b) curvilinear. (c) linear, positive. (d) no correlation.

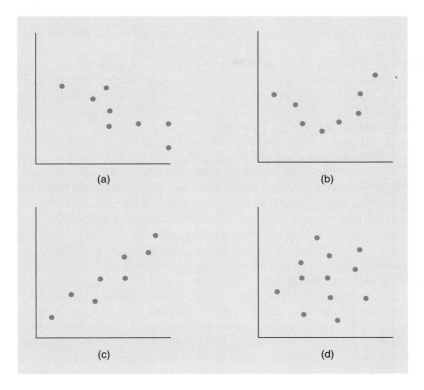

FIGURE 3–10   *Scatter diagrams for "How Are You Doing?" question 4.*

5. Identifying whether it is linear or not tells you whether it is appropriate to use the standard procedures for figuring a linear correlation. If it is linear, identifying the direction and approximate degree of correlation before doing the figuring lets you check the results of your figuring when you are done.

THE DEGREE OF LINEAR CORRELATION: THE CORRELATION COEFFICIENT

Looking at a scatter diagram gives a rough idea of the type and degree of relationship between two variables. But it is not a very precise approach. What you need is a number that gives the precise degree of correlation.

DEGREE OF CORRELATION

What we mean by the *degree of correlation* is how much there is a clear pattern of some particular relationship between the two variables. For example, we saw that a positive linear correlation is when high scores go with highs, mediums with mediums, lows with lows. The degree of such a correlation, then, is how much highs go with highs, and so on. Similarly, the degree of negative linear correlation is how much highs on one variable go with lows on the other, and so forth. As you just learned, in terms of a scatter diagram, a large linear correlation means that the dots fall close to a straight line (the line sloping up or down depending on whether the linear correlation is positive or negative). A perfect linear correlation means all the dots fall exactly on the straight line.

LOGIC OF FIGURING THE DEGREE
OF LINEAR CORRELATION

The first thing you need to figure the degree of correlation is some way to gauge what is a high score and what is a low score—and how high a high score is and how low a low score is. This means comparing scores on different variables in a consistent way. As we saw in Chapter 2, you can solve this problem of comparing apples and oranges by using Z scores.

To review, a Z score is the number of standard deviations a score is from the mean. Whatever the range of values of the variable, if you change your raw scores to Z scores, a raw score that is high (that is, above the mean of the scores on that variable) will always have a positive Z score, and a raw score that is low (below the mean) will always have a negative Z score. Furthermore, regardless of the particular measure used, Z scores tell you in a very standard way just how high or low each score is. A Z score of 1 is always exactly 1 standard deviation above the mean, and a Z score of 2 is twice as many standard deviations above the mean. Z scores on one variable are directly comparable to Z scores on another variable.

There is an additional reason why Z scores are so useful when figuring the degree of correlation. It has to do with what happens if you multiply a score on one variable by a score on the other variable, which is called a *cross-product*. When using Z scores, this is called a **cross-product of Z scores.** If you multiply a high Z score by a high Z score, you will always get a positive cross-product. This is because no matter what the variable, scores above the mean are positive Z scores, and a positive multiplied by a positive is a positive. Furthermore—and here is where it gets interesting—if you multiply a low Z score by a low Z score, you also always get a positive cross-product. This is because no matter what the variable, scores below the mean are negative Z scores, and a negative multiplied by a negative gives a positive.

cross-product of Z scores

If highs on one variable go with highs on the other, and lows on one go with lows on the other, the cross-products of Z scores always will be positive. Considering a whole distribution of scores, suppose you take each person's Z score on one variable and multiply it by that person's Z score on the other variable. The result of doing this when highs go with highs and lows with lows is that the multiplications all come out positive. If you add up these cross-products of Z scores, which are all positive, for all the people in the study, you will end up with a big positive number.

On the other hand, with a negative correlation, highs go with lows and lows with highs. In terms of Z scores, this would mean positives with negatives and negatives with positives. Multiplied out, that gives all negative cross-products. If you add all these negative cross-products together, you get a large negative number.

Finally, suppose there is no linear correlation. In this situation, for some people highs on one variable would go with highs on the other variable (and some lows would go with lows), making positive cross-products. For other people, highs on one variable would go with lows on the other variable (and some lows would go with highs), making negative cross-products. Adding up these cross-products for all the people in the study would result in the positive cross-products and the negative cross-products cancelling each other out, giving a result of 0.

In each situation, we changed all the scores to Z scores, multiplied each person's two Z scores by each other, and added up these cross-products. The result was a large positive number if there was a positive linear correlation, a large negative number if there was a negative linear correlation, and a number near 0 if there was no linear correlation.

However, you are still left with the problem of figuring the *degree* of a positive or negative correlation. The larger the number, the bigger the correlation. But how large is large, and how large is not very large? You can't judge the degree of correlation from the sum of the cross-products alone, which gets bigger just by adding the cross-products of more people together. (That is, a study with 100 people would have a larger sum of cross-products than the same study with only 25 people.)

The solution is to divide this sum of the cross-products by the number of people in the study. That is, you figure the *average of the cross-products of Z scores*. It turns out that because of the nature of Z scores, this average can never be more than +1 which would be a positive linear **perfect correlation.** It can never be less than −1 which would be a negative linear perfect correlation. In the situation of no linear correlation, the average of the cross-products of Z scores is 0.

For a positive linear correlation that is not perfect, which is the usual situation, the average of the cross-products of Z scores is between 0 and +1 To put it another way, if the general trend of the dots is upward and to the right, but they do not fall exactly on a single straight line, this number is between 0 and +1 The same rule holds for negative correlations: They fall between 0 and −1.

perfect correlation

Tip for Success

If you figure a correlation coefficient to be larger than +1 or less than −1 you have made an error in your figuring.

THE CORRELATION COEFFICIENT

The average of the cross-products of Z scores is called the **correlation coefficient (r).** It is also called the *Pearson correlation coefficient* (or the *Pearson product–moment correlation coefficient,* to be very traditional). It is named after Karl Pearson (whom you will meet in Box 11–1). Pearson, along with Francis Galton (see Box 3–1), played a major role in developing the correlation coefficient. The correlation coefficient is abbreviated by the letter *r,* which is short for *regression,* a concept closely related to correlation. (We discuss regression later in the chapter.)

correlation coefficient (*r*)

The sign (+ or −) of a correlation coefficient tells you the general trend, in terms of whether the scores go up and to the right (a positive correlation), or down and to the right (a negative correlation). The actual value of the correlation coefficient—from a low of 0 to a high of 1, ignoring the sign of the correlation coefficient—tells you the strength of the linear correlation. So, a correlation coefficient of +.85 represents a stronger linear correlation than a correlation of +.42. However, a correlation of −.90 represents a stronger linear correlation than +.85 (since .90 is bigger than .85). In a scatter diagram, the closer the dots are to falling on a single straight line, the stronger the linear correlation. Figure 3–11 shows the scatter diagrams from Figure 3–9, with the correlation coefficient shown for each scatter diagram.

Web Links

http://noppa5.pc.helsinki.fi/koe/corr/cor7.html. See a visual demonstration of the scatter diagram and degree of linear correlation.

http://www.stat.uiuc.edu/~stat100/java/guess/GCApplet.html. Guess the degree of linear correlation shown in scatter diagrams.

http://www.uvm.edu/~dhowell/SeeingStatisticsApplets/CorrelationPoints.html. Make your own scatter diagram and see the degree of linear correlation.

FORMULA FOR THE CORRELATION COEFFICIENT

The correlation coefficient, as we have seen, is the average of the cross-products of Z scores. Put as a formula,

(3-1)
$$r = \frac{\Sigma Z_X Z_Y}{N}$$

The correlation coefficient is the sum, over all the people in the study, of the product of each person's two Z scores divided by the number of people.

r is the correlation coefficient. Z_X is the Z score for each person on the X variable and Z_Y is the Z score for each person on the Y variable. $Z_X Z_Y$ is Z_X multiplied by Z_Y (the cross-product of the Z scores) for each person and $\Sigma Z_X Z_Y$ is the sum of the

FIGURE 3–11
Examples of scatter diagrams and correlation coefficients for different degrees of correlation.

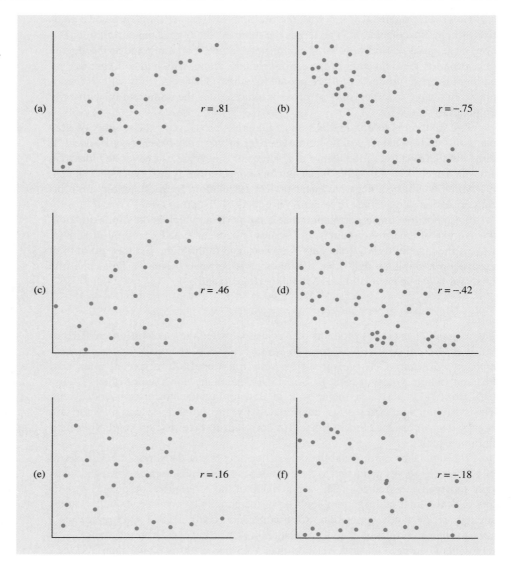

Tip for Success

When changing the raw scores to Z scores, it is easiest (and you will make fewer errors) if you do all the Z scores for one variable and then all the Z scores for the other variable. Also, to make sure you have done it correctly, when you finish all the Z scores for a variable, add them up—they should add up to 0 (within rounding error).

cross-products of Z scores over all the people in the study. N is the number of people in the study.[1]

STEPS FOR FIGURING THE CORRELATION COEFFICIENT

Here are the four steps for figuring the correlation coefficient.

❶ **Change all scores to Z scores.** This requires figuring the mean and the standard deviation of each variable, then changing each raw score to a Z score (using the method from Chapter 2).

[1]There is also a "computational" version of this formula, which is mathematically equivalent and thus gives the same result:

$$r = \frac{N\Sigma(XY) - \Sigma X \Sigma Y}{\sqrt{[N\Sigma X^2 - (\Sigma X)^2]}\sqrt{[N\Sigma Y^2 - (\Sigma Y)^2]}} \tag{3-2}$$

BOX 3–1   Galton: Gentleman Genius

Francis Galton is credited with inventing the correlation coefficient. (Karl Pearson worked out the formulas, but Pearson was a student of Galton and gave Galton all the credit.) Statistics at this time (around the end of the 19th century) was a tight little British club. In fact, most of science was an only slightly larger club. Galton also was influenced greatly by his own cousin, Charles Darwin.

Galton was a typical, eccentric, independently wealthy gentleman scientist. Aside from his work in statistics, he possessed a medical degree, had explored "darkest Africa," invented glasses for reading underwater, experimented with stereoscopic maps, dabbled in meteorology and anthropology, and wrote a paper about receiving intelligible signals from the stars.

Above all, Galton was a compulsive counter. Some of his counts are rather infamous. Once while attending a lecture, he counted the fidgets of an audience per minute, looking for variations with the boringness of the subject matter. While twice having his picture painted, he counted the artist's brushstrokes per hour, concluding that each portrait required an average of 20,000 strokes. While walking the streets of various towns in the British Isles, he classified the beauty of the female inhabitants by fingering a recording device in his pocket to register "good," "medium," or "bad."

Galton's consuming interest, however, was the counting of geniuses, criminals, and other types in families. He wanted to understand how each type was produced so that science could improve the human race by encouraging governments to enforce eugenics—selective breeding for intelligence, proper moral behavior, and other qualities—to be determined, of course, by the eugenicists. (Eugenics has since been generally discredited.) The concept of correlation came directly from his first simple efforts in this area, the study of the relation of the height of children to their parents.

At first, Galton's method of exactly measuring the tendency for "one thing to go with another" seemed almost the same as proving the cause of something. For example, if it could be shown mathematically that most of the brightest people came from a few highborn British families and most of the least intelligent people came from poor families, that would prove that intelligence was caused by the inheritance of certain genes (provided that you were prejudiced enough to overlook the differences in educational opportunities). The same study might prove more convincingly that if you were a member of one of those better British families, history would make you a prime example of how easy it is to misinterpret the meaning of a correlation.

You can learn more about Galton on the following Web page: *http://www_gap.dcs.st_and.ac.uk/~history/mathematicians/Galton.html.*

Sources: Peters (1987); Salsburg (2001); Tankard (1984).

❷ **Figure the cross-product of the Z scores for each person.** That is, for each person, multiply the person's Z score on one variable by the person's Z score on the other variable.

❸ **Add up all the cross-products of the Z scores.**

❹ **Divide by the number of people in the study.**

This formula is easier to use when figuring by hand when you have a large number of people in the study, because you don't have to first figure out all the Z scores. However, as we emphasized in Chapter 2, researchers rarely use computational formulas like this any more because most of the actual figuring is done by a computer. As a student learning statistics, it is better to use the definitional formula (3–1). This is because when solving problems using the definitional formula, you are strengthening your understanding of what the correlation coefficient means. In all examples in this chapter, we use the definitional formula and we urge you to use it in doing the chapter's practice problems.

Tip for Success

When figuring the cross-products of the Z scores, pay careful attention to the sign of each Z score. As you know, a negative score multiplied by a negative score produces a positive score. Students frequently make errors at this step, so do your figuring carefully.

AN EXAMPLE

Let us try these steps with the sleep and mood example.

❶ **Change all scores to Z scores.** Starting with the number of hours slept last night, the mean is 8 (sum of 80 divided by 10 students), and the standard deviation is 1.10 (sum of squared deviations, 12, divided by 10 students, for a variance of 1.2, the square root of which is 1.10). For the first student, then, a number of hours slept of 7 is 1 hour below the mean of 8, and -1 divided by 1.10 is $-.91$. Thus the first score is .91 standard deviations below the mean, or a Z score of $-.91$. We figured the rest of the Z scores in the same way and show them in the appropriate columns in Table 3–2.

❷ **Figure the cross-product of the Z scores for each person.** For the first student, multiply $-.91$ by 0. This gives .00. The cross-products for all the students are shown in the last column of Table 3–2.

❸ **Add up all the cross-products of the Z scores.** Adding up all the cross-products of Z scores, as shown in Table 3–2, gives a sum of 8.42.

❹ **Divide by the number of people in the study.** Dividing 8.42 by 10 (the number of students in the study) gives a result of .842. This rounds off to .84. This is the correlation coefficient.

In terms of the correlation coefficient formula,

$$r = \frac{\Sigma Z_X Z_Y}{N} = \frac{8.42}{10} = .842$$

Because this correlation coefficient is positive and near 1, the highest possible value, this is a very strong positive linear correlation.

TABLE 3–2 Figuring the Correlation Coefficient for the Sleep and Mood Study (Fictional Data)

Number of Hours Slept (X)				Happy Mood (Y)				Cross-Products
	Deviation	Dev Squared	Z Scores ❶		Deviation	Dev Squared	Z Scores ❶	❷
X	X − M	$(X-M)^2$	Z_X	Y	Y − M	$(Y-M)^2$	Z_Y	$Z_X Z_Y$
7	-1	1	$-.91$	4	0	0	0	.00
9	1	1	.91	5	1	1	.58	.53
8	0	0	.00	3	-1	1	$-.58$	.00
9	1	1	.91	7	3	9	1.73	1.57
8	0	0	.00	4	0	0	.00	.00
6	-2	4	-1.82	1	-3	9	-1.73	3.15
8	0	0	.00	3	-1	1	$-.58$	.00
7	-1	1	$-.91$	2	-2	4	-1.16	1.06
10	2	4	1.82	6	2	4	1.16	2.11
8	0	0	.00	5	1	1	.58	.00
$\Sigma = 80$	$\Sigma (X-M)^2 = 12$			$\Sigma = 40$	$\Sigma (Y-M)^2 = 30$			$\Sigma Z_X Z_Y = 8.42$ ❸
$M = 8$	$SD^2 = 1.20$			$M = 4$	$SD^2 = 3.00$			$r = .842/10 = .84$ ❹
	$SD = 1.10$				$SD = 1.73$			

TABLE 3–3	Average Class Size and Achievement Test Scores in Five Elementary Schools (Fictional Data)	
Elementary School	Class Size	Achievement Test Score
Main Street	25	80
Casat	14	98
Harland	33	50
Shady Grove	28	82
Jefferson	20	90

AN EXAMPLE OF GRAPHING AND COMPUTING A CORRELATION

In this example, we put together the steps of making a scatter diagram and computing the correlation coefficient.

Suppose that an educational researcher knows the average class size and average achievement test score from the five elementary schools in a particular small school district, as shown in Table 3–3. (Again, it would be very rare in actual research practice to do a study or figure a correlation with only five cases. We have kept the numbers low here to make it easier for you to follow the steps of the example.) The question he then asks is, what is the relationship between these two variables?

The first thing he must do is to make a scatter diagram. This requires three steps.

❶ **Draw the axes and decide which variable goes on which axis.** Because it seems more reasonable to think of class size as affecting achievement test scores rather than the other way around, we will draw the axes with class size along the bottom.

❷ **Determine the range of values to use for each variable and mark them on the axes.** We will assume that the achievement test scores go from 0 to 100. Class size has to be at least 1 and in this example we guessed that it would be unlikely to be more than 50.

❸ **Mark a dot for each person's pair of scores.** (In this example, of course, we have schools instead of people.) The completed scatter diagram is shown in Figure 3–12.

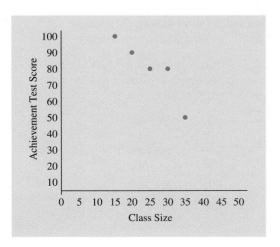

FIGURE 3–12 *Scatter diagram for the scores in Table 3–3.*

In any correlation problem, before figuring the correlation coefficient, it is a good idea to look at the scatter diagram to be sure that the pattern is not curvilinear. In this example, the pattern of dots is roughly a straight line, so you can assume that the pattern is linear (and not curvilinear). It is also wise to make a rough estimate of the direction and degree of correlation. This serves as a check against making a major mistake in figuring. In this example, the basic pattern is one in which the dots go down and to the right fairly consistently. This suggests a strong negative correlation. Now we can proceed to figure the correlation coefficient, following the usual steps.

❶ **Change all scores to Z scores.** The mean for class size is 24, and the standard deviation is 6.54. The Z score for the first class size, of 25, is .15. That is, $(25 - 24)/6.54 = .15$. All of the Z scores are shown in the appropriate columns of Table 3–4.

❷ **Figure the cross-product of the Z scores for each person.** For the first cross-product, multiply .15 by 0, which is 0. The second is -1.53 multiplied by 1.10, which is -1.68. All of the cross-products of Z scores are shown in the last column of Table 3–4.

❸ **Add up all the cross-products of the Z scores.** The total is -4.52.

❹ **Divide by the number of people in the study.** The sum of the cross-products of Z scores (-4.52) divided by the number of people (5) is $-.90$. That is, $r = -.90$.

In terms of the correlation coefficient formula,

$$r = \frac{\Sigma Z_X Z_Y}{N} = \frac{-4.52}{5} = -.90$$

This correlation coefficient of $-.90$ agrees well with our original estimate of a strong negative correlation.

HOW ARE YOU DOING?

1. Give two reasons why we use Z scores for figuring the degree of linear correlation between two variables, thinking of correlation as how much highs go with highs and lows go with lows (or vice versa for negative correlations).
2. When figuring the correlation coefficient, why do you divide the sum of cross-products of Z scores by the number of people in the study?
3. Write the formula for the correlation coefficient and define each of the symbols.

TABLE 3–4 **Figuring the Correlation Coefficient for Average Class Size and Achievement Test Scores in Five Elementary Schools (Fictional Data)**

School	Class Size		Achievement Test Score		Cross-Products
	X	Z_X ❶	Y	Z_Y ❶	$Z_X Z_Y$ ❷
Main Street	25	.15	80	.00	.00
Casat	14	-1.53	98	1.10	-1.68
Harland	33	1.38	50	-1.84	-2.54
Shady Grove	28	.61	82	.12	.07
Jefferson	20	$-.61$	90	.61	$-.37$
Σ:	120		400		-4.52 ❸
M:	24		80		$r = -.90$ ❹
$SD =$	$\sqrt{214/5} = 6.54$		$\sqrt{1{,}328/5} = 16.30$		

4. Figure the correlation coefficient for the Z scores shown below for three people who were each tested on two variables, X and Y.

Person	Z_X	Z_Y
K	.5	$-.7$
L	-1.4	$-.8$
M	.9	1.5

ANSWERS:

1. First, Z scores put both variables on the same scale of measurement so that a high or low score (and how much it is high or low) means the same thing for both variables. Second, high Z scores are positive and low are negative. Thus, if highs go with highs and lows with lows, the cross-products will all be positive. Similarly, with a negative correlation where highs go with lows and lows with highs, the cross-products will all be negative.
2. Otherwise, the more people in the study, the bigger the sum of the cross-products, even if the degree of correlation is the same. Dividing by the number of people corrects for this.
3. $r = \Sigma Z_X Z_Y / N$. r is the correlation coefficient. Σ is the symbol for sum of—add up all the scores that follow (in this formula, you add up all the cross-products that follow). Z_X is the Z score for each person's raw score on one of the variables (the one labeled X) and Z_Y is the Z score for each person's raw score on the other variable (labeled Y). N is the number of people in the study.
4. $r = \Sigma Z_X Z_Y / N = [(.5)(-.7) + (-1.4)(-.8) + (.9)(1.5)]/3 = [-.35 + 1.12 + 1.35]/3 = 2.12/3 = .71$

ISSUES IN INTERPRETING THE CORRELATION COEFFICIENT

There are some subtle cautions in interpreting a correlation coefficient.

CAUSALITY AND CORRELATION

If two variables have a clear linear correlation, we normally assume that there is something causing them to go together. However, you can't know the **direction of causality** (what is causing what) just from the fact that the two variables are correlated.

direction of causality

THREE POSSIBLE DIRECTIONS OF CAUSALITY

Consider the example with which we started the chapter, the correlation between doing exciting activities with your partner and satisfaction with the relationship. There are three possible directions of causality for these two variables:

1. It could be that doing exciting activities together causes the partners to be more satisfied with their relationship.
2. It could also be that people who are more satisfied with their relationship choose to do more exciting activities together.
3. Another possibility is that something like having less pressure (versus more pressure) at work makes people happier in their marriage and also gives them more time and energy to do exciting activities with their partner.

These three possible directions of causality are shown in Figure 3–13a.

The principle is that for any correlation between variables X and Y, there are at least three possible directions of causality:

1. X could be causing Y
2. Y could be causing X
3. Some third factor could be causing both X and Y.

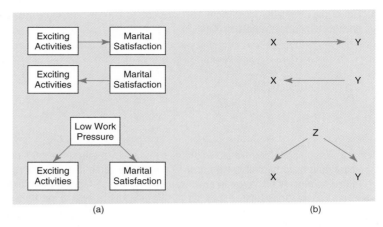

FIGURE 3–13 *Three possible directions of causality (shown with arrows) for a correlation for (a) the exciting activities and marital satisfaction example and (b) the general principle for any two variables X and Y.*

These three possible directions of causality are shown in Figure 3–13b.

It is also possible (and often likely) that there is more than one direction of causality making two variables correlated.

RULING OUT SOME POSSIBLE DIRECTIONS OF CAUSALITY

Sometimes you can rule out one or more of these possible directions of causality based on additional knowledge of the situation. For example, the correlation between high school grades and college grades cannot be due to college grades causing high school grades—causality doesn't go backward in time. But we still do not know whether the high school grades somehow caused the college grades (for example, by giving the students greater confidence), or some third factor, such as a tendency to study hard, makes for good grades in both high school and college.

In the social and behavioral sciences, one major strategy to rule out at least one direction of causality is to do studies where people are measured at two different points in time. This is called a **longitudinal study.** (For example, we might measure a couple's level of exciting activities at one time and then examine the quality of their marriage a year later.)

Another major way we can rule out alternative directions of causality is by conducting a **true experiment.** In a true experiment, participants are randomly assigned (say, by flipping a coin) to a particular level of a variable and then measured on another variable. For example, Aron et al. (2000) followed up their survey studies of married couples with a series of true experiments. Married couples came to their laboratory, spent 10 minutes doing a structured activity together, and then filled out a marital satisfaction questionnaire. What made this a true experiment is that half of the couples were randomly assigned (by flipping a coin) to do an activity that was exciting and the other half did an activity that was pleasant but not particularly exciting. The finding was that when those who had done the exciting activities filled out the marital satisfaction questionnaires, they reported substantially higher levels of marital satisfaction than did those who had done the pleasant but not exciting activities. As a result of this experiment, we can be confident that at least under these kinds of conditions, there is a direction of causality from the activities to marital satisfaction.

longitudinal study

true experiment

The main point to remember from all this is that just knowing that two variables are correlated, by itself, does not tell you anything about the direction of causality between them. *Understanding this principle is perhaps the single most important indication of sophistication in understanding social and behavioral science research!*

THE STATISTICAL SIGNIFICANCE OF A CORRELATION COEFFICIENT

The correlation coefficient by itself is a descriptive statistic. It describes the degree and direction (positive or negative) of linear correlation in the particular group of people studied. However, when doing research, you often are more interested in a particular group of scores as representing some larger group that you have not studied directly. For example, the researcher studying sleep and mood tested only 10 individuals. But the researcher's intention in such a study is that the scores from these 10 people would tell us something about sleep and mood for people more generally. (In practice, you would want a much larger group than 10 for this purpose. We used small numbers of people in our examples to make them easier to learn from.)

There is a problem, however, in studying only some of the people in the larger group you want to know about. It is possible that, by chance, the ones you pick to study happen to be just those people for whom highs happen to go with highs and lows with lows—even though, had you studied all the people in the larger population, there might really be no correlation.

We say that a correlation is **statistically significant** if it is unlikely that you could have gotten a correlation as big as you did if in fact the overall group had no correlation. Specifically, you figure out whether that likelihood is less than some small degree of probability (p), such as .05 (5%) or .01 (1%). If the probability is that small, we say that the correlation is "statistically significant" with "$p < .05$ or "$p < .01$ (spoken as "p less than point oh five" or "p less than point oh one").

The method and logic of figuring *statistical significance* is the main focus of this book, starting with Chapter 4. We would be jumping ahead to try to explain it fully now. However, by the time you complete the later chapters, the details will be quite clear. (The needed details for applying the general principles of statistical significance you learn in those chapters to figuring statistical significance of a correlation coefficient is in the Appendix to this chapter. But we suggest that you leave this Appendix at least until you have completed Chapter 8.) We bring up this topic now only to give you a general idea of what is being talked about if you see mentions of statistical significance, $p < .05$ or some such phrase, when reading a research article that reports correlation coefficients.

statistically significant

HOW ARE YOU DOING?

1. If anxiety and depression are correlated, what are three possible directions of causality that might explain this correlation?
2. A researcher randomly assigns participants to eat either zero or four cookies and then asks them how full they feel. The number of cookies eaten and feeling full are highly correlated. What directions of causality can and cannot be ruled out?
3. What does it mean to say that a particular correlation coefficient is statistically significant?

ANSWERS:

1. Being depressed can cause a person to be anxious; being anxious can cause a person to be depressed; some third variable (such as some aspect of heredity or childhood traumas) could be causing both anxiety and depression.

2. Eating more cookies can cause participants to feel full. Feeling full cannot have caused participants to have eaten more cookies, because how many cookies were eaten was determined randomly. Third variables can't cause both, because how many cookies were eaten was determined randomly.

3. The probability is very low of getting a correlation this big between these two variables in the group of people studied if in fact there is no correlation between these two variables for people in general.

PREDICTION

One important use of correlations is to help in making predictions. Social and behavioral scientists of various kinds are called on to make informed (and precise) guesses about many different things. For example, a college admissions officer might want to use an applicant's score on one variable, such as the applicant's SAT score, to predict what the applicant's score would be on another variable, such as the applicant's likely college grade point average (GPA). Similarly, a personnel manager might want to use the score on a job application examination to predict whether the applicant will be successful on the job; a parole officer might want to use the number of rule violations to predict whether a prisoner will commit a crime if released; a public health official might want to use tomorrow's expected high temperature to predict the number of people likely to have heat-related health problems; and so forth.

We first consider procedures for making predictions about one variable, such as college GPA, based on information about another variable, such as SAT scores. We then introduce situations in which predictions about one variable, such as college GPA, are made based on information about two or more other variables, such as using both SAT scores and high school GPA.

PREDICTOR (X) AND CRITERION (Y) VARIABLES

predictor variable

criterion variable

With correlation it does not matter much which variable is which. But with prediction you have to decide which variable is being predicted from and which variable is being predicted to. The variable being predicted from is called the **predictor variable.** The variable being predicted to is called the **criterion variable.** In equations the predictor variable is usually labeled X, the criterion variable, Y. That is, X predicts Y. In the example we just considered, SAT scores would be the predictor variable or X and college GPA would be the criterion variable or Y. (See Table 3–5.)

PREDICTION USING Z SCORES

It is easier to learn about prediction if we first consider prediction using Z scores. (We will get to prediction using ordinary scores shortly.)

TABLE 3–5	Predictor and Criterion Variables	
Name	Variable Predicted From	Variable Predicted To
	Predictor variable	Criterion variable
Symbol	X	Y
Example	SAT scores	College GPA

THE PREDICTION MODEL

The **prediction model,** or *prediction rule,* to make predictions with Z scores is as follows: A person's predicted Z score on the criterion variable is found by multiplying a particular number, called a **standardized regression coefficient,** by that person's Z score on the predictor variable. The standardized regression coefficient is symbolized by the Greek letter beta (β).

Beta (β) is called a standardized regression *coefficient* because a coefficient is a number you multiply by another number. It is called a standardized *regression* coefficient because the statistical method for prediction is sometimes called regression (for reasons we discuss later in the chapter). Finally, it is called a *standardized* regression coefficient because you are working with Z scores, which are also called standard scores.

prediction model

standardized regression coefficient

FORMULA FOR THE PREDICTION MODEL USING Z SCORES

Here is the formula for the prediction model using Z scores (also known as the Z-score prediction model):

(3-3)
$$\text{Predicted } Z_Y = (\beta)(Z_X)$$

A person's predicted Z score on the criterion variable is the standardized regression coefficient multiplied by that person's Z score on the predictor variable.

In this formula, Predicted Z_Y is the predicted value of the particular person's Z score on the criterion variable Y. (The predicted value of a score often is written with a hat symbol. Thus $\hat{Z}_Y$ means Predicted Z_Y.) β is the standardized regression coefficient. Z_X is the particular person's Z score on the predictor variable X. Thus, $(\beta)(Z_X)$ means multiplying the standardized regression coefficient by the person's Z score on the predictor variable.

For example, suppose that at your school the standardized regression coefficient (β) is .3 for predicting college GPA at graduation from SAT at admission. So, the Z-score prediction model for predicting college GPA from high school SAT score is:

$$\text{Predicted } Z_Y = (.3)(Z_X)$$

A person applying to your school has an SAT score that is 2 standard deviations above the mean (that is, a Z score of +2). The predicted Z score for this person's GPA would be .3 multiplied by 2, which is .6. That is, this person's predicted Z score for their college GPA is .6 standard deviations above the mean. In terms of the prediction model (formula 3–3),

$$\text{Predicted } Z_Y = (\beta)(Z_X) = (.3)(2) = .6$$

STEPS FOR THE PREDICTION MODEL USING Z SCORES

Here are the steps for the prediction model using Z scores.

❶ **Determine the standardized regression coefficient (β).**
❷ **Multiply the standardized regression coefficient (β) by the person's Z score on the predictor variable.**

We can illustrate the steps using the same example as above for predicting college GPA of a person at your school with an entering SAT 2 standard deviations above the mean.

❶ **Determine the standardized regression coefficient (β).** In the example, it was .3.

❷ **Multiply the standardized regression coefficient (β) by the person's Z score on the predictor variable.** In the example, the person's Z score on the predictor variable is +2. Multiplying .3 by 2 gives .6. Thus, .6 is the person's predicted Z score on the criterion variable (college GPA).

THE STANDARDIZED REGRESSION COEFFICIENT (β)

It can be proved mathematically that the best number to use for the standardized regression coefficient (β) when predicting one variable from another is the correlation coefficient. That is, when predicting one variable from another using Z scores, $\beta = r$.

AN EXAMPLE

Consider again the sleep and mood example from earlier in the chapter. In this example, 10 students had a correlation of .84 between number of hours slept the night before and happy mood that day. Because the correlation is .84, the standardized regression coefficient (β) is also .84. That is, $r = .84$ thus $\beta = .84$. This means that the model for predicting a person's Z score for happy mood is to multiply .84 by the person's Z score for the number of hours slept the night before.

Suppose you were thinking about staying up so late one night you would get only 5 hours' sleep. This would be a Z score of -2.73 on numbers of hours slept—that is, nearly 3 standard deviations less sleep than the mean. (We changed 5 hours to a Z score using the mean and standard deviation for the scores in this example and applying the procedure you learned in Chapter 2 for changing raw scores to Z scores: $Z = (X - M)/SD$). We could then predict your Z score on happy mood the next day by multiplying .84 by -2.73. The result comes out to -2.29. This means that based on the results of our little study, if you sleep only 5 hours tonight, tomorrow we would expect you to have a happy mood that is more than 2 standard deviations below the mean (that is, you would be very unhappy). In terms of the formula,

$$\text{Predicted } Z_Y = (\beta)(Z_X) = (.84)\,(-2.73) = -2.29$$

In terms of the steps,

❶ **Determine the standardized regression coefficient (β).** Because the correlation coefficient is .84, the standardized regression coefficient (β) is also .84.

❷ **Multiply the standardized regression coefficient (β) by the person's Z score on the predictor variable.** Your Z score on the predictor variable is -2.73. Multiplying .84 by -2.73 gives a predicted Z score on happy mood of -2.29.

By contrast, if you planned to get 9 hours' sleep, the prediction model would predict that tomorrow you would have a Z score for happy mood of .84 multiplied by .91 (the Z score when the number of hours slept is 9), which is +.76. You would be somewhat happier than the average. In terms of the formula,

$$\text{Predicted } Z_Y = (\beta)(Z_X) = (.84)\,(.91) = .76$$

(Incidentally, it is not a good idea to make predictions that involve values of the predictor variable very far from those in the original study. For example, you should not conclude that sleeping 20 hours would make you extremely happy the next day!)

WHY PREDICTION IS ALSO CALLED REGRESSION

Social and behavioral scientists often call this kind of prediction *regression*. Regression means, literally, going back or returning. We use the term regression here because in the usual situation in which there is less than a perfect correlation between two variables, the criterion variable Z score is some fraction of the predictor variable Z score. This fraction is β (the standardized regression coefficient). In our sleep and mood example, $\beta = .84$ thus the fraction is 84/100. This means that a person's predicted Z score on the criterion variable is 84/100 of the person's Z score on the predictor variable. As a result, the predicted Z score on the criterion variable is closer to the mean of 0 than is the Z score on the predictor variable. (In our sleep and mood example, when the Z score on the predictor variable was .91, the Z score predicted for the criterion variable was .76, a number closer to 0 than .91.) That is, the Z score on the criterion variable regresses, or goes back, toward a Z of 0.

Tip for Success

When making predictions using Z scores, you can check your work by being sure that a person's predicted Z score on the criterion variable is closer to 0 than the person's Z score on the predictor variable.

HOW ARE YOU DOING?

1. In words, what is the prediction model using Z scores?
2. Why does the standardized regression coefficient have this name? That is, explain the meaning of each of the three words that make up the term: standardized, regression, and coefficient.
3. Write the formula for the prediction model using Z scores, and define each of the symbols.
4. Figure the predicted Z score on the criterion variable (Y) in each of the following situations:

Situation	r	Z_X
a	.2	1.2
b	.5	2.0
c	.8	1.2

ANSWERS:

1. A person's predicted Z score on the variable being predicted about (the criterion variable) is the standardized regression coefficient (β) multiplied by the person's Z score on the variable being predicted from (the predictor variable).
2. It is called *standardized* because you are predicting with Z scores, which are also called standard scores. It is called a *regression* coefficient because it is used in prediction, which is also called regression. (Prediction is called regression because the result of the prediction process is a predicted score on the criterion variable that is closer to the mean—goes back toward the mean—than is the score on the predictor variable.) It is called a *coefficient* because it is a number you multiply by another number.
3. Predicted $Z_Y = (\beta)(Z_X)$. Predicted Z_Y is the predicted Z score on the criterion variable. β is the standardized regression coefficient. Z_X is the Z score on the predictor variable.
4. (a) (.2) (1.2) = .24
   (b) (.5) (2.0) = 1.00
   (c) (.8) (1.2) = .96

PREDICTION USING RAW SCORES

Based on what you have learned, you can now also make predictions involving raw scores. To do this, change the raw score on the predictor variable to a Z score, make the prediction using the prediction model with Z scores, and then change the predicted Z score on the criterion variable to a raw score.

STEPS OF RAW-SCORE PREDICTION

❶ **Change the person's raw score on the predictor variable to a Z score.** That is, change X to Z_X. Based on the formula from Chapter 2, $Z_X = (X - M_X)/SD_X$.

❷ **Multiply the standardized regression coefficient (β) by the person's Z score on the predictor variable.** That is, multiply β (which is the same as r) by Z_X. This gives the predicted Z score on the criterion variable. This is formula (3–3):

$$\text{Predicted } Z_Y = (\beta)(Z_X)$$

❸ **Change the person's predicted Z score on the criterion variable to a raw score.**[2] That is, change the Predicted Z_Y to Y. Based on the formula from Chapter 2,

$$\text{Predicted } Y = (SD_Y)(\text{Predicted } Z_Y) + M_Y$$

AN EXAMPLE

Recall our example from the sleep and mood study in which we wanted to predict your mood the next day if you sleep 5 hours the night before. In this example, the mean for sleep was 8 and the standard deviation was 1.10; for happy mood, the mean was 4 and the standard deviation was 1.73. The correlation between sleep and mood was .84.

❶ **Change the person's raw score on the predictor variable to a Z score.** $Z_X = (X - M_X)/SD_X = (5 - 8)/1.10 = -3/1.10 = -2.73$. That is, as we saw earlier, the Z score for 5 hours' sleep is -2.73.

❷ **Multiply the standardized regression coefficient (β) by the person's Z score on the predictor variable.** Predicted $Z_Y = (\beta)(Z_X) = (.84)(-2.73) = -2.29$. That is, as we also saw earlier, your predicted Z score for mood if you sleep only 5 hours is -2.29.

❸ **Change the person's predicted Z score on the criterion variable to a raw score.** Predicted $Y = (SD_Y)(\text{Predicted } Z_Y) + M_Y = (1.73)(-2.29) + 4 = -3.96 + 4 = .04$. In other words, using the prediction model based on the study of 10 students, we would predict that if you sleep only 5 hours tonight, tomorrow you will rate your happy mood as about a zero!

Table 3–6 shows these steps worked out for sleeping 9 hours tonight.

Tip for Success

In using these steps, be careful when changing raw scores to Z scores and Z scores to raw scores to use the mean and standard deviation for the correct variable. In Step 1, you are working only with the score, mean, and standard deviation for the predictor variable (X). In Step 3, you are working only with the score, mean, and standard deviation for the criterion variable (Y).

TABLE 3–6 Steps, Formulas, and Example of Raw-Score Prediction

Step	Formula	Example
❶	$Z_X = (X - M_X)/SD_X$	$Z_X = (9-8)/1.10 = .91$
❷	Predicted $Z_Y = (\beta)(Z_X)$	Predicted $Z_Y = (.84)(.91) = .76$
❸	Predicted $Y = (SD_Y)(\text{Predicted } Z_Y) + M_Y$	Predicted $Y = (.76)(1.73) + 4 = 5.31$

[2]In practice, if you are going to make predictions for many different people, you would use a *raw-score prediction formula* that allows you to just plug in a particular person's raw score on the predictor variable and then solve directly to get the person's predicted raw score on the criterion variable. What the raw score prediction formula amounts to is taking the usual Z-score prediction formula, but substituting for the Z scores the formula for getting a Z score from a raw score. If you know the mean and standard deviation for both variables and the correlation coefficient, this whole thing can then be reduced algebraically to give the raw-score prediction formula. This raw-score prediction formula is of the form Predicted $Y = a + (b)(X)$ where a is called the *regression constant* (because this number that is added into the prediction does not change regardless of the value of X) and b is called the *raw-score regression coefficient* (because it is the number multiplied by the raw-score value of X and then added to a to get the predicted value of Y). You will sometimes see these terms referred to in research reports. However, since the logic of regression and its relation to correlation is most directly appreciated from the Z-score prediction formula, that is our emphasis in this introductory text.

1. Explain the principle behind prediction using raw scores.
2. List the steps of making predictions using raw scores.
3. For a variable X, the mean is 10 and the standard deviation is 3. For a variable Y, the mean is 100 and the standard deviation is 10. The correlation of X and Y is .6. (a) Predict the score on Y for a person who has a score on X of 16. (b) Predict the score on Y for a person who has a score on X of 7.
4. For a variable X, the mean is 20 and the standard deviation is 5. For a variable Y, the mean is 6 and the standard deviation is 2. The correlation of X and Y is .8. (a) Predict the score on Y for a person who has a score on X of 20. (b) Predict the score on Y for a person who has a score on X of 25.

ANSWERS:

1. The principle is that you first change the raw score you are predicting from to a Z score, then make the prediction using the prediction model with Z scores, then change the predicted Z score to a predicted raw score.
2. ❶ **Change the person's raw score on the predictor variable to a Z score.**
   ❷ **Multiply the standardized regression coefficient (β) by the person's Z score on the predictor variable.**

   ❸ **Change the person's predicted Z score on the criterion variable to a raw score.**
3. (a) $Z_X = (X - M_X)/SD_X = (16 - 10)/3 = 6/3 = 2$.
   Predicted $Z_Y = (\beta)(Z_X) = (.6)(2) = 1.2$
   Predicted $Y = (SD_Y)(\text{Predicted} Z_Y) + M_Y = (10)(1.2) + 100 = 12 + 100 = 112$.
   (b) $Z_X = (X - M_X)/SD_X = (7 - 10)/3 = -3/3 = -1$.
   Predicted $Z_Y = (\beta)(Z_X) = (.6)(-1) = -.6$.
   Predicted $Y = (SD_Y)(\text{Predicted} Z_Y) + M_Y = (10)(-.6) + 100 = -6 + 100 = 94$.
4. (a) $Z_X = (X - M_X)/SD_X = (20 - 20)/5 = 0/5 = 0$.
   Predicted $Z_Y = (\beta)(Z_X) = (.8)(0) = 0$.
   Predicted $Y = (SD_Y)(\text{Predicted} Z_Y) + M_Y = (2)(0) + 6 = 0 + 6 = 6$.
   (b) $Z_X = (X - M_X)/SD_X = (25 - 20)/5 = 5/5 = 1$.
   Predicted $Z_Y = (\beta)(Z_X) = (.8)(1) = .8$.
   Predicted $Y = (SD_Y)(\text{Predicted} Z_Y) + M_Y = (2)(.8) + 6 = 1.6 + 6 = 7.6$.

MULTIPLE REGRESSION AND MULTIPLE CORRELATION

So far, we have predicted a person's score on a criterion variable using the person's score on a single predictor variable. Suppose you could use more than one predictor variable? For example, in predicting happy mood, all you had to work with was the number of hours slept the night before. Suppose you also knew how well the person slept or how many dreams the person had. With this added information, you might be able to make a much more accurate prediction of mood.

The association between a criterion variable and two or more predictor variables is called **multiple correlation.** Making predictions in this situation is called **multiple regression.**

We explore these topics only briefly because the details are beyond the level of an introductory book. However, multiple regression and correlation are frequently used in research articles in the social and behavioral sciences, so it is valuable for you to have a general understanding of them.

multiple correlation

multiple regression

MULTIPLE REGRESSION PREDICTION MODELS

In multiple regression, each predictor variable has its own regression coefficient. The predicted Z score of the criterion variable is found by multiplying the Z score for each predictor variable by its standardized regression coefficient and then adding up the results. For example, here is the Z-score multiple regression formula with three predictor variables

> The predicted Z score for the criterion variable is the standardized regression coefficient for the first predictor variable multiplied by the person's Z score on the first predictor variable, plus the standardized regression coefficient for the second predictor variable multiplied by the person's Z score on the second predictor variable, plus the standardized regression coefficient for the third predictor variable multiplied by the person's Z score on the third predictor variable.

$$\text{Predicted } Z_Y = (\beta_1)(Z_{X_1}) + (\beta_2)(Z_{X_2}) + (\beta_3)(Z_{X_3}) \qquad (3\text{-}4)$$

Predicted Z_Y is the person's predicted score on the criterion variable. β_1 is the standardized regression coefficient for the first predictor variable; β_2 and β_3 are the standardized regression coefficients for the second and third predictor variables. Z_{X_1} is the person's Z score for the first predictor variable; Z_{X_2} and Z_{X_3} are the person's Z scores for the second and third predictor variables. $(\beta_1)(Z_{X1})$ means multiplying β_1 by Z_{X_1} and so forth.

For example, in the sleep and mood study, a multiple regression model for predicting happy mood (Y) using the predictor variables of number of hours slept, which we could now call X_1 and also a rating of how well you slept (X_2) and number of dreams during the night (X_3) might turn out to be as follows:

$$\text{Predicted } Z_Y = (.53)(Z_{X_1}) + (.28)(Z_{X_2}) + (.03)(Z_{X_3})$$

Suppose you were asked to predict the mood of a student who had a Z score of -1.82 for number of hours slept, a Z score of 2.34 for how well she slept, and a Z score of .94 for number of dreams during the night. That is, the student did not sleep very long, slept very well, and had a few more dreams than average. You would figure the predicted Z score for happy mood by multiplying .53 by the number-of-hours slept Z score, multiplying .28 by the how-well-slept Z score, and multiplying .03 by the number-of-dreams Z score, then adding up the results:

$$\text{Predicted } Z_Y = (.53)(-1.82) + (.28)(2.34) + (.03)(.94)$$

$$= -.96 + .66 + .03 = -.27$$

Thus, under these conditions, you would predict a happy mood Z score of $-.27$. This means a happy mood about one-quarter of a standard deviation below the mean. You can see that how well the student slept partially offset getting fewer hours' sleep. Given the very low standardized regression coefficient (β_3) for dreams in this model, once you have take into account the number of hours slept and how well you slept, number of dreams (no matter how many or how few) would in general make very little difference in mood the next day.

In general terms, the size of the standardized regression coefficient for a predictor variable shows the amount of influence that variable has when predicting a score on the criterion variable. The larger the standardized regression coefficient for a predictor variable, the more influence that variable has when predicting a score on the criterion variable.

An Important Difference between Multiple Regression and Prediction Using One Predictor Variable

There is one particularly important difference between multiple regression and prediction when using only one predictor variable. In prediction when using one predictor variable, $\beta = r$. That is, the standardized regression coefficient is the same as the correlation coefficient. But in multiple regression, the standardized regression coefficient (β) for a predictor variable is *not* the same as the ordinary correlation coefficient (r) of that predictor with the criterion variable.

Usually, a β will be closer to 0 than r. The reason is that part of what makes any one predictor successful in predicting the criterion will usually overlap with what makes the other predictors successful in predicting the criterion variable. In multiple regression, the standardized regression coefficient is about the unique, distinctive contribution of the predictor variable, excluding any overlap with other predictor variables.

Consider the sleep and mood example. When we were predicting mood using just the number of hours slept, β was the same as the correlation coefficient of .84. Now, with multiple regression, the β for number of hours slept is only .53. It is less because part of what makes number of hours slept predict mood overlaps with what makes sleeping well predict mood (in this fictional example, people who sleep more hours usually sleep well).

In multiple regression, the overall correlation between the criterion variable and all the predictor variables is called the **multiple correlation coefficient** and is symbolized as R. However, because of the usual overlap among the predictor variables, the multiple correlation (R) is usually smaller than the sum of the individual rs of each predictor variable with the criterion variable.

multiple correlation coefficient

HOW ARE YOU DOING?

1. What is multiple regression?
2. Write the multiple regression prediction model with two predictors, and define each of the symbols.
3. In a multiple regression model, the standardized regression coefficient for the first predictor variable is .4 and for the second predictor variable is .7. What is the predicted criterion variable Z score for (a) a person with a Z score of +1 on the first predictor variable and a Z score of +2 on the second predictor variable, and (b) a person with a Z score of +2 on the first predictor variable and a Z score of +1 on the second predictor variable?
4. In multiple regression, why are the standardized regression coefficients for each predictor variable often smaller than the ordinary correlation coefficient of that predictor variable with the criterion variable?

ANSWERS:

1. The procedure for predicting a criterion variable from a prediction rule that includes more than one predictor variable.
2. Predicted $Z_Y = (\beta_1)(Z_{X_1}) + (\beta_2)(Z_{X_2})$
   Predicted Z_Y is the person's predicted score on the criterion variable. β_1 is the standardized regression coefficient for the first predictor variable, β_2 is the standardized regression coefficient for the second predictor variable. Z_{X_1} is the person's Z score for the first predictor variable, and Z_{X_2} is the person's Z score for the second predictor variable.
3. (a) Predicted $Z_Y = (.4)(Z_{X_1}) + (.7)(Z_{X_2}) = (.4)(1) + (.7)(2) = .4 + 1.4 = 1.8$.
   (b) Predicted $Z_Y = (.4)(Z_{X_1}) + (.7)(Z_{X_2}) = (.4)(2) + (.7)(1) = .8 + .7 = 1.5$.
4. In multiple regression, a predictor variable's association with the criterion variable usually overlaps with the other predictor variables' association with the criterion variable. Thus, the unique association of a predictor variable with the criterion variable (the standardized

regression coefficient) is usually smaller than the ordinary correlation of the predictor variable with the criterion variable.

THE CORRELATION COEFFICIENT AND THE PROPORTION OF VARIANCE ACCOUNTED FOR

A correlation coefficient tells you the strength of a linear relationship. As you learned earlier in the chapter, bigger rs (values farther from 0) mean a higher degree of correlation. So, an r of .4 is a stronger correlation than an r of .2. However, an r of .4 is *more than* twice as strong as an r of .2. To compare correlations with each other, you have to square each correlation (that is, you use r^2 instead of r). The correlation squared is called the **proportion of variance accounted for (r^2)**.[3]

proportion of variance accounted for (r^2)

For example, a correlation of .2 is equivalent to an r^2 of .04, and a correlation of .4 is equivalent to an r^2 of .16. A correlation of .2 actually means a relationship between X and Y that is only one-quarter as strong as a correlation of .4.

This all works the same way in multiple regression. In multiple regression, the proportion of variance in the criterion variable accounted for by all the predictor variables taken together is the multiple correlation squared, R^2.

CORRELATION AND PREDICTION IN RESEARCH ARTICLES

Scatter diagrams are occasionally reported in research articles. For example, in an article published in *Social Science Quarterly,* DeSart and Holbrook (2003) looked at the relationship between the results of trial-heat presidential election polls in each state and the actual U.S. presidential election results in each state in 2000. In each of the 50 states, trial-heat polls were carried out in September 2000, just over one month before the actual election. DeSart and Holbrook were interested in the correlation between the percentage of votes that Al Gore received in each state in the September trial-heat poll and the percentage of votes he received in each state in the actual election. Their results are shown in Figure 3–14. As shown in the scatter diagram, there was a clear, strong linear positive trend—notice that the dots fall very close to a straight line that goes up and to the right. This is consistent with the very large r of .96. So, these results show that the September polls in each state did a very good job of predicting the actual election results in each state.

---

[3]The reason r^2 is called proportion of variance accounted for can be understood as follows: Suppose you used the prediction formula to predict each person's score on Y. Unless the correlation between X and Y was perfect (1.0), the variance of those predicted Y scores would be smaller than the variance of the original Y scores. There is less variance in the predicted Y scores because these predicted scores are on average closer to the mean than are the original scores. (We discussed this in the section on why prediction is called regression.) However, the more accurate the prediction, the more the predicted scores are like the actual scores. Thus, the more accurate the prediction, the closer the variance of the predicted scores is to the variance of the actual scores. Now suppose you divide the variance of the predicted Y scores by the variance of the original Y scores. The result of this division is the proportion of variance in the actual scores "accounted for" by the variance in the predicted scores. This proportion turns out (for reasons beyond what we can cover in this book) to be r^2.

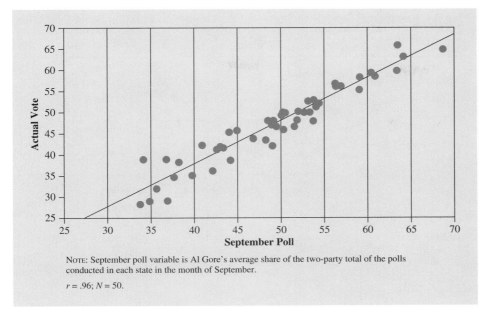

NOTE: September poll variable is Al Gore's average share of the two-party total of the polls conducted in each state in the month of September.

$r = .96$; $N = 50$.

FIGURE 3–14 *September Statewide Polls and Actual Results 2000 U.S. Presidential Election.*
Source: DeSart, J. A., & Holbrook, T. M. (2003). Statewide trial-heat polls and the 2000 presidential election: A forecast model. *Social Science Quarterly, 84,* 561–573. Copyright © 2003 by the Southwestern Social Science Association. Reprinted by permission.

Research articles usually give correlation coefficients either in the text of research articles or in tables. The result with which we started the chapter would be described as follows: There was a positive correlation ($r = .51$) between excitement of activities done with partner and marital satisfaction. (Often the "significance level" of the correlation will also be reported—in this example it would be $r = .51$, $p < .05$.)

Tables of correlations are common when several variables are involved. Usually, the table is set up so that each variable is listed down the left and also across the top. The correlation of each pair of variables is shown inside the table. This is called a **correlation matrix.**

correlation matrix

Table 3–7 is from a study published by Buboltz, Johnson, and Woller (2003) in the *Journal of Counseling and Development.* The participants in the study were 311 college students. The study looked at the relationship between various characteristics of students' families and students' level of psychological reactance. The researchers defined psychological reactance as a personality characteristic consisting of the tendency to react in an extreme way when an individual's behavior is restricted in some way. The students completed a self-report questionnaire measure of psychological reactance called the Therapeutic Reactance Scale. They also completed a measure called the Family Environment Scale. This self-report questionnaire was used to measure various characteristics of each student's family. These characteristics included the level of cohesion, conflict, and expressiveness in the family. In the table, the family characteristics are referred to as "subscales" of the Family Environment Scale.

This example shows several features that are typical of the way correlation matrixes are laid out. First, notice that the correlation of a variable with itself is not

TABLE 3–7 Intercorrelations among the Therapeutic Reactance Scale and the Family Environment Scale Subscales

Scale	1	2	3	4	5	6	7	8	9	10	11
1. Therapeutic Reactance Scale	—	.41**	−.39**	.27**	.34**	.50**	.11	.22**	.51**	.09	.08
Family Environment Scale subscales											
2. Cohesion		—	−.62**	.41**	.40**	.31**	.42**	.41**	.46**	.39**	−.03
3. Conflict			—	−.36**	−.40**	−.20**	−.37**	−.27**	−.32**	−.25**	.10
4. Expressiveness				—	.30**	.19**	.28**	.36**	.29**	.16**	−.11*
5. Independence					—	.32**	.27**	.26**	.25**	.13*	−.08
6. Achievement Orientation						—	.16**	.22**	.40**	.26**	.23**
7. Intellectual-Cultural Orientation							—	.35**	.22**	.20**	−.01
8. Active-Recreational Orientation								—	.32**	.18**	−.04
9. Moral-Religious Emphasis									—	.20**	.15**
10. Organization										—	.23**
11. Control											—

*p < .05, **p < .01

Source: Buboltz, W. C., Jr., Johnson, P., & Woller, K. M. P. (2003). Psychological reactance in college students: Family-of-origin predictors. *Journal of Counseling and Development, 81,* 311–317. Copyright © ACA. Reprinted by permission. No further reproduction authorized without written permission of the American Counseling Association.

given. In this example, a short line is put in instead; sometimes they are just left blank. Also notice that only the upper triangle of the table is filled in. This is because the lower left triangle would contain exactly the same information. For example, the correlation of psychological reactance (which was measured using the Therapeutic Reactance Scale) and conflict (which is −.39) has to be the same as the correlation of conflict and psychological reactance (so there is no point putting −.39 again in the lower part of the table). Another shortcut saves space across the page: The names of the variables are listed only on the side of the table, with the numbers for them put across the top. The asterisks—* and **—after some of the correlation coefficients indicate correlation coefficients that are statistically significant. As noted in the bottom left corner of the table, one asterisk (*) means that the correlation coefficient is statistically significant at $p < .05$ and two asterisks (**) means it is statistically significant at $p < .01$.

Looking at this example, among other results, you can see that there were quite a few positive linear correlations between family characteristics (such as cohesion, expressiveness, independence, and moral-religious emphasis) and psychological reactance. There was a negative linear correlation between one of the family characteristics—conflict—and psychological reactance. These results suggest that there is a relationship between certain family characteristics and students' levels of psychological reactance.

When prediction models are given in research articles, they are usually for multiple regression. Multiple regression results are common in research articles in the social and behavioral sciences and are often reported in tables. Consider again Buboltz and colleagues' (2003) study of the relationship between family characteristics and psychological reactance among college students. In addition to the corre-

TABLE 3–8	Summary of Regression Analysis Assessing the Unique Effects of Each Relationship Dimension Predicting Psychological Reactance		
Relationship Dimension	B	$SE\ B$	β
Conflict	-1.71	0.49	-0.23***
Cohesion	1.46	0.45	0.22***
Expressiveness	0.90	0.52	0.10

Note: Beta coefficients for each predictor are over and above the other predictors.
*$p < .05$, **$p < .01$, ***$p < .001$.
Source: Buboltz, W. C., Jr., Johnson, P., & Woller, K. M. P. (2003). Psychological reactance in college students: Family-of-origin predictors. *Journal of Counseling and Development, 81*, 311–317. Copyright © 2003 by Copyright © ACA. Reprinted by permission. No further reproduction authorized without written permission of the American Counseling Association.

lation matrix, the researchers presented the results of a multiple regression model for predicting psychological reactance from three of the family characteristics: conflict, cohesion, and expressiveness. Each of these three characteristics represents a different dimension of the relationship among family members. The standardized regression coefficients for this multiple regression model are shown in Table 3–8 (in the β column). You can see that family conflict had a negative standardized regression coefficient and family cohesion and family expressiveness each had a positive standardized regression coefficient. Looking at the β column, you can also see that the standardized regression coefficients for conflict and cohesion were larger than the standardized regression coefficient for expressiveness. This tells you that family conflict and family cohesion were more important unique predictors of psychological reactance than family expressiveness.

The table also includes the unstandardized regression coefficients (labeled with a capital B here). Finally, for each B, it gives what is called its standard error (*SE B*). These have to do with the accuracy of estimation of these coefficients in the population in general. You will have a better understanding of these after Chapter 6.

SUMMARY

1. When two variables are associated in a clear pattern, for example, when high scores on one consistently go with high scores on the other, and lows on one go with lows on the other, the two variables are correlated.

2. A scatter diagram shows the relation between two variables. The lowest to highest possible values of one variable (the one you are predicting from, if they are distinguishable) are marked on the horizontal axis. The lowest to highest possible values of the other variable are marked on the vertical axis. Each individual's pair of scores is shown as a dot.

3. When the dots in the scatter diagram generally follow a straight line, this is called a linear correlation. In a curvilinear correlation, the dots follow a line pattern other than a simple straight line. No correlation exists when the dots do not follow any kind of line. In a positive linear correlation, the line goes upward to the right (so that low scores go with lows and highs with highs). In a negative linear correlation, the line goes downward to the right (so that low scores go with highs and highs with lows).

4. The correlation coefficient (r) gives the degree of linear correlation. It is the average of the cross-products of Z scores. The correlation coefficient is highly positive when there is a strong positive linear correlation. This is because positive Z scores are multiplied by positive, and negative Z scores by negative. The correlation coefficient is highly negative when there is a strong negative linear correlation. This is because positive Z scores are multiplied by negative and negative Z scores by positive. The coefficient is 0 when there is no linear correlation. This is because positive Z scores are sometimes multiplied by positive and sometimes by negative Z scores and negative Z scores are sometimes multiplied by negative and sometimes by positive. Thus, positive and negative cross-products cancel each other out.

5. The maximum positive value of r is +1. $r = +1$ when there is a perfect positive linear correlation. The maximum negative value of r is -1. $r = -1$ when there is a perfect negative linear correlation.

6. The actual value of the correlation coefficient—from a low of 0 to a high of 1, ignoring the sign of the correlation coefficient—tells you the strength of the linear correlation. The closer a correlation coefficient is to 1, the stronger the linear correlation.

7. Correlation does not tell you the direction of causation. If two variables, X and Y, are correlated, this could be because X is causing Y, Y is causing X, or a third factor is causing both X and Y.

8. A correlation figured using scores from a particular group of people is often intended to apply to people in general. A correlation is statistically significant when statistical procedures (taught later in this book) make it highly unlikely that you would get a correlation as big as the one found with the group of people studied, if in fact there were no correlation between these two variables among people in general.

9. Prediction (or regression) makes predictions about scores on a criterion variable based on scores on a predictor variable. The prediction model for predicting a person's Z score on the criterion variable is to multiply the standardized regression coefficient (β) by the person's Z score on the predictor variable. The best number to use for the standardized regression coefficient in this situation is the correlation coefficient (r).

10. Predictions with raw scores can be made by changing a person's score on the predictor variable to a Z score, multiplying it by the standardized regression coefficient (β) and then changing the predicted criterion variable Z score to a raw score.

11. In multiple regression, a criterion variable is predicted from two or more predictor variables. In a multiple regression model, each predictor variable is multiplied by its own standardized regression coefficient, and the results are added up to make the prediction. However, because the predictor variables overlap in their influence on the criterion variable, each of the regression coefficients generally is smaller than the variable's correlation coefficient with the criterion variable. The multiple correlation coefficient (R) is the overall degree of association between the criterion variable and the predictor variables taken together.

12. Comparisons of the degree of linear correlation are considered most accurate in terms of the correlation coefficient squared (r^2 or R^2), the proportion of variance accounted for.

13. Correlational results are usually presented in research articles either in the text with the value of r (and sometimes the significance level) or in a special table (a correlation matrix) showing the correlations among several variables. Results of prediction in which a criterion variable is predicted from a single variable are rarely described directly in research articles. Multiple regressions are commonly reported in articles, often in a table that includes the regression coefficients.

KEY TERMS

correlation (p. 58)
scatter diagram (p. 59)
linear correlation (p. 60)
curvilinear correlation
  (p. 61)
no correlation (p. 63)
positive correlation
  (p. 64)
negative correlation
  (p. 64)
cross-product of Z scores
  (p. 68)
perfect correlation
  (p. 69)

correlation coefficient (r)
  (p. 69)
direction of causality
  (p. 75)
longitudinal study
  (p. 76)
true experiment (p. 76)
statistically significant
  (p. 77)
predictor variable (p. 78)
criterion variable (p. 78)
prediction model (p. 79)
standardized regression
  coefficient (β) (p. 79)

multiple correlation
  (p. 83)
multiple regression
  (p. 83)
multiple correlation coefficient (R) (p. 85)
proportion of variance accounted for (r^2) (p. 86)
correlation matrix (p. 87)

EXAMPLE WORKED-OUT PROBLEMS

MAKING A SCATTER DIAGRAM AND DESCRIBING THE GENERAL PATTERN OF ASSOCIATION

Based on the number of hours studied and the test score for the five students shown below, make a scatter diagram and describe in words the general pattern of association.

Student	Hours Studied	Test Score
A	0	52
B	10	92
C	6	75
D	8	71
E	6	64

ANSWER

The steps of solving the problem are described below; Figure 3–15 shows the scatter diagram with markers for each step.

❶ **Draw the axes and decide which variable goes on which axis.** Since studying comes before the test score, we will draw the axes with number of hours studied along the bottom.

❷ **Determine the range of values to use for each variable and mark them on the axes.** We will assume that the test scores go from 0 to 100. We do not know the maximum possible for the number of hours studied, but let us assume a maximum of 10 in this example.

❸ **Mark a dot for each person's pair of scores.** For example, to mark the dot for student D, you go across to 8 and up to 71.

The general pattern is roughly linear. Its direction is positive (it goes up and to the right, with more hours studied going with larger test scores and vice versa). It is a quite strong correlation, since the dots all fall fairly close to a straight line—it should be fairly close to +1. In words, it is a strong, linear, positive correlation.

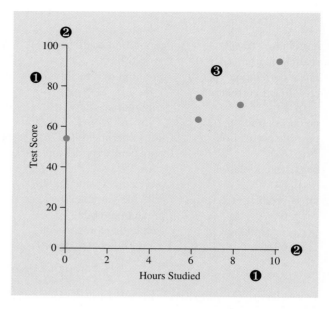

FIGURE 3–15 *Scatter diagram for scores in Example Worked-Out Problem.* ❶ *Draw the axes and decide which variable goes on which axis.* ❷ *Determine the range of values to use for each variable and mark them on the axes.* ❸ *Mark a dot for each person's pair of scores.*

FIGURING THE CORRELATION COEFFICIENT

Figure the correlation coefficient for the hours studied and test score example given above.

ANSWER

You can figure the correlation using either the formula or the steps. The basic figuring is shown in Table 3–9 with markers for each of the steps.

Using the formula,

$$r = \Sigma Z_X Z_Y / N = 4.49/5 = .90.$$

TABLE 3–9 Figuring Correlation Coefficient for Answer to Example Worked-Out Problem

	Hours Studied		Test Score		Cross-Products
	X	Z_X ❶	Y	Z_Y ❶	$Z_X Z_Y$ ❷
	0	−1.79	52	−1.43	2.56
	10	1.19	92	1.61	1.92
	6	.00	75	.32	.00
	8	.60	71	.02	.01
	6	.00	64	−.52	0
Σ:	30		354		4.49 ❸
M:	6		70.8		$r = 4.49/5 = .90$ ❹
SD:	$\sqrt{56/5} = 3.35$		$\sqrt{866.8/5} = 13.17$		

Using the steps,

❶ **Change all scores to Z scores.** For example, the mean for hours studied is 6, and the standard deviation is 3.35; thus, the Z score for student A, who studied for 0 hours, is $(0 - 6)/3.35 = -1.79$.

❷ **Figure the cross-product of the Z scores for each person.** For example, for student A, the cross-product is -1.79 multiplied by -1.43 which is 2.56; for student B, it is 1.19 multiplied by 1.61, which equals 1.92.

❸ **Add up all the cross-products of the Z scores.** The total is 4.49.

❹ **Divide by the number of people in the study.** The sum (4.49) divided by 5 is .90; that is, $r = -.90$.

PREDICTION USING Z SCORES

Based on the data shown below (which are the same data used for an example earlier in the chapter), predict the Z scores for achievement for schools that have class sizes with Z scores of $-2, -1, 0, +1, +2$.

Elementary School	Class Size	Achievement Test Score
Main Street	25	80
Casat	14	98
Harland	33	50
Shady Grove	28	82
Jefferson	20	90
M	24	80
SD	6.54	16.30

$r = -.90$

ANSWER

This can be done using either the formula or the steps. Using the formula Predicted $Z_Y = (\beta)(Z_X)$ the Z-score prediction model for this problem is,

$$\text{Predicted } Z_Y = (-.90)\,(Z_X) = (-.90)\,(-2) = 1.80.$$
$$(-.90)\,(-1) = .90.$$
$$(-.90)\,(0) = 0.$$
$$(-.90)\,(+1) = -.90.$$
$$(-.90)\,(+2) = -1.80.$$

Using the steps,

❶ **Determine the standardized regression coefficient (β).** Because the correlation coefficient is $-.90$, the same as r. Thus, $\beta = -.90$.

❷ **Multiply the standardized regression coefficient by the person's Z score on the predictor variable.** $-.90 \times -2 = 1.80$; $-.90 \times -1 = .90$; $-.90 \times 0 = 0$; $-.90 \times 1 = -.90$; $-.90 \times 2 = -1.80$.

PREDICTION USING RAW SCORES

Using the data from the example above on class size and achievement test score, predict the raw scores for achievement for a school that has a class size of 27.

ANSWER

Using the steps,

❶ **Change the person's raw score on the predictor variable to a Z score (note that in this example, we have a school's raw score).** $Z_X = (X - M_X)/SD_X = (27 - 24)/6.54 = 3/6.54 = .46$.

❷ **Multiply the standardized regression coefficient (β) by the person's predictor variable Z score.** Predicted $Z_Y = (\beta)(Z_X) = (-.90)(.46) = -.41$. That is, the predicted Z score for this school is $-.41$.

❸ **Change the person's predicted Z score on the criterion variable to a raw score.** Predicted $Y = (SD_Y)$ (Predicted $Z_Y) + M_Y = (16.30)(-.41) + 80 = -6.68 + 80 = 73.32$. In other words, using the prediction model based on the study of 5 schools, we would predict that a school with an average class size of 27 students will have an average achievement test score of 73.32.

MULTIPLE REGRESSION PREDICTIONS

A (fictional) researcher studied the talkativeness of children in families with a mother, father, and one grandparent. The researcher found that the child's talkativeness score depended on the quality of the child's relationship with each of these people. The multiple regression prediction model using Z scores is as follows:

> Predicted talkativeness Z score of the child = (.32) (Z mother) + (.21) (Z father) + (.11) (Z grandparent)

Predict a child's talkativeness Z score who had Z scores for relationship quality of .48 with mother, $-.63$ with father, and 1.25 with grandparent.

ANSWER

Predicted talkativeness Z score of the child = (.32) (Z mother) + (.21) (Z father) + (.11) (Z grandparent).
= (.32) (.48) + (.21) (−.63) + (.11) (1.25) = .15 + −.13 + .14 = .16

PRACTICE PROBLEMS

These problems involve figuring. Most real-life statistics problems are done on a computer with special statistical software. Even if you have such software, do these problems by hand (with the help of a calculator) to ingrain the method in your mind. Also, in all problems involving figuring, be sure to show your work.

For practice in using a computer to solve statistics problems, refer to the computer section of each chapter of the *Student's Study Guide and Computer Workbook* that accompanies this text.

All data are fictional unless an actual citation is given.

For answers to Set I problems, see pp. 424–26.

SET I

1. For each of the following scatter diagrams, indicate whether the pattern is linear, curvilinear, or no correlation; if it is linear, indicate whether it is positive or negative and aproximately how strong the correlation is (strong, moderate, weak).

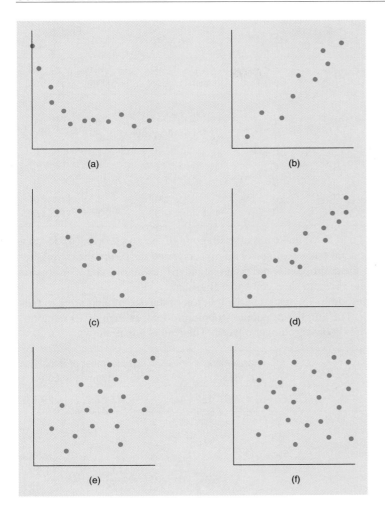

(a) (b) (c) (d) (e) (f)

2. The following have been prepared so that data sets B through D are slightly modified versions of data set A. Make scatter diagrams and figure the correlation coefficients for each data set.

Data Set A X Y	Data Set B X Y	Data Set C X Y	Data Set D X Y
1 1	1 1	1 5	1 1
2 2	2 2	2 2	2 4
3 3	3 3	3 3	3 3
4 4	4 5	4 4	4 2
5 5	5 4	5 1	5 5

3. A researcher is interested in whether a new drug affects the development of a cold. Eight people are tested: Four take the drug and four do not. (Those who take it are rated 1; those who don't, 0.) Whether they get a cold (rated 1) or not (0) is recorded. Four possible results are shown. Figure the correlation coefficient for each possibility (A, B, C, and D).

Possibility A		Possibility B		Possibility C		Possibility D	
Take Drug	Get Cold	Take Drug	Get Cold	Take Drug	Get Cold	Take Drug	Get Cold
0	1	0	1	0	1	0	1
0	1	0	1	0	1	0	1
0	1	0	1	0	0	0	1
0	1	0	0	0	0	0	0
1	0	1	1	1	1	1	0
1	0	1	0	1	1	1	0
1	0	1	0	1	0	1	0
1	0	1	0	1	0	1	0

For problems 4 and 5, (a) make a scatter diagram of the raw scores; (b) describe in words the general pattern of correlation, if any; and (c) figure the correlation coefficient. In these problems, the mean, standard deviation, and Z scores for each variable are given to save you some figuring.

4. The Louvre Museum is interested in the relation of the age of a painting to public interest in it. The number of people stopping to look at each of 10 randomly selected paintings is observed over a week. The results are as shown:

Painting Title	Approximate Age (Years) ($M = 253.4$, $SD = 152.74$)		Number of People Stopping to Look ($M = 88.2$, $SD = 29.13$)	
	X	Z_X	Y	Z_Y
The Entombment	465	1.39	68	−.69
Mys Mar Ste Catherine	515	1.71	71	−.59
The Bathers	240	−.09	123	1.19
The Toilette	107	−.96	112	.82
Portrait of Castiglione	376	.80	48	−1.38
Charles I of England	355	.67	84	−.14
Crispin and Scapin	140	−.75	66	−.76
Nude in the Sun	115	−.91	148	2.05
The Balcony	122	−.86	71	−.59
The Circus	99	−1.01	91	.10

5. A schoolteacher thought that he had observed that students who dressed more neatly were generally better students. To test this idea, the teacher had a friend rate each of the students for neatness of dress. Following are the ratings for neatness, along with each student's score on a standardized school achievement test.

Child	Neatness Rating ($M = 19.6$, $SD = 3.07$)		Score on Achievement Test ($M = 63.1$, $SD = 4.70$)	
	X	Z_X	Y	Z_Y
Janet	18	−.52	60	−.66
Gareth	24	1.43	58	−1.09
Grove	14	−1.82	70	1.47

Kevin	19	−.20	58	−1.09
Joshua	20	.13	66	.62
Nicole	23	1.11	68	1.04
Susan	20	.13	65	.40
Drew	22	.78	68	1.04
Marie	15	−1.50	56	−1.51
Chad	21	.46	62	−.23

For problems 6 and 7, do the following: (a) Make a scatter diagram of the raw scores; (b) describe in words the general pattern of correlation, if any; (c) figure the correlation coefficient; (d) explain the logic of what you have done, writing as if you are speaking to someone who has never had a statistics course (but who does understand the mean, standard deviation, and Z scores); (e) give three logically possible directions of causality, saying for each whether it is a reasonable direction in light of the variables involved (and why); (f) make raw score predictions on the criterion variable for persons with Z scores on the predictor variable of −2, −1, 0, +1, +2; and (g) give the proportion of variance accounted for (r^2).

6. Four young children were monitored closely over a period of several weeks to measure how much they watched violent television programs and their amount of violent behavior toward their playmates. (For part (f), assume that hours watching violent television is the predictor variable.) The results were as follows:

Child's Code Number	Weekly Viewing of Violent TV (hours)	Number of Violent or Aggressive Acts toward Playmates
G3368	14	9
R8904	8	6
C9890	6	1
L8722	12	8

7. A political scientist studied the relation between the number of town-hall meetings held by the four candidates for mayor in a small town and the percentage of people in the town who could name each candidate. (For part (f), assume that the number of town-hall meetings is the predictor variable.) Here are the results:

Mayor Candidate	Number of Town-Hall Meetings	Percentage of People Who Can Name Candidate
A	4	70
B	5	94
C	2	36
D	1	48

8. Chapman, Hobfoll, and Ritter (1997) interviewed 68 inner-city pregnant women and their husbands (or boyfriends) twice during their pregnancy, once between 3 and 6 months into the pregnancy and again between 6 and 9 months into the pregnancy. Table 3–10 shows the correlations among several of their measures. ("Zero-Order Correlations" means the same thing as ordinary corre-

TABLE 3–10 Zero-Order Correlations for Study Variables

Variable	1	2	3	4	5	6	7	8	9	10
1. Women's report of stress	—									
2. Men's report of women's stress	.17	—								
3. Partner Support 1	−.28*	−.18	—							
4. Partner Support 2	−.27*	−.18	.44***	—						
5. Depressed Mood 1	.23*	.10	−.34**	−.17	—					
6. Depressed Mood 2	−.50***	.14	−.42***	−.41***	.55***	—				
7. Women's age	.06	.16	.04	−.24*	−.35*	−.09	—			
8. Women's ethnicity	−.19	−.09	−.16	−.14	.11	.13	−.02	—		
9. Women's marital status	−.18	.01	.12	.24*	−.04	−.20	.05	−.34**	—	
10. Parity	.19	.13	−.11	−.17	.10	.16	.26*	.31*	−.12	—

$*p < .05$, $**p < .01$, $***p < .001$.

Source: Chapman, H. A., Hobfoll, S. E., & Ritter, C. (1997). Partners' stress underestimations lead to women's distress: A study of pregnant inner-city women. *Journal of Personality and Social Psychology, 73*, 418–425. Copyright © 1997 by the American Psychological Association. Reprinted by permission.

lations.) Most important in this table are the correlations among women's reports of their own stress, men's reports of their partners' stress, women's perception of their partners' support at the first and at the second interviews, and women's depression at the first and at the second interviews.

Explain the results on these measures as if you were writing to a person who has never had a course in statistics. Specifically, (a) explain what is meant by a correlation coefficient using one of the correlations as an example; (b) study the table and then comment on the patterns of results in terms of which variables are relatively strongly correlated and which are not very strongly correlated; and (c) comment on the limitations of making conclusions about direction of causality based on these data, using a specific correlation as an example (noting at least one plausible alternative causal direction and why that alternative is plausible).

9. A researcher working with hockey players found that knowledge of fitness training principles correlates .4 with number of injuries received over the subsequent year. The researcher now plans to test all new athletes for their knowledge of fitness training principles and use this information to predict the number of injuries they are likely to receive. Indicate the (a) predictor variable, (b) criterion variable, and (c) standardized regression coefficient. (d) Write the Z-score prediction model. Indicate the predicted Z scores for number of injuries for athletes whose Z scores on the principles of fitness training test are (e) −2, (f) −1, (g) 0, (h) +1, and (i) +2.

10. Gunn, Biglan, Smolkowski, and Ary (2000) studied reading in a group of Hispanic and non-Hispanic third graders. As part of this study, they did an analysis predicting reading comprehension (called "passage comprehension") from three more specific measures of reading ability: "Letter-Word Identification" (ability to read irregular words), "Word Attack" (ability to use phonic and structural analysis), and "Oral Reading Fluency" (correct words per minute). The results are shown in Table 3–11. Explain the results as if you were writing to a person who understands correlation but has never learned anything about

TABLE 3–11 Multiple Regression Predicting Comprehension from Decoding Skill and Oral Reading Fluency

Variable	Beta	t	p	R^2	F	p
Passage Comprehension raw score						
Letter-Word Identification	−.227	−2.78	.006			
Word Attack	.299	3.75	.001			
Oral Reading Fluency—	.671	9.97	.001			
Correct words per minute				.534	57.70	.001

Source: Gunn, B., Biglan, A., Smolkowski, K., & Ary, D. (2000). The efficacy of supplemental instruction in decoding skills for Hispanic and non-Hispanic students in early elementary school. *Journal of Special Education, 34*, 90–103. Reprinted by permission.

regression or multiple regression analysis. (Ignore the columns for *t*, *p*, *F*, and *p*. These have to do with statistical significance.)

11. Based on Table 3–11 (from Gunn et al., 2000), (a) determine the Z score multiple regression formula, and (b) calculate the predicted passage comprehension Z score for each of the following third graders (figures are Z scores):

Third Grader	Letter-Word Identification	Word Attack	Oral Reading Fluency
A	1	1	1
B	0	0	0
C	−1	−1	−1
D	1	0	0
E	0	1	0
F	0	0	1
G	3	1	1
H	1	3	1
I	3	1	3

SET II

12. For each of the scatter diagrams on the following page, indicate whether the pattern is linear, curvilinear, or no correlation; if it is linear, indicate whether it is positive or negative and approximately how strong the correlation is (strong, moderate, weak).

13. Make up a scatter diagram with 10 dots for each of the following situations: (a) perfect positive linear correlation, (b) strong but not perfect positive linear correlation, (c) weak positive linear correlation, (d) strong but not perfect negative linear correlation, (e) no correlation, (f) clear curvilinear correlation.

    For problems 14 and 15, (a) make a scatter diagram of the raw scores; (b) describe in words the general pattern of correlation, if any; and (c) figure the correlation coefficient.

14. A researcher studying people in their 80s was interested in the relation between number of very close friends and overall health (on a scale from 0 to 100). The scores for six research participants are shown on the following page.

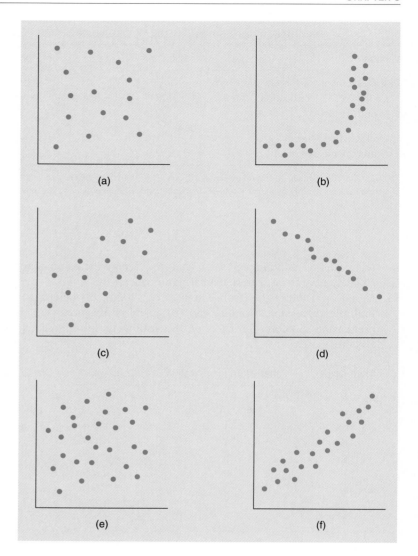

(a) (b)

(c) (d)

(e) (f)

Research Participant	Number of Friends	Overall Health
A	2	41
B	4	72
C	0	37
D	3	84
E	2	52
F	1	49

15. In a study of people first getting acquainted with each other, researchers reasoned the amount of self-disclosure of one's partner (on a scale from 1 to 30) and one's liking for one's partner (on a scale from 1 to 10). The Z scores for the variables are given to save you some figuring. Here are the results:

Partner's Self-Disclosure		Liking for Partner	
Actual Score	Z Score	Actual Score	Z Score
18	.37	8	1.10
17	.17	9	1.47
20	.80	6	.37
8	−1.72	1	−1.47
13	−.67	7	.74
24	1.63	1	−1.47
11	−1.09	3	−.74
12	−.88	5	.0
18	.38	7	.74
21	1.00	3	−.74

For problems 16 and 17, do the following: (a) Make a scatter diagram of the raw scores; (b) describe in words the general pattern of correlation, if any; (c) figure the correlation coefficient; (d) explain the logic of what you have done, writing as if you are speaking to someone who has never had a statistics course (but who does understand the mean, standard deviation, and Z scores); (e) give three logically possible directions of causality, saying for each whether it is a reasonable direction in light of the variables involved (and why); (f) make raw score predictions on the criterion variable for persons with Z scores on the predictor variable of −2, −1, 0, +1, +2, and (g) give the proportion of variance accounted for (r^2).

16. Four research participants take a test of manual dexterity (high scores mean better dexterity) and an anxiety test (high scores mean more anxiety). (For part (f), assume that dexterity is the predictor variable.) The scores are as follows:

Person	Dexterity	Anxiety
A	1	10
B	1	8
C	2	4
D	4	−2

17. Five college students were asked about how important a goal it is to them to have a family and about how important a goal it is for them to be highly successful in their work. Each variable was measured on a scale from 0 "Not at all important goal" to 10 "Very important goal." (For part (f), assume that the family goal is the predictor variable.) The scores are as follows:

Student	Family Goal	Work Goal
A	7	5
B	6	4
C	8	2
D	3	9
E	4	1

18. As part of a larger study, Speed and Gangestad (1997) collected ratings and nominations on a number of characteristics for 66 fraternity men from their fellow fraternity members. The following paragraph is taken from their "Results" section:

> . . . men's romantic popularity significantly correlated with several characteristics: best dressed ($r = .48$), most physically attractive ($r = .47$), most outgoing ($r = .47$), most self-confident ($r = .44$), best trendsetters ($r = .38$), funniest ($r = .37$), most satisfied ($r = .32$), and most independent ($r = .28$). Unexpectedly, however, men's potential for financial success did not significantly correlate with romantic popularity ($r = .10$). (p. 931)

Explain these results as if you were writing to a person who has never had a course in statistics. Specifically, (a) explain what is meant by a correlation coefficient using one of the correlations as an example; (b) explain in a general way what is meant by "significantly" and "not significantly," referring to at least one specific example; and (c) speculate on the meaning of the pattern of results, taking into account the issue of direction of causality.

19. Gable and Lutz (2000) studied 65 children, 3 to 10 years old, and their parents. One of their results was: "Parental control of child eating showed a negative association with children's participation in extracurricular activities ($r = .34$; $p < .01$)" (p. 296). Another result was: "Parents who held less appropriate beliefs about children's nutrition reported that their children watched more hours of television per day ($r = .36$; $p < .01$)" (p. 296).

Explain these results as if you were writing to a person who has never had a course in statistics. Be sure to comment on possible directions of causality for each result.

20. Arbitrarily select eight people, each from a different page of the telephone directory. Do each of the following: (a) make a scatter diagram for the relation between the number of letters in each person's first and last name, (b) figure the correlation coefficient for the relation between the number of letters in each person's first and last name, (c) describe the result in words, and (d) suggest a possible interpretation for your results.

21. A researcher studying adjustment to the job of new employees found a correlation of .3 between amount of employees' education and rating by job supervisors 2 months later. The researcher now plans to use amount of education to predict supervisors' later ratings of employees. Indicate the (a) predictor variable, (b) criterion variable, and (c) the standardized regression coefficient (β). (d) Write the Z-score prediction model. Give the predicted Z scores for supervisor ratings for employees with amount of education Z scores of (e) -1.5, (f) -1, (g) $-.5$, (h) 0, (i) $+.5$, (j) $+1$, and (k) $+1.5$.

22. Researchers studying criminal justice issues have long been interested in what influences people's attitudes about punishment of criminal offenders. Graham, Weiner, and Zucker (1997) took advantage of the very public trial of U.S. football star O. J. Simpson to test some basic issues in this area. In the first few days after Simpson was accused of having murdered his ex-wife, the researchers asked people a series of questions about the case. The researchers were mainly interested in the responses of the 177 individuals who believed Simpson was probably guilty, particularly their belief about retribution—how much they agreed or disagreed with the statement, "The punishment should make O. J. suffer as he made others suffer." The researchers were interested in a number of possible influences on this belief. These included "control" (how much control they believed Simpson had over his actions at the time of the crime), "responsibility" (how much they believed he was responsible for the crime), "anger" they felt toward him, "sympa-

thy" they felt for him, "stability" (how much they believed his actions represented a stable versus temporary way of behaving), and "expectancy" (if they thought he would commit such a crime again). Graham and her colleagues reported:

... Table [3–12] reveals partial support for our hypotheses. As expected, the strongest predictors of the retributive goal of making Simpson suffer were inferences about responsibility and the moral emotions of anger and sympathy. Stability and expectancy ... were relatively weak [predictors]. (p. 337)

Explain these results as if you were writing to a person who understands correlation but has never had any exposure to prediction or multiple regression analysis. (Refer only to the retribution part of the table. You may ignore the *t* column, which is about statistical significance of the results.)

23. Based on Table 3–12 from problem 22, (a) write out the Z-score multiple regression formula for predicting retribution, and (b) figure the predicted Z score for retribution for persons A through J, whose Z scores on each predictor variable are shown below.

Person	Control	Responsibility	Anger	Sympathy	Stability	Expectancy
		Predictor Variable				
A	1	0	0	0	0	0
B	0	1	0	0	0	0
C	0	0	1	0	0	0
D	0	0	0	1	0	0
E	0	0	0	0	1	0
F	0	0	0	0	0	1
G	1	1	1	0	0	0
H	0	0	1	1	0	0
I	1	1	1	1	1	1
J	−1	−1	−1	−1	−1	−1

TABLE 3–12 **Multiple Regressions Predicting Punishment Goals From the Attributional Variables, Study 1**

	Retribution		Rehabilitation		Protection		Deterrence	
				Punishment Goal				
Predictors	β	t	β	t	β	t	β	t
Control	−.05	<1	−.05	<1	−.03	<1	.15	1.90
Responsibility	.17	2.07*	−.00	<1	−.04	<1	.19	2.15*
Anger	.30	4.04***	.11	1.54	−.03	<1	−.04	<1
Sympathy	−.30	−3.68***	.39	5.18***	−.07	<1	−.13	−1.54
Stability	−.01	<1	−.34	−4.85***	−.19	2.33*	.04	<1
Expectancy	−.10	−1.33	−.06	<1	−.27	3.36***	.08	1.04
R^2		.27		.37		.17		.18

Note: β = standardized regression coefficient.
*$p < .05$; ***$p < .001$.
Source: Graham, S., Weiner, B., & Zucker, G. S. (1997). An attributional analysis of punishment goals and public reactions to O. J. Simpson. *Personality and Social Psychology Bulletin, 23*, 331–346. Copyright © 1997 by the Society for Personality and Social Psychology, Inc. Reprinted by permission of Sage Publications, Inc.

24. Ask five other students of the same gender as yourself (each from different families) to give you their own height and also their mother's height. Based on the numbers these five people give you, (a) figure the correlation coefficient, and (b) determine the Z-score prediction model for predicting a person's height from his or her mother's height. Finally, based on your prediction model, predict the height of a person of your gender whose mother's height is (c) 5 feet, (d) 5 feet 6 inches, and (e) 6 feet. (Note: Either convert inches to decimals of feet or do the whole problem using inches.)

CHAPTER APPENDIX: HYPOTHESIS TESTS AND POWER FOR THE CORRELATION COEFFICIENT

This material is for students who have already completed at least through Chapter 8 and are now returning to this chapter.

SIGNIFICANCE OF A CORRELATION COEFFICIENT

Hypothesis testing of a correlation coefficient follows the usual steps of hypothesis testing. However, there are four important points to note.

1. Usually, the null hypothesis is that the correlation in a population like that studied is no different from a population in which the true correlation is 0.
2. If the data meet assumptions (explained below), the comparison distribution is a t distribution with degrees of freedom equal to the number of people minus 2.
3. You figure the correlation coefficient's score on that t distribution using the formula

The t score is the correlation coefficient multiplied by the square root of 2 less than the number of people in the study, divided by the square root of 1 minus the correlation coefficient squared.

$$t = \frac{(r)(\sqrt{[N-2]})}{\sqrt{(1-r^2)}}$$
(3-5)

4. Note that significance tests of a correlation, like a t test, can be either one-tailed or two-tailed. A one-tailed test means that the researcher has predicted the sign (positive or negative) of the correlation.

Assumptions for the significance test of a correlation coefficient are that (a) the populations for both variables are normally distributed, and (b) in the population, the distribution of each variable at each point of the other variable has about equal variance. However, as with the t test and analysis of variance (Chapter 10), moderate violations of these assumptions are not fatal.

AN EXAMPLE

Here is an example using the sleep and mood study example. Let's suppose that the researchers predicted a positive correlation between number of employees supervised and stress, to be tested at the .05 level.

❶ **Restate the question as a research hypothesis and a null hypothesis about the populations.** There are two populations:

Population 1: People like those in this study.

Population 2: People for whom there is no correlation between number of hours slept the night before and mood the next day.

The null hypothesis is that the two populations have the same correlation. The research hypothesis is that Population 1 has a higher correlation than Population 2. (That is, the prediction is for a population correlation greater than 0.)

❷ **Determine the characteristics of the comparison distribution.** Assuming we meet the assumptions (in practice, it would be hard to tell with only 10 people in the study), the comparison distribution is a t distribution with $df = 8$. (That is, $df = N - 2 = 10 - 2 = 8$.)

❸ **Determine the cutoff sample score on the comparison distribution at which the null hypothesis should be rejected.** The t table (Table A–2 in the Appendix) shows that for a one-tailed test at the .05 level, with 8 degrees of freedom, you need a t of at least 1.860.

❹ **Determine your sample's score on the comparison distribution.** We figured a correlation of $r = .84$. Applying the formula to find the equivalent t, we get

$$t = \frac{(r)(\sqrt{[N-2]})}{\sqrt{[1-r^2]}} = \frac{(.84)(\sqrt{8})}{\sqrt{(1-.71)}} = \frac{(.84)(2.83)}{\sqrt{.29}} = \frac{2.38}{.54} = 4.41$$

TABLE 3–13 Approximate Power of Studies Using the Correlation Coefficient (r) for Testing Hypotheses at the .05 Level of Significance

		Effect Size		
		Small ($r = .10$)	Medium ($r = .30$)	Large ($r = .50$)
Two-tailed				
Total N:	10	.06	.13	.33
	20	.07	.25	.64
	30	.08	.37	.83
	40	.09	.48	.92
	50	.11	.57	.97
	100	.17	.86	a
One-tailed				
Total N:	10	.08	.22	.46
	20	.11	.37	.75
	30	.13	.50	.90
	40	.15	.60	.96
	50	.17	.69	.98
	100	.26	.92	a

[a]Nearly 1.00.

❺ **Decide whether to reject the null hypothesis.** The t score of 4.41 for our sample correlation is more extreme than the minimum needed t score of 1.860. Thus, you can reject the null hypothesis, and the research hypothesis is supported.

EFFECT SIZE AND POWER

The correlation coefficient itself is a measure of effect size. (Thus, in the example, effect size is $r = .84$.) Cohen's (1988) conventions for the correlation coefficient are .10 for a small effect size, .30 for a medium effect size, and .50 for a large effect size. Table 3–13 gives approximate power, and Table 3–14 gives minimum sample size for 80% power. (More complete tables are provided in Cohen, 1988, pp. 84–95, 101–102.)

TABLE 3–14 Approximate Number of Participants Needed for 80% Power for a Study Using the Correlation Coefficient (r) for Testing a Hypothesis at the .05 Significance Level

	Effect Size		
	Small ($r = .10$)	Medium ($r = .30$)	Large ($r = .50$)
Two-tailed	783	85	28
One-tailed	617	68	22

CHAPTER 4

Some Key Ingredients for Inferential Statistics

The Normal Curve, Probability, and Population Versus Sample

Ordinarily, social and behavioral scientists do a research study to test some theoretical principle or the effectiveness of some practical procedure. For example, an educational researcher might compare reading speeds of students taught with two different methods to examine a theory of teaching. A sociologist might examine the effectiveness of a program of neighborhood meetings intended to promote water conservation. Such studies are carried out with a particular group of research participants. But the researchers usually want to make more general conclusions about the theoretical principle or procedure being studied—conclusions that go beyond the particular group of research participants studied. To do this, researchers use inferential statistics.

This chapter and Chapters 5, 6, and 7 introduce inferential statistics. In this chapter, we consider three topics: the normal curve, probability, and population versus sample. This is a comparatively short chapter, preparing the way for the next ones, which are more demanding.

Tip for Success

Before beginning this chapter, be sure you have mastered the material in Chapter 1 on the shapes of distributions and the material in Chapter 2 on mean, standard deviation, and Z scores.

THE NORMAL DISTRIBUTION

As we noted in Chapter 1, the graphs of many of the distributions of variables that social and behavioral scientists study (as well as many other distributions in nature) follow a unimodal, roughly symmetrical, bell-shaped distribution. These bell-shaped histograms or frequency polygons approximate a precise and important

FIGURE 4–1   *A normal curve.*

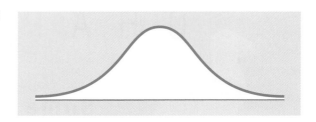

normal distribution

normal curve

mathematical distribution called the **normal distribution** or, more simply, the **normal curve.** An example of the normal curve is shown in Figure 4–1.

WHY THE NORMAL CURVE IS SO COMMON IN NATURE

Take, for example, the number of different letters a particular person can remember accurately on various testings (with different random letters each time). On some testings, the number of letters remembered may be high, on others low, and on most somewhere in between. That is, the number of different letters a person can recall on various testings probably approximately follows a normal curve. Suppose that the person has a basic ability to recall, say, seven letters in this kind of memory task. Nevertheless, on any particular testing, the actual number recalled will be affected by various influences—noisiness of the room, the person's mood at the moment, a combination of random letters unwittingly confused with a familiar name, and so on.

These various influences add up to make the person recall more than seven on some testings and less than seven on others. However, the particular combination of such influences that come up at any testing is essentially random. Thus, on most testings, positive and negative influences should cancel out. The chances are not very good of all the negative influences happening to come together on a testing when none of the positive influences show up. Thus, in general, the person remembers a middle amount, an amount in which all the opposing influences cancel each other out. Very high or very low scores are much less common.

This creates a unimodal distribution—most of the scores near the middle and fewer at the extremes. It also creates a distribution that is symmetrical, because the number of letters recalled is as likely to be above as below the middle. Being a unimodal symmetrical curve does not guarantee that it will be a normal curve; it could be too flat or too peaked. However, it can be shown mathematically that in the long run, if the influences are truly random and the number of different influences being combined is large, a precise normal curve results. Mathematical statisticians call this principle the *central limit theorem.* We have more to say about this principle in Chapter 6.

THE NORMAL CURVE AND THE PERCENTAGE OF SCORES BETWEEN THE MEAN AND 1 AND 2 STANDARD DEVIATIONS FROM THE MEAN

The shape of the normal curve is standard. Thus, there is a known percentage of scores above or below any particular point. For example, exactly 50% of the scores are below the mean, because in any symmetrical distribution, half the scores are below the mean. More interestingly, as shown in Figure 4–2, approximately 34% of the scores are always between the mean and 1 standard deviation from the mean. (Notice, incidentally, that in Figure 4–2 the 1 standard deviation point on the normal curve is at the place the curve starts going more out than down.)

Web Link

http://members.aol.com/discanner/ balldrop.html. See a graphic illustration of the normal curve.

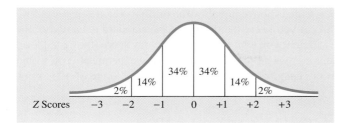

FIGURE 4–2 *Normal curve with approximate percentages of scores between the mean and 1 and 2 standard deviations above and below the mean.*

Consider IQ scores. On many widely used intelligence tests, the mean IQ is 100, the standard deviation is 16, and the distribution of IQs is roughly normal (see Figure 4–3). Knowing about the normal curve and the percentages of scores between the mean and 1 standard deviation above the mean allows us to know that about 34% of people have IQs between 100, the mean, and 116, the IQ score that is 1 standard deviation above the mean. Similarly, because the normal curve is symmetrical, about 34% of people have IQs between 100 and 84 (the score that is 1 standard deviation below the mean), and 68% (34% + 34%) have IQs between 84 and 116.

As you can also see from looking at the normal curve, there are many fewer scores between 1 and 2 standard deviations from the mean than there are between the mean and 1 standard deviation from the mean. It turns out that about 14% of the scores are between 1 and 2 standard deviations above the mean (see Figure 4–2). (Similarly, because the normal curve is symmetrical, about 14% of the scores are between 1 and 2 standard deviations below the mean.) Thus, about 14% of people have IQs between 116 (1 standard deviation above the mean) and 132 (2 standard deviations above the mean).

You will find it very useful to remember the 34% and 14% figures. These figures tell you the percentage of people above and below any particular score whenever you know that score's number of standard deviations above or below the mean. You can also reverse this approach and figure out a person's number of standard deviations from the mean from a percentage. Suppose a laboratory test showed that a particular archaeological sample of ceramics was in the top 2% of all the samples in the excavation for containing iron, and it is known that the distribution of iron in such samples is roughly normal. In this situation, the sample must have a level of iron that is at least 2 standard deviations above the mean level of iron. This is because a total of 50% of the scores are above the mean. There are 34% between the mean and 1 *SD* and another 14% between 1 and 2 *SD*s above the mean, leaving a remainder of 2% of scores that are 2 *SD*s above the mean. Remember from Chapter 2 that a *Z* score is the num-

FIGURE 4–3 *Distribution of IQ scores on many standard intelligence tests (with a mean of 100 and a standard deviation of 16).*

ber of standard deviations a score is above or below the mean—which is just what we are talking about here. Thus, if you knew the mean and the standard deviation of the iron concentrations in the samples, you could figure out the raw score (the actual level of iron in this sample) that is equivalent to being two *SD*s above the mean. You would do this using the methods of changing *Z* scores (in this case, a *Z* score of +2) to raw scores and vice versa that you learned in Chapter 2, which are

$$X = (Z)(SD) + M \text{ and } Z = (X - M)/SD$$

THE NORMAL CURVE TABLE AND *Z* SCORES

The 50%, 34%, and 14% figures are important practical rules for working with scores that have a normal distribution. However, in many research and applied situations, social and behavioral scientists need more precise information. Because the normal curve is mathematically exact, you can figure the exact percentage of scores between any two points on the normal curve, not just those that happen to be right at 1 or 2 standard deviations from the mean. For example, exactly 68.59% of scores have a *Z* score between +.62 and −1.68; exactly 2.81% of scores have a *Z* score between +.79 and +.89, and so forth.

    You can figure these percentages using calculus, based on the formula for the normal curve (which you can look up in a mathematical statistics text). However, you can also do this much more simply. Statisticians have worked out tables for the normal curve that give the percentage of scores between the mean (a *Z* score of 0) and any other *Z* score. Suppose you want to know the percentage of scores between the mean and a *Z* score of .62. You just look up .62 in the table, and it tells you that 23.24% of the scores, in a perfect normal distribution, fall between the mean and this *Z* score.

normal curve table

    We have included such a **normal curve table** in the Appendix (Table A–1, pp. 413–15). Table 4–1 shows the first part of the full table. The leftmost column in the table lists the *Z* score and the column next to it gives the percentage of scores between the mean and that *Z* score. Notice that the table lists only positive *Z* scores. It is unnecessary to list the negative *Z* scores because the normal curve is perfectly symmetrical; thus, the percentage of scores between the mean and, say, a *Z* of +.62 is exactly the same as the percentage of scores between the mean and a *Z* of −.62.

Tip for Success

Remember that negative Z scores are scores below the mean and positive Z scores are scores above the mean.

    In our example, you would find .62 in the "*Z*" column and then, right next to it in the "% Mean to *Z*" column, you would find 23.24.

    You also can reverse the process and use the table to find the *Z* score for a particular percentage of scores. For example, suppose you were told that Janice's creativity score was in the top 30% of ninth-grade students. Assuming that creativity scores follow a normal curve, you could figure out her *Z* score as follows: First, you would reason that if she is in the top 30%, then 20% of students have scores between her score and the mean. That is, there are 50% above the mean, and she is in the top 30% of scores overall, which leaves 20% between her score and the mean. This is all shown in Figure 4–4. Then you would look at the "% Mean to *Z*" column of the table until you found a percentage that was very close to 20%. In this example, the closest you could come would be 19.85%. Finally, you would look at the "*Z*" column to the left of this percentage. The *Z* score for 19.85% is .52. Thus, Janice's *Z* score for her level of creativity (as measured on this test) is .52. If you know the mean and standard deviation for ninth-grade students' creativity scores, you can figure out Janice's actual raw score on the test by changing this *Z* score of .52 to a raw score using the usual method of changing *Z* scores to raw scores.

TABLE 4–1 Normal Curve Areas: Percentage of the Normal Curve between the Mean and the *Z* Scores Shown (First part of table only: full table in Appendix)

Z	% Mean to *Z*	*Z*	% Mean to *Z*	*Z*	% Mean to *Z*
.00	.00	.45	17.36	.90	31.59
.01	.40	.46	17.72	.91	31.86
.02	.80	.47	18.08	.92	32.12
.03	1.20	.48	18.44	.93	32.38
.04	1.60	.49	18.79	.94	32.64
.05	1.99	.50	19.15	.95	32.89
.06	2.39	.51	19.50	.96	33.15
.07	2.79	.52	19.85	.97	33.40
.08	3.19	.53	20.19	.98	33.65
.09	3.59	.54	20.54	.99	33.89
.10	3.98	.55	20.88	1.00	34.13
.11	4.38	.56	21.23	1.01	34.38
.12	4.78	.57	21.57	1.02	34.61
.13	5.17	.58	21.90	1.03	34.85
.14	5.57	.59	22.24	1.04	35.08
.15	5.96	.60	22.57	1.05	35.31
.16	6.36	.61	22.91	1.06	35.54
.17	6.75	.62	23.24	1.07	35.77
.18	7.14	.63	23.57	1.08	35.99
.19	7.53	.64	23.89	1.09	36.21
.20	7.93	.65	24.22	1.10	36.43
.21	8.32	.66	24.54	1.11	36.65
.22	8.71	.67	24.86	1.12	36.86
.23	9.10	.68	25.17	1.13	37.08
.24	9.48	.69	25.49	1.14	37.29
.25	9.87	.70	25.80	1.15	37.49
.26	10.26	.71	26.11	1.16	37.70
.27	10.64	.72	26.42	1.17	37.90
.28	11.03	.73	26.73	1.18	38.10
.29	11.41	.74	27.04	1.19	38.30
.30	11.79	.75	27.34	1.20	38.49
.31	12.17	.76	27.64	1.21	38.69
.32	12.55	.77	27.94	1.22	38.88
.33	12.93	.78	28.23	1.23	39.07
.34	13.31	.79	28.52	1.24	39.25
.35	13.68	.80	28.81	1.25	39.44
.36	14.06	.81	29.10	1.26	39.62
.37	14.43	.82	29.39	1.27	39.80
.38	14.80	.83	29.67	1.28	39.97
.39	15.17	.84	29.95	1.29	40.15
.40	15.54	.85	30.23	1.30	40.32
.41	15.91	.86	30.51	1.31	40.49
.42	16.28	.87	30.78	1.32	40.66
.43	16.64	.88	31.06	1.33	40.82
.44	17.00	.89	31.33	1.34	40.99

Tip for Success

Notice that the table repeats the basic two columns several times on the page. Be sure to look across only one column.

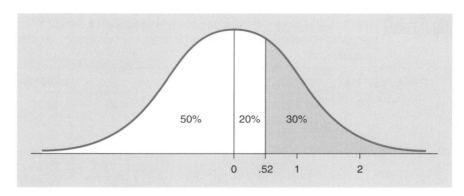

FIGURE 4–4 *Distribution of creativity test scores showing area for top 30% and Z score where this area begins.*

STEPS FOR FIGURING THE PERCENTAGE OF SCORES ABOVE OR BELOW A PARTICULAR RAW SCORE OR Z SCORE USING THE NORMAL CURVE TABLE

Here are the six steps for figuring percentage of scores.

❶ **If you are beginning with a raw score, first change it to a Z score.** Use the usual formula, $Z = (X - M)/SD$.

❷ **Draw a picture of the normal curve, where the Z score falls on it, and shade in the area for which you are finding the percentage.** (When marking where the Z score falls on the normal curve, be sure to put it in the right place above or below the mean according to whether it is a positive or negative Z score.)

❸ **Make a rough estimate of the shaded area's percentage based on the 50%–34%–14% percentages.** You don't need to be very exact—it is enough just to estimate a range in which the shaded area has to fall, figuring it is between two particular whole Z scores.

❹ **Find the exact percentage using the normal curve table.** Look up the Z score in the "Z" column of Table A–1 and find the percentage in the "% Mean to Z" column next to it. If you want the percent of scores between the mean and this Z score, this would be your final answer.

❺ **If needed, add or subtract 50% from this percentage.** Often you need to add 50% to the percentage figured in Step 4. You need to do this if the Z score is positive and you want the total percent below this Z score, or if the Z score is negative and you want the total percent above this Z score. Other times, you have to subtract this percentage from 50%. You have to do this if the Z score is positive and you want the percent higher than it (as in the creativity test example above), or if the Z score is negative and you want the percent lower than it. However, don't try to memorize rules about adding or subtracting the 50%. It is much easier to make a picture for the problem and reason out whether the percentage you have from the table is correct as is, or if you need to add or subtract 50%.

❻ **Check that your exact percentage is similar to your rough estimate from Step 3.**

EXAMPLES

Here are two examples using IQ scores where $M = 100$ and $SD = 16$.

Example 1: If a person has an IQ of 125, what percentage of people have higher IQs?

❶ **If you are beginning with a raw score, first change it to a Z score.** Using the usual formula, $Z = (125 - 100)/16 = +1.56$.

❷ **Draw a picture of the normal curve, where the Z score falls on it, and shade in the area for which you are finding the percentage.** This is shown in Figure 4–5 (along with the exact percentages figured later).

❸ **Make a rough estimate of the shaded area's percentage based on the 50%–34%–14% percentages.** If the shaded area started at a Z score of 1, it would include 16%. If it started at a Z score of 2, it would include only 2%. So, with a Z score of 1.56, it has to be somewhere between 16% and 2%.

❹ **Find the exact percentage using the normal curve table.** In Table A–1, 1.56 in the "Z" column goes with 44.06 in the "% mean to Z" column. Thus, 44.06% of people have IQ scores between the mean IQ and an IQ of 125 (Z score of +1.56).

❺ **If needed, add or subtract 50% from this percentage.** Because 50% of people are above the mean on any normal curve and 44.06% of the people above the mean are below this person's IQ, that leaves 5.94% above this person's score (that is, $50\% - 44.06\% = 5.94\%$). This is the answer to our problem.

❻ **Check that your exact percentage is similar to your rough estimate from Step 3.** Our result, 5.94%, is within the 16% to 2% range we estimated.

Example 2: If a person has an IQ of 95, what percentage of people have lower IQs?

❶ **If you are beginning with a raw score, first change it to a Z score.** Using the usual formula, $Z = (95 - 100)/16 = -.31$.

❷ **Draw a picture of the normal curve, where the Z score falls on it, and shade in the area for which you are finding the percentage.** This is shown in Figure 4–6 (along with the exact percentages figured later).

❸ **Make a rough estimate of the shaded area's percentage based on the 50%–34%–14% percentages.** You know that 50% of the curve is below the mean. So, the shaded area has to be less than 50%. You can also figure that 16% of the curve is below a Z score of −1. (This is because 34% is between 0 and −1, leaving 16% below −1.) Thus, our Z score of −.31 has to have between 50% and 16% at the scores below it.

❹ **Find the exact percentage using the normal curve table.** The table shows that 12.17% of scores are between the mean and a Z score of .31.

❺ **If needed, add or subtract 50% from this percentage.** The percentage below a Z score of −.31 is the total of 50% below the mean, less the 12.17% between the mean and −.31, leaving 37.83% (that is, $50\% - 12.17\% = 37.83\%$).

❻ **Check that your exact percentage is similar to your rough estimate from Step 3.** Our result, 37.83%, is within the 50% to 16% range.

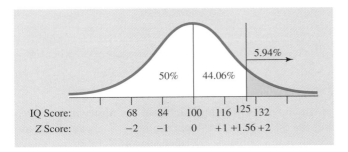

FIGURE 4–5 *Distribution of IQ scores showing percentage of scores above an IQ scores of 125 (shaded area).*

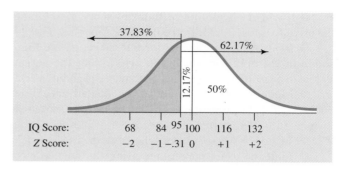

FIGURE 4–6   *Distribution of IQ scores showing percentage of scores below an IQ score of 95 (shaded area).*

FIGURING Z SCORES AND RAW SCORES FROM PERCENTAGES USING THE NORMAL CURVE TABLE

Going from a percentage to a Z score or raw score is similar to going from a Z score or raw score to a percentage. However, you just use the reverse procedure for the part of figuring the exact percentage. Also, any necessary conversion between a Z score and raw score is done at the end. Here are the five steps.

❶ Draw a picture of the normal curve and shade in the approximate area for your percentage using the 50%–34%–14% percentages.

❷ Make a rough estimate of the Z score where the shaded area starts.

❸ Find the exact Z score using the normal curve table (including adding or subtracting 50%, if necessary, before looking it up). Looking at your picture, figure out the percentage between the mean and where the shading starts or ends. For example, if your percentage is the top 8%, then the percentage from the mean to where that shading starts is 42% (that is, 50%−8% = 42%). If your percentage is the bottom 35%, then the percentage from where the shading starts is 15% (that is, 50%−35% = 15%). If your percentage is the top 83%, then the percentage from the mean to where the shading stops is 33% (that is, 83%−50% = 33%).

Once you have the percentage from the mean to where the shading starts or stops, look up the closest number you can find to it in the "% Mean to Z" column of the normal curve table and find the Z score in the "Z" column next to it. That Z will be your answer—except it may be negative. The best way to tell if it is positive or negative is by looking at your picture.

❹ Check that your exact Z score is similar to your rough estimate from Step 2.

❺ If you want to find a raw score, change it from the Z score. Use the usual formula, $X = (Z)(SD) + M$

EXAMPLES

Here are three examples. Once again, we will use IQ for our examples, where $M = 100$ and $SD = 16$.

Example 1: What IQ score would a person need to be in the top 5%?

❶ Draw a picture of the normal curve and shade in the approximate area for your percentage using the 50%–34%–14% percentages. We wanted the top 5%. Thus, the shading has to begin above 1 *SD* (there are 16% of scores above 1 *SD*). However, it cannot start above 2 *SD* because only 2% of all the scores are

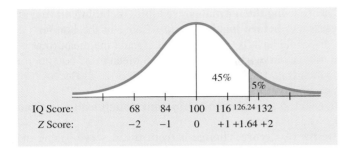

FIGURE 4-7   *Finding the Z score and IQ raw score for where the top 5% start.*

above 2 *SD*. But 5% is a lot closer to 2% than to 16%. Thus, you would start shading a small way to the left of the 2 *SD* point. This is shown in Figure 4–7.

❷ **Make a rough estimate of the Z score where the shaded area starts.** The *Z* score has to be between +1 and +2.

❸ **Find the exact Z score using the normal curve table (including adding or subtracting 50%, if necessary, before looking it up).** Because 50% of people have IQs above the mean, at least 45% have IQs between this person and the mean (that is, 50%−5% = 45%). Looking in the "% Mean to Z" column of the normal curve table, the closest figure to 45% is 44.95% (or you could use 45.05%). This goes with a *Z* score of 1.64 in the "*Z*" column.

❹ **Check that your exact Z score is similar to your rough estimate from Step 2.** +1.64 is between +1 and +2.

❺ **If you want to find a raw score, change it from the Z score.** Using the usual formula, $X = (1.64)(16) + 100 = 126.24$. In sum, to be in the top 5%, a person would need an IQ of at least 126.24.

Example 2: What IQ score would a person need to be in the lowest 1%?

❶ **Draw a picture of the normal curve and shade in the approximate area for your percentage using the 50%–34%–14% percentages.** You want the bottom 1%. There are 2% of scores below −2 *SD*. So, the shading has to begin below (to the left of) −2 *SD*. Thus, you would start shading to the left of (below) the 2 *SD* point. This is shown in Figure 4–8.

❷ **Make a rough estimate of the Z score where the shaded area starts.** The *Z* score has to be below −2.

FIGURE 4-8   *Finding the Z score and IQ raw score for where the bottom 1% start (going down).*

❸ **Find the exact Z score using the normal curve table (including adding or subtracting 50%, if necessary, before looking it up).** Being in the bottom 1% means that at least 49% of people have IQs between this IQ and the mean (that is, 50% − 1% = 49%). In the normal curve table, 49% in the "% Mean to Z" column (or as close as you can get, which is 49.01%) goes with a Z score of 2.33. Because we are below the mean, this becomes −2.33.

❹ **Check that your exact Z score is similar to your rough estimate from Step 2.** As we estimated, −2.33 is below −2.

❺ **If you want to find a raw score, change it from the Z score.** Using the usual formula, X = (−2.33) (16) + 100 = 62.72. So, a person in the bottom 1% on IQ has a score that is 62.72 or below.

Example 3: What range of IQ scores includes the 95% of people in the middle range of IQ scores?

This kind of problem, of finding the middle percentage, may seem odd. However, it is actually a very common type of situation in some procedures you will learn about in later chapters.

The best way to think of this kind of problem is in terms of finding the particular scores that go with the upper and lower ends of this percentage. Thus, in this example, you are really trying to find the points where the bottom 2.5% ends and the top 2.5% begins (which, out of 100%, leaves the middle 95%).

❶ **Draw a picture of the normal curve and shade in the approximate area for your percentage using the 50%–34%–14% percentages.** Let's begin with the point where the top 2.5% begins. This has to be higher than 1 *SD* (there are 16% of scores higher than 1 *SD*). However, it cannot start above 2 *SD* because there are only 2% of scores above 2 *SD*. But 2.5% is very close to 2%. Thus, you would figure that the top 2.5% starts just to the left of the 2 *SD* point. Similarly, the point where the bottom 2.5% comes in would be just to the right of −2 *SD*. The result of all this is that we will shade in the area starting just above −2 *SD* and continuing up to just below +2 *SD*. This is shown in Figure 4–9.

❷ **Make a rough estimate of the Z score or raw score where the shaded area starts.** You can see from the picture that the Z score for the upper limit of the shaded area has to be between +1 and +2, but quite close to +2. Similarly, the lower limit of the shaded area has to be between −1 and −2, but quite close to −2.

❸ **Find the exact Z score using the normal curve table (including adding or subtracting 50%, if necessary, before looking it up).** Being in the top 2.5% means that at least 47.5% of people have IQs between this IQ and the mean (that is,

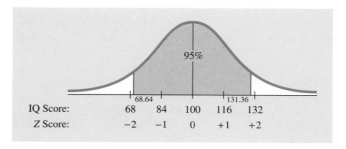

FIGURE 4–9   *Finding the Z scores and IQ raw scores for where the middle 95% of IQ scores begin and end.*

50%−2.5% = 47.5%). In the normal curve table, 47.5% in the "% Mean to Z" column goes with a Z score of 1.96. The normal curve is entirely symmetrical. Thus, the Z score for the bottom 2.5% is −1.96.

❹ **Check that your exact Z score is similar to your rough estimate from Step 2.** As we estimated, 1.96 is between 1 and 2 and is very close to 2 and −1.96 is between −1 and −2 and very close to −2.

❺ **If you want to find a raw score, change it from the Z score.** For the high end, using the usual formula, $X = (1.96)(16) + 100 = 131.36$. For the low end, again using the usual formula, $X = (−1.96)(16) + 100 = 68.64$. In sum, the middle 95% of IQ scores run from 68.64 to 131.36.

HOW ARE YOU DOING?

1. Why is the normal curve (or at least a curve that is symmetrical and unimodal) so common in nature?
2. Without using a normal curve table, about what percentage of scores on a normal curve are (a) above the mean, (b) between the mean and 1 *SD* above the mean, (c) between 1 and 2 SDs above the mean, (d) below the mean, (e) between the mean and 1 *SD* below the mean, and (f) between 1 and 2 SDs below the mean?
3. Without using a normal curve table, about what percentage of scores on a normal curve are (a) between the mean and 2 SDs above the mean, (b) below 1 SD above the mean, (c) above 2 SDs below the mean?
4. Without using a normal curve table, about what Z score would a person have who is at the start of the top (a) 50%, (b) 16%, (c) 84%, (d) 2%?
5. Using the normal curve table, what percentage of scores are (a) between the mean and a Z score of 2.14, (b) above 2.14, (c) below 2.14?
6. Using the normal curve table, what Z score would you have if (a) 20% are above you, (b) 80% are below you?

ANSWERS:

1. It is common because any particular score is the result of the random combination of many effects, some of which make the score larger and some of which make the score smaller. Thus, on average these effects balance out to produce scores near the middle, with relatively few scores at each extreme, because it is unlikely for most of the increasing and decreasing effects to come out in the same direction.
2. (a) 50%, (b) 34%, (c) 14%, (d) 50%, (e) 34%, (f) 14%.
3. (a) 48%, (b) 84%, (c) 98%.
4. (a) 0, (b) 1, (c) −1, (d) 2.
5. (a) 48.38%, (b) 1.62%, (c) 98.38%.
6. (a) .84, (b) .84.

PROBABILITY

The purpose of most research in the social and behavioral sciences is to examine the truth of a theory or the effectiveness of a procedure. But scientific research of any kind can only make that truth or effectiveness seem more or less likely; it cannot give us the luxury of knowing for certain. Probability is very important in science. In particular, probability is very important in inferential statistics, the methods social and behavioral scientists use to go from results of research studies to conclusions about theories or applied procedures.

Probability has been studied for centuries by mathematicians and philosophers. Yet even today, the topic is full of controversy. Fortunately, however, you need to know only a few key ideas to understand and carry out the inferential statistical procedures you learn in this book.[1] These few key points are not very difficult—indeed, some students find them obvious.

probability

outcome

expected relative frequency

long-run relative-frequency interpretation of probability

In statistics, we usually define **probability** as the expected relative frequency of a particular outcome. An **outcome** is the result of an experiment (or just about any situation in which the result is not known in advance, such as a coin coming up heads or it raining tomorrow). *Frequency* is how many times something happens. The *relative frequency* is the number of times something happens relative to the number of times it could have happened. That is, relative frequency is the proportion of times it happens. (A coin might come up heads 8 times out of 12 flips, for a relative frequency of 8/12, or 2/3.) **Expected relative frequency** is what you expect to get in the long run, if you repeated the experiment many times. (In the case of a coin, in the long run you expect to get 1/2 heads.) This is called the **long-run relative-frequency interpretation of probability.**

FIGURING PROBABILITIES

Probabilities are usually figured as the proportion of successful possible outcomes—the number of possible successful outcomes divided by the number of *all* possible outcomes. That is,

$$\text{Probability} = \frac{\text{Possible successful outcomes}}{\text{All possible outcomes}}$$

Consider the probability of getting heads when flipping a coin. There is one possible successful outcome (getting heads) out of two possible outcomes (getting heads or getting tails). This makes a probability of 1/2, or .5. In a throw of a single die, the probability of a 2 (or any other particular side of the die) is 1/6, or .17. This is because there is one possible successful outcome out of six possible outcomes of any kind. The probability of throwing a die and getting a number 3 or lower is 3/6, or .5. There are three possible successful outcomes (a 1, a 2, or a 3) out of six possible outcomes.

Now consider a slightly more complicated example. Suppose a class has 200 people in it, and 30 are seniors. If you were to pick someone from the class at random, the probability of picking a senior would be 30/200, or .15. This is because there are 30 possible successful outcomes (getting a senior) out of 200 possible outcomes.

STEPS FOR FIGURING PROBABILITIES

Here are the three steps for figuring probabilities.

❶ **Determine the number of possible successful outcomes.**
❷ **Determine the number of all possible outcomes.**
❸ **Divide the number of possible successful outcomes (Step 1) by the number of all possible outcomes (Step 2).**

Applying these three steps to the probability of getting a number 3 or lower on a throw of a die,

❶ **Determine the number of possible successful outcomes.** There are three outcomes of 3 or lower—a 1, 2, or 3.

---

[1]There are, of course, many probability topics that are not related to statistics and other topics related to statistics that are not important for the kinds of statistics used in the social and behavioral sciences. For example, computing joint and conditional probabilities, which is covered in many statistics books, is not covered here because it is rarely seen in published research in the social and behavioral sciences and is not necessary for an intuitive grasp of the logic of the major inferential statistical methods covered in this book.

❷ **Determine the number of possible outcomes.** There are six possible outcomes in the throw of a die—a 1, 2, 3, 4, 5, or 6.

❸ **Divide the number of possible successful outcomes (Step 1) by the number of all possible outcomes (Step 2).** 3/6 = .5.

RANGE OF PROBABILITIES

A probability is a proportion, the number of possible successful outcomes to the total number of possible outcomes. A proportion cannot be less than 0 or greater than 1. Probabilities and proportions can also be thought of in terms of percentages, ranging from 0% to 100%. (To change a probability or proportion into a percentage, multiply by 100. To change a percentage into a probability or proportion, divide by 100.) Something that has no chance of happening has a probability of 0, and something that is certain to happen has a probability of 1. Notice that when the probability of an event is 0, the event is completely *impossible;* it cannot happen. But when the probability of an event is low, say .05 (5%) or even .01 (1%), the event is *improbable* or *unlikely,* but not impossible.

PROBABILITIES EXPRESSED AS SYMBOLS

Probability usually is symbolized by the letter p. The actual probability number is usually given as a decimal, though sometimes fractions are used. A 50–50 chance is usually written as $p = .5$, but it could also be written as $p = 1/2$. It is also common to see a probability written as being less than some number using the "less than" sign. For example, $p < .05$ means "the probability is less than .05."

PROBABILITY AND THE NORMAL DISTRIBUTION

So far, we have mainly discussed probabilities of specific events that might or might not happen. We also can talk about a range of events that might or might not happen. The throw of a die coming out 3 or lower is an example (it includes the range 1, 2, and 3). Another example is the probability of selecting someone on a city street who is between the ages of 30 and 40.

If you think of probability in terms of proportion of scores, probability fits in well with frequency distributions (see Chapter 1). In the frequency distribution shown in Figure 4–10, 10 of the total of 50 people scored 7 or higher. If you were selecting people from this group of 50 at random, there would be 10 chances (possible successful outcomes) out of 50 (all possible outcomes) of selecting one that was 7 or higher, so $p = 10/50 = .2$.

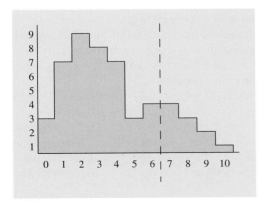

FIGURE 4–10 *Frequency distribution (shown as a histogram) of 50 people in which $p = .2$ (10/50) of randomly selecting a person with a score of 7 or higher.*

You can also think of the normal distribution as a probability distribution. With a normal curve, the proportion of scores between any two Z scores is known. As we are seeing, the percentage of scores between any two Z scores is the same as the probability of selecting a score between those two Z scores. As you saw earlier in this chapter, approximately 34% of scores are between the mean and 1 standard deviation from the mean. You should therefore not be surprised to learn that the probability of a score being between the mean and a Z score of +1 (1 standard deviation above the mean) is .34 (that is, $p = .34$).

In a sense, it is merely a technical point that the normal curve can be seen as either a frequency distribution or a probability distribution. We mention this only so that you will not be confused when we refer later to the probability of a score coming from a particular portion of the normal curve.

HOW ARE YOU DOING?

1. The probability of an event is defined as the expected relative frequency of a particular outcome. Explain what is meant by (a) relative frequency and (b) outcome.
2. Suppose you have 400 pennies in a jar and 40 of them are more than 9 years old. You then mix up the pennies and pull one out. (a) What is the probability of getting one that is more than 9 years old? In this problem, (b) what is the number of possible successful outcomes? and (c) what is the number of all possible outcomes?
3. Suppose people's scores on a particular measure are normally distributed with a mean of 50 and a standard deviation of 10. If you were to pick a person completely at random, what is the probability you would pick someone with a score on this measure higher than 60?
4. What is meant by $p < .01$?

ANSWERS:

1. (a) Relative frequency is the number of times something happens in relation to the number of times it could have happened.
   (b) An outcome is the result of an experiment—what happens in a situation where what will happen is not known in advance.
2. (a) $p = 40/400 = .10$. (b) 40. (c) 400.
3. $p = .16$ (since 16% of the scores are more than 1 standard deviation above the mean).
4. The probability is less than .01.

SAMPLE AND POPULATION

We are going to introduce you to some important ideas by thinking of beans. Suppose you are cooking a pot of beans and taste a spoonful to see if they are done. In this example, the pot of beans is a **population,** the entire set of things of interest. The spoonful is a **sample,** the part of the population about which you actually have information. This is shown in Figure 4–11a. Figures 4–11b and 4–11c are other ways of illustrating the relation of a sample to a population.

In social and behavioral science research, we typically study samples not of beans but of individuals to make inferences about some larger group. A sample might consist of 50 Canadian women who participate in a particular experiment, whereas the population might be intended to be all Canadian women. In an opinion survey, 1,000 people might be selected from the voting-age population and asked for whom they plan to vote. The opinions of these 1,000 people are the sample. The

population

sample

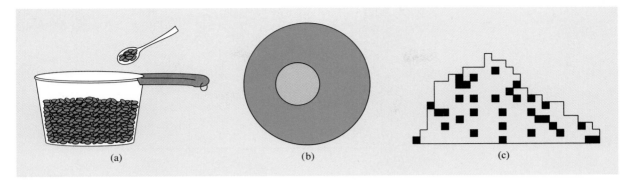

FIGURE 4–11   *Populations and samples: In (a), the entire pot of beans is the popula-tion and the spoonful is a sample. In (b), the entire larger circle is the population and the cir-cle within it is the sample. In (c), the histogram is of the population and the particular shaded scores together make up the sample.*

opinions of the larger voting public, to which the pollsters hope to apply their re-sults, is the population (see Figure 4–12).[2]

WHY SAMPLES INSTEAD OF POPULATIONS ARE STUDIED

If you want to know something about a population, your results would be most ac-curate if you could study the entire population rather than a subgroup from that population. However, in most research situations this is not practical. More impor-tant, the whole point of research is usually to be able to make generalizations or predictions about events beyond our reach. We would not call it research if you tested three particular cars to see which gets better gas mileage—unless you hoped to say something about the gas mileage of those models of cars in general. In other words, a researcher might do an experiment on the effect of a particular new method of teaching geography using 40 eighth-grade students as participants in the experiment. But the purpose of the experiment is not to find out how these particu-lar 40 students respond to the experimental condition. Rather, the purpose is to learn something about how eighth-grade students in general respond to the new method of teaching geography.

The strategy in almost all social and behavioral science research is to study a sample of individuals who are believed to be representative of the general popula-tion (or of some particular population of interest). More realistically, researchers try to study people who do not differ from the general population in any systematic way that should matter for that topic of research.

The sample is what is studied, and the population is an unknown that re-searchers draw conclusions about on the basis of the sample. Most of what you learn in the rest of this book is about the important work of drawing conclusions about populations based on information from samples.

---

[2]Strictly speaking, *population* and *sample* refer to scores (numbers or measurements), not to the people who have those scores. In the first example, the sample is really the scores of the 50 Canadian women, not the 50 women themselves, and the population is really what the *scores* would be if all Canadian women were tested.

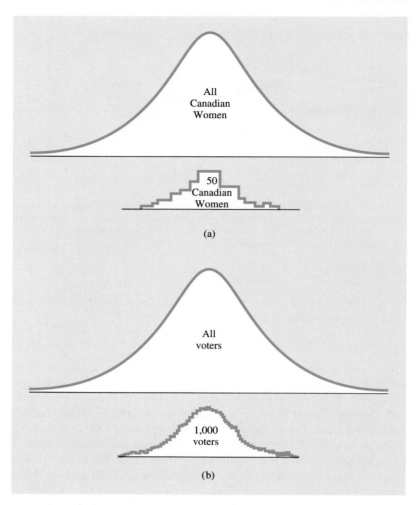

FIGURE 4–12   *Additional examples of populations and samples. In (a), the population is the scores of all Canadian women, and a sample consists of the scores of the 50 particular Canadian women studied. In (b), the population is the voting preferences of the entire voting-age population, and a sample consists of the voting preferences of the 1,000 voting-age people who were surveyed.*

METHODS OF SAMPLING

random selection

Usually, the ideal method of picking out a sample to study is called **random selection.** The researcher starts with a complete list of the population and randomly selects some of them to study. An example of a random method of selection would be to put each name on a table tennis ball, put all the balls into a big hopper, shake it up, and have a blindfolded person select as many as are needed. (In practice, most researchers use a computer-generated list of random numbers.)

haphazard selection

    It is important not to confuse truly random selection with what might be called **haphazard selection;** for example, just taking whoever is available or happens to be first on a list. When using haphazard selection, it is surprisingly easy to accidentally pick a group of people to study that is really quite different from the population as a whole. Consider a survey of attitudes about your statistics instructor. Suppose you give your questionnaire only to other students sitting near you in class. Such a survey would be affected by all the things that influence where students choose to sit, some of which have to do with just what you are studying—how much they like the instructor or the class. (Thus, asking students who sit near you would likely result in opinions more like your own than a truly random sample would.)

Unfortunately, it is often impractical or impossible to study a truly random sample. One problem is that we do not usually have a complete list of the full population. Another problem is that not everyone a researcher approaches agrees to participate in the study. Yet another problem is the cost and difficulty of tracking down people who live in remote places. For these and other reasons as well, social and behavioral scientists use various approximations to truly random samples that are more practical. However, researchers are consistently careful to rule out, as much as possible in advance, any systematic influence on who gets selected. Once the study has begun, researchers are constantly on the alert for any ways in which the sample may be systematically different from the population. For example, in much experimental research in education and psychology, it is common to use volunteer college students as the participants in the study. This is done for practical reasons and because often the topics studied in these experiments (for example, how short-term memory works) are thought to be relatively consistent across different types of people. Yet even in these cases, researchers avoid, for example, selecting people with a special interest in their research topic. Such researchers are also very aware that their results may not apply beyond college students, volunteers, people from their region, and so forth.

STATISTICAL TERMINOLOGY FOR SAMPLES AND POPULATIONS

The mean, variance, and standard deviation of a population are called **population parameters.** A population parameter usually is unknown and can only be estimated from what you know about a sample taken from that population. You do not taste all the beans, just the spoonful. "The beans are done" is an inference about the whole pot.

In this book, when referring to the population mean, standard deviation, or variance, even in formulas, we use the word "Population" (or the abbreviated "Pop")[3] before the M, SD^2, or SD. The mean, variance, and standard deviation you figure for the scores in a sample are called **sample statistics.** A sample statistic is figured from known information. Sample statistics are what we have been calculating all along. Sample statistics use the symbols we have been using all along: M, SD^2 and SD.

population parameters

sample statistics

HOW ARE YOU DOING?

1. Explain the difference between the population and a sample in relation to a research study.
2. Why do social and behavioral scientists usually study samples and not populations?
3. Explain the difference between random sampling and haphazard sampling.
4. Explain the difference between a population parameter and a sample statistic.

ANSWERS:

1. The population is the entire group to which results of a study are intended to apply. The sample is the particular, smaller group of individuals actually studied.

---

[3]In statistics writing, it is common to use Greek letters to refer to population parameters. For example, the population mean is μ and the population standard deviation is σ. However, we have not used these symbols in this text, wanting to make it easier for students to grasp the formulas without also having to deal with Greek letters.

BOX 4–1   Surveys, Polls, and 1948's Costly "Free Sample"

It is time to make you a more informed reader of polls in the media. Usually the results of properly done public polls will be accompanied, somewhere in fine print, by a statement like "From a telephone poll of 1,000 American adults taken on June 4 and 5. Sampling error ±3%." What does all this mean?

The Gallup poll is as good an example as any (Gallup, 1972; see also *http://www.gallup.com*), and there is no better place to begin than 1948, when all three of the major polling organizations—Gallup, Crossley (for Hearst papers), and Roper (for *Fortune*)—wrongly predicted Thomas Dewey's victory over Harry Truman for the U.S. presidency. Yet Gallup's prediction was based on 50,000 interviews and Roper's on 15,000. By contrast, to predict George H. W. Bush's 1988 victory, Gallup used only 4,089. Since 1952, the pollsters have never used more than 8,144—but with very small error and no outright mistakes. What has changed?

The method used before 1948, and never repeated since, was called "quota sampling." Interviewers were assigned a fixed number of persons to interview, with strict quotas to fill in all the categories that seemed important, such as residence, sex, age, race, and economic status. Within these specifics, however, they were free to interview whomever they liked. Republicans generally tended to be easier to interview. They were more likely to have telephones and permanent addresses and to live in better houses and better neighborhoods. This slight bias had not mattered prior to 1948. Democrats had been winning for years anyway. In 1948, the election was very close, and the Republican bias produced the embarrassing mistake that changed survey methods forever.

Since 1948, all survey organizations have used what is called a "probability method." Simple random sampling is the purest case of the probability method, but simple random sampling for a survey about a U.S. presidential election would require drawing names from a list of all the eligible voters in the nation—a lot of people. Each person selected would have to be found, in diversely scattered locales. So instead, "multistage cluster sampling" is used. The United States is divided into seven size-of-community groupings, from large cities to rural open country; these groupings are divided into seven geographic regions (New England, Middle Atlantic, and so on), after which smaller equal-sized groups are zoned, and then city blocks are drawn from the zones, with the probability of selection being proportional to the size of the population or number of dwelling units. Finally, an interviewer is given a randomly selected starting point on the map and is required to follow a given direction, take households in sequence, and ask for the youngest man 18 or older or, if no man is at home, the oldest woman 18 or older. (This has been found to compensate best for the tendencies for young men, and then all men, and then older women, in that order, to be not at home and hence underrepresented.)

Actually, telephoning is often the favored method for polling today. Phone surveys cost about one-third of door-to-door polls. Since most people now own phones, this method is less biased than in Truman's time. Phoning also allows computers to randomly dial phone numbers and, unlike telephone directories, this method calls unlisted numbers.

Whether the survey is by telephone or face to face, there will be about 35% nonrespondents after three attempts. This creates yet another bias, dealt with through questions about how much time a person spends at home, so that a slight extra weight can be given to the responses of those reached but usually at home less, to make up for those missed entirely.

What happened in the 2000 presidential election? Obviously, polls lost some of their credibility. Actually, the polls before the election were quite accurate, predicting Al Gore winning the national popular vote over George W. Bush by a very slight margin—which he did. The exit polls may not have been completed with as much care—the issue is still being debated.

Now you know quite a bit about opinion polls, but we have left two important questions unanswered: Why are only about 1,000 included in a poll meant to describe all U.S. adults, and what does the term *sampling error* mean? For these answers, you must wait for Chapter 6 (Box 6–1).

2. It is not practical in most cases to study the entire population.
3. In random sampling, the sample is chosen from among the population using a completely random method, so that any particular individual has an equal chance of being included in the sample. In haphazard sampling, the researcher selects to be studied whoever is available or convenient.
4. A population parameter is about the population (such as the mean of all the scores in the population); a sample statistic is about a particular sample (such as the mean of the scores of the people in the sample).

NORMAL CURVES, PROBABILITIES, SAMPLES, AND POPULATIONS IN RESEARCH ARTICLES

You need to understand the topics we covered in this chapter to learn what comes next. However, the topics of this chapter are rarely mentioned directly in research articles (except articles *about* methods or statistics). Sometimes you will see the normal curve mentioned, usually when a researcher is describing the pattern of scores on a particular variable. (We talk more about this and give some examples from published articles in Chapter 11, where we consider circumstances in which the scores do not follow a normal curve.)

Probability is also rarely discussed directly, except in relation to statistical significance, a topic we mentioned briefly in Chapter 3. In almost any article you look at, the Results section will have many descriptions of various methods associated with statistical significance, followed by something like "$p < .05$" or "$p < .01$." The p refers to probability, but the probability of what? That is the main topic of our discussion of statistical significance in Chapter 5.

Finally, you will sometimes see a brief mention of the method of selecting the sample from the population. For example, Schuster and colleagues (2001) conducted a national survey of stress reactions of U.S. adults after the September 11, 2001, terrorist attacks. Their report was published in the *New England Journal of Medicine*. They summarized the method of their study as follows: "Using random-digit dialing three to five days after September 11, we interviewed a nationally representative sample of 560 U.S. adults about their reactions to the terrorist attacks and their perceptions of their children's reactions" (p. 1507). Whenever possible, researchers check whether their sample is similar to the population as a whole, based on any information they may have about the overall population. In this study, the researchers compared their sample to 2001 census records and reported that the "sample slightly overrepresented women, non-Hispanic whites, and persons with higher levels of education and income" (p. 1507). Schuster and colleagues went on to note that overrepresentation of these groups "is typical of samples selected by means of random-digit dialing" (pp. 1507–1508).

SUMMARY

1. The scores on many variables in social science research approximately follow a bell-shaped, symmetrical, unimodal distribution called the normal curve. Because the shape of this curve follows an exact mathematical formula, there is a specific percentage of scores between any two points on a normal curve.
2. A useful working rule for normal curves is that 50% of the scores are above the mean, 34% are between the mean and 1 standard deviation above the mean, and 14% are between 1 and 2 standard deviations above the mean.

3. A normal curve table gives the percentage of scores between the mean and any particular positive Z score. Using this table, and knowing that the curve is symmetrical and that 50% of the scores are above the mean, you can figure the percentage of scores above or below any particular Z score. You can also use the table to figure the Z score for the point where a particular percentage of scores begins or ends.

4. Most social and behavioral scientists consider the probability of an event to be its expected relative frequency. Probability is usually figured as the proportion of successful outcomes to total possible outcomes. It is symbolized by *p* and has a range from 0 (event is impossible) to 1 (event is certain). The normal curve provides a way to know the probabilities of scores' being within particular ranges of values.

5. A sample is an individual or group that is studied—usually as representative of a larger group or population that cannot be studied in its entirety. Ideally, the sample is selected from a population using a strictly random procedure. The mean, variance, and so forth of a sample are called *sample statistics*. When of a population, they are called *population parameters*.

6. Research articles rarely discuss normal curves (except briefly when the variable being studied seems not to follow a normal curve) or probability (except in relation to statistical significance). Procedures of sampling are sometimes described, particularly when the study is a survey, and the representativeness of a sample may also be discussed.

KEY TERMS

normal distribution (p. 108)
normal curve (p. 108)
normal curve table (p. 110)
probability (*p*) (p. 118)
outcome (p. 118)

expected relative frequency (p. 118)
long-run relative-frequency interpretation of probability (p. 118)
population (p. 120)

sample (p. 120)
random selection (p. 122)
haphazard selection (p. 122)
population parameters (p. 123)
sample statistics (p. 123)

EXAMPLE WORKED-OUT PROBLEMS

FIGURING THE PERCENTAGE ABOVE OR BELOW A PARTICULAR RAW SCORE OR Z SCORE

Suppose a test of sensitivity to violence is known to have a mean of 20, a standard deviation of 3, and to follow a normal curve. What percentage of people have scores above 24?

ANSWER

❶ **If you are beginning with a raw score, first change it to a Z score.** Using the usual formula, $Z = (X - M)/SD$, $Z = (24 - 20)/3 = 1.33$.

❷ **Draw a picture of the normal curve, where the Z score falls on it, and shade in the area for which you are finding the percentage.** This is shown in Figure 4–13.

❸ **Make a rough estimate of the shaded area's percentage based on the 50%–34%–14% percentages.** If the shaded area started at a Z score of 1, it would

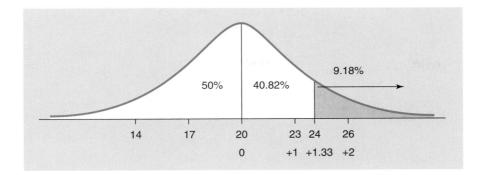

FIGURE 4–13 *Distribution of sensitivity to violence scores showing percentage of scores above a score of 24 (shaded area).*

include 16%. If it started at a *Z* score of 2, it would include only 2%. So with a *Z* score of 1.33, it has to be somewhere between 16% and 2%.

❹ **Find the exact percentage using the normal curve table.** In Table A–1 (in the Appendix), 1.33 in the "*Z*" column goes with 40.82 in the "% Mean to *Z*" column.

❺ **If needed, add or subtract 50% from this percentage.** Because 50% of people are above the mean on any normal curve, and 40.82% of the people above the mean are below this score, that leaves 9.18% above this person's score (that is, 50%−40.82% = 9.18%). That is the answer to the problem: 9.18% of people have a higher score than 24 on the sensitivity to violence measure.

❻ **Check that your exact percentage is within the range of your rough estimate from Step 3.** Our result, 9.18%, is within the 16% to 2% range estimated.

Note: If the problem involves *Z* scores that are all 0, 1, or 2 (or −1 or −2), you can work the problem using the 50%–34%–14% figures and without using the normal curve table. The only steps are making the figure and adding or subtracting 50% as necessary.

FIGURING *Z* SCORES AND RAW SCORES FROM PERCENTAGES

Consider the same situation: A test of sensitivity to violence is known to have a mean of 20, a standard deviation of 3, and to follow a normal curve. What is the minimum score a person needs to be in the top 75%?

ANSWER

❶ **Draw a picture of the normal curve and shade in the approximate area for your percentage using the 50%–34%–14% percentages.** The shading has to begin between the mean and 1 *SD* below the mean. (There are 50% above the mean and 84% above 1 *SD* below the mean.) This is shown in Figure 4–14.

❷ **Make a rough estimate of the *Z* score where the shaded area starts.** The *Z* score has to be between −1 and 0.

❸ **Find the exact *Z* score using the normal curve table (including adding or subtracting 50%, if necessary, before looking it up).** Since 50% of people have IQs above the mean, for the top 75% you need to include the 25% below the mean. Looking in the "% Mean to *Z*" of the normal curve table, the closest figure to 25% is 24.86, which goes with a *Z* of .67. Since we are interested in below the mean, we want −.67.

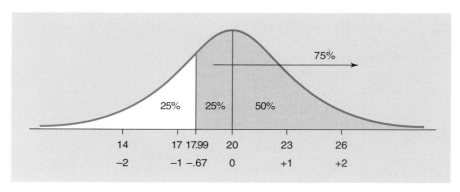

FIGURE 4–14 *Finding the Z score and sensitivity to violence raw score for where the top 75% start.*

❹ **Check that your exact** *Z* **score is similar to your rough estimate from Step 2.** $-.67$ is between 0 and -1.

❺ **If you want to find a raw score, change it from the** *Z* **score.** Using the usual formula, $X = (Z)(SD) + M$, $X = (-.67)(3) + 20 = -2.01 + 20 = 17.99$. That is, to be in the top 75%, a person would need to have a score on this test of at least 18.

Note: If the problem instructs you not to use a normal curve table, you should be able to work the problem using the 50%–34%–14% figures. The only steps are making the figure, adding or subtracting 50% as necessary, and possibly changing the results to raw scores.

FINDING A PROBABILITY

A candy dish has four kinds of fruit-flavored candy: 20 apple, 20 strawberry, 5 cherry, and 5 grape. If you close your eyes and pick one piece of candy at random, what is the probability it will be either cherry or grape?

ANSWER

❶ **Determine the number of possible successful outcomes.** There are 10 possible successful outcomes—5 cherry and 5 grape.

❷ **Determine the number of all possible outcomes.** There are 50 possible outcomes overall: $20 + 20 + 5 + 5 = 50$.

❸ **Divide the number of possible successful outcomes (Step 1) by the number of all possible outcomes (Step 2).** $10/50 = .2$. Thus, the probability of picking either a cherry or grape candy is .2.

PRACTICE PROBLEMS

These problems involve figuring. Most real-life statistics problems are done on a computer with special statistical software. Even if you have such software, do these problems by hand (with the help of a calculator) to ingrain the method in your mind. Also, in all problems involving figuring, be sure to show your work.

For practice in using a computer to solve statistics problems, refer to the computer section of each chapter of the *Student's Study Guide and Computer Workbook* that accompanies this text.

All data are fictional unless an actual citation is given.

For answers to Set I problems, see pp. 426–27.

SET I

1. Suppose the people living in a particular city have a mean score of 40 and a standard deviation of 5 on a measure of concern about the environment. Assume that these concern scores are normally distributed. Approximately what percentage of people in this city have a score (a) above 40, (b) above 45, (c) above 30, (d) above 35, (e) below 40, (f) below 45, (g) below 30, (h) below 35? (Do not use a normal curve table; use the 50%–34%–14% figures for this problem.)

2. Using the information in problem 1, what is the minimum score a person has to have to be in the top (a) 2%, (b) 16%, (c) 50%, (d) 84%, and (e) 98%? (Do not use a normal curve table; use the 50%–34%–14% figures for this problem.)

3. An education researcher has been studying test anxiety using a particular measure, which she administers to students prior to midterm exams. On this measure, she has found that the distribution follows a normal curve. Using a normal curve table, what percentage of students have Z scores (a) below 1.5, (b) above 1.5, (c) below -1.5, (d) above -1.5, (e) above 2.10, (f) below 2.10, (g) above .45, (h) below -1.78, and (i) above 1.68?

4. In the previous problem, the measure of test anxiety has a mean of 15 and a standard deviation of 5. Using a normal curve table, what percentage of students have scores (a) above 16, (b) above 17, (c) above 18, (d) below 18, (e) below 14?

5. In the test anxiety example of problems 3 and 4, using a normal curve table, what score on the test anxiety measure would a person need to have to be in (a) the top 40%, (b) the top 30%, (c) the top 20%?

6. Using a normal curve table, give the percent of scores between the mean and a Z score of (a) .58, (b) .59, (c) 1.46, (d) 1.56, (e) $-.58$.

7. Assuming a normal curve, (a) if a student is in the bottom 30% of the class on Spanish ability, what is the highest Z score this person could have? (b) If the person is in the bottom 3%, what would be the highest Z score this person could have?

8. Assuming a normal curve, (a) if a person is in the top 10% of the country on mathematics ability, what is the lowest Z score this person could have? (b) If the person is in the top 1%, what would be the lowest Z score this person could have?

9. Consider a test of coordination that has a normal distribution, a mean of 50, and a standard deviation of 10. (a) How high a score would a person need to be in the top 5%? (b) Explain your answer to someone who has never had a course in statistics.

10. The following numbers of employees in a company received special assistance from the personnel department last year:

Drug/alcohol	10
Family crisis counseling	20
Other	20
Total	50

If you were to select a score at random from the records for last year, what is the probability that it would be in each of the following categories? (a) drug/alcohol, (b) family, (c) drug/alcohol or family, (d) any category except "Other," (e) any of the three categories? (f) Explain your answer to part (a) to someone who has never had a course in statistics.

11. A research article is concerned with the level of self-esteem of Australian high school students. The methods section emphasizes that a "random sample" of Australian high school students was surveyed. Explain to a person who has never had a course in statistics what this means and why it is important.

12. Altman, Levine, Howard, and Hamilton (1997) conducted a telephone survey of the attitudes of the U.S. adult public toward tobacco farmers. In the method section of their article, they explained that their respondents were "randomly selected from a nationwide list of telephone numbers" (p. 117). Explain to a person who has never had a course in statistics or research methods what this means and why it is important.

SET II

13. Consider a test that has a normal distribution, a mean of 100, and a standard deviation of 14. How high a score would a person need to be in the top (a) 1%, and (b) 5%?

14. The length of time it takes to complete a word puzzle is found to be normally distributed with a mean of 80 seconds and a standard deviation of 10 seconds. Approximately what percentage of scores (on time to complete the word puzzle) will be (a) above 100, (b) below 100, (c) above 90, (d) below 90, (e) above 80, (f) below 80, (g) above 70, (h) below 70, (i) above 60, and (j) below 60? (Do not use a normal curve table; use the 50%–34%–14% figures for this problem.)

15. Using the information in problem 14, what is the longest time to complete the word puzzle a person can have and still be in the bottom (a) 2%, (b) 16%, (c) 50%, (d) 84%, and (e) 98%? (Do not use a normal curve table; use the 50%–34%–14% figures for this problem.)

16. Suppose that the scores of architects on a particular creativity test are normally distributed. Using a normal curve table, what percentage of architects have Z scores (a) above .10, (b) below .10, (c) above .20, (d) below .20, (e) above 1.10, (f) below 1.10, (g) above −.10, and (h) below −.10?

17. In the example in problem 16, using a normal curve table, what is the minimum Z score an architect can have on the creativity test to be in the (a) top 50%, (b) top 40%, (c) top 60%, (d) top 30%, and (e) top 20%?

18. In the example in problem 16, assume that the mean is 300 and the standard deviation is 25. Using a normal curve table, what scores would be the top and bottom score to find (a) the middle 50% of architects, (b) the middle 90% of architects, and (c) the middle 99% of architects?

19. Suppose that you are designing an instrument panel for a large industrial machine. The machine requires the person using it to reach 2 feet from a particular position. The reach from this position for adult women is known to have a mean of 2.8 feet with a standard deviation of .5. The reach for adult men is known to have a mean of 3.1 feet with a standard deviation of .6. Both women's and men's reach from this position is normally distributed. If this design is implemented, (a) what percentage of women will not be able to work on this instrument panel? (b) What percentage of men will not be able to work on

this instrument panel? (c) Explain your answers to a person who has never had a course in statistics.

20. You are conducting a survey at a college with 800 students, 50 faculty members, and 150 administrative staff members. Each of these 1,000 individuals has a single listing in the campus phone directory. Suppose you were to cut up the directory and pull out one listing at random to contact. What is the probability it would be (a) a student, (b) a faculty member, (c) an administrative staff member, (d) a faculty or administrative staff member, and (e) anyone except an administrative staff member? (f) Explain your answer to part (d) to someone who has never had a course in statistics.

21. You apply to 20 graduate programs, 10 of which are in the United States, 5 of which are in Canada, and 5 of which are in Australia. You get a message from home that you have a letter from one of the programs you applied to, but nothing is said about which one. Give the probability it is from (a) a program in the United States, (b) a program in Canada, (c) from any program other than in Australia. (d) Explain your answer to (c) to someone who has never had a course in statistics.

22. Suppose you want to conduct a survey of the voting preference of undergraduate students. One approach would be to contact every undergraduate student you know and ask them to fill out a questionnaire. (a) What kind of sampling method is this? (b) What is a major limitation of this kind of approach?

23. A large study of how people make future plans and its relation to their life satisfaction (Prenda & Lachman, 2001) obtained their participants "through random-digit dialing procedures." These are procedures in which phone numbers to call potential participants are randomly generated by a computer. Explain to a person who has never had a course in statistics (a) why this method of sampling might be used and (b) why it may be a problem if not everyone called agreed to be interviewed.

24. Suppose that you were going to conduct a survey of visitors to your campus. You want the survey to be as representative as possible. (a) How would you select the people to survey? (b) Why would that be your best method?

C H A P T E R

Introduction to Hypothesis Testing

hypothesis testing

Tip for Success

The material in this chapter builds upon what you learned in Chapter 4 and the chapters it is based upon, particularly the material in Chapter 2 on mean, standard deviation, and Z scores. We strongly urge you not to proceed to this chapter until you are confident you have mastered this earlier material.

In Chapter 4, you learned about the normal curve, probability, and the difference between a sample and a population. In this chapter, we introduce the crucial topic of **hypothesis testing.** Hypothesis testing is a systematic procedure for deciding whether the results of a research study, which examines a sample, supports a particular theory or practical innovation, which applies to a population. Hypothesis testing is the central theme in all the remaining chapters of this book, as it is in most social and behavioral science research.

We should warn you at this point that many students find the most difficult part of the course to be mastering the basic logic of this chapter and the next two. This chapter in particular requires some mental gymnastics. Even if you follow everything the first time through, you will be wise to review it thoroughly. Hypothesis testing involves a group of ideas that make little sense covered separately, so this chapter covers a fairly large number of ideas all at once. However, a benefit of this is that once you understand the material in this chapter and the two that follow, your mind will be used to this sort of thing, and the rest of the course should seem easier.

At the same time, we have kept this introduction to hypothesis testing as simple as possible, putting off what we could for later chapters. For example, real-life social and behavioral science research almost always involves samples of many individuals. However, to simplify how much you have to learn at one time, all of the examples in this chapter are about studies in which the sample is a single individual. To do this, we had to create some odd examples. Just remember that you are building a foundation that will, by Chapter 8, prepare you to understand hypothesis testing as it is actually carried out.

A HYPOTHESIS-TESTING EXAMPLE

Here is our first necessarily odd example that we made up to keep this introduction to hypothesis testing as straightforward as possible. A large research project has been going on for several years. In this project, new babies are given a special vitamin and then the research team follows their development during the first 2 years of life. So far, the vitamin has not speeded up babies' development. The ages at which these and all other babies start to walk is shown in Figure 5–1. Notice that the mean is 14 months, the standard deviation is 3 months, and the ages follow a normal curve. Looking at the distribution, you can see that less than 2% start walking before 8 months of age; these are the babies who are 2 standard deviations below the mean. (This fictional distribution actually is close to the true distribution researchers have found for European babies, although that true distribution is slightly skewed to the right [Hindley, Filliozat, Klackenberg, Nicolet-Meister, & Sand, 1966].)

One of the researchers working on the project has an idea. If the vitamin the babies are taking could be more highly refined, perhaps the effect of the vitamin would be dramatically greater: Babies taking the highly purified version should start walking much earlier than other babies. (We will assume that the purification process could not possibly make the vitamin harmful.) However, refining the vitamin in this way is extremely expensive for each dose, so the research team decides to try the procedure with just enough highly purified doses for only one baby. A newborn in the project is then randomly selected to take the highly purified version of the vitamin, and the researchers then follow this baby's progress for 2 years. What kind of result should lead the researchers to conclude that the highly purified vitamin allows babies to walk earlier?

This is an example of a hypothesis-testing problem. The researchers want to draw a general conclusion about whether the purified vitamin allows babies in general to walk earlier. The conclusion about babies in general, however, will be based on results of studying only a sample. In this example, the sample is of a single baby.

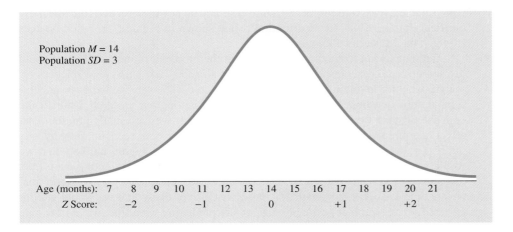

Population $M = 14$
Population $SD = 3$

Age (months):	7	8	9	10	11	12	13	14	15	16	17	18	19	20	21
Z Score:		−2			−1			0			+1			+2	

FIGURE 5–1   *Distribution of when babies begin to walk (fictional data).*

THE CORE LOGIC OF HYPOTHESIS TESTING

There is a standard way researchers approach a hypothesis-testing problem like this one. They use the following reasoning. Ordinarily, among babies that are not given the specially purified vitamin, the chance of a baby's starting to walk at age 8 months or earlier would be less than 2%. Thus, walking at 8 months or earlier is highly unlikely among such babies. But what if the randomly selected baby in our study does start walking by 8 months? If the specially purified vitamin had no effect on this particular baby's walking age (which means that the baby's walking age should be similar to that of babies that were not given the vitamin), it is highly unlikely (less than a 2% chance) that the particular baby we selected at random would start walking by 8 months. So, if the baby in our study does in fact start walking by 8 months, that allows us to *reject* the idea that the specially purified vitamin has *no* effect. If we reject the idea that the specially purified vitamin has no effect, then we must also *accept* the idea that the specially purified vitamin *does* have an effect. Thus, our explanation for the baby's early walking age is that the specially purified vitamin speeded up the baby's development.

The researchers first spelled out what would have to happen for them to conclude that the special purification procedure makes a difference. Having laid this out in advance, the researchers can then go on to carry out their study. In this example, carrying out the study means giving the specially purified vitamin to a randomly selected baby and watching to see how early that baby walks. Suppose the result of the study shows that the baby starts walking before 8 months. They would then conclude that it is unlikely the specially purified vitamin makes no difference and thus also conclude that it does make a difference.

This kind of testing the opposite-of-what-you-predict, roundabout reasoning is at the heart of inferential statistics in social and behavioral sciences. It is something like a double negative. One reason for this approach is that we have the information to figure the probability of getting a particular experimental result if the situation of there being no difference is true. In the purified vitamin example, the researchers know what the probabilities are of babies walking at different ages if the specially purified vitamin does not have any effect. It is the probability of babies walking at various ages that is already known from studies of babies in general—that is, babies who have not received the specially purified vitamin. (Suppose the specially purified vitamin has no effect. In that situation, the age at which babies start walking is the same whether or not they receive the specially purified vitamin. Thus, the distribution is that shown in Figure 5–1, based on ages at which babies start walking in general.)

Without such a tortuous way of going at the problem, in most cases you could just not do hypothesis testing at all. In almost all social and behavioral sciences research, whether involving experiments, surveys, or whatever, we base our conclusions on this question: What is the probability of getting our research results if the opposite of what we are predicting were true? That is, we are usually predicting an effect of some kind. However, we decide on whether there *is* such an effect by seeing if it is unlikely that there is *not* such an effect. If it is highly unlikely that we would get our research results if the opposite of what we are predicting were true, that allows us to reject that opposite prediction. If we reject that opposite prediction, we are able to accept our prediction. However, if it is likely that we would get our research results if the opposite of what we are predicting were true, we are not able to reject that opposite prediction. If we are not able to reject that opposite prediction, we are not able to accept our prediction.

Tip for Success

This section, "The Core Logic of Hypothesis Testing," is central to everything else we do in the book. Thus, you may want to read it a few times. You should also be certain that you understand the logic of hypothesis testing before reading later chapters.

THE HYPOTHESIS-TESTING PROCESS

Let's look at our example, going over each step in some detail. Along the way, we cover the special terminology of hypothesis testing. Most important, we introduce five steps of hypothesis testing you use for the rest of this book.

STEP 1: RESTATE THE QUESTION AS A RESEARCH HYPOTHESIS AND A NULL HYPOTHESIS ABOUT THE POPULATIONS

First, note that the researchers are interested in the effects on babies in general (not just this particular baby). That is, the purpose of studying any sample is to know about populations. Thus, it is useful to restate the research question in terms of populations. In the present example, we can think of two populations of babies:

Population 1: Babies who take the specially purified vitamin.

Population 2: Babies who do not take the specially purified vitamin.

Population 1 are those who receive the experimental treatment. In our example, there is only one real-life baby in Population 1. Yet this one baby represents an as-yet-unborn future group of many babies to whom the researchers want to apply their results. Population 2 is a kind of baseline of what is already known.

The prediction of the research team is that Population 1 babies (those who take the specially purified vitamin) will on the average walk earlier than Population 2 babies (those who do not take the specially purified vitamin). This prediction is based on the researchers' theory of how these vitamins work. A prediction like this about the difference between populations is called a **research hypothesis.** Put more formally, the prediction is that the mean of Population 1 is lower (babies receiving the special vitamin walk earlier) than the mean of Population 2.   **research hypothesis**

The opposite of the research hypothesis is that the populations are not different in the way predicted. Under this scenario, Population 1 babies (those who take the specially purified vitamin) will on the average *not* walk earlier than Population 2 babies (those who do not take the specially purified vitamin). That is, this prediction is that there is no difference in when Population 1 and Population 2 babies start walking. They start at the same time. A statement like this, about a lack of difference between populations, is the crucial *opposite* of the research hypothesis. It is called a **null hypothesis.** It has this name because it states the situation in which   **null hypothesis** there is no difference (the difference is "null") between the populations.[1]

The research hypothesis and the null hypothesis are complete opposites. If one is true, the other cannot be true. In fact, the research hypothesis is sometimes called the *alternative hypothesis*—that is, it is the alternative to the null hypothesis. This is actually a bit ironic. As researchers, we care most about the research hypothesis. But when doing the steps of hypothesis testing, we use this roundabout method of seeing whether or not we can reject the null hypothesis so that we can decide about its alternative (the research hypothesis).

---

[1]We are oversimplifying a bit here to make the initial learning easier. The research hypothesis is that one population will walk earlier than the other. Thus, to be precise, its opposite is that the other group will either walk at the same time or walk later. That is, the opposite of the research hypothesis in this example includes both no difference and a difference in the direction opposite to what we predicted. We discuss this issue in some detail later in the chapter.

STEP 2: DETERMINE THE CHARACTERISTICS OF THE COMPARISON DISTRIBUTION

Recall that the overall logic of hypothesis testing involves figuring out the probability of getting a particular result if the null hypothesis is true. Thus, you need to know about what the situation would be if the null hypothesis were true. In our example, we start out knowing all about Population 2 (see Figure 5–1). For example, we know that Population $M = 14$ and Population $SD = 3$. (We use the term "Population" before M and SD because we are referring to the mean and standard deviation of a population.) If the null hypothesis is true, Population 1 and Population 2 are the same—in our example, this means Populations 1 and 2 both follow a normal curve, have a mean of 14 months, and a standard deviation of 3 months.

comparison distribution

In the hypothesis-testing process, you want to find out the probability that you could have gotten a sample score as extreme as what you got (say, a baby walking very early) if your sample were from a distribution of the sort you would have if the null hypothesis were true. Thus, in this book we call this distribution a **comparison distribution.** (The comparison distribution is sometimes called a *statistical model* or a *sampling distribution*—an idea we discuss in Chapter 6.) That is, in the hypothesis-testing process, you compare the actual sample's score to this comparison distribution.

STEP 3: DETERMINE THE CUTOFF SAMPLE SCORE ON THE COMPARISON DISTRIBUTION AT WHICH THE NULL HYPOTHESIS SHOULD BE REJECTED

Ideally, well before conducting a study, researchers set a target against which they will compare their result—how extreme a sample score they would need to draw a confident conclusion. Specifically, they determine the score the sample would need to have in order to decide against the null hypothesis—how extreme it would have to be for it to be too unlikely that they could get such an extreme score if the null hypothesis were true. This is called the **cutoff sample score.** The cutoff sample score is also known as the *critical value*.

cutoff sample score

Consider our purified vitamin example in which the null hypothesis is that it doesn't matter whether a baby is fed the specially purified vitamin. The researchers might decide that if the null hypothesis were true, a randomly selected baby walking by 8 months would be very unlikely. With a normal distribution, being 2 or more standard deviations below the mean (walking at 8 months) could occur less than 2% of the time. Thus, based on the comparison distribution, the researchers set their cutoff sample score even before doing the study. They decide in advance that *if* the result of their study is a baby who walks by 8 months, they will reject the null hypothesis.

On the other hand, what if the baby does not start walking until after 8 months? If that happens, the researchers will not be able to reject the null hypothesis.

When setting in advance how extreme a score needs to be to reject the null hypothesis, researchers use Z scores and percentages. In our purified vitamin example, the researchers might decide that if a result were less likely than 2%, they would reject the null hypothesis. Being in the bottom 2% of a normal curve means having a Z score of about -2 or lower. Thus, the researchers would set -2 as their Z-score cutoff point on the comparison distribution for deciding that a result is extreme enough to reject the null hypothesis. So, if the actual sample Z score is -2 or lower, the researchers will reject the null hypothesis. However, if the actual sample Z score is greater than -2, the researchers will not reject the null hypothesis.

Suppose that the researchers are even more cautious about too easily rejecting the null hypothesis. They might decide that they will reject the null hypothesis only

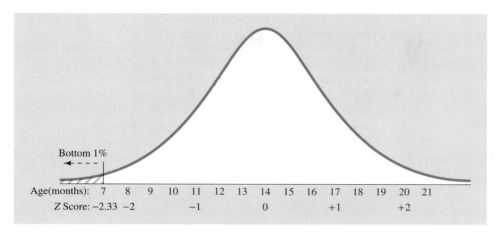

FIGURE 5–2 *Distribution of when babies begin to walk, with bottom 1% shaded (fictional data).*

if they get a result that could occur by chance 1% of the time or less. They could then figure out the Z-score cutoff for 1%. Using the normal curve table, to have a score in the lower 1% of a normal curve, you need a Z score of −2.33 or less. (In our example, a Z score of −2.33 means 7 months.) In Figure 5–2, we have shaded the 1% of the comparison distribution in which a sample would be considered so extreme that the possibility that it came from a distribution like this would be rejected. So, now the researchers will only reject the null hypothesis if the actual sample Z score is −2.33 or lower—that is, if it falls in the shaded area in Figure 5–2.

In general, social and behavioral science researchers use a cutoff on the comparison distribution with a probability of 5% that a score will be at least that extreme (if the null hypothesis were true). That is, researchers reject the null hypothesis if the probability of getting a result this extreme (if the null hypothesis were true) is less than 5%. This probability is usually written as $p < .05$. However, in some areas of research, or when researchers want to be especially cautious, they use a cutoff of 1% ($p < .01$).[2] These are called **conventional levels of significance.** They are described as the *.05 significance level* and the *.01 significance level* (we also refer to them as the 5% significance level and the 1% significance level). (We discuss in more detail in Chapter 7 the issues in deciding on the significance level to use.) When a sample score is so extreme that researchers reject the null hypothesis, the result is said to be **statistically significant** (or *significant,* as it is often abbreviated).

conventional levels of significance ($p < .05, p < .01$)

statistically significant

STEP 4: DETERMINE YOUR SAMPLE'S SCORE ON THE COMPARISON DISTRIBUTION

The next step is to carry out the study and get the actual result for your sample. Once you have the results for the sample, you figure the Z score for the sample's raw score based on the population mean and standard deviation of the comparison distribution.

[2]These days, when hypothesis testing is usually done on the computer, you have to decide in advance only on the cutoff probability. The computer prints out the exact probability of getting your result if the null hypothesis were true. You then just compare the printed-out probability to see if it is less than the cutoff probability level you set in advance. However, to *understand* what these probability levels mean, you need to learn the entire process, including how to figure the Z score for a particular cutoff probability.

Assume that the researchers did the study and the baby who was given the specially purified vitamin started walking at 6 months. The mean of the comparison distribution to which we are comparing these results is 14 months and the standard deviation is 3 months. That is, Population $M = 14$ and Population $SD = 3$. Thus a baby who walks at 6 months is 8 months below the population mean, which puts this baby 2⅔ standard deviations below the population mean. The Z score for this sample baby on the comparison distribution is thus -2.67 ($Z = [6 - 14]/3$). Figure 5–3 shows the score of our sample baby on the comparison distribution.

STEP 5: DECIDE WHETHER TO REJECT THE NULL HYPOTHESIS

To decide whether to reject the null hypothesis, you compare your actual sample's Z score (from Step 4) to the cutoff Z score (from Step 3). In our example, the actual sample's Z score was -2.67. Let's suppose the researchers had decided in advance that they would reject the null hypothesis if the sample's Z score was below -2. Since -2.67 is below -2, the researchers would reject the null hypothesis.

Or, suppose the researchers had used the more conservative 1% significance level. The needed Z score to reject the null hypothesis would then have been -2.33 or lower. But, again, the actual Z for the randomly selected baby was -2.67 (a more extreme score than -2.33). Thus, even with this more conservative cutoff, they would still reject the null hypothesis. This situation is shown in Figure 5–3. As you can see in the figure, the bottom 1% of the distribution is shaded. We recommend that you always draw such a picture of the distribution. Be sure to shade in the part of the distribution that is *more extreme* than the cutoff sample score. If your actual sample Z score falls within the shaded region, you can reject the null hypothesis. Since the sample Z score (of -2.67) in this example falls within the shaded region, the researchers can reject the null hypothesis.

If the researchers reject the null hypothesis, what remains is the research hypothesis. In this example, the research team can conclude that the results of their study support the research hypothesis, that babies who take the specially purified vitamin walk earlier than other babies.

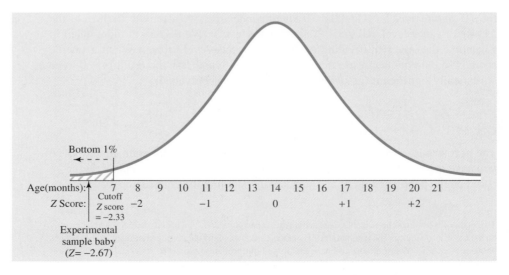

F I G U R E 5 – 3 *Distribution of when babies begin to walk, indicating both the bottom 1% and the single baby that is the sample studied (fictional data).*

IMPLICATIONS OF REJECTING OR FAILING TO REJECT THE NULL HYPOTHESIS

It is important to emphasize two points about the conclusions you can make from the hypothesis-testing process. First, suppose you reject the null hypothesis. Therefore, your results support the research hypothesis (as in our example). You would still not say that the results *prove* the research hypothesis or that the results show that the research hypothesis is *true*. This would be too strong because the results of research studies are based on probabilities. Specifically, they are based on the probability being low of getting your result if the null hypothesis were true. Proven and true are okay in logic and mathematics, but to use these words in conclusions from scientific research is inappropriate. (It is okay to use *true* when speaking hypothetically—for example, "*if* this hypothesis *were* true, then . . ."—but not when speaking of conclusions about an actual result.) What you do say when you reject the null hypothesis is that the results are *statistically significant*.

Second, when a result is not extreme enough to reject the null hypothesis, you do not say that the result *supports* the null hypothesis. You simply say the result is *not statistically significant*. A result that is not strong enough to reject the null hypothesis means only that the study was inconclusive. The results may not be extreme enough to reject the null hypothesis, but the null hypothesis might still be false (and the research hypothesis true). Suppose that in our example the specially purified vitamin had only a slight but still real effect. In that case, we would not expect to find any single baby given the purified vitamin to be walking a lot earlier than other babies. Thus, we would not be able to reject the null hypothesis, even though it is false.

Showing that the null hypothesis is true would mean showing that there is absolutely no difference between the populations. It is always possible that there is a difference between the populations, but that the difference is much smaller than what the particular study was able to detect. Therefore, when a result is not extreme enough to reject the null hypothesis, the results are inconclusive. Sometimes, however, if studies have been done using large numbers and accurate measuring procedures, evidence may build up in support of something close to the null hypothesis—that there is at most very little difference between the populations. (We have more to say on this important issue later in this chapter and in Chapter 7.)

SUMMARY OF THE STEPS OF HYPOTHESIS TESTING

Here is a summary of the five steps of hypothesis testing:

❶ **Restate the question as a research hypothesis and a null hypothesis about the populations.**

❷ **Determine the characteristics of the comparison distribution.**

❸ **Determine the cutoff sample score on the comparison distribution at which the null hypothesis should be rejected.**

❹ **Determine your sample's score on the comparison distribution.**

❺ **Decide whether to reject the null hypothesis.**

HOW ARE YOU DOING?

1. A sample is given an experimental treatment intended to make them score higher than the general public on a particular measure. State (a) the null hypothesis and (b) the research hypothesis.
2. (a) What is a comparison distribution? (b) What role does it play in hypothesis testing?
3. What is the cutoff sample score?
4. Why do we say that hypothesis testing involves a double negative logic?

5. What can you conclude when (a) a result is so extreme that you reject the null hypothesis, and (b) a result is not so extreme that you can reject the null hypothesis?

6. A training program to increase friendliness is tried on one individual randomly selected from the general public. Among the general public (who do not get this procedure) the mean on the friendliness measure is 30 with a standard deviation of 4. The researchers want to test their hypothesis at the 5% significance level. After going through the procedure, this individual's score on the friendliness measure is 40. What should the researchers conclude?

ANSWERS:

1. (a) The population of people like those who get the experimental treatment do not score higher than the population of individuals who do not get the experimental treatment. (b) The population of people like those who get the experimental treatment score higher than the population of people who do not get the experimental treatment.

2. (a) A distribution to which you compare the results of your study. (b) In hypothesis testing, the comparison distribution is the distribution for the situation when the null hypothesis is true. To decide whether to reject the null hypothesis, you check how extreme the score of your sample is on this comparison distribution—how likely it would be to get a sample with a score this extreme if your sample came from this comparison distribution.

3. The Z score at which, if the sample's Z score is more extreme than it on the comparison distribution, you reject the null hypothesis.

4. Because we are interested in the research hypothesis, but we test whether it is true by seeing if we can reject its opposite, the null hypothesis.

5. (a) The research hypothesis is supported; the result is statistically significant. (b) The result is not statistically significant; the result is inconclusive.

6. The cutoff sample Z score is 1.64. The actual sample's Z score is 2.5. Reject the null hypothesis; the research hypothesis is supported; the result is statistically significant. Thus, the training program increases friendliness.

ONE-TAILED AND TWO-TAILED HYPOTHESIS TESTS

In the baby-walking example, the researchers were interested in only one direction of result. Specifically, they tested whether babies given the specially purified vitamin would walk *earlier* than other babies. The researchers in this study were not really interested in the possibility that giving the specially purified vitamins would cause babies to start walking later.

DIRECTIONAL HYPOTHESES AND ONE-TAILED TESTS

directional hypothesis

The baby-walking study is an example of a **directional hypothesis.** The study focused on a specific direction of effect. When a researcher makes a directional hypothesis, the null hypothesis is also, in a sense, directional. Suppose the research hypothesis is that taking the specially purified vitamin will make babies walk earlier. The null hypothesis, then, is that the specially purified vitamin will either have no effect or make babies walk later. Thus, in Figure 5–2, for the null hypothesis to be rejected, the sample had to have a score in one particular tail of the comparison distribution—the lower extreme or tail (in this example, the bottom 1%) of the comparison distribution. (When it comes to rejecting the null hypothesis with a directional hypothesis, a score at the other tail would be the same as a score in the middle—that is, it would not allow you to reject the null hypothesis.) For this reason, the test of a

one-tailed test

directional hypothesis is called a **one-tailed test.** A one-tailed test can be one-tailed in either direction. In this example, the prediction was that the baby would walk early—

a prediction in the direction of a low score on months before walking. Thus, the cutoff region was at the low end (left side) of the comparison distribution. In other research situations with a directional hypothesis, the cutoff may be at the high end (right side) of the comparison distribution. That is, in these situations, the researchers would be predicting that the experimental procedure will produce a high score.

NONDIRECTIONAL HYPOTHESES AND TWO-TAILED TESTS

Sometimes, a research hypothesis states that an experimental procedure will have an effect, without specifying whether it will produce a very high score or a very low score. For example, a researcher may be interested in the impact of a new social-skills program on worker productivity. The program could improve productivity by making the working environment more pleasant. Or, the program could hurt productivity by encouraging people to socialize instead of work. The research hypothesis is that the skills program *changes* the level of productivity. The null hypothesis is that the program does not change productivity one way or the other.

When a research hypothesis predicts an effect but does not predict a particular direction for the effect, it is called a **nondirectional hypothesis.** To test the significance of a nondirectional hypothesis, you have to take into account the possibility that the sample could be extreme at either tail of the comparison distribution. Thus, this is called a **two-tailed test.**

nondirectional hypothesis

two-tailed test

DETERMINING CUTOFF POINTS WITH TWO-TAILED TESTS

There is a special complication in a two-tailed test. You have to divide up the significance percentage between the two tails. For example, with a 5% significance level, you would reject a null hypothesis only if the sample was so extreme that it was in either the top 2.5% or the bottom 2.5%. In this way, the overall level of significance is kept at a total of 5%.

Note that a two-tailed test makes the cutoff Z scores for the 5% level +1.96 and -1.96. For a one-tailed test at the 5% level, the cutoff was not so extreme—only +1.64 or -1.64, but only one side of the distribution was considered. These situations are shown in Figure 5–4a.

Using the 1% significance level, a two-tailed test (.5% at each tail) has cutoffs of +2.58 and -2.58, while a one-tailed test's cutoff is either +2.33 or -2.33. These situations are shown in Figure 5–4b.

WHEN TO USE ONE-TAILED OR TWO-TAILED TESTS

If the researcher decides in advance to use a one-tailed test, then the sample's score does not need to be so extreme to be significant as it would need with a two-tailed test. Yet there is a price: With a one-tailed test, if the result is extreme in the direction opposite to what was predicted, no matter how extreme, the result cannot be considered statistically significant.

In principle, you plan to use a one-tailed test when you have a clearly directional hypothesis and a two-tailed test when you have a clearly nondirectional hypothesis. In practice, it is not so simple. Even when a theory clearly predicts a particular result, the actual result may come out opposite to what you expected. Sometimes, this opposite result may be even more interesting than what you had predicted. By using one-tailed tests, we risk having to ignore possibly important results.

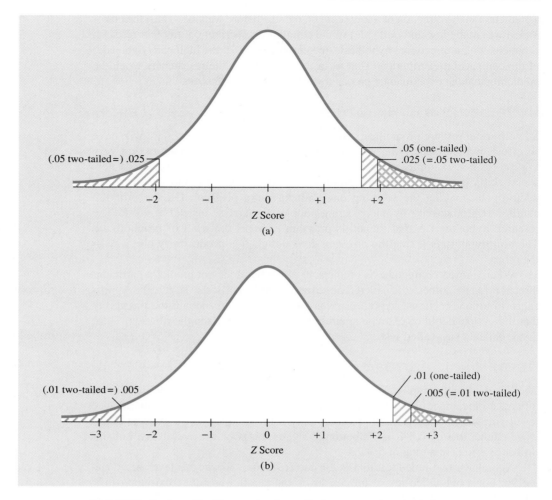

FIGURE 5-4   *Significance level cutoffs for one- and two-tailed tests: (a) .05 signifi-*
cance level; (b) .01 significance level. (The one-tailed tests in these examples assume the pre-
diction was for a high score. You could instead have a one-tailed test where the prediction is
for the lower, left tail.)

For these reasons, researchers disagree about whether one-tailed tests should
be used, even when there is a clearly directional hypothesis. To be safe, many researchers use two-tailed tests for both nondirectional and directional hypotheses. If
the two-tailed test is significant, then the researcher looks at the result to see the direction and considers the study significant in that direction. In practice, this is a
conservative procedure, because the cutoff scores are more extreme for a two-
tailed test, so it is less likely a two-tailed test will give a significant result. Thus, if
you do get a significant result with a two-tailed test, you are more confident about
the conclusion. In fact, in most social and behavioral sciences research articles, unless the researcher specifically states that a one-tailed test was used, it is assumed
that it was a two-tailed test.

In practice, however, it is our experience that most research results are either
so extreme that they will be significant whether you use a one-tailed or two-tailed

test or so far from extreme that they would not be significant no matter what you use. But what happens when a result is less certain? The researcher's decision about one-tailed or two-tailed tests now can make a big difference. In this situation the researcher tries to use the method that will give the most accurate and noncontroversial conclusion. The idea is to let nature—and not a researcher's decisions—determine the conclusion as much as possible. Furthermore, whenever a result is less than completely clear one way or the other, most researchers will not be comfortable drawing strong conclusions until more research is done.

BOX 5-1   To Be or Not to Be—But Can Not Being Be? The Problem of Whether and When to Accept the Null Hypothesis

The null hypothesis states that there is no difference between populations represented by different groups or experimental conditions. As we have seen, the usual rule in statistics is that a study cannot find the null hypothesis to be true. A study can only tell you that you cannot reject the null hypothesis. That is, a study that fails to reject the null hypothesis is simply uninformative. Such studies tend not to be published, obviously. However, much work could be avoided if people knew what interventions, measures, or experiments had not worked. Indeed, Greenwald (1975) reports that sometimes ideas have been assumed too long to be true just because a few studies found results supporting them, while many more, unreported, had not.

Frick (1995), has pointed out yet another serious problem with being rigidly uninterested in the null hypothesis: Sometimes it may be true that one thing has no effect on another. This does not mean that there would be a zero relationship of no correlation or no difference at all—a result that is almost impossible in many situations. It would only mean that the effect was so small that it probably represented no real, or at least no important, relationship or difference.

The problem is knowing when to conclude that the null hypothesis (or something close to it) might be true. Frick (1995) gives three criteria. First, the null hypothesis should seem possible. Second, the results in the study should be consistent with the null hypoth-

esis and not easily interpreted any other way. Third, and most important, the researcher has to have made a strong effort to find the effect that he or she wants to conclude is not there. Among other things, this means studying a large sample and having very thorough and sensitive measurement. If the study is an experiment, the experimenter should have tried to produce the difference by using a strong manipulation and rigorous conditions of testing.

Frick (1995) points out that all of this leaves a subjective element to the acceptance of the null hypothesis. Who decides when a researcher's effort was strong enough? Subjective judgments are a part of science, like it or not. For example, reviewers of articles submitted for publication in the top scientific journals have to decide if a topic is important enough to compete for limited space in those journals. Furthermore, the null hypothesis is being accepted all the time anyway. (For example, many social and behavioral scientists accept the null hypothesis about the effect of extrasensory perception.) It is better to discuss our basis for accepting the null hypothesis than just to accept it.

What are we to make of all this? It is clear that just failing to reject the null hypothesis is not the same as supporting it. Indeed, equating these is a serious mistake. But Frick (1995) reminds us that there are situations in which the evidence ought to convince us that something like the null hypothesis is likely to be the case.

AN EXAMPLE OF HYPOTHESIS TESTING WITH A TWO-TAILED TEST

Here is another fictional example, this time using a two-tailed test. A researcher is interested in the effect of going through a natural disaster on the attitude of police chiefs about the goodness of the people in their city. The researcher believes that after a disaster, the police chief is likely to have a more positive attitude about the people of the city (because the chief will have seen many acts of heroism and helping of neighbors after the event). However, it is also possible that a disaster will lead to police chiefs having more negative attitudes, because there may be cases of looting and other dishonest behavior after the disaster. Thus, the researcher will make a nondirectional hypothesis.

Let us assume that there is considerable previous research on the attitudes of police chiefs about the goodness of the people in their cities and that on a standard questionnaire, the mean attitude rating is 69.5 with a standard deviation of 14.1, and the attitude scores follow a normal curve. Let us also assume that a major earthquake has just occurred in an isolated city and shortly afterward the researcher is able to give the standard questionnaire to the police chief of that city. The researchers then carry out the hypothesis-testing procedure:

❶ **Restate the question as a research hypothesis and a null hypothesis about the populations.** There are two populations of interest:

Population 1: Police chiefs whose city has just been through a disaster.
Population 2: Police chiefs in general.

The research hypothesis is that when measured on their attitude toward the goodness of the people of their city, police chiefs whose city has just been through a disaster (Population 1) score differently from police chiefs in general (Population 2). The opposite of the research hypothesis, the null hypothesis, is that police chiefs whose city has just been through a disaster have the same attitude as police chiefs in general. (That is, the null hypothesis is that the attitudes of Populations 1 and 2 are the same.)

❷ **Determine the characteristics of the comparison distribution.** If the null hypothesis is true, the distributions of Populations 1 and 2 are the same. We know the distribution of Population 2, so we can use it as our comparison distribution. As noted, it follows a normal curve, with Population $M = 69.5$ and Population $SD = 14.1$.

❸ **Determine the cutoff sample score on the comparison distribution at which the null hypothesis should be rejected.** The researcher selects the 5% significance level. The researcher has made a nondirectional hypothesis and will therefore use a two-tailed test. Thus, the researcher will reject the null hypothesis only if the police chief's attitude score is in either the top or bottom 2.5% of the comparison distribution. In terms of Z scores, these cutoffs are $+1.96$ and -1.96 (see Figure 5–5).

❹ **Determine your sample's score on the comparison distribution.** The police chief who went through the earthquake took the standard attitude questionnaire and had a score of 41. This corresponds to a Z score on the comparison distribution of -2.02. That is, $Z = (41 - 69.5)/14.1 = -2.02$.

❺ **Decide whether to reject the null hypothesis.** A Z score of -2.02 is slightly more extreme than the Z score of -1.96, which is where the lower 2.5% of the comparison distribution begins. Notice in Figure 5–5 that the Z score of -2.02 falls within the shaded area in the left tail of the comparison distribution.

This is a result so extreme that it is unlikely to have occurred if this police chief were from a population no different than Population 2. Therefore, the researcher rejects the null hypothesis. This result supports the research hypothesis that going

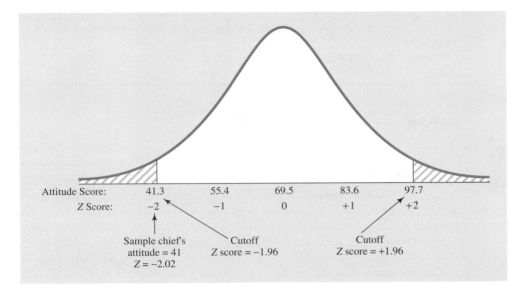

FIGURE 5–5 *Distribution of attitudes of police chiefs toward goodness of people in their cities with upper and lower 2.5% shaded and showing the sample police chief whose city has just been through a disaster (fictional data).*

Tip for Success

When carrying out the five steps of hypothesis testing, always draw a figure like Figure 5–5. Be sure to include the cutoff score(s) and shade the appropriate tail(s). If the sample score falls within a shaded tail region, the null hypothesis can be rejected and the result is statistically significant. If the sample score does not fall within a shaded tail region, the null hypothesis cannot be rejected.

through a disaster does indeed change police chiefs' attitudes toward their city. In this case, the results would mean that the effect is one of making the chief less positive about the city's people. (Remember, however, that this is a fictional study.)

HOW ARE YOU DOING?

1. What is a nondirectional hypothesis test?
2. What is a two-tailed test?
3. Why do you use a two-tailed test when testing a nondirectional hypothesis?
4. What is the advantage of using a one-tailed test when your theory predicts a particular direction of result?
5. Why might you use a two-tailed test even when your theory predicts a particular direction of result?
6. A researcher predicts that making a person hungry will affect how he or she does on a coordination test. A randomly selected person agrees not to eat for 24 hours before taking a standard coordination test and gets a score of 400. For people in general of this age group and gender tested under normal conditions, coordination scores are normally distributed with a mean of 500 and a standard deviation of 40. Using the .01 significance level, what should the researchers conclude?

ANSWERS:

1. A nondirectional hypothesis test is a hypothesis test in which you do not predict a particular direction of difference.
2. A two-tailed test is one in which the overall percentage for the cutoff is evenly divided between the two tails of the comparison distribution. A two-tailed test is used to test the significance of a nondirectional hypothesis.
3. You use a two-tailed test when testing a nondirectional hypothesis because an extreme result in either direction would support the research hypothesis.
4. The cutoff for a one-tailed test is not so extreme; thus, if your result comes out in the predicted direction, it is more likely to be significant. The cutoff is not so extreme because the entire percentage (say 5%) is put in one tail instead of being divided between two.

5. It lets you count as significant an extreme result in either direction; if you used a one-tailed test and the result came out opposite to your prediction, it could not be called statistically significant.

6. The cutoffs are +2.58 and −2.58. The sample person's Z score is $(400 − 500)/40 = −2.5$. The result is not significant; the study is inconclusive.

HYPOTHESIS TESTS AS REPORTED IN RESEARCH ARTICLES

In general, hypothesis testing is reported in research articles as part of one of the specific methods you learn in later chapters. For each result of interest, the researcher usually first says whether the result was statistically significant. Next, the researcher usually gives the symbol associated with the specific method used in figuring the probabilities, such as t, F, or χ^2 (these procedures are covered in Chapters 8–12). Finally, there will be an indication of the significance level, such as $p < .05$ or $p < .01$. (The researcher will usually also provide much other information, such as sample scores and relevant means and standard deviations.) For example, Schimel, Greenberg, and Martens (2003) conducted two experiments to test the hypothesis that projecting one's own negative personal traits (such as dishonesty or anger) on other people reduces one's concerns about having those traits. (The results of the experiments supported this hypothesis.) As part of one experiment, Schimel et al. tested whether the research participants found it more threatening to get feedback that they had a high level of anger (which the researchers called the "high-anger form") compared to a low level of anger ("low-anger form"). The results supported this hypothesis and the researchers reported that "A t test performed on the threat measure for high- versus low-anger forms . . . revealed a significant effect, $t(21) = 3.75$, $p < .001$, indicating that participants thought the high-anger feedback was more threatening than the low-anger feedback (Ms = 12.8 and 7.27, SD = 3.29 and 4.51, respectively)" (p. 975). There is a lot here that you will learn about in later chapters, but the key thing to understand now about this result is the "$p < .001$." This means that the probability of their results if the null hypothesis (of no difference between the populations their groups represent) were true is less than .001 (.1%).

When a result is close, but does not reach the significance level chosen, it may be reported as a "near significant trend" or as having "approached significance," with $p < .10$, for example. When a result is not even close to being extreme enough to reject the null hypothesis, it may be reported as "not significant" or the abbreviation ns will be used. Whether or not a result is significant, it is increasingly common for researchers to report the exact p level—such as $p = .03$ or $p = .27$. In addition, if a one-tailed test were used, that usually will be noted. Again, when reading research articles, assume a two-tailed test if nothing is said otherwise. Even though a researcher has chosen a significance level in advance, such as .05, results that meet more rigorous standards may be noted as such. Thus, in the same article you may see results in which some are noted as "$p < .05$," others as "$p < .01$," and still others as "$p < .001$," for example.

Finally, in many cases the results of hypothesis testing are shown simply as asterisks in a table of results. In such tables, a result with an asterisk is significant, while a result without one is not.

In reporting results of significance testing, researchers rarely make explicit the research hypothesis or the null hypothesis, or describe any of the other steps of the process in any detail. It is assumed that the reader understands all of this very well.

SUMMARY

1. Hypothesis testing considers the probability that the result of a study could have come about even if the experimental procedure had no effect. If this probability is low, the scenario of no effect is rejected and the theory behind the experimental procedure is supported.

2. The expectation of an effect is the research hypothesis, and the hypothetical situation of no effect is the null hypothesis.

3. When a result (that is, a sample score) is so extreme that the result would be very unlikely if the null hypothesis were true, the null hypothesis is rejected and the research hypothesis supported. If the result is not that extreme, the study is inconclusive.

4. Social and behavioral scientists usually consider a result too extreme if it is less likely than 5% (that is, a significance level of .05) to have come about, if the null hypothesis were true. Sometimes a more stringent 1% (.01 significance level), or even .1% (.001 significance level), cutoff is used.

5. The cutoff percentages are the probability of the result being extreme in a predicted direction in a directional or one-tailed test. The cutoff percentages are the probability of the result being extreme in either direction in a nondirectional or two-tailed test.

6. The five steps of hypothesis testing are:
   ❶ **Restate the question as a research hypothesis and a null hypothesis about the populations.**
   ❷ **Determine the characteristics of the comparison distribution.**
   ❸ **Determine the cutoff sample score on the comparison distribution at which the null hypothesis should be rejected.**
   ❹ **Determine your sample's score on the comparison distribution.**
   ❺ **Decide whether to reject the null hypothesis.**

7. Research articles typically report the results of hypothesis testing by saying a result was or was not significant and giving the probability level cutoff (usually 5% or 1%) the decision was based on.

KEY TERMS

hypothesis testing (p. 132)
research hypothesis
   (p. 135)
null hypothesis (p. 135)
comparison distribution
   (p. 136)
cutoff sample score
   (p. 136)

conventional levels of
   significance ($p < .05$,
   $p < .01$) (p. 137)
statistically significant
   (p. 137)
directional hypothesis
   (p. 140)
one-tailed test (p. 140)

nondirectional hypothesis
   (p. 141)
two-tailed test (p. 141)

EXAMPLE WORKED-OUT PROBLEM

A randomly selected individual, after going through an experimental treatment, has a score of 27 on a particular measure. The scores of people in general on this measure are normally distributed with a mean of 19 and a standard deviation of 4. The researcher predicts an effect, but does not predict a particular direction of effect. Using the 5% significance level, what should you conclude? Solve this problem explicitly using all five steps of hypothesis testing and illustrate your answer with a sketch showing the comparison distribution, the cutoff (or cutoffs), and the score of the sample on this distribution.

ANSWER

❶ **Restate the question as a research hypothesis and a null hypothesis about the populations.** There are two populations of interest:

> **Population 1:** People who go through the experimental procedure.
> **Population 2:** People in general (that is, people who do not go through the experimental procedure).

The research hypothesis is that Population 1 will score differently than Population 2 on the particular measure. The null hypothesis is that the two populations are not different on the measure.

❷ **Determine the characteristics of the comparison distribution:** Population $M = 19$, Population $SD = 4$, normally distributed.

❸ **Determine the cutoff sample score on the comparison distribution at which the null hypothesis should be rejected.** For a two-tailed test at the 5% level (2.5% at each tail), the cutoff sample scores are $+1.96$ and -1.96.

❹ **Determine your sample's score on the comparison distribution.** $Z = (27 - 19)/4 = 2$.

❺ **Decide whether to reject the null hypothesis.** A Z score of 2 is more extreme than the cutoff Z of $+1.96$. Reject the null hypothesis; the result is significant. The experimental procedure affects scores on this measure. The diagram is shown in Figure 5–6.

| Raw Score | 11 | 15 | 19 | 23 | 27 |
| Z Score | −2 | −1 | 0 | +1 | +2 |

Sample Individual
Raw Score = 27
Z Score = 2

FIGURE 5–6 *Diagram for Example Worked-Out Problem showing comparison distribution, cutoffs (2.5% shaded area on each tail), and sample score.*

PRACTICE PROBLEMS

These problems involve figuring. Most real-life statistics problems are done on a computer with special statistical software. Even if you have such software, do these problems by hand (with the help of a calculator) to ingrain the method in your mind. Also, in all problems involving figuring, be sure to show your work.

For practice in using a computer to solve statistics problems, refer to the computer section of each chapter of the *Student's Study Guide and Computer Workbook* that accompanies this text.

All data are fictional unless an actual citation is given.

For answers to Set I problems, see pp. 427–28.

SET I

1. Define the following terms in your own words: (a) hypothesis testing procedure, (b) .05 significance level, and (c) two-tailed test.
2. When a result is not extreme enough to reject the null hypothesis, explain why it is wrong to conclude that your result supports the null hypothesis.
3. For each of the following, (a) say what two populations are being compared, (b) state the research hypothesis, (c) state the null hypothesis, and (d) say whether you should use a one-tailed or two-tailed test and why.

    i. Do Canadian children whose parents are librarians score higher than Canadian children in general on reading ability?
    ii. Is the level of income for residents of a particular city different from the level of income for people in the region?
    iii. Do people who have experienced an earthquake have more or less self-confidence than the general population?

4. Based on the information given for each of the following studies, decide whether to reject the null hypothesis. For each, give the Z-score cutoff (or cutoffs) on the comparison distribution at which the null hypothesis should be rejected, the Z score on the comparison distribution for the sample score, and conclusion. Assume that all populations are normally distributed.

Study	Population M	SD	Sample Score	p	Tails of Test
A	10	2	14	.05	1 (high predicted)
B	10	2	14	.05	2
C	10	2	14	.01	1 (high predicted)
D	10	2	14	.01	2
E	10	4	14	.05	1 (high predicted)

5. Based on the information given for each of the following studies, decide whether to reject the null hypothesis. For each, give the Z-score cutoff (or cutoffs) on the comparison distribution at which the null hypothesis should be rejected, the Z score on the comparison distribution for the sample score, and conclusion. Assume that all populations are normally distributed.

Study	Population M	SD	Sample Score	p	Tails of Test
A	70	4	74	.05	1 (high predicted)
B	70	1	74	.01	2
C	70	2	76	.01	2
D	70	2	77	.01	2
E	70	2	68	.05	1 (high predicted)

6. A researcher studying the senses of taste and smell has carried out many studies in which students are given each of 20 different foods (apricot, chocolate, cherry, coffee, garlic, and so on). She administers each food by dropping a liquid on the tongue. Based on her past research, she knows that for students overall at the university, the mean number of these 20 foods that students can identify correctly is 14, with a standard deviation of 4, and the distribution of scores follows a normal curve. The researcher wants to know whether people's accuracy on this task has more to do with smell than with taste. In other words, she wants to test whether people do *worse* on the task when they are only able to taste the liquid compared to when they can both taste and smell the liquid (note that this is a directional hypothesis). Thus, she sets up special procedures that keep a person from being able to use the sense of smell during the task. The researcher then tries the procedure on one randomly selected student. This student is able to identify only five correctly. Using the .05 significance level, what should the researcher conclude? Solve this problem explicitly using all five steps of hypothesis testing and illustrate your answer with a sketch showing the comparison distribution, the cutoff (or cutoffs), and the score of the sample on this distribution. Then explain your answer to someone who has never had a course in statistics (but who is familiar with mean, standard deviation, and Z scores).

7. A nursing researcher is working with people who have had a particular type of major surgery. This researcher proposes that people will recover from the operation more quickly if friends and family are in the room with them for the first 48 hours after the operation. It is known that time to recover from this kind of surgery is normally distributed with a mean of 12 days and a standard deviation of 5 days. The procedure of having friends and family in the room for the period after the surgery is tried with a randomly selected patient. This patient recovers in 18 days. Using the .01 significance level, what should the researcher conclude? Solve this problem explicitly using all five steps of hypothesis testing and illustrate your answer with a sketch showing the comparison distribution, the cutoff (or cutoffs), and the score of the sample on this distribution. Then explain your answer to someone who has never had a course in statistics (but who is familiar with mean, standard deviation, and Z scores).

8. Robins and John (1997) carried out a study on narcissism (self-love), comparing people who scored high versus low on a narcissism questionnaire. (An example item was "If I ruled the world it would be a better place.") They also had other questionnaires, including one that had an item about how many times the participant looked in the mirror on a typical day. In their results section, the researchers noted ". . . as predicted, high-narcissism individuals reported looking at themselves in the mirror more frequently than did low narcissism individuals ($Ms = 5.7$ vs. 4.8), . . . $p < .05$" (p. 39). Explain this result to a person who has never had a course in statistics. (Focus on the meaning of this result in terms of the general logic of hypothesis testing and statistical significance.)

9. Reber and Kotovsky (1997), in a study of problem solving, described one of their results comparing a specific group of participants within their overall control condition as follows: "This group took an average of 179 moves to solve the puzzle, whereas the rest of the control participants took an average of 74 moves, $t(19) = 3.31, p < .01$" (p. 183). Explain this result to a person who has never had a course in statistics. (Focus on the meaning of this result in terms of the general logic of hypothesis testing and statistical significance.)

SET II

10. List the five steps of hypothesis testing and explain the procedure and logic of each.
11. When a result is significant, explain why is it wrong to say the result "proves" the research hypothesis?
12. For each of the following, (a) say what two populations are being compared, (b) state the research hypothesis, (c) state the null hypothesis, and (d) say whether you should use a one-tailed or two-tailed test and why.

    i. In an experiment, people are told to solve a problem by focusing on the details. Is the speed of solving the problem different for people who get such instructions compared to people who are given no special instructions?

    ii. Based on anthropological reports in which the status of women is scored on a 10-point scale, the mean and standard deviation across many cultures are known. A new culture is found in which there is an unusual family arrangement. The status of women is also rated in this culture. Do cultures with the unusual family arrangement provide higher status to women than cultures in general?

    iii. Do people who live in big cities develop more stress-related conditions than people in general?

13. Based on the information given for each of the following studies, decide whether to reject the null hypothesis. For each, give the Z-score cutoff (or cutoffs) on the comparison distribution at which the null hypothesis should be rejected, the Z score on the comparison distribution for the sample score, and conclusion. Assume that all populations are normally distributed.

| | Population | | Sample | | Tails |
Study	M	SD	Score	p	of Test
A	5	1	7	.05	1 (high predicted)
B	5	1	7	.05	2
C	5	1	7	.01	1 (high predicted)
D	5	1	7	.01	2

14. Based on the information given for each of the following studies, decide whether to reject the null hypothesis. For each, give the Z-score cutoff (or cutoffs) on the comparison distribution at which the null hypothesis should be rejected, the Z score on the comparison distribution for the sample score, and conclusion. Assume that all populations are normally distributed.

Study	Population M	SD	Sample Score	p	Tails of Test
A	100.0	10.0	80	.05	1 (low predicted)
B	100.0	20.0	80	.01	2
C	74.3	11.8	80	.01	2
D	16.9	1.2	80	.05	1 (low predicted)
E	88.1	12.7	80	.05	2

15. A researcher wants to test whether certain sounds will make rats do worse on learning tasks. It is known that an ordinary rat can learn to run a particular maze correctly in 18 trials, with a standard deviation of 6. (The number of trials to learn this maze is normally distributed.) The researcher now tries an ordinary rat on the maze, but with the sound. The rat takes 38 trials to learn the maze. Using the .05 level, what should the researcher conclude? Solve this problem explicitly using all five steps of hypothesis testing and illustrate your answer with a sketch showing the comparison distribution, the cutoff (or cutoffs), and the score of the sample on this distribution. Then explain your answer to someone who has never had a course in statistics (but who is familiar with mean, standard deviation, and Z scores).

16. A researcher developed an elaborate training program to reduce the stress of childless men who marry women with adolescent children. It is known from previous research that such men, 1 month after moving in with their new wife and her children, have a stress level of 85 with a standard deviation of 15, and the stress levels are normally distributed. The training program is tried on one man randomly selected from all those in a particular city who during the preceding month have married a woman with an adolescent child. After the training program, this man's stress level is 60. Using the .05 level, what should the researcher conclude? Solve this problem explicitly using all five steps of hypothesis testing and illustrate your answer with a sketch showing the comparison distribution, the cutoff (or cutoffs), and the score of the sample on this distribution. Then explain your answer to someone who has never had a course in statistics (but who is familiar with mean, standard deviation, and Z scores).

17. A researcher predicts that listening to music while solving math problems will make a particular brain area more active. To test this, a research participant has her brain scanned while listening to music and solving math problems, and the brain area of interest has a percent signal change of 5.8. From many previous studies with this same math-problems procedure (but not listening to music), it is known that the signal change in this brain area is normally distributed with a mean of 3.5 and a standard deviation of 1.0. Using the .01 level, what should the researcher conclude? Solve this problem explicitly using all five steps of hypothesis testing and illustrate your answer with a sketch showing the comparison distribution, the cutoff (or cutoffs), and the score of the sample on this distribution. Then explain your answer to someone who has never had a course in statistics (but who is familiar with mean, standard deviation, and Z scores).

18. Pecukonis (1990), as part of a larger study, measured ego development (a measure of overall maturity) and ability to empathize with others among a group of

TABLE 5–1 Selected Indicators of Change in Tobacco Use, ETS Exposure, and Public Attitudes toward Tobacco Control Policies—Massachusetts, 1993–1995

	1993	1995
Adult Smoking Behavior		
Percentage smoking >25 cigarettes daily	24	10*
Percentage smoking <15 cigarettes daily	31	49*
Percentage smoking within 30 minutes of waking	54	41
Environmental Tobacco Smoke Exposure		
Percentage of workers reporting a smoke free worksite	53	65*
Mean hours of ETS exposure at work during prior week	4.2	2.3*
Percentage of homes in which smoking is banned	41	51*
Attitudes Toward Tobacco Control Policies		
Percentage supporting further increase in tax on tobacco with funds earmarked for tobacco control	78	81
Percentage believing ETS is harmful	90	84
Percentage supporting ban on vending machines	54	64*
Percentage supporting ban on support of sports and cultural events by tobacco companies	59	53*

*$p < .05$

Source: Siegel, M., & Biener, L. (1997). Evaluating the impact of statewide anti-tobacco campaigns: The Massachusetts and California tobacco control programs. *Journal of Social Issues, 53,* 147–168. Reprinted by permission of Blackwell Publishers Journals.

24 aggressive adolescent girls in a residential treatment center. The girls were divided into high and low ego development groups, and the empathy ("cognitive empathy") scores of these two groups were compared. In his results section, Pecukonis reported, "The average score on cognitive empathy for subjects scoring high on ego development was 22.1 as compared with 16.3 for low scorers, . . . $p < .005$" (p. 68). Explain this result to a person who has never had a course in statistics. (Focus on the meaning of this result in terms of the general logic of hypothesis testing and statistical significance.)

19. In an article about anti-tobacco campaigns, Siegel and Biener (1997) discuss the results of a survey of tobacco usage and attitudes conducted in Massachusetts in 1993 and 1995; Table 5–1 shows the results of this survey. Focusing on just the first line (the percentage smoking >25 cigarettes daily), explain what this result means to a person who has never had a course in statistics. (Focus on the meaning of this result in terms of the general logic of hypothesis testing and statistical significance.)

C H A P T E R

Hypothesis Tests
with Means of Samples

Tip for Success

It is important that you understand Chapter 5 quite solidly before going on to this chapter.

In Chapter 5, we introduced the basic logic of hypothesis testing. The studies we used as examples had a sample of a single individual. As we noted, however, in actual practice, social and behavioral science research almost always involves samples of many individuals. In this chapter, we build on what you have learned so far and consider hypothesis testing involving a sample of more than one individual. Mainly, this requires examining in some detail a new kind of distribution, called a distribution of means.

THE DISTRIBUTION OF MEANS

Hypothesis testing in the usual research situation, where you are studying a sample of many individuals, is exactly the same as you learned in Chapter 5—with an important exception. When you have more than one person in your sample, there is a special problem with Step 2, determining the characteristics of the comparison distribution. In each of our examples so far, the comparison distribution has been a distribution of *individual scores* (such as the population of ages when individual babies start walking). The distribution of individual scores has been the appropriate comparison distribution, because we have used examples with a sample of *one individual*. So, there has been consistency between the type of sample score we have been dealing with (a score from *one individual*) and the comparison distribution (a distribution of *individual scores*).

Now, consider the situation when you have a sample of, say, 50 individuals. You now have a *group of 50 scores*. As you will recall from Chapter 2, the mean is a very useful representative value of a group of scores. Thus, the score you care about when there is more than one individual in your sample is the *mean of the group of scores*. In this example, you would focus on the mean of the 50 individuals. If you were to compare the mean of this sample of 50 individuals to a distribution of a population of individual scores, this would be a mismatch—like comparing apples to oranges. Instead, when you are interested in the mean of a sample of 50 scores, you need a comparison distribution that is a distribution of means of samples of 50 scores. We call such a comparison distribution a **distribution of means.** So, the scores in a distribution of means are means, not scores of individuals.

distribution of means

A distribution of means is a distribution of the means of each of a very large number of samples of the same size, with each sample randomly taken from the same population of individuals. (Statisticians also call this distribution of means a *sampling distribution of the mean*. In this book, however, we use the term *distribution of means* to make it clear that we are talking about populations of *means*, not samples or some kind of distribution of samples.)

The distribution of means is the proper comparison distribution when there is more than one person in a sample. Thus, in most research situations, determining the characteristics of a distribution of means is necessary for Step 2 of the hypothesis-testing procedure (determining the characteristics of the comparison distribution).

BUILDING A DISTRIBUTION OF MEANS

To help you understand the idea of a distribution of means, we consider how you could build up such a distribution from an ordinary population distribution of individuals. Suppose our population of individuals was the grade levels of the 90,000 elementary and junior high school children in a particular region. Suppose further (to keep the example simple) that there are exactly 10,000 children at each grade level, from first through ninth grade. This population distribution would be rectangular, with a mean of 5, a variance of 6.67, and a standard deviation of 2.58 (see Figure 6–1).

Next, suppose that you wrote each child's grade level on a table tennis ball and put all 90,000 balls into a giant tub. The tub would have 10,000 balls with a 1 on them, 10,000 with a 2 on them, and so forth. Stir up the balls in the tub, and then take two of them out. You have taken a random sample of two balls. Suppose one ball has a 2 on it and the other has a 9 on it. The mean grade level of this sample of two children's grade levels is 5.5, the average of 2 and 9. Now you put the balls back, mix up all the balls, and select two balls again. Maybe this time you get two 4s, making the mean of your second sample 4. Then you try again; this time you get a 2 and a 7, making your mean 4.5. So far you have three means: 5.5, 4, and 4.5.

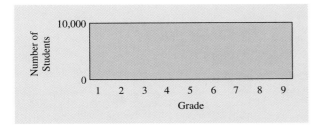

FIGURE 6–1   *Distribution of grade levels among 90,000 school children (fictional data).*

These three numbers (each a mean of a sample of grade levels of two school-children) can be thought of as a small distribution in its own right. The mean of this little distribution of three numbers is 4.67 (the sum of 5.5, 4, and 4.5 divided by 3). The variance of this distribution is .39 (the variance of 5.5, 4, and 4.5). The standard deviation is .62 (the square root of .39). A histogram of this distribution of three means is shown in Figure 6–2.

If you continued the process of selecting samples of two balls and taking the mean of the numbers on the two balls, the histogram of means would continue to grow. Figure 6–3a shows an example after 10 samples, each of two randomly drawn balls. Figure 6–3b shows the histogram of the distribution of means after 20 samples, each of two randomly drawn balls. After 100 such samples, the histogram of the distribution of the means might look like that in Figure 6–3c; after 1,000, like Figure 6–3d. (We actually made the histograms shown in Figure 6–3 using a computer to make the random selections, instead of using 90,000 table tennis balls and a giant tub.)

In practice, researchers almost never take many different samples from a population. It is quite a lot of work to come up with a single sample and study the people in that sample. Fortunately, however, you can figure out the characteristics of a distribution of means directly, using some simple rules, without taking even one sample. The only information you need is (a) the characteristics of the distribution of the population of individuals and (b) the number of scores in each sample. (Don't worry for now about how you could know the characteristics of the population of individuals.) The laborious method of building up a distribution of means in the way we have just considered and the concise method you will learn shortly give the same result. We have had you think of the process in terms of the painstaking method only because it helps you understand the idea of a distribution of means.

CHARACTERISTICS OF A DISTRIBUTION OF MEANS

Recall that Step 2 of hypothesis testing involves determining the characteristics of the comparison distribution. The three key characteristics of the comparison distribution that you need to determine are: its mean, its spread (which you can measure using the variance and standard deviation), and its shape.

Notice three things about the distribution of means we built up in our example, as shown in Figure 6–3d.

1. The mean of the distribution of means is about the same as the mean of the original population of individuals (both are 5).
2. The spread of the distribution of means is less than the spread of the distribution of the population of individuals.
3. The shape of the distribution of means is approximately normal.

The first two characteristics, regarding the mean and the spread, are true for all distributions of means. The third, regarding the shape, is true for most distributions

FIGURE 6–2 *Distribution of the means of three randomly taken samples of two schoolchildren's grade levels, each from a population of grade levels of 90,000 schoolchildren (fictional data).*

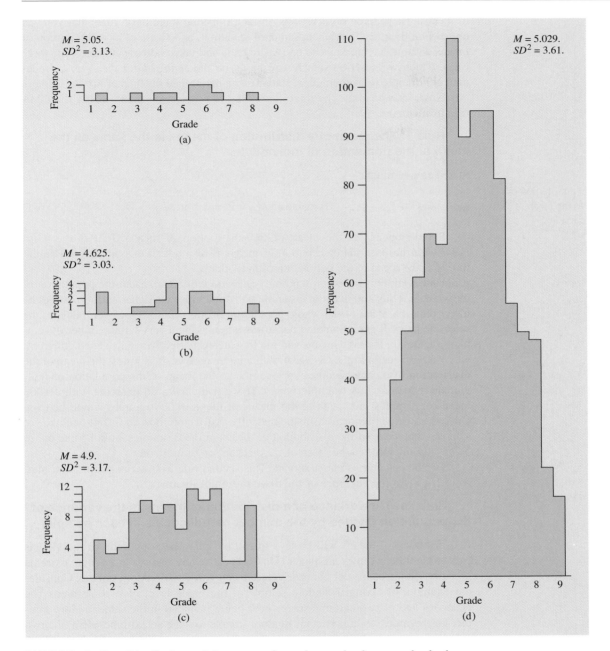

FIGURE 6–3 *Distributions of the means of samples, each of two randomly drawn balls, from a population of 90,000 balls, consisting of 10,000 with each of the numbers from 1 through 9. Numbers of sample means in each distribution shown are (a) 10 sample means, (b) 20 sample means, (c) 100 sample means, and (d) 1,000 sample means. (Actual sampling simulated by computer.)*

of means. These three observations, in fact, illustrate three basic rules that you can use to find the mean, variance, standard deviation, and shape of any distribution of means without having to write on plastic balls and take endless samples. (The three rules, which we describe shortly, are based on the *central limit theorem,* a fundamental principle in mathematical statistics we mentioned in Chapter 4.)

mean of the distribution of means

Now, let's examine the three rules. The first is for the **mean of the distribution of means.**

Rule 1: The mean of a distribution of means is the same as the mean of the population of individuals.

Stated as a formula,

> The mean of the distribution of means is equal to the mean of the population of individuals.

$$\text{Population } M_M = \text{Population } M \qquad (6\text{-}1)$$

Population M_M is the mean of the distribution of means. It uses the word *Population* because the distribution of means is also a kind of population. Population M is the mean of the population of individuals.

Each sample is based on randomly selected individuals from the population of individuals. Thus, the mean of a sample will sometimes be higher and sometimes be lower than the mean of the whole population of individuals. However, because the selection process is random and because we are taking a very large number of samples, eventually the high means and the low means perfectly balance each other out.

You can see in Figure 6–3 that with a large number of samples, the mean of the distribution of means becomes very similar to the mean of the population of individuals, which in this example was 5. If we had shown an example with 10,000 means of samples, the mean of the means of these 10,000 samples would be even closer to 5. It can be proven mathematically that if you took an infinite number of samples, the mean of the distribution of means of these samples would come out to be exactly the same as the mean of the distribution of individuals.

variance of the distribution of means

The second rule is about spread. This second rule has two parts: the first part, Rule 2A, is for the **variance of the distribution of means.**

Rule 2a: The variance of a distribution of means is the variance of the population divided by the number of individuals in each sample.

A distribution of means will be less spread out than the population of individuals from which the samples are taken. This is because any one score, even an extreme score, has some chance of being selected in any particular random sample. Consider our example of taking a random sample of the grade level of two children. The chance is less of two extreme scores both being included in the same random sample. Furthermore, for a particular random sample to have an extreme mean, the two extreme scores would both have to be extreme in the same direction (both very high or both very low). Thus, having more than a single score in each sample has a moderating effect on the mean of such samples. In any one sample, the extremes tend to be balanced out by a middle score or by an extreme in the opposite direction. This makes each sample mean tend toward the middle and away from extreme values. With fewer extreme means, there is less spread, and the variance of the means is less than the variance of the population of individuals.

Consider again our example. There were plenty of 1s and 9s in the population, making a fair amount of spread. That is, about a ninth of the time, if you were taking samples of single scores, you would get a 1, and a ninth of the time you would get a 9. If you are taking samples of two at a time, you would get a sample with a mean of 1 (that is, in which both balls were 1s) or a mean of 9 (both balls 9s) much less often. Getting two balls that average out to a middle value such as 5 is much more likely. (This is because several combinations could give this result—a 1 and a 9, a 2 and an 8, a 3 and a 7, a 4 and a 6, or two 5s.)

The more individuals in each sample, the less spread out will be the means of those samples. This is because the more scores in each sample, the rarer it will be for extremes in any particular sample not to be balanced out by middle scores or extremes in the other direction. In terms of the plastic balls in our example, we rarely got a mean of 1 when taking samples of two balls at a time. If we were taking three balls at a time, getting a sample with a mean of 1 (all three balls would have to be 1s) is even less likely. Getting middle values for the means becomes more likely.

Using samples of two balls at a time, the variance of the distribution of means came out to about 3.33. This is half of the variance of the population of individuals, which was 6.67. If we had built up a distribution of means using samples of three balls each, the variance of the distribution of means would have been 2.22. This is one third of the variance of the population of individuals. Had we randomly selected five balls for each sample, the variance of the distribution of means would have been one fifth of the variance of the population of individuals.

These examples follow a general rule—our Rule 2a for the distribution of means: the variance of a distribution of means is the variance of the distribution of the population divided by the number of individuals in each of the samples. This rule holds in all situations and can be proven mathematically.

Here is rule 2a stated as a formula:

(6-2)
$$\text{Population } SD_M^2 = \frac{\text{Population } SD^2}{N}$$

> The variance of a distribution of means is the variance of the population of individuals divided by the number of individuals in each sample.

Population SD_M^2 is the variance of the distribution of means, Population SD^2 is the variance of the population of individuals, and N is the number of individuals in each sample.

In our example, the variance of the population of individual children's grade levels was 6.67, and there were two children's grade levels in each sample. Thus,

$$\text{Population } SD_M^2 = \frac{\text{Population } SD^2}{N} = \frac{6.67}{2} = 3.34$$

To use a different example, suppose a population had a variance of 400 and you wanted to know the variance of a distribution of means of 25 individuals each:

$$\text{Population } SD_M^2 = \frac{\text{Population } SD^2}{N} = \frac{400}{25} = 16$$

The second rule also tells us about the **standard deviation of a distribution of means.**

standard deviation of a distribution of means

Rule 2b: The standard deviation of a distribution of means is the square root of the variance of the distribution of means.

Stated as a formula,

(6-3)
$$\text{Population } SD_M = \sqrt{\text{Population } SD_M^2}$$

> The standard deviation of a distribution of means is the square root of the variance of the distribution of means.

Population SD_M is the standard deviation of the distribution of means.

standard error (*SE*)

The standard deviation of the distribution of means also has a special name of its own, the the **standard error (*SE*)** (or *standard error of the mean*, abbreviated *SEM*). It has this name because it tells you how much the means of samples are typically "in error" as estimates of the mean of the population of individuals. That is, it tells you how much the particular means in the distribution of means deviate from the mean of the population. We will have more to say about this idea in the discussion of confidence intervals at the end of the chapter.

Finally, the third rule for finding the characteristics of a distribution of means focuses on its shape.

Rule 3: The shape of a distribution of means is approximately normal if either (a) each sample is of 30 or more individuals or (b) the distribution of the population of individuals is normal.

shape of the distribution of means

Whatever the shape of the distribution of the population of individuals, the distribution of means tends to be unimodal and symmetrical. In the grade-level example, the population distribution was rectangular. (It had an equal number at each grade level.) However, the **shape of the distribution of means** (Figure 6–3d) was roughly that of a bell—unimodal and symmetrical. Had we taken many more than 1,000 samples, the shape would have been even more clearly unimodal and symmetrical.

A distribution of means tends to be unimodal because of the same basic process of extremes balancing each other out that we noted in the discussion of the variance: Middle scores for means are more likely, and extreme means are less likely. A distribution of means tends to be symmetrical because lack of symmetry (skew) is caused by extremes. With fewer extremes, there is less asymmetry. In our grade-level example, the distribution of means we built up also came out so clearly symmetrical because the population distribution of individual grade levels was symmetrical. Had the population distribution of individuals been skewed to one side, the distribution of means would have still been skewed, but not as much.

The more individuals in each sample, the closer the distribution of means will be to a normal curve. In fact, with samples of 30 or more individuals, even with a non-normal population of individuals, the approximation of the distribution of means to a normal curve is very close and the percentages in the normal curve table will be extremely accurate.[1,2] Finally, whenever the population distribution of individuals is normal, the distribution of means will be normal, regardless of the number of individuals in each sample.

---

[1]We have ignored that a normal curve is a smooth theoretical distribution. However, in most real-life distributions, scores are only at specific numbers, such as a child being in a particular grade and not in a fraction of a grade. So, one difference between our example distribution of means and a normal curve is that the normal curve is smooth. However, in social and behavioral science research, even when our measurements are at specific numbers, we usually assume that the underlying thing being measured is continuous.

[2]We have already considered this principle of a distribution of means tending toward a normal curve in Chapter 4. Though we had not yet discussed the distribution of means, we still used this principle to explain why the distribution of so many things in nature follows a normal curve. In that chapter, we explained it as the various influences balancing each other out, to make an averaged influence come out with most of the scores near the center and a few at each extreme. Now we have made the same point using the terminology of a distribution of means. Think of any distribution of individual scores in nature as about a situation in which each score is actually an average of a random set of influences on that individual. Consider the distribution of weights of pebbles. Each pebble's weight is a kind of average of all the different forces that went into making the pebble have a particular weight.

SUMMARY OF RULES AND FORMULAS FOR DETERMINING THE CHARACTERISTICS OF A DISTRIBUTION OF MEANS

Rule 1: The mean of a distribution of means is the same as the mean of the distribution of the population of individuals:

$$\text{Population } M_M = \text{Population } M$$

Rule 2a: The variance of a distribution of means is the variance of the population of individuals divided by the number of individuals in each sample:

$$\text{Population } SD_M^2 = \frac{\text{Population } SD^2}{N}$$

Rule 2b: The standard deviation of a distribution of means is the square root of the variance of the distribution of means:

$$\text{Population } SD_M = \sqrt{\text{Population } SD_M^2}$$

Rule 3: The shape of a distribution of means is approximately normal if either (a) each sample is of 30 or more individuals or (b) the distribution of the population of individuals is normal.

Figure 6–4 shows these three rules graphically.

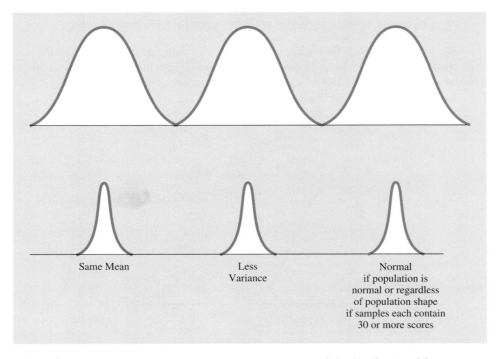

Same Mean

Less
Variance

Normal
if population is
normal or regardless
of population shape
if samples each contain
30 or more scores

FIGURE 6–4 *The distribution of means (lower curves) and the distribution of the population of individuals (upper curves).*

EXAMPLE OF DETERMINING THE CHARACTERISTICS OF A DISTRIBUTION OF MEANS

Consider the population of scores of students who have taken the Graduate Record Examinations (GREs): Suppose the distribution is approximately normal with a mean of 500 and a standard deviation of 100. What will be the characteristics of the distribution of means of samples of 50 students?

Rule 1: The mean of a distribution of means is the same as the mean of the population of individuals. The mean of the population is 500. Thus, the mean of the distribution of means will also be 500. That is, Population M_M = Population M = 500.

Rule 2a: The variance of a distribution of means is the variance of the population of individuals divided by the number of individuals in each sample.

Rule 2b: The standard deviation of a distribution of means is the square root of the variance of the distribution of means. The standard deviation of the population of individuals is 100; thus, the variance of the population of individuals is 10,000. The variance of the distribution of means is therefore 10,000 divided by 50 (the size of the sample). This comes out to 200. That is, Population SD_M^2 = Population SD^2/N = $100^2/50$ = 200. The standard deviation of the distribution of means is the square root of 200, which is 14.14. That is, Population SD_M = $\sqrt{\text{Population } SD_M^2}$ = $\sqrt{200}$ = 14.14.

Rule 3: The shape of a distribution of means is approximately normal if either (a) each sample is of 30 or more individuals or (b) the distribution of the population of individuals is normal. Our situation meets both of these conditions— the sample of 50 students is more than 30, and the population of individuals follows a normal distribution. Thus, the distribution of means will follow a normal curve. (It would have been enough even if only one of the two conditions had been met.)

REVIEW OF THE THREE KINDS OF DISTRIBUTIONS

We have considered three different kinds of distributions: (a) the distribution of a population of individuals, (b) the distribution of a particular sample of individuals taken from that population, and (c) the distribution of means. Figure 6–5 shows these three kinds of distributions graphically and Table 6–1 describes them.

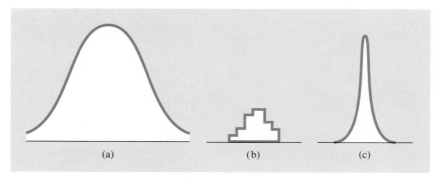

FIGURE 6–5 *Three kinds of distributions: (a) the distribution of a population of individuals, (b) the distribution of a particular sample taken from that population, and (c) the distribution of means.*

TABLE 6–1	**Comparison of Three Types of Distributions**		
	Population's Distribution	Particular Sample's Distribution	Distribution of Means
Content	Scores of all individuals in the population	Scores of the individuals in a single sample	Means of samples randomly taken from the population
Shape	Could be any shape; often normal	Could be any shape	Approximately normal if samples have ≥ 30 individuals in each or if population is normal
Mean	Population M	$M = \Sigma X / N$ figured from scores of those in the sample	Population M_M = Population M
Variance	Population SD^2	$SD^2 = \Sigma(X - M)^2 / N$	Population SD_M^2 = Population SD^2 / N
Standard Deviation	Population SD	$SD = \sqrt{SD^2}$	Population SD_M = $\sqrt{\text{Population } SD_M^2}$

Tip for Success

Be sure you fully understand the different types of distribution shown in Table 6–1 before you move on to later chapters. To check your understanding, cover up portions of the table and then try to recall the information that is covered up.

HOW ARE YOU DOING?

1. What is a distribution of means?
2. Explain how you could create a distribution of means by taking a large number of samples of four individuals each.
3. (a) Why is the mean of the distribution of means the same as the mean of the population of individuals? (b) Why is the variance of a distribution of means smaller than the variance of the distribution of the population of individuals?
4. Write the formula for the variance of the distribution of means and define each of the symbols.
5. (a) What is the standard error (*SE*)? (b) Why does it have this name?
6. A population of individuals has a normal distribution, a mean of 60, and a standard deviation of 10. What are the characteristics of a distribution of means from this population for samples of four each?

ANSWERS:

1. It is a distribution of the means of a very large number of samples of the same size randomly taken from the population of individuals.
2. Take a random sample of four from the population and figure its mean. Repeat this a very large number of times. Make a distribution of these means.
3. (a) With randomly taken samples, some will have higher means and some lower means than those of the population of individuals; these should balance out. (b) You are less likely to get a sample of several scores with an extreme mean than you are to get a single extreme score. This is because in any random sample it is highly unlikely to get several extremes in the same direction—extreme scores tend to be balanced out by middle scores or extremes in the opposite direction.
4. Population SD_M^2 = Population SD^2 / N. Population SD_M^2 is the variance of the distribution of means; Population SD^2 is the variance of the population of individuals; N is the number of individuals in your sample.
5. (a) The standard deviation of the distribution of means. (b) It tells you about how much means of samples typically (standardly) differ from the population mean, and thus the typical amount that means of samples are in error as estimates of the population mean.
6. Population M_M = Population M = 60. Population SD_M^2 = Population SD^2 / N = $10^2 / 4$ = 25. Population SD_M = 5. Shape = normal.

HYPOTHESIS TESTING WITH A DISTRIBUTION OF MEANS

Now we are ready to turn to hypothesis testing when there is more than one individual in the study's sample.

THE DISTRIBUTION OF MEANS AS THE COMPARISON DISTRIBUTION IN HYPOTHESIS TESTING

In the usual research situation in the social and behavioral sciences, a researcher studies a sample of more than one person. In this situation, the distribution of means is the comparison distribution. It is the distribution whose characteristics need to be determined in Step 2 of the hypothesis-testing process. The distribution of means is the distribution to which you compare your sample's mean to see how likely it is that you could have selected a sample with a mean that extreme if the null hypothesis were true.

FIGURING THE Z SCORE OF A SAMPLE'S MEAN ON THE DISTRIBUTION OF MEANS

There can be some confusion in figuring the location of your sample on the comparison distribution in hypothesis testing with a sample of more than one. In this situation, you are finding a Z score of your sample's mean on a distribution of means. (Before, you were finding the Z score of a single individual on a distribution of a population of single individuals.) The method of changing the sample's mean to a Z score is the same as the usual way of changing a raw score to a Z score. However, you have to be careful not to get mixed up because more than one mean is involved. It is important to remember that you are treating the sample mean like a single score. Recall that the ordinary formula (from Chapter 2) for changing a raw score to a Z score is $Z = (X - M)/SD$. In the present situation, you are actually using the following conceptually identical formula:

> The Z score for the sample's mean on the distribution of means is the sample's mean minus the mean of the distribution of means, divided by the standard deviation of the distribution of means.

$$Z = \frac{(M - \text{Population } M_M)}{\text{Population } SD_M} \qquad (6\text{-}4)$$

For example, suppose your sample's mean is 18 and the distribution of means has a mean of 10 and a standard deviation of 4. The Z score of this sample mean is +2. Using the formula,

$$Z = \frac{(M - \text{Population } M_M)}{\text{Population } SD_M} = \frac{(18 - 10)}{4} = \frac{8}{4} = 2$$

This is shown in Figure 6–6.

EXAMPLE

Suppose a team of educational researchers is interested in the effects of instructions on timed school achievement tests. These educational researchers have a theory that predicts that people will do better on a test if they are told to answer each question with the first response that comes to mind. To test this theory, the researchers give a standard school achievement test to 64 randomly selected fifth-grade schoolchildren. They give the test in the usual way, except that they add to the instructions a statement that children are to answer each question with the first response that comes to mind.

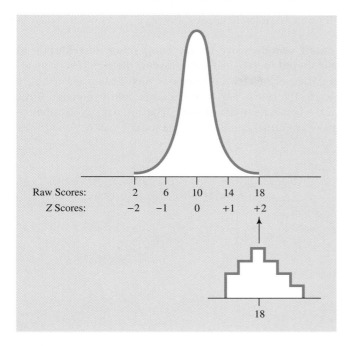

Raw Scores: 2   6   10   14   18
Z Scores: −2   −1   0   +1   +2

FIGURE 6–6   *Z score for the mean of a particular sample on the distribution of means.*

When given in the usual way, the test is known to have a mean of 200, a standard deviation of 48, and an approximately normal distribution. This distribution is shown in Figure 6–7a.

Now let's follow the five steps of hypothesis testing you learned in Chapter 6.

❶ **Restate the question as a research hypothesis and a null hypothesis about the populations.** The two populations are these:

> **Population 1:** Fifth graders who get the special instructions.
>
> **Population 2:** Fifth graders who do not get the special instructions.

The research hypothesis is that the population of fifth graders who takes the test with the special instructions will on the average have higher scores than the population of fifth graders who take the test in the normal way. The null hypothesis is that Population 1's scores will not on average be higher than Population 2's. Note that these are directional hypotheses. The researchers want to know if their special instructions will increase test scores; results in the opposite direction would be irrelevant.

❷ **Determine the characteristics of the comparison distribution.** The result of the study will be a mean of a sample of 64 individuals (of fifth graders in this case). Thus, the comparison distribution has to be the distribution of means of samples of 64 individuals each. This comparison distribution of means will have a mean of 200 (the same as the population mean). That is, Population $M_M = 200$. Its variance will be the population variance divided by the number of individuals in the sample. The population variance, Population SD^2, is 2,304 (the population standard deviation of 48 squared); the sample size is 64. Thus, the variance of the distribution of means, Population SD_M^2, will be 36 (that is, 2,304/64). The standard deviation of the distribution of means, Population SD_M, is 6 (the square root of 36). Finally, because there are more than 30 individuals in the sample, the shape of the distribution of means will be approximately normal. Figure 6–7b shows this distribution of means.

❸ **Determine the cutoff sample score on the comparison distribution at which the null hypothesis should be rejected.** Let's assume the researchers decide to use the standard 5% significance level. As we noted in Step 1, they are making a directional prediction. Hence, the researchers will reject the null hypothesis if the result is in the top 5% of the comparison distribution. The comparison distribution (the distribution of means) is a normal curve. Thus, the top 5% can be found from

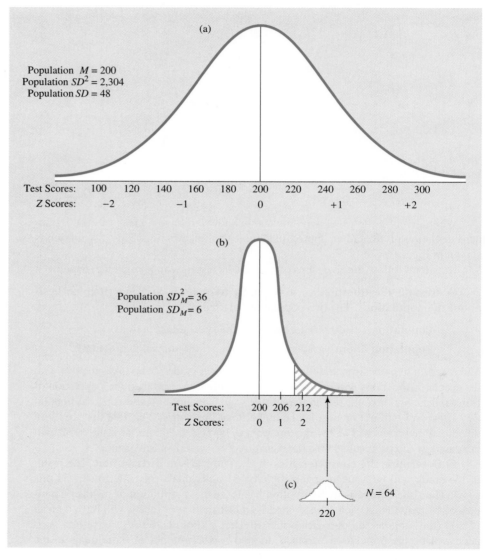

FIGURE 6–7 *For the fictional study of performance on a standard school achievement test, (a) the distribution of the population of individuals, (b) the distribution of means (the comparison distribution), and (c) the sample's distribution. The shaded area in the distribution of means is the rejection region—the area in which the null hypothesis will be rejected if the study's sample's mean turns out to be in that area.*

the normal curve table. It starts at a Z of +1.64. This top 5% is shown as the shaded area in Figure 6–7b.

❹ **Determine your sample's score on the comparison distribution.** Let's suppose the result of the (fictional) study is that the 64 fifth graders given the special instructions had a mean of 220. (This sample's distribution is shown in Figure 6–7c.) A mean of 220 is 3.33 standard deviations above the mean of the distribution of means:

$$Z = \frac{(M - \text{Population } M_M)}{\text{Population } SD_M} = \frac{(220 - 200)}{6} = \frac{20}{6} = 3.33$$

❺ **Decide whether to reject the null hypothesis.** We set the minimum Z score to reject the null hypothesis at +1.64. The Z score of the sample's mean is +3.33. Thus, the educational researchers can reject the null hypothesis and conclude that the research hypothesis is supported. To put this another way, the result is statistically significant at the $p < .05$ level. You can see this in Figure 6–7b. Note how extreme the sample's mean is on the distribution of means (the distribution that would apply if the null hypothesis were true). The final conclusion is that among fifth graders like those studied, the special instructions do improve test scores.

HOW ARE YOU DOING?

1. How is hypothesis testing with a sample of more than one person different from hypothesis testing with a sample of a single person?
2. How do you find the Z score for the sample's mean on the distribution of means?
3. A researcher predicts that showing a certain film will change people's attitudes toward alcohol. The researchers then randomly select 36 people, show them the film, and give them an attitude questionnaire. The mean score on the attitude test for these 36 people is 70. The score for people in general on this test is 75, with a standard deviation of 12. Using the five steps of hypothesis testing and the 5% significance level, does showing the film change people's attitudes toward alcohol?

ANSWERS:

1. In hypothesis testing with a sample of more than one person, the comparison distribution is a distribution of means.
2. You use the normal formula for changing a raw score to a Z score, using the mean and standard deviation of the distribution of means.
3. ❶ **Restate the question as a research hypothesis and a null hypothesis about the populations.** The two populations are these:

Population 1: People shown the film.

Population 2: People in general.

The research hypothesis is that the population shown the film have different average attitude scores than the population of people in general; the null hypothesis is that the populations have the same average attitude score.

❷ **Determine the characteristics of the comparison distribution.** Population M_M = Population M = 70. Population SD_M^2 = Population SD^2/N = $12^2/36$ = 4. Population SD_M = 2. Shape is normal.

❸ **Determine the cutoff sample score on the comparison distribution at which the null hypothesis should be rejected.** Two-tailed cutoffs, 5% significance level, are +1.96 and −1.96.

❹ **Determine your sample's score on the comparison distribution.** Z = $(70 - 75)/2 = -2.5$.

❺ Decide whether to reject the null hypothesis. The *Z* score of the sample's mean is −2.5, which is more extreme than −1.96; reject the null hypothesis. Seeing the film does change attitudes toward alcohol.

ESTIMATION AND CONFIDENCE INTERVALS

Hypothesis testing is our main focus in this book. However, there is another kind of statistical question related to the distribution of means that is also important in the social and behavioral sciences: estimating an unknown population mean based on the scores in a sample. Traditionally, this has been very important in survey research. In recent years it is also becoming important in experimental research and can even serve as an alternative approach to hypothesis testing.

ESTIMATING THE MEAN: POINT ESTIMATES

The best estimate of the population mean is the sample mean. In the study of fifth graders who were given the special instructions, the mean score for the sample of 64 fifth graders was 220. Thus, 220 is the best estimate of the mean for the unknown population of fifth graders who would ever receive the special instructions.

The mean of the sample is the best estimate, because you are more likely to get a sample mean of 220 from a population with a mean of 220 than from a population with any other mean. Consider Figure 6–8. Suppose the true distribution of means has the same mean as our sample, as would be the case in this figure if the true distribution of means was distribution c. In this situation, it is very likely that a mean

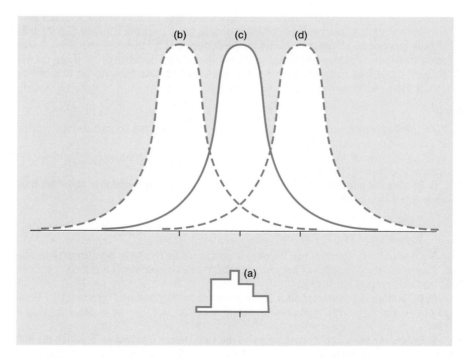

FIGURE 6–8   *A sample and three distributions of sample means. The mean of a particular sample (a) is more likely to have come from a distribution of means with the same mean (c) than from any other distribution of means (such as b and d).*

from this distribution of means would be close to our sample's mean. But suppose the true distribution of means was like distribution d. In this case, many fewer means are near to our sample's mean.

In this example, you are estimating the specific value of the population mean. When you estimate a specific value of a population parameter, it is called a **point estimate.**

point estimate

THE ACCURACY OF A POINT ESTIMATE

How accurate is this point estimate of the mean? A way to get at this question is to ask, how much do means from a distribution of means vary? One indication of such variation, we know, is the standard deviation of the distribution of means. Like any standard deviation, it tells you how much scores in the distribution typically vary. In this case, the "scores" are sample means. Because our interest is in making an estimate of the population mean, any variation is error. Thus, the amount of variation is the amount you can expect means of scores from a population like the one we studied to be in error as an estimate of the true, unknown population mean.[3] As we briefly noted earlier when introducing the standard deviation of the distribution of means, this is why it is also known as the standard error of the mean, or the standard error (*SE*) for short. The accuracy of our estimate of 220 for the mean of the population of fifth graders who get the special instructions would be the standard deviation of the distribution of means, which we figured earlier to be 6.

INTERVAL ESTIMATES

You can also estimate the *range* of possible means that are likely to include the population mean. This is called an **interval estimate.**

interval estimate

Consider our point estimate of 220 with a standard error of 6. It seems reasonable that a mean between 220 and 226 (one standard error above 220) is 34% likely. This is because the distribution of means is a normal curve, the standard error is 1 standard deviation on that curve, and 34% of a normal curve is between the mean and 1 standard deviation above the mean. From this reasoning, we could also figure that another 34% should be between 220 and 214 (1 standard error below 220). Putting this together, we have a region from 214 to 226 that we are 68% confident should include the population mean. (See Figure 6–9a.) This is an example of a **confidence interval (CI).** We would call it the "68% confidence interval." The upper and lower ends of a confidence interval are called **confidence limits.** In this example, the confidence limits for the 68% confidence interval are 214 and 226.

confidence interval (CI)

confidence limits

Normally, however, you would want to be more than 68% confident about your estimates. Thus, it is standard when figuring confidence intervals to use 95% or even 99% confidence intervals. These are figured based on the distribution of means for the area that includes the middle 95% or middle 99%. For the **95% confidence interval,** you want the area in a normal curve on each side between the mean and the Z score that includes 47.5%. The normal curve table shows this to be 1.96.

95% confidence interval

---

[3]You don't know the true distribution of means for the population your sample comes from. But in the examples we have considered in this chapter, you do know the variance and shape of the distribution of means for a similar population (Population 2). It is reasonable to assume that even if the mean is different, the variance and shape of the distribution of the population your sample comes from is the same. Thus, you can use this distribution of means to estimate the amount that a sample mean from any population with the same variance and shape is likely to vary from its population mean.

Thus, in terms of Z scores, the 95% confidence interval is from -1.96 to $+1.96$ on the distribution of means. Changing these Z scores to raw scores for the school achievement test example gives an interval of 208.24 to 231.76 (see Figure 6–9b). That is, for the lower confidence limit, $(-1.96)(6) + 220 = -11.76 + 220 = 208.24$; for the upper confidence limit, $(1.96)(6) + 220 = 11.76 + 220 = 231.76$. In sum, based on the sample of 64 fifth graders who get the special instructions, you can be 95% confident that the true population mean for such fifth graders is between 208.24 and 231.76.

99% confidence interval

For a **99% confidence interval,** you use the Z scores for the middle 99% of the normal curve (the part that includes 49.5% above and below the mean). This comes out to $+2.57$ and -2.57. Changing these Z scores to raw scores, the 99% confidence interval is from 204.58 to 235.42 (see Figure 6–9c).

Notice in Figure 6–9 that the greater the confidence, the broader the confidence interval. In our example, you could be 68% confident that the true population mean is between 214 and 226; but you could be 95% confident that it is between 208.24 and 231.76 and 99% confident it is between 204.58 and 235.42. This is a general principle. It makes sense that you need a wider range of possibility to be more sure you are right.

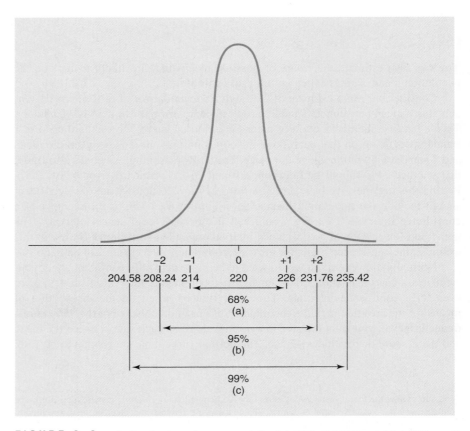

FIGURE 6–9 *A distribution of means and the (a) 68%, (b) 95%, and (c) 99% confidence intervals for fifth graders taking a test with special instructions (fictional data).*

Steps for Figuring the 95% and 99% Confidence Intervals

Here are three steps for figuring a confidence interval. These steps assume that the distribution of means is approximately a normal distribution.

❶ **Estimate the population mean and figure the standard deviation of the distribution of means.** The best estimate of the population mean is the sample mean. Next, find the variance of the distribution of means in the usual way: Population SD_M^2 = Population SD^2/N. Take the square root of the variance of the distribution of means to find the standard deviation of the distribution of means:

$$\text{Population } SD_M = \sqrt{\text{Population } SD_M^2}$$

❷ **Find the Z scores that go with the confidence limits you want.** For the 95% confidence interval, the Z scores are +1.96 and −1.96. For the 99% confidence interval, the Z scores are +2.57 and −2.57.

❸ **To find the confidence interval, change these Z scores to raw scores.** To find the lower limit, multiply −1.96 (for the 95% confidence interval) or −2.57 (for the 99% confidence interval) by the standard deviation of the distribution of means (Population SD_M) and add this to the population mean. To find the upper limit, multiply +1.96 (for the 95% confidence interval) or +2.57 (for the 99% confidence interval) by the standard deviation of the distribution of means (Population SD_M) and add this to the population mean.

Example

Let's return again to the study of 64 fifth graders who were given special instructions on a test. We figured the 99% confidence limit earlier, but now we are going to do the figuring using the three steps:

❶ **Estimate the population mean and figure the standard deviation of the distribution of means.** The best estimate of the population mean is the sample mean of 220. Population SD_M^2 = Population $SD^2/N = 48^2/64 = 36$. Thus,

$$\text{Population } SD_M = \sqrt{\text{Population } SD_M^2} = \sqrt{36} = 6.$$

❷ **Find the Z scores that go with the confidence limits you want.** For the 99% confidence interval, the Z scores are +2.57 and −2.57.

❸ **To find the confidence interval, change these Z scores to raw scores.** Lower confidence limit = $(-2.57)(6) + 220 = -15.42 + 220 = 204.58$; upper confidence limit = $(+2.57)(6) + 220 = 15.42 + 220 = 235.42$. The 99% confidence interval is from 204.58 to 235.42. Thus, based on the sample of 64 fifth graders, you can be 99% confident that an interval from 204.58 to 235.42 includes the true population mean.

Confidence Intervals and Hypothesis Testing

You can also use confidence intervals as a way to do hypothesis testing. If the confidence interval does not include the mean of the null hypothesis distribution, then the result is significant. For example, in the fifth-grader study, the 95% confidence interval for those who got the special instructions was from 208.24 to 231.76. However, the population that did not get the special instructions had a mean of 200. This population mean is outside the range of the confidence interval. Thus, if you are 95% confident that the true range is 208.24 to 231.76 and the population mean for those who didn't get the special instructions is not in this range, you are 95% confident that that population is not the same as the one your sample came from.

Another way to understand this is in terms of the idea that the confidence limits are the points at which a more extreme true population would not include your sample mean 95% of the time. The population mean for those getting the special instructions was 200. If this were the true mean also for the group that got the special instructions, 95% of the time it would not produce a sample as high as the one we got.

Most social and behavioral science research uses ordinary hypothesis testing. However, sometimes you will see the confidence-interval method used instead. And sometimes you will see both.

HOW ARE YOU DOING?

1. (a) What is the best estimate of a population mean, and (b) why?
2. (a) What number is used to indicate the accuracy of an estimate of the population mean, and (b) why?
3. What is a 95% confidence interval?
4. A researcher predicts that showing a certain film will change people's attitudes toward alcohol. The researchers then randomly select 36 people, show them the film, and give them an attitude questionnaire. The mean score on the attitude test for these 36 people is 70. The score for people in general on this test is 75, with a standard deviation of 12. (a) Find the best point estimate of the mean of people who see the film and (b) its 95% confidence interval. (c) Compare this result to the conclusion you drew when you used this example in the "how are you doing?" section for hypothesis testing with a distribution of means.

ANSWERS:

1. (a) The sample mean. (b) It is more likely to have come from a population with the same mean than from any other population.
2. (a) The standard deviation of the distribution of means. (b) The standard deviation of the distribution of means is roughly the average amount that means vary from the mean of the distribution of means.
3. The range of values that you are 95% confident includes the population mean, estimated based on the scores in a sample.
4. (a) Best estimate is the sample mean: 70.
   (b) Population SD_M^2 = Population SD^2/N = $12^2/36$ = 4. Thus, the standard deviation of the distribution of means, Population SD_M = $\sqrt{\text{Population } SD_M^2}$ = $\sqrt{4}$ = 2. Lower confidence limit = (-1.96) (2) + 70 = -3.92 + 70 = 66.08; upper confidence limit = $(+1.96)$ (2) + 70 = 3.92 + 70 = 73.92. The 95% confidence interval is 66.08 to 73.92.
   (c) The 95% confidence interval does not include the mean of the general population (which was 75). Thus, you can reject the null hypothesis that the two populations are the same. This is the same conclusion as when using this example for hypothesis testing.

HYPOTHESIS TESTS ABOUT MEANS
OF SAMPLES AND CONFIDENCE INTERVALS
IN RESEARCH ARTICLES

As we have noted several times, research in which there is a known population mean and standard deviation is rare in social and behavioral science research. We have asked you to learn about this situation mainly as a building block for understanding hypothesis testing in more common research situations. In the rare case in which research with a known population distribution is conducted, the hypothesis

---

BOX 6–1   More about Polls: Sampling Errors and Errors in Thinking about Samples

If you think back to Box 4–1 on surveys and the Gallup poll, you will recall that we left two important questions unanswered about fine print with the results of a poll, saying something like "From a telephone poll of 1,000 American adults taken on June 4 and 5. Sampling error ±3%." First, you might wonder how such small numbers like 1,000 (but rarely much less) can be used to predict the opinion of the entire U.S. population. Second, after working through the material in this chapter on the standard deviation of the distribution of means, you may wonder what a "sampling error" means when a sample is not randomly sampled but rather selected by the complicated probability method used for polls.

Regarding sample size, you know from this chapter that large sample sizes, like 1,000, greatly reduce the standard deviation of the distribution of means. That is, the curve becomes very high and narrow, gathered all around the population mean. The mean of any sample of that size is very close to being the population mean.

Still, you might persist in an intuitive feeling that the number required to represent all of the huge U.S. public might need to be larger than just 1,000. However, if you think about it, when a sample is only a small part of a very large population, the sample's absolute size is the only determiner of accuracy. This absolute size determines the impact of the random errors of measurement and selection. What remains important is reducing bias or systematic error, which can be done only by careful planning.

As for the term *sampling error,* when simple random sampling is not used, sampling error is not quite the same as the standard deviation of a distribution of means, or the confidence interval based on it, as described in this chapter. Instead, the sampling error for polls is worked out according to past experience with the sampling procedures used. It is expressed in tables for different sample sizes (usually below 1,000, because that is where error increases dramatically).

So now you understand opinion polls even better. The number of people polled is not very important (provided that it is at least 1,000 or so). What matters very much, however, is the method of sampling and estimating error, which will not be reported even in the fine print in the detail necessary to judge if the results are reliable. The reputation of the organization doing the survey is probably the best criterion. If the sampling and error-estimating approach is not revealed, be cautious. For more information about how polls are conducted, see the following website (note that sampling error is referred to as "margin of error" on the website): *http://www.gallup.com/help/FAQs /poll1.asp.* (As for the 2000 U.S. presidential election between George W. Bush and Al Gore, the TV networks claim that the organizations doing the exit polls for the media did not do a good job.)

---

test is called a **Z test** (or a *Z test for a single sample*), because it is the Z score that is   *Z test*
checked against the normal curve.

Here is an example. As part of a larger study, Wiseman (1997) gave a loneliness test to a group of college students in Israel. As a first step in examining the results, Wiseman checked that the average score on the loneliness test was not significantly different from a known population distribution based on a large U.S. study of university students that had been conducted earlier by Russell, Peplau, and Cutrona (1980). Wiseman reported:

> . . . [T]he mean loneliness scores of the current Israeli sample were similar to those of Russell et al.'s (1980) university sample for both males (Israeli: $M = 38.74$, $SD = 9.30$; Russell: $M = 37.06$, $SD = 10.91$; $z = 1.09$, NS) and females (Israeli: $M = 36.39$, $SD = 8.87$; Russell: $M = 36.06$, $SD = 10.11$; $z = .25$, NS). (p. 291)

In this example, the researcher gives the standard deviation for both the sample studied (the Israeli group) and the population (the data from Russell). However, in the steps of figuring each Z (the sample's score on the distribution of means), the researcher would have used the standard deviation only of the population. Notice also that the researcher took the nonsignificance of the difference as support for the sample means being "similar" to the population means. However, the researcher was very careful not to claim that these results showed there was no difference.

Of the topics we have covered in this chapter, the one you are most likely to see discussed in a research article is the standard deviation of the distribution of means, used to describe the amount of variation that might be expected among means of samples of a given size from this population. In this context, it is usually called the *standard error,* abbreviated *SE* (or *SEM*, for standard error of the mean). Standard errors are often shown in research articles as the lines that go above (and sometimes also below) the tops of the bars in a bar graph. For example, Perna, Antoni, Baum, Gordon, and Schneiderman (2003) tested whether a stress management intervention could reduce injury and illness among college athletes. In their study—which was published in the *Annals of Behavioral Medicine*—34 college athletes were randomly assigned to be in one of two groups: (1) a stress management intervention group: this group received a cognitive behavioral stress management (CBSM) intervention during preseason training; (2) a control group: this group did not receive the intervention. At the end of the season, for each athlete, the researchers recorded the number of health center visits (including visits to the athletic training center) and the number of days of illness or injury during the season. The results are shown in Figure 6–10, which includes error bars.

FIGURE 6–10 *Mean (+SE) number of accumulated days injured or ill and athletic training room and health center office visits for cognitive behavioral stress management (CBSM) (n = 18) and control groups (n = 16) from study entry to season's end.*
Source: Perna, F. M., Antoni, M. H., Baum, A., Gordon, P., & Schneiderman, N. (2003). Cognitive behavioral stress management effects on injury and illness among competitive athletes: A randomized clinical trial. *Annals of Behavioral Medicine, 25,* 66–73. Copyright © Lawrence Erlbaum Associates, Inc. Reprinted by permission.

Be careful to read the fine print when you see lines above the tops of bars in a bar graph. Sometimes the lines are not standard error bars, but instead represent standard deviations or confidence intervals! In Figure 6–10, the "(+SE)" in the figure caption tells you that the bars represent the standard error. In some research articles, you would only know by reading the text what the bars represent.

Confidence intervals (usually abbreviated as CI), while far from standard, are becoming increasingly common in research articles. A researcher might explain that the average number of overtime hours worked in a particular industry is 3.7 with a 95% confidence interval of 2.5 to 4.9. This would tell you that the true average number of overtime hours is probably somewhere between 2.5 and 4.9. For example, in an article published in the *Journal of the American Medical Association*, Hu, Colditz, Willett, and Manson (2003) reported that "Each 1 hour per day of brisk walking was associated with a 24% (95% CI, 19%–29%) reduction in obesity" (p. 1785). This means that we can be 95% certain that the true reduction in obesity was between 19% and 29%.

SUMMARY

1. When studying a sample of more than one individual, the comparison distribution in the hypothesis-testing process is a distribution of means. It can be thought of as what would result from (a) taking a very large number of samples, each of the same number of scores taken randomly from the population of individuals, and then (b) making a distribution of the means of these samples.

2. The distribution of means has the same mean as the population of individuals. However, it has a smaller variance because the means of samples are less likely to be extreme than individual scores. (In any one sample, extreme scores are likely to be balanced by middle scores or extremes in the other direction.) Specifically, the variance of the distribution of means is the variance of the population divided by the number of individuals in each sample. Its standard deviation is the square root of its variance. The shape of the distribution of means approximates a normal curve if either (a) the samples are each of 30 or more individuals or (b) the population of individuals follows a normal curve.

3. Hypothesis tests with a single sample of more than one individual and a known population are done in the same way as the hypothesis tests of Chapter 5 (where the studies were of a single individual compared to a population of individual scores). The main exception is that the comparison distribution in a hypothesis test with a single sample of more than one individual and a known population is a distribution of means.

4. The best point estimate for the population mean is the sample mean. Its accuracy is the standard deviation of the distribution of means (also known as the standard error, *SE*), which tells you roughly the amount means vary. You can figure an interval estimate of the population mean based on the distribution of means. If we assume the distribution of means follows a normal curve, the 95% confidence interval includes the range from 1.96 standard deviations below the sample mean (the lower confidence limit) to 1.96 standard deviations above the sample mean (the upper confidence limit). The 99% confidence interval includes the range from 2.57 standard deviations below the sample mean (the lower confidence limit) to 2.57 standard deviations above the sample mean (the upper confidence limit).

5. The kind of hypothesis test described in this chapter (the *Z* test) is rarely used in research practice; you have learned it as a stepping stone. The standard deviation of the distribution of means (the standard error, *SE*), is often used to describe the expected variability of means, particularly in bar graphs in which the standard error may be shown as the length of a line above (and sometimes below) the top of each bar. Confidence intervals are sometimes reported in research articles, usually with the abbreviation CI.

KEY TERMS

distribution of means (p. 155)

mean of a distribution of means (Population M_M) (p. 158)

variance of a distribution of means (Population SD_M^2) (p. 158)

standard deviation of a distribution of means

(Population SD_M) (p. 159)

standard error (*SE*) (p. 160)

shape of the distribution of means (p. 160)

point estimate (p. 169)

interval estimate (p. 169)

confidence interval (CI) (p. 169)

confidence limits (p. 169)

95% confidence interval (p. 169)

99% confidence interval (p. 170)

Z test (p. 173)

EXAMPLE WORKED-OUT PROBLEMS

FIGURE THE STANDARD DEVIATION OF THE DISTRIBUTION OF MEANS

Find the standard deviation of the distribution of means for a population with Population *SD* = 13 and a sample size of 20.

ANSWER

Using Rules 2a and 2b for the characteristics of a distribution of means: **the variance of a distribution of means is the variance of the population of individuals divided by the number of individuals in each sample; the standard deviation of a distribution of means is the square root of the variance of the distribution of means.** The variance of the population is 169 (that is, 13 squared is 169); 169 divided by 20 gives a variance of the distribution of means of 8.45. The square root of this, 2.91, is the standard deviation of the distribution of means.

Using the formulas,

$$\text{Population } SD_M^2 = \text{Population } SD^2/N = 13^2/20 = 8.45.$$

$$\text{Population } SD_M = \sqrt{\text{Population } SD_M^2} = \sqrt{8.45} = 2.91.$$

HYPOTHESIS TESTING WITH A SAMPLE OF MORE THAN ONE

A sample of 75 given an experimental treatment had a mean of 16 on a particular measure. The general population of individuals has a mean of 15 on this measure and a standard deviation of 5. Carry out the full five steps of hypothesis testing with a two-tailed test at the 5% significance level and make a drawing of the distributions involved.

ANSWER

❶ Restate the question as a research hypothesis and a null hypothesis about the populations. The two populations are these:

> **Population 1:** Those given the experimental treatment.
>
> **Population 2:** The general population (those not given the experimental treatment).

The research hypothesis is that the population given the experimental treatment will score differently on the particular measure used than the population in general (those not given the experimental treatment). The null hypothesis is that the populations have the same average score on this measure.

❷ Determine the characteristics of the comparison distribution. Population M_M = Population M = 15. Population SD_M^2 = Population SD^2/N = $5^2/75$ = .33; Population SD_M = $\sqrt{\text{Population } SD_M^2}$ = $\sqrt{.33}$ = .57; shape is normal (sample size is greater than 30).

❸ Determine the cutoff sample score on the comparison distribution at which the null hypothesis should be rejected. Two-tailed cutoffs, 5% significance level, are +1.96 and −1.96.

❹ Determine your sample's score on the comparison distribution. Using the formula $Z = (M - \text{Population } M_M)/\text{Population } SD_M$, $Z = (16 - 15)/.57 = 1/.57 = 1.75$.

❺ Decide whether to reject the null hypothesis. The result, 1.75, is *not* more extreme than the cutoffs of +1.96 and −1.96; do not reject the null hypothesis. Results are inconclusive. The distributions involved are shown in Figure 6–11.

FINDING CONFIDENCE INTERVALS

Find the 99% confidence interval for the sample mean in the study described above.

ANSWER

❶ Estimate the population mean and figure the standard deviation of the distribution of means. The best estimate of the population mean in the problem above is the sample mean of 16. The standard deviation of the distribution of means, Population SD_M, in the problem above was .57.

❷ Find the Z scores that go with the confidence limits you want. For the 99% confidence interval, the Z scores are +2.57 and −2.57.

❸ To find the confidence interval, change these Z scores to raw scores. Lower confidence limit = (−2.57) (.57) + 16 = −1.46 + 16 = 14.54; upper confidence limit = (+2.57) (.57) + 16 = 1.46 + 16 = 17.46. The 99% confidence interval is from 14.54 to 17.46.

PRACTICE PROBLEMS

These problems involve figuring. Most real-life statistics problems are done on a computer with special statistical software. Even if you have such software, do these problems by hand (with the help of a calculator) to ingrain the method in your mind. Also, in all problems involving figuring, be sure to show your work.

For practice in using a computer to solve statistics problems, refer to the computer section of each chapter of the *Student's Study Guide and Computer Workbook* that accompanies this text.

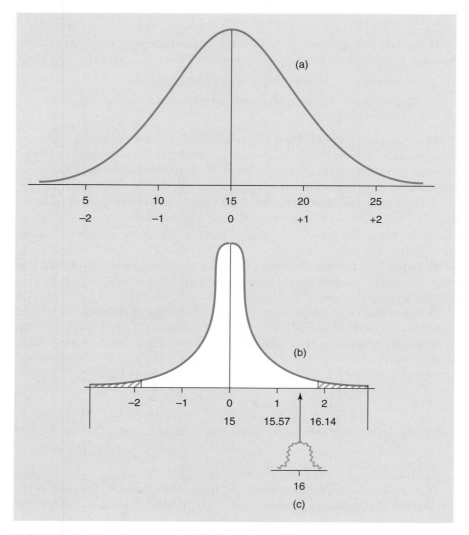

FIGURE 6–11   *Answer to hypothesis-testing problem in Example Worked-Out Problems: (a) the distribution of the population of individuals, (b) the distribution of means (the comparison distribution), and (c) the sample's distribution.*

All data are fictional unless an actual citation is given.
For answers to Set I problems, see pp. 428–30.

SET I

1. Why is the standard deviation of the distribution of means generally smaller than the standard deviation of the distribution of the population of individuals?
2. For a population that has a standard deviation of 10, figure the standard deviation of the distribution of means for samples of size (a) 2, (b) 3, (c) 4, and (d) 9.
3. For a population that has a standard deviation of 20, figure the standard deviation of the distribution of means for samples of size (a) 2, (b) 3, (c) 4, and (d) 9.
4. Figure the 95% confidence interval (that is, the lower and upper confidence limits) for each part of problem 2. Assume that in each case the researcher's

sample has a mean of 100 and that the population of individuals is known to follow a normal curve.

5. Figure the 99% confidence interval (that is, the lower and upper confidence limits) for each part of problem 3. Assume that in each case the researcher's sample has a mean of 10 and that the population of individuals is known to follow a normal curve.

6. For each of the following samples that were given an experimental treatment, test whether they are different from the general population: (a) a sample of 10 with a mean of 44, (b) a sample of 1 with a mean of 48. The general population of individuals has a mean of 40, a standard deviation of 6, and follows a normal curve. Carry out the full five steps of hypothesis testing with a two-tailed test at the .05 significance level, make a drawing of the distributions involved, and figure the 95% confidence interval.

7. For each of the following samples that were given an experimental treatment, test whether they scored significantly higher than the general population: (a) a sample of 100 with a mean of 82, (b) a sample of 10 with a mean of 84. The general population of individuals has a mean of 81, a standard deviation of 8, and follows a normal curve. For each sample, carry out the full five steps of hypothesis testing with a one-tailed test at the .01 significance level, make a drawing of the distributions involved, and figure the 99% confidence interval.

8. Twenty-five women between the ages of 70 and 80 were randomly selected from the general population of women their age to take part in a special program to decrease reaction time (speed). After the course, the women had an average reaction time of 1.5 seconds. Assume that the mean reaction time for the general population of women of this age group is 1.8, with a standard deviation of .5 seconds. (Also assume that the population is approximately normal.) What should you conclude about the effectiveness of the course? (a) Using the .01 significance level, carry out the steps of hypothesis testing. (b) Make a drawing of the distributions involved. (c) Figure the 99% confidence interval. (d) Explain your answer to someone who is familiar with the general logic of hypothesis testing, the normal curve, Z scores, and probability, but is not familiar with the idea of a distribution of means or confidence intervals.

9. A large number of people were shown a particular film of an automobile collision between a moving car and a stopped car. Each person then filled out a questionnaire about how likely it was that the driver of the moving car was at fault, on a scale from 0 = *not at fault* to 10 = *completely at fault*. The distribution of ratings under ordinary conditions follows a normal curve with Population $M = 5.5$ and Population $SD = .8$. Sixteen randomly selected individuals are tested in a condition in which the wording of the question is changed so the question asks, "How likely is it that the driver of the car who crashed into the other was at fault?" (The difference is that in this changed condition, instead of describing the event in a neutral way, the question uses the phrase "crashed into.") Using the changed instruction, these 16 research participants gave a mean at-fault rating of 5.9. Did the changed instructions significantly increase the rating of being at fault? (a) Carry out the steps of hypothesis testing (use the .05 level). (b) Make a drawing of the distributions involved. (c) Figure the 95% confidence interval. (d) Explain your answer to someone who has never taken statistics.

10. Lee, Byatt, and Rhodes (2000) tested a theory of the role of distinctiveness in face perception. In their study, participants indicated whether or not they recognized each of 48 faces of male celebrities when they were shown rapidly on a computer screen. A third of the faces were shown in caricature form, in which facial features

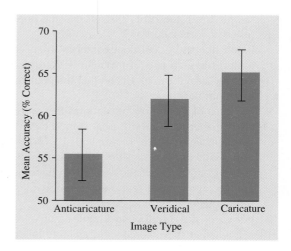

FIGURE 6–12 *Identification accuracy as a function of image type. Standard error bars are shown.*
Source: Lee, K., Byatt, G., & Rhodes, G. (2000). Caricature effects, distinctiveness, and identification: Testing the face-space framework. *Psychological Science, 11,* September 2000, p. 381. Reprinted by permission of Blackwell Publishers Journals.

were electronically modified so that distinctive features were slightly exaggerated; a third were shown in veridical form, in which the faces were not modified at all; and a third were shown in anticaricature form, in which facial features were modified to be slightly more like the average of the celebrities' faces. The average percent correct across their participants is shown in Figure 6–12. Explain the meaning of the error bars in this figure to a person who understands mean, standard deviation, and variance, but nothing else about statistics.

11. Chiu, Hong, and Dweck (1997) studied the tendency of some individuals to believe that people's traits are fixed; they labeled these individuals as "entity theorists" because they see other people as fixed entities. In particular, the researchers wanted to test whether entity theorists would be more likely to take a single event as evidence that a person has a fixed trait. As part of the study, they described to the research participants a situation in which one person behaved in a more friendly way than another, and then asked them which person would be more likely to be friendly in the future. Chiu et al. reported one of their findings about entity theorists as follows: "For them, if one person was found to be friendlier than another person in a particular situation, this relation would more likely than not generalize to a completely different situation" (p. 23). The statistical support for this was described as follows: "Entity theorists' overall prediction [of how likely the person was to be friendly] was significantly greater than .50 (95% CI = .5583 ± .0348)" (p. 23). Explain what "95% CI = .5583 ± .0348" means to a person who understands hypothesis testing with the mean of a sample of more than one but has never heard of confidence intervals.

Set II

12. Under what conditions is it reasonable to assume that a distribution of means will follow a normal curve?
13. Indicate the mean and the standard deviation of the distribution of means for each of the following situations.

	Population		Sample Size
	M	SD^2	N
(a)	100	40	10
(b)	100	30	10
(c)	100	20	10
(d)	100	10	10
(e)	50	10	10
(f)	100	40	20
(g)	100	10	20

14. Figure the standard deviation of the distribution of means for a population with a standard deviation of 20 and sample sizes of (a) 10, (b) 11, (c) 100, and (d) 101.

15. For each of the following studies, the samples were given an experimental treatment and the researchers compared their results to the general population. For each, carry out the full five steps of hypothesis testing for a two-tailed test, make a drawing of the distributions involved, and figure the 95% confidence interval. (Assume all populations are normally distributed.)

	Population		Sample Size	Sample Mean	Significance Level
	M	SD	N		
(a)	36	8	16	38	.05
(b)	36	6	16	38	.05
(c)	36	4	16	38	.05
(d)	36	4	16	38	.01
(e)	34	4	16	38	.01

16. For each of the following studies, the samples were given an experimental treatment and the researchers compared their results to the general population. For each, carry out the full five steps of hypothesis testing for a two-tailed test at the .01 level, make a drawing of the distributions involved, and figure the 99% confidence interval.

	Population		Sample Size	Sample Mean
	M	SD	N	
(a)	10	2	50	12
(b)	10	2	100	12
(c)	12	4	50	12
(d)	14	4	100	12

17. Figure the 95% confidence interval (that is, the lower and upper confidence limits) for each part of problem 13. Assume that in each case the population of individuals is known to follow a normal curve.

18. Figure the 99% confidence interval (that is, the lower and upper confidence limits) for each part of problem 14. Assume that in each case the researcher's sample has a mean of 50 and that the population of individuals is known to follow a normal curve.

19. A researcher is interested in whether North Americans are able to identify emotions correctly in people from other cultures. It is known that, using a particular method of measurement, the accuracy ratings of adult North Americans in general are normally distributed with a mean of 82 and a variance of 20. This distribution is based on ratings made of emotions expressed by other North Americans. In the present study, however, the researcher arranges to test 50 adult North Americans rating emotions of individuals from Indonesia. The mean accuracy for these 50 individuals was 78. Using a two-tailed test and the .05 significance level, what should the researcher conclude? (a) Carry out the steps of hypothesis testing. (b) Make a drawing of the distributions involved. (c) Figure the 95% confidence interval. (d) Explain your answer to someone who knows about hypothesis testing with a sample of a single individual but knows nothing about hypothesis testing with a sample of more than one individual or about confidence intervals.

20. A researcher is interested in the conditions that affect the number of dreams per month that people report in which they are alone. We will assume that based on extensive previous research, it is known that in the general population the number of such dreams per month follows a normal curve, with Population $M = 5$ and Population $SD = 4$. The researcher wants to test the prediction that the number of such dreams will be greater among people who have recently experienced a traumatic event. Thus, the researcher studies 36 individuals who have recently experienced a traumatic event, having them keep a record of their dreams for a month. Their mean number of alone dreams is 8. Should you conclude that people who have recently had a traumatic experience have a significantly different number of dreams in which they are alone? (a) Carry out the steps of hypothesis testing (use the .05 level). (b) Make a drawing of the distributions involved. (c) Figure the 95% confidence interval. (d) Explain your answer to a person who has never had a course in statistics.

21. A government-sponsored telephone counseling service for adolescents tested whether the length of calls would be affected by a special telephone system that had a better sound quality. Over the past several years, the lengths of telephone calls (in minutes) were normally distributed with Population $M = 18$ and Population $SD = 8$. They arranged to have the special phone system loaned to them for one day. On that day, the mean length of the 46 calls they received was 21 minutes. Test whether the length of calls has changed using the 5% significance level. (a) Carry out the steps of hypothesis testing. (b) Make a drawing of the distributions involved. (c) Figure the 95% confidence interval. (d) Explain your answer to someone who knows about hypothesis testing with a sample of a single individual but knows nothing about hypothesis testing with samples of more than one individual or about confidence intervals.

22. Li, Linderberger, Freund, and Baltes (2001) compared older (aged 60 to 75) and younger (aged 20 to 30) adults on the impact on memory of making some aspect of what they were doing more difficult. Figure 6–13 shows some of their results. In the figure caption they note that "Error bars represent ± 1 *SEM*" (standard error of the mean). This tells you that the line above and below the top of each bar represents the standard error. Explain the meaning of the statement, "Error bars represent ± 1 *SEM*," using one of the error bars as an example, to a person who understands mean and standard deviation, but knows nothing else about statistics.

23. Bushman and Anderson (2001) studied news reports of the effects of media violence on aggression over a 30-year period. Some of their results are shown in

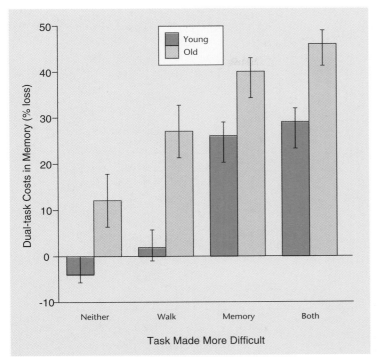

FIGURE 6–13   *Dual-task costs in memory recall as a function of age group and difficulty condition. Error bars represent ±1 SEM.*
Source: Li, K. Z. H., Lindenberger, U., Freund, A. M., & Baltes, P. B. (2001). Walking while memorizing: Age-related differences in compensatory behavior. *Psychological Science, 12,* 230–237.

Figure 6–14. In the figure caption they note that "Capped vertical bars denote 95% confidence intervals." Explain what this means, using one of the vertical bars as an example, to a person who understands standard error bars but has never heard of confidence intervals.

24. Cut up 90 small slips of paper, and write each number from 1 to 9 on 10 slips each. Put the slips in a large bowl and mix them up. (a) Take out a slip, write down the number on it, and put it back. Do this 20 times. Make a histogram, and figure the mean and the variance of the result. You should get an approximately rectangular distribution. (b) Take two slips out, figure out their mean, write it down, and put the slips back.[4] Repeat this process 20 times. Make a histogram, then figure the mean and the variance of this distribution of means. The variance should be about half of the variance of this distribution of means. (c) Repeat the process again, this time taking three slips at a time. Again, make a histogram and figure the mean and the variance of the distribution of means.

[4]Technically, when taking the samples of two slips, this should be done by taking one, writing it down, putting it back, then taking the next, writing it down, and putting it back. You would consider these two scores as one sample for which you figure a mean. The same applies for samples of three slips. This is called sampling with replacement. However, with 90 slips in the bowl, taking two or three slips at a time and putting them back, will be a close enough approximation for this exercise and will save you some time.

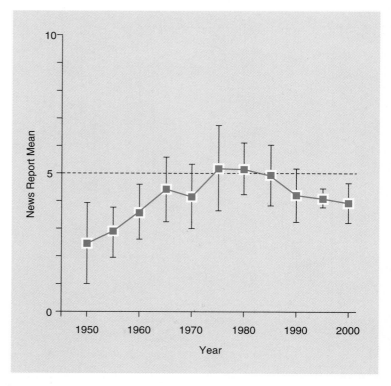

FIGURE 6–14   *News reports of the effect of media violence on aggression. Note: News report means are the average rated conclusions of newspaper and magazine articles. A rating of 0 indicates that the article said there was no relationship between violent media and aggression. A rating of 5 indicates that the article urged parents to discourage their children from consuming violent media. A rating of 10 indicates that the article said that viewing violence caused an increase in aggression. Capped vertical bars denote 95% confidence intervals.*
Source: Bushman, B. J., & Anderson, C. A. (2001). Media violence and the American public: Scientific facts versus media misinformation. *American Psychologist, 56,* 477–489.

The distribution of means of three slips each should have a variance of about a third of the distribution of samples of one slip each. Also note that as the sample size increases, your distributions are getting closer to normal. (Had you begun with a normally distributed distribution of slips, your distributions of means would have been fairly close to normal regardless of the number of slips in each sample.)

C H A P T E R 7

Making Sense of Statistical Significance: Decision Errors, Effect Size, and Statistical Power

Statistical significance is extremely important in social and behavioral science research, but it can also be misused. Sophisticated researchers and readers of research understand that there is more to the story of a research result than $p < .05$ or *ns*. This chapter helps you become sophisticated about statistical significance. Gaining this sophistication means learning about three closely interrelated issues: decision errors, effect size, and statistical power.

Tip for Success

This chapter builds very directly on Chapters 5 and 6. We do not recommend embarking on this chapter until you have a strong grasp of the key material in those chapters, especially hypothesis testing and the distribution of means.

DECISION ERRORS

A crucial topic for making sense of statistical significance is the kind of errors that are possible in the hypothesis-testing procedure. The kind of errors we consider here are about how, in spite of doing all your figuring correctly, your conclusions from hypothesis testing can still be incorrect. It is *not* about making mistakes in calculations or even about using the wrong procedures. That is, **decision errors** are a situation in which the *right procedures* lead to the *wrong decisions*.

Decision errors are possible in hypothesis testing because you are making decisions about populations based on information in samples. The whole hypothesis-testing process is based on probabilities. The hypothesis-testing process is set up to make the probability of decision errors as small as possible. For example, we only decide to reject the null hypothesis if a sample's mean is so extreme that there is a very

decision errors

small probability (say, less than 5%) that we could have gotten such an extreme sample if the null hypothesis is true. But a very small probability is not the same as a zero probability! Thus, in spite of your best intentions, decision errors are always possible.

There are two kinds of decision errors in hypothesis testing: Type I error and Type II error.

TYPE I ERROR

Type I error

You make a **Type I error** if you reject the null hypothesis when in fact the null hypothesis is true. Or, to put it in terms of the research hypothesis, you make a Type I error when you conclude that the study supports the research hypothesis when in reality the research hypothesis is false.

Suppose you carried out a study in which you had set the significance level cutoff at a very lenient probability level, such as 20%. This would mean that it would not take a very extreme result to reject the null hypothesis. If you did many studies like this, you would often (about 20% of the time) be deciding to consider the research hypothesis supported when you should not. That is, you would have a 20% chance of making a Type I error.

Even when you set the probability at the conventional .05 or .01, you will still make a Type I error sometimes (to be precise, 5% or 1% of the time). Consider again the example from the last chapter of giving special instructions intended to make fifth graders perform better on a standard achievement test. Suppose the special instructions in reality make no difference whatsoever. However, in randomly picking a sample of fifth graders to study, the researchers might just happen to pick a group of fifth graders to be in the study who would do unusually well on the test, no matter what kind of instructions they received. Randomly selecting a sample like this is unlikely, because in general a random sample, especially one of 64 individuals, will have a mean that is close to the population mean. But such extreme samples are possible, and should this happen, the researchers would reject the null hypothesis and conclude that the special instructions do make a difference. Their decision to reject the null hypothesis would be wrong—a Type I error. Of course, the researchers could not know they had made a decision error of this kind. What reassures researchers is that they know from the logic of hypothesis testing that the probability of making such a decision error is kept low (less than 5% if you use the .05 significance level).

Still, the fact that Type I errors can happen at all is of serious concern to social and behavioral scientists, who might construct entire theories and research programs, not to mention practical applications, based on a conclusion from hypothesis testing that is in fact mistaken. It is because these errors are of such serious concern that they are called Type I.

As we have noted, researchers cannot tell when they have made a Type I error. However, they can try to carry out studies so that the chance of making a Type I error is as small as possible.

What is the chance of making a Type I error? It is the same as the significance level we set. If you set the significance level at $p < .05$, you are saying you will reject the null hypothesis if there is less than a 5% (.05) chance that you could have gotten your result if the null hypothesis were true. When rejecting the null hypothesis in this way, you are allowing up to a 5% chance that you got your results even though the null hypothesis was actually true. That is, you are allowing a 5% chance of a Type I error. (You will sometimes see the significance level, the chance of making a Type I error, referred to as *alpha,* the Greek letter α.)

Again, the significance level is the same as the chance of making a Type I error. Thus, the lower probability we set for the significance level, the smaller the chance of a Type I error. Researchers who do not want to take a lot of risk set the significance level lower than .05, such as $p < .001$. In this way the result of a study has to be very extreme in order for the hypothesis-testing process to reject the null hypothesis.

Using a .001 significance level is like buying insurance against making a Type I error. However, as when buying insurance, the better the protection, the higher the cost. There is a cost in setting the significance level at too extreme a level. We turn to that cost next.

TYPE II ERROR

If you set a very stringent significance level, such as .001, you run a different kind of risk. With a very stringent significance level, you may carry out a study in which in reality the research hypothesis is true, but the result does not come out extreme enough to reject the null hypothesis. Thus, the decision error you would make is in *not* rejecting the null hypothesis when in fact the null hypothesis is false. To put this in terms of the research hypothesis, you make this kind of decision error when the hypothesis-testing procedure leads you to decide that the results of the study are inconclusive when in reality the research hypothesis is true. This is called a **Type II error.**

Type II error

Consider again our fifth grader example. Suppose that, in truth, giving the special instructions *does* make fifth graders do better on the test. However, in conducting your particular study, the results are not strong enough to allow you to reject the null hypothesis. Perhaps the random sample that you selected to try out the new instructions happened to include mainly fifth graders who do very poorly on this kind of test regardless of the instructions given. As we have seen, even though the special instructions might help them do better than they would have otherwise, their scores may still not be much higher than the average of all fifth graders. The results would not be significant. Having decided not to reject the null hypothesis, and thus refusing to draw a conclusion, would be a Type II error.

Type II errors especially concern social and behavioral scientists interested in practical applications, because a Type II error could mean that a valuable practical procedure is not used.

As with a Type I error, you cannot know when you have made a Type II error. But researchers can try to carry out studies so as to reduce the probability of making one. One way of buying insurance against a Type II error is to set a very lenient significance level, such as $p < .10$ or even $p < .20$. In this way, even if a study results in only a very small effect, the results have a good chance of being significant. There is a cost to this insurance policy too.

Tip for Success

It is very easy to get confused between a Type I error and a Type II error. Be sure you understand each type of error (and the difference between them) before moving on to the section on effect size.

RELATION OF TYPE I AND TYPE II ERRORS

When it comes to setting significance levels, protecting against one kind of decision error increases the chance of making the other. The insurance policy against Type I error (setting a significance level of, say, .001) has the cost of increasing the chance of making a Type II error. (This is because with a stringent significance level like .001, even if the research hypothesis is true, the results have to be quite strong to be extreme enough to reject the null hypothesis.) The insurance policy against Type II error (setting a significance level of, say, .20) has the cost that you increase the chance of making a Type I error. (This is because with a level of significance like .20, even if the null hypothesis is true, it is fairly easy to get a significant result just by accidentally getting a sample that is higher or lower than the general population before doing the study.)

The trade-off between these two conflicting concerns usually is worked out by compromise—thus the standard 5% and 1% significance levels.

SUMMARY OF POSSIBLE OUTCOMES OF HYPOTHESIS TESTING

The entire issue of possible correct and mistaken conclusions in hypothesis testing is shown in Table 7–1. Along the top of this table are the two possibilities about whether the null hypothesis or the research hypothesis is really true. (Remember, you never actually know this.) Along the side is whether, after hypothesis testing, you decide that the research hypothesis is supported (reject the null hypothesis) or decide that the results are inconclusive (do not reject the null hypothesis). Table 7–1 shows that there are two ways to be correct and two ways to be in error in any hypothesis-testing situation. We will have more to say about these possibilities after we consider the topic of statistical power.

HOW ARE YOU DOING?

1. What is a decision error?
2. (a) What is a Type I error? (b) Why is it possible? (c) What is its probability?
3. (a) What is a Type II error? (b) Why is it possible?
4. If you set a lenient significance level (say .25), what is the effect on the probability of (a) Type I error and (b) Type II error?
5. If you set a stringent signifiance level (say .001) , what is the effect on the probability of (a) Type I error and (b) Type II error?

ANSWERS:

1. A decision error is a conclusion from hypothesis testing that does not match reality.
2. (a) Rejecting the null hypothesis (and thus supporting the research hypothesis) when the null hypothesis is actually true (and the research hypothesis false) is a Type I error. (b) You reject the null hypothesis when a sample's result is so extreme it is unlikely you would have gotten that result if the null hypothesis is true. However, even though it is unlikely, it is still possible that the null hypothesis is true. (c) Its probability is the significance level (such as .05).
3. (a) Failing to reject the null hypothesis (and thus failing to support the research hypothesis) when the null hypothesis is actually false (and the research hypothesis true) is a Type II error. (b) You reject the null hypothesis when a sample's result is so extreme it is unlikely you would have gotten that result if the null hypothesis is true. However, the null hypothesis could be false, but the sample mean may not be extreme enough to reject the null hypothesis.
4. (a) It is high; (b) it is low.
5. (a) It is low; (b) it is high.

TABLE 7–1   Possible Correct and Incorrect Decisions in Hypothesis Testing

		Real Situation (in practice, unknown)	
		Null Hypothesis True	Research Hypothesis True
Conclusion Using Hypothesis-testing Procedure	Research hypothesis supported (reject null hypothesis)	Error (Type I)	Correct decision
	Study is inconclusive (do not reject null hypothesis)	Correct decision	Error (Type II)

EFFECT SIZE

Consider again the example from Chapter 6 of giving special instructions to fifth graders taking a standard achievement test. In the hypothesis-testing process for this example, we compared two populations:

Population 1: Fifth graders receiving special instructions.

Population 2: Fifth graders not receiving special instructions.

The research hypothesis was that Population 1 would score higher than Population 2. Population 2 (that is, how fifth graders perform on this test when given in the usual way) is known to have a mean of 200. In the example, we said the researchers found that their sample of 64 fifth graders who were given the special instructions had a mean score on the test of 220. Following the hypothesis-testing procedure, we rejected the null hypothesis that the two populations are the same, because it was extremely unlikely that we would get a sample with a score as high as 220 from a population like Population 2. (See Figure 7–1, which is the same as Figure 6–7 from the last chapter.) Thus, we could conclude the result is "statistically significant." In this example, the best estimate of the mean of Population 1 is the sample's mean, which is 220. Thus, we can estimate that giving the special instructions has an average effect of increasing a fifth grader's score by 20 points.

Now look again at Figure 7–1. Suppose the sample's score had been only 210. This would have had a Z score of 1.67 ([210 – 200]/6). This is more extreme than the cutoff in this example, which was 1.64, so the result would still have been significant. However, in this situation we would estimate that the average effect of the special instructions was only 10 points.

Notice that both results are significant, but in one example the effect is twice as big as in the other example. The point is that knowing statistical significance does not give you much information about the size of the effect. Significance tells us that the results of the experiment should convince us that there is an effect (that it is not "due to chance"). But significance does not tell us how big this nonchance effect is.

Put another way, **effect size** is the amount that two populations do *not* overlap—that is, how much they are separated. In the fifth-grader example, Population 2 (the known population) had a mean of 200; based on our original sample's mean of 220, we estimated that Population 1 (those getting the special instructions) would have a mean of 220. The left curve in Figure 7–2 is the distribution (*of individual scores*) for Population 2; the right curve is the distribution for Population 1. Now look at Figure 7–3. Again, the left curve is for Population 2 and is the same as in Figure 7–2. However, this time the right curve for Population 1 is estimated based on a sample getting the special instructions with a mean of 210. Here you can see that the effect size is smaller, and the two populations overlap even more. The amount that two populations do not overlap is called the effect size because it is the extent to which the experimental procedure has an *effect* of separating the two populations.

effect size

We often very much want to know not just whether a result is significant, but how big the effect is. As we will discuss later, an effect could well be statistically significant, but not of much practical significance. (That is, suppose an increase of only 10 points on the test is not considered important.) Also, as you will see later in the chapter, effect size plays an important role in two other important statistical topics: meta-analysis and power.

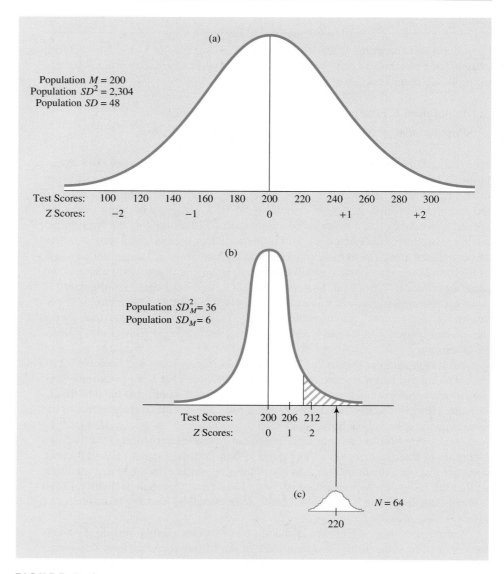

FIGURE 7–1 *For the fictional study of fifth graders' performance on a standard school achievement test, (a) the distribution of the population of individuals, (b) the distribution of means (the comparison distribution), and (c) the sample's distribution. The shaded area in the distribution of means is the rejection region—the area in which the null hypothesis will be rejected if the study's sample's mean turns out to be in that area. (See discussion in Chapter 6.)*

FIGURING EFFECT SIZE

In the example we just looked at, we considered the effect size of a completed research study. Effect size is also often considered when you are planning a research study. In either situation, the figuring is the same.

Effect size is based on two numbers. The first number is the researcher's prediction of the difference between the means of the two populations. In the situations we have considered so far, the mean of Population 2 (the known population) is known in advance. However, you don't know the mean of Population 1 in hypothesis-

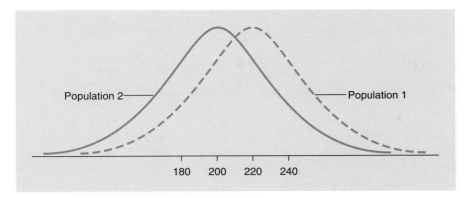

FIGURE 7–2   *For the fictional study of fifth graders' performance on a standard school achievement test, distribution of individuals for Population 1, those given the special instructions (right curve), and for Population 2, those not given special instructions (left curve). Population 1's mean is estimated based on the sample mean of 220, as originally described in Chapter 6; its standard deviation of 48 is assumed to be the same as Population 2's, which is known.*

testing situations. When you are figuring the effect size of a completed research study, you use your best estimate of the mean of Population 1, which is the sample mean. (Therefore, you are actually figuring an *estimated* effect size.) When you are figuring the effect size of a planned research study, you have to make a prediction of the mean of Population 1. This prediction is based on some precise theory, on previous experience with research of this kind, or on what would be the smallest difference that would be useful. The second number that the effect size is based on is the population standard deviation. In the situations we have considered so far, the population standard deviation (or the variance) is known in advance.

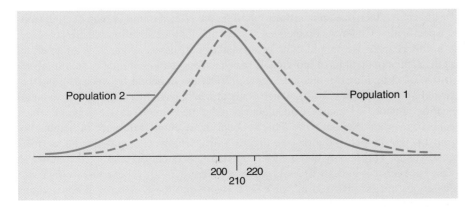

FIGURE 7–3   *For the fictional study of fifth graders' performance on a standard school achievement test, distribution of individuals for Population 1, those given the special instructions (right curve), and for Population 2, those not given special instructions (left curve). Population 1's mean is estimated based on a sample with a mean of 210; its standard deviation of 48 is assumed to be the same as Population 2's, which is known.*

Here is the rule for calculating effect size: Divide the predicted difference between the means by the population standard deviation.[1] Stated as a formula,

> The effect size is the difference between the population means divided by the population's standard deviation.

$$\text{Effect Size} = \frac{\text{Population 1 } M - \text{Population 2 } M}{\text{Population } SD} \qquad (7\text{-}1)$$

Notice that when figuring effect size you don't use the standard deviation of the distribution of means. Instead, you use the standard deviation of the population of individuals. Also notice that you are concerned with only one population's SD. This is because in hypothesis testing you usually assume that both populations have the same standard deviation. (We will say more about this in later chapters.)

Consider again the fifth-grader example shown in Figure 7–1. The best estimate of the mean of Population 1 is the sample mean, which was 220. The mean of Population 2 was 200, and the population standard deviation was 48. The difference between the two population means is 20 and the standard deviation of the populations of individuals is 48. Thus, the effect size is 20/48, or .42. In terms of the formula,

$$\text{Effect Size} = \frac{\text{Population 1 } M - \text{Population 2 } M}{\text{Population } SD} = \frac{220 - 200}{48} = \frac{20}{48} = .42$$

For the example in which the sample mean was 210, we would estimate Population 1's mean to be 210. Thus,

$$\text{Effect Size} = \frac{\text{Population 1 } M - \text{Population 2 } M}{\text{Population } SD} = \frac{210 - 200}{48} = \frac{10}{48} = .21$$

In both of these examples, the effect size is positive. If the effect size is negative, it just means that the mean of Population 1 is smaller than the mean of Population 2.

EFFECT SIZE CONVENTIONS

What should you consider to be a "big" effect, and what is a "small" effect? Jacob Cohen (1988, 1992), a researcher who developed the effect size measure among other major contributions to statistical methods, has helped solve this problem. Cohen came up with some **effect size conventions** based on the effects found in many actual studies. Specifically, Cohen recommended that for the kind of situation we are considering in this chapter, we should think of a small effect size as about .2. With an effect size of .2, the populations of individuals have an overlap of about 85%. This small effect size of .2 is, for example, the average difference in height between 15- and 16-year-old girls (see Figure 7–4a), which is about a half-inch difference with a standard deviation of about 2.1 inches. Cohen considered a medium effect size to be .5, which means an overlap of about 67%. This is about the average difference in heights between 14- and 18-year-old girls (see Figure 7–4b). Finally, Cohen defined a large effect size as .8. This is only about a 53% overlap. It is about the average difference in height between 13- and 18-year-old girls (see Figure 7–4c). These three effect size conventions are summarized in Table 7–2. (Note that these effect size conventions apply in the same way to both positive and negative effect sizes. So, $-.2$ is a small effect size, $-.5$ is a medium effect size, and $-.8$ is a large effect size.)

effect size conventions

TABLE 7–2 Summary of Cohen's Effect Size Conventions for Mean Differences

Verbal Description	Effect Size
Small	.2
Medium	.5
Large	.8

[1]This procedure gives a measure of effect size called "Cohen's *d*." It is the preferred method for the kind of hypothesis testing you have learned so far. (In later chapters, you learn of other measures of effect size that are appropriate to other hypothesis-testing situtations.)

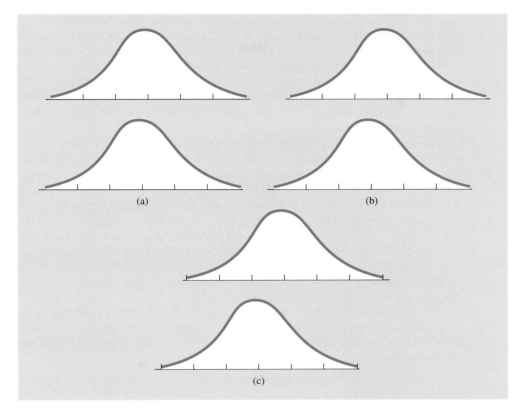

FIGURE 7-4   *Comparisons of pairs of population distributions of individuals showing Cohen's conventions for effect size: (a) small effect size (.2), (b) medium effect size (.5), (c) large effect size (.8).*

Consider another example. As we noted earlier in the book, many IQ tests have a standard deviation of 16 points. An experimental procedure with a small effect size would be an increase of 3.2 IQ points. (A difference of 3.2 IQ points between the mean of the population who goes through the experimental procedure and the mean of the population that does not, divided by the population standard deviation of 16, gives an effect size of .2.) An experimental procedure with a medium effect size would increase IQ by 8 points. An experimental procedure with a large effect size would increase IQ by 12.8 points.

A MORE GENERAL IMPORTANCE OF EFFECT SIZE

Effect size, as we have seen, is the difference between means divided by the population standard deviation. This division by the population standard deviation standardizes the difference between means, in the same way that a Z score gives a standard for comparison to other scores, even scores on different scales. Especially by using the standard deviation of the population of individuals, we bypass the variation from study to study of different sample sizes, making comparison even easier and effect size even more of a standard.

Knowing the effect size of a study lets you compare results with effect sizes found in other studies, even when the other studies have different sample sizes. Equally important, knowing the effect size lets you compare studies using different measures, even if those measures have different means and variances.

Also, within a particular study, our general knowledge of what is a small or a large effect size helps you evaluate the overall importance of a result. For example, a result may be statistically significant but not very large. Or a result that is not statistically significant (perhaps due to a small sample) may have just as large an effect size as another study (perhaps one with a larger sample) where the result was significant. Knowing the effect sizes of the studies helps us make better sense of such results. We examine both of these important implications of effect size in later sections of this chapter.

meta-analysis

An important development in statistics in recent years is a procedure called **meta-analysis.** This procedure combines results from different studies, even results using different methods of measurement. When combining results, the crucial thing combined is the effect sizes. As an example, a sociologist might be interested in the effects of cross-race friendships on prejudice, a topic on which there has been a large number of studies. Using meta-analysis, the sociologist could combine the results of these studies. This would provide an overall average effect size. It would also tell how the average effect sizes differ for studies done in different countries or about prejudice toward different ethnic groups. (For an example of such a study, see Pettigrew & Meertens [1995]. For another example of meta-analysis, see Box 7–1.)

Reviews of the collection of studies on a particular topic that use meta-analysis are an alternative to the traditional "narrative" literature review article. Such traditional reviews describe and evaluate each study and then attempt to draw some overall conclusion.

HOW ARE YOU DOING?

1. What does effect size add to just knowing whether or not a result is significant?
2. Write the formula for effect size in the situation we have been considering.
3. On a standard test, the population is known to have a mean of 500 and a standard deviation of 100. Those receiving an experimental treatment have a mean of 540. What is the effect size?
4. What are the effect size conventions?
5. (a) What is meta-analysis? (b) What is the role of effect size in a meta-analysis?

ANSWERS:

1. A significant result can be just barely big enough to be significant or much bigger than necessary to be significant. Thus, knowing effect size tells you how big the effect is.
2. Effect Size = (Population 1 M − Population 2 M)/Population SD
3. Effect Size = (Population 1 M − Population 2 M)/Population SD = (540 − 500)/100 = .4.
4. Small = .2, medium = .5, large = .8.
5. (a) A systematic procedure for combining results of different studies. (b) Meta-analyses usually come up with an average effect size across studies and also sometimes compare average effect sizes for different subgroups of studies.

STATISTICAL POWER

Power is the ability to achieve your goals. A goal of a researcher conducting a study is to get a significant result—but only *if* the research hypothesis really is true. The **statistical power** of a research study is the probability that the study will produce a statistically significant result if the research hypothesis is true. Power is *not* the probability that a study will produce a statistically significant result. The power of a study is the probability that it will produce a statistically significant result, *if the re-*

statistical power

BOX 7-1   Effect Sizes for Relaxation and Meditation: A Restful Meta-Analysis

In the 1970s and 1980s, the results of research on meditation and relaxation were the subject of considerable controversy. Eppley, Abrams, and Shear (1989) decided to look at the issue systematically by conducting a meta-analysis of the effects of various relaxation techniques on trait anxiety (that is, ongoing anxiety as opposed to a temporary state). Eppley and colleagues chose trait anxiety for their meta-analysis because it is a definite problem related to many other mental health issues, yet in itself is fairly consistent from test to test with the same measure and from one measure to another measure of it.

Following the usual procedure, the researchers searched the scientific literature for studies—not only research journals but also books and unpublished doctoral dissertations. Finding all the relevant research is one of the most difficult parts of meta-analysis.

To find the "bottom line," Eppley et al. (1989) compared effect sizes for each of the four main methods of meditation and relaxation that have been studied in systematic research. The result was that the average effect size for the 35 transcendental meditation (TM) studies was .70 (meaning an average difference of .70 standard deviation in anxiety scores between those who practiced this meditation procedure versus those in the control groups). This effect size was significantly larger than the average effect size of .28 for the 44 studies on all other types of meditation, the average effect size of .38 for the 30 "progressive relaxation" studies (a widely used method by clinical psychologists), and the average

effect size of .40 for the 37 studies on other forms of relaxation.

But the meta-analysis had really just begun. There were many subvariables of interest. For example, looking at different populations of research participants, they discovered that people who were screened to be highly anxious contributed more to the effect size, and prison populations and younger subjects seemed to gain more from TM. There was no impact on effect size of the skill of the instructors, expectations of the subjects, whether subjects had volunteered or been randomly assigned to conditions, experimenter bias (the TM results were actually stronger when any apparently pro-TM researchers' data were eliminated), the various measures of anxiety, and the research designs.

The researchers thought that one clue to TM's high performance might be that techniques involving concentration produced a significantly smaller effect, whereas TM makes a point of teaching an "effortless, spontaneous" method. Also, TM uses Sanskrit mantras (special sounds) said to come from a very old tradition and selected for each student by the instructor. Results were lower for methods employing randomly selected Sanskrit sounds or personally selected English words.

Whatever the reasons, Eppley et al. (1989) concluded that there are "grounds for optimism that at least some current treatment procedures can effectively reduce trait anxiety" (p. 973). So if you are prone to worry about matters like statistics exams, consider these results.

search hypothesis is true. If the research hypothesis is false, you do not want to get significant results. (That would be a Type I error.) Remember, however, even if the research hypothesis is true, an experiment will not automatically give a significant result—the particular sample that happens to be selected from the population may not turn out to be extreme enough to reject the null hypothesis.

Statistical power is important for several reasons. As you will learn later in the chapter, figuring power when planning a study helps you determine how many participants you need. Also, understanding power is extremely important when you read a research article, particularly for making sense of results that are not significant or results that are statistically but not practically significant.

Consider once again our example of the effects of giving special instructions to fifth graders taking a standard achievement test. Recall that we compared two populations:

Population 1: Fifth graders receiving special instructions.

Population 2: Fifth graders not receiving special instructions.

Also recall that the research hypothesis was that Population 1 would score higher than Population 2.

The top curve in Figure 7–5 shows the distribution of means for one possible situation the researchers might predict in which this research hypothesis would be true. The bottom curve shows the distribution of means for Population 2. (Be careful: When discussing effect size, we showed figures, such as Figures 7–2 and 7–3, for populations of individuals; now we are back to focusing on distributions of means.)

The bottom distribution of means is a comparison distribution, the distribution of means that you would expect for both populations if the null hypothesis were true. The shaded part of this bottom distribution is the area where you would reject

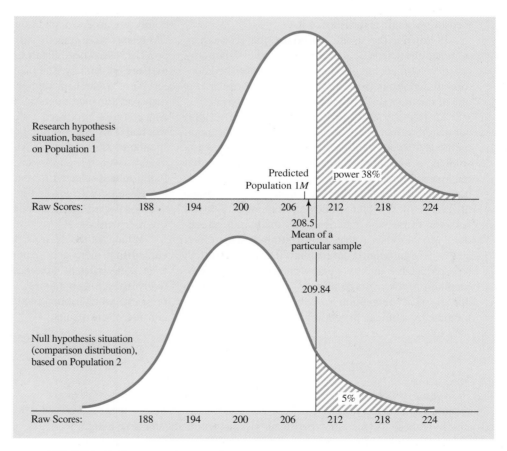

FIGURE 7–5   *Distributions of mean test scores of 64 fifth graders from a fictional study of fifth graders taking a standard achievement test. The lower distribution of means is based on a known distribution of individual test scores of fifth graders who do not receive any special instructions (Population 2). The upper distribution of means is based on a predicted distribution of individual test scores of fifth graders who receive the special instructions (Population 1). The researchers predict a mean of 208 for this population. Shaded sections of both distributions are the area in which the null hypothesis will be rejected. Power = 38%.*

the null hypothesis if, as a result of your study, the mean of your sample was in this area. The shaded rejection area begins at 209.84 (a *Z* score of 1.64), taking up 5% of this comparison distribution.

The top curve is the distribution of means that the researchers *predict* for the population receiving special instructions (Population 1). We have never considered this predicted distribution before. This was partly because this population is quite imaginary—*unless* the research hypothesis is true. If the null hypothesis is true, the true distribution for Population 1 is the same as the distribution based on Population 2. The Population 1 distribution would not be set off to the right (or the left).

However, to learn about power, we now consider the situation in which the researchers predict the research hypothesis to be true. In this situation, the researchers predict the mean of Population 1 to be 208. So, for this example, the mean of Population 1 is to the right of the mean of Population 2 (in other situations, the mean of Population 1 may be to the left of the mean of Population 2). The upper distribution of means (for predicted Population 1) is shown with a mean of 208. The comparison distribution's mean is only 200. Thus, the population receiving the special instructions (Population 1) is predicted to have, on the average, scores that are 8 points higher.

Now, suppose the researchers carry out the study. They give the special instructions to a randomly selected group of 64 fifth graders and find their mean score on the test. Remember, if the research hypothesis is true as they predict, the mean of their group of 64 students is from a distribution like the upper distribution of means.

In this example, however, this upper distribution of means (from the researchers' prediction about Population 1) is only slightly to the right of the comparison distribution. That is, the researchers are predicting that the special instructions will produce only a small increase in scores (8 points). The shaded sections of both distributions are the area in which the null hypothesis will be rejected. So, if the sample mean in your study falls in the shaded area, you will reject the null hypothesis. What this picture tells us is that most of the means from this upper distribution will not be far enough to the right on the lower distribution to reject the null hypothesis. Less than half of the upper distribution is shaded. Put another way, if the research hypothesis is true (as the researchers predict), the sample we study is a random sample from the distribution shown here based on Population 1. However, there is less than a 50–50 chance that the random sample from this distribution will be in the shaded area.

Recall that the statistical power of a study is the probability that the study will produce a statistically significant result, if the research hypothesis is true. Since the research hypothesis is true in this example, the shaded region in the upper distribution represents the power of the study. It turns out that the power for this situation (shown in Figure 7–5) is only 38%.

Suppose that the particular sample of 64 fifth graders studied had a mean of 208.5, as shown by the arrow under this distribution in the figure. However, you need a mean of at least 209.84 to reject the null hypothesis. Thus, the result of this study would not be statistically significant. It would not be significant, even though the research hypothesis really is true. This is how you would come to make a Type II error.

It is entirely possible that the researchers might happen to select a sample from Population 1 with a mean far enough to the right (that is, with a high enough mean test score) to be in the shaded area. However, given the way we have set up this particular example, there is a better-than-even chance that the study will *not* turn out significant, *even though we know the research hypothesis is true.* (Of course, once again, the researcher would not know this.) When a study like the one in this example has only a small chance of being significant even if the research hypothesis is true, we say the study has *low power.*

Suppose, on the other hand, the situation was one in which the upper curve was expected to be way to the right of the lower curve, so that almost any sample taken from the upper curve would be in the shaded rejection area in the lower curve. (Figure 7–6, below, is an example of this kind.) In that situation, the study would have high power.

FIGURING STATISTICAL POWER

The statistical power of a study can be figured. In a situation like the fifth-grader-testing example, figuring power involves figuring out the area of the shaded portion of the upper distribution in Figure 7–5. However, the figuring is somewhat laborious. Furthermore, the figuring becomes quite complex once we consider, starting in the next chapter, more realistic hypothesis-testing situations. Thus, instead of figuring power themselves, researchers usually find the power of a study using special charts called **power tables.** (Such tables have been prepared by Cohen, 1988, and

power tables

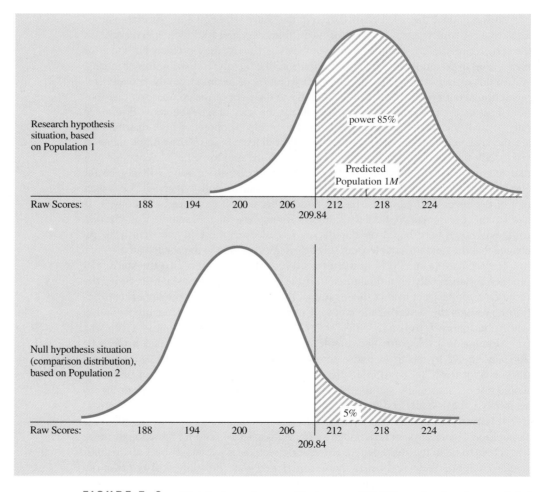

FIGURE 7–6 *Distributions of means of test scores of 64 fifth graders based on predicted (upper) and known (lower) distributions of populations of individuals. (From a fictional study of fifth graders taking a standard achievement test.) Scores are shown on both distributions for the significance cutoff on the lower distribution (the significance cutoff is based on p < .05, one-tailed). In this example, the predicted mean of the upper distribution is 216. Power = 85%.*

Kraemer & Thiemann, 1987, among others.) In the following chapters, with each method you learn, we will provide basic power tables and discuss how to use them. Table A–5 in the Appendix is an index to these tables.

1. (a) What is statistical power? (b) How is it different from just the probability of getting a significant result?
2. What is the probability of getting a significant result if the research hypothesis is false?
3. Give two reasons why statistical power is important.
4. (a) What is a power table? (b) Why are power tables widely used?

ANSWERS:

1. (a) Statistical power is the probability of getting a significant result if the research hypothesis is true. (b) It is the probability *if the research hypothesis is true.*
2. The significance level (that is, the probability of making a Type I error).
3. Statistical power can help you determine how many participants are needed for a study you are planning. Also, understanding power can help you make sense of results that are not significant or results that are statistically but not practically significant.
4. (a) A table that gives the power of a study without having to do any figuring. (b) In common hypothesis-testing situations, figuring power is very complicated.

WHAT DETERMINES THE POWER OF A STUDY?

It is very important that you understand what power is about. It is especially important to understand the factors that affect the power of a study and how to use power when planning a study and when making sense of a study you read.

The statistical power of a study depends on two main factors: how big an effect (the effect size) the research hypothesis predicts and how many participants are in the study (the sample size). Power is also affected by the significance level chosen, whether a one-tailed or two-tailed test is used, and the kind of hypothesis-testing procedure used.

EFFECT SIZE

Figure 7–5 shows the situation in our special test-instructions example in which the researchers predicted that those who got the special instructions (Population 1, the top curve) would have a mean score 8 points higher than fifth graders in general (Population 2, the bottom curve). Figure 7–6 shows the same study for a situation in which the researchers predicted that those who got the special instructions would have a mean 16 points higher than fifth graders in general. Compare Figure 7–6 to Figure 7–5. You are more likely to get a significant result in the situation shown in Figure 7–6. This is because there is more overlap of the top curve with the shaded area on the comparison distribution. Recall that the probability of getting a significant result (the power) for the situation in Figure 7–5, in which the researchers predict a mean of 208, is only 38%. However, for the situation in Figure 7–6, in which the researchers predict a mean of 216, the power is 85%. In any study, the bigger the difference you expect between the means of the two populations, the more power in the study.

The difference in means between populations we saw earlier is part of what goes in to effect size. Thus, the bigger the effect size, the greater the power. The effect size for the situation in Figure 7–5, in which the researchers predicted Population 1 to have a mean of 208, is .17. That is, Effect Size = (Population 1 M − Population 2 M)/Population SD = (208 − 200)/48 = 8/48 = .17. The effect size for the situation in Figure 7–6, in which the researchers predicted Population 1 to have a mean of 216, is .33. That is, Effect Size = (Population 1 M − Population 2 M)/Population SD = (216 − 200)/48 = 16/48 = .33.

Effect size is also affected by the population standard deviation. The smaller the standard deviation, the bigger the effect size. In terms of the effect size formula, this is because if you divide by a smaller number, the result is bigger. In terms of the actual distributions, this is because if two distributions that are separated are narrower, they overlap less. Figure 7–7 shows two distributions of

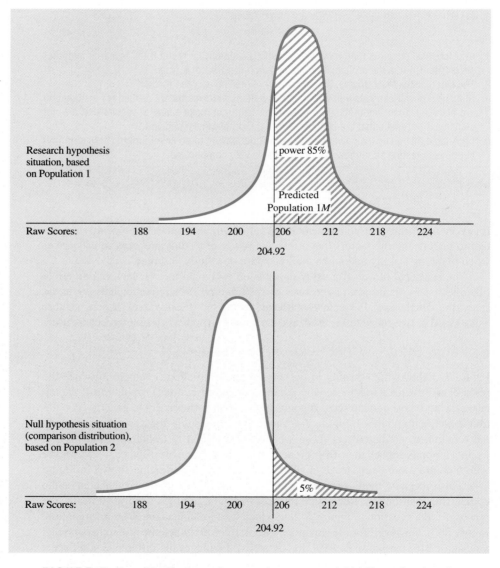

FIGURE 7–7   *Distributions of means of test scores of 64 fifth graders based on predicted (upper) and known (lower) distributions of populations of individuals. (From a fictional study of fifth graders taking a standard achievement test.) Scores are shown on both distributions for the significance cutoff on the lower distribution (the significance cutoff is based on p < .05, one-tailed). In this example, the population standard deviation is half as large as that shown in the original example in Figure 7–5. Power = 85%.*

means based on the same example. However, this time we have changed the example so that the variance is much smaller (the standard deviation in the distribution of means is exactly half of what it was in Figure 7–5). In this version, the predicted mean is the original 208. However, both distributions of means are much narrower. Therefore, there is much less overlap between the upper curve and the lower curve (the comparison distribution). The result is that the power is 85%, much higher than in the original situation (where it was only 38%). The idea here is that the smaller the population variance (and standard deviation), the greater the power.

Overall, these examples illustrate the general principle that the less overlap between the two distributions, the more likely that a study will give a significant result. Two distributions might have little overlap overall either because there is a large difference between their means (as in Figure 7–6) or because they have so little variance that even with a small mean difference they do not overlap much (as in Figure 7–7). This principle is summarized more generally in Figure 7–8.

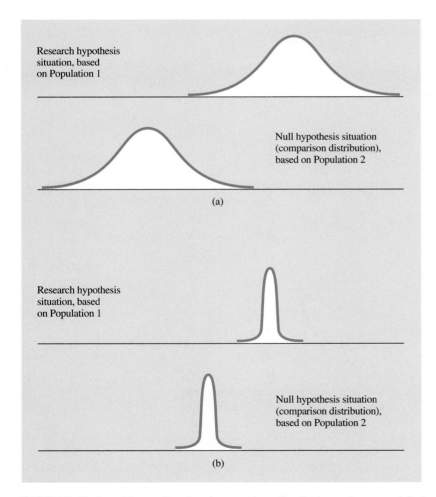

FIGURE 7–8   *The predicted and comparison distributions of means might have little overlap (and thus the study would have high power) because either (a) the two means are very different or (b) the variance is very small.*

SAMPLE SIZE

The other major influence on power, besides effect size, is the number of people in the sample that is studied, the sample size. Basically, the more people there are in the study, the more power.

Sample size affects power because the larger the sample size, the smaller the standard deviation of the distribution of means. If these distributions have a smaller standard deviation, they are narrower. And if they are narrower, there is less overlap between them. Figure 7–9 shows the situation for our fifth-grader example if the study included 100 fifth graders instead of the 64 in the original example, with a predicted mean of 208 and a population standard deviation of 48. The power now is 51%. (It was 38% with 64 fifth graders.) With 500 participants in the study, power is 98% (see Figure 7–10).

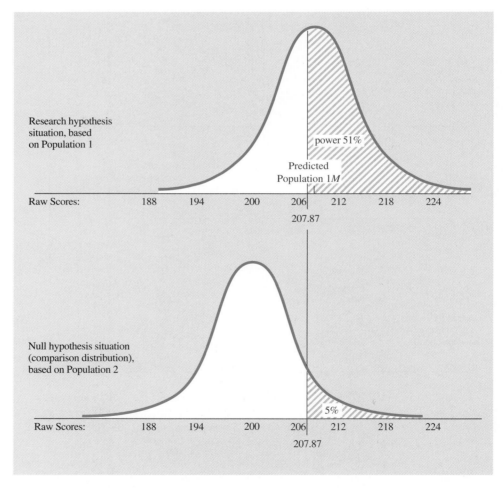

FIGURE 7–9 *Distributions of means of test scores of 100 fifth graders based on predicted (upper) and known (lower) distributions of populations of individuals. (From a fictional study of fifth graders taking a standard achievement test.) Scores are shown on both distributions for the significance cutoff on the lower distribution (the significance cutoff is based on p < .05, one-tailed). Power = 51%. Compare this example to the original example (in Figure 7–5) in which the sample size was 64 (and power was 38%).*

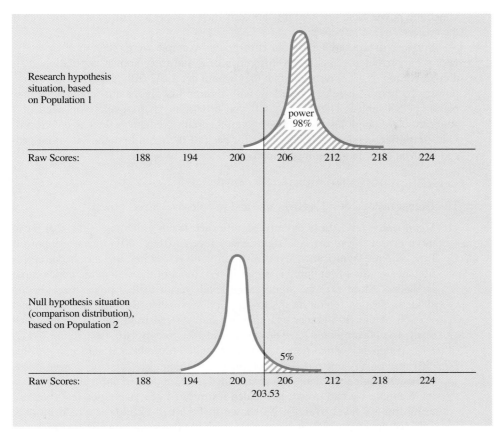

FIGURE 7–10   *Distributions of means of test scores of 500 fifth graders based on pre-dicted (upper) and known (lower) distributions of populations of individuals. (From a fic-tional study of fifth graders taking a standard achievement test.) Scores are shown on both distributions for the significance cutoff on the lower distribution (the significance cutoff is based on p < .05, one-tailed). Power = 98%. Compare this example to the original example in Figure 7–5 in which the sample size was 64 (and power was 38%) and the example in Figure 7–6 in which the sample size was 100 (and power was 51%).*

Don't get mixed up. The distributions of means can be narrow (and thus have less overlap and more power) for two very different reasons. One reason is that the populations of individuals may have small standard deviations. This reason has to do with effect size. The other reason is that the sample size is large. This reason is completely separate. Sample size has nothing to do with effect size. Both effect size and sample size influence power. However, as we will see shortly, these two differ-ent influences on power lead to completely different kinds of practical steps for in-creasing power when planning a study.

FIGURING NEEDED SAMPLE SIZE FOR A GIVEN LEVEL OF POWER

When planning a study, the main reason researchers figure power is to help decide how many people to include in the study. Sample size has an important influence on power. Thus, a researcher wants to be sure to have enough people in the study for the study to have fairly high power. (Too often, researchers carry out studies in which the power is so low that it is unlikely they will get a significant result even if the research hypothesis is true.)

Suppose the researchers in our fifth-grader example were planning their study, with their predicted effect mean difference of 8 and their known population standard deviation of 48. It turns out that they would need 222 fifth graders to have 80% power. To help researchers come up with figures like this, statisticians have prepared special tables. These tables tell you how many participants you need in a study to have a high level of power, given a certain predicted effect size. We provide simplified versions of such tables for each of the main hypothesis-testing procedures you learn in upcoming chapters.

OTHER INFLUENCES ON POWER

Three other factors (besides effect size and sample size) affect power:

1. *Significance level.* Less extreme significance levels (such as .10 or .20) mean more power. More extreme significance levels (.01 or .001) mean less power. Less extreme significance levels result in more power because the shaded rejection area on the lower curve is bigger. Thus, more of the area in the upper curve is shaded. More extreme significance levels result in less power because the shaded rejection region on the lower curve is smaller. Suppose in our original version of the fifth-grader example, we had instead used the .01 significance level. The power would have dropped from 38% to only 16% (see Figure 7–11).

2. *One- versus two-tailed tests.* Using a two-tailed test makes it harder to get significance on any one tail. Thus, keeping everything else the same, power is less with a two-tailed test than with a one-tailed test. Suppose in our fifth-grader testing example we had used a two-tailed test instead of a one-tailed test (but still using the 5% level overall). As shown in Figure 7–12, power would be only 26% (compared to 38% in the original one-tailed version shown in Figure 7–5).

3. *Type of hypothesis-testing procedure.* Sometimes the researcher has a choice of more than one hypothesis-testing procedure to use for a particular study. We have not considered any such situations so far in this book but we will do so in Chapter 11.

SUMMARY OF INFLUENCES ON POWER

Table 7–3 summarizes the effects of various factors on the power of a study.

HOW ARE YOU DOING?

1. (a) What are the two factors that determine effect size? For each (b and c), explain how and why it affects power.
2. (a) How and (b) why does sample size affect power?
3. (a) How and (b) why does the significance level used affect power?
4. (a) How and (b) why does using a one-tailed versus a two-tailed test affect power?

ANSWERS:

1. (a) The two ways are the difference between the population means and the population standard deviation.
   (b) The more difference between the population means, the larger the effect size, the more power. This is because it makes the distribution of means further apart and thus have less overlap. Therefore, the area in the predicted distribution more extreme than the cutoff in the known distribution is greater.
   (c) The smaller the population standard deviation, the larger the effect size, the more power. This is because it makes the distribution of means narrower and thus have less overlap.

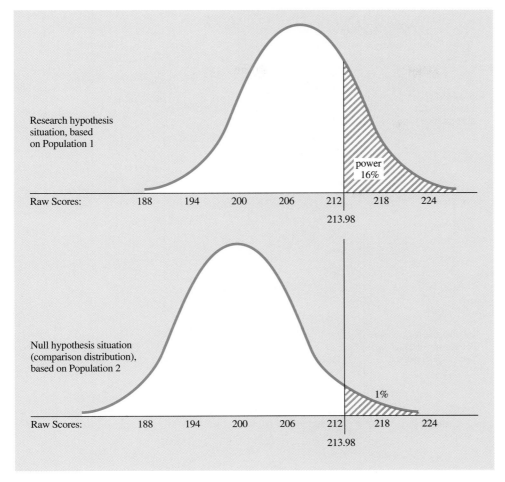

FIGURE 7–11   *Distributions of means of test scores of 64 fifth graders based on pre-dicted (upper) and known (lower) distributions of populations of individuals. (From a fictional study of fifth graders taking a standard achievement test.) Scores are shown on both distributions for the significance cutoff on the lower distribution. The significance cutoff is based on p < .01, one-tailed. Power = 16%. Compare this example to the original example (in Figure 7–5) in which the significance cutoff was p < .05 (and power was 38%).*

Thus, the area in the predicted distribution more extreme than the cutoff in the known distribution is greater.

2. (a) The larger the sample size, the more power. (b) This is because it makes the distribution of means narrower (because the standard deviation of the distribution of means is the population variance divided by the sample size) and thus have less overlap, so the area in the predicted distribution more extreme than the cutoff in the known distribution is greater.

3. The more liberal the significance level (for example, .10 versus .05), the more power. (b) This is because it makes the cutoff in the known distribution less extreme, so the corresponding area more extreme than this cutoff in the predicted distribution of means is larger.

4. A study with a one-tailed test has more power (for a result in the predicted direction) than a two-tailed test. (b) This is because with a one-tailed test, the cutoff in the predicted direction in the known distribution is less extreme, so the corresponding area more extreme than this cutoff in the predicted distribution of means is larger. There is an added cutoff in the opposite side, but this is so far out on the distribution that it has little effect on power.

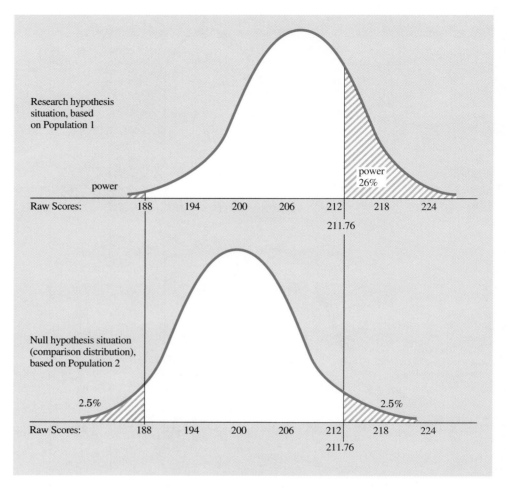

FIGURE 7–12 *Distributions of means of test scores of 64 fifth graders based on predicted (upper) and known (lower) distributions of populations of individuals. (From a fictional study of fifth graders taking a standard achievement test.) Scores are shown on both distributions for the significance cutoff on the lower distribution. The significance cutoff is based on p < .05, two-tailed. Power = 26%. Compare this example to the original example (in Figure 7–5) in which the significance test was one-tailed (and power was 38%).*

THE ROLE OF POWER WHEN PLANNING A STUDY

Determining power is very important when planning a study. If you do a study in which the power is low, even if the research hypothesis is true, the study will probably not give statistically significant results. Thus, the time and expense of carrying out the study, as it is currently planned, would probably not be worthwhile. So when the power of a planned study is found to be low, researchers look for practical ways to increase the power to an acceptable level.

What is an acceptable level of power? A widely used rule is that a study should have 80% power to be worth doing (see Cohen, 1988). Power of 80% means that there is an 80% (8 out of 10) chance that the study will produce a statistically significant result, if the research hypothesis is true. Obviously, the more power the better. However, the costs of greater power, such as studying more people, often make even 80% power beyond your reach.

TABLE 7–3 Influences on Power		
Feature of the Study	Increases Power	Decreases Power
Effect size	Large	Small
Effect size combines the following two features:		
Predicted difference between population means	Large Differences	Small Differences
Population standard deviation	Small Population *SD*	Large Population *SD*
Sample size (*N*)	Large *N*	Small *N*
Significance level	Lenient (such as .10)	Stringent (such as .01)
One-tailed versus two-tailed test	One-tailed	Two-tailed
Type of hypothesis-testing procedure used	Varies	Varies

How can you increase the power of a planned study? In principle, you can increase the power of a planned study by changing any of the factors summarized in Table 7–3. Let's consider each.

1. *Increase the effect size by increasing the predicted difference between population means.* You can't just arbitrarily predict a bigger difference. There has to be a basis for your prediction. Thus, to increase the predicted difference, your method in carrying out the study must make it reasonable to expect a bigger difference. Consider again our example of the experiment about the impact of special instructions on fifth graders' test scores. One way to increase the expected mean difference would be to make the instructions more elaborate, spending more time explaining them, perhaps allowing time for practice, and so forth. In some studies, you may be able to increase the expected mean difference by using a more intense experimental procedure. A disadvantage of this approach of increasing the impact of the experimental procedure is that it can be difficult or costly. Another disadvantage is that you may have to use an experimental procedure that is not like the one to which you want the results of your study to apply.

2. *Increase effect size by decreasing the population standard deviation.* You can decrease the population standard deviation in a planned study in at least two ways. One way is to use a population that has less variation within it than the one originally planned. With the fifth-grader testing example, you might only use fifth graders in a particular suburban school system. The disadvantage is that your results will then apply only to the more limited population.

   Another way to decrease the population standard deviation is to use conditions of testing that are more standardized and measures that are more precise. For example, testing in a controlled laboratory setting usually makes for smaller overall variation among scores in results (meaning a smaller standard deviation). Similarly, using tests with very clear wording and clear procedures for marking answers also reduces variation. When practical, this is an excellent way to increase power, but often the study is already as rigorous as it can be.

3. *Increase the sample size.* The most straightforward way to increase power in a study is to study more people. Of course, if you are studying astronauts who have walked on the moon, there is a limit to how many are available. In most research situations, though, sample size is the main way to change a planned study to raise its power.

4. *Use a less-stringent level of significance.* Ordinarily, the level of significance you use should be the least stringent that reasonably protects against Type I error. Normally, this will be .05. It is rare that much can be done to improve power in this way.

5. *Use a one-tailed test.* Whether you use a one- or a two-tailed test depends on the logic of the hypothesis being studied. As with significance level, it is rare that you have much of a choice about this factor.

6. *Use a more sensitive hypothesis-testing procedure.* This is fine if alternatives are available. We consider some options of this kind in Chapter 11. Usually, however, the researcher begins with the most sensitive method available, so little more can be done.

Table 7–4 summarizes some practical ways to increase the power of a planned experiment.

THE ROLE OF POWER WHEN INTERPRETING THE RESULTS OF A STUDY

Understanding statistical power and what affects it is very important in drawing conclusions from the results of research.

ROLE OF POWER WHEN A RESULT IS STATISTICALLY SIGNIFICANT: STATISTICAL SIGNIFICANCE VERSUS PRACTICAL SIGNIFICANCE

You have learned that a study with a larger effect size is more likely to come out statistically significant. It also is possible for a study with a very small effect size to come out significant. This is likely to happen when a study has high power due to other factors, especially a large sample size. Consider a study in which among all

---

TABLE 7–4 Summary of Practical Ways of Increasing the Power of a Planned Experiment

Feature of the Study	Practical Way of Raising Power	Disadvantages
Predicted difference between population means	Increase the intensity of experimental procedure.	May not be practical or may distort study's meaning.
Population standard deviation	Use a less diverse population.	May not be available; decreases generalizability.
	Use standardized, controlled circumstances of testing or more precise measurement.	Not always practical.
Sample size (N)	Use a larger sample size.	Not always practical; can be costly.
Significance level	Use a more lenient level of significance (such as .1).	Raises the probability of Type I error.
One-tailed versus two-tailed test	Use a one-tailed test.	May not be appropriate to the logic of the study.
Type of hypothesis-testing procedure	Use a more sensitive procedure	None may be available or appropriate.

students who take the Scholastic Aptitude Test (SAT) in a particular year, a sample of 10,000 whose first name begins with a particular letter are randomly selected. Suppose that their mean Verbal SAT is 504, compared to the overall population's mean Verbal SAT of 500 (Population $SD = 100$). This result would be significant at the .001 level. Its effect size is a tiny .04. That is, the significance test tells you that you can be confident there is a real difference—that the population of students whose first name begins with this letter have higher Verbal SAT scores than the general population of students. At the same time, the difference is not very important. The effect size makes it clear that this difference is very small. The distributions of the two populations overlap so much that it would be of little use to know what letter a person's first name begins with.

The message here is that in judging a study's results, there are two questions. First, is the result statistically significant? If it is, you can consider there to be a real effect. The next question then is whether the effect size is large enough for the result to be useful or interesting. This second question is especially important if the study has practical implications. (Sometimes, in a study testing purely theoretical issues, it may be enough just to be confident there is an effect at all in a particular direction.)

If the sample was small, you can assume that a statistically significant result is probably also practically significant. On the other hand, if the sample size is very large, you must consider the effect size directly, as it is quite possible that the effect size is too small to be useful.

The implications of what we just said may seem a bit of a paradox. Most people assume that the more participants in the study, the more important its results. In a sense, just the reverse is true. All other things being equal, if a study with only a few participants manages to be significant, that significance must be due to a large effect size. A study with a large number of people in it that is statistically significant may or may not have a large effect size.

Notice that it is not usually a good idea to compare the significance level of two studies to see which has the more important result. For example, a study with a small number of participants that is significant at the .05 level might well have a large effect size. At the same time, a study with a large number of participants that is significant at the .001 level might well have a small effect size.

The most important lesson from all this is that the word *significant* in statistically significant has a very special meaning. It means that you can be pretty confident that there is some real effect. But it does *not* mean that the effect is significant in a practical sense, that it is important or noteworthy.

ROLE OF POWER WHEN A RESULT IS NOT STATISTICALLY SIGNIFICANT

We saw in Chapter 5 that a result that is not statistically significant is inconclusive. Often, however, we really would like to conclude that there is little or no difference between the populations. Can we ever do that?

Consider the relation of power to a nonsignificant result. Suppose you carried out a study that had low power and did not get a significant result. In this situation, the result is entirely inconclusive. Not getting a significant result may have come about because the research hypothesis was false or because the study had too little power (for example, because it had too few participants).

On the other hand, suppose you carried out a study that had high power and you did not get a significant result. In this situation, it seems unlikely that the research hypothesis is true. In this situation (where there is high power), a nonsignificant result is a fairly strong argument against the research hypothesis. This does not mean that all versions of the research hypothesis are false. For example, it is possible that the research hypothesis is true and the populations are only very slightly different (and you figured power based on predicting a large difference).

In sum, a nonsignificant result from a study with low power is truly inconclusive. However, a nonsignificant result from a study with high power does suggest that either the research hypothesis is false or that there is less of an effect than was predicted when figuring power.

SUMMARY OF THE ROLE OF SIGNIFICANCE AND SAMPLE SIZE IN INTERPRETING RESEARCH RESULTS

Table 7–5 summarizes the role of significance and sample size in interpreting research results.

HOW ARE YOU DOING?

1. (a) What are the two basic ways of increasing the effect size of a planned study? For each (b) and (c), how can it be done, and what are the disadvantages?
2. What is usually the easiest way to increase the power of a planned study?
3. What are the disadvantages of increasing the power of a planned study by (a) using a more lenient significance level, or (b) using a one-tailed test rather than a two-tailed test?
4. Why is statistical significance not the same as practical importance?
5. You are comparing two studies in which one is significant at $p < .01$ and the other is significant at $p < .05$. (a) What can you conclude about the two studies? (b) What can you not conclude about the two studies?
6. When a result is significant, what can you conclude about effect size if the study had (a) a very large sample size or (b) a very small sample size?
7. When a result is not significant, what can you conclude about the truth of the research hypothesis if the study had (a) a very large sample size or (b) a very small sample size?

ANSWERS:

1. (a) Increase the predicted difference between the population means and reduce the population standard deviation.
(b) You can increase the predicted difference between the population means by increasing the intensity of the experimental procedure. The disadvantages are that it might not be practical and it may change the meaning of the procedure you really want to study.
(c) You can decrease the population standard deviation by using a less diverse population. This has the disadvantage of not permitting you to apply your results to a more general population. Another way to decrease the population standard deviation is to use more standardized procedures or more accurate measurement. However, this may not be practical.
2. Increase the sample size.

TABLE 7–5 Role of Significance and Sample Size in Interpreting Experimental Results

Result Statistically Significant	Sample Size	Conclusion
Yes	Small	Important result
Yes	Large	Might or might not have practical importance
No	Small	Inconclusive
No	Large	Research hypothesis probably false

3. (a) It increases the probability of a Type I error. (b) This may not be appropriate to the logic of the study, and if the result comes out opposite to predictions, in principle, it would have to be considered nonsignificant.

4. A statistically significant result means that you can be confident the effect did not occur by chance; it does not, however, mean it is a large or substantial effect.

5. (a) We can be more confident that the first study's result is not due to chance. (b) We cannot conclude which one has the bigger effect size.

6. (a) The effect size could be small or large. (b) The effect size is probably large.

7. (a) The research hypothesis is probably not true (or has a much smaller effect size than predicted). (b) You can conclude very little about the truth of the research hypothesis.

DECISION ERRORS, EFFECT SIZE, AND POWER IN RESEARCH ARTICLES

You mainly think about decision errors when planning research and interpreting the results of a research study. It is rare that you will read about decision errors in research articles. It is increasingly common, however, for articles to mention effect size. For example, Moorehouse and Tobler (2000) studied the effectiveness of an intervention program for "high-risk, multiproblem, inner-city, primarily African-American and Latino youth." The authors reported "Youth who received 5–30 hours of intervention ([the high dosage group], $n = 101$) were compared with those who received 1–4 hours (the low-dosage group, $n = 31$). . . . The difference between the groups in terms of reduction in [alcohol and drug] use was highly significant. A between-groups effect size of .68 was achieved for the high-dosage group when compared with the low-dosage group." (Their wording about the study is a bit confusing—they are using "dosage" here to mean the amount of intervention, not the amount of drugs anyone was taking!) The meaning of the .68 effect size is that the group getting 5–30 hours of intervention was .68 standard deviations higher in terms of reduction on their drug and alcohol use than the group getting only 1–4 hours of the intervention. This is a medium to large effect size. Effect sizes are also commonly reported in meta-analyses, in which results from different articles are being combined and compared (for an example, see Box 7–1).

As was the case with decision errors, you usually think about power when planning research and evaluating the results of a research study. (Power, for example, is often a major topic in grant proposals requesting funding for research and in thesis proposals.) As for research articles, power is sometimes mentioned in the final section of an article where the author discusses the meaning of the results or in discussions of results of other studies. In either situation, the emphasis tends to be on the meaning of nonsignificant results. Also, when power is discussed, it may be explained in some detail. This is because it has been only recently that most social and behavioral scientists have begun to be knowledgeable about power.

For example, Denenberg (1999), in discussing the basis for his own study, makes the following comments about a relevant previous study by Mody, Studdert-Kennedy, and Brady (1997) that had not found significant results.

> [T]hey were confronted with the serious problem of having to accept the null hypothesis. . . . we can view this issue in terms of statistical power. . . . A minimal statistical power of .80 is required before one can consider the argument that the lack of significance may be interpreted as evidence that Ho [the null hypothesis] is true. To conduct a power analysis, it is necessary to specify an expected mean difference, the alpha [significance] level, and whether a one-tailed or two-tailed test will be used. Given a power requirement of .8, one can then determine the N necessary. Once these

conditions are satisfied, if the experiment fails to find a significant difference, then one can make the following kind of a statement: "We have designed an experiment with a .8 probability of finding a significant difference, if such exists in the population. Because we failed to find a significant effect, we think it quite unlikely that one exists. Even if it does exist, its contribution would appear to be minimal. . . ."

Mody et al. never discussed power, even though they interpreted negative findings as evidence for the validity of the null hypothesis in all of their experiments. . . . Because the participants were split in this experiment, the *n*s [sample sizes] were reduced to 10 per group. Under such conditions one would not expect to find a significant difference, unless the experimental variable was very powerful. In other words it is more difficult to reject the null hypothesis when working with small *n*s [sample sizes]. The only meaningful conclusion that can be drawn from this study is that no meaningful interpretation can be made of the lack of findings. . . . (pp. 380–381)

SUMMARY

1. There are two kinds of decision errors one can make in hypothesis testing. A Type I error occurs when a researcher rejects the null hypothesis, but the null hypothesis is actually true. A Type II error occurs when a researcher does not reject the null hypothesis, but the null hypothesis is actually false.

2. Effect size is the degree of separation of the known population and the population that is given the experimental treatment. The effect size is figured by dividing the difference between population means by the population standard deviation. Cohen's effect size conventions consider a small effect to be .2, a medium effect to be .5, and a large effect to be .8. Effect size is important in its own right in interpreting results of studies. It is also used to compare and combine results of studies, as in meta-analysis, and to compare different results within a study.

3. The statistical power of a study is the probability that it will produce a statistically significant result if the research hypothesis is true. Researchers usually look up the power of a study on special tables.

4. The larger the effect size, the greater the power. This is because the greater the difference between means or the smaller the population standard deviation (the two ingredients in effect size), the less overlap between the known and predicted populations' distributions of means. Thus, the area in the predicted distribution more extreme than the cutoff in the known distribution is greater.

5. The larger the sample size, the greater the power. This is because the larger the sample, the smaller the variance of the distribution of means. So, for a given effect size, there is less overlap between distributions of means.

6. Power is also affected by significance level (the more extreme, such as .01, the lower the power), by whether a one- or two-tailed test is used (with less power for a two-tailed test), and by the type of hypothesis-testing procedure used (in the occasional situation where there is a choice of procedure).

7. Statistically significant results from a study with high power (such as one with a large sample size) may not have practical importance. Results that are not statistically significant from a study with low power (such as one with a small sample size) leave open the possibility that statistically significant results might show up if power were increased.

8. Research articles rarely include discussions of decision errors. Mentions of effect size are increasingly common in research articles. Research articles sometimes include discussions of power, especially when evaluating nonsignificant results.

KEY TERMS

decision errors (p. 185)   effect size (p. 189)   meta-analysis (p. 194)
Type I error (p. 186)   effect size conventions   statistical power (p. 194)
Type II error (p. 187)   (p. 192)   power tables (p. 198)

EXAMPLE WORKED-OUT PROBLEM

In a known population with a normal distribution, Population $M = 40$ and Population $SD = 10$. A sample given an experimental treatment has a mean of 37. What is the effect size? Is this approximately small, medium, or large?

ANSWER

Effect Size = (Population 1 M − Population 2 M)/Population SD = $(37 - 40)/10$ = $-.3/10 = -.3$. Approximately small.

PRACTICE PROBLEMS

These problems involve figuring. Most real-life statistics problems are done on a computer with special statistical software. Even if you have such software, do these problems by hand (with the help of a calculator) to ingrain the method in your mind. Also, in all problems involving figuring, be sure to show your work.

For practice in using a computer to solve statistics problems, refer to the computer section of each chapter of the *Student's Study Guide and Computer Workbook* that accompanies this text.

All data are fictional unless an actual citation is given.

For answers to Set I problems, see pp. 430–31.

SET I

1. For each of the following studies, make a chart of the four possible correct and incorrect decisions, and explain what each would mean. (Each chart should be laid out like Table 7–1, but you should put into the boxes the possible results, using the names of the variables involved in the study.)

   (a) A study of whether increasing the amount of recess time improves school-children's in-class behavior.
   (b) A study of whether color-blind individuals can distinguish gray shades better than the population at large.
   (c) A study comparing individuals who have ever been in psychotherapy to the general public to see if they are more tolerant of other people's upsets than is the general population.

2. You conduct a research study. How can you know (a) if you have made a Type I error? and (b) if you have made a Type II error?

3. In a completed study, there is a known population with a normal distribution, Population $M = 25$, and Population $SD = 12$. What is the estimated effect size if a sample given an experimental procedure has a mean of (a) 19, (b) 22, (c) 25, (d) 30, and (e) 35? For each part, also indicate whether the effect is approximately small, medium, or large.

4. In a planned study, there is a known population with a normal distribution, Population $M = 50$, and Population $SD = 5$. What is the predicted effect size if

the researchers predict that those given an experimental treatment have a mean of (a) 50, (b) 52, (c) 54, (d) 56, and (e) 47? For each part, also indicate whether the effect is approximately small, medium, or large.

5. Here is information about several possible versions of a planned study, each involving a single sample. Figure the predicted effect size for each study:

| | Population 2 | | Predicted |
	M	SD	Population 1 M
(a)	90	4	91
(b)	90	4	92
(c)	90	4	94
(d)	90	4	86

6. You read a study in which the result is significant ($p < .05$). You then look at the size of the sample. If the sample is very large (rather than very small), how should this affect your interpretation of (a) the probability that the null hypothesis is actually true and (b) the practical importance of the result? (c) Explain your answers to a person who understands hypothesis testing but has never learned about effect size or power.

7. Aron et al. (1997) placed strangers in pairs and asked them to talk together following a series of instructions designed to help them become close. At the end of 45 minutes, individuals privately answered some questions about how close they now felt to their partners. (The researchers combined the answers into a "closeness composite.") One key question was whether closeness would be affected by either (a) matching strangers based on their attitude agreement or (b) leading participants to believe that they had been put together with someone who would like them. The result for both agreement and expecting to be liked was that "there was no significant differences on the closeness composite" (p. 367). The researchers went on to argue that the results suggested that there was little true effect of these variables on closeness (note that the symbol d in the text below means effect size):

There was about 90% power in this study of achieving significant effects . . . for the two manipulated variables if in fact there were a large effect of this kind (d [effect size] = .8). Indeed, the power is about 90% for finding at least a near-significant (p <.10) medium-sized effect (d [effect size] = .5). Thus, it seems unlikely that we would have obtained the present results if in fact there is more than a small effect. . . . (p. 367)

Explain this result to a person who understands hypothesis testing but has never learned about effect size or power.

8. How does each of the following affect the power of a planned study?

   (a) A larger predicted difference between the means of the populations
   (b) A larger population standard deviation
   (c) A larger sample size
   (d) Using a more stringent significance level (e.g., .01 instead of .05)
   (e) Using a two-tailed test instead of a one-tailed test

9. List two situations in which it is useful to consider power, indicating what the use is for each.

SET II

10. For each of the following studies, make a chart of the four possible correct and incorrect decisions, and explain what each would mean. (Each chart should be laid out like Table 7–1, but put into the boxes the possible results, using the names of the variables involved in the study.)

    (a) A study of whether infants born prematurely begin to recognize faces later than do infants in general.
    (b) A study of whether high school students who receive an AIDS prevention program in their school are more likely to practice safe sex than are other high school students.
    (c) A study of whether memory for abstract ideas is reduced if the information is presented in distracting colors.

11. In a completed study, there is a known population with a normal distribution, Population $M = 122$, and Population $SD = 8$. What is the estimated effect size if a sample given an experimental procedure has a mean of (a) 100, (b) 110, (c) 120, (d) 130, and (e) 140? For each part, also indicate whether the effect is approximately small, medium, or large.

12. In a planned study, there is a known population with a normal distribution, Population $M = 0$, and Population $SD = 10$. What is the predicted effect size if the researchers predict that those given an experimental treatment have a mean of (a) -8, (b) -5, (c) -2, (d) 0, and (e) 10? For each part, also indicate whether the effect is approximately small, medium, or large.

13. Here is information about several possible versions of a planned study, each involving a single sample. Figure the predicted effect size for each study:

| | Population 2 | | Predicted |
	M	SD	Population 1 M
(a)	90	2	91
(b)	90	1	91
(c)	90	2	92
(d)	90	2	94
(e)	90	2	86

14. What is meant by effect size? (Write your answer for a lay person.)
15. What is meant by the statistical power of an experiment? (Write your answer for a lay person.)
16. You read a study in which the result is not statistically significant. You then look at the size of the sample. If the sample is very large (rather than very small), how should this affect your judgment of (a) the probability that the null hypothesis is actually true and (b) the probability that the null hypothesis is actually false? (c) Explain your answers to a person who understands hypothesis testing but has never learned about power.
17. Caspi et al. (1997) analyzed results from a large-scale longitudinal study of a sample of children born around 1972 in Dunedin, New Zealand. As one part of their study, Caspi et al. compared the 94 in their sample who were, at age 21, alcohol dependent (clearly alcoholic) versus the 863 who were not alcohol dependent. The researchers compared these two groups in terms of personality

test scores from when they were 18 years old. After noting that all results were significant, they reported the following results (note that the symbol d in the text below means effect size):

Young adults who were alcohol dependent at age 21 scored lower at age 18 on Traditionalism ($d = .49$), harm avoidance ($d = .44$), Control ($d = .64$), and Social Closeness ($d = .40$), and higher on Aggression ($d = .86$), Alienation ($d = .66$), and Stress Reaction ($d = .50$).

Explain these results, including why it was especially important for the researchers in this study to give effect sizes, to a person who understands hypothesis testing but has never learned about effect size or power.

18. You are planning a study that you determine from a power table as having quite low power. Name six things that you might do to increase power.

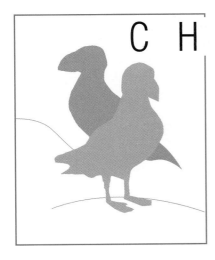

C H A P T E R 8

Introduction to the *t* Test

Chapter Outline

At this point, you may think you know all about hypothesis testing. Here's a surprise: What you know so far will not help you much as a researcher. Why? The procedures for testing hypotheses described up to this point were, of course, absolutely necessary for what you will now learn. However, these procedures involved comparing a group of scores to a known population. In real research practice, you often compare two or more groups of scores to each other, without any direct information about populations. For example, you may have two scores for a group of people, such as a score on a test of attitudes toward the courts before and after having gone through a law suit. Or you might have one score per person for two groups of people, such as an experimental group and a control group in a study of the effect of a new method of training teachers.

These kinds of research situations are very common in social and behavioral science research, where usually the only information available is from the samples. Nothing is known about the populations that the samples are supposed to come from. In particular, the researcher does not know the variance of the populations involved, which is a crucial ingredient in Step 2 of the hypothesis-testing process (determining the characteristics of the comparison distribution).

In this chapter, we first examine the solution to the problem of not knowing the population variance by focusing on a special situation: the comparison of the mean of a single sample to a population with a *known* mean but an *unknown* variance. Then, after describing how to handle this problem of not knowing the population variance, we go on to consider the situation in which there is no known population at all—the situation in which all you have are two scores for each of a number of people.

t tests

Tip for Success

In order to understand this chapter, you will need to know well the material in Chapters 5, 6, and 7, especially the logic and procedures for hypothesis testing and the distribution of means.

t test for a single sample

The hypothesis-testing procedures you learn in this chapter, those in which the population variance is unknown, are examples of what are called *t* **tests.** The *t* test is sometimes called "Student's *t*" because its main principles were originally developed by William S. Gosset, who published his articles anonymously using the name "Student" (see Box 8–1).

THE *t* TEST FOR A SINGLE SAMPLE

Let's begin with the following situation. You conduct a study that gives you scores for a sample of individuals and you want to compare the mean of this sample to a population for which the mean is known but the variance is unknown. Hypothesis testing in this situation is called a *t* **test for a single sample.** (It is also called a *one-sample t test.*)

The *t* test for a single sample works basically the same way as the procedure you learned in Chapter 6. In the studies we considered in Chapter 6, you had scores for a sample of individuals (such as a group of 64 fifth graders who had taken a standard test with special instructions) and you wanted to compare the mean of this sample to a population (such as fifth graders in general). However, in the studies we considered in Chapter 6, you knew both the mean and variance of the general population to which you were going to compare your sample. In the situations we are now going to consider, everything is the same, but you don't know the population variance. This presents two important new wrinkles, having to do with the details of how you carry out two of the steps of the hypothesis-testing process.

The first important new wrinkle is in Step 2. Because the population variance is not known, you have to estimate it. So the first new wrinkle we consider is how to estimate an unknown population variance. The other important new wrinkle affects both Steps 2 and 3. When the population variance has to be estimated, the shape of the comparison distribution is not a normal curve. So the second new wrinkle we consider is the shape of the comparison distribution (for Step 2) and how to use a special table to find the cutoff (Step 3) on what is a slightly differently shaped distribution.

AN EXAMPLE

Suppose your college newspaper reports an informal survey showing that students at your college study an average of 2.5 hours each day. However, you think the students in *your* dormitory study much more than that. You randomly pick 16 students from your dormitory and ask them how much they study each day. (We will assume that they are all honest and accurate.) Your result is that these 16 students study an average of 3.2 hours per day. Should you conclude that students in general in your dormitory study more than the college average? Or should you conclude that your results are so close to the college average that the small difference of .7 hours might well be due to your having picked, purely by chance, 16 of the more studious residents of your dormitory?

Step 1 of the hypothesis-testing process is to restate the problem as hypotheses about populations.

There are two populations:

Population 1: The kind of students who live in your dormitory.
Population 2: The kind of students at your college generally.

The research hypothesis is that Population 1 students study more than Population 2 students; the null hypothesis is that Population 1 students do not study more than Population 2 students. So far the problem is no different from those in Chapter 6.

BOX 8–1   William S. Gosset, alias "Student": Not a Mathematician, but a Practical Man

William S. Gosset graduated from Oxford in 1899 with a degree in mathematics and chemistry. It happened that in the same year the Guinness brewers in Dublin, Ireland, were seeking a few young scientists to take a first-ever scientific look at beer making. Gosset took one of these jobs and soon had immersed himself in barley, hops, and vats of brew.

The problem was how to make beer of a consistently high quality. Scientists, such as Gosset, wanted to make the quality of beer less variable, and were especially interested in finding the cause of bad batches. A proper scientist would say, "Conduct experiments!" But a business such as a brewery could not afford to waste money on experiments involving large numbers of vats, some of which any brewer worth his hops knew would fail. So Gosset was forced to contemplate the probability of, say, a certain strain of barley producing terrible beer when the experiment could consist of only a few batches of each strain. Adding to the problem was that he had no idea of the variability of a given strain of barley—perhaps some fields planted with the same strain grew better barley. (Does this sound familiar? Poor Gosset, like today's researchers, had no idea of his population's variance.)

Gosset was up to the task, although at the time only he knew that. To his colleagues at the brewery, he was a professor of mathematics and not a proper brewer at all. To his statistical colleagues, mainly at the Biometric Laboratory at University College in London, he was a mere brewer and not a proper mathematician. In short, Gosset was the sort of scientist who was not above applying his talents to real life.

In fact, he seemed to revel in real life: raising pears, fishing, golfing, building boats, skiing, cycling, and lawn bowling (after he broke his leg by driving his car, a two-seater Model T Ford that he called "The Flying Bedstead," into a lamppost). And especially he reveled in simple tools that could be applied to anything and simple formulas that he could compute in his head. (A friend described him as an expert carpenter but claimed that Gosset did almost all of his finer woodwork with nothing but a penknife!)

So Gosset discovered the *t* distribution and invented the *t* test—simplicity itself (compared to most of statistics)—for situations when samples are small and the variability of the larger population is unknown. Most of his work was done on the backs of envelopes, with plenty of minor errors in arithmetic that he had to weed out later. Characteristically, he published his paper on his "brewery methods" only when editors of scientific journals demanded it. However, the Guinness brewery did not allow its scientists to publish papers, because one Guinness scientist had revealed brewery secrets. To this day, most statisticians call the *t* distribution "Student's *t*" because Gosset wrote under the anonymous name "Student" so that the Guinness brewery would not know about his writings or be identified through his being known to be its employee. A few of his fellow statisticians knew who "student" was, but apparently meetings with others involved secrecy worthy of a spy novel. Supposedly, the brewery learned of his scientific fame only at his death, when colleagues wanted to honor him.

In spite of his great achievements, Gosset often wrote in letters that his own work provided "only a rough idea of the thing" or so-and-so "really worked out the complete mathematics." He was remembered as a thoughtful, kind, humble man, sensitive to others' feelings. Gosset's friendliness and generosity with his time and ideas also resulted in many students and younger colleagues making major breakthroughs based on his help. And it led to his becoming the mediator in a famous feud between two less humble giants in the field, Karl Pearson and Ronald Fisher, whom you will meet later.

Sources: Peters (1987); Salsburg (2001); Stigler (1986); Tankard (1984).

Step 2 is to determine the characteristics of the comparison distribution. In this example, its mean will be 2.5, what the survey found for students at your college generally (Population 2).

The next part of Step 2 is finding the variance of the distribution of means. Now you face a problem. Up to now in this book, you have always known the variance of the population of individuals. Using that variance, you then figured the variance of the distribution of means. However, in the present example, the variance of the number of hours studied for students at your college (the Population 2 students) was not reported in the newspaper article. So you email the paper. Unfortunately, the reporter did not calculate the variance, and the original survey results are no longer available. What to do?

BASIC PRINCIPLE OF THE *t* TEST: ESTIMATING THE POPULATION VARIANCE FROM THE SAMPLE SCORES

If you do not know the variance of the population of individuals, you can estimate it from what you do know—the scores of the people in your sample.

In the logic of hypothesis testing, the group of people you study is considered to be a random sample from a particular population. The variance of this sample ought to reflect the variance of that population. If the scores in the population have a lot of variation, then the scores in a sample randomly selected from that population should also have a lot of variation. If the population has very little variation, the scores in samples from that population should also not have much variation. Thus, it should be possible to use the variation among the scores in a sample to make an informed guess about the variation of the scores in the population. That is, you could figure the variance of the sample's scores, and that should be similar to the variance of the scores in the population (see Figure 8–1).

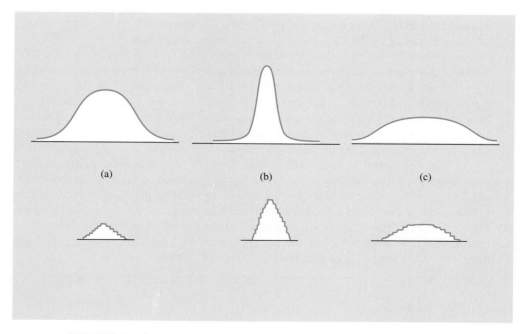

FIGURE 8–1   *Variation in samples (lower distributions) and variation in the populations they are taken from (upper distributions).*

There is, however, one small hitch. The variance of a sample will generally be slightly smaller than the variance of the population from which it is taken. For this reason, the variance of the sample is a **biased estimate** of the population variance.[1]

Fortunately, you can figure an **unbiased estimate of the population variance** by slightly changing the ordinary variance formula. The ordinary variance formula is the sum of the squared deviation scores divided by the number of scores. The changed procedure still starts with the sum of the squared deviation scores, but divides this sum by the number of scores *minus 1*. Dividing by a slightly smaller number makes the result slightly bigger. Dividing by the number of scores minus 1 makes the resulting variance just enough bigger to make it an unbiased estimate of the population variance. "Unbiased," incidentally, means that the estimate is equally likely to be too high as it is to be too low. It does *not* mean that your estimate will be exactly the true population variance.

The symbol we will use for the unbiased estimate of the population variance is S^2. The formula is the usual variance formula, but now dividing by $N - 1$ (instead of by N):

biased estimate

unbiased estimate of the population variance (S^2)

(8-1)
$$S^2 = \frac{\Sigma(X - M)^2}{N - 1}$$

| The estimated population variance is the sum of the squared deviation scores divided by the number of scores minus 1. |

Let's return to our example of hours spent studying and figure the estimated population variance from the sample's 16 scores. First, you figure the sum of squared deviation scores. (Subtract the mean from each of the scores, square those deviation scores, and add them.) Presume in our example that this comes out to 9.6. To get the estimated population variance, you divide this sum of squared deviation scores by the number of scores minus 1. That is, you divide 9.6 by $16 - 1$; 9.6 divided by 15 comes out to .64. In terms of the formula,

$$S^2 = \frac{\Sigma(X - M)^2}{N - 1} = \frac{9.6}{16 - 1} = \frac{9.6}{15} = .64$$

DEGREES OF FREEDOM

The number you divide by (the number of scores minus 1) to get the estimated population variance has a special name. It is called the **degrees of freedom (*df*).** It has this name because it is the number of scores in a sample that are "free to vary." The idea is that, when figuring the variance, you first have to know the mean. If you know the mean and all but one of the scores in the sample, you can figure out the one you don't know with a little arithmetic. Thus, once you know the mean, one of the scores in the sample is not free to have any possible value. So in this kind of situation the degrees of freedom is the number of scores minus 1. In terms of a formula,

degrees of freedom (*df*)

(8-2)
$$df = N - 1$$

| The degrees of freedom is the number of scores in the sample minus 1. |

[1]A sample's variance is slightly smaller than the population's because it is based on deviations from the sample's mean. A sample's mean is the optimal balance point for its scores. Thus, deviations of a sample's scores from its mean will be smaller than deviations from any other number. The mean of a sample generally is not exactly the same as the mean of the population it comes from. Thus, deviations of a sample's scores from its mean will generally be smaller than deviations of that sample's scores from the population mean.

In our example, $df = 16 - 1 = 15$. (In some situations you learn about in later chapters, the degrees of freedom are figured a bit differently. This is because in those situations, the number of scores free to vary is different. For all the situations you learn about in this chapter, $df = N - 1$.) The formula for the estimated population variance is often written using df instead of $N - 1$.

> The estimated population variance is the sum of squared deviation scores divided by the degrees of freedom.

$$S^2 = \frac{\Sigma(X - M)^2}{df}$$ (8-3)

THE STANDARD DEVIATION OF THE DISTRIBUTION OF MEANS

Once you have figured the estimated population variance, you can figure the standard deviation of the comparison distribution using the same procedures you learned in Chapter 6. As always, when you have a sample of more than one, the comparison distribution is a distribution of means. And the variance of a distribution of means is the variance of the population of individuals divided by the sample size. You have just estimated the variance of the population. Thus, you can estimate the variance of the distribution of means by dividing the estimated population variance by the sample size. The standard deviation of the distribution of means is the square root of its variance. Stated as formulas,

> The variance of the distribution of means based on an estimated population variance is the estimated population variance divided by the number of scores in the sample.

$$S_M^2 = \frac{S^2}{N}$$ (8-4)

> The standard deviation of the distribution of means based on an estimated population variance is the square root of the variance of the distribution of means based on an estimated population variance.

$$S_M = \sqrt{S_M^2}$$ (8-5)

Note that with an estimated population variance, the symbols for the variance and standard deviation of the distribution of means use S instead of Population SD.

In our example, the sample size was 16 and we worked out the estimated population variance to be .64.

The variance of the distribution of means, based on that estimate, will be .04. That is, .64 divided by 16 equals .04. The standard deviation is .2, the square root of .04. In terms of the formulas,

$$S_M^2 = \frac{S^2}{N} = \frac{.64}{16} = .04$$

$$S_M = \sqrt{S_M^2} = \sqrt{.04} = .2$$

THE SHAPE OF THE COMPARISON DISTRIBUTION WHEN USING AN ESTIMATED POPULATION VARIANCE: THE t DISTRIBUTION

In Chapter 6 you learned that when the population distribution follows a normal curve, the shape of the distribution of means will also be a normal curve. However, this changes when you do hypothesis testing using an estimated population variance. When you are using an estimated population variance, you have less true information and more room for error. The mathematical effect is that there are likely to be slightly more extreme means than in an exact normal curve. Furthermore, the smaller your sample size, the bigger this tendency. This is because, with a smaller sample size, your estimate of the population variance is based on less information.

The result of all of this is that, when doing hypothesis testing using an estimated variance, your comparison distribution will not be a normal curve. Instead, the comparison distribution will be a slightly different curve, called a **t distribution.**

t distribution

Actually, there is a whole family of *t* distributions. They vary in shape according to the degrees of freedom in the sample used to estimate the population variance. However, for any particular degrees of freedom, there is only one *t* distribution.

Generally, *t* distributions look to the eye like a normal curve—bell-shaped, completely symmetrical, and unimodal. A *t* distribution differs subtly in having heavier tails (that is, slightly more scores at the extremes). Figure 8–2 shows the shape of a *t* distribution compared to a normal curve.

This slight difference in shape affects how extreme a score you need to reject the null hypothesis. As always, to reject the null hypothesis, your sample mean has to be in an extreme section of the comparison distribution of means, such as the top 5%. However, if the comparison distribution has more of its means in the tails than a normal curve would have, then the point where the top 5% begins has to be further out on this comparison distribution. Thus, it takes a slightly more extreme sample mean to get a significant result when using a *t* distribution than when using a normal curve.

Just how much the *t* distribution differs from the normal curve depends on the degrees of freedom, the amount of information used in estimating the population variance. The *t* distribution differs most from the normal curve when the degrees of freedom are low (because your estimate of the population variance is based on a very small sample). For example, using the normal curve, you may recall that 1.64 is the cutoff for a one-tailed test at the .05 level. On a *t* distribution with 7 degrees of freedom (that is, with a sample size of 8), the cutoff is 1.895 for a one-tailed test at the .05 level. If the estimate is based on a larger sample, say, a sample of 25 (so that $df = 24$), the cutoff is 1.711, a cutoff much closer to that for the normal curve. If your sample size is infinite, the *t* distribution is the same as the normal curve. (Of course, if your sample size were infinite, it would include the entire population!) But even with sample sizes of 30 or more, the *t* distribution is nearly identical to the normal curve.

Shortly you will learn how to find the cutoff using a *t* distribution, but let's first return briefly to the example of how much students in your dormitory study each night. You finally have everything you need for Step 2 about the characteristics of the comparison distribution. We have already seen that the distribution of means in

FIGURE 8–2   *A t distribution (dashed line) compared to the normal curve (solid line).*

this example has a mean of 2.5 hours and a standard deviation of .2. You can now add that the shape of the comparison distribution will be a *t* distribution with 15 degrees of freedom.[2]

THE CUTOFF SAMPLE SCORE FOR REJECTING THE NULL HYPOTHESIS: USING THE *t* TABLE

t table

Step 3 of hypothesis testing is determining the cutoff for rejecting the null hypothesis. There is a different *t* distribution for any particular degrees of freedom. However, to avoid taking up pages and pages with tables for each different *t* distribution, you use a simplified table that gives only the crucial cutoff points. We have included such a **_t_ table** in the Appendix (Table A–2). Just as with the normal curve table, the *t* table only shows positive *t* scores. If you have a one-tailed test, you need to decide if your cutoff score is a positive *t* score or a negative *t* score. If your one-tailed test is testing whether the mean of Population 1 is greater than the mean of Population 2, the cutoff *t* score is positive. However, if your one-tailed test is testing whether the mean of Population 1 is less than the mean of Population 2, the cutoff *t* score is negative.

In the hours-studied example, you have a one-tailed test. (You want to know whether students in your dormitory study *more* than students in general at your college study.) You will probably want to use the 5% significance level because the cost of a Type I error (mistakenly rejecting the null hypothesis) is not great. You have 16 people, making 15 degrees of freedom for your estimate of the population variance.

Table 8–1 shows a portion of the *t* table from Table A–2 in the Appendix. Find the column for the .05 significance level for one-tailed tests and move down to the row for 15 degrees of freedom. The crucial cutoff is 1.753. Just as with the normal curve table, the *t* table only shows positive *t* scores. So, if you have a one-tailed test, you need to decide if your cutoff score is a positive *t* score or a negative *t* score. In this example, you are testing whether students in your dormitory (Population 1) study *more* than students in general at your college (Population 2). In other words, you are testing whether students in your dormitory have a higher *t* score than students in general. This means that the cutoff *t* score is positive. You will reject the null hypothesis if your sample's mean is 1.753 or more standard deviations above the mean on the comparison distribution. (If you were using a known variance, you would have found your cutoff from a normal curve table. The Z score needed to reject the null hypothesis based on the normal curve would have been 1.645.)

One other point about using the *t* table: In the full *t* table in the Appendix, there are rows for each degree of freedom from 1 through 30, then for 35, 40, 45, and so on, up to 100. Suppose your study has degrees of freedom between two of these higher values. To be safe, you should use the nearest degrees of freedom to your's that is given in the table that is *less* than yours. For example, in a study with 43 degrees of freedom, you would use the cutoff for *df* = 40.

---

[2]Statisticians make a subtle distinction in this situation between the comparison distribution and the distribution of means. (We avoid this distinction to simplify your learning of what is already fairly difficult.) The general procedure of hypothesis testing with means of samples, as you learned it in Chapter 6, can be described as figuring a Z score for your sample's mean, and then comparing this Z score to a cutoff Z score from the normal curve table. We described this process as using the distribution of means as your comparison distribution. Statisticians would say that actually you are comparing your computed Z score to a distribution of Z scores (which is simply an ordinary normal curve). Similarly, for a *t* test, you will see shortly that we figure what is called a *t* score in the same way as a Z score, but using a standard deviation of the distribution of means based on an estimated population variance. The *t* score is then compared to a cutoff *t* score from a *t* distribution table. According to the formal statistical logic, you can think of this process as involving a comparison distribution of *t* scores, not of means.

| TABLE 8–1 | Cutoff Scores for *t* Distributions with 1 Through 17 Degrees of Freedom (Highlighting Cutoff for Hours Studied Example) |

	One-Tailed Tests			Two-Tailed Tests		
df	.10	.05	.01	.10	.05	.01
1	3.078	6.314	31.821	6.314	12.706	63.657
2	1.886	2.920	6.965	2.920	4.303	9.925
3	1.638	2.353	4.541	2.353	3.182	5.841
4	1.533	2.132	3.747	2.132	2.776	4.604
5	1.476	2.015	3.365	2.015	2.571	4.032
6	1.440	1.943	3.143	1.943	2.447	3.708
7	1.415	1.895	2.998	1.895	2.365	3.500
8	1.397	1.860	2.897	1.860	2.306	3.356
9	1.383	1.833	2.822	1.833	2.262	3.250
10	1.372	1.813	2.764	1.813	2.228	3.170
11	1.364	1.796	2.718	1.796	2.201	3.106
12	1.356	1.783	2.681	1.783	2.179	3.055
13	1.350	1.771	2.651	1.771	2.161	3.013
14	1.345	1.762	2.625	1.762	2.145	2.977
15	1.341	1.753	2.603	1.753	2.132	2.947
16	1.337	1.746	2.584	1.746	2.120	2.921
17	1.334	1.740	2.567	1.740	2.110	2.898

THE SAMPLE MEAN'S SCORE ON THE COMPARISON DISTRIBUTION: THE *t* SCORE

Step 4 of hypothesis testing is figuring your sample mean's score on the comparison distribution. In Chapter 6, this meant finding the *Z* score on the comparison distribution—the number of standard deviations your sample's mean is from the mean on the comparison distribution. You do exactly the same thing when your comparison distribution is a *t* distribution. The only difference is that, instead of calling this a *Z* score, because it is from a *t* distribution, you call it a **t score.** In terms of a formula,

t score

The *t* score is your sample's mean minus the population mean, divided by the standard deviation of the distribution of means.

$$(8\text{-}6) \qquad t = \frac{M - \text{Population } M}{S_M}$$

In the example, your sample's mean of 3.2 is .7 hours from the mean of the distribution of means, which amounts to 3.5 standard deviations from the mean (.7 hours divided by the standard deviation of .2 hours). That is, the *t* score in the example is 3.5. In terms of the formula,

$$t = \frac{M - \text{Population } M}{S_M} = \frac{3.2 - 2.5}{.2} = \frac{.7}{.2} = 3.5$$

DECIDING WHETHER TO REJECT THE NULL HYPOTHESIS

Step 5 of hypothesis testing is deciding whether to reject the null hypothesis. This step is exactly the same with a *t* test as it was in those discussed in previous chapters. You compare the cutoff score from Step 3 with the sample's score on the

FIGURE 8–3 *Distributions for the hours studied example.*

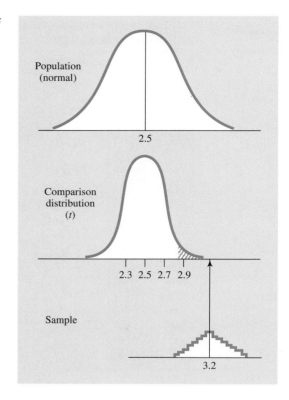

comparison distribution from Step 4. In the example, the cutoff *t* score was 1.753 and the actual *t* score for our sample was 3.5. Conclusion: Reject the null hypothesis. The research hypothesis is supported that students in your dormitory study more than students in the college overall.

Figure 8–3 shows the various distributions for this example.

SUMMARY OF HYPOTHESIS TESTING WHEN THE POPULATION VARIANCE IS NOT KNOWN

Table 8–2 compares the hypothesis-testing procedure we just considered (for a *t* test for a single sample) with the hypothesis testing procedure from Chapter 6 (for a *Z* test for a single sample). That is, we are comparing the current situation in which you know the population's mean but not its variance to the Chapter 6 situation where you knew the population's mean *and* variance. Table 8–3 summarizes the steps of hypothesis testing for the *t* test for a single sample.

HOW ARE YOU DOING?

1. In what sense is a sample's variance a biased estimate of the variance of the population the sample is taken from? That is, in what way does the sample's variance typically differ from the population's?
2. What is the difference between the usual formula for figuring the variance and the formula for estimating a population's variance from the scores in a sample?
3. (a) What are degrees of freedom? (b) How do you figure the degrees of freedom in a *t* test for a single sample? (c) What do they have to do with estimating the population variance? (d) What do they have to do with the *t* distribution?

TABLE 8–2 Hypothesis Testing with a Single Sample Mean When Population Variance Is Unknown (*t* Test for a Single Sample) Compared to When Population Variance is Known (*Z* Test for a Single Sample)

Steps in Hypothesis Testing	Difference From When Population Variance Is Known
❶ Restate the question as a research hypothesis and a null hypothesis about the populations.	No difference in method.
❷ Determine the characteristics of the comparison distribution:	
Population mean	No difference in method.
Population variance	Estimate from the sample.
Standard deviation of the distribution of sample means	No difference in method (but based on estimated population variance).
Shape of the comparison distribution	Use the *t* distribution with $df = N - 1$.
❸ Determine the significance cutoff.	Use the *t* table.
❹ Determine your sample's score on the comparison distribution.	No difference in method (but called at *t* score).
❺ Decide whether to reject the null hypothesis.	No difference in method.

4. (a) How does a *t* distribution differ from a normal curve? (b) How do degrees of freedom affect this? (c) What is the effect of the difference on hypothesis testing?
5. List three differences in how you do hypothesis testing for a *t* test for a single sample versus for a *Z* test for a single sample (what you learned in Chapter 6).
6. A population has a mean of 23. A sample of 4 is given an experimental procedure and has scores of 20, 22, 22, and 20. Test the hypothesis that the procedure produces a lower score. Use the .05 significance level. (a) Use the steps of hypothesis testing and (b) make a sketch of the distributions involved.

ANSWERS:

1. The sample's variance will in general be smaller than the variance of the population the sample is taken from.

TABLE 8–3 Steps for a *t* Test for a Single Sample

❶ **Restate the question as a research hypothesis and a null hypothesis about the populations.**

❷ **Determine the characteristics of the comparison distribution.**

   a. The mean is the same as the known population mean.
   b. The standard deviation is figured as follows:
      ❹ Figure the estimated population variance: $S^2 = \Sigma (X - M)^2/df$
      ❺ Figure the variance of the distribution of means: $S_M^2 = S^2/N$
      ❻ Figure the standard deviation of the distribution of means: $S_M = \sqrt{S_M^2}$
   c. The shape is a *t* distribution with $N - 1$ degrees of freedom.

❸ **Determine the cutoff sample score on the comparison distribution at which the null hypothesis should be rejected.**

   a. Decide the significance level and whether to use a one-tailed or a two-tailed test.
   b. Look up the appropriate cutoff in a *t* table.

❹ **Determine your sample's score on the comparison distribution:** $t = (M - \text{Population } M)/S_M$

❺ **Decide whether to reject the null hypothesis:** Compare the scores from Steps 3 and 4.

2. In the usual formula you divide by the number of participants (N); in the formula for estimating a population's variance from the scores in a sample, you divide by the number of participants in the sample minus 1 ($N - 1$).

3. (a) The number of scores free to vary. (b) The number of scores in the sample minus 1. (c) In estimating the population variance, the formula is the sum of squared deviations divided by the degrees of freedom. (d) t distributions differ slightly from each other according to the degrees of freedom.

4. (a) It has heavier tails; that is, more scores at the extremes. (b) The more degrees of freedom, the closer the shape (including the tails) to a normal curve. (c) The cutoffs for significance are more extreme for a t distribution than for a normal curve.

5. In the t test you (a) estimate the population variance from the sample (it is not known in advance); (b) you look up the cutoff on a t table in which you also have to take into account the degrees of freedom (you don't use a normal curve table); and (c) your sample's score on the comparison distribution, which is a t distribution (not a normal curve), is a t score (not a Z score).

6. (a) Steps of hypothesis testing:

❶ **Restate the question as a research hypothesis and a null hypothesis about the populations.** There are two populations:

Population 1: People who are given the experimental procedure.

Population 2: The general population.

The research hypothesis is that Population 1 will score lower than Population 2. The null hypothesis is that Population 1 will not score lower than Population 2.

❷ **Determine the characteristics of the comparison distribution.**
a. The mean of the distribution of means is 23.
b. The standard deviation is figured as follows:
   ❹ Figure the estimated population variance. You first need to figure the sample mean, which is $(20 + 22 + 22 + 20)/4 = 84/4 = 21$. The estimated population variance is $S^2 = \Sigma(X - M)^2/(df) = [(20 - 21)^2 + (22 - 21)^2 + (22 - 21)^2 + (20 - 21)^2]/(4 - 1) = (-1^2 + 1^2 + 1^2 + -1^2)/3 = (1 + 1 + 1 + 1)/3 = 4/3 = 1.33$.
   ❺ Figure the variance of the distribution of means:
$$S_M^2 = S^2/N = 1.33/4 = .33.$$
   ❻ Figure the standard deviation of the distribution of means:
$$S_M = \sqrt{S_M^2} = \sqrt{.33} = .57.$$
c. The shape of the comparison distribution will be a t distribution with $df = 3$.

❸ **Determine the cutoff sample score on the comparison distribution at which the null hypothesis should be rejected.** From Table A–2, the cutoff for a one-tailed t test at the .05 level for $df = 3$ is -2.353. The cutoff t score is negative, since the hypothesis is that the procedure produces a *lower* score.

❹ **Determine your sample's score on the comparison distribution.** $t = (M - $ Population $M)/S_M = (21 - 23)/.57 = -2/.57 = -3.51$.

❺ **Decide whether to reject the null hypothesis.** The t of -3.51 is more extreme than the cutoff t of -2.353. Therefore, reject the null hypothesis; the research hypothesis is supported.

(b) Sketches of distributions are shown in Figure 8–4.

THE t TEST FOR DEPENDENT MEANS

The situation you just learned about (the t test for a single sample) is for when you know the population mean but not its variance, and where you have a single sample of scores. It turns out that in most research you do not even know the population's *mean*; plus, in most research situations, you usually have not one set but *two* sets of

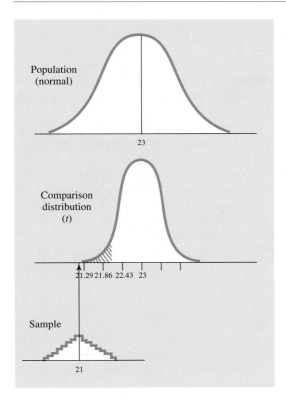

FIGURE 8–4 *Distributions for answer to "How Are You Doing?" question 6b.*

scores. These two things, not knowing the population mean and having two sets of scores, almost always go together. This situation is very common.

The rest of this chapter focuses specifically on the important research situation in which you have two scores from each person in your sample. This kind of research situation is called a **repeated-measures design** (also known as a *within-subjects design*). A common example is when you measure the same people before and after some social or psychological intervention. For example, an organizational specialist might measure days missed from work for 80 workers before and after a new health promotion program was introduced.

The hypothesis-testing procedure for the situation in which each person is measured twice is called a ***t* test for dependent means.** It has the name *dependent means* because the mean for each group of scores (for example, a group of before-scores and a group of after-scores) are dependent on each other in that they are both from the same people. (In Chapter 9, we consider the situation in which you compare scores from two different groups of people, a research design analyzed by a *t* test for *independent* means.)

The *t* test for dependent means is also called a *t test for paired samples*, a *t test for correlated means*, and a *t test for matched samples*. Each of these names comes from the same idea that in this kind of *t* test you are comparing two sets of scores that are related to each other in a direct way, such as each person being tested before and after some procedure.

You do a *t* test for dependent means in exactly the same way as a *t* test for a single sample, except that (a) you use something called *difference scores* and (b) you assume that the population mean (of the difference scores) is 0.

repeated-measures design

***t* test for dependent means**

DIFFERENCE SCORES

difference scores

With a repeated-measures design, your sample includes two scores for each person instead of just one. The way you handle this is to make the two scores per person into one score per person! You do this magic by creating **difference scores:** For each person, you subtract one score from the other. If the difference is before versus after, difference scores are also called *change scores*.

Consider the health-promotion, absence-from-work example. The organizational specialist subtracts the number of days missed from work for the month before the program from the number of days missed during the month after the program. This gives an after-minus-before difference score for each employee. When the two scores are a before-score and an after-score, you usually take the after-score minus the before-score to indicate the *change*.

Once you have the difference score for each person in the study, you do the rest of the hypothesis testing with difference scores. That is, you treat the study as if there were a single sample of scores (scores that in this situation happen to be difference scores).[3]

POPULATION OF DIFFERENCE SCORES WITH A MEAN OF 0

So far in the research situations we have considered in this book, you have always known the mean of the population to which you compared your sample's mean. For example, in the college dormitory survey of hours studied, you knew the population mean was 2.5 hours. However, now we are using difference scores, and we usually don't know the mean of the population of difference scores.

Here is the solution. Ordinarily, the null hypothesis in a repeated-measures design is that on the average there is no difference between the two groups of scores. For example, the null hypothesis in the health promotion study is that on average there is no difference between absences from work before and after the health promotion program is started. What does *no difference* mean? Saying there is on average no difference is the same as saying that the mean of the population of the difference scores is 0. Therefore, when working with difference scores, you are comparing the population of difference scores that your sample of difference scores comes from to a population of difference scores with a mean of 0. In other words, with a *t* test for dependent means, what we call Population 2 will ordinarily have a mean of 0.

EXAMPLE OF A *t* TEST FOR DEPENDENT MEANS

Olthoff (1989) tested the communication quality of engaged couples 3 months before and again 3 months after marriage. One group studied was 19 couples who received ordinary premarital counseling from the ministers who were going to marry them. (To keep the example simple, we will focus on just this one group, and only on the husbands in the group. Scores for wives were similar, though somewhat more varied, making it a more complicated example for learning the *t* test procedure.)

---

[3]You can also use a *t* test for dependent means when you have scores from pairs of research participants. You consider each pair as if it were one person and figure a difference score for each pair. For example, suppose you have 30 married couples and want to test whether husbands are consistently older than wives. You could figure for each couple a difference score of husband's age minus wife's age. The rest of the figuring would then be exactly the same as for an ordinary *t* test for dependent means. When the *t* test for dependent means is used in this way, it is sometimes called a *t test for matched pairs*.

TABLE 8–4 *t* Test for Communication Quality Scores Before and After Marriage for 19 Husbands Who Received No Special Communication Training

Husband	Communication Quality		Difference (After – Before)	Deviation (Difference – M)	Squared Deviation
	Before	*After*			
A	126	115	− 11	1.05	1.1
B	133	125	− 8	4.05	16.4
C	126	96	− 30	−17.95	322.2
D	115	115	0	12.05	145.2
E	108	119	11	23.05	531.3
F	109	82	− 27	−14.95	233.5
G	124	93	− 31	−18.95	359.1
H	98	109	11	23.05	531.3
I	95	72	− 23	−10.95	119.9
J	120	104	− 16	− 3.95	15.6
K	118	107	− 11	1.05	1.1
L	126	118	− 8	4.05	16.4
M	121	102	− 19	− 6.95	48.3
N	116	115	− 1	11.05	122.1
O	94	83	− 11	1.05	1.1
P	105	87	− 18	− 5.95	35.4
Q	123	121	− 2	10.05	101.0
R	125	100	− 25	−12.95	167.7
S	128	118	− 10	2.05	4.2
Σ:	2,210	1,981	−229		2,772.9

For difference scores:

$M = -229/19 = -12.05$.

Population $M = 0$ (assumed as a no-change baseline of comparison).

$S^2 = \Sigma(X - M)^2/df = 2,772.9/(19 - 1) = 154.05$.

$S_M^2 = S^2/N = 154.05/19 = 8.11$.

$S_M = \sqrt{S_M^2} = \sqrt{8.11} = 2.85$.

t with $df = 18$ needed for 5% level, two-tailed $= \pm 2.101$.

$t = (M - \text{Population } M)/S_M = (-12.05 - 0)/2.85 = -4.23$.

Decision: Reject the null hypothesis.

Source: Data from Olthoff (1989).

The scores for the 19 husbands are listed in the "Before" and "After" columns in Table 8–4, followed by all the *t* test figuring. The crucial column for starting the analysis is the difference scores. For example, the first husband, whose communication quality was 126 before marriage and 115 after, had a difference of −11. (You usually figure after minus before, so that an increase is positive and a decrease, as for this husband, is negative.) The mean of the difference scores is −12.05. That is, on the average, these 19 husbands' communication quality decreased by about 12 points.

Is this decrease significant? In other words, how likely is it that this sample of difference scores is a random sample from a population of change scores whose

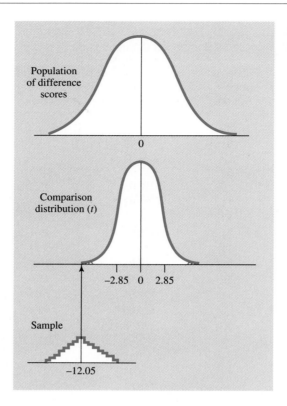

FIGURE 8-5 *Distributions for the Olthoff (1989) example of a t test for dependent means.*

mean is 0? Let's carry out the hypothesis-testing procedure. (The distributions involved are shown in Figure 8–5.)

❶ Restate the question as a research hypothesis and a null hypothesis about the populations. There are two populations:

> **Population 1:** Husbands who receive ordinary premarital counseling.
>
> **Population 2:** Husbands whose communication quality does not change from before to after marriage.

The research hypothesis is that Population 1's mean difference score (communication quality after marriage minus communication quality before marriage) is different from Population 2's mean difference score. That is, the research hypothesis is that husbands who receive ordinary premarital counseling (such as the husbands Olthoff studied) *do* change in communication quality from before to after marriage. The null hypothesis is that the populations are the same. That is, the null hypothesis is that the husbands who receive ordinary premarital counseling do *not* change in their communication quality from before to after marriage.

Notice that you have no actual information about Population 2 husbands. The husbands in the study are a sample of Population 1 husbands. In fact, if the research hypothesis is correct, Population 2 husbands do not even really exist. For the purposes of hypothesis testing, you set up Population 2 as a kind of straw man comparison group. That is, you set up a comparison group for purposes of the analysis of husbands who, if measured before and after marriage, would on average show no difference.

❷ **Determine the characteristics of the comparison distribution.** If the null hypothesis is true, the mean of the population of difference scores is 0. The variance of the population of difference scores can be estimated from the sample of difference scores. As shown in Table 8–4, the sum of squared deviations of the difference scores from the mean of the difference scores is 2,772.9. With 19 husbands in the study, there are 18 degrees of freedom. Dividing the sum of squared deviation scores by the degrees of freedom gives an estimated population variance of difference scores of 154.05.

The distribution of means of difference scores has a mean of 0, the same as the mean of the population of difference scores. The variance of the distribution of means of difference scores is the estimated population variance of difference scores (154.05) divided by the sample size (19), which gives 8.11. The standard deviation of the distribution of means of difference scores is 2.85, the square root of 8.11.

Because Olthoff was using an estimated population variance, the comparison distribution is a *t* distribution. The estimate of the population variance of difference scores is based on 18 degrees of freedom, so this comparison distribution is a *t* distribution for 18 degrees of freedom.

❸ **Determine the cutoff sample score on the comparison distribution at which the null hypothesis should be rejected.** Olthoff used a two-tailed test to allow for either an increase or a decrease in communication quality. Using the .05 significance level, and 18 degrees of freedom, Table A–2 shows that to reject the null hypothesis you need a *t* score of +2.101 or above, or a *t* score of −2.101 or below.

❹ **Determine your sample's score on the comparison distribution.** Olthoff's sample had a mean difference score of −12.05. That is, the mean was 12.05 points below the mean of 0 on the distribution of means of difference scores. The standard deviation of the distribution of means of difference scores is 2.85. Thus, the mean of the difference scores of −12.05 is 4.23 standard deviations below the mean of the distribution of means of difference scores. So Olthoff's sample of difference scores has a *t* score of −4.23.

❺ **Decide whether to reject the null hypothesis.** The *t* of −4.23 for the sample of difference scores is more extreme than the needed *t* of ± 2.101. Thus, Olthoff could reject the null hypothesis. This suggests that the husbands are from a population in which husbands' communication quality is different after marriage from what it was before (it got lower).

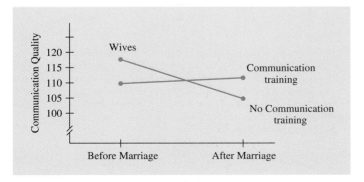

FIGURE 8–6 *Communication skills of wives given premarital communications training and wives not given such training. (Based on Olthoff, 1989.)*

Olthoff's actual study was more complex. You may be interested to know that he found that the wives also showed this decrease in communication quality after marriage. But a group of similar engaged couples who were given special communication-skills training by their ministers (much more than the usual short sessions) had no significant decline in marital communication quality after marriage (see Figure 8–6). In fact, there is now a great deal of research showing that relationship quality of all kinds on the average declines from before to after marriage (e.g., Karney & Bradbury, 1997) and that intensive communication skills training can be very helpful in reducing or eliminating this decline (Markman, Renick, Floyd, Stanley, & Clements, 1993).

SUMMARY OF STEPS FOR A t TEST FOR DEPENDENT MEANS

Table 8–5 summarizes the steps for a t test for dependent means.[4]

TABLE 8–5 **Steps for a t Test for Dependent Means**

❶ **Restate the question as a research hypothesis and a null hypothesis about the populations.**

❷ **Determine the characteristics of the comparison distribution.**
   a. Make each person's two scores into a difference score. Do all the remaining steps using these difference scores.
   b. Figure the mean of the difference scores.
   c. Assume a mean of the distribution of means of difference scores of 0.
   d. The standard deviation of the distribution of means of difference scores is figured as follows:

   ❹ Figure the estimated population variance of difference scores: $S^2 = \Sigma(X - M)^2/df$
   ❽ Figure the variance of the distribution of means of difference scores: $S_M^2 = S^2/N$
   ❿ Figure the standard deviation of the distribution of means of difference scores:
   $$S_M = \sqrt{S_M^2}$$

   e. The shape is a t distribution with $N - 1$ degrees of freedom.

❸ **Determine the cutoff sample score on the comparison distribution at which the null hypothesis should be rejected.**
   a. Decide the significance level and whether to use a one-tailed or a two-tailed test.
   b. Look up the appropriate cutoff in a t table.

❹ **Determine your sample's score on the comparison distribution:** $t = (M - \text{Population } M)/S_M$

❺ **Decide whether to reject the null hypothesis:** Compare the scores from Steps 3 and 4.

---

[4]The usual steps of carrying out a t test for dependent means can be somewhat combined into computational formulas for S and t based on difference scores. For purposes of learning the ideas, we strongly recommend that you use the regular procedures as we have discussed them in this chapter when doing the practice problems. In a real research situation, the figuring is usually done by computer. However, if you ever have to do a t test for dependent means for an actual research study by hand (without a computer), you may find these formulas useful.

D in the formulas below is for difference score:

$$S = \sqrt{\frac{\Sigma D^2 - ((\Sigma D)^2/N)}{N - 1}} \qquad (8\text{-}7)$$

$$t = \frac{\Sigma D/N}{S/\sqrt{N}} \qquad (8\text{-}8)$$

A Second Example of a *t* Test for Dependent Means

Here is another example. A researcher is studying a theory that predicts that people feel more positively toward their government during a war. To test this idea, the researcher surveys a randomly selected group of nine people about their attitudes toward their government while their country is at war and then surveys them again a year after the war is over. (In a real study, the researcher would use a much larger sample. We have made the sample size small to keep the example simple.) The prediction was that people are more pro-government during the war.

Table 8–6 shows the results of this fictional study. It also shows the figuring of difference scores and all the other figuring for the *t* test for dependent means. Figure 8–7 shows the distributions involved. Using the steps shown in Table 8–5, here are the steps of hypothesis testing:

❶ **Restate the question as a research hypothesis and a null hypothesis about the populations.** There are two populations:

> **Population 1:** People in the country studied.

> **Population 2:** People who are not more pro-government during a war than they are one year after a war.

The research hypothesis is that Population 1's mean difference score (pro-government attitudes during war minus pro-government after war) is greater than

TABLE 8–6 *t* Test for a Study of Pro-Government Attitudes During versus One Year After a War (Fictional Data)

Survey Respondent	Conditions		Difference	Deviation	Squared Deviation
	During War	1 Year After	(During – After)	(Difference – *M*)	
1	18	12	6	6−2 = 4	16
2	21	21	0	−2	4
3	19	16	3	1	1
4	21	16	5	3	9
5	17	19	−2	−4	16
6	20	19	1	−1	1
7	18	16	2	0	0
8	16	17	−1	−3	9
9	20	16	4	2	4
Σ:	170	152	18	0	60

For difference scores:

$M = 18/9 = 2.0$.

Population $M = 0$ (assumed as a no-change baseline of comparison).

$S^2 = \Sigma(X - M)^2/df = 60/(9 - 1) = 60/8 = 7.5$.

$S_M^2 = S^2/N = 7.50/9 = .83$.

$S_M = \sqrt{S_M^2} = \sqrt{.83} = .91$.

t for $df = 8$ needed for 5% significance level, one-tailed = 1.860.

$t = (M - \text{Population } M)/S_M = (2.00 - 0)/.91 = 2.20$.

Decision: Reject the null hypothesis.

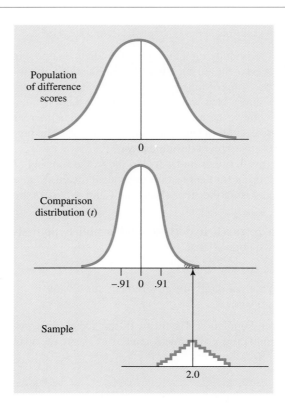

Population 2's.[5] That is, the research hypothesis is that people in the country studied *are* more pro-government during a war than one year after. The null hypothesis is that Population 1's mean difference score is not greater than Population 2's mean difference score. That is, the null hypothesis is that people in the country studied are not more pro-government during a war than they are one year after a war.

❷ **Determine the characteristics of the comparison distribution.**
   a. Make each person's two scores into a difference score. This is shown in the column labeled "Difference" in Table 8–6. Do all the remaining steps using these difference scores.
   b. Figure the mean of the difference scores. The sum of the difference scores (18) divided by the number of difference scores (9) gives a mean of the difference scores of 2.0: $M = 2.0$.
   c. Assume a mean of the distribution of means of difference scores of 0: Population $M = 0$.
   d. The standard deviation of the distribution of means of difference scores is figured as follows:

[5]You could also have thought of this example in terms of difference scores of pro-government attitudes *after* the war minus pro-government attitudes *during* the war. This would not change the end result of the hypothesis testing. However, the research hypothesis would be a little different. In this case, the research hypothesis would be that Population 1's mean difference score is *less than* Population 2's. This is because the researcher predicts lower pro-government attitudes after the war than during the war. The sample's mean difference score would be -2.0 (compared to the $+2.0$ shown in Table 8–6). Also, the cutoff t score would be -1.860 (not $+1.860$) and the sample's t score would come out to be -2.20 (not $+2.20$), allowing the null hypothesis to be rejected.

❹ Figure the estimated population variance of difference scores: $S^2 = \Sigma (X - M)^2/(df) = 60/(9 - 1) = 7.50$.

❺ Figure the variance of the distribution of means of difference scores: $S_M^2 = S^2/N = 7.50/9 = .83$.

❻ Figure the standard deviation of the distribution of means of difference scores: $S_M = \sqrt{S_M^2} = \sqrt{.83} = .91$.

e. The shape is a *t* distribution with $df = N - 1$. Therefore, the comparison distribution is a *t* distribution for 8 degrees of freedom. It is a *t* distribution because we figured its variance based on an estimated population variance. It has 8 degrees of freedom because there were 8 degrees of freedom in the estimate of the population variance.

❸ **Determine the cutoff sample score on the comparison distribution at which the null hypothesis should be rejected.**

a. We will use the standard .05 significance level. This is a one-tailed test because there was a reasonable basis for predicting the direction of the difference.

b. Using the .05 significance level with 8 degrees of freedom, Table A–2 shows a cutoff *t* of 1.860.

❹ **Determine your sample's score on the comparison distribution.** $t = (M - \text{Population } M)/S_M = (2.0 - 0)/.91 = 2.20$. The sample's mean difference of 2.0 is 2.20 standard deviations (of .91 each) above the mean of 0 on the distribution of means of difference scores.

❺ **Decide whether to reject the null hypothesis.** The sample's *t* score of 2.20 is more extreme than the cutoff *t* of 1.860. You can reject the null hypothesis. People in the country studied have a more positive attitude toward their government in war time.

You may be interested to know that McLeod, Everland, and Signorielli (1994) did an actual study of this kind. They surveyed 167 people in the United States by telephone during the 1991 Persian Gulf War and then surveyed these same people again one year after the war. Their results, like the fictional example here, showed significantly greater pro-government attitudes during the war than after.

HOW ARE YOU DOING?

---

1. Describe the situation in which you would use a *t* test for dependent means.
2. When doing a *t* test for dependent means, what do you do with the two scores you have for each participant?
3. In a *t* test for dependent means, (a) what is usually considered to be the mean of the "known" population (Population 2), and (b) why?
4. Five individuals are tested before and after an experimental procedure; their scores are given below. Test the hypothesis that there is no change, using the .05 significance level. (a) Use the steps of hypothesis testing and (b) sketch the distributions involved.

Person	Before	After
1	20	30
2	30	50
3	20	10
4	40	30
5	30	40

| TABLE 8–7 | Figuring for Answer to "How Are You Doing?" Question 4 |

Person	Score		Difference	Deviation	Squared Deviation
	Before	After	(After − Before)	(Difference − M)	
1	20	30	10	6	36
2	30	50	20	16	256
3	20	10	−10	−14	196
4	40	30	−10	−14	196
5	30	40	10	6	36
Σ:	140	160	20		720

For difference scores:

$M = 20/5 = 4.$

Population $M = 0$.

$S^2 = \Sigma(X - M)^2/df = 720/(5 - 1) = 720/4 = 180.$

$S_M^2 = S^2/N = 180/5 = 36.$

$S_M = \sqrt{S_M^2} = \sqrt{36} = 6.$

t for $df = 4$ needed for 5% significance level, two-tailed = ± 2.776.

$t = (M - \text{Population } M)/S_M = (4 - 0)/6 = .67$

Decision: Do not reject the null hypothesis.

ANSWERS:

1. It is used when you are doing hypothesis testing and you have two scores for each participant (such as a before-score and an after-score) and the population variance is unknown.
2. Subtract one from the other to create a difference (or change) score for each person. The t test is then done with these difference (or change) scores.
3. (a) 0. (b) Because you are comparing your sample to a situation in which there is no difference—a population of difference scores in which the average difference is 0.
4. (a) Steps of hypothesis testing (all figuring is shown in Table 8–7):

    ❶ **Restate the question as a research hypothesis and a null hypothesis about the populations.** There are two populations:

    Population 1: People like those tested before and after the experimental procedure.

    Population 2: People whose scores are the same before and after the experimental procedure.

    The research hypothesis is that Population 1's mean change scores (after minus before) is different than Population 2's. The null hypothesis is that Population 1's change is the same as Population 2's.

    ❷ **Determine the characteristics of the comparison distribution.** The mean of the distribution of means of difference scores (the comparison distribution) is 0. The standard deviation of the distribution of means of difference scores is 6. It is a t distribution with 4 degrees of freedom.

    ❸ **Determine the cutoff sample score on the comparison distribution at which the null hypothesis should be rejected.** For a two-tailed test at the .05 level, the cutoff sample t scores are 2.776 and −2.776.

    ❹ **Determine your sample's score on the comparison distribution.** $t = (4 - 0)/6 = .67$.

    ❺ **Decide whether to reject the null hypothesis.** The sample's t score of .67 is not more extreme than the cutoff t of ± 2.776. Therefore, do *not* reject the null hypothesis.

    (b) The distributions are shown in Figure 8–8.

FIGURE 8–8 *Distributions for answer to "How Are You Doing?" question 4.*

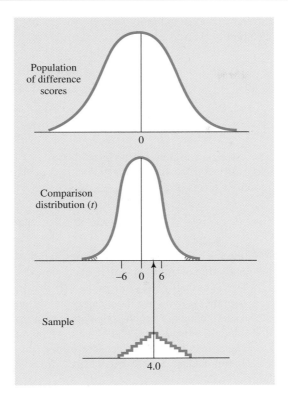

ASSUMPTIONS OF THE *t* TEST

As you have seen, when using an estimated population variance, the comparison distribution is a *t* distribution. However, the comparison distribution will be exactly a *t* distribution only if the distribution of individuals follows a normal curve. Otherwise, the comparison distribution will follow some other (usually unknown) shape.

Thus, strictly speaking, a normal population is a requirement within the logic and mathematics of the *t* test. A requirement like this for a hypothesis-testing procedure is called an **assumption.** That is, a normal population distribution is one assumption of the *t* test. You can think of an assumption as a requirement that you must meet for the results of a hypothesis testing procedure to be accurate. In this case, the effect of this assumption of a normal population is that if the population distribution is not normal, the comparison distribution will be some unknown shape other than a *t* distribution—and thus the cutoffs on the *t* table will be incorrect.

Unfortunately, when you do a *t* test, you don't know whether the population is normal. This is because when doing a *t* test, usually all you have are the scores in your sample. Fortunately, however, as you saw in Chapter 4, distributions in the social and behavioral sciences quite often do approximate a normal curve. (This also applies to distributions of difference scores.) Also, statisticians have found that in practice, you get reasonably accurate results with *t* tests even when the population is rather far from normal. The only very common situation in which using a *t* test for dependent means is likely to give a seriously distorted result is when you are using a one-tailed test and the population is highly skewed (that is, it is very asymmetrical, with a much longer tail on one side than the other). Thus, you need to be cautious about your conclusions when doing a one-tailed test if the sample of

assumption

difference scores is highly skewed, suggesting that the population it comes from is also highly skewed.

EFFECT SIZE AND POWER FOR THE t TEST FOR DEPENDENT MEANS[6]

EFFECT SIZE

The estimated effect size for a study using a t test is the mean of the difference scores divided by the estimated standard deviation of the population of difference scores. In terms of a formula,

$$\text{Estimated Effect Size} = M / S \qquad (8\text{-}9)$$

M is the mean of the difference scores and S is the estimated standard deviation of the population of individual difference scores.

This is basically the same as the way you learned to figure effect size in Chapter 7, except that (a) you use the mean of the difference scores instead of the difference of the sample mean from the population mean, and (b) you use an estimated population standard deviation instead of a known population standard deviation.

The conventions for effect size are the same as you learned for the situation we considered in Chapter 7: A small effect size is .20, a medium effect size is .50, and a large effect size is .80.

Consider our first example of a t test for dependent means, the study of husbands' change in communication quality. In that study, the mean of the difference scores was -12.05. The estimated population standard deviation of the difference scores would be 12.41. That is, we figured the estimated variance of the difference scores (S^2) to be 154.05; $S = \sqrt{S^2} = 12.41$. Therefore, the effect size is -12.05 divided by 12.41, which is $-.97$. This is a very large effect size. (The negative sign for the effect size means that the large effect was a decrease.)

POWER

Table 8–8 gives the approximate power at the .05 significance level for small, medium, and large effect sizes and one- or two-tailed tests.

Suppose a researcher plans a study using the .05 significance level, two-tailed, with 20 participants. The predicted effect size is about .5 (a medium effect size). The table shows the study would have a power of .59. This means that, if the research hypothesis is true and has a medium effect size, there is a 59% chance that this study will come out significant.

The power table (Table 8–8) is also useful when you are reading about a nonsignificant result in a published study. Suppose that a study using a t test for dependent means has a nonsignificant result. The study tested significance at the .05 level, was two-tailed, and had 10 participants. Should you conclude that there is in fact no difference at all between the populations? Probably not. Even assuming a medium effect size, Table 8–8 shows that there is only a 32% chance of getting a significant result in this study.

---

[6]Note that effect size and power for the t test for a single sample are determined in the same way as for the t test for dependent means.

TABLE 8–8   **Approximate Power for Studies Using the *t* Test for Dependent Means for Testing Hypothesis at the .05 Significance Level**

Difference Scores in Sample (*N*)	Effect Size		
	Small (.20)	Medium (.50)	Large (.80)
One-tailed test			
10	.15	.46	.78
20	.22	.71	.96
30	.29	.86	*
40	.35	.93	*
50	.40	.97	*
100	.63	*	*
Two-tailed test			
10	.09	.32	.66
20	.14	.59	.93
30	.19	.77	.99
40	.24	.88	*
50	.29	.94	*
100	.55	*	*

*Power is nearly 1.

Consider another study that was not significant. This study also used the .05 significance level, one-tailed. This study had 100 research participants. Table 8–8 tells you that there would be a 63% chance of the study's coming out significant if there were even a true small effect size in the population. If there were a medium effect size in the population, the table indicates that there is almost a 100% chance that this study would have come out significant. In this study with 100 participants, you could conclude from the results of this study that in the population there is probably at most a small difference.

To keep Table 8–8 simple, we have given power figures for only a few different numbers of participants (10, 20, 30, 40, 50, and 100). This should be adequate for the kinds of rough evaluations you need to make when evaluating results of research articles.[7]

PLANNING SAMPLE SIZE

Table 8–9 gives the approximate number of participants needed to have 80% power for a planned study. (Eighty percent is a common figure used by researchers for the minimum power to make a study worth doing.) The table gives the number of participants needed based on predicted small, medium, and large effect sizes, using

[7]Cohen (1988, pp. 28–39) provides more detailed tables in terms of numbers of participants, levels of effect size, and significance levels. If you use his tables, note that the *d* referred to is actually based on a *t* test for independent means (the situation we consider in Chapter 9). To use these tables for a *t* test for dependent means, first multiply your effect size by 1.4. For example, if your effect size is .30, for purposes of using Cohen's tables, you would consider it to be .42 (that is, .30 × 1.4 = .42). The only other difference from our table is that Cohen describes the significance level by the letter *a* (for "alpha level"), with a subscript of either 1 or 2, referring to a one-tailed or two-tailed test. For example, a table that refers to "$a_1 = .05$" at the top means that this is the table for $p < .05$, one-tailed.

TABLE 8–9 Approximate Number of Research Participants Needed for 80% Power for the *t* Test for Dependent Means in Testing Hypotheses at the .05 Significance Level

	Effect Size		
	Small (.20)	Medium (.50)	Large (.80)
One-tailed	156	26	12
Two-tailed	196	33	14

one- and two-tailed tests, for the .05 significance levels. Suppose you plan a study in which you expect a large effect size and will use the .05 significance level, two-tailed. The table shows that for 80% power you would need only 14 participants to have 80% power. On the other hand, a study using the same significance level, also two-tailed, but in which you expect only a small effect size, would need 196 participants for 80% power.[8]

THE POWER OF STUDIES USING THE *t* TEST FOR DEPENDENT MEANS

Studies using difference scores (that is, studies using a repeated-measures design) often have much larger effect sizes for the same amount of expected difference between means than have other kinds of research designs. That is, testing each of a group of participants twice (once under one condition and once under a different condition) usually produces a high-power type of study. In particular, this kind of study gives more power than dividing the participants up into two groups and testing each group once (one group tested under one condition and the other tested under the other condition). In fact, studies using difference scores usually have even more power than those in which you have twice as many participants, but tested each only once.

Why do repeated-measures designs have so much power? The reason is that the standard deviation of difference scores is usually quite low. This produces a larger effect size, which increases the power. (The standard deviation of difference scores is what you divide by to get the effect size when using difference scores.) In a repeated measures design, the only variation is in the difference scores. Variation among participants on each testing's scores are not part of the variation involved in the analysis. This is because difference scores are all comparing participants to themselves. The effect of all this is that studies using difference scores often have quite large effect sizes (and thus high power) even with a small number of people in the study.

However, although it has advantages from the point of view of power, the kind of repeated-measures study discussed in this chapter (testing a group of people before and after an experimental procedure, without any kind of control group that does not go through the procedure) often has disadvantages from the point of view

---

[8]More detailed tables, giving needed numbers of participants for levels of power other than 80% (and also for effect sizes other than .20, .50, and .80 and for other significance levels), are provided in Cohen (1988, pp. 54–55). However, see footnote 7 in this chapter about using Cohen's tables for a *t* test for dependent means.

of the meaning of the results. For example, consider a study where people are tested before and after some experimental procedure. Even if such a study produces a significant difference, it leaves many alternative explanations for that difference. For example, the research participants might have improved during that period anyway, or perhaps other events happened in between, or the participants not getting benefits may have dropped out. It is even possible that the initial test itself caused changes. The limitations of this kind of research are discussed in detail in research methods textbooks.

HOW ARE YOU DOING?

1. (a) What is an assumption in hypothesis testing? (b) Describe a specific assumption for a *t* test for dependent means. (c) What is the effect of violating this assumption? (d) When is the *t* test for dependent means likely to give a very distorted result?
2. (a) Write the formula for estimated effect size, and (b) describe each of its terms.
3. You are planning a study in which you predict an effect size of .5. You plan to test significance using a *t* test for dependent means, one-tailed, with an alpha of .05. (a) What is the power of this study if you carry it out with 20 participants? (b) How many participants would you need to have 80% power?
4. (a) Why do repeated-measures designs have so much power? (b) What is the main disadvantage of the kind of repeated-measures study discussed in this chapter?

ANSWERS:

1. (a) It is a requirement that you must meet for the results of the hypothesis-testing procedure to be accurate.
   (b) The population of individuals' difference scores is assumed to be a normal distribution.
   (c) The significance level cutoff from the *t* table is not accurate.
   (d) When doing a one-tailed test and the population distribution is highly skewed.
2. (a) Estimated Effect Size = M/S
   (b) M is the mean of the difference scores. S is the estimated standard deviation of the population of individual difference scores.
3. (a) .71. (b) 26.
4. (a) Because the standard deviation of the difference scores is usually quite low (which makes the effect size relatively high, thereby increasing power).
   (b) Even if a study produces a significant difference, there are alternative explanations for that difference.

t TESTS IN RESEARCH ARTICLES

Research articles usually describe *t* tests in a fairly standard format that includes the degrees of freedom, the *t* score, and the significance level. For example, $t(24) = 2.80$, $p < .05$ tells you that the researcher used a *t* test with 24 degrees of freedom, found a *t* score of 2.80, and the result was significant at the .05 level. Whether a one- or two-tailed test was used may also be noted. (If not, assume that it was two-tailed.) Usually the means, and sometimes the standard deviations, are given for each testing. Rarely is the standard deviation of the difference scores reported.

   Had our student in the dormitory example reported the results in a research article, she would have written something like this: "The sample from my dormitory studied a mean of 3.2 hours ($SD = .80$). Based on a *t* test for a single sample, this was significantly different from the known mean of 2.5 for the college as a whole, $t(15) = 3.50$, $p < .01$, one-tailed."

As we noted earlier, social and behavioral scientists only occasionally use the *t* test for a single sample. We introduced it mainly as a stepping stone to the more widely used *t* test for dependent means. Olthoff (1989) might have reported the results of his study of husbands' communication quality as follows: "There was a significant decline in communication quality, dropping from a mean of 116.32 before marriage to a mean of 104.26 after marriage, $t(18) = 2.76$, $p < .05$, two-tailed." Here is how McLeod et al. (1994) reported some of the results of their study of pro-government attitudes during and after the 1991 Persian Gulf War:

> Confidence in the president declined from 2.57 (out of a possible 3) to 2.17 ($t[165] = 4.32$, $p < .001$). The decline in confidence in people running Congress was even steeper, falling from 2.23 during the war to 1.74 one year later ($t[165] = 5.26$, $p < .001$). (p. 25)

Results of *t* tests are sometimes given in tables. For example, Table 8–10 reproduces the table from the McLeod et al. (1994) article. As you can see, the same pattern of pro-government (and also pro-war) attitudes was consistent over almost all the questions asked. Notice, incidentally, the method of using asterisks to indicate the level of significance. This is a common procedure; in fact, sometimes the *t* value itself is not given, just the asterisks (with the note at the bottom as to the exact *p* levels to which they refer).

TABLE 8–10 *t* Tests for Differences between Time 1 and 2 Responses

	During War Mean	1-Year Later Mean	*T*-Value
War-related attitude scales (Maximum = 5.0)			
War is justified	3.41	3.11	2.11[*]
War is correct option	3.61	3.44	2.47[**]
Institutional confidence variables (Maximum = 3.0)			
Confidence in president	2.57	2.17	4.32[***]
Confidence in Congress	2.23	1.74	5.26[***]
Confidence in military	2.83	2.69	1.64[*]
Confidence in TV	2.16	2.18	−0.24
Confidence in newspapers	2.39	2.34	0.36
Media roles variables (Maximum = 7.0)			
Providing information	6.10	6.42	−2.38[**]
Explaining significance	5.60	5.71	−0.83
Building solidarity	5.58	5.01	3.26[***]
Reducing tension	5.07	4.47	3.18[***]
Restrictive attitude scales (Maximum = 3.0)			
Anti-war gore	2.39	2.12	3.59[***]
Anti-protest	2.95	2.77	3.38[***]

$N = 167$
[*]$p < .05$ [**]$p < .01$ [***]$p < .001$

Source: Conflict and public opinion: Rallying effects of the Persian Gulf War. McLeod, D. M., Eveland, W. P., & Signorelli, N. (1994). *Journalism Quarterly, 71*, 20–31. Copyright © 1994 by the Association for Education in Journalism and Mass Communication. Reprinted by permission.

SUMMARY

1. You use the standard five steps of hypothesis testing even when you don't know the population variance. However, in this situation you have to estimate the population variance from the scores in the sample, using a formula that divides the sum of squared deviation scores by the degrees of freedom ($df = N - 1$).

2. When the population variance is estimated, the comparison distribution of means is a *t* distribution (with cutoffs given in a *t* table). A *t* distribution has slightly heavier tails than a normal curve (just how much heavier depends on how few degrees of freedom). Also, in this situation, a sample's number of standard deviations from the mean of the comparison distribution is called a *t* score.

3. You use a *t* test for a single sample when a sample mean is being compared to a known population mean and the population variance is unknown.

4. You use a *t* test for dependent means in studies where each participant has two scores, such as a before-score and an after-score, or a score in each of two experimental conditions. In this *t* test, you first figure a difference score for each participant, then go through the usual 5 steps of hypothesis testing with the modifications described in summary points 1 and 2 above and making Population 2 a population of difference scores with a mean of 0 (no difference).

5. An assumption of the *t* test is that the population distribution is a normal curve. However, even when it is not, the *t* test is usually fairly accurate.

6. The effect size of a study using a *t* test for dependent means is the mean of the difference scores divided by the standard deviation of the difference scores. Power and needed sample size for 80% power can be looked up in special tables.

7. The power of studies using difference scores is usually much higher than that of studies using other designs with the same number of participants. However, research using a single group tested before and after some intervening event, without a control group, allows for alternative explanations of any observed changes.

8. *t* tests are reported in research articles using a standard format. For example, "$t(24) = 2.80, p < .05$."

KEY TERMS

t tests (p. 218)
t test for a single sample (p. 218)
biased estimate (p. 221)
unbiased estimate of the population variance (S^2) (p. 221)

degrees of freedom (*df*) (p. 221)
t distribution (p. 223)
t table (p. 224)
t score (p. 225)
repeated-measures design (p. 229)

t test for dependent means (p. 229)
difference scores (p. 230)
assumption (p. 239)

EXAMPLE WORKED-OUT PROBLEMS

t TEST FOR A SINGLE SAMPLE

Eight participants are tested after being given an experimental procedure. Their scores are 14, 8, 6, 5, 13, 10, 10, and 6. The population (of people not given this procedure) is normally distributed with a mean of 6. Using the .05 level, two-tailed, does the experimental procedure make a difference? (a) Use the steps of hypothesis testing and (b) sketch the distributions involved.

ANSWER

(a) Steps of hypothesis testing:

❶ **Restate the question as a research hypothesis and a null hypothesis about the populations.** There are two populations:

> **Population 1:** People who are given the experimental procedure.
>
> **Population 2:** The general population.

The research hypothesis is that Population 1 will score differently than Population 2. The null hypothesis is that Population 1 will not score differently than Population 2.

❷ **Determine the characteristics of the comparison distribution.** The mean of the distribution of means is 6 (the known population mean). To figure the estimated population variance, you first need to figure the sample mean, which is $(14 + 8 + 6 + 5 + 13 + 10 + 10 + 6)/8 = 72/8 = 9$. The estimated population variance is $S^2 = \Sigma(X - M)^2/df = 78/7 = 11.14$; the variance of the distribution of means is $S_M^2 = S^2/N = 11.14/8 = 1.39$. The standard deviation of the distribution of means is $S_M = \sqrt{S_M^2} = \sqrt{1.39} = 1.18$. Its shape will be a t distribution for $df = 7$.

❸ **Determine the cutoff sample score on the comparison distribution at which the null hypothesis should be rejected.** From Table A–2, the cutoffs for a two-tailed t test at the .05 level for $df = 7$ are 2.365 and −2.365.

❹ **Determine your sample's score on the comparison distribution.** $t = (M - \text{Population } M)/S_M = (9 - 6)/1.18 = 3/1.18 = 2.54$.

❺ **Decide whether to reject the null hypothesis.** The t of 2.54 is more extreme than the needed t of ± 2.365. Therefore, reject the null hypothesis; the research hypothesis is supported. The experimental procedure does make a difference.

(b) Sketches of distributions are shown in Figure 8–9.

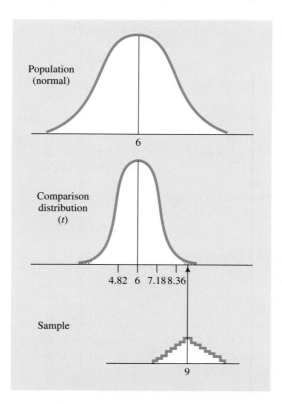

FIGURE 8–9 *Distributions for answer to Example Worked-Out Problems for t test for a single sample.*

t TEST FOR DEPENDENT MEANS

A researcher tests 10 individuals before and after an experimental procedure. The results were as follows:

Participant	Before	After
1	10.4	10.8
2	12.6	12.1
3	11.2	12.1
4	10.9	11.4
5	14.3	13.9
6	13.2	13.5
7	9.7	10.9
8	11.5	11.5
9	10.8	10.4
10	13.1	12.5

Test the hypothesis that there is an increase in scores, using the .05 significance level. (a) Use the steps of hypothesis testing and (b) sketch the distributions involved.

ANSWER

(a) Table 8–11 shows the results, including the figuring of difference scores and all the other figuring for the *t* test for dependent means. Here are the steps of hypothesis testing:

TABLE 8–11 Figuring for Answer to Example Worked-Out Problems for *t* Test for Dependent Means

Participant	Score		Difference	Deviation	Squared Deviation
	Before	*After*	*(After – Before)*	*(Difference – M)*	
1	10.4	10.8	.4	.26	.07
2	12.6	12.1	−.5	−.64	.41
3	11.2	12.1	.9	.76	.58
4	10.9	11.4	.5	.36	.13
5	14.3	13.9	−.4	−.54	.29
6	13.2	13.5	.3	.16	.03
7	9.7	10.9	1.2	1.06	1.12
8	11.5	11.5	0.0	−.14	.02
9	10.8	10.4	−.4	−.54	.29
10	13.1	12.5	−.6	−.74	.55
Σ:	117.7	119.1	1.4	0	3.49

For difference scores:

$M = 1.4/10 = .14.$

Population $M = 0$.

$S^2 = \Sigma(X - M)^2/df = 3.49/(10 - 1) = 3.49/9 = .39.$

$S_M^2 = S^2/N = .39/10 = .039.$

$S_M = \sqrt{S_M^2} = \sqrt{.039} = .20.$

t for $df = 9$ needed for 5% significance level, one-tailed = 1.833.

$t = (M - \text{Population } M)/S_M = (.14 - 0)/.20 = .70.$

Decision: Do not reject the null hypothesis.

❶ **Restate the question as a research hypothesis and a null hypothesis about the populations.** There are two populations:

> **Population 1:** People like those who are given the experimental procedure.
>
> **Population 2:** People who show no change from before to after.

The research hypothesis is that Population 1's mean difference score (after minus before) is greater than Population 2's. The null hypothesis is that Population 1's mean difference (after minus before) is not greater than Population 2's.

❷ **Determine the characteristics of the comparison distribution.** Its population mean is 0 change. The estimated population variance of difference scores is shown in Table 8–11 to be .39. The standard deviation of the distribution of means of difference scores is .20. Therefore, the comparison distribution has a mean of 0 and a standard deviation of .20. It will be a t distribution for $df = 9$.

❸ **Determine the cutoff sample score on the comparison distribution at which the null hypothesis should be rejected.** For a one-tailed test at the .05 level with $df = 9$, the cutoff is 1.833.

❹ **Determine your sample's score on the comparison distribution.** The sample's mean change of .14 is .70 standard deviations (of .20 each) on the distribution of means above that distribution's mean of 0. That is, $t = (M - \text{Population } M)/S_M = (.14 - 0)/.20 = .70$.

❺ **Decide whether to reject the null hypothesis.** The sample's t of .70 is less extreme than the needed t of 1.833. Thus, you cannot reject the null hypothesis. The study is inconclusive.

(b) Sketches of distributions are shown in Figure 8–10.

FIGURE 8–10 *Distributions for answer to Example Worked-Out Problems for t test for dependent means.*

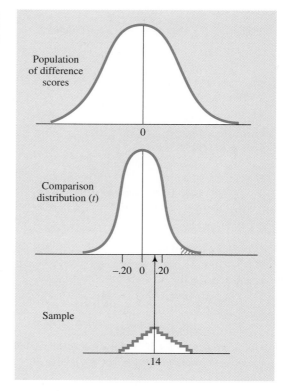

PRACTICE PROBLEMS

These problems involve figuring. Most real-life statistics problems are done on a computer with special statistical software. Even if you have such software, do these problems by hand (with the help of a calculator) to ingrain the method in your mind. Also, in all problems involving figuring, be sure to show your work.

For practice in using a computer to solve statistics problems, refer to the computer section of each chapter of the *Student's Study Guide and Computer Workbook* that accompanies this text.

All data are fictional unless an actual citation is given.

For answers to Set I problems, see pp. 431–33.

SET I

1. In each of the following studies, a single sample's mean is being compared to a population with a known mean but an unknown variance. For each study, decide whether the result is significant. (Be sure to show all of your calculations.)

	Sample Size (N)	Population Mean	Estimated Population Variance (S^2)	Sample Mean (M)	Tails	Significance Level
(a)	64	12.40	9.00	11.00	1 (low predicted)	.05
(b)	49	1,006.35	317.91	1,009.72	2	.01
(c)	400	52.00	7.02	52.41	1 (high predicted)	.01

2. Suppose a candidate running for sheriff claims that she will reduce the average speed of emergency response to less than 30 minutes. (30 minutes is thought to be the average response time with the current sheriff.) There are no past records, so the actual standard deviation of such response times cannot be determined. Thanks to this campaign, she is elected sheriff, and careful records are now kept. The response times for the first month are 26, 30, 28, 29, 25, 28, 32, 35, 24, and 23 min.

    Using the .05 significance level, did she keep her promise? (a) Go through the five steps of hypothesis testing. (b) Sketch the distributions involved. (c) Explain your answer to someone who has never taken a course in statistics.

3. A researcher tests five individuals who have seen paid political ads about a particular issue. These individuals take a multiple-choice test about the issue in which people in general (who know nothing about the issue) usually get 40 questions correct. The number correct for these five individuals was 48, 41, 40, 51, and 50.

    Using the .05 level of significance, two-tailed, do people who see the ads do better on this test? (a) Use the steps of hypothesis testing. (b) Sketch the distributions involved. (c) Explain your answer to someone who is familiar with the *Z* test (from Chapter 6), but is unfamiliar with *t* tests.

4. For each of the following studies using difference scores, test the significance using a *t* test for dependent means. Also, figure the estimated effect size for each study.

	Number of Difference Scores in Sample	Mean of Difference Scores in Sample	Estimated Population Variance of Difference Scores	Tails	Significance Level
(a)	20	1.7	8.29	1 (high predicted)	.05
(b)	164	2.3	414.53	2	.05
(c)	15	−2.2	4.00	1 (low predicted)	.01

5. A program to decrease littering was carried out in four cities in California's Central Valley starting in August 2003. The amount of litter in the streets (average pounds of litter collected per block per day) was measured during the July before the program was started and then the next July, after the program had been in effect for a year. The results were as follows:

City	July 2003	July 2004
Fresno	9	2
Merced	10	4
Bakersfield	8	9
Stockton	9	1

Using the 1% level of significance, was there a significant decrease in the amount of litter? (a) Use the five steps of hypothesis testing. (b) Sketch the distributions involved. (c) Explain your answer to someone who understands mean, standard deviation, and variance, but knows nothing else about statistics.

6. A researcher assesses the level of a particular hormone in the blood in five patients before and after they begin taking a hormone treatment program. Results for the five are as follows:

Patient	Before	After
A	.20	.18
B	.16	.16
C	.24	.23
D	.22	.19
E	.17	.16

Using the 5% significance level, was there a significant change in the level of this hormone? (a) Use the steps of hypothesis testing. (b) Sketch the distributions involved. (c) Explain your answer to someone who understands the t test for a single sample but is unfamiliar with the t test for dependent means.

7. Figure the estimated effect size and indicate whether it is approximately small, medium, or large, for each of the following studies:

Study	Mean Change	S
(a)	20	32
(b)	5	10
(c)	.1	.4
(d)	100	500

8. What is the power of each of the following studies, using a *t* test for dependent means (based on the .05 significance level)?

Effect Size	N	Tails
(a) Small	20	One
(b) Medium	20	One
(c) Medium	30	One
(d) Medium	30	Two
(e) Large	30	Two

9. About how many participants are needed for 80% power in each of the following planned studies that will use a *t* test for dependent means with *p* < .05?

Predicted Effect Size	Tails
(a) Medium	Two
(b) Large	One
(c) Small	One

10. Weller and Weller (1997) conducted a study of the tendency for the menstrual cycles of women who live together (such as sisters) to become synchronized. For their statistical analysis, they compared scores on a measure of synchronization of pairs of sisters living together versus the degree of synchronization that would be expected by chance (lower scores mean more synchronization). Their key results (reported in a table not reproduced here) were synchrony scores of 6.32 for the 30 roommate sister pairs in their sample compared to an expected synchrony score of 7.76; they then reported a *t* score of 2.27 for this difference. This result is statistically significant at *p* < .05. Explain this result to a person who is familiar with hypothesis testing with a known population variance, but not with the *t* test for a single sample.

11. A researcher conducts a study of perceptual illusions under two different lighting conditions. Twenty participants were each tested under both of the two different conditions. The experimenter reported: "The mean number of effective illusions was 6.72 under the bright conditions and 6.85 under the dimly lit conditions, a difference that was not significant, $t(19) = 1.62$." Explain this result to a person who has never had a course in statistics. Be sure to use sketches of the distributions in your answer.

Set II

12. In each of the following studies, a single sample's mean is being compared to a population with a known mean but an unknown variance. For each study, decide whether the result is significant.

	Sample Size (N)	Population Mean	Estimated Population Standard Deviation (S)	Sample Mean (M)	Tails	Significance Level
(a)	16	100.31	2.00	100.98	1 (high predicted)	.05
(b)	16	.47	4.00	.00	2	.05
(c)	16	68.90	9.00	34.00	1 (low predicted)	.01

13. Evolutionary theories often emphasize that humans have adapted to their physical environment. One such theory hypothesizes that people should spontaneously follow a 24-hour cycle of sleeping and waking—even if they are not exposed to the usual pattern of sunlight. To test this notion, eight paid volunteers were placed (individually) in a room in which there was no light from the outside and no clocks or other indications of time. They could turn the lights on and off as they wished. After a month in the room, each individual tended to develop a steady cycle. Their cycles at the end of the study were as follows: 25, 27, 25, 23, 24, 25, 26, and 25.

    Using the 5% level of significance, what should we conclude about the theory that 24 hours is the natural cycle? (That is, does the average cycle length under these conditions differ significantly from 24 hours?) (a) Use the steps of hypothesis testing. (b) Sketch the distributions involved. (c) Explain your answer to someone who has never taken a course in statistics.

14. In a particular country, it is known that college seniors report falling in love an average of 2.2 times during their college years. A sample of five seniors, originally from that country but who have spent their entire college career in the United States, were asked how many times they had fallen in love during their college years. Their numbers were 2, 3, 5, 5, and 2. Using the .05 significance level, do students like these who go to college in the United States fall in love more often than those from their country who go to college in their own country? (a) Use the steps of hypothesis testing. (b) Sketch the distributions involved. (c) Explain your answer to someone who is familiar with hypothesis testing with a known population variance, but not with the t test for a single sample.

15. For each of the following studies using difference scores, test the significance using a t test for dependent means.

Number of Difference Scores in Sample	Mean of Difference Scores in Sample	Estimated Population Variance of Difference Scores	Tails	Significance Level
(a) 10	3.8	50	One (high)	.05
(b) 100	3.8	50	One (high)	.05

(c) 100	1.9	50	One (high)	.05
(d) 100	1.9	50	Two	.05
(e) 100	1.9	25	Two	.05

16. Four individuals with high levels of cholesterol went on a special diet, avoiding high-cholesterol foods and taking special supplements. Their total cholesterol levels before and after the diet were as follows:

Participant	Before	After
J. K.	287	255
L. M. M.	305	269
A. K.	243	245
R. O. S.	309	247

Using the 5% level of significance, was there a significant change in cholesterol level? (a) Use the steps of hypothesis testing. (b) Sketch the distributions involved. (c) Explain your answer to someone who has never taken a course in statistics.

17. Five people who were convicted of speeding were ordered by the court to attend a workshop. A special device put into their cars kept records of their speeds for 2 weeks before and after the workshop. The maximum speeds for each person during the 2 weeks before and the 2 weeks after the workshop follow.

Participant	Before	After
L. B.	65	58
J. K.	62	65
R .C.	60	56
R. T.	70	66
J. M.	68	60

Using the 5% significance level, should we conclude that people are likely to drive more slowly after such a workshop? (a) Use the steps of hypothesis testing. (b) Sketch the distributions involved. (c) Explain your answer to someone who is familiar with hypothesis testing involving known populations, but has never learned anything about *t* tests.

18. Five sophomores were given an English achievement test before and after receiving instruction in basic grammar. Their scores are shown below.

Student	Before	After
A	20	18
B	18	22
C	17	15
D	16	17
E	12	9

Is it reasonable to conclude that future students would show higher scores after instruction? Use the 5% significance level. (a) Use the steps of hypothesis testing. (b) Sketch the distributions involved. (c) Explain your answer to someone who understands mean, standard deviation, and variance, but knows nothing else about statistics.

19. Figure the estimated effect size and indicate whether it is approximately small, medium, or large, for each of the following studies:

Study	Mean Change	S
(a)	8	30
(b)	8	10
(c)	16	30
(d)	16	10

20. What is the power of each of the following studies, using a t test for dependent means (based on the .05 significance level)?

Effect Size	N	Tails
(a) Small	50	Two
(b) Medium	50	Two
(c) Large	50	Two
(d) Small	10	Two
(e) Small	40	Two
(f) Small	100	Two
(g) Small	100	One

21. About how many participants are needed for 80% power in each of the following planned studies that will use a t test for dependent means with $p < .05$?

Predicted Effect Size	Tails
(a) Small	Two
(b) Medium	One
(c) Large	Two

22. A study compared union activity of employees in 10 plants during two different decades. The researchers reported "a significant increase in union activity, $t(9) = 3.28$, $p < .01$." Explain this result to a person who has never had a course in statistics. Be sure to use sketches of the distributions in your answer.

23. Holden, Thompson, Zambarano, and Marshall (1997) compared mothers' reported attitudes toward corporal punishment of their children from before to 3 years after having their first child. "The average change in the women's prior-to-current attitudes was significant, $t(107) = 10.32$, $p < .001$" (p. 485). (The change was that they felt more negatively about corporal punishment after having their child.) Explain this result to someone who is familiar with the t test for a single sample, but not with the t test for dependent means.

24. Table 8–12 (reproduced from Table 4 of Larson, Dworkin, & Verma, 2001) shows ratings of various aspects of work and home life of 100 middle-class men in India who were fathers. Pick three rows of interest to you and explain the results to someone who is familiar with the mean, variance, and Z scores, but knows nothing else about statistics.

| TABLE 8–12 | Comparison of Fathers' Mean Psychological States in the Job and Home Spheres ($N = 100$) | | | |

| | | Sphere | | |
Scale	Range	Work	Home	Work vs. home
Important	0–9	5.98	5.06	6.86***
Attention	0–9	6.15	5.13	7.96***
Challenge	0–9	4.11	2.41	11.49***
Choice	0–9	4.28	4.74	−3.38***
Wish doing else	0–9	1.50	1.44	0.61
Hurried	0–3	1.80	1.39	3.21**
Social anxiety	0–3	0.81	0.64	3.17**
Affect	1–7	4.84	4.98	−2.64**
Social climate	1–7	5.64	5.95	4.17***

Note: Values for column 3 are *t* scores; *df* = 99 for all *t* tests.
**$p < .01$, ***$p < .001$.

Source: Larson, R., Dworkin, J., & Verna, S. (2001). Men's work and family lives in India: The daily organization of time and emotions. *Journal of Family Psychology, 15,* 206–224. Copyright © The American Psychological Association. Reprinted with permission of the authors and The American Psychological Association.

CHAPTER 9

The *t* Test for Independent Means

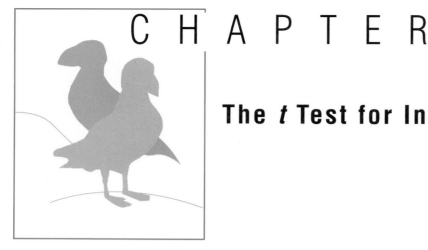

t test for independent means

Tip for Success

You should be thoroughly comfortable with the material in Chapter 8, particularly the basic logic and procedures of the t *test, before going on to the material in this chapter.*

This chapter examines hypothesis testing in the very common situation of comparing two samples, such as an experimental group and a control group (or a group of men and a group of women). This is a *t* test situation because you don't know the population variances (so they must be estimated). In the previous chapter, you learned how to use the *t* test for dependent means to compare two groups of scores from a *single group of people* (such as the same people measured before and after a health promotion education program). In this chapter, you learn how to compare two groups of scores from *two entirely separate groups of people*. The scores of these two groups are independent of each other, so the test you will learn is called a *t* **test for independent means.**

In the previous chapter, you learned the logic and figuring for the *t* test for dependent means. In that chapter, the same group of people had a score in each of the two groups, which meant you had a pair of scores for each person. This allowed you to create a difference score for each person. You then carried out the hypothesis-testing procedure using these difference scores. The comparison distribution you used for this hypothesis testing was a distribution of means of difference scores.

In the situation you face in this chapter, the scores in one group are for a different group of people than the scores in the other group. So, you don't have any pairs of scores as you did when the same group of people had a score in each of the two groups. So, it wouldn't make sense to create difference scores, and you can't use difference scores for the hypothesis-testing procedure in this chapter. Instead, when the scores in one group are for a different group of people than the scores in the other group, what you can compare is the *mean* of one group to the *mean* of the other group. So, the key focus in the *t* test for independent means becomes the *difference between the means* of the two groups. The hypothesis-testing procedure, however, works just like the hypothesis-testing procedures you have already learned. Since the focus is now on the difference between means, the comparison distribution is a **distribution of differences between means.**

THE DISTRIBUTION OF DIFFERENCES BETWEEN MEANS

WHAT IS IN A DISTRIBUTION OF DIFFERENCES BETWEEN MEANS?

This special distribution is, in a sense, two steps removed from the populations of individuals: First, there is a distribution of means from each population of individuals. Second, there is a distribution of differences between pairs of means, one of each pair from each of these distributions of means.

   Think of this distribution of differences between means as being built up as follows: (a) Randomly select one mean from the distribution of means for Population 1, (b) randomly select one mean from the distribution of means for Population 2, and (c) subtract. (That is, take the mean from the first distribution of means minus the mean from the second distribution of means.) This gives a difference score between the two selected means. Then repeat the process. This creates a second difference, a difference between the two newly selected means. Repeating this process a large number of times creates a distribution of differences between means. You would never actually create a distribution of differences between means using this lengthy method. But it shows clearly what the distribution is made up of.

THE LOGIC

Figure 9–1 shows the entire logical construction involved in a distribution of differences between means. At the top are the two population distributions. We do not know the characteristics of these population distributions. But we do know that if the null hypothesis is true, the two population means are the same. That is, the null hypothesis is that Population M_1 = Population M_2. We also can estimate the

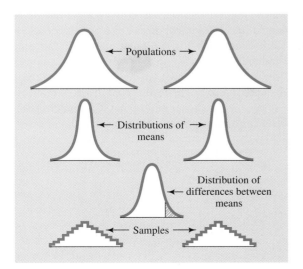

FIGURE 9–1   *A diagram of the logic of a distribution of differences between means.*

variance of these populations based on the sample information (these estimated variances will be S_1^2 and S_2^2).

Below each population distribution is the distribution of means for that population. Using the estimated population variance and knowing the size of each sample, you can figure the variance of each distribution of means in the usual way. (It is the variance of its parent population divided by the size of the sample.)

Below these two distributions of means, and built from them, is the crucial distribution of differences between means. This distribution's variance is ultimately based on estimated population variances. Thus, we can think of it as a t distribution. The goal of a t test for independent means is to decide whether the difference between the means of your two actual samples is a more extreme difference than the cutoff difference on this distribution of differences between means. The two actual samples are shown (as histograms) at the bottom.

Remember, this whole procedure is really a kind of complicated castle in the air. It exists only in our minds to help us make decisions based on the results of an actual experiment. The only concrete reality in all of this is the actual scores in the two samples. You estimate the population variances from these sample scores. The variances of the two distributions of means are based entirely on these estimated population variances (and the sample sizes). And, as you will see shortly, the characteristics of the distribution of differences between means is based on these two distributions of means.

Still, the procedure is a powerful one. It has the power of mathematics and logic behind it. It helps you develop general knowledge based on the specifics of a particular study.

With this overview of the basic logic, we now turn to five key details: (1) the mean of the distribution of differences between means, (2) the estimated population variance and the variance of the two distributions of means, (3) the variance and standard deviation of the distribution of differences between means, (4) the shape of the distribution of differences between means, and (5) the t score for the difference between the particular two means being compared.

MEAN OF THE DISTRIBUTION OF DIFFERENCES BETWEEN MEANS

In a t test for independent means, you are considering two populations—for example, one population from which an experimental group is taken and one population from which a control group is taken. In practice, you don't know the mean of either population. You do know that if the null hypothesis is true, these two populations have equal means. Also, if these two populations have equal means, the two distributions of means have equal means. (This is because each distribution of means has the same mean as its parent population of individuals.) Finally, if you take random samples from two distributions with equal means, the differences between the means of these random samples, in the long run, balance out to 0. The result of all this is the following: Whatever the specifics of the study, the researcher knows that if the null hypothesis is true, the distribution of differences between means has a mean of 0.

ESTIMATING THE POPULATION VARIANCE AND THE VARIANCE OF THE TWO DISTRIBUTIONS OF MEANS

In Chapter 8, you learned to estimate the population variance from the scores in your sample. It is the sum of squared deviation scores divided by the degrees of freedom (the number in the sample minus 1). To do a t test for independent means, it has to be reasonable to assume that the populations the two samples come from have the same variance. (If the null hypothesis is true, they also have the same mean. However, whether or not the null hypothesis is true, you must be able to assume the two populations have the same variance.) Therefore, when you estimate the population variance from the scores in either sample, you are getting two separate estimates of what should be the same number. In practice, the two estimates will almost never be exactly identical. Since they are both supposed to be estimating the same thing, the best solution is to average the two estimates to get the best single overall estimate. This is called the **pooled estimate of the population variance** (S^2_{Pooled}).

pooled estimate of the population variance (S^2_{Pooled})

In making this average, however, you also have to take into account that the two samples may not be the same size. If one sample is larger than the other, the estimate it provides is likely to be more accurate (because it is based on more information). If both samples are exactly the same size, you could just take an ordinary average of the two estimates. On the other hand, when they are not the same size, you need to make some adjustment in the averaging to give more weight to the larger sample. That is, you need a **weighted average,** an average weighted by the amount of information each sample provides.

weighted average

Also, to be precise, the amount of information each sample provides is not its number of scores but its degrees of freedom (its number of scores minus 1). Thus, your weighted average needs to be based on the degrees of freedom each sample provides. To find the weighted average you figure out what proportion of the total degrees of freedom each sample contributes, and multiply that proportion by the population variance estimate from that sample. Finally, you add up the two results and that is your weighted, pooled estimate. In terms of a formula:

> The pooled estimate of the population variance is the degrees of freedom in the first sample divided by the total degrees of freedom (from both samples) times the population estimate based on the first sample, plus the degrees of freedom in the second sample divided by the total degrees of freedom times the population estimate based on the second sample.

(9-1)
$$S^2_{\text{Pooled}} = \frac{df_1}{df_{\text{Total}}}(S^2_1) + \frac{df_2}{df_{\text{Total}}}(S^2_2)$$

In this formula, S^2_{Pooled} is the pooled estimate of the population variance. df_1 is the degrees of freedom in the sample for Population 1, and df_2 is the degrees of freedom in the sample for Population 2. (Remember, each sample's df is its number of scores minus 1.) df_{Total} is the total degrees of freedom ($df_{\text{Total}} = df_1 + df_2$). S^2_1 is the estimate of the population variance based on the scores in the sample from Population 1; S^2_2 is the estimate based on the scores in the sample from Population 2.

Consider a study in which the population variance estimate based on an experimental group of 11 participants is 60, and the population variance estimate based on a control group of 31 participants is 80. The estimate from the experimental group is based on 10 degrees of freedom (11 participants minus 1), and the estimate from the control group is based on 30 degrees of freedom (31 minus 1). The total information on which the estimate is based is the total degrees of freedom—in this example, 40 (10 + 30). Thus, the experimental group provides one quarter of the information (10/40 = 1/4), and the control group provides three quarters of the information (30/40 = 3/4).

You then multiply the estimate from the experimental group by 1/4, making 15 (that is, $60 \times 1/4 = 15$). You multiply the estimate from the control group by 3/4, making 60 (that is, $80 \times 3/4 = 60$). Adding the two, this gives an overall estimate of 15 plus 60, which is 75. Using the formula,

$$S^2_{\text{Pooled}} = \frac{df_1}{df_{\text{Total}}}(S^2_1) + \frac{df_2}{df_{\text{Total}}}(S^2_2) = \frac{10}{40}(60) + \frac{30}{40}(80)$$

$$= \frac{1}{4}(60) + \frac{3}{4}(80) = 15 + 60 = 75$$

Tip for Success

You know you have made a mistake in figuring S_{Pooled}^2 *if it does not come out between the two estimates. (You also know you have made a mistake if it does not come out closer to the estimate from the larger sample.)*

Notice that this procedure does not give the same result as ordinary averaging (without weighting). Ordinary averaging would give an estimate of 70 (that is, $[60 + 80]/2 = 70$). Your weighted, pooled estimate of 75 is closer to the estimate based on the control group alone than to the estimate based on the experimental group alone. This is as it should be, because the control group estimate in this example was based on more information.

The pooled estimate of the population variance is the best estimate for both populations. (Remember, to do a t test for independent means, you have to be able to assume that the two populations have the same variance.) However, even though the two populations have the same variance, if the samples are not the same size, the distributions of means taken from them do not have the same variance. That is because the variance of a distribution of means is the population variance divided by the sample size. In terms of formulas,

The variance of the distribution of means for the first population (based on an estimated population variance) is the pooled estimate of the population variance divided by the number of participants in the sample from the first population.

$$S_{M_1}^2 = \frac{S_{Pooled}^2}{N_1} \tag{9-2}$$

The variance of the distribution of means for the second population (based on an estimated population variance) is the pooled estimate of the population variance divided by the number of participants in the sample from the second population.

$$S_{M_2}^2 = \frac{S_{Pooled}^2}{N_2} \tag{9-3}$$

Consider again the study with 11 in the experimental group and 31 in the control group. We figured the pooled estimate of the population variance to be 75. So for the experimental group, the variance of the distribution of means would be 75/11, which is 6.82. For the control group, the variance would be 75/31, which is 2.42.

In terms of formulas,

Tip for Success

Remember that when figuring estimated variances you divide by the degrees of freedom. But when figuring the variance of a distribution of means, which does not involve any additional estimation, you divide by the actual number in the sample.

$$S_{M_1}^2 = \frac{S_{Pooled}^2}{N_1} = \frac{75}{11} = 6.82$$

$$S_{M_2}^2 = \frac{S_{Pooled}^2}{N_2} = \frac{75}{31} = 2.42$$

variance of the distribution of differences between means $(S_{Difference}^2)$

VARIANCE AND STANDARD DEVIATION OF THE DISTRIBUTION OF DIFFERENCES BETWEEN MEANS

The variance of the distribution of differences between means is the variance of the distribution of means for the first population (based on an estimated population variance) plus the variance of the distribution of means for the second population (based on an estimated population variance).

The **variance of the distribution of differences between means** $(S_{Difference}^2)$ is the variance of Population 1's distribution of means plus the variance of Population 2's distribution of means. (This is because in a difference between two numbers, the variation in each contributes to the overall variation in their difference. It is like subtracting a moving number from a moving target.) Stated as a formula,

$$S_{Difference}^2 = S_{M_1}^2 + S_{M_2}^2 \tag{9-4}$$

standard deviation of the distribution of differences between means $(S_{Difference})$

The **standard deviation of the distribution of differences between means** $(S_{Difference})$ is the square root of the variance:

(9-5)

$$S_{\text{Difference}} = \sqrt{S^2_{\text{Difference}}}$$

The standard deviation of the distribution of differences between means is the square root of the variance of the distribution of differences between means.

In the example we have been considering, the variance of the distribution of means for the experimental group was 6.82, and the variance of the distribution of means for the control group was 2.42. The variance of the distribution of the difference between means is thus 6.82 plus 2.42, which is 9.24. This makes the standard deviation of this distribution the square root of 9.24, which is 3.04. In terms of the formulas,

$$S^2_{\text{Difference}} = S^2_{M_1} + S^2_{M_2} = 6.82 + 2.42 = 9.24$$

$$S_{\text{Difference}} = \sqrt{S^2_{\text{Difference}}} = \sqrt{9.24} = 3.04$$

STEPS TO FIND THE STANDARD DEVIATION OF DIFFERENCES BETWEEN MEANS

❶ Figure the estimated population variances based on each sample. That is, figure one estimate for each population using the formula $S^2 = \Sigma(X - M)^2/(N - 1)$.

❷ Figure the pooled estimate of the population variance:

$$S^2_{\text{Pooled}} = \frac{df_1}{df_{\text{Total}}}(S^2_1) + \frac{df_2}{df_{\text{Total}}}(S^2_2)$$

$$(df_1 = N_1 - 1 \text{ and } df_2 = N_2 - 1; df_{\text{Total}} = df_1 + df_2)$$

❸ Figure the variance of each distribution of means:

$$S^2_{M_1} = S^2_{\text{Pooled}}/N_1$$

and

$$S^2_{M_2} = S^2_{\text{Pooled}}/N_2$$

❹ Figure the variance of the distribution of differences between means:

$$S^2_{\text{Difference}} = S^2_{M_1} + S^2_{M_2}$$

❺ Figure the standard deviation of the distribution of differences between means:

$$S_{\text{Difference}} = \sqrt{S^2_{\text{Difference}}}$$

SHAPE OF THE DISTRIBUTION OF DIFFERENCES BETWEEN MEANS

The distribution of differences between means is based on estimated population variances. Thus, the distribution of differences between means (the comparison distribution) is a t distribution. The variance of this distribution is figured based on population variance estimates from two samples. Therefore, the degrees of freedom for this t distribution are the sum of the degrees of freedom of the two samples. In terms of a formula,

(9-6)

$$df_{\text{Total}} = df_1 + df_2$$

The total degrees of freedom is the degrees of freedom in the first sample plus the degrees of freedom in the second sample.

In the example we have been considering with an experimental group of 11 and a control group of 31, we saw earlier that the total degrees of freedom is 40 ($11 - 1 = 10$; $31 - 1 = 30$; and $10 + 30 = 40$). To determine the t score needed for significance, you look up the cutoff point in the t table in the row with 40 degrees of freedom. Suppose you were conducting a one-tailed test using the .05 significance level. The t table in the Appendix (Table A–2) shows a cutoff of 1.684 for 40 degrees of freedom. That is, for a result to be significant, the difference between the means has to be at least 1.684 standard deviations above the mean difference of 0 on the distribution of differences between means.

THE t SCORE FOR THE DIFFERENCE BETWEEN THE TWO ACTUAL MEANS

Here is how you figure the t score for Step 4 of the hypothesis testing: First, figure the difference between your two samples' means. (That is, subtract one from the other.) Then, figure out where this difference is on the distribution of differences between means. You do this by dividing your difference by the standard deviation of this distribution. In terms of a formula,

> The t score is the difference between the two sample means divided by the standard deviation of the distribution of differences between means.

$$t = \frac{M_1 - M_2}{S_{\text{Difference}}} \qquad (9\text{-}7)$$

For our example, suppose the mean of the first sample is 198 and the mean of the second sample is 190. The difference between these two means is 8 (that is, $198 - 190 = 8$). Earlier we figured the standard deviation of the distribution of differences between means in this example to be 3.04. That would make a t score of 2.63 (that is, $8/3.04 = 2.63$). In other words, in this example the difference between the two means is 2.63 standard deviations above the mean of the distribution of differences between means. In terms of the formula,

$$t = \frac{M_1 - M_2}{S_{\text{Difference}}} = \frac{198 - 190}{3.04} = \frac{8}{3.04} = 2.63$$

HOW ARE YOU DOING?

1. (a) When would you carry out a t test for independent means? (b) How is this different from the situation in which you would carry out a t test for dependent means?
2. (a) What is the comparison distribution in a t test for independent means? (b) Explain the logic of going from scores in two samples to an estimate of the variance of this comparison distribution. (c) Illustrate your answer with sketches of the distributions involved. (d) Why is the mean of this distribution 0?
3. Write the formula for each of the following: (a) pooled estimate of the population variance, (b) variance of the distribution of means for the first population, (c) variance of the distribution of differences between means, and (d) t score in a t test for independent means. (e) Define all the symbols used in these formulas.
4. Explain (a) why a t test for independent means uses a single pooled estimate of the population variance, (b) why, and (c) how this estimate is "weighted."
5. For a particular study comparing means of two samples, the first sample has 21 participants and an estimated population variance of 100; the second sample has 31 participants and an estimated population variance of 200. (a) What is the standard deviation of the distribution of differences between means? (b) What is its mean? (c) What will be its shape? (d) Illustrate your answer with sketches of the distributions involved.

ANSWERS:

1. (a) When you have done a study in which you have scores from two samples of different individuals and you do not know the population variance. (b) In a t test for dependent means you have two scores from each of several individuals.

2. (a) A distribution of differences between means. (b) You estimate the population variance from each sample's scores. Since you assume the populations have the same variance, you then pool these two estimates (giving proportionately more weight in this averaging to the sample that has more degrees of freedom in its estimate). Using this pooled estimate, you figure the variance of the distribution of means for each sample's population by dividing this pooled estimate by the sample's number of participants. Finally, since your interest is in a difference between means, you create a comparison distribution of differences between means. This comparison distribution will have a variance equal to the sum of the variances of the two distributions of means. (Because the distribution of differences between means is made up of pairs of means, one taken from each distribution of means, the variance of both of these distribution of means contribute to the variance of the comparison distribution.) (c) Your sketch should look like Figure 9–1. (d) It will have a mean of zero because if the null hypothesis is true, the two populations have the same mean. So, differences between means would on the average come out to zero.

3. (a) $S^2_{Pooled} = \dfrac{df_1}{df_{Total}}(S^2_1) + \dfrac{df_2}{df_{Total}}(S^2_2)$

(b) $S^2_{M_1} = \dfrac{S^2_{Pooled}}{N_1}$

(c) $S^2_{Difference} = S^2_{M_1} + S^2_{M_2}$

(d) $t = \dfrac{M_1 - M_2}{S_{Difference}}$

(e) S^2_{Pooled} is the pooled estimate of the population variance; df_1 and df_2 are the degrees of freedom in the samples from the first and second populations, respectively; df_{Total} is the total degrees of freedom (the sum of df_1 and df_2); S^2_1 and S^2_2 are the population variance estimates based on the samples from the first and second populations, respectively; $S^2_{M_1}$ is the variance of the distribution of means for the first population based on an estimated variance of the population of individuals; N_1 is the number of participants in the sample from the first population; $S^2_{Difference}$ is the variance of the distribution of differences between means based on estimated variances of the populations of individuals; t is the t score for a t test for independent means (the number of standard deviations from the mean on the distribution of differences between means); M_1 and M_2 are the means of the samples from the first and second populations, respectively; and $S_{Difference}$ is the standard deviation of the distribution of differences between means based on estimated variances of the populations of individuals.

4. (a) You assume that both populations have the same variance; thus the estimates from the two samples should be estimates of the same number. (b) We weight (give more influence to) an estimate from a larger sample because, being based on more information, it is likely to be more accurate. (c) The actual weighting is done by multiplying each sample's estimate by the degrees of freedom for that sample divided by the total degrees of freedom; you then sum these two products.

5. (a) $S^2_{Pooled} = (20/50)(100) + (30/50)(200) = 40 + 120 = 160$
$S^2_{M_1} = 160/21 = 7.62$; $S^2_{M_2} = 160/31 = 5.16$;
$S^2_{Difference} = 7.62 + 5.16 = 12.78$; $S_{Difference} = \sqrt{12.78} = 3.57$

(b) 0; (c) t distribution with $df = 50$; (d) Should look like Figure 9–1 with numbers written in (see Figure 9–2 for an example).

HYPOTHESIS TESTING WITH A *t* TEST FOR INDEPENDENT MEANS

Considering the five steps of hypothesis testing, there are three new wrinkles for a *t* test for independent means: (a) The comparison distribution is now a distribution of differences between means (this affects Step 2); (b) the degrees of freedom for

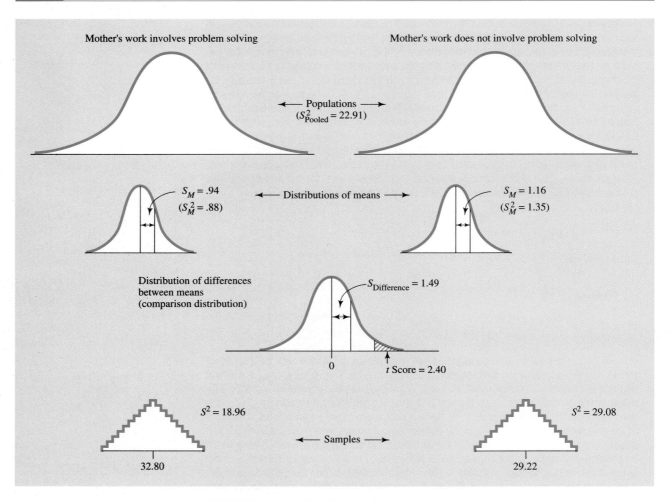

Mother's work involves problem solving

Mother's work does not involve problem solving

← Populations →
$(S_{Pooled}^2 = 22.91)$

$S_M = .94$
$(S_M^2 = .88)$

← Distributions of means →

$S_M = 1.16$
$(S_M^2 = 1.35)$

Distribution of differences
between means
(comparison distribution)

$S_{Difference} = 1.49$

0

t Score = 2.40

$S^2 = 18.96$

← Samples →

$S^2 = 29.08$

32.80

29.22

FIGURE 9–2 *The distributions in the example of a* t *test for independent means. (Data from Moorehouse & Sanders, 1992)*

finding the cutoff on the *t* table is based on two samples (this affects Step 3); and (c) your sample's score on the comparison distribution is based on the difference between your two means (this affects Step 4).

EXAMPLE OF A *t* TEST FOR INDEPENDENT MEANS

Moorehouse and Sanders (1992) studied whether an adolescent boy's sense of how well he is doing in school is related to his mother's work situation. The boys were all in seventh to ninth grades and were all from families in which the mother worked full time. For purposes of this analysis, the boys were divided into two groups: those in which the mother's work gave her opportunities to solve problems (26 boys) and those in which the mother's work did not give her opportunities to solve problems (17 boys). All 43 boys were given a standard test of perceived academic competence (how successful they see themselves as being at school).

The scores and figuring for the *t* test are shown in Table 9–1. The distributions involved are shown in Figure 9–2. Let's go through the five steps of hypothesis testing.

TABLE 9–1 **t Test for Independent Means for a Study of the Relation of the Work Situation of the Mothers of Adolescent Boys to the Boys' Perceived Academic Competence**

Boys Whose Mothers' Work Involves Problem Solving			Boys Whose Mothers' Work Does Not Involve Problem Solving		
Score	Deviation From Mean	Squared Deviation From Mean	Score	Deviation From Mean	Squared Deviation From Mean
36.9	4.1	16.81	23.5	−5.7	32.49
34.6	1.8	16.81	22.5	−6.7	44.89
26.4	−6.4	40.96	36.4	7.2	51.84
33.3	.5	.25	40.0	10.8	116.64
35.4	2.6	6.76	30.6	1.4	1.96
34.8	2.0	4.00	30.5	1.3	1.69
32.3	−4.5	.25	34.5	5.3	28.09
34.5	1.7	2.89	31.3	2.1	4.41
36.0	3.2	10.24	19.4	−9.8	96.04
24.5	−8.3	68.89	29.6	.4	.16
31.6	−1.2	1.44	24.8	−4.4	19.36
36.1	3.3	10.89	25.0	−4.2	17.64
36.8	4.0	16.00	28.8	−.4	.16
27.9	−4.9	24.01	32.5	3.3	10.89
34.4	1.6	2.56	33.3	4.1	16.81
33.8	1.0	1.00	29.6	.4	.16
36.9	4.1	16.81	24.5	−4.7	22.09
34.4	1.6	2.56			
31.7	−1.1	1.21			
29.4	−3.4	11.56			
34.1	1.3	1.69			
18.2	−14.6	213.16			
34.5	1.7	2.89			
35.3	2.5	6.25			
35.5	2.7	7.29			
33.4	.6	.36			
Σ: 852.7		473.97	496.8		465.32

$M_1 = 32.80$; $S_1^2 = 473.97/25 = 18.96$; $M_2 = 29.22$; $S_2^2 = 465.32/16 = 29.08$

$N_1 = 26$; $df_1 = N_1 - 1 = 25$; $N_2 = 17$; $df_2 = N_2 - 1 = 16$

$df_{\text{Total}} = df_1 + df_2 = 25 + 16 = 41$

$$S_{\text{Pooled}}^2 = \frac{df_1}{df_{\text{Total}}}(S_1^2) + \frac{df_2}{df_{\text{Total}}}(S_2^2) = \frac{25}{41}(18.96) + \frac{16}{41}(29.08)$$

$$= .61(18.96) + .39(29.08) = 11.57 + 11.34 = 22.91$$

$S_{M_1}^2 = S_{\text{Pooled}}^2/N_1 = 22.91/26 = .88$

$S_{M_2}^2 = S_{\text{Pooled}}^2/N_2 = 22.91/17 = 1.35$

$S_{\text{Difference}}^2 = S_{M_1}^2 + S_{M_2}^2 = .88 + 1.35 = 2.23$

$S_{\text{Difference}} = \sqrt{S_{\text{Difference}}^2} = \sqrt{2.23} = 1.49$

Needed t with $df = 41$ (using $df = 40$ in table), 5% level, one tailed = 1.684

$t = (M_1 - M_2)/S_{\text{Difference}} = (32.80 - 29.22)/1.49 = 3.58/1.49 = 2.40$

Conclusion: Reject the null hypothesis; the research hypothesis is supported.

Source: Data from Moorehouse & Sanders (1992).

❶ **Restate the question as a research hypothesis and a null hypothesis about the populations.** There are two populations:

> **Population 1:** Boys whose mothers' work involves solving problems.
>
> **Population 2:** Boys whose mothers' work does not involve solving problems.

Based on theory and previous research, Moorehouse and Sanders expected that boys whose mothers' work involved solving problems would have higher scores on the test of perceived academic competence. The research hypothesis was that Population 1 boys would score higher than Population 2 boys. (That is, this was a directional hypothesis.) The null hypothesis was that the Population 1 boys would not score higher than the Population 2 boys.

❷ **Determine the characteristics of the comparison distribution.** The comparison distribution is a distribution of differences between means. Its mean is 0 (as it almost always is in a t test for independent means, because we are interested in whether there is more than 0 difference between the two populations). Regarding its standard deviation,

❹ **Figure the estimated population variances based on each sample.** As shown in Table 9–1, S_1^2 comes out to 18.96 and $S_2^2 = 29.08$.

❺ **Figure the pooled estimate of the population variance.** As shown in Table 9–1, the figuring for S_{Pooled}^2 gives a result of 22.91.

❻ **Figure the variance of each distribution of means.** Dividing S_{Pooled}^2 by the N in each sample, as shown in Table 9–1, gives $S_{M_1}^2 = .88$ and $S_{M_2}^2 = 1.35$.

❼ **Figure the variance of the distribution of differences between means.** Adding up the variances of the two distributions of means, as shown in Table 9–1, comes out to $S_{Difference}^2 = 2.23$.

❽ **Figure the standard deviation of the distribution of differences between means.** $\sqrt{2.23} = 1.49$.

The shape of this comparison distribution will be a t distribution with a total of 41 degrees of freedom.

❸ **Determine the cutoff sample score on the comparison distribution at which the null hypothesis should be rejected.** This requires a one-tailed test because a particular direction of difference between the two populations was predicted. Since the t table in the Appendix (Table A–2) does not have exactly 41 degrees of freedom, you use the next lowest (40). At the .05 level, you need a t of at least 1.684. (The cutoff t score is +1.684, as the research hypothesis is that Population 1 boys would score *higher* than Population 2 boys.)

❹ **Determine your sample's score on the comparison distribution.** The t score is the difference between the two sample means ($32.80 - 29.22$, which is 3.58), divided by the standard deviation of the distribution of differences between means (which is 1.49). This comes out to 2.40.

❺ **Decide whether to reject the null hypothesis.** The t score of 2.40 for the difference between the two actual means is larger than the needed t score of 1.684. You can reject the null hypothesis. The research hypothesis is supported: Boys whose mothers' work involves solving problems see themselves as better at schoolwork than boys whose mothers' work does not involve solving problems.

SUMMARY OF STEPS FOR CONDUCTING A *t* TEST FOR INDEPENDENT MEANS

Table 9–2 summarizes the steps for a *t* test for independent means.[1]

A SECOND EXAMPLE OF A *t* TEST FOR INDEPENDENT MEANS

Suppose a researcher wants to study the effectiveness of a new job skills training program for people who have not been able to hold a job. Fourteen people who have not been able to hold a job agree to be in the study. The researcher randomly picks

---

TABLE 9–2   Steps for a *t* Test for Independent Means

❶ **Restate the question as a research hypothesis and a null hypothesis about the populations.**
❷ **Determine the characteristics of the comparison distribution.**
   a. Its mean will be 0.
   b. Figure its standard deviation.
      ❹ **Figure the estimated population variances based on each sample.** For each population, $S^2 = \Sigma(X - M)^2/(N - 1)$.
      ❺ **Figure the pooled estimate of the population variance:**

$$S^2_{\text{Pooled}} = \frac{df_1}{df_{\text{Total}}}(S^2_1) + \frac{df_2}{df_{\text{Total}}}(S^2_2)$$

$$(df_1 = N_1 - 1 \text{ and } df_2 = N_2 - 1; df_{\text{Total}} = df_1 + df_2)$$

      ❻ **Figure the variance of each distribution of means:** $S^2_{M_1} = S^2_{\text{Pooled}}/N_1$ and $S^2_{M_2} = S^2_{\text{Pooled}}/N_2$
      ❼ **Figure the variance of the distribution of differences between means:**
$$S^2_{\text{Difference}} = S^2_{M_1} + S^2_{M_2}$$
      ❽ **Figure the standard deviation of the distribution of differences between means:** $S_{\text{Difference}} = \sqrt{S^2_{\text{Difference}}}$
   c. It will be a *t* distribution with df_{Total} degrees of freedom.
❸ **Determine the cutoff sample score on the comparison distribution at which the null hypothesis should be rejected.**
   a. Determine the degrees of freedom (df_{Total}), desired significance level, and tails in the test (one or two).
   b. Look up the appropriate cutoff in a *t* table. If the exact *df* is not given, use the *df* below it.
❹ **Determine your sample's score on the comparison distribution:**
   $t = (M_1 - M_2)/S_{\text{Difference}}$
❺ **Decide whether to reject the null hypothesis:** Compare the scores from Steps 3 and 4.

---

[1]The steps of figuring the standard deviation of the distribution of differences between means can be combined into a single overall computational formula:

(9-8) $$S_{\text{Difference}} = \sqrt{\frac{(N_1 - 1)(S^2_1) + (N_2 - 1)(S^2_2)}{N_1 + N_2 - 2}\left(\frac{1}{N_1} + \frac{1}{N_2}\right)}$$

As usual, we urge you to use the full set of steps and the regular, definitional formulas in your figuring when doing the practice problems in this book. Those steps help you learn the basic principles. However, this computational formula will be useful if statistics software is not available and you have to figure by hand a *t* test for independent means on scores from a real study with many participants in each group.

seven of these volunteers to be an experimental group that will go through the special training program. The other seven volunteers are put in a control group that will go through an ordinary job skills training program. After finishing their training program (of whichever type), all 14 are placed in similar jobs.

A month later, each volunteer's employer is asked to rate how well the new employee is doing using a 9-point scale. The scores and figuring for the t test are shown in Table 9–3. The distributions involved are shown in Figure 9–3. Let's carry out the analysis, following the steps of hypothesis testing.

❶ **Restate the question as a research hypothesis and a null hypothesis about the populations.** There are two populations:

> **Population 1:** Individuals who could not hold a job who then participate in the special job skills program
>
> **Population 2:** Individuals who could not hold a job who then participate in an ordinary job skills program

It is possible for the special program to have either a positive or a negative effect compared to the ordinary program, and either result would be of interest. Thus,

TABLE 9–3 Figuring for a t Test for Independent Means for the Job Skills Example

Experimental Group (Receiving Special Program)			Control Group (Receiving Ordinary Program)		
Score	Deviation From Mean	Squared Deviation From Mean	Score	Deviation From Mean	Squared Deviation From Mean
6	0	0	6	3	9
4	−2	4	1	−2	4
9	3	9	5	2	4
7	1	1	3	0	0
7	1	1	1	−2	4
3	−3	9	1	−2	4
6	0	0	4	1	1
Σ: 42	0	24	21	0	26

$M_1 = 6; S_1^2 = 24/6 = 4; M_2 = 3; S_2^2 = 26/6 = 4.33$

$N_1 = 7; df_1 = N_1 - 1 = 6; N_2 = 7; df_2 = N_2 - 1 = 6$

$df_{Total} = df_1 + df_2 = 6 + 6 = 12$

$S_{Pooled}^2 = \dfrac{df_1}{df_{Total}}(S_1^2) + \dfrac{df_2}{df_{Total}}(S_2^2) = \dfrac{6}{12}(4) + \dfrac{6}{12}(4.33) = .5(4) + .5(4.33) = 2.00 + 2.17 = 4.17$

$S_{M_1}^2 = S_{Pooled}^2/N_1 = 4.17/7 = .60$

$S_{M_2}^2 = S_{Pooled}^2/N_2 = 4.17/7 = .60$

$S_{Difference}^2 = S_{M_1}^2 + S_{M_2}^2 = .60 + .60 = 1.20$

$S_{Difference} = \sqrt{S_{Difference}^2} = \sqrt{1.20} = 1.10$

Needed t with $df = 12$, 5% level, two-tailed $= \pm 2.179$

$t = (M_1 - M_2)/S_{Difference} = (6.00 - 3.00)/1.10 = 3.00/1.10 = 2.73$

Conclusion: Reject the null hypothesis, the research hypothesis is supported.

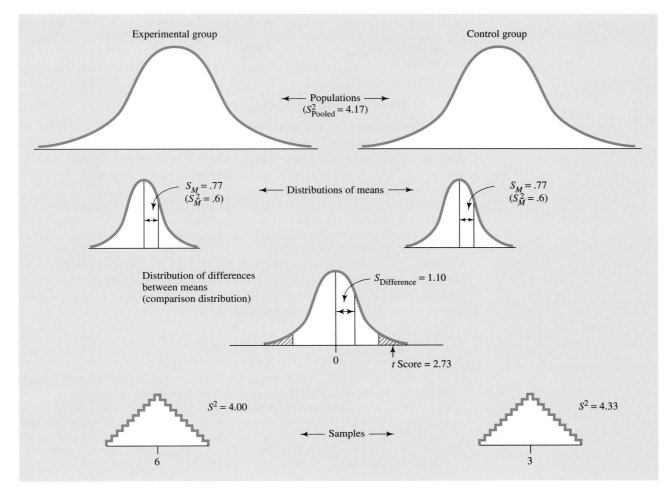

FIGURE 9–3   *The distributions involved in the job skills example of a* t *test for independent means.*

the research hypothesis is that the means of Population 1 and Population 2 are different. This is a nondirectional hypothesis. The null hypothesis is that the means of Population 1 and Population 2 are the same.

❷ **Determine the characteristics of the comparison distribution.**

    a. Its mean will be 0.

    b. Figure its standard deviation. See Table 9–3 for the figuring for each step below.

        ❶ **Figure the estimated population variances based on each sample.** $S_1^2 = 4$ and $S_2^2 = 4.33$.

        ❷ **Figure the pooled estimate of the population variance.** $S_{Pooled}^2 = 4.17$.

        ❸ **Figure the variance of each distribution of means.** Dividing S_{Pooled}^2 by the N in each sample gives $S_{M_1}^2 = .60$ and $S_{M_2}^2 = .60$.

Tip for Success

In this example, note that $S_{M_1}^2$ is the same value as $S_{M_2}^2$. This is because there are the same number of people in each of the samples. When the number of people in the two samples is not the same, $S_{M_1}^2$ and $S_{M_2}^2$ will have different values.

❶ **Figure the variance of the distribution of differences between means.** Adding up the variances of the two distribution of means comes out to $S^2_{\text{Difference}} = 1.20$.

❷ **Figure the standard deviation of the distribution of differences between means.** $S_{\text{Difference}} = \sqrt{1.20} = 1.10$.

  c. It is a t distribution with $df_{\text{Total}} = 12$.

❸ **Determine the cutoff sample score on the comparison distribution at which the null hypothesis should be rejected.** The cutoff you need is for a two-tailed test (because the hypothesis is nondirectional) at the usual .05 level, with 12 degrees of freedom. Looking this up on the t table in the Appendix, the cutoff t scores are 2.179 and −2.179.

❹ **Determine your sample's score on the comparison distribution.** The t score is the difference between the two sample means divided by the standard deviation of the distribution of differences between means. This comes out to a t of 2.73. (That is, $t = 3.0/1.10 = 2.73$.)

❺ **Decide whether to reject the null hypothesis.** The t score of 2.73 is more extreme than the cutoff t score of 2.179. Thus, the researchers can reject the null hypothesis. The research hypothesis is supported: The new special job skills program is more effective than the ordinary job skills program.

HOW ARE YOU DOING?

1. List the ways in which hypothesis testing for a t test for independent means is different from a t test for dependent means in terms of (a) Step 2, (b) Step 3, and (c) Step 4.
2. Using the .05 significance level, two-tailed, figure a t test for independent means for an experiment comparing an experimental to a control condition. For the experimental condition, with 26 participants, $M = 5, S^2 = 10$; for the control condition, with 36 participants, $M = 8, S^2 = 12$. (a) Use the steps of hypothesis testing. (b) Sketch the distributions involved.

ANSWERS:

1. (a) The comparison distribution for a t test for independent means is a distribution of differences between means.
(b) The degrees of freedom for a t test for independent means is the sum of the degrees of freedom for the two samples.
(c) The t score for a t test for independent means is based on differences between means (divided by the standard deviation of the distribution of differences between means).
2. (a) Steps of hypothesis testing:
    ❶ **Restate the question as a research hypothesis and a null hypothesis about the populations.** There are two populations.

    Population 1: People given the experimental procedure.
    Population 2: People given the control procedure.

The research hypothesis is that the mean of Population 1 is different than the mean of Population 2. The null hypothesis is that the mean of Population 1 is the same as the mean of Population 2.
    ❷ **Determine the characteristics of the comparison distribution.**
    a. Its mean will be 0.
    b. Figure its standard deviation.
        ❶ **Figure the estimated population variances based on each sample.** $S^2_1 = 10$ and $S^2_2 = 12$.

❶ Figure the pooled estimate of the population variance.
$S^2_{Pooled} = (25/60)(10) + (35/60)(12) = 4.17 + 7.00 = 11.17$.
 ❶ Figure the variance of each distribution of means. $S^2_{M_1} = 11.17/26 = .43$
and $S^2_{M_2} = 11.17/36 = .31$.
 ❶ Figure the variance of the distribution of differences between means.
$S^2_{Difference} = .43 + .31 = .74$.
 **❶ Figure the standard deviation of the distribution of differences between
means.** $S_{Difference} = \sqrt{.74} = .86$.
c. It is a *t* distribution with $df_{Total} = 60$.
 **❸ Determine the cutoff sample score on the comparison distribution at which the
null hypothesis should be rejected.** The *t* cutoffs for .05 level, two-tailed, $df = 60$ are
2.001 and −2.001.
 ❹ Determine your sample's score on the comparison distribution.
$t = (5 − 8)/.86 = −3.49$.
 ❺ Decide whether to reject the null hypothesis. The *t* of −3.49 is more extreme than
the needed *t* of ±2.001. Therefore, reject the null hypothesis.
b. The distributions involved are shown in Figure 9–4.

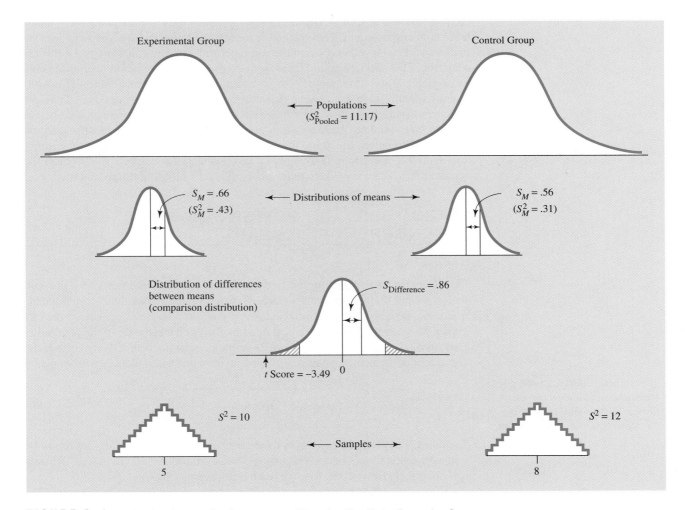

FIGURE 9–4   *The distributions for the answer to "How Are You Doing" question 2.*

ASSUMPTIONS OF THE *t* TEST FOR INDEPENDENT MEANS

The first assumption for a *t* test for independent means is the same as that for any *t* test: Each of the population distributions is assumed to follow a normal curve. In practice, this is only a problem if you have reason to think that the two populations are dramatically skewed distributions, and in opposite directions. The *t* test holds up well even when the shape of the population distributions is fairly far from normal.

In a *t* test for independent means, you also have to be able to assume that the two populations have the same variance. (You take advantage of this assumption when you average the estimates from each of the two samples.) Once again, however, it turns out that in practice the *t* test gives pretty accurate results even when there are fairly large differences in the population variances, particularly when there are equal or near equal numbers of scores in the two samples.

However, the *t* test can give quite misleading results if (a) the scores in the samples suggest that the populations are very far from normal, (b) the variances are very different, or (c) there are both problems. In these situations, there are alternatives to the ordinary *t* test procedure, some of which we will consider in Chapter 11.

Many computer programs for figuring the *t* test for independent means actually provide two sets of results. One set of results figures the *t* test assuming the population variances are equal. This method is the standard one, the one you have learned in this chapter. The other method the computer program uses does not make this assumption. This special method takes into account that the population variances may be unequal. (But it still assumes the populations follow a normal curve.) However, in most situations we can assume that the population variances are equal. Thus, researchers usually use the standard method. Using the special approach has the advantage that you don't have to worry about whether you met the equal population variance assumption. But it has the disadvantage that if you have met that assumption, with this special method you have less power. That is, when you do meet the assumption, you are less likely to get a significant result using the special method.

EFFECT SIZE AND POWER FOR THE *t* TEST FOR INDEPENDENT MEANS

EFFECT SIZE

The effect size for the *t* test for independent means is the difference between the population means divided by the standard deviation of the population of individuals. When you have results of a completed study, you estimate the effect size as the difference between the sample means divided by the pooled estimate of the population standard deviation. (The pooled estimate of the population standard deviation is the square root of the pooled estimate of the population variance.) Stated as a formula,

> The estimated effect size is the difference between the sample means divided by the pooled estimate of the population's standard deviation.

$$\text{Estimated Effect Size} = \frac{M_1 - M_2}{S_{\text{Pooled}}} \tag{9-9}$$

Cohen's (1988) conventions for the *t* test for independent means are the same as in all the situations we have considered so far: .20 for a small effect size, .50 for a medium effect size, and .80 for a large effect size.

Consider our example of the effectiveness of a special job skills program. The mean for the sample of individuals who participated in the special job skills program was 6.00. The mean for the sample of individuals who participated in the ordinary job skills program was 3.00. We figured the pooled estimate of the population variance to be 4.17; the pooled estimate of the population's standard deviation is thus 2.04. The difference in means of 3.00, divided by 2.04, gives an effect size of 1.47. This is a very large effect size. In terms of the formula,

$$\text{Estimated Effect Size} = \frac{M_1 - M_2}{S_{\text{Pooled}}} = \frac{6.00 - 3.00}{2.04} = 1.47$$

POWER

Table 9–4 gives the approximate power for the .05 significance level for small, medium, and large effect sizes, and one-tailed or two-tailed tests.[2]

For example, suppose you have read a study using a *t* test for independent means that had a nonsignificant result using the .05 significance level, two-tailed. There were 40 participants in each group. Should you conclude that there is in fact no difference at all in the populations? This conclusion seems quite unjustified. Table 9–4 shows a power of only .14 for a small effect size. This suggests that if such a small effect really exists in the populations, this study would probably not come out significant. Still, we can also conclude that if there is a true difference in the populations, it is probably not large. Table 9–4 shows a power of .94 for a large effect size. This suggests that if a large effect exists, it almost surely would have produced a significant result.

TABLE 9–4 Approximate Power for Studies Using the *t* Test for Independent Means Testing Hypotheses at the .05 Significance Level

Number of Participants in Each Group	Effect Size		
	Small (.20)	Medium (.50)	Large (.80)
One-tailed test			
10	.11	.29	.53
20	.15	.46	.80
30	.19	.61	.92
40	.22	.72	.97
50	.26	.80	.99
100	.41	.97	*
Two-tailed test			
10	.07	.18	.39
20	.09	.33	.69
30	.12	.47	.86
40	.14	.60	.94
50	.17	.70	.98
100	.29	.94	*

*Nearly 1.

[2]Cohen (1988, pp. 28–39) provides more detailed tables in terms of number of participants, levels of effect size, and significance levels. Note that Cohen describes the significance level by the letter *a* (for "alpha level"), with a subscript of either 1 or 2, referring to a one-tailed or two-tailed test. For example, a table that refers to "$a_1 = .05$" at the top means that this is the table for $p < .05$, one-tailed.

BOX 9–1   Two Women Make a Point about Gender and Statistics

One of the most useful advanced statistics books written so far is *Using Multivariate Statistics* by Barbara Tabachnick and Linda Fidell (2001), two experimental psychologists at California State University at Northridge. These two met at a faculty luncheon soon after Tabachnick was hired. Fidell recalls:

> I had this enormous data set to analyze, and out came lots of pretty numbers in nice neat little columns, but I was not sure what all of it meant, or even whether my data had violated any critical assumptions. That was in 1975. I had been trained at the University of Michigan; I knew statistics up through the analysis of variance. But none of us were taught the multivariate analysis of variance at that time. Then along came these statistical packages to do it. But how to comprehend them?

(You will be introduced to the multivariate analysis of variance in Chapter 12.)

Both Fidell and Tabachnick had gone out and learned on their own, taking the necessary courses, reading, asking others who knew the programs better, trying out what would happen if they did this with the data, what would happen if they did that. Now the two women asked each other, why must this be so hard? Were others reinventing this same wheel at the very same time? They decided to put their wheel into a book.

"And so began fifteen years of conflict-free collaboration," reports Fidell. (That is something to compare to the feuds recounted in other boxes in this book.) The authors had no trouble finding a publisher, and the book, now in its fourth edition, has sold "nicely." In Fidell's opinion, statistics is a field in which women seem particularly to excel and feel comfortable. It is a branch of mathematics that, according to Fidell, women often come to find "perfectly logical, perfectly reasonable—and then, with time, something they can truly enjoy."

In teaching new students, the math-shy ones in particular, she finds that once she can "get them to relax," they often find that they thoroughly enjoy statistics. She tells them, "I intend to win you over. And if you will give me half a chance, I will do it."

Source: Personal interview with Linda Fidell.

POWER WHEN SAMPLE SIZES ARE NOT EQUAL

For a study with any given total number of participants, power is greatest when the participants are divided into two equal groups. Recall the example from the start of this chapter where the 42 participants were divided into 11 in the experimental group and 31 in the control group. This study has much less power than it would have if the researchers had been able to divide their 42 participants into 21 in each group.

There is a practical problem in figuring power from tables when sample sizes are not equal. Like most power tables, Table 9–4 assumes equal numbers in each of the two groups. What do you do when your two samples have different numbers of people in them? It turns out that in terms of power, the **harmonic mean** of the numbers of participants in two unequal sample sizes gives the equivalent sample size for what you would have with two equal samples. The harmonic mean sample size is given by this formula:

harmonic mean

> The harmonic mean is 2 times the first sample size times the second sample size, all divided by the sum of the two sample sizes.

$$\text{Harmonic Mean} = \frac{(2)(N_1)(N_2)}{N_1 + N_2} \tag{9-10}$$

In our example with 11 in one group and 31 in the other, the harmonic mean is 16.24:

$$\text{Harmonic Mean} = \frac{(2)(N_1)(N_2)}{N_1 + N_2} = \frac{(2)(11)(31)}{11 + 31} = \frac{682}{42} = 16.24$$

Thus, even though you have a total of 42 participants, the study has the power of a study with equal sample sizes of only about 16 in each group. (This means that a study with a total of 32 participants divided equally would have had about the same power.)

PLANNING SAMPLE SIZE

Table 9–5 gives the approximate number of participants needed for 80% power for estimated small, medium, and large effect sizes, using one-tailed and two-tailed tests, all using the .05 significance level.[3] Suppose you plan a study in which you expect a medium effect size and will use the .05 significance level, one-tailed. Based on Table 9–5, you need 50 people in each group (100 total) to have 80% power. However, if you did a study using the same significance level but expected a large effect size, you would need only 20 people in each group (40 total).

HOW ARE YOU DOING?

1. List two assumptions for the *t* test for independent means. For each, give the situations in which violations of these assumptions would be seriously problematic.
2. Why do you need to assume the populations have the same variance?
3. What is the predicted effect size for a study in which the sample drawn from Population 1 has a mean of 17, Population 2's sample mean is 25, and the pooled estimate of the population standard deviation is 20?
4. What is the power of a study using a *t* test for independent means, with a two-tailed test at the .05 significance level, in which the researchers predict a large effect size and there are 20 participants in each group?
5. What is the approximate power of a study using a *t* test for independent means, with a two-tailed test at the .05 significance level, in which the researchers predict a large effect size, and there are 6 participants in one group and 34 participants in the other group?
6. How many participants do you need in each group for 80% power in a planned study in which you predict a small effect size and will be using a *t* test for independent means, one-tailed, at the .05 significance level?

ANSWERS:

1. One assumption is that the two populations are normally distributed; this is mainly a problem if you have reason to think the two populations are strongly skewed in opposite directions. A second assumption is that the two populations have the same variance; this is mainly a problem if you believe the two distributions have quite different variances *and* the sample sizes are different.

TABLE 9–5 Approximate Number of Participants Needed in Each Group (Assuming Equal Sample Sizes) for 80% Power for the *t* Test for Independent Means, Testing Hypotheses at the .05 Significance Level

	Effect Size		
	Small (.20)	Medium (.50)	Large (.80)
One-tailed	310	50	20
Two-tailed	393	64	26

[3]Cohen (1988, pp. 54–55) provides fuller tables, indicating needed numbers of participants for levels of power other than 80%; for effect sizes other than .20, .50, and .80; and for other significance levels.

2. Because you make a pooled estimate of the population variance. The pooling would not make sense if the estimates from the two samples were for populations with different variances.
3. Predicted effect size $= (17 - 25)/20 = -8/20 = -.4$.
4. .69.
5. Harmonic mean $= (2)(6)(34)/(6 + 34) = 408/40 = 10.2$. Power for a study like this with 10 in each group $= .39$.
6. 310.

THE t TEST FOR INDEPENDENT MEANS IN RESEARCH ARTICLES

A t test for independent means is usually described in research articles by giving the means (and sometimes the standard deviations) of the two samples, plus the usual way of reporting any kind of t test—for example, $t(18) = 4.72$, $p < .01$ (recall that the number in parentheses is the degrees of freedom).

The result of the Moorehouse and Sanders (1992) example might be written up as follows: "The mean perceived academic competence for the boys whose mothers' work involved problem solving was 32.8 ($SD = 4.27$), and the mean for the boys whose mothers' work did not involve problem solving was 29.2 ($SD = 5.23$); $t(41) = 2.42$, $p < .05$, one-tailed."

Table 9–6 is an example in which the results are given in a table. This table is taken from a study conducted by Frisch, Shamsuddin, and Kurtz (1995) in which 293 female medical students in Malaysia were surveyed on their views about smok-

TABLE 9–6	**t Tests for Means on Passive Smoking Knowledge, Attitude, and Efforts According to Smoking Status, for Total Group and Men and Women**			
	Brother Smoker	Brother Nonsmoker	t-Value	Sig.
Total Group	$N = 41$	$N = 73$		
Knowledge	2.03 (96)	1.88 (140)	2.61	.01
Attitude	1.95 (94)	1.70 (137)	3.29	.001
Efforts	2.36 (92)	2.23 (133)	1.88	.061
Phys. Resp.*	1.78 (95)	1.61 (142)	2.02	.04
Men				
Knowledge	2.15 (54)	1.92 (69)	2.97	.004
Attitude	2.08 (54)	1.83 (67)	2.12	.036
Efforts	2.50 (52)	2.31 (66)	1.87	.064
Phys. Resp.*	1.81 (54)	1.65 (69)	1.27	.207
Women				
Knowledge	1.87 (42)	1.85 (71)	.30	.767
Attitude	1.77 (40)	1.57 (70)	2.43	.018
Efforts	2.17 (40)	2.15 (67)	.26	.797
Phys. Resp.*	1.76 (41)	1.58 (73)	1.51	.136

*Physician's responsibility.
Source: Frisch, A. S., Shamsuddin, K., & Kurtz, M. (1995). Family factors and knowledge: Attitudes and efforts concerning exposure to environmental tobacco among Malaysian medical students. *Journal of Asian and African Studies, 30*, 68–79. Reprinted by permission.

ing and on whether their family members and friends smoked. This table compares those students who have brothers who smoke to those who have brothers who don't smoke. The measures were Knowledge (of the health risks of being around smokers), Attitude (toward being around smokers), Efforts (to avoid being around smokers), and Physician's Responsibility (to inform patients of health risks of being around smokers). All scales were scored so that higher scores were pro-smoking. Lower scores meant more concern about the health risks.

The first line of the table shows that those with a brother who smokes scored higher on the Knowledge scale. This means that such students have less knowledge about the health risks of being around smokers. The second line shows that those with a brother who smokes have a more positive attitude toward being around smokers (that is, they do not see it as being as much of a health risk).

Note that some of these results were not significant. What should we conclude? Consider the students' beliefs about a physician's responsibility. In this comparison, there were 41 with smoker brothers and 73 with nonsmoker brothers. The formula for the harmonic mean indicates that for purposes of determining power, there are 52.5 participants per group. That is,

$$\text{Harmonic Mean} = \frac{(2)(N_1)(N_2)}{N_1 + N_2} = \frac{(2)(41)(73)}{41 + 73} = \frac{5,986}{114} = 52.5$$

Once you know the sample size to use, you can look up power in Table 9–4, using 50 participants (the nearest number of participants in the table to 52.5) and a two-tailed test. From the table, the power of this study to find significance for a small effect size is only .17. On the other hand, the power of the study to find a medium effect size is .70 and a large effect size, .98. Thus, if in fact there is a small effect for having a brother who is a smoker, this would probably not have shown up in this study. On the other hand, suppose there was in fact a medium effect of this kind. In that case, the result of this study probably would have been significant. Almost certainly if there were a large effect, the study would have come out significant. Thus, we can fairly confidently take from this study that having a brother who is a smoker probably does not make a large difference for Malaysian female medical students' beliefs about a physician's responsibility to inform their patients about the risks of being around smokers. However, we cannot conclude that there might not be a small effect of this kind.

SUMMARY

1. A *t* test for independent means is used for hypothesis testing with two samples of scores. The main difference from a *t* test for a single sample is that the comparison distribution is a distribution of differences between means of samples. This distribution can be thought of as being built up in two steps: Each population of individuals produces a distribution of means, and then a new distribution is created of differences between pairs of means selected from these two distributions of means.

2. The distribution of differences between means has a mean of 0 and is a *t* distribution with the total of the degrees of freedom from the two samples. Its standard deviation is figured in several steps:
   - **Ⓐ Figure the estimated population variances based on each sample.**
   - **Ⓑ Figure the pooled estimate of the population variance.**
   - **Ⓒ Figure the variance of each distribution of means.**

⟠ **Figure the variance of the distribution of differences between means.**
⟡ **Figure the standard deviation of the distribution of differences between means.**

3. The assumptions of the *t* test for independent means are that the two populations are normally distributed and have the same variance. However, the *t* test gives fairly accurate results when the true situation is moderately different from the assumptions.

4. Estimated effect size for a *t* test for independent means is the difference between the sample means divided by the pooled estimate of the population standard deviation. Power is greatest when the sample sizes of the two groups are equal. When they are not equal, you use the harmonic mean of the two sample sizes when looking up power on a table.

5. *t* tests for independent means are usually reported in research articles with the means of the two groups plus the degrees of freedom, *t* score, and significance level. Results may also be reported in a table where each significant difference is shown by asterisks.

KEY TERMS

t test for independent
  means (p. 256)
distribution of differences
  between means (p. 257)
pooled estimate of the
  population variance
  (S^2_{Pooled}) (p. 259)

weighted average
  (p. 259)
variance of the distribution
  of differences between
  means $(S^2_{Difference})$
  (p. 260)

standard deviation of the
  distribution of differ-
  ences between means
  $S_{Difference}$ (p. 260)
harmonic mean (p. 274)

EXAMPLE WORKED-OUT PROBLEMS

FIGURING THE STANDARD DEVIATION OF THE DISTRIBUTION OF DIFFERENCES BETWEEN MEANS

Figure $S_{Difference}$ for the following study: $N_1 = 40$, $S^2_1 = 15$; $N_2 = 60$; $S^2_2 = 12$.

ANSWER

⟠ **Figure the estimated population variances based on each sample:** $S^2_1 = 15$; $S^2_2 = 12$.

⟡ **Figure the pooled estimate of the population variance:**
$$df_1 = N_1 - 1 = 40 - 1 = 39; df_2 = N_2 - 1 = 60 - 1 = 59;$$
$$df_{Total} = df_1 + df_2 = 39 + 59 = 98.$$
$$S^2_{Pooled} = \frac{df_1}{df_{Total}}(S^2_1) + \frac{df_2}{df_{Total}}(S^2_2) = (39/98)(15) + (59/98)(12)$$
$$= 5.97 + 7.22 = 13.19$$

⟢ **Figure the variance of each distribution of means:**
$$S^2_{M_1} = S^2_{Pooled}/N_1 = 13.19/40 = .33$$
$$S^2_{M_2} = S^2_{Pooled}/N_2 = 13.19/60 = .22$$

⟣ **Figure the variance of the distribution of differences between means:**
$$S^2_{Difference} = S^2_{M_1} + S^2_{M_2} = .33 + .22 = .55$$

❷ Figure the standard deviation of the distribution of differences between means:

$$S_{\text{Difference}} = \sqrt{S^2_{\text{Difference}}} = \sqrt{.55} = .74$$

HYPOTHESIS TESTING USING THE t TEST FOR INDEPENDENT MEANS

A researcher randomly assigns five individuals to receive a new experimental procedure and five to a control condition. At the end of the study, all 10 are measured. Scores for those in the experimental group were 7, 6, 9, 7, and 6. Scores for those in the control group were 5, 2, 4, 3, and 6. Carry out a t test for independent means using the .05 level of significance, two-tailed. Use the steps of hypothesis testing and sketch the distributions involved.

ANSWER

The figuring is shown in Table 9–7; the distributions are shown in Figure 9–5. Here are the steps of hypothesis testing.

❶ Restate the question as a research hypothesis and a null hypothesis about the populations. There are two populations:

>   **Population 1:** People like those who receive the experimental procedure.
>   **Population 2:** People like those who receive the control procedure.

TABLE 9–7   **Figuring for Example Worked-Out Problem for Hypothesis Testing Using the t Test Independent Means**

	Experimental Group			Control Group	
Score	Deviation From Mean	Squared Deviation From Mean	Score	Deviation From Mean	Squared Deviation From Mean
7	0	0	5	1	1
6	−1	1	2	−2	4
9	2	4	4	0	0
7	0	0	3	−1	1
6	−1	1	6	2	4
Σ: 35	0	6	20	0	10

$M_1 = 7; S^2_1 = 6/4 = 1.5; M_2 = 4; S^2_2 = 10/4 = 2.5$

$N_1 = 5; df_1 = N_1 - 1 = 4; N_2 = 5; df_2 = N_2 - 1 = 4$

$df_{\text{Total}} = df_1 + df_2 = 4 + 4 = 8$

$S^2_{\text{Pooled}} = \dfrac{df_1}{df_{\text{Total}}}(S^2_1) + \dfrac{df_2}{df_{\text{Total}}}(S^2_2) = \dfrac{4}{8}(1.5) + \dfrac{4}{8}(2.5) = .75 + 1.25 = 2.00$

$S^2_{M_1} = S^2_{\text{Pooled}}/N_1 = 2.00/5 = .40$

$S^2_{M_2} = S^2_{\text{pooled}}/N_2 = 2.00/5 = .40$

$S^2_{\text{Difference}} = S^2_{M_1} + S^2_{M_2} = .40 + .40 = .80$

$S_{\text{Difference}} = \sqrt{S^2_{\text{Difference}}} = \sqrt{.80} = .89$

Needed t with $df = 8$, 5% level, two-tailed $= \pm 2.306$

$t = (M_1 - M_2)/S_{\text{Difference}} = (7 - 4)/.89 = 3/.89 = 3.37$

Conclusion: Reject the null hypothesis; the research hypothesis is supported.

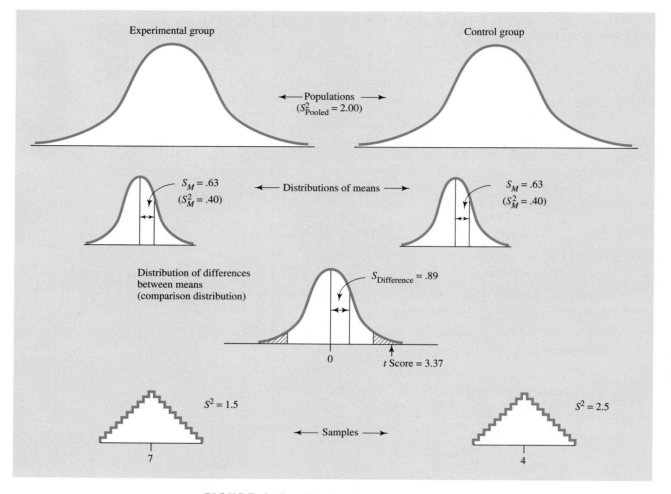

FIGURE 9–5 *The distributions in the Example Worked-Out Problem for hypothesis testing using the* t *test for independent means.*

The research hypothesis is that the means of the two populations are different. The null hypothesis is that the means of the two populations are the same.

❷ **Determine the characteristics of the comparison distribution.**

    a. The distribution of differences between means has a mean of 0.

    b. Figure its standard deviation.

        ❶ Figure the estimated population variances based on each sample: $S_1^2 = 1.5$; $S_2^2 = 2.5$

        ❷ Figure the pooled estimate of the population variance: $S_{Pooled}^2 = 2.00$

        ❸ Figure the variance of each distribution of means: $S_{M1}^2 = .40$; $S_{M2}^2 = .40$

        ❹ Figure the variance of the distribution of differences between means: $S_{Difference}^2 = .80$

    ❶ **Figure the standard deviation of the distribution of differences between means:** $S_{\text{Difference}} = .89$

    c. It is a *t* distribution with $df = 8$.

    ❸ **Determine the cutoff sample score on the comparison distribution at which the null hypothesis should be rejected.** With $df = 8$, .05 significance level, two-tailed test, the cutoffs are 2.306 and -2.306.

    ❹ **Determine the sample's score on the comparison distribution.** $t = (7 - 4)/.89 = 3.37$.

    ❺ **Decide whether to reject the null hypothesis.** The *t* of 3.37 is more extreme than ± 2.306. Thus, you can reject the null hypothesis. The research hypothesis is supported.

FINDING POWER WHEN SAMPLE SIZES ARE UNEQUAL

A planned study with a predicted small effect size has 22 in one group and 51 in the other. What is the approximate power for a one-tailed test at the .05 significance level?

ANSWER

$$\text{Harmonic Mean} = \frac{(2)(N_1)(N_2)}{N_1 + N_2} = \frac{(2)(22)(51)}{22 + 51} = \frac{2244}{73} = 30.7$$

From Table 9–4, for a one-tailed test with 30 participants in each group, power for a small effect size is .19.

PRACTICE PROBLEMS

These problems involve figuring. Most real-life statistics problems are done on a computer with special statistical software. Even if you have such software, do these problems by hand (with the help of a calculator) to ingrain the method in your mind. Also, in all problems involving figuring, be sure to show your work.

    For practice in using a computer to solve statistics problems, refer to the computer section of each chapter of the *Student's Study Guide and Computer Workbook* that accompanies this text. All data are fictional unless an actual citation is given. For answers to Set I problems, see pp. 433–35.

SET I

1. For each of the following studies, say whether you would use a *t* test for dependent means or a *t* test for independent means.

    (a) An education researcher randomly assigns a group of 47 fourth-grade students to receive a new after-school math program and 48 other fourth-grade students to receive the standard after-school math program, and then measures how well they all do on a math test.

    (b) A marketing researcher measures 100 doctors' reports of the number of their patients asking them about a particular drug during the month before and the month after a major advertising campaign.

    (c) A researcher tests reaction time of each of a group of 14 individuals twice, once while in a very hot room and once while in a normal-temperature room.

2. Figure $S_{\text{Difference}}$ for each of the following studies:

	N_1	S_1^2	N_2	S_2^2
(a)	20	1	20	2
(b)	20	1	40	2
(c)	40	1	20	2
(d)	40	1	40	2
(e)	40	1	40	4

3. For each of the following experiments, decide if the difference between conditions is statistically significant at the .05 level (two-tailed).

	Experimental Group			Control Group		
	N	M	S^2	N	M	S^2
(a)	30	12.0	2.4	30	11.1	2.8
(b)	20	12.0	2.4	40	11.1	2.8
(c)	30	12.0	2.2	30	11.1	3.0

4. A communication researcher randomly assigned 82 volunteers to one of two experimental groups. Sixty-one were instructed to get their news for a month only from television, and 21 were instructed to get their news for a month only from the radio. (Why the researcher didn't assign equal numbers to the two conditions is a mystery!) After the month was up, all participants were tested on their knowledge of several political issues. The researcher did not have a prediction as to which news source would make people more knowledgeable. That is, the researcher simply predicted that there is some kind of difference. These were the results of the study. TV group: $M = 24$, $S^2 = 4$; radio group: $M = 26$, $S^2 = 6$. Using the .01 level, what should the researcher conclude? (a) Use the steps of hypothesis testing; (b) sketch the distributions involved; and (c) explain your answers to someone who is familiar with the t test for a single sample, but not with the t test for independent means.

5. A teacher was interested in whether using a student's own name in a story affected children's attention span while reading. Six children were randomly assigned to read a story under ordinary conditions (using names like Dick and Jane). Five other children read versions of the same story, but with each child's own name substituted for one of the children in the story. The teacher kept a careful measure of how long it took each child to read the story. The results are shown below. Using the .05 level, does including the child's name make any difference? (a) Use the steps of hypothesis testing; (b) sketch the distributions involved; and (c) explain your answers to someone who has never had a course in statistics.

Ordinary Story		Own-Name Story	
Student	Reading Time	Student	Reading Time
A	2	G	4
B	5	H	16
C	7	I	11
D	9	J	9
E	6	K	8
F	7		

6. A developmental researcher compares 4-year-olds and 8-year-olds on their ability to understand the analogies used in stories. The scores for the five 4-year-olds tested were 7, 6, 2, 3, and 8. The scores for the three 8-year-olds tested were 9, 2, and 5. Using the .05 level, do older children do better? (a) Use the steps of hypothesis testing; (b) sketch the distributions involved; and (c) explain your answers to someone who understands the *t* test for a single sample, but does not know anything about the *t* test for independent means.

7. Figure the estimated effect size for problems (a) 4, (b) 5, and (c) 6. (d) Explain what you have done in part (a) to someone who understands the *t* test for independent means but knows nothing about effect size.

8. Figure the approximate power of each of the following planned studies, all using a *t* test for independent means at the .05 significance level, one-tailed, with a predicted small effect size:

	N_1	N_2
(a)	3	57
(b)	10	50
(c)	20	40
(d)	30	30

9. What are the approximate numbers of participants needed for each of the following planned studies to have 80% power, assuming equal numbers in the two groups and all using the .05 significance level? (Be sure to give the total number of participants needed, not just the number needed for each group.)

	Expected Means		Expected	
Study	M_1	M_2	Population *SD*	Tails
(a)	107	149	84	1
(b)	22.5	16.2	31.5	2
(c)	14	12	2.5	1
(d)	480	520	50	2

10. Van Aken and Asendorpf (1997) studied 139 German 12-year-olds. All of the children completed a general self-worth questionnaire and were interviewed about the supportiveness they experienced from their mothers, fathers, and classmates. The researchers then compared the self-worth of those with high and low levels of support of each type. The researchers reported that "lower general self-worth was found for children with a low-supportive mother ($t(137) = 4.52, p < .001, d$[effect size] $= 0.78$) and with a low-supportive father ($t(137) = 4.03, p < .001, d$[effect size] $= 0.69$). . . . A lower general self-worth was also found for children with only low supportive classmates ($t(137) = 2.04, p < .05, d$[effect size] $= 0.35$)." ("*d*" in the above is a symbol for effect size.) (a) Explain what these results mean to a person who has never had a course in statistics. (b) Include a discussion of effect size and power. (When figuring power, you can assume that the two groups in each comparison had about equal sample sizes.)

11. Gallagher-Thompson, Dal Canto, Jacob, and Thompson (2001) compared 27 wives who were caring for their husbands who had Alzheimer's disease to 27 wives in which neither partner had Alzheimer's disease. The two groups of wives were otherwise similar in terms of age, number of years married, and

TABLE 9–8 Comparison of Caregiving and Noncaregiving Wives on Select Psychosocial Variables

	Caregiving Wives ($n = 27$)			Noncaregiving Wives ($n = 27$)				
	M	SD	Range	M	SD	Range	t	p
Geriatric Depression Scale[a]	9.42	6.59	1–25	2.37	2.54	0–8	5.14	.0001
Perceived Stress Scale[b]	22.29	8.34	6–36	15.33	6.36	7–30	3.44	.001
Hope questionnaire[c]								
Agency	11.88	1.63	9–16	13.23	1.39	10–16	3.20	.002
Resilience	11.89	0.91	10–14	13.08	1.60	10–16	3.31	.002
Total	23.77	2.03	21–29	26.31	2.56	22–31	3.97	.0001
Mutuality Scale[d]								
Closeness	3.51	.81	.33–4	3.70	.41	2.67–4	−1.02	.315
Reciprocity	2.25	1.19	.17–4	3.25	.55	1.67–4	−3.68	.001
Shared pleasures	2.65	1.00	0–4	3.52	.61	1.75–4	−3.66	.001
Shared values	3.15	.89	0–4	3.46	.45	2.4–4	−1.51	.138

Note: For all measures, higher scores indicate more of the construct being measured.
[a]Maximum score is 30.
[b]Maximum score is 56.
[c]Four questions in each subscale, with a maximum total score of 32.
[d]Maximum mean for each subscale is 4.
Source: Gallagher-Thompson, D., Dal Canto, P. G., Jacob, T., & Thompson, L. W. (2001). A comparison of marital interaction patterns between couples in which the husband does or does not have Alzheimer's disease. *The Journals of Gerontology Series B: Psychological Sciences and Social Sciences, 56,* 5140–5150. Reprinted by permission of The Gerontological Society of America.

social economic status. Table 9–8 (reproduced from their Table 1) shows some of their results. Focusing on the Geriatric Depression Scale (the first row of the table) and the Mutuality Scale for Shared Values (the last row in the table), explain these results to a person who knows about the *t* test for a single sample, but is unfamiliar with the *t* test for independent means.

SET II

12. Make up two examples of studies (not in the book or from your lectures) that would be tested with a *t* test for independent means.
13. For each of the following studies, say whether you would use a *t* test for dependent means or a *t* test for independent means.

(a) A researcher measures the heights of 40 college students who are the firstborn in their families and compares the 15 who come from large families to the 25 who come from smaller families.
(b) A researcher tests performance on a math skills test of each of 250 individuals before and after they complete a one-day seminar on managing test anxiety.
(c) A researcher compares the resting heart rate of 15 individuals who have been taking a particular drug to the resting heart rate of 48 other individuals who have not been taking this drug.

14. Figure $S_{Difference}$ for each of the following studies:

	N_1	S_1^2	N_2	S_2^2
(a)	30	5	20	4
(b)	30	5	30	4
(c)	30	5	50	4
(d)	20	5	30	4
(e)	30	5	20	2

15. For each of the following experiments, decide if the difference between conditions is statistically significant at the .05 level (two-tailed).

	Experimental Group			Control Group		
	N	M	S^2	N	M	S^2
(a)	10	604	60	10	607	50
(b)	40	604	60	40	607	50
(c)	10	604	20	40	607	16

16. A researcher theorized that people can hear better when they have just eaten a large meal. Six individuals were randomly assigned to eat either a large meal or a small meal. After eating the meal, their hearing was tested. The hearing ability scores (high numbers indicate greater ability) are given below. Using the .05 level, do the results support the researcher's theory? (a) Use the steps of hypothesis testing, (b) sketch the distributions involved, and (c) explain your answers to someone who has never had a course in statistics.

Big Meal Group		Small Meal Group	
Subject	Hearing	Subject	Hearing
A	22	D	19
B	25	E	23
C	25	F	21

17. Twenty students randomly assigned to an experimental group receive an instructional program; 30 in a control group do not. After 6 months, both groups are tested on their knowledge. The experimental group has a mean of 38 on the test (with an estimated population standard deviation of 3); the control group has a mean of 35 (with an estimated population standard deviation of 5). Using the .05 level, what should the experimenter conclude? (a) Use the steps of hypothesis testing, (b) sketch the distributions involved, and (c) explain your answer to someone who is familiar with the *t* test for a single sample, but not with the *t* test for independent means.

18. A study of the effects of color on easing anxiety compared anxiety test scores of participants who completed the test printed on either soft yellow paper or on harsh green paper. The scores for five participants who completed the test printed on the yellow paper were 17, 19, 28, 21, and 18. The scores for four participants who completed the test on the green paper were 20, 26, 17, and 24. Using the .05 level, one-tailed (predicting lower anxiety scores for the yellow paper), what should the researcher conclude? (a) Use the steps of hypothesis testing, (b) sketch the

distributions involved, and (c) explain your answers to someone who is familiar with the t test for a single sample, but not with the t test for independent means.

19. Figure the estimated effect size for problems (a) 16, (b) 17, and (c) 18. (d) Explain your answer to part (a) to a person who understands the t test for independent means but is unfamiliar with effect size.

20. What is the approximate power of each of the following planned studies, all using a t test for independent means at the .05 significance level, two-tailed, with a predicted medium effect size?

	N_1	N_2
(a)	90	10
(b)	50	50
(c)	6	34
(d)	20	20

21. What are the approximate numbers of participants needed for each of the following planned studies to have 80% power, assuming equal numbers in the two groups and all using the .05 significance level? (Be sure to give the total number of participants needed, not just the number needed for each group.)

Study	Expected Means M_1	Expected Means M_2	Expected Population SD	Tails
(a)	10	15	25	1
(b)	10	30	25	1
(c)	10	30	40	1
(d)	10	15	25	2

22. Escudero, Rogers, and Gutierrez (1997) videotaped 30 couples discussing a marital problem in their laboratory. The videotapes were later systematically rated for various aspects of the couple's communication, such as domineeringness and the positive or negative quality of affect (emotion) expressed between them. A major interest of their study was to compare couples who were having relationship problems with those who were not. The 18 couples in the group having problems were recruited from those who had gone to a marital clinic for help; they were called the Clinic group. The group not having problems were recruited through advertisements, and were called the Nonclinic group. (The two groups in fact had dramatically different scores on a standard test of marital satisfaction.) Table 9–9 presents some of their results. (You can ignore the arrows and plus and minus signs, which have to do with how they rated the interactions. Also, ignore the note at the bottom about "arcsine transformation.") (a) Focusing on Domineeringness and Submissiveness, explain these results to a person who has never had a course in statistics. (b) Include a discussion of effect size and power. (When figuring power, you can assume that the two groups in each comparison had about equal sample sizes.)

23. Jackson, Ervin, Gardner, and Schmitt (2001) gave a questionnaire about Internet usage to college students. Table 9–10 (their Table 1) shows their results comparing men and women. (a) Select one significant and one nonsignificant result and explain these two results to a person who understands the t test for a

TABLE 9–9 Base-Rate Differences between Clinic and Nonclinic Couples on Relational Control and Nonverbal Affect Codes Expressed in Proportions (*SD*s in Parentheses)

	Couple Status		Between-Group Differences
	Clinic Mean	Nonclinic Mean	*t*
Domineeringness ($\uparrow$)	.452 (107)	.307 (.152)	3.06*
Levelingness ($\rightarrow$)	.305 (.061)	.438 (.065)	5.77**
Submissiveness ($\downarrow$)	.183 (.097)	.226 (.111)	1.12
Double-codes	.050 (.028)	.024 (.017)	2.92*
Positive affect (+)	.127 (.090)	.280 (.173)	3.22*
Negative affect (−)	.509 (.192)	.127 (.133)	5.38**
Neutral affect (0)	.344 (.110)	.582 (.089)	6.44**
Double-codes (+/−)	.019 (.028)	.008 (.017)	2.96*

Note: Proportions of each control and affect code were converted using arcsine transformation for use in between-group comparisons. $^*p < .01,$ $^{**}p < .001,$ (d.f. = 28).
Source: Escudero, V., Rogers, L. E., & Gutierrez, E. (1997). Patterns of relational control and nonverbal affect in clinic and nonclinic couples. *Journal of Social and Personal Relationships, 14,* 5–29. Copyright © 1997 by the Society for Personality and Social Psychology, Inc. Reprinted by permission of Sage Publications.

TABLE 9–10 Gender Differences in Internet Use and Potential Mediators

	Males[a]	Females[b]	*t*-value	*df*	*p*-value
E-mail use	4.16 (0.66)	4.30 (0.57)	2.81	626	.005
Web use	3.57 (0.67)	3.30 (0.67)	−4.84	627	.000
Overall internet use	3.86 (0.58)	3.80 (0.53)	−1.44	627	.130
Computer anxiety	1.67 (0.56)	1.80 (0.57)	4.03	612	.000
Computer self-efficacy	3.89 (0.52)	3.71 (0.62)	−3.49	608	.001
Loneliness	2.06 (0.64)	1.96 (0.64)	−1.88	607	.061
Depression	1.22 (0.32)	1.28 (0.34)	2.36	609	.019
E-mail privacy	4.04 (0.78)	4.10 (0.69)	−0.97	609	.516
E-mail trust	3.50 (0.77)	3.46 (0.75)	−0.65	610	.516
Web privacy	4.06 (0.74)	4.09 (0.71)	0.62	623	.534
Web trust	3.14 (0.73)	3.12 (0.73)	−0.28	624	.780
Web search success	4.05 (0.85)	4.13 (0.81)	1.12	568	.262
Importance of computer skills	2.54 (1.03)	2.31 (0.90)	−2.57	477	.011
Computers cause health problems	2.67 (1.00)	3.00 (1.08)	3.36	476	.001
Gender stereotypes about computer skills	3.45 (1.15)	4.33 (0.96)	−8.95	476	.000
Racial/ethnic stereotypes about computer skills	3.63 (1.17)	3.99 (1.07)	3.40	477	.001
Computers are taking over	3.08 (1.19)	2.87 (1.08)	−1.89	476	.059

Note: For the attitude items, 1 = strongly agree, 2 = strongly disagree. For gender, 1 = male, 2 = female. Numbers in parentheses are standard deviations.
[a] *n* = 227.
[b] *n* = 403.
Source: Jackson, L. A., Ervin, K. S., Gardner, P. D., & Schmitt, N. (2001). Gender and the Internet: Women communicating and men searching. *Sex Roles, 44,* 363–379. Reprinted with permission.

single sample but does not know anything about the t test for independent means. (b) Include a discussion of effect size and power.

24. Do men or women have longer first names? Take out a phone book and use the random numbers given below to select the pages. On the first page (page 12), look for the first clearly female name, and write down how many letters it has. Do the same thing (find the page for the number, etc.) 16 times. Then continue, getting lengths for 16 male names. (You will have to exclude names for which you cannot tell the gender.) Carry out a t test for independent means using these two samples. (Be sure to note the city and year of the telephone book you used.) 12, 79, 10, 97, 53, 74, 15, 55, 41, 128, 57, 93, 94, 31, 68, 516, 60, 56, 7, 93, 43, 91, 57, 58, 38, 120, 14, 38, 57, 743, 98, 471, 38, 66, 20, 32, 60, 43, 78, 29, 39, 17, 31, 12, 61, 100, 80, 35, 31, 99, 22

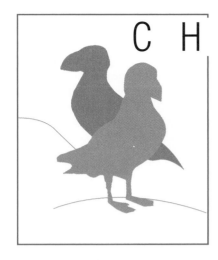

CHAPTER 10

Introduction to the Analysis of Variance

Cindy Hazan and Philip Shaver (1987) arranged to have the *Rocky Mountain News,* a large Denver area newspaper, print a mail-in survey. The survey included the question shown in Table 10–1 to measure what is called attachment style. Those who selected the first choice are "secure"; those who selected the second, "avoidant"; and those who selected the third, "anxious-ambivalent." These attachment styles are thought to be different ways of behaving and thinking in close relationships that develop from a person's experience with early caretakers (e.g.,

TABLE 10–1	Question Used in Hazan and Shaver (1987) Newspaper Survey

Which of the following best describes your feelings. [Check One]

[ ] I find it relatively easy to get close to others and am comfortable depending on them and having them depend on me. I don't often worry about being abandoned or about someone getting too close to me.

[ ] I am somewhat uncomfortable being close to others; I find it difficult to trust them completely, difficult to allow myself to depend on them. I am nervous when anyone gets too close, and often, love partners want me to be more intimate than I feel comfortable being.

[ ] I find that others are reluctant to get as close as I would like. I often worry that my partner doesn't really love me or won't want to stay with me. I want to merge completely with another person, and this desire sometimes scares people away.

Source: From Hazan & Shaver (1987), p. 515.

analysis of variance
(ANOVA)

Tip for Success

This chapter assumes you understand hypothesis testing and the t *test, particularly the material on the distribution of means. So be sure you understand the relevant material in Chapters 5, 6, 8, and 9, before starting this chapter.*

within-groups estimate of the population variance

Mickelson, Kessler, & Shaver, 1997). Readers also answered questions about various aspects of love, including amount of jealousy. Hazan and Shaver then compared the amount of jealousy reported by people with the three different attachment styles.

With a *t* test, Hazan and Shaver could have compared the mean jealousy scores of any two of the attachment styles. Instead, they were interested in differences among all three attachment styles. The statistical procedure for testing variation among the means of more than two groups is called the **analysis of variance,** abbreviated as **ANOVA.** (You could use the analysis of variance for a study with only two groups, but the simpler *t* test gives the same result.)

In this chapter, we introduce the analysis of variance, focusing on the fundamental logic, how to carry out an analysis of variance in the most basic situation, and how to make sense of more complicated forms of the analysis of variance when reading about them in research articles.

BASIC LOGIC OF THE ANALYSIS OF VARIANCE

The null hypothesis in an analysis of variance is that the several populations being compared all have the same mean. For example, in the attachment style example, the null hypothesis is that the populations of secure, avoidant, and anxious-ambivalent people all have the same average degree of jealousy. The research hypothesis would be that the degree of jealousy differs among these three populations.

Hypothesis testing in analysis of variance is about whether the means of the samples differ more than you would expect if the null hypothesis were true. This question about *means* is answered, surprisingly, by analyzing *variances* (hence the name *analysis of variance*). Among other reasons, you focus on variances because when you want to know how several means differ, you are asking about the variation among those means.

Thus, to understand the logic of analysis of variance, we consider variances. In particular, we begin by discussing two different ways of estimating population variances. As you will see, the analysis of variance is about a comparison of the results of these two different ways of estimating population variances.

ESTIMATING POPULATION VARIANCE FROM VARIATION WITHIN EACH SAMPLE

With the analysis of variance, as with the *t* test, you do not know the true population variances. However, as with the *t* test, you can estimate the variance of each of the populations from the scores in the samples. Also, as with the *t* test, you assume in the analysis of variance that all populations have the *same* variance. This allows you to average the estimates from each sample into a single pooled estimate, called the **within-groups estimate of the population variance.** It is an average of estimates figured entirely from the scores *within* each of the samples.

One of the most important things to remember about this within-groups estimate is that it is not affected by whether or not the null hypothesis is true. This estimate comes out the same whether the means of the populations are all the same (the null hypothesis is true) or whether the means of the populations are very different (the null hypothesis is false). This estimate comes out the same, because it focuses only on the variation inside of each population. Thus, it doesn't matter how far apart the means of the different populations are.

ESTIMATING THE POPULATION VARIANCE FROM VARIATION BETWEEN THE MEANS OF THE SAMPLES

There is also a second way to estimate the population variance. Each sample's mean is a number in its own right. If there are several samples, there are several such numbers, and these numbers will have some variation among them. The variation among these means gives another way to estimate the variance in the populations that the samples come from. Just how this works is a bit tricky, so follow the next two sections closely.

When the Null Hypothesis Is True. First, consider the situation in which the null hypothesis is true. In this situation, all samples come from populations that have the same mean. Remember, we are always assuming that all populations have the same variance (and also that they are all normal curves). Thus, if the null hypothesis is true, all populations are identical. (They have the same mean, variance, and shape.)

However, even when the populations are identical, the samples will each be a little different, and their means will each be a little different. How different can the sample means be? That depends on how much variation there is within each population. If a population has very little variation in the scores within it, then the means of samples from that population (or any identical population) will tend to be very similar to each other.

What if several identical populations (with the same population mean) have a lot of variation in the scores within each? In that situation, if you take one sample from each population, the means of those samples could easily be very different from each other. Being very different, the variance of these means will be large.

The point is that the more variance within each of several identical populations, the more variance there will be among the means of samples when you take a random sample from each population.

Suppose you were studying samples of six children from each of three large playgrounds (the populations in this example). If each playground had children who were all either 7 or 8 years old, the means of your three samples would all be between 7 and 8. Thus, there would not be much variance among those means. However, if each playground had children ranging from 3 to 12 years old, the means of the three samples would probably vary quite a bit. What this shows is that the variation among the means of samples is related directly to the amount of variation within each of the populations from which the samples are taken. The more variation within each population, the more variation among the means of samples taken from those populations.

This principle is shown in Figure 10–1. The three identical populations on the left have small variances and the three identical populations on the right have large variances. In each set of three identical populations, even though the *means of the populations* are exactly the same, the *means of the samples* from those populations are not exactly the same. Most important, the means from the populations with less variance are closer together (have less variance among them). The means from the populations with more variance are more spread out (have more variance among them).

We have now seen that the variation among the means of samples taken from identical populations is related directly to the variation of the scores within each of those populations. This has a very important implication: It should be possible to estimate the variance within each population from the variation among the means of our samples.

Such an estimate is called a **between-groups estimate of the population variance.** (It has this name because it is based on the variation between the means of the samples, the "groups." Grammatically, it ought to be *among* groups; but *between* groups is traditional.) You will learn how to actually figure this estimate later in the chapter.

between-groups estimate of the population variance

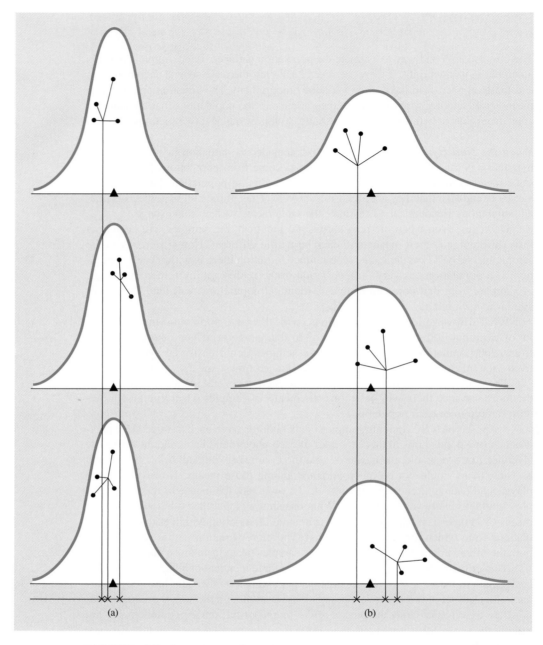

FIGURE 10-1   *Means of samples from identical populations will not be identical.*
(a) Sample means from populations with less variation will vary less. (b) Sample means
from populations with more variation will vary more. (Population means are indicated by a trian-
gle, sample means by an X.)

So far, all of this logic we have considered has assumed that the null hypothesis is true, so that there is no variation among the means of the *populations*. Let's now consider what happens when the null hypothesis is not true, and instead the research hypothesis is true.

When the Null Hypothesis Is Not True. If the null hypothesis is not true and the research hypothesis is true, the populations themselves have different means. In this situation, variation among means of samples taken from these populations is still caused by the variation within the populations. So, the larger the variation within the populations, the larger the variation among the means of sample taken from the populations. However, in this situation in which the research hypothesis is true, variation among the means of the samples *also* is caused by the variation among the population means. That is, in this situation the means of the samples are spread out for two different reasons: (a) because of variation within each of the populations and (b) because of variation among the means of the population. The left side of Figure 10–2 shows populations with the same means and the means of samples taken from them. (This is the same situation as in both sides of Figure 10–1.) The right side of Figure 10–2 shows three populations with different means and the means of samples taken from them. (This is the situation we have just been discussing.) Notice that the means of the samples are more spread out in the situation on the right side of Figure 10–2. This is true even though the variations within the populations are the same for the situation on both sides of Figure 10–2. The additional spread (variance) for the means on the right side of the figure is due to the populations having different means. (You may want to read this paragraph again to ensure that you fully understand the logic we are presenting.)

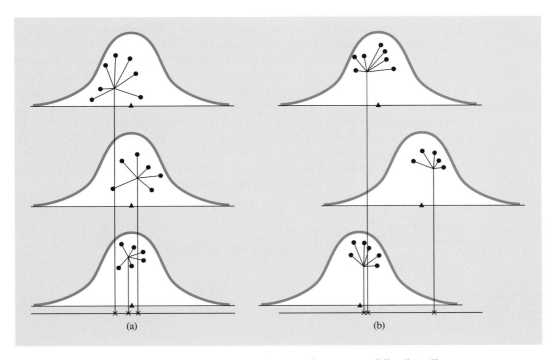

(a) (b)

FIGURE 10–2 *Means of samples from populations whose means differ (b) will vary more than sample means taken from populations whose means are the same (a). (Population means are indicated by a triangle, sample means by an X.)*

In summary, the between-groups estimate of the population variance is figured based on the variation among the means of the samples. If the null hypothesis is true, this estimate gives an accurate indication of the variation within the populations. But if the null hypothesis is false, this method of estimating the population variance is influenced both by the variation within the populations and the variation among the population means. It will not give an accurate estimate of the variation within the populations, because it also will be affected by the variation among the populations. This difference has important implications. It is what makes the analysis of variance a method of testing hypotheses about whether there is a difference among means of groups.

COMPARING THE WITHIN-GROUPS AND BETWEEN-GROUPS ESTIMATES OF POPULATION VARIANCE

Table 10–2 summarizes what we have seen so far about the within-groups and between-groups estimates of population variance, both when the null hypothesis is true and when the research hypothesis is true. When the null hypothesis is true, the within-groups and between-groups estimates are based on the same thing (that is, the variation within populations). Literally, they are estimates of the same population variance. When the null hypothesis is true, both estimates should be about the same. (Only *about* the same—these are estimates.) Here is another way of describing this similarity of the between-groups estimate and the within-groups estimate when the null hypothesis is true. In this situation, the ratio of the between-groups estimate to the within-groups estimate should be approximately 1 to 1. For example, if the within-groups estimate is 107.5, the between-groups estimate should be around 107.5, so that the ratio would be about 1. (A ratio is found by dividing one number by the other.)

The situation is quite different when the null hypothesis is not true. As shown in Table 10–2, when the research hypothesis is true, the between-groups estimate is influenced by two sources of variation: (a) the variation of the scores within each population, and (b) the variation of the means of the populations from each other. Yet even when the research hypothesis is true, the within-groups estimate still is influenced *only* by the variation within the populations. Therefore, when the research hypothesis is true, the between-groups estimate should be larger than the within-groups estimate. In this situation, the ratio of the between-groups estimate to the within-groups estimate should be greater than 1. For example, the between-groups estimate might be 638.9 and the within-groups estimate 107.5, making a ratio of 638.9 to 107.5 or 5.94. That is, when we divide the larger, the between-groups estimate, by the smaller, the within-groups estimate, we get not 1 but more than 1. In this example the between-groups estimate is nearly six times bigger than the within-groups estimate.

Tip for Success

Table 10–2 provides a useful summary of the logic of the analysis of variance. Test your understanding of this logic by trying to explain Table 10–2 without referring to the book. You might try writing your answer down and swapping it with someone else in your class.

TABLE 10–2	Sources of Variation in Within-Group and Between-Group Variance Estimates		
		Variation Within Populations	Variation Between Populations
Null hypothesis is true			
Within-groups estimate reflects		✓	
Between-groups estimate reflects		✓	
Research hypothesis is true			
Within-groups estimate reflects		✓	
Between-groups estimate reflects		✓	✓

This is the central principle of the analysis of variance: *When the null hypothesis is true, the ratio of the between-groups population variance estimate to the within-groups population variance estimate should be about 1. When the research hypothesis is true, this ratio should be greater than 1.* If you figure this ratio and it comes out much bigger than 1, you can reject the null hypothesis. That is, it is unlikely that the null hypothesis could be true and the between-groups estimate be a lot bigger than the within-groups estimate.

THE *F* RATIO

This crucial ratio of the between-groups to the within-groups population variance estimate is called an **F ratio.** (The *F* is for Sir Ronald Fisher, an eminent statistician who developed the analysis of variance; see Box 10–1.)

F ratio

THE *F* DISTRIBUTION AND THE *F* TABLE

We have said that if the crucial ratio of between-groups estimate to within-groups estimate (the *F* ratio) is a lot larger than 1, you can reject the null hypothesis. The next question is, just how much bigger than 1?

Statisticians have developed the mathematics of an **F distribution** and have prepared tables of *F* ratios. For any given situation, you merely look up in an **F table** how extreme an *F* ratio is needed to reject the null hypothesis at, say, the .05 level. (You learn to use the *F* table later in the chapter.)

F distribution

F table

For an example of an *F* ratio, let's return to the attachment style study. The results of that study, for jealousy, were as follows: The between-groups population variance estimate was 23.19 and the within-groups population variance estimate was .53. (You will learn shortly how to figure these estimates on your own.) The ratio of the between-groups to the within-groups variance estimates (23.19/.53) came out to 43.75; that is, $F = 43.75$. This *F* ratio is considerably larger than 1. The *F* ratio needed to reject the null hypothesis at the .05 level in this study is only 3.01. Thus, the researchers confidently rejected the null hypothesis and concluded that amount of jealousy is different among the three attachment styles. (Mean jealousy ratings were 2.17 for secures, 2.57 for avoidants, and 2.88 for anxious-ambivalents.)

AN ANALOGY

Some students find an analogy helpful in understanding the analysis of variance. The analogy is to what engineers call the signal-to-noise ratio. For example, your ability to make out the words in a staticky cell-phone conversation depends on the strength of the signal versus the amount of random noise. With the *F* ratio in the analysis of variance, the difference among the means of the samples is like the signal; it is the information of interest. The variation within the samples is like the noise. When the variation among the samples is sufficiently great in comparison to the variation within the samples, you conclude that there is a significant effect.

HOW ARE YOU DOING?

1. When do you use an analysis of variance?
2. (a) What is the within-groups population variance estimate based on? (b) How and (c) why is it affected by the null hypothesis being true or not?
3. (a) What is the between-groups population variance estimate based on? (b) How and (c) why is it affected by the null hypothesis being true or not?
4. What are two sources of variation that can contribute to the between-groups population variance estimate?
5. (a) What is the *F* ratio; (b) why is it usually about 1 when the null hypothesis is true; and (c) why is it usually larger than 1 when the null hypothesis is false?

Tip for Success

These "How Are You Doing" questions and answers provide a useful summary of the logic of the analysis of variance. Be sure to review them (and the relevant sections in the text) as many times as necessary to fully understand this logic.

BOX 10-1   Sir Ronald Fisher, Caustic Genius at Statistics

Ronald A. Fisher, a contemporary of William Gosset (see Chapter 8, Box 8–1) and Karl Pearson (see Chapter 11, Box 11–1), was probably the brightest and certainly the most productive of this close-knit group of British statisticians. In the process of writing 300 papers and 7 books, he developed many of the modern field's key concepts: variance, analysis of variance, statistics (in the sense of describing a sample, as opposed to parameters of a population), significance levels, the null hypothesis, and almost all of our basic ideas of research design, including the fundamental importance of randomization.

It is one of those family legends that little Ronald, born in 1890 in East Finchley, a northern suburb of London, was so fascinated by math that one day, at age 3, when put into his highchair for breakfast, he asked his nurse, "What is a half of a half?" Told it was a quarter, he asked, "What's half of a quarter?" To that answer he wanted to know what was half of an eighth. At the next answer he purportedly thought a moment and said, "Then I suppose that a half of a sixteenth must be a thirty-toof." Ah, baby stories.

As a grown man, however, Fisher seems to have been anything but darling. Some observers ascribe this to a cold and unemotional mother, but whatever the reason, throughout his life he was embroiled in bitter feuds, even with scholars who had previously been his closest allies and who certainly ought to have been comrades in research. When he was teased, apparently he responded with dead seriousness; when others were anxious, he joked. William G. Cochran (a well-known statistician in his own right) reported a tale of their crossing a street together at a moment that was obviously unsafe. When Cochran hesitated, Fisher supposedly chided him: "Oh come on, a spot of natural selection won't hurt us." And Cochran sheepishly risked his neck.

Fisher's thin ration of compassion extended to his readers as well—not only was his writing hopelessly obscure, but it often simply failed to supply important assumptions and proofs. Gosset said that when Fisher began a sentence with "Evidently," it meant 2 hours of hard work before one could hope to see why the point was evident. Another statistician sought to excuse him, however, saying that, "Fisher was talking on a plane barely understood by the rest of humanity." It is true that he was invariably admired and respected for his work, if not for his manners.

Indeed, his lack of empathy extended to all of humankind. Like Galton, Fisher was fond of eugenics, favoring anything that might increase the birthrate of the upper and professional classes and skilled artisans. Not only did he see contraception as a poor idea—fearing that the least desirable persons would use it least—but he defended infanticide as serving an evolutionary function. It may be just as well that his opportunities to experiment with breeding never extended beyond the raising of his own children and some crops of potatoes and wheat.

The greatest influence on Fisher was probably his 14 years working at an agricultural experimental station called Rothamsted, in Hertfordshire, 25 miles north of London. At Rothamsted, Fisher, like Gosset at his brewery in Dublin, faced all sorts of practical problems, such as whether yearly applications of manure improved the yield of a field in the long run or was the cause of mysterious declines in production after many decades. Perhaps it was even this isolation from the personality disputes among London academics and this closeness to real issues that helped Fisher concentrate on developing statistics as a powerful research tool.

Although Fisher eventually became the Galton Professor of Eugenics at University College, his most influential appointment probably came when he was invited to Iowa State College in Ames for the summers of 1931 and 1936 (where he was said to be so put out with the terrible heat that he stored his sheets in the refrigerator all day). At Ames, Fisher greatly impressed George Snedecor, an American professor of mathematics also working on agricultural problems. Consequently, Snedecor wrote a textbook of statistics for agriculture that borrowed heavily from Fisher's work at Rothamsted. The book so popularized Fisher's ideas about statistics and research design that its second edition sold 100,000 copies.

While Fisher was at Ames, he also won over E. F. Lindquist, professor of education at the University of Iowa in Iowa City. Lindquist filled his next textbook with Fisher's ideas, introducing them to the fields of education and psychology, where they have played a major role to this day.

You can learn more about Fisher at the following website: *http://www-history.mcs.st-and.ac.uk/~history/Mathematicians/Fisher.html.*

Sources: Peters (1987); Salsburg (2001); Stigler (1986); Tankard (1984).

ANSWERS:

1. Analysis of variance is used when you are comparing means of samples from more than two populations.
2. (a) The variation of scores within each of the samples. (b) It is not affected. (c) Whether or not the null hypothesis is true has to do with whether or not the means of the populations differ. Thus, the within-groups estimate is not affected by whether or not the null hypothesis is true, because the variation *within* each population (which is the basis for the variation within each sample) is not affected by whether or not the population means differ.
3. (a) The variation among the means of the samples. (b) It is larger when the null hypothesis is false. (c) Whether or not the null hypothesis is true has to do with whether or not the means of the populations differ. When the null hypothesis is false, the means of the populations differ. Thus, the between-groups estimate is bigger when the null hypothesis is false, because the variation among the means of the populations (which is one basis for the variation among the means of the samples) is greater when the population means differ.
4. Variation among the scores within each of the populations and variation among the means of the populations.
5. (a) The ratio of the between-groups population variance estimate to the within-groups population variance estimate. (b) Because both estimates are based entirely on the same source of variation—the variation of the scores within each of the populations. (c) Because the between-groups estimate is also influenced by the variation among the means of the populations, while the within-groups estimate is not. Thus, when the null hypothesis is false (meaning that the means of the populations differ), the between-groups estimate will be bigger than the within-groups estimate.

CARRYING OUT AN ANALYSIS OF VARIANCE

Having considered the basic logic of the analysis of variance, we will go through an example to illustrate the details. (We use a fictional study to keep the numbers simple.)

Suppose a researcher is interested in the influence of knowledge of previous criminal record on juries' perceptions of the guilt or innocence of defendants. The researcher recruits 15 volunteers who have been selected for jury duty (but have not yet served at a trial). The researcher shows them a videotape of a 4-hour trial in which a woman is accused of passing bad checks. Before viewing the tape, however, all of the research participants are given a "background sheet" with age, marital status, education, and other such information about the accused woman. The sheet is the same for all 15 participants, with one difference. For five of the participants, the last section of the sheet says that the woman has been convicted several times before for passing bad checks—we will call these participants the *Criminal Record Group*. For five other participants, the last section of the sheet says the woman has a completely clean criminal record—the *Clean Record Group*. For the remaining five participants, the sheet does not mention anything about criminal record one way or the other—the *No Information Group*.

The participants are randomly assigned to groups. After viewing the tape of the trial, all 15 participants make a rating on a 10-point scale, which runs from completely sure she is innocent (1) to completely sure she is guilty (10). The results of this fictional study are shown in Table 10–3. As you can see, the means of the three groups are different (8, 4, and 5). Yet there is also quite a bit of variation within each of the three groups. Population variance estimates from the scores within each of these three groups are 4.5, 5.0, and 6.5.

You need to figure three numbers to test the hypothesis that the three populations are different: (a) a population variance estimate based on the variation of the scores within each of the samples, (b) a population variance estimate based on the differences among the group means, and (c) the ratio of the two, the F ratio. (In addition, we need the significance cutoff from an F table.)

TABLE 10–3 | **Results of the Criminal Record Study (Fictional Data)**

Criminal Record Group			Clean Record Group			No Information Group		
Rating	Deviation from Mean	Squared Deviation from Mean	Rating	Deviation from Mean	Squared Deviation from Mean	Rating	Deviation from Mean	Squared Deviation from Mean
10	2	4	5	1	1	4	−1	1
7	−1	1	1	−3	9	6	1	1
5	−3	9	3	−1	1	9	4	16
10	2	4	7	3	9	3	−2	4
8	0	0	4	0	0	3	−2	4
Σ: 40	0	18	20	0	20	25	0	26

$M = 40/5 = 8.$
$S^2 = 18/4 = 4.5.$

$M = 20/5 = 4.$
$S^2 = 20/4 = 5.0.$

$M = 25/5 = 5.$
$S^2 = 26/4 = 6.5.$

ESTIMATING POPULATION VARIANCE FROM THE VARIATION OF SCORES WITHIN EACH GROUP

You can estimate the population variance from any one group (that is, from any one sample) using the usual method of estimating a population variance from a sample. First, you figure the sum of the squared deviation scores. That is, you take the deviation of each score from its group's mean, square that deviation score, and sum all the squared deviation scores. Second, you divide that sum of squared deviation scores by that group's degrees of freedom. (The degrees of freedom for a group are the number of scores in the group minus 1.) For the example, as shown in Table 10–3, this gives an estimated population variance of 4.5 based on the Criminal Record Group's scores, an estimate of 5.0 based on the Clean Record Group's scores, and an estimate of 6.5 based on the No Information Group's scores.

Once again, in the analysis of variance, as with the t test, we assume that the populations have the same variance. The estimates based on each sample's scores are all estimating the same true population variance. The sample sizes are equal in this example so that the estimate for each group is based on an equal amount of information. Thus, you can pool these variance estimates by straight averaging. This gives an overall estimate of the population variance based on the variation within groups of 5.33 (that is, the sum of 4.5, 5.0, and 6.5, which is 16, divided by 3, the number of groups).

The estimated population variance based on the variation of the scores within each of the groups is the within-groups variance estimate. This is symbolized as S^2_{Within}. In terms of a formula,

> The within-groups population variance estimate is the sum of the population variance estimates based on each sample, divided by the number of groups.

$$S^2_{\text{Within}} = \frac{S^2_1 + S^2_2 + \cdots + S^2_{\text{Last}}}{N_{\text{Groups}}} \tag{10-1}$$

In this formula, S^2_1 is the estimated population variance based on the scores in the first group (the group from Population 1), S^2_2 is the estimated population variance based on the scores in the second group, S^2_{Last} is the estimated population variance based on the scores in the last group. (The dots, or ellipses, in the formula show that you are to fill in the population variance estimate for as many other groups as there are in the analysis.) N_{Groups} is the number of groups. Using this formula for our figuring, we get

$$S^2_{\text{Within}} = \frac{S_1^2 + S_2^2 + \cdots + S_{\text{Last}}^2}{N_{\text{Groups}}} = \frac{4.5 + 5.0 + 6.5}{3} = \frac{16}{3} = 5.33$$

ESTIMATING POPULATION VARIANCE FROM THE DIFFERENCES BETWEEN GROUP MEANS

To figure the between-groups estimate of the population variance involves two steps. You first estimate from the means of your samples the variance of a distribution of means. Second, based on the variance of this distribution of means, you figure the variance of the population of individuals. Here are the two steps in more detail:

❹ Estimate the variance of the distribution of means: Sum the sample means' squared deviations from the grand mean and divide this by the number of means minus 1.

You can think of the means of your samples as taken from a distribution of means. You follow the standard procedure of using the scores in a sample to estimate the variance of the population from which these scores are taken. In this situation, you think of the means of your samples as the scores and the distribution of means as the population from which these scores come. What this all boils down to are the following procedures. You begin by figuring the sum of squared deviations. (You find the mean of your sample means, figure the deviation of each sample mean from this mean of means, square each of these deviations, and then sum these squared deviations.) Then, divide this sum of squared deviations by the degrees of freedom, which is the number of means minus 1. In terms of a formula (when sample sizes are all equal),

(10-2)
$$S_M^2 = \frac{\Sigma (M - GM)^2}{df_{\text{Between}}}$$

> The estimated variance of the distribution of means is the sum of each sample mean's squared deviation from the overall mean, divided by the degrees of freedom for the between-groups population variance estimate.

In this formula, S_M^2 is the estimated variance of the distribution of means (estimated based on the means of the samples in your study). M is the mean of each of your samples. GM is the **grand mean,** the overall mean of all your scores, which is also the mean of your means. df_{Between} is the degrees of freedom in the between-groups estimate, the number of groups minus 1. Stated as a formula,

grand mean (GM)

(10-3)
$$df_{\text{Between}} = N_{\text{Groups}} - 1$$

> The degrees of freedom for the between-groups population variance estimate is the number of groups minus 1.

In the criminal-record example, the three means are 8, 4, and 5. The figuring of S_M^2 is shown in Table 10–4.

❺ Figure the estimated variance of the population of individual scores: Multiply the variance of the distribution of means by the number of scores in each group.

What we have just figured in Step A, from a sample of a few means, is the estimated variance of a distribution of means. From this we want to make an estimation of the variance of the population (the distribution of individuals) on which the distribution of means is based. We saw in Chapter 6 that the variance of a distribution of means is smaller than the variance of the population (the distribution of individuals)

TABLE 10–4 Estimated Variance of the Distribution of Means Based on Means of the Three Experimental Groups in the Criminal Record Study (Fictional Data)

Sample Means	Deviation from Grand Mean	Squared Deviation from Grand Mean
(M)	(M − GM)	(M − GM)²
4	−1.67	2.79
8	2.33	5.43
5	− .67	.45
Σ: 17	−0.01	8.67

$GM = \Sigma M / N_{\text{Groups}} = 17/3 = 5.67; \; S^2_M = \Sigma (M - GM)^2 / df_{\text{Between}} = 8.67/2 = 4.34.$

that it is based on. This is because means are less likely to be extreme than are individual scores (because several scores that are extreme in the same direction are unlikely to be included in any one sample). Specifically, you learned in Chapter 6 that the variance of a distribution of means is the variance of the distribution of individual scores divided by the number of scores in each sample.

Now, however, we are going to reverse what we did in Chapter 6. In Chapter 6 you figured the variance of the distribution of means by *dividing* the variance of the distribution of individuals by the sample size. Now you are going to figure the variance of the distribution of individuals by *multiplying* the variance of the distribution of means by the sample size (see Table 10–5). That is, to come up with the variance of the population of individuals, you multiply your estimate of the variance of the distribution of means by the sample size. The result of all this is the between-groups population variance estimate. Stated as a formula (for when sample sizes are equal),

> The between-groups population variance estimate is the estimated variance of the distribution of means multiplied by the number of scores in each group.

$$S^2_{\text{Between}} = (S^2_M)(n) \qquad (10\text{-}4)$$

In this formula, S^2_{Between} is the estimate of the population variance based on the variation among the means (the between-groups population variance estimate). n is the number of participants in each sample.

Let's return to our example in which there were five participants in each sample and an estimated variance of the distribution of means of 4.34. In this example, multiplying 4.34 by 5 gives a between-groups population variance estimate of 21.7. In terms of the formula,

$$S^2_{\text{Between}} = (S^2_M)(n) = (4.34)(5) = 21.7$$

TABLE 10–5 Comparison of Figuring the Variance of a Distribution of Means from the Variance of a Distribution of Individuals, and the Reverse

*From distribution of individuals to distribution of means: $S^2_M = S^2/N$
*From distribution of means to distribution of individuals: $S^2 = (S^2_M)(N)$

To summarize, the procedure of estimating the population variance based on the differences between group means is (a) figure the estimated variance of the distribution of means and then (b) multiply that estimated variance by the number of scores in each group.

FIGURING THE *F* RATIO

The *F* ratio is the ratio of the between-groups estimate of the population variance to the within-groups estimate of the population variance. Stated as a formula,

(10-5)

$$F = \frac{S^2_{\text{Between}}}{S^2_{\text{Within}}}$$

The *F* ratio is the between-groups population variance estimate divided by the within-groups population variance estimate.

In the example, the ratio of between and within is 21.7 to 5.33. Carrying out the division gives an *F* ratio of 4.07. In terms of the formula,

$$F = \frac{S^2_{\text{Between}}}{S^2_{\text{Within}}} = \frac{21.7}{5.33} = 4.07$$

Tip for Success

A very common mistake when figuring the F ratio is to turn the formula upside down. Just remember it is as simple as Black and White, so it is Between divided by Within.

THE *F* DISTRIBUTION

You are not quite done. You still need to find the cutoff for the *F* that is large enough to reject the null hypothesis. This requires a distribution of *F* ratios that you can use to figure out what is an extreme *F* ratio.

In practice, you simply look up the needed cutoff on a table. To understand from where that number on the table comes, you need to understand the *F* distribution. The easiest way to understand this distribution is to think about how you would go about making one.

Start with three identical populations. Next, randomly select five scores from each. Then, on the basis of these three samples (of five scores each), figure the *F* ratio. (That is, you use these scores to make a between-groups estimate and a within-groups estimate and divide the first by the second.) Let's say that you do this and the *F* ratio you come up with is 1.36. Now you select three new random samples of five scores each and figure the *F* ratio using these three samples. Perhaps you get an *F* of .93. If you do this whole process many, many times, you will eventually get a lot of *F* ratios. The distribution of all possible *F* ratios figured in this way (from random samples from identical populations) is called the *F* distribution. Figure 10–3 shows an example of an *F* distribution. (There are many different *F* distributions and each has a slightly different shape. The exact shape depends on how many samples you take each time and how many scores are in each sample. The general shape is like that shown in the figure.)

No one actually goes about making *F* distributions in this way. It is a mathematical distribution whose exact characteristics can be found from a formula. Statisticians can also prove that if you had the patience to follow this procedure of taking random samples and figuring the *F* ratio of each for a very long time, you would get the same result.

As you can see in Figure 10–3, the *F* distribution is not symmetrical, but has a long tail on the right. The reason for this positive skew is that an *F* distribution is a distribution of ratios of variances. Variances are always positive numbers. (A variance is an average of squared deviations, and anything squared is a positive

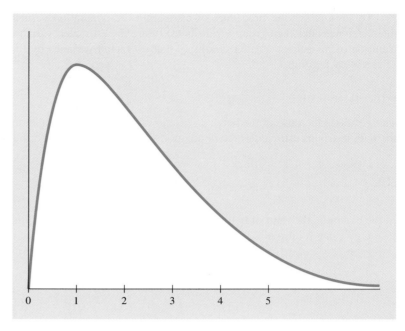

FIGURE 10–3   *An F distribution.*

number.) A ratio of a positive number to a positive number can never be less than 0. Yet there is nothing to stop a ratio from being a very high number. Thus, the *F* ratios' distribution cannot be lower than 0 and can rise quite high. (Most *F* ratios pile up near 1, but they spread out more on the positive side, where they have more room to spread out.)

THE *F* TABLE

between-groups degrees of freedom (df_{between})

numerator degrees of freedom (df_{between})

within-groups degrees of freedom (df_{within})

denominator degrees of freedom (df_{within})

The *F* table is a little more complicated than the *t* table. This is because there is a different *F* distribution according to both the degrees of freedom used in the between-groups variance estimate and the degrees of freedom used in the within-groups variance estimate. That is, you have to take into account two different degrees of freedom to look up the needed cutoff. One is the **between-groups degrees of freedom.** It is also called the **numerator degrees of freedom.** This is the degrees of freedom you use in the between-groups variance estimate, the numerator of the *F* ratio. As shown earlier in Formula 10–3, the degrees of freedom for the between-groups population variance estimate is the number of groups minus 1 ($N_{\text{Groups}} - 1$).

The other type of degrees of freedom is the **within-groups degrees of freedom,** also called the **denominator degrees of freedom.** This is the sum of the degrees of freedom from each sample you use when figuring out the within-groups variance estimate, the denominator of the *F* ratio. Stated as a formula,

> The degrees of freedom for the within-groups population variance estimate is the sum of the degrees of freedom used in making estimates of the population variance from each sample.

$$df_{\text{Within}} = df_1 + df_2 + \cdots + df_{\text{Last}}$$ (10-6)

| TABLE 10–6 | Cutoffs for the *F* Distribution (Portion) | | | | | | |

Denominator Degrees of Freedom	Significance Level	Numerator Degrees of Freedom					
		1	*2*	*3*	*4*	*5*	*6*
10	.01	10.05	7.56	6.55	6.00	5.64	5.39
	.05	4.97	4.10	3.71	3.48	3.33	3.22
	.10	3.29	2.93	2.73	2.61	2.52	2.46
11	.01	9.65	7.21	6.22	5.67	5.32	5.07
	.05	4.85	3.98	3.59	3.36	3.20	3.10
	.10	3.23	2.86	2.66	2.54	2.45	2.39
12	.01	9.33	6.93	5.95	5.41	5.07	4.82
	.05	4.75	3.89	3.49	3.26	3.11	3.00
	.10	3.18	2.81	2.61	2.48	2.40	2.33
13	.01	9.07	6.70	5.74	5.21	4.86	4.62
	.05	4.67	3.81	3.41	3.18	3.03	2.92
	.10	3.14	2.76	2.56	2.43	2.35	2.28

Note: Full table is Table A–3 in the Appendix.

In the criminal record experiment example, the between-groups degrees of freedom is 2. (There are 3 means, minus 1.) In terms of the formula,

$$df_{\text{Between}} = N_{\text{Groups}} - 1 = 3 - 1 = 2$$

The denominator degrees of freedom is 12. This is because each of the groups has 4 degrees of freedom on which the estimate is based (5 scores minus 1) and there are 3 groups overall, making a total of 12 degrees of freedom. In terms of the formula,

$$df_{\text{Within}} = df_1 + df_2 + \cdots + df_{\text{Last}} = (5 - 1) + (5 - 1) + (5 - 1) = 4 + 4 + 4 = 12$$

You would look up the cutoff for an *F* distribution "with 2 and 12" degrees of freedom. As shown in Table 10–6, for the .05 level, you need an *F* ratio of 3.89 to reject the null hypothesis. (The full *F* table is Table A–3 in the Appendix.)

HOW ARE YOU DOING?

For part (c) of each question, use the following scores involving three samples: The scores in Sample A are 5 and 7 (*M* = 6), the scores in Sample B are 6 and 10 (*M* = 8), and the scores in Sample C are 8 and 9 (*M* = 8.5).

1. (a) Write the formula for the within-groups population variance estimate and (b) define each of the symbols. (c) Figure the within-groups population variance estimate for the above scores.
2. (a) Write the formula for the variance of the distribution of means when using it as part of an analysis of variance and (b) define each of the symbols. (c) Figure the variance of the distribution of means for the above scores.
3. (a) Write the formula for the between-groups population variance estimate based on the variance of the distribution of means and (b) define each of the symbols. (c) Figure the

between-groups population variance estimate for the above scores. (d) Explain the logic behind this formula.

4. (a) Write the formula for the F ratio and (b) define each of the symbols. (c) Figure the F ratio for the above scores.

5. (a) Write the formulas for the between-groups and within-groups degrees of freedom and (b) define each of the symbols. (c) Figure the between-groups and within-groups degrees of freedom for the above scores.

6. (a) What is the F distribution? (b) Why is it skewed to the right? (c) What is the cutoff F for the above scores for the .05 significance level?

ANSWERS:

1. (a) $S^2_{Within} = (S^2_1 + S^2_2 + \cdots + S^2_{Last})/N_{groups}$.

(b) S^2_{Within} is the within-groups population variance estimate; S^2_1 is the estimated population variance based on the scores in the first group; S^2_2 is the estimated population variance based on the scores in the second group; S^2_{Last} is the estimated population variance based on the scores in the last group; the dots show that you are to fill in the population variance estimate for as many other groups as there are in the analysis; N_{Groups} is the number of groups.

(c) $S^2_1 = ([5 - 6]^2 + [7 - 6]^2)/(2 - 1) = (1 + 1)/1 = 2$;

$S^2_2 = ([6 - 8]^2 + [10 - 8]^2)/(2 - 1) = (4 + 4)/1 = 8$;

$S^2_3 = ([8 - 8.5]^2 + [9 - 8.5]^2)/(2 - 1) = (.25 + .25)/1 = .5$;

$S^2_{Within} = (S^2_1 + S^2_2 + \cdots + S^2_{Last})/N_{Groups} = (2 + 8 + .5)/3 = 10.5/3 = 3.5$.

2. (a) $S^2_M = \Sigma(M - GM)^2/df_{Between}$.

(b) S^2_M is the estimated variance of the distribution of means (estimated based on the means of the samples in your study). M is the mean of each of your samples. GM is the grand mean, the overall mean of all your scores, which is also the mean of your means. $df_{Between}$ is the degrees of freedom in the between-groups estimate, the number of groups minus 1.

(c) Grand mean is $(6 + 8 + 8.5)/3 = 7.5$.

$$S^2_M = \Sigma(M - GM)^2/df_{Between} = ([6 - 7.5]^2 + [8 - 7.5]^2 + [8.5 - 7.5]^2)/(3 - 1)$$

$$= (2.25 + .25 + 1)/2 = 3.5/2 = 1.75.$$

3. (a) $S^2_{Between} = (S^2_M)(n)$.

(b) $S^2_{Between}$ is the between-groups population variance estimate; S^2_M is the estimated variance of the distribution of means (estimated based on the means of the samples in your study); n is the number of participants in each sample.

(c) $S^2_{Between} = (S^2_M)(n) = (1.75)(2) = 3.5$.

(d) The goal is to have a variance of a distribution of individuals based on the variation among the means of the groups. S^2_M is the estimate of the variance of a distribution of means from the overall population based on the means of the samples. To go from the variance of a distribution of means to the variance of a distribution of individuals, you multiply by the size of each sample. This is because the variance of the distribution of means is always smaller than the distribution of individuals (because means of samples are less likely to be extreme than are individual scores); the exact relation is that the variance of the distribution of means is the variance of the distribution of individuals divided by the sample size; thus you reverse that process here.

4. (a) $F = S^2_{Between}/S^2_{Within}$

(b) F is the F ratio; $S^2_{Between}$ is the between-groups population variance estimate; S^2_{Within} is the within-groups population variance estimate.

(c) $F = S^2_{Between}/S^2_{Within} = 3.5/3.5 = 1.0$.

5. (a) $df_{Between} = N_{Groups} - 1$ and $df_{Within} = df_1 + df_2 + \ldots + df_{Last}$.

(b) $df_{Between}$ is the between-groups degrees of freedom; N_{Groups} is the number of groups; df_{Within} is the within-groups degrees of freedom; df_1 is the degrees of freedom for the population variance estimate based on the scores in the first sample; df_2 is the degrees of freedom for the population variance estimate based on the scores in the second sample; df_{Last} is the degrees of freedom for the population variance estimate based on the scores in the last sample; the dots show that you are to fill in the population degrees of freedom for as many other samples as there are in the analysis.

(c) $df_{Between} = N_{Groups} - 1 = 3 - 1 = 2$; $df_{Within} = df_1 + df_2 + \ldots + df_{Last} = 1 + 1 + 1 = 3$.

6. (a) The distribution of F ratios you would expect by chance. (b) F ratios, because they are a ratio of variances (which as averages of squared numbers have to be positive), are ratios of two positive numbers, which always have to be positive. Thus, they can't be less than 0. But there is no limit to how high an F ratio can be. Thus, the scores bunch up at the left (near 0) and spread out to the right. (c) 9.55.

HYPOTHESIS TESTING WITH THE ANALYSIS OF VARIANCE

Here are the steps of hypothesis testing for the criminal record experiment.

❶ **Restate the question as a research hypothesis and a null hypothesis about the populations.** There are three populations:

> **Population 1:** Jurors told that the defendant has a criminal record.
>
> **Population 2:** Jurors told that the defendant has a clean record.
>
> **Population 3:** Jurors given no information of the defendant's record.

The null hypothesis is that these three populations have the same mean. The research hypothesis is that the populations' means differ.

❷ **Determine the characteristics of the comparison distribution.** The comparison distribution is an F distribution with 2 and 12 degrees of freedom.

❸ **Determine the cutoff sample score on the comparison distribution at which the null hypothesis should be rejected.** Using the F table for the .05 significance level, the needed F ratio is 3.89.

❹ **Determine your sample's score on the comparison distribution.** In the analysis of variance, the comparison distribution is an F distribution, and the sample's score on that distribution is thus its F ratio. In the example, the F ratio was 4.07.

❺ **Decide whether to reject the null hypothesis.** In the example, the F ratio of 4.07 is more extreme than the .05 significance level cutoff of 3.89. Thus, the researcher would reject the null hypothesis that the three groups come from populations with the same mean. This suggests that they come from populations with different means: that people exposed to different kinds of information (or no information) about the criminal record of a defendant in a situation of this kind will differ in their ratings of the defendant's guilt.

You may be interested to know that several real studies have looked at whether knowing a defendant's prior criminal record affects the likelihood of conviction. The overall conclusion seems to be reasonably consistent with that of the fictional study described here. For a review of such studies, see Dane and Wrightsman (1982).

SUMMARY OF STEPS FOR HYPOTHESIS TESTING USING THE ANALYSIS OF VARIANCE

Table 10–7 summarizes the steps of an analysis of variance of the kind we have been considering in this chapter.[1]

ASSUMPTIONS IN THE ANALYSIS OF VARIANCE

The assumptions for the analysis of variance are basically the same as for the t test for independent means. That is, you get strictly accurate results only when the populations follow a normal curve and have equal variances. As with the t test, in practice you get quite acceptable results even when your populations are moderately far from normal and have moderately different variances. As a general rule, if the variance estimate of the group with the largest estimate is no more than 4 or 5 times that of the smallest and the sample sizes are equal, the conclusions using the F distribution should be adequately accurate. In Chapter 11, we consider what to do when you have reason to think that your populations are a long way from meeting these assumptions.

COMPARING EACH GROUP TO EACH OTHER GROUP

When you reject the null hypothesis in an analysis of variance, this implies that the population means are not all the same. What is not clear, however, is which population means differ from which. For example, in the criminal record study, the Criminal Record group jurors had the highest ratings for the defendant's guilt ($M = 8$); the No Information group jurors, the second highest ($M = 5$); and the Clean Record group jurors, the lowest ($M = 4$). From the analysis of variance results, we concluded that the true means of the three populations these groups represent are not all the same. (That is, the overall analysis of variance was significant.) However, we do not know which particular populations' means are *significantly different* from each other.

For this reason, researchers often do not stop after getting a significant result with an analysis of variance. Instead, they may go on to compare each population to

---

[1]There are some computational formulas that are helpful if you have to do an analysis of variance for a real study by hand (without a computer). Also, the procedure you have learned to do in the chapter works (without modification) only if you have equal numbers of scores in each group. The computational formulas below also work when there are unequal numbers of scores in each group. These formulas require that you first figure an intermediary for the two variance estimates, called "sum of squares," or SS for short. For the between-groups estimate, $S^2_{\text{Between}} = SS_{\text{Between}}/df_{\text{Between}}$. The formula for SS_{Between} is as follows:

$$SS_{\text{Between}} = \frac{\left(\Sigma X_1\right)^2}{n_1} + \frac{\left(\Sigma X_2\right)^2}{n_2} + \cdots + \frac{\left(\Sigma X_{\text{Last}}\right)^2}{n_{\text{Last}}} - \frac{\left(\Sigma X\right)^2}{N} \tag{10-7}$$

For the within-groups estimate, $S^2_{\text{Within}} = SS_{\text{Within}}/df_{\text{Within}}$. The formula for SS_{Within} is as follows:

$$SS_{\text{Within}} = \Sigma X^2 - \frac{\left(\Sigma X\right)^2}{N} - SS_{\text{Between}} \tag{10-8}$$

However, as usual, we urge you to use the definitional formulas we have presented in the chapter to work out the practice problems. The definitional formulas are closely related to the meaning of the procedures. Using the definitional formulas to work out the problems helps you learn the meaning of the analysis of variance.

TABLE 10–7	Steps for the Analysis of Variance (When Sample Sizes Are Equal)

❶ **Restate the question as a research hypothesis and a null hypothesis about the populations.**

❷ **Determine the characteristics of the comparison distribution.**
   a. The comparison distribution is an F distribution.
   b. The between-groups degrees of freedom is the number of groups minus 1: $df_{Between} = N_{Groups} - 1$.
   c. The within-groups degrees of freedom is the sum of the degrees of freedom in each group (the number in the group minus 1): $df_{Within} = df_1 + df_2 + \ldots + df_{Last}$.

❸ **Determine the cutoff sample score on the comparison distribution at which the null hypothesis should be rejected.**
   a. Decide the significance level.
   b. Look up the appropriate cutoff in an F table, using the degrees of freedom from Step 2.

❹ **Determine your sample's score on the comparison distribution.** This will be an F ratio.
   a. Figure the between-groups population variance estimate $(S^2_{Between})$.
      i. Figure the mean of each group
      ❹ **Estimate the variance of the distribution of means:**
         $S^2_M = \Sigma(M - GM)^2/df_{Between}$.
      ❺ **Figure the estimated variance of the population of individual scores:**
         $S^2_{Between} = (S^2_M)(n)$.
   b. Figure the within-groups population variance estimate (S^2_{Within})
      i. Figure population variance estimates based on each group's scores: For each group, $S^2 = \Sigma(X - M)^2/(n - 1)$.
      ii. Average these variance estimates:
         S^2_{Within} or $MS_{Within} = (S^2_1 + S^2_2 + \cdots + S^2_{Last})/N_{Groups}$.
   c. Figure the F ratio: $F = S^2_{Between}/S^2_{Within}$.

❺ **Decide whether to reject the null hypothesis:** Compare the scores from Steps 3 and 4.

each other population. For example, with three groups, you would compare group 1 to group 2, group 1 to group 3, and group 2 to group 3. You could do each of these comparisons using ordinary t tests for independent means. However, there is a problem with using ordinary t tests like this. The problem is that you are making three comparisons, each at the .05 level. The overall chance of at least one of them being significant just by chance is more like .15.

Some statisticians argue that it is all right to do three t tests in this situation because we have first checked that the overall analysis of variance is significant. These are called **protected t tests.** We are protected from making too big an error by the overall analysis of variance being significant. However, most statisticians believe that the protected t test is not enough protection. Advanced statistics texts give procedures that provide even more protection. (Also, most standard statistics software have options as part of the analysis of variance that provide various ways to compare means that provide strong protection of this kind. One widely used method is called *Tukey's HSD* test.)

protected t tests

HOW ARE YOU DOING?

1. A study compares the effects of three experimental treatments, A, B, and C, by giving each treatment to 16 participants and then assessing their performance on a standard measure. The results on the standard measure are, Treatment A group: $M = 20$, $S^2 = 8$; Treatment B group: $M = 22$, $S^2 = 9$; Treatment C group: $M = 18$, $S^2 = 7$. Use the steps of hypothesis testing (with the .01 significance level) to test whether the three experimental treatments create any difference among the populations these groups represent.

2. Give the two main assumptions for the analysis of variance.
3. Why do we need the equal variance assumption?
4. What is the general rule about when violations of the equal variance assumption are likely to lead to serious inaccuracies in results?
5. After getting a significant result with an analysis of variance, why do researchers usually go on to compare each population to each other population?

ANSWERS:

1. Steps of hypothesis testing:

   ❶ **Restate the question as a research hypothesis and a null hypothesis about the populations.** There are three populations:

   > **Population 1:** People given experimental treatment A.
   >
   > **Population 2:** People given experimental treatment B.
   >
   > **Population 3:** People given experimental treatment C.

   The null hypothesis is that these three populations have the same mean. The research hypothesis is that their means differ.

   ❷ **Determine the characteristics of the comparison distribution.** The comparison distribution will be an F distribution. Its degrees of freedom are figured as follows: The between-groups variance estimate is based on three groups, making 2 degrees of freedom. The within-groups estimate is based on 15 degrees of freedom (16 participants) in each of the three groups, for a total of 45 degrees of freedom.

   ❸ **Determine the cutoff sample score on the comparison distribution at which the null hypothesis should be rejected.** Using Table A–3 in the Appendix, the cutoff for $df = 2, 45$ at the .01 level is 5.11.

   ❹ **Determine your sample's score on the comparison distribution.**
   a. Figure the between-groups population variance estimate ($S^2_{Between}$):
      i. Figure the mean of each group. The group means are 20, 22, and 18.

      ❹ **Estimate the variance of the distribution of means:** Sum the sample means' squared deviations from the grand mean and divide by the number of means minus 1:

      $$S^2_M = [(20-20)^2 + (22-20)^2 + (18-20)^2]/(3-1) = (0+4+4)/2 = 4.$$

      ❽ **Figure the estimated variance of the population of individual scores:** Multiply the variance of the distribution of means by the number of scores in each group:

      $$S^2_{Between} = (4)(16) = 64.$$

   b. Figure the within-groups population variance estimate (S^2_{Within}):
      i. Figure population variance estimates based on each group's scores. Treatment A group, $S^2 = 8$; Treatment B group, $S^2 = 9$; Treatment C group, $S^2 = 7$.

      ii. Average these variance estimates. $S^2_{Within} = (8 + 9 + 7)/3 = 8$.

   The F ratio is the between-groups estimate divided by the within-groups estimate: $F = 64/8 = 8.00$.

   ❺ **Decide whether to reject the null hypothesis.** The F of 8.00 is more extreme than the .01 cutoff of 5.11. Therefore, reject the null hypothesis. The research hypothesis is supported; the different experimental treatments do produce different effects on the standard performance measure.

2. The populations are assumed to be normally distributed with equal variances.
3. We need the equal variance assumption in order to be able to justify averaging the estimates from each sample into an overall within-groups population variance estimate.
4. The analysis can lead to inaccurate results when the variance estimate from the group with the largest estimate is more than four or five times the smallest variance estimate.
5. To find out which populations' means are significantly different from each other.

EFFECT SIZE AND POWER FOR
THE ANALYSIS OF VARIANCE

EFFECT SIZE

Effect size for the analysis of variance is a little more complex than for a t test. With the t test, you took the difference between the two means and divide by the pooled population standard deviation. In the analysis of variance, you still can divide by the population standard deviation—you can use the square root of the within-groups population variance estimate. However, in analysis of variance, we have more than two means, so it is not obvious just what is the equivalent to the difference between the means—the numerator in figuring effect size. Cohen (1988) suggests that in the analysis of variance, we should think of the equivalent of the difference between means as the variation among the means. Specifically, Cohen recommends using the standard deviation of the distribution of means. (This is the square root of the variance you figure as the first step of finding the between-groups population variance estimate.) Thus, Cohen defines the **effect size for the analysis of variance** as the standard deviation of the distribution of means divided by the standard deviation of the population of individuals. Stated as a formula in terms of estimated variances,

effect size for the analysis of variance

> The estimated effect size for the analysis of variance is the standard deviation of the distribution of means divided by the standard deviation of the population of individuals.

(10-9)
$$\text{Estimated Effect Size} = \frac{S_M}{S_{\text{Within}}}$$

Cohen's conventions for effect size for analysis of variance are .10 for a small effect, .25 for a medium effect, and .40 for a large effect size.

Consider our criminal-record experiment. We figured S_M^2, the estimated variance of the distribution of means based on the means of our three samples, to be 4.34. S_M, the square root of S_M^2, is 2.08. We figured S_{Within}^2, the estimate of the variance of each population of individuals, based on the variance estimates using each group's scores, to be 5.33. S_{Within}, the square root of S_{Within}^2, is 2.31. Applying the formula,

$$\text{Estimated Effect Size} = \frac{S_M}{S_{\text{Within}}} = \frac{2.08}{2.31} = .90$$

This is a very large effect size (thanks to our fictional data).

With a bit of algebraic manipulation, it turns out that the effect size using estimated variances can be figured directly from knowing the F and the number of scores in each group. The formula is:

> The estimated effect size for the analysis of variance is the square root of the F ratio divided by the square root of the number of scores in each group.

(10-10)
$$\text{Estimated Effect Size} = \frac{\sqrt{F}}{\sqrt{n}}$$

For example, in the criminal record study we had calculated F to be 4.07 and there were five people in each group. Using the formula,

$$\text{Estimated Effect Size} = \frac{\sqrt{F}}{\sqrt{n}} = \frac{\sqrt{4.07}}{\sqrt{5}} = \frac{2.02}{2.24} = .90$$

This formula is very helpful when figuring the effect size of a completed study reported in a published research article.

POWER

Table 10–8 shows the approximate power for the .05 significance level for small, medium, and large effect sizes; sample size of 10, 20, 30, 40, 50, and 100 per group; and three, four, and five groups.[2]

Consider a planned study with five groups of 10 participants each and an expected large effect size (.40). Using the .05 significance level, the study would have a power of .56. Thus, even if the research hypothesis is in fact true and has a large effect size, there is only a little greater than even chance (56%) that the study will come out significant.

As we have noted in previous chapters, determining power is especially useful when interpreting the practical implication of a nonsignificant result. For example, suppose that you have read a study using an analysis of variance with four groups of 30 participants each in which the researcher reports a nonsignificant result at the .05 level. Table 10–8 shows a power of only .13 for a small effect size. This suggests that even if such a small effect exists in the population, this study would be very unlikely to have come out significant. But the table shows a power of .96 for a large

TABLE 10–8 Approximate Power for Studies Using the Analysis of Variance Testing Hypotheses at the .05 Significance Level

Participants per Group (n)	Effect Size		
	Small (.10)	Medium (.25)	Large (.40)
Three groups ($df_{Between} = 2$)			
10	.07	.20	.45
20	.09	.38	.78
30	.12	.55	.93
40	.15	.68	.98
50	.18	.79	.99
100	.32	.98	*
Four groups ($df_{Between} = 3$)			
10	.07	.21	.51
20	.10	.43	.85
30	.13	.61	.96
40	.16	.76	.99
50	.19	.85	*
100	.36	.99	*
Five groups ($df_{Between} = 4$)			
10	.07	.23	.56
20	.10	.47	.90
30	.13	.67	.98
40	.17	.81	*
50	.21	.90	*
100	.40	*	*

*Nearly 1.

[2]More detailed tables are provided in Cohen (1988, pp. 289–354). When using these tables, note that the value of u at the top of each table refers to $df_{between}$, which for a one-way analysis of variance is the number of groups minus 1, not the number of groups as used in our Table 10–8.

effect size. This suggests that if a large effect existed in the population, it almost surely would have shown up in that study.

PLANNING SAMPLE SIZE

Table 10–9 gives the approximate number of participants you need in each group for 80% power at the .05 significance level for estimated small, medium, and large effect sizes for studies with three, four, and five groups.[3]

For example, suppose you are planning a study involving four groups and you expect a small effect size (and will use the .05 significance level). For 80% power, you would need 274 participants in each group, a total of 1,096 in all. However, suppose you could adjust the research plan so that it was now reasonable to predict a large effect size (perhaps by using more accurate measures and a more powerful experimental procedure). Now you would need only 18 in each of the four groups, for a total of 72.

HOW ARE YOU DOING?

1. (a) Write the formula for effect size in analysis of variance using standard deviations; (b) define each of the symbols; and (c) figure the effect size for a study in which $S_M = 3.79$ and $S_{Within} = 19.21$.
2. (a) Write the formula for effect size in analysis of variance using the F ratio; (b) define each of the symbols; and (c) figure the effect size for a study in which $F = 4.33$ and $n = 80$.
3. What is the power of a study with four groups of 40 participants each to be tested at the .05 significance level, in which the researchers predict a large effect size?
4. About how many participants do you need in each group for 80% power in a planned study with five groups in which you predict a medium effect size and will be using the .05 significance level?

ANSWERS:

1. (a) Estimated effect size $= S_M/S_{Within}$. (b) S_M is the standard deviation of the distribution of means; S_{Within} is the standard deviation of the distribution of individuals. (c) 3.79/19.21 = .20.
2. (a) Estimated effect size $= \sqrt{F}/\sqrt{n}$. (b) F is the F ratio; n is the number of scores in each group. (c) $\sqrt{4.33}/\sqrt{80} = .23$.
3. .99.
4. 39.

TABLE 10–9 **Approximate Number of Participants Needed in Each Group (Assuming Equal Sample Sizes) for 80% Power for the One-Way Analysis of Variance Testing Hypotheses at the .05 Significance Level**

	Effect Size		
	Small (.10)	Medium (.25)	Large (.40)
Three groups ($df_{Between} = 2$)	322	52	21
Four groups ($df_{Between} = 3$)	274	45	18
Five groups ($df_{Between} = 4$)	240	39	16

---

[3]More detailed tables are provided in Cohen (1988, pp. 381–389). If you use these, see footnote 2 in this chapter.

FACTORIAL ANALYSIS OF VARIANCE

factorial analysis of variance

Factorial analysis of variance is an extension of the procedures you just learned. It is a wonderfully flexible and efficient approach that handles many types of experimental studies. The actual figuring of a factorial analysis of variance is beyond what we can cover in an introductory book. Our goal in this section is to help you understand the basic approach and the terminology so that you can make sense of research articles that use it.

We will introduce factorial analysis of variance with an example. Lambert, Khan, Lickel, and Fricke (1997) were interested in how stereotypes affect the evaluations we make of others. For example, people often use age or gender stereotypes to evaluate whether someone will be successful in a particular job. Lambert et al. were especially interested in how the influence of stereotypes is affected (a) by awareness that a stereotype is inappropriate for a particular circumstance and (b) by mood. They believed that people are less affected by a stereotype when it is inappropriate and are particularly unaffected by stereotypes when in a sad mood.

Thus, Lambert et al. did the following experiment. Participants were asked to put themselves in the position of a job interviewer. Their task was to "form a preliminary evaluation of the suitability of an individual for a particular job" (1997, p. 1010)—which for all participants was that of a flight attendant. The participants were then given a resume of an applicant that included a photo of a very attractive woman. Based on this information, the participants were asked how likely it was they would hire her, using a scale from 0 (not at all) to 10 (extremely). This experiment used the *attractiveness stereotype*, a stereotype that includes the tendency to think that good-looking people are especially competent.

The researchers put half the participants in a sad mood prior to reading the resume, supposedly as part of a separate experiment. These participants were asked to think about "an episode in your life that made you feel very sad and continues to make you sad whenever you think about it, even today" (p. 1004). This was the *Sad Mood* condition. The other half of the participants were not given any particular instructions. This was the *Neutral Mood* condition.

The other influence of interest to the researchers was appropriateness of the stereotype. Participants were given a description of a good flight attendant that differed according to how important attractiveness was for the job. For half the participants in each of the mood groups, the description emphasized the ability "to solve and analyze problems in a rational and analytic fashion" (p. 1010); this was the *Stereotype Inappropriate* condition. For the other participants, the description emphasized passenger satisfaction and how appearance contributed to it; this was the *Stereotype Appropriate* condition.

In sum, there were two experimental manipulations: sad mood versus neutral mood and the job description being stereotype appropriate versus stereotype inappropriate.

Lambert and his colleagues could have conducted two studies, one comparing participants put in a sad versus a neutral mood and one comparing participants given the stereotype appropriate versus inappropriate job descriptions. Instead, they studied the effects of both mood and stereotype appropriateness in a single study. They considered four groups of participants (see Table 10–10): (a) those in the sad mood and stereotype-appropriate conditions, (b) those in the sad mood and stereotype-inappropriate conditions, (c) those in the neutral mood and stereotype-appropriate conditions, and (d) those in the neutral mood and stereotype-inappropriate conditions.

TABLE 10–10 Factorial Design Employed by Lambert et al. (1997)

	Mood	
Stereotype	Sad	Neutral
Appropriate	a	c
Inappropriate	b	d

FACTORIAL RESEARCH DESIGN DEFINED

The Lambert et al. (1997) study is an example of a **factorial research design** study. In a factorial research design the effect of two or more variables are examined at once by making groupings of every combination of the variables. In this example, there are two levels of mood (sad and neutral) and two levels of stereotype appropriateness (appropriate and inappropriate). This allows four possible combinations, and Lambert et al. used all of them in their study.

A factorial research design has a major advantage over doing separate studies of each variable—efficiency. With a factorial design you can study both variables at once, without needing twice as many participants. In the example, Lambert et al. were able to use a single group of participants to study the effects of mood and stereotype appropriateness.

INTERACTION EFFECTS

There is an even more important advantage of a factorial research design. A factorial design lets you study the effects of combining two or more variables. In this example, mood and stereotype appropriateness might affect hiring in a simple additive way. By additive, we mean that their combined influence is the sum of their separate influences—if you are more of one and also more of the other, then the overall effect is the total of the two individual effects. For example, suppose being sad makes you more willing to hire someone; similarly, the stereotype being appropriate makes you more willing to hire a person. If these two effects are additive, then participants in the sad, stereotype-appropriate group will be most willing to hire the person; participants in the neutral, stereotype-inappropriate group will be least likely to hire the person; and those in the other two conditions would have an intermediate likelihood of hiring the person.

It could also be that one variable but not the other has an effect. Or perhaps neither variable has any effect. In the additive situation, or the one in which only one variable or neither has an effect, looking at the two variables in combination does not give any interesting additional information.

However, it is also possible that the combination of the two variables changes the result. In fact, Lambert et al. (1997) predicted that the effect of stereotype inappropriateness would be especially strong in the sad mood condition. This prediction was based on the notion that when in a sad mood, we are more willing to revise our initial, unthinking, stereotype-based reactions.

A situation where the *combination* of variables has a special effect is called an **interaction effect.** An interaction effect is an effect in which the impact of one variable depends on the level of the other variable. In the Lambert et al. (1997) study, there was an interaction effect. Look at Table 10–11. The result was that the participants in the Appropriate-Sad group were most likely to hire the applicant, the Inappropriate-Neutral group was the next most likely, and the two other groups were least likely (to about an equal extent). Consider the bottom row of the results, the Inappropriate Stereotype group. This part of the result supported the researchers' theory that when in a sad mood, people are able to counteract their stereotypes. (What about the appropriate-sad being the most likely to hire? The researchers acknowledged that this result was "unexpected and difficult to explain" [p. 1011].)

Suppose the researchers had studied stereotype appropriateness and mood in two separate studies. They would have concluded that each factor had only a slight effect. The average likelihood of hiring for the appropriate is 6.77 (that is, the average of 5.8 and 7.73 comes out to 6.77) and for inappropriate is 6.29. The average likelihood of hiring for those in the sad-mood condition was 6.78 versus 6.28 for

factorial research design

interaction effect

| TABLE 10–11 | Mean Likelihood of Hiring in the Lambert et al. (1997) Study |

Stereotype		Mood	
		Sad	Neutral
	Appropriate	7.73	5.80
	Inappropriate	5.83	6.75

those in the neutral-mood condition. Thus, following the approach of two separate studies, they would have completely missed the important result. The most important results had to do with the combination of the two factors.

SOME TERMINOLOGY

The Lambert et al. study would be analyzed with what is called a **two-way analysis of variance** (it uses a **two-way factorial research design**). By contrast, the situations we considered earlier (such as the attachment style study or the criminal record experiment) were examples of studies analyzed using a **one-way analysis of variance.** Such studies are called one-way because they consider the effect of only one variable that separates groups (such as a person's attachment style or information about a defendant's criminal record).

In a two-way analysis, each variable or "way" (each dimension in the diagram) is a possible **main effect.** If the result for a variable, averaging across the other variable or variables, is significant, it is a main effect. This is entirely different from an interaction effect, which is based on the combination of variables. In the two-way Lambert et al. study, there was a possibility of two main effects and one interaction effect. The two possible main effects are one for stereotype appropriateness and one for mood. The possible interaction effect is for the combination of stereotype appropriateness and mood. In a two-way analysis of variance, you are always testing two possible main effects and one possible interaction.

Each grouping combination in a factorial design is called a **cell.** The mean of the scores in each grouping is called a **cell mean.** In the Lambert et al. study, there are four cells. Thus, there are four cell means, one for each combination of the levels of stereotype appropriateness and mood. That is, one cell is Stereotype Appropriate and Sad Mood (as shown in Table 10–11, its mean is 7.33); one cell is Stereotype Inappropriate and Sad Mood (5.83); one cell is Stereotype Appropriate and Neutral Mood (5.80); and one cell is Stereotype Inappropriate and Neutral Mood (6.75).

The means of one variable alone are called **marginal means.** For example, in the Lambert et al. study there are four marginal means, one mean for all the stereotype-appropriate participants (as we saw earlier, 6.77), one for all the stereotype-inappropriate participants (6.29), one for all the sad-mood participants (6.78), and one for all the neutral-mood participants (6.28). (Because we were mainly interested in the interaction, we did not show these marginal means in the tables.)

To look at a main effect, you focus on the marginal means. To look at the interaction effect, you focus on the pattern of individual cell means.

HOW ARE YOU DOING?

1. (a) What is a factorial design? (b) and (c) Give two advantages of a factorial design over doing two separate experiments.
2. In a factorial design, (a) what is a main effect, and (b) what is an interaction effect?
3. Below are the means from a study in which participants rated the originality of paintings under various conditions. For each mean, indicate its grouping and whether it is a cell or marginal mean.

	Contemporary	Rennaissance	Overall
Landscape	6.5	5.5	6
Portrait	3.5	2.5	3
Overall	5	4	

4. In each of the following studies, participants' performance on a coordination task was measured under various conditions or compared for different groups. For each study, make a diagram of the design and indicate whether it is a one-way or two-way design: (a) a study in which people are assigned to either a high-stress condition or a low-stress condition, and within each of these conditions, half are assigned to work alone and half to work in a room with other people; (b) a study comparing students majoring in physics, chemistry, or engineering; (c) a study comparing people doing a task in a hot room versus a cold room, with half in each room doing the task with their right hand and half with their left hand.

ANSWERS:

1. (a) A research design in which the effect of two or more variables is examined at once by making groupings of every combination of the variables.
   (b) It is more efficient. For example, you can study the effects of two variables at once with only a single group of participants.
   (c) It makes it possible to see if there are interaction effects.
2. (a) The effect of one of the variables ignoring the pattern of results on the other variable.
   (b) The different effect of one variable according to the level of the other variable.
3. 6.5 = cell mean for Contemporary/Landscape group; 5.5 = cell mean for Rennaissance/Landscape group; 6 = marginal mean for Landscape groups; 3.5 = cell mean for Contemporary/Portrait groups; 2.5 = cell mean for Rennaissance/Portrait group; 3 = marginal mean for Portrait group; 5 = marginal mean for Contemporary groups; and 4 = marginal mean for Rennaissance groups.
4. (a) Two-way.

| | Stress | |
	High	Low
Alone		
With Others		

(b) One-way.

Physics	Chemistry	Engineering

(c) Two-way.

| | Room | |
	Hot	Cold
Right		
Left		

RECOGNIZING AND INTERPRETING INTERACTION EFFECTS

It is very important to understand interaction effects. In many experiments the interaction effect is the main point of the research. As we have seen, an interaction effect is an effect in which the impact of one variable depends on the level of another variable. The Lambert et al. study results (Table 10–11) show an interaction effect. This is because the impact of stereotype appropriateness is different with a sad mood than with a neutral mood. You can think out and describe an interaction effect in three ways: in words, in numbers, or in a graph.

IDENTIFYING INTERACTION EFFECTS IN WORDS AND NUMBERS

You can think out an interaction effect in words by saying that an interaction effect occurs when the effect of one variable depends on the level of another variable. In the Lambert et al. example, the effect of stereotype appropriateness depends on the level of mood. (You can also say that the effect of mood depends on the level of stereotype appropriateness. Interaction effects are completely symmetrical, in that you can describe them from the point of view of either variable.) Another way of saying this is that the effect of stereotype appropriateness varies according to the level of mood (the impact of stereotype appropriateness is different with a sad mood than with a neutral mood).

You can see an interaction effect numerically by looking at the pattern of cell means. If there is an interaction effect, the differences in cell means across one row will not be the same as the differences in cell means across another row. Consider the Lambert et al. example. In the Stereotype Appropriate row, the Sad Mood participants rated how likely they were to hire (7.33) much *higher* than the Neutral Mood participants (5.80). This was a positive difference of 1.93 (that is, 7.73 − 5.80 = 1.93). However, look at the Stereotype Inappropriate row. Those in a sad mood rated their likelihood of hiring (5.83) *lower* than those in the neutral mood (6.75). The difference for sad versus neutral mood for stereotype-inappropriate participants was −.92.

Table 10–12 gives cell and marginal means for six possible results of a fictional two-way factorial study on the relation of age and education to income. Age has two levels (younger, such as 25 to 29, versus older, such as 30 to 34) and education has two levels (high school versus college). These fictional results are exaggerated, to make clear when there are interactions and main effects.

TABLE 10–12 Possible Means for Results of a Study of the Relation of Age and Education to Income

	Result A			Result B			Result C		
	High School	College	Overall	High School	College	Overall	High School	College	Overall
Younger	40	40	40	60	40	50	20	60	40
Older	40	60	50	40	60	50	40	80	60
Overall	40	50		50	50		30	70	

	Result D			Result E			Result F		
	High School	College	Overall	High School	College	Overall	High School	College	Overall
Younger	20	20	20	40	60	50	40	60	50
Older	120	120	120	40	80	60	60	100	80
Overall	70	70		40	70		50	80	

In Result A there is an interaction. Note that in the Younger row, education makes no difference, but in the Older row, the college cell mean is much higher than the high-school cell mean. One way to say this is that for the younger group, education is unrelated to income; but for the older group, people with a college education earn much more than those with less education.

Result B is also an interaction. This is because in the Younger row the high-school mean income is higher than the college mean income, but in the Older row the high-school mean income is lower. Put in words, among younger people, those with only a high-school education make more money (perhaps because they entered the workplace earlier or the kinds of jobs they have start out at a higher level); but among older people, those with a college education make more money.

Result C is *not* an interaction effect. In the Younger row, the high-school mean is 40 lower than the college mean, and the same is true in the Older row. In words, whether young or old, people with college educations earn $40,000 more.

In Result D, there is also no interaction—in neither row is there any difference. Regardless of education, older people earn $100,000 more.

Result E is an interaction. In the Younger row, the college mean is 20 higher, but in the Older row, the college mean is 40 higher. So among young people, college-educated people earn a little more, but among older people, those with a college education earn much more.

Finally, Result F is also an interaction effect—there is a smaller difference in the Younger row than in the Older row. As with Result E, for people with a college education, income increases more with age than it does for those with only a high-school education.[4]

IDENTIFYING INTERACTION EFFECTS GRAPHICALLY

Another common way of making sense of interaction effects is by graphing the pattern of cell means. This is usually done with a bar graph.[5] Figure 10–4 is reproduced from Lambert et al.'s (1997) article. The graphs in Figure 10–5 show the graphs for the fictional age and education results we just considered (the ones shown in Table 10–12).

One thing to notice about such graphs is this: Whenever there is an interaction, the patterns of bars on one section of the graph is different from the pattern on the other section of the graph. Thus, in Figure 10–4, the pattern for inappropriate is a step down, but the pattern for appropriate is a step up. The bars having a different pattern is just a graphic way of saying that the pattern of differences between the cell means from row to row is not the same.

Consider Figure 10–5. First, look at Results C and D. In Result C the younger and older sets of bars have the same pattern—both step up by 40. In Result D, both are flat. Within both Results C and D, the younger bars and the older bars have the same pattern. These were the examples that did not have interactions. All the other results, which did have interactions, have patterns of bars that are not parallel. For example, in Result A, the two younger bars are flat but the older bars show a step up. In Result B,

---

[4]Based on 1990 statistics from the U.S. Department of Education, the actual situation in the United States is closest to Result F, though not as extreme. People with a college education earn more than those with only a high-school education in both age groups, but the difference is somewhat greater for the older group. However, it is important to keep in mind that whether or not people receive a college education is also related to the social class of their parents and other factors that may affect income as much or more than education does.

[5]The use of bar graphs to show analysis of variance cell means where there is an interaction effect has become the standard in recent years. Prior to this, it was more common to use line graphs.

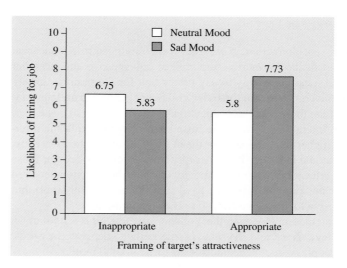

FIGURE 10-4   *Judgments of the physically attractive job candidate as a function of framing attractiveness (inappropriate vs. appropriate) and manipulated mood (sad vs. neutral), Experiment 3. Higher numbers indicate a greater likelihood of hiring the target for the job.*
Source: Lambert, A. J., Khan, S. R., Lickel, B. A., & Fricke, K. (1997). Mood and the correlation of positive versus negative stereotypes. *Journal of Personality and Social Psychology, 72,* 1002–1016. Copyright © 1997 by the American Psychological Association. Reprinted by permission.

FIGURE 10-5   *Graphs for the results of the fictional data shown in Table 10–11.*

the younger bars show a step down from high school to college, but the older bars show a step up from high school to college. In Results E and F, both younger and older bars show a step up, but the younger bars show a smaller step up than the older bars.

You can also see main effects from these graphs. In Figure 10–5, a main effect for age would be shown by the bars for younger being overall higher or lower than the bars for older. For example, in Result C, the bars for older are clearly higher than the bars for younger. What about the main effect for the bars that are not grouped together—college versus high school in this example? With these bars, you have to see whether the overall step pattern goes up or down. For example, in Result C, there is also a main effect for education, because the general pattern of the bars for high school to college goes up, and it does this for both the younger and older bars. Result D shows a main effect for age (the older bars are higher than the younger bars). But Result D does not show a main effect for education—the pattern is flat for both the older and younger bars.

RELATION OF INTERACTION AND MAIN EFFECTS

Any combination of main and interaction effects can be significant. For example, they may all be significant, as in the pattern in Result F of Table 10–12. In this result, older students earn more (a main effect for age), college students earn more (a main effect for level of education), and how much more college students earn depends on age (the interaction effect).

There can also be an interaction effect with no main effects. Result B of Table 10–12 is an example. The average level of income is the same for younger and older (no main effect for age), and it is the same for college and high school (no main effect for level of education).

There can also be one main effect significant along with an interaction, one main effect significant by itself, or for there to be no significant main or interaction effects. See how many of these possibilities you can find in the fictional results in Table 10–12.

When there is no interaction, a main effect has a straightforward meaning. However, when there is an interaction along with a main effect, you have to be cautious in drawing conclusions about the main effect. This is because the main effect may be created by just one of the levels of the variable. For example, in Result A the main effect for education (40 vs. 50) is entirely due to the difference for older people. It would be misleading to say that education makes a difference without noting that it really only matters when you are older.

Sometimes the main effect clearly holds up over and above any interaction. For example, in Result F in the age and education example, it seems clear that the main effect for age holds up over and above the interaction. That is, it is true for both people with and without a college education that older people earn more. (There is still an interaction, of course, because how much more older people earn depends on education.)

EXTENSIONS AND SPECIAL CASES OF THE FACTORIAL ANALYSIS OF VARIANCE

Analysis of variance is very versatile. Factorial designs can be extended into three-way and higher designs. There are also procedures to handle situations in which the same participants are tested more than once. This is like the *t* test for dependent means but works with more than two testings. It is called a *repeated measures analysis of variance.*

HOW ARE YOU DOING?

Questions 1 to 3 are based on the results shown below of a fictional study of the effects of vividness and length of examples on number of examples recalled.

	Vividness		
	Low	High	Overall
Short	5	7	6
Long	3	1	2
Overall	4	4	

1. Describe the pattern of results in words.
2. Explain the pattern in terms of numbers.
3. Make two graphs of these results: one graph should show vividness (low and high) on the horizontal axis, with bars for short and long example length; another graph should show example length (short and long) on the horinzontal axis, with bars for low and high vividness.
4. For a two-way factorial design, what are the possible combinations of main and interaction effects?
5. When there is both a main and an interaction effect, (a) under what conditions must you be cautious in interpreting the main effect, and (b) under what conditions can you still be confident in the overall main effect?

ANSWERS:

1. There is a main effect in which short examples are recalled better and an interaction effect such that there is a bigger advantage of short over long examples when they are highly vivid.
2. The main effect is that on the average people recall six short examples but only two long examples. The interaction effect is that for low vivid examples, people recall two more short than long; but for highly vivid examples, they recall six more short than long.
3. See Figure 10–6.

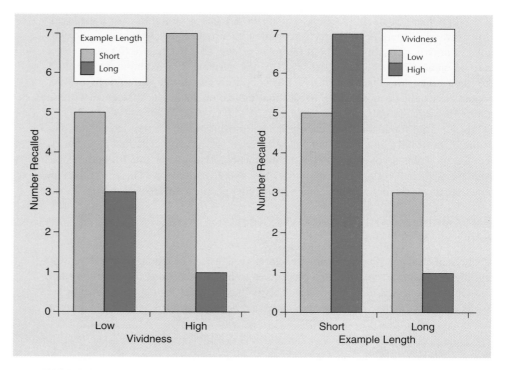

FIGURE 10–6   *Answer to "How Are You Doing?" question 3.*

4. All possible combinations: no main or interaction effects, either main effect only, the interaction only, both main effects but no interaction effect, an interaction effect with either main effect, or an interaction effect with both main effects.
5. (a) When the main effect is found for only one level of the other variable.
   (b) When the main effect holds at each level of the other variable.

ANALYSES OF VARIANCE IN RESEARCH ARTICLES

A one-way analysis of variance is usually described in a research article by giving the F, the degrees of freedom, and the significance level. For example, $F(3, 68) = 5.21$, $p < .01$. The means for the groups usually are given in a table. However, if there are only a few groups and only one or a few measures, the means may be given in the regular text of the article. Returning to the criminal-record experiment example, we could describe the analysis of variance results this way: "The means for the Criminal Record, Clean Record, and No Information conditions were 7.0, 4.0, and 5.0, respectively, $F(2, 12) = 4.07$, $p < .05$."

In a factorial analysis of variance, researchers usually give a description in the text plus a table. The text gives the F ratio and the information that goes with it for each main and interaction effect. The table gives the cell means and sometimes also the marginal means. If there is an interaction effect, there may also be a graph. For example, Lambert et al. (1997) described the result we used for our example as follows:

> Analysis of participants' intention to hire the target revealed only one significant effect, the predicted Mood X Job Type interaction, $F(1, 57) = 11.46$, $p < .001$. Data relevant to this interaction are displayed in Figure [10–4]. (p. 101)

SUMMARY

1. The analysis of variance (ANOVA) is used to test hypotheses based on differences among means of more than two samples. The procedure compares two estimates of population variance. One, the within-groups estimate, is figured by averaging the population variance estimates from each of the samples. The other, the between-groups estimate, is based on the variation among the means of the samples.

2. The F ratio is the between-groups estimate divided by the within-groups estimate. The null hypothesis is that all the samples come from populations with the same mean. If the null hypothesis is true, the F ratio should be about 1. This is because the two population variance estimates are based on the same thing, the variation within each of the populations. If the research hypothesis is true, so that the samples come from populations with different means, the F ratio should be larger than 1. This is because the between-groups estimate is now influenced by the variation both within the populations and among them. But the within-groups estimate is still affected only by the variation within each of the populations.

3. When the samples are of equal size, the within-groups population variance estimate is the ordinary average of the estimates of the population variance figured from each sample. The between-groups population variance estimate is done in two steps. First, you estimate the variance of the distribution of means based on the means of your samples. (This is figured with the usual formula for estimating population variance from sample scores.) Second, you multiply this estimate by the number of participants in each group. This step takes you from the variance of the distribution of means to the variance of the distribution of individual scores.

4. The distribution of F ratios when the null hypothesis is true is a mathematically defined distribution that is skewed to the right. Significance cutoffs are given on an F table according to the degrees of freedom for each population variance estimate: the between-groups (numerator) estimate is based on the number of groups minus 1 and the within-groups (denominator) estimate is based on the sum of the degrees of freedom within all samples.

5. The assumptions for the analysis of variance are the same as for the t test. The populations must be normally distributed, with equal variances. Like the t test, the analysis of variance is adequately accurate even when there are moderate violations of these assumptions.

6. Estimated effect size in the analysis of variance can be figured as the standard deviation of the distribution of means (S_M) divided by the standard deviation of the distribution of individuals (S_{Within}). Estimated effect size can also be figured as the square root of F divided by the square root of the number of participants in each group. Power depends on effect size, number of people in the study, significance level, and number of groups.

7. In a factorial research design, participants are put into groupings according to the combinations of the variables whose effects are being studied. In such designs, you can study the effects of two variables without needing twice as many participants. Also, such designs allow you to study the effects of combinations of the two variables.

8. An interaction effect is when the impact of one variable depends on the level of the other variable. A main effect is the impact of one variable, ignoring the effect of the other variable. Interaction effects and main effects can be described verbally, numerically, and graphically (usually on a graph with bars for each combination of the variables that divide the groups, with the height of the bar being the score on the measured variable).

9. Analysis of variance results are reported in a standard fashion in research articles, such as $F(3, 68) = 5.81$, $p < .01$. In a factorial analysis of variance, there is usually a description in the text plus a table. A graph may also be used to show any significant interactions.

KEY TERMS

analysis of variance (ANOVA) (p. 290)

within-groups estimate of the population variance (S^2_{Within}) (p. 290)

between-groups estimate of the population variance (S^2_{Between}) (p. 291)

F ratio (p. 295)

F distribution (p. 295)

F table (p. 295)

grand mean (GM) (p. 299)

between-groups degrees of freedom (df_{between}) (p. 302)

numerator degrees of freedom (df_{between}) (p. 302)

within-groups degrees of freedom (df_{within}) (p. 302)

denominator degrees of freedom (df_{within}) (p. 302)

protected t tests (p. 307)

effect size for the analysis of variance (p. 309)

factorial analysis of variance (p. 312)

factorial research design (p. 313)

interaction effect (p. 313)

two-way analysis of variance (p. 314)

two-way factorial design (p. 314)

one-way analysis of variance (p. 314)

main effect (p. 314)

cell (p. 314)

cell mean (p. 314)

marginal means (p. 314)

EXAMPLE WORKED-OUT PROBLEMS

OVERALL ANALYSIS OF VARIANCE

An experiment compares the effects of four treatments, giving each treatment to 20 participants and then assessing their performance on a standard measure. The results on the standard measure are Treatment 1: $M = 15$, $S^2 = 20$; Treatment 2: $M = 12$, $S^2 = 25$; Treatment 3: $M = 18$, $S^2 = 14$; Treatment 4: $M = 15$, $S^2 = 27$. Use the five steps of hypothesis testing (and the .05 significance level) to determine whether treatment matters.

ANSWER

Steps of hypothesis testing:

❶ **Restate the question as a research hypothesis and a null hypothesis about the populations.** There are four populations:

> **Population 1:** People given experimental treatment 1.
>
> **Population 2:** People given experimental treatment 2.
>
> **Population 3:** People given experimental treatment 3.
>
> **Population 4:** People given experimental treatment 4.

The null hypothesis is that these four populations have the same mean. The research hypothesis is that their means differ.

❷ **Determine the characteristics of the comparison distribution.** The comparison distribution will be an F distribution.

$df_{Between} = N_{Groups} - 1 = 4 - 1 = 3$; $df_{Within} = df_1 + df_2 + \ldots + df_{Last} = 19 + 19 + 19 + 19 = 76$.

❸ **Determine the cutoff sample score on the comparison distribution at which the null hypothesis should be rejected.** Using Table A–3 in the Appendix for $df = 3, 75$ (the closest below 3, 76) at the .05 level, the cutoff is 2.73.

❹ **Determine your sample's score on the comparison distribution.**

a. Figure the between-groups population variance estimate ($S^2_{Between}$):

   i. Figure the mean of each group. The group means are 15, 12, 18, and 15.

   ❹ **Estimate the variance of the distribution of means:** Sum the sample means' squared deviations from the grand mean and divide by the number of means minus 1:

$GM = (15 + 12 + 18 + 15)/4 = 15.$
$S^2_M = \Sigma(M - GM)^2/df_{Between}$
$\quad = ([15 - 15]^2 + [12 - 15]^2 + [18 - 15]^2 + [15 - 15]^2)/(4 - 1)$
$\quad = (0 + 9 + 9 + 0)/3 = 18/3 = 6.$

   ❺ **Figure the estimated variance of the population of individual scores:** Multiply the variance of the distribution of means by the number of scores in each group.

$$S^2_{Between} = (S^2_M)(n) = (6)(20) = 120.$$

b. Figure the within-groups population variance estimate (S^2_{Within}):

   i. Figure population variance estimates based on each group's scores. Treatment 1 group, $S^2 = 20$; Treatment 2 group, $S^2 = 25$; Treatment 3 group, $S^2 = 14$; Treatment 4 group, $S^2 = 27$.

ii.   Average these variance estimates.

$$S^2_{\text{Within}} = (20 + 25 + 14 + 27)/4 = 86/4 = 21.5.$$
$$F = S^2_{\text{Between}}/S^2_{\text{Within}} = 120/21.5 = 5.58$$

❺ **Decide whether to reject the null hypothesis.** The F of 5.58 is more extreme than the .05 cutoff of 2.73. Therefore, reject the null hypothesis. The research hypothesis is supported; the different experimental treatments do produce different effects on the standard performance measure.

FIGURING EFFECT SIZE FROM STANDARD DEVIATIONS

Figure the effect size from the standard deviations in the analysis of variance question above.

ANSWER

Estimated effect size $= S_M/S_{\text{Within}} = \sqrt{6}/\sqrt{21.5} = .53$.

FIGURING EFFECT SIZE FROM THE F RATIO AND SAMPLE SIZE

Figure the effect size from the F ratio and sample size in the analysis of variance question above.

ANSWER

Estimated effect size $= \sqrt{F}/\sqrt{n} = \sqrt{5.58}/\sqrt{20} = .53$.

PRACTICE PROBLEMS

These problems involve figuring. Most real-life statistics problems are done on a computer with special statistical software. Even if you have such software, do these problems by hand (with the help of a calculator) to ingrain the method in your mind. Also, in all problems involving figuring, be sure to show your work.

For practice in using a computer to solve statistics problems, refer to the computer section of each chapter of the *Student's Study Guide and Computer Workbook* that accompanies this text. All data are fictional unless an actual citation is given. For answers to Set I problems, see pp. 435–37.

SET I

1. For each of the following studies, decide whether you can reject the null hypothesis that the groups come from identical populations. Use the .05 level. In addition, figure the estimated effect size and approximate power for each. (Note that studies (b) and (c) provide S, not S^2.)

(a)	Group 1	Group 2	Group 3
n	10	10	10
M	7.4	6.8	6.8
S^2	.82	.90	.80

(b)	Group 1	Group 2	Group 3	Group 4
n	25	25	25	25
M	94	101	124	105
S	24	28	31	25

(c)	Group 1	Group 2	Group 3	Group 4	Group 5
n	25	25	25	25	25
M	94	101	124	105	106
S	24	28	31	25	27

2. For each of the following studies, decide whether you can reject the null hypothesis that the groups come from identical populations. Use the .01 level. In addition, figure the estimated effect size for each. (Be sure to show your calculations throughout.)

(a)	Group 1	Group 2	Group 3
	8	6	4
	8	6	4
	7	5	3
	9	7	5

(b)	Group 1	Group 2	Group 3
	12	10	8
	4	2	0
	12	10	8
	4	2	0

3. A social worker at a small mental hospital was asked to determine whether there was any clear difference in the length of stay of patients with different categories of diagnosis. Looking at the last four clients in each of the three major categories, the results (in terms of weeks of stay) were as follows:

Diagnosis Category		
Affective Disorders	Cognitive Disorders	Drug-Related Conditions
7	12	8
6	8	10
5	9	12
6	11	10

Using the .05 level, is there a significant difference in length of stay among diagnosis categories? (a) Use the five steps of hypothesis testing; (b) figure estimated effect size; and (c) explain your answer to (a) to someone who understands everything involved in conducting a t test for independent means but who is unfamiliar with the analysis of variance.

4. A study compared the felt intensity of unrequited love among three groups: 50 individuals who were currently experiencing unrequited love, who had a mean experienced intensity = 3.5, $S^2 = 5.2$; 50 who had previously experienced unrequited love and described their experiences retrospectively, $M = 3.2$, $S^2 = 5.8$; and 50 who had never experienced unrequited love but described how they thought they would feel if they were to experience it, $M = 3.8$, $S^2 = 4.8$. Determine the significance of the difference among groups, using the 5% level. (a) Use the steps of hypothesis testing; (b) figure estimated effect size and approximate power; and (c) explain your answer (d) to someone who has never had a course in statistics.

5. A researcher studying genetic influences on learning compares the maze performance of four genetically different strains of rats, using eight rats per strain. Performance for the four strains were as follows:

Strain	Mean	S
J	41	3.5
M	38	4.6
Q	14	3.8
W	37	4.9

Using the .01 significance level, is there an overall difference in maze performance among the four strains? (a) Use the steps of hypothesis testing; and (b) explain your answer to someone who is familiar with hypothesis testing with known populations, but is unfamiliar with the t test or the analysis of variance.

6. What is the power of each of the following planned studies, using the analysis of variance with $p < .05$?

	Predicted Effect Size	Number of Groups	Participants in Each Group
(a)	Small	3	20
(b)	Small	3	30
(c)	Small	4	20
(d)	Medium	3	20

7. About how many participants do you need in each group for 80% power in each of the following planned studies, using the analysis of variance with $p < .05$?

	Predicted Effect Size	Number of Groups
(a)	Small	3
(b)	Large	3
(c)	Small	4
(d)	Medium	3

8. Each of the following is a table of means showing results of a study using a factorial design. Assuming that any differences are statistically significant, for each table, (a) and (b) make two bar graphs showing the results (in one graph grouping the bars according to one variable and in the other graph grouping the bars according to the other variable); (c) indicate which effects (main and interaction), if any, are found; and (d) describe the meaning of the pattern of means (that is, any main or interaction effects or the lack thereof) in words.

i. Measured variable: Income (thousands of dollars)

	Age	
	Young	Old
Lower	20	35
Upper	25	100

(Class)

ii. Measured variable: Grade point average

	Major	
	Science	Arts
Community	2.1	2.8
Liberal Arts	2.8	2.1

(College)

iii. Measured variable: Days sick per month

	Gender	
	Females	Males
Exercisers	2.0	2.5
Controls	3.1	3.6

(Group)

9. Each of the following is a table of means showing results of a study using a factorial design. Assuming that any differences are statistically significant, for each table, (a) and (b) make two bar graphs showing the results (in one graph grouping the bars according to one variable and in the other graph grouping the bars according to the other variable); (c) indicate which effects (main and interaction), if any, are found; and (d) describe the meaning of the pattern of means (that is, any main or interaction effects or the lack thereof) in words.

i. Measured variable: Conversation length

	Topic	
	Nonpersonal	Personal
Friend	16	20
Parent	10	6

(Relationship)

ii. Measured variable: Rated restaurant quality

	City		
	New York	Chicago	Vancouver
Expensive	9	5	7
Moderate	6	4	6
Inexpensive	4	3	5

(Cost)

iii. Measured variable: Ratings of flavor

	Coffee Brand		
	X	Y	Z
Regular	7	4	6
Decaf	5	2	6

(Type)

10. Grilo, Walker, Becker, Edell, and McGlashan (1997) are researchers interested in the relation of depression and substance use to personality disorders. Personality disorders are persistent, problematic traits and behaviors that exceed the usual range of individual differences. The researchers conducted interviews assessing personality disorders with adolescents who were psychiatric inpatients and had one of three diagnoses: those with major depression, those with

substance abuse, and those with both major depression and substance abuse. The mean number of disorders was as follows: major depression, $M = 1.0$; substance abuse, $M = .7$; those with both conditions, $M = 1.9$. The researchers reported, "The three study groups differed in the average number of diagnosed personality disorders, $F(2,112) = 10.18$, $p < .0001$." Explain this result to someone who is familiar with hypothesis testing with known populations, but is unfamiliar with the t test or the analysis of variance.

11. A researcher wants to know if the need for health care among prisoners varies according to the different types of prison facilities. The researcher randomly selects 40 prisoners from each of the three main types of prisons in a particular Canadian province and conducts exams to determine their need for health care. In the article describing the results, the researcher reported the means for each group and then added: "The need for health care among prisoners in the three types of prison systems appeared to be clearly different, $F(2, 117) = 5.62$, $p < .01$". Explain this result to a person who has never had a course in statistics.

12. Do different types of English words—such as nouns, verbs, and adjectives—vary in length? Go to your dictionary, turn to random pages (using the random numbers listed below), and go down the column until you come to a noun. Note its length (in number of letters). Do this for 10 different nouns. Do the same for 10 verbs and then for 10 adjectives. Using the .05 significance level, carry out an analysis of variance comparing the three types of words. (Be sure also to give the full bibliographic information on your dictionary—authors, title, year published, publisher, city.)

651, 73, 950, 320, 564, 666, 736, 768, 661, 484, 990, 379, 323, 219, 715, 472, 176, 811, 167, 612, 102, 452, 849, 615, 228, 352, 851, 981, 821, 834, 719, 525, 907, 448, 4, 335, 671, 118, 403.

SET II

13. For each of the following studies, decide if you can reject the null hypothesis that the groups come from identical populations. Use the .05 level.

(a)	Group 1	Group 2	Group 3
n	5	5	5
M	10	12	14
S^2	4	6	5

(b)	Group 1	Group 2	Group 3
n	10	10	10
M	10	12	14
S^2	4	6	5

(c)	Group 1	Group 2	Group 3
n	5	5	5
M	10	14	18
S^2	4	6	5

(d)	Group 1	Group 2	Group 3
n	5	5	5
M	10	12	14
S^2	2	3	2.5

14. For each of the following studies, decide whether you can reject the null hypothesis that the groups come from identical populations. Use the .01 level.

(a)

Group 1	Group 2	Group 3
1	1	8
2	2	7
1	1	8
2	2	7

(b)

Group 1	Group 2	Group 3
1	4	8
2	5	7
1	4	8
2	5	7

15. An organizational researcher was interested in whether individuals working in different sectors of a company differed in their attitudes toward the company. The results for the three people surveyed in engineering were 10, 12, and 11; for the three in the marketing department, 6, 6, and 8; for the three in accounting, 7, 4, and 4; and for the three in production, 14, 16, and 13 (higher numbers mean more positive attitudes). Was there a significant difference in attitude toward the company among employees working in different sectors of the company at the .05 level? (a) Carry out the five steps of hypothesis testing; (b) figure the estimated effect size; and (c) explain your answer to someone who understands everything involved in conducting a t test for independent means, but is unfamiliar with the analysis of variance.

16. Do students at various colleges differ in how sociable they are? Twenty-five students were randomly selected from each of three colleges in a particular region and were asked to report on the amount of time they spent socializing each day with other students. The results for College X was a mean of 5 and an estimated population variance of 2; for College Y, $M = 4$, $S^2 = 1.5$; and for College Z, $M = 6$, $S^2 = 2.5$. What should you conclude? Use the .05 level. (a) Use the steps of hypothesis testing; (b) figure estimated effect size; and (c) explain your answer to someone who understands everything involved in conducting a t test for independent means but who has never heard of the analysis of variance.

17. A researcher studying artistic preference randomly assigns a group of 45 participants to one of three conditions in which they view a series of unfamiliar abstract paintings. The 15 participants in the Famous condition are led to believe that these are each famous paintings; their mean rating for liking the paintings is 6.5 ($S = 3.5$). The 15 in the Critically Acclaimed condition are led to believe that these are paintings that are not famous but are very highly thought of by a group of professional art critics; their mean rating is 8.5 ($S = 4.2$). The 15 in the Control condition are given no special information about the paintings; their mean rating is 3.1 ($S = 2.9$). Does what people are told about paintings make a difference in how well they are liked? Use the .05 level. (a) Use the steps of hypothesis testing; (b) figure estimated effect size; and (c) explain your answer to someone who is familiar with the t test for independent means, but is unfamiliar with analysis of variance.

18. What is the power of each of the following planned studies, using the analysis of variance with $p < .05$?

	Predicted Effect Size	Number of Groups	Participants in Each Group
(a)	Small	4	50
(b)	Medium	4	50
(c)	Large	4	50
(d)	Medium	5	50

19. About how many participants do you need in each group for 80% power in each of the following planned studies, using the analysis of variance with $p < .05$?

	Predicted Effect Size	Number of Groups
(a)	Small	5
(b)	Medium	5
(c)	Large	5
(d)	Medium	3

20. Each of the following is a table of means showing results of a study using a factorial design. Assuming that any differences are statistically significant, for each table (a) and (b), make two bar graphs showing the results (in one graph grouping the bars according to one variable and in the other graph grouping the bars according to the other variable); (c) indicate which effects (main and interaction), if any, are found; and (d) describe the meaning of the pattern of means (that is, any main or interaction effects or the lack thereof) in words.

   i. Measured variable: Degree of envy of another person's success

Degree of Success

Status of Other		Great	Small
	Friend	8	5
	Stranger	1	4

   ii. Measured variable: Observed engagement in the activity

Play Activity

Situation		Blocks	Dress Up
	Alone	4.5	2.5
	With playmate	2.5	4.5

   iii. Measured variable: Intensity of attention

Program

Type of Balletgoer		The Nutcracker	Modern
	Regular	20	15
	Sometime	15	15
	Novice	10	5

21. Each of the following is a table of means showing results of a study using a factorial design. Assuming that any differences are statistically significant, for each table (a) and (b), make two bar graphs showing the results (in one graph grouping the bars according to one variable and in the other graph grouping the

bars according to the other variable); (c) indicate which effects (main and inter-action), if any, are found; and (d) describe the meaning of the pattern of means (that is, any main or interaction effects or the lack thereof) in words.

i. Measured variable: Right frontal neural activity in brain during mem-ory task

Items Remembered

Times Presented	Words	Pictures
Once	45	68
Twice	30	30

ii. Measured variable: Approval rating of the U.S. president

Region

Class	West	East	Midwest	South
Middle	70	45	55	50
Lower	50	25	35	30

iii. Measured variable: Satisfaction with education

Gender

Time After Obtaining BA	Females	Males
1 month	3	3
1 year	4	4
5 years	9	9

22. An experiment is conducted in which 60 participants each fill out a personality test, but not according to the way the participants see themselves. Instead, 15 are randomly assigned to fill it out according to the way they think their moth-ers see them (that is, the way they think their mothers would fill it out to de-scribe the participants); 15 as their fathers would fill it out for them; 15 as their best friends would fill it out for them; and 15 as the professors they know best would fill it out for them. The main results appear in Table 10–13. Explain these results to a person who has never had a course in statistics.

23. Sinclair and Kunda (2000) tested the idea that if you want to think well of someone (for example, because they have said positive things about you), you are less influenced by the normal stereotypes when evaluating them. Partici-pants filled out a questionnaire on their social skills and then received feedback from either a male or female "manager in training." The study was rigged so that the managers gave half the participants positive feedback and half negative

TABLE 10–13 Means for Main Personality Scales for Each Experimental Condition (Fictional Data)

Scale	Mother	Father	Friend	Professor	$F(3, 56)$
Conformity	24	21	12	16	4.21[**]
Extroversion	14	13	15	13	2.05
Maturity	15	15	22	19	3.11[*]
Self-confidence	38	42	27	32	3.58[*]

[*]$p < .05$, [**]$p < .01$.

feedback. The participants then rated the managers for their skill at evaluating them. The question was whether the usual tendency to stereotype women as less skillful managers would be undermined when people got positive ratings. Sinclair and Kunda described their results as follows:

> Participants' ratings of the manager's skill at evaluating them were analyzed with a 2 (feedback) $\times$ 2 (manager gender) [two-way] ANOVA. Managers who had provided positive feedback ($M = 9.08$) were rated more highly than were managers who had provided negative feedback ($M = 7.46$), F(1,46) = 19.44, $p < .0001$. However, as may be seen in . . . [Figure 10–7], the effect was qualified by a significant interaction, $F(1, 46) = 4.71, p < .05$. . . . (pp. 1335–1336)

Describe the meaning of these results to a person who has never had a course in statistics. (Do not go into the details of the figuring, just the basic logic of the pattern of means, and the meaning of any significant results.)

24. Cut up 100 little pieces of paper of about the same size and write "1" on 16, "2" on 34, "3" on 34, and "4" on 16 of them. (You are creating an approximately normal distribution.) Put the slips into a bowl or hat, mix them up, draw out two, write the numbers on them down, and put them back. Then draw out another two, write down their numbers, and put them back, and finally another two, write down their numbers, and put them back. (Strictly speaking, you should sample "with replacement." That means putting each one, not two, back after writing its number down. But we want to save you a little time, and it should not make much difference in this case.) Figure an analysis of variance for these three randomly selected groups of two each. Write down the F ratio, and repeat the entire drawing process and analysis of variance again. Do this entire process at least 20 times, and make a frequency polygon of your results. You are creating an F distribution for 2 (3 groups − 1) and 3 (2 − 1 in each of three groups) degrees of freedom. At what point do the top 5% of your F scores begin? Compare that to the 5% cutoff given in Table A-3 in the Appendix for 2 and 3 degrees of freedom.

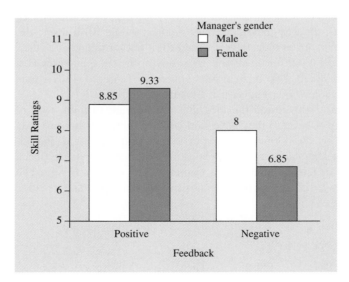

FIGURE 10–7   *Participants' ratings of the manager's skill at evaluating them as a function of feedback favorability and the manager's gender (Study 2).*
Source: Sinclair, L., & Kunda, Z. (2000). Motivated stereotyping of women: She's fine if she praised me but incompetent if she criticized me. *Personality and Social Psychology Bulletin, 26, No. 11,* 1329–1342. Copyright © 1997 by the Society for Personality and Social Psychology, Inc. Reprinted by permission of Sage Publications, Inc.

C H A P T E R 11

Chi-Square Tests and Strategies When Population Distributions Are Not Normal

The hypothesis-testing procedures you have learned in the last few chapters (the *t* test and the analysis of variance) are very versatile, but there are many research situations in which these methods cannot be used. One such situation is hypothesis testing for variables whose values are categories—such as a person's region of the country, religious preference, or hair color. The *t* test and the analysis of variance all require that the measured variable have scores that are quantitative, such as rating on a 7-point scale or number of years served as mayor. Another research situation in which the ordinary *t* test and analysis of variance do not apply is when the populations do not clearly follow a normal curve.

This chapter examines hypothesis testing in these two situations in which the ordinary hypothesis-testing procedures cannot be used properly. The first half of the chapter focuses on chi-square tests. **Chi-square tests** are used when the scores are on a nominal variable (that is, a variable with values that are categories). The second half of the chapter focuses on strategies for hypothesis testing when you cannot assume that the population distributions are even roughly normal.

chi-square tests

Tip for Success

This chapter assumes you have a solid command of hypothesis testing and are familiar with the t test and analysis of variance, and in particular the assumptions required for their use. In addition, you should review the Chapter 1 material on kinds of variables and on shapes of distributions.

CHI-SQUARE TESTS

Consider an example. Harter et al. (1997) were interested in three styles of relating to romantic partners: a self-focused autonomy style, an other-focused connection style, and a mutuality style. Harter et al. conducted a newspaper survey that included items about the respondents' styles and also the respondents' perceptions of their partners' styles. One of the researchers' predictions was that men who described themselves as having the self-focused autonomy style would be most likely to describe their partners as having the other-focused style. And sure enough, of the 101 self-focused men in their study, 49.5% "reported the predicted pairing, compared to 25.5% who reported self-focused autonomous partners and 24.5% who reported partners displaying mutuality" (p. 156). In terms of raw numbers, of the 101 self-focused men, 50 had other-focused partners, 26 had self-focused partners, and 25 had mutuality-style partners.

Suppose the partners of these men had been equally likely to be of each of the three relationship styles. If that were the situation, then about 33.66 (1/3 of the 101) of the partners of these men should have been of each style. This information is laid out in the "Observed Frequency" and "Expected Frequency" columns of Table 11–1. The Observed Frequency column shows the breakdown of relationship styles of partners actually *observed* and the Expected Frequency column shows the breakdown you would *expect* if the different partner styles had been exactly equally likely. (Note that it won't always be the case that you expect an equal breakdown across the categories. In other situations, the expected frequency for each category may be based on theory, or on a distribution in another study or circumstance.)

Clearly, there is a discrepancy between what was actually observed and the breakdown you would expect if the partner styles were equally likely. The question is this: Should you assume that this discrepancy is no more than what we would expect just by chance for a sample of this size? Suppose that self-focused men in general (the population) are equally likely to have partners of the three styles. Still, in any particular sample from that population, you would not expect a perfectly equal breakdown of partners' styles. But if the breakdown in the sample is a long way from equal, you would doubt that the partner styles in the population really are equal. In other words, we are in a hypothesis-testing situation, much like the ones we have been considering all along. But with a big difference too.

In the situations in previous chapters, the scores have all been numerical values on some dimension, such as a score on a standard achievement test, length of time in a relationship, an employer's rating of an employee's job effectiveness on a 9-point scale, and so forth. By contrast, relationship style of a man's partner is an example of what in Chapter 1 we called a *nominal variable* (or a *categorical variable*). A nominal variable is one in which the information is the number of people in each category. These are called nominal variables because the different categories or levels of the variable have names instead of numbers.

TABLE 11–1 Observed and Expected Frequencies for Relationship Styles of Partners of Self-Focused Autonomous Men

Partner Style	Observed Frequency[a] (O)	Expected Frequency (E)	Difference $(O-E)$	Difference Squared $(O-E)^2$	Difference Squared Weighted by Expected Frequency $(O-E)^2/E$
Other-Focused Connection	50	33.67	16.33	266.67	7.92
Self-Focused Autonomous	26	33.67	−7.67	58.83	1.75
Mutuality	25	33.67	−8.67	75.17	2.23

[a]Data from Harter et al. (1997).

Hypothesis testing with nominal variables uses what are called chi-square tests. (Chi is the Greek letter χ; it is pronounced *ki,* rhyming with high and pie.) The chi-square test was originally developed by Karl Pearson (see Box 11–1) and is sometimes called the *Pearson chi-square.*

THE CHI-SQUARE STATISTIC AND THE CHI-SQUARE TEST FOR GOODNESS OF FIT

The basic idea of any chi-square test is that you compare how well an observed breakdown of people over various categories fits some expected breakdown (such as an equal breakdown). In terms of the relationship style example, you are comparing the observed breakdown of 50, 26, and 25 to the expected breakdown of about 34 (33.67) for each style. A breakdown of numbers of people expected in each category is actually a frequency distribution, as you learned in Chapter 1. Thus, a chi-square test is more formally described as comparing an **observed frequency** distribution to an **expected frequency** distribution. Overall, what the hypothesis testing involves is first figuring a number for the amount of mismatch between the observed frequency and the expected frequency and then seeing whether that number is for a greater mismatch than you would expect by chance.

observed frequency
expected frequency

Let's start with how you would come up with that mismatch number for the observed versus expected frequencies. The mismatch between observed and expected for any one category is just the observed frequency minus the expected frequency. For example, consider again the Harter et al. (1997) study. For self-focused men with an other-focused partner, the observed frequency of 50 is 16.33 more than the expected frequency of 33.67 (recall the expected frequency is 1/3 of the 101 total). For the second category, the difference is -7.67. For the third, -8.67. These differences are shown in the Difference column of Table 11–1.

You do not use these differences directly. One reason is that some differences are positive and some are negative. Thus, they would cancel each other out. To get around this, you square each difference. (This is the same strategy we used in Chapter 2 to deal with difference scores in figuring the variance.) In the relationship-style example, the squared difference for those with other-focused partners is 16.33 squared, or 266.67. For those with self-focused partners, it is 58.83. For those with mutuality-style partners, 75.17. These squared differences are shown in the Difference Squared column of Table 11–1.

In the Harter et al. (1997) example, the expected frequencies are the same in each category. But in other research situations, expected frequencies for the different categories may not be the same. A particular amount of difference between observed and expected has a different importance according to the size of the expected frequency. For example, a difference of eight people between observed and expected is a much bigger mismatch if the expected frequency is 10 than if the expected frequency is 1,000. If the expected frequency is 10, a difference of 8 would mean that the observed frequency was 18 or 2, frequencies that are dramatically different from 10. But if the expected frequency is 1,000, a difference of 8 is only a slight mismatch. This would mean that the observed frequency was 1,008 or 992, frequencies that are only slightly different from 1,000.

How can you adjust the mismatch (the squared difference) between observed and expected for a particular category? What you need to do is adjust or weight the mismatch to take into account the expected frequency for that category. You can do this by dividing your squared difference for a category by the expected frequency

BOX 11–1　Karl Pearson: Inventor of Chi-Square and Center of Controversy

Karl Pearson, sometimes hailed as the founder of the science of statistics, was born in 1857, the son of a Yorkshire barrister. Most of both his virtues and his vices are revealed in what he reported to his colleague Julia Bell as his earliest memory: He was sitting in his highchair, sucking his thumb, when he was told to stop or his thumb would wither away. Pearson looked at his two thumbs and silently concluded, "I can't see that the thumb I suck is any smaller than the other. I wonder if she could be lying to me." Here we see Pearson's faith in himself and in observational evidence and his rejection of authority. We also see his tendency to doubt the character of people with whom he disagreed.

Pearson studied mathematics on a scholarship at Cambridge. Soon after he arrived, he requested to be excused from compulsory divinity lectures and chapel. As soon as his request was granted, however, he appeared in chapel. The dean summoned him for an explanation, and Pearson declared that he had asked to be excused not from chapel "but from *compulsory* chapel."

After graduation, Pearson traveled and studied in Germany, becoming a socialist and a self-described "free-thinker." Returning to England, he changed his name from Carl to Karl (in honor of Karl Marx) and wrote an attack on Christianity under a pen name. In 1885 he founded a "Men and Women's Club" to promote equality between the sexes. The club died out, but through it he met his wife, Maria Sharp.

Pearson eventually turned to statistics out of his interest in proving the theory of evolution, being especially influenced by Sir Francis Galton's work (see Box 3–1). Most of Pearson's research from 1893 to 1901 focused on the laws of heredity and evolution, but he needed better statistical methods for his work, leading to his most famous contribution, the chi-square

test. Pearson also invented the method of computing correlation used today and coined the terms *histogram, skew,* and *spurious correlation.* When he felt that biology journals failed to appreciate his work properly, he founded the famous journal of statistics called *Biometrika.* In short, he led statistics from its early position as a matter largely ignored to one central to the scientific method, especially in the natural sciences.

Unfortunately, Pearson was a great fan of eugenics, the "improvement" of the human race through selective breeding, and his work was later used by the Nazis as justification for their treatment of Jews and other ethnic minorities. Toward the end of his life he fought back, writing a paper using clear logic and data on Jews and Gentiles from all over the world to demonstrate that there was no Jewish or Aryan race and that the Nazis' ideas were sheer nonsense.

Indeed, throughout his life, Pearson's strong opinions led to a few devoted friendships and a long list of enemies, especially as other, younger statisticians passed him by, while he refused to publish their work in *Biometrika.* William S. Gosset (see Box 8–1), inventor of the *t* test, was one of his friends. Sir Ronald Fisher, inventor of the analysis of variance and a man associated with even more extreme attitudes (as described in Chapter 10, Box 10–1), was one of Pearson's worst enemies. The kindly, peaceable Gosset, friends of both, was always trying to smooth matters between them. In 1933, Pearson finally retired, and Fisher, of all persons, took over his chair, the Galton Professorship of Eugenics at University College in London. In 1936, the two entered into their bitterest argument yet; Pearson died the same year.

Sources: Peters (1987); Salsburg (2001); Stigler (1986); Tankard (1984).

for that category. Thus, if the expected frequency for a particular category is 10, you divide the squared difference by 10. If the expected frequency for the category is 1,000, you divide the squared difference by 1,000. In this way, you weight each squared difference by the expected frequency. This weighting puts the squared difference onto a more appropriate scale of comparison.

Let's return to our example. For men with an other-focused partner, you would weight the mismatch by dividing the squared difference of 266.67 by 33.67, giving

7.92. For those with a self-focused partner, 58.83 divided by 33.67 gives 1.75. For those with a mutuality-style partner, 75.17 divided by 33.67 gives 2.23. These adjusted mismatches (squared differences divided by expected frequencies) are shown in the right-most column of Table 11–1.

What remains is to get an overall figure for the mismatch between observed and expected frequencies. This final step is done by adding up the mismatch for all the categories. That is, you take the result of the squared difference divided by the expected frequency for the first category, add the result of the squared difference divided by the expected frequency for the second category, and so on. In the Harter et al. example, this would be 7.92 plus 1.75 plus 2.23, for a total of 11.90. This final number (the sum of the weighted squared differences) is an overall indication of the amount of mismatch between the expected and observed frequencies. It is called the **chi-square statistic.** In terms of a formula,

(11-1)
$$\chi^2 = \Sigma \frac{(O - E)^2}{E}$$

chi-square statistic

> Chi-square is the sum, over all the categories, of the squared difference between observed and expected frequencies divided by the expected frequency.

In this formula, χ^2 is the chi-square statistic. Σ is the summation sign, telling you to sum over all the different categories. O is the observed frequency for a category (the number of people actually found in that category in the study). E is the expected frequency for a category. (In this example, it is based on what we would expect if there were equal numbers in each category.) Applying the formula to the Harter et al. example,

$$\chi^2 = \Sigma \frac{(O - E)^2}{E} = \frac{(50 - 33.67)^2}{33.67} + \frac{(26 - 33.67)^2}{33.67} + \frac{(25 - 33.67)^2}{33.67} = 11.90$$

STEPS FOR FIGURING THE CHI-SQUARE STATISTIC

Here is a summary of what we've said so far in terms of steps:

- **A** **Determine the actual, observed frequencies in each category.**
- **B** **Determine the expected frequencies in each category.**
- **C** **In each category, take observed minus expected frequencies.**
- **D** **Square each of these differences.**
- **E** **Divide each squared difference by the expected frequency for its category.**
- **F** **Add up the results of Step E for all the categories.**

THE CHI-SQUARE DISTRIBUTION

Now we turn to the question of whether the chi-square statistic you have figured is a bigger mismatch than you would expect by chance. To answer that, you need to know how likely it is to get chi-square statistics of various sizes by chance. That is, you need the distribution of chi-square statistics that would arise by chance. As long as you have a reasonable number of people in the study, the distribution of the chi-square statistic follows quite closely a known mathematical distribution—the **chi-square distribution.**

chi-square distribution

The exact shape of the chi-square distribution depends on the degrees of freedom. For a chi-square test, the degrees of freedom are the number of categories that are free to vary, given the totals. In the partners' relationship-style example, there are three categories. If you know the total number of people and you know the number in any two categories, you could figure out the number in the third category—so only two are free to vary. That is, in a study like this one, if there are three categories, there are two degrees of freedom.

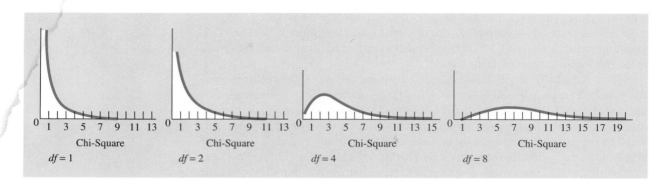

FIGURE 11–1   *Examples of chi-square distributions for different degrees of freedom.*

Chi-square distributions for several different degrees of freedom are shown in Figure 11–1. Notice that the distributions are all skewed to the right. This is because the chi-square statistic cannot be less than 0 but can have very high values. (Chi-square must be positive because it is figured by adding a group of fractions, in each of which the numerator and denominator both have to be positive. The numerator has to be positive because it is squared. The denominator has to be positive because the number of people expected in a given category can't be a negative number—you can't expect less than no one!)

THE CHI-SQUARE TABLE

chi-square table

What matters most about the chi-square distribution for hypothesis testing is the cutoff for a chi-square to be extreme enough to reject the null hypothesis. For example, suppose you are using the .05 significance level. In that situation, you want to know the point on the chi-square distribution where 5% of the chi-square statistics are above that point. A **chi-square table** gives the cutoff chi-square for different significance levels and various degrees of freedom. Table 11–2 shows a portion of a chi-square table like the one in the Appendix (Table A–4). For our example, where there were two degrees of freedom, the table shows that the cutoff chi-square for the .05 level is 5.992.

| TABLE 11–2 | Portion of a Chi-Square Table |

	Significance Level		
df	.10	.05	.01
1	2.706	3.841	6.635
2	4.605	5.992	9.211
3	6.252	7.815	11.345
4	7.780	9.488	13.277
5	9.237	11.071	15.087

Note: Full table is Table A-4 in the Appendix.

chi-square test for goodness of fit

THE CHI-SQUARE TEST FOR GOODNESS OF FIT

In the Harter et al. example, we figured a chi-square of 11.90. This is clearly larger than the chi-square cutoff for this example (using the .05 significance level) of 5.992 (see Figure 11–2). Thus, the researchers rejected the null hypothesis. That is, they rejected as too unlikely that the mismatch they observed could have come about if in the population of self-focused men there were an equal number of partners of each relationship style. It seemed more reasonable to conclude that there truly were different proportions of relationship styles of the partners of such men.

We have just carried out a full hypothesis-testing procedure for the Harter et al. example. This example involved differing numbers of people at three levels of a particular nominal variable (the relationship style of partners of self-focused men). This kind of chi-square test involving levels of a single nominal variable is called a **chi-square test for goodness of fit.**

FIGURE 11–2 *For the Harter et al. (1997) example, the chi-square distribution (df = 2) showing the cutoff for rejecting the null hypothesis at the .05 level and the sample's chi-square.*

STEPS OF HYPOTHESIS TESTING

Let us review the chi-square test for goodness of fit. We will use the same example, but this time systematically follow our standard five steps. In the process we also consider some fine points.

❶ **Restate the question as a research hypothesis and a null hypothesis about the populations.** There are two populations:

> **Population 1:** Self-focused men like those in the study.

> **Population 2:** Self-focused men whose partners are equally of the three relationship styles.

The research hypothesis is that the distribution of people over categories in the two populations is different; the null hypothesis is that they are the same.

❷ **Determine the characteristics of the comparison distribution.** The comparison distribution here is a chi-square distribution with 2 degrees of freedom. (Once you know the total, there are only two category numbers still free to vary.)

❸ **Determine the cutoff on the comparison distribution at which the null hypothesis should be rejected.** You do this by looking up the cutoff on the chi-square table for your significance level and the study's degrees of freedom. In the present example, we used the .05 significance level, and we determined in Step 2 that there were 2 degrees of freedom. Based on the table, this gives a cutoff chi-square of 5.992.

❹ **Determine your sample's score on the comparison distribution.** Your sample's score is the chi-square figured from the sample. In other words, this is where you do all the figuring.

> ❹ **Determine the actual, observed frequencies in each category.** These are shown in the first column of Table 11–1.

> ❺ **Determine the expected frequencies in each category.** We figured these each to be 33.67 based on expecting an equal distribution of the 101 partners.

> ❻ **In each category, take observed minus expected frequencies.** These are shown in the third column of Table 11–1.

> ❼ **Square each of these differences.** These are shown in the fourth column of Table 11–1.

> ❽ **Divide each squared difference by the expected frequency for its category.** These are shown in the fifth column of Table 11–1.

> ❾ **Add up the results of step E for all the categories.** The result we figured earlier (11.90) is the chi-square statistic for the sample. It is shown in Figure 11–2.

❺ **Decide whether to reject the null hypothesis.** The chi-square cutoff to reject the null hypothesis (from Step 3) is 5.992 and the chi-square of the sample (from Step 4) is 11.90. Thus, you can reject the null hypothesis. The research

Tip for Success

It is important not to be confused by the terminology here. The comparison distribution is the distribution to which we compare the number that summarizes the whole pattern of the result. With a t test, this number is the t score and we use a t distribution. With an analysis of variance, it is the F ratio and we use an F distribution. Accordingly, with a chi-square test, our comparison distribution is a distribution of the chi-square statistic. This can be confusing because when preparing to use the chi-square distribution, we compare a distribution of observed frequencies to a distribution of expected frequencies. Yet the distribution of expected frequencies is not a comparison distribution in the sense that we use this term in Step 2 of hypothesis testing.

hypothesis that the two populations are different is supported. That is, Harter et al. could conclude that the partners of self-focused men are not equally likely to be of the three relationship styles.

HOW ARE YOU DOING?

1. In what situation do you use a chi-square test for goodness of fit?
2. List the steps for figuring the chi-square statistic and explain the logic behind each step.
3. Write the formula for the chi-square statistic and define each of the symbols.
4. (a) What is a chi-square distribution? (b) What is its shape? (c) Why does it have that shape?
5. Use the steps of hypothesis testing to carry out a chi-square test for goodness of fit (using the .05 significance level) for a sample in which one category has 15 people, the other has 35 people, and the categories are expected to have equal frequencies.

ANSWERS:

1. When you want to test whether a sample's distribution of people across categories represents a population that is significantly different from a population with an expected distribution of people across categories.

2. ❶ **Determine the actual, observed frequencies in each category.** This is the key information for the sample studied.
   ❷ **Determine the expected frequencies in each category.** Having these numbers makes it possible to make a direct comparison of what is expected to the observed frequencies.
   ❸ **In each category, take observed minus expected frequencies.** This is the direct comparison of the distribution for the sample versus the distribution representing the expected population.
   ❹ **Square each of these differences.** This gets rid of the direction of the difference (since the interest is only in how much difference there is).
   ❺ **Divide each squared difference by the expected frequency for its category.** This adjusts the degree of difference for the absolute size of the expected frequencies.
   ❻ **Add up the results of step E for all the categories.** This gives you a statistic for the overall degree of discrepancy.

3. $\chi^2 = \Sigma \dfrac{(O - E)^2}{E}$

   χ^2 is the chi-square statistic; Σ tells you to sum over all the different categories; O is the observed frequency for a category; E is the expected frequency for a category.

4. a. For any particular number of categories, the distribution you would expect if you figured a very large number of chi-square statistics for samples from a population in which the distribution of people over categories is the expected distribution.
   b. It is skewed to the right.
   c. It has this shape because a chi-square statistic can't be less than 0 (since the numerator, a squared score, has to be positive, and its denominator, an expected number of individuals, also has to be positive), but there is no limit to how large it can be.

5. ❶ **Restate the question as a research hypothesis and a null hypothesis about the populations.** There are two populations:

   Population 1: People like those in the sample.

   Population 2: People who have an equal distribution of the two categories.

   The research hypothesis is that the distribution of numbers of people over categories is different in the two populations; the null hypothesis is that it is the same.
   ❷ **Determine the characteristics of the comparison distribution.** The comparison distribution is a chi-square distribution with 1 degree of freedom (that is, 2 categories −1 = 1).
   ❸ **Determine the cutoff sample score on the comparison distribution at which the null hypothesis should be rejected.** At the .05 level with $df = 1$, cutoff is 3.841.

❹ **Determine your sample's score on the comparison distribution.**

    Ⓐ **Determine the actual, observed frequencies in each category.** As given in the problem, these are 15 and 35.

    Ⓑ **Determine the expected frequencies in each category.** With 50 people total and expecting an even breakdown, the expected frequencies are 25 and 25.

    Ⓒ **In each category, take observed minus expected frequencies.** These come out to -10 (that is, $15 - 25 = -10$) and 10 (that is, $35 - 25 = 10$).

    Ⓓ **Square each of these differences.** Both come out to 100 (that is, $-10^2 = 100$ and $10^2 = 100$).

    Ⓔ **Divide each squared difference by the expected frequency for its category.** These both come out to 4 (that is, $100/25 = 4$).

    Ⓕ **Add up the results of step E for all the categories.** $4 + 4 = 8$.

❺ **Decide whether to reject the null hypothesis.** The sample's chi-square of 8 is more extreme than the cutoff of 3.841. Reject the null hypothesis; people like those in the sample are different from the expected even breakdown.

THE CHI-SQUARE TEST FOR INDEPENDENCE

So far, we have looked at the distribution of one nominal variable with several categories, such as the relationship style of men's partners. In fact, this kind of situation is fairly rare in research. We began with an example of this kind mainly as a stepping stone to a more common actual research situation, to which we now turn.

The most common use of chi-square is one in which there are *two nominal variables,* each with several categories. For example, Harter et al. (1997) might have been interested in whether the breakdown of partners of self-focused men was the same as the breakdown of partners of other-focused men. If that were their purpose, we would have had two nominal variables. Relationship style of partners would be the first nominal variable. Men's own relationship style would be the second nominal variable. Hypothesis testing in this kind of situation is called a **chi-square test for independence.** You will learn shortly why it has this name.

chi-square test for independence

Suppose researchers at a large university survey 200 staff members. The staff members are asked about the kind of transportation they use to get to work, as well as whether they are "morning people" (prefer to go to bed early and awaken early) or "night people" (go to bed late and awaken late). Table 11–3 shows the results. Notice the two nominal variables: type of transportation (with three levels) and sleep tendency (with two levels).

TABLE 11–3	Contingency Table of Observed Frequencies of Morning and Night People Using Different Types of Transportation (Fictional Data)

		Transportation			Total	
		Bus	Carpool	Own Car		
Sleep Tendency	Morning	60	30	30	120	(60%)
	Night	20	20	40	80	(40%)
	Total	80	50	70	200	(100%)

CONTINGENCY TABLES

contingency table

Table 11–3 is a **contingency table**—a table in which the distributions of two nominal variables are set up so that you have the frequencies of their combinations, as well as the totals. Thus, in Table 11–3, the 60 in the bus–morning combination is how many morning people ride the bus. (A contingency table is similar to the tables in factorial analysis of variance that you learned about in Chapter 10; but in a contingency table, the number in each cell is a *number of people,* not a *mean.*)

Table 11–3 is called a 3 × 2 contingency table because it has three levels of one variable crossed with two levels of the other. (Which dimension is named first does not matter.) It is also possible to have larger contingency tables, such as a 4 × 7 or a 6 × 18 table. Smaller tables, 2 × 2 contingency tables, are especially common.

INDEPENDENCE

independence

The question in this example is whether there is any relation between the type of transportation people use and whether they are morning or night people. If there is no relation, the *proportion* of morning and night people is the same among bus riders, carpoolers, and those who drive their own cars. Or to put it the other way, if there is no relation, the *proportion* of bus riders, carpoolers, and own car drivers is the same for morning and night people. However you describe it, the situation of no relation between the variables in a contingency table is called **independence.**[1]

SAMPLE AND POPULATION

In the observed survey results in the example, the proportions of night and morning people in the sample vary with different types of transportation. For example, the bus riders are split 60–20, so three-fourths of the bus riders are morning people. Among people who drive their own cars, the split is 30–40. Thus, a slight majority are night people. Still, the sample is only of 200. It is possible that in the larger population, the type of transportation a person uses is independent of the person's being a morning or a night person. The big question is whether the lack of independence in the sample is large enough to reject the null hypothesis of independence in the population. That is, you need to do a chi-square test.

DETERMINING EXPECTED FREQUENCIES

cell

One thing that is new in a chi-square test for independence is that you now have to figure differences between observed and expected for each *combination* of categories—that is, for each **cell** of the contingency table. (When there was only one nominal variable, you figured these differences just for each category of that single nominal variable.) Table 11–4 is the contingency table for the example survey.

The key consideration in figuring expected frequencies in a contingency table is that "expected" is based on the two variables being independent. If they are independent, then the proportions up and down the cells of each column should be the same. In the example, overall, there are 60% morning people and 40% night people; thus, if transportation method is independent of being a morning or night person, this 60%–40% split should hold for each column (each transportation type). First, the 60%–40% overall split should hold for the bus group. This would make an ex-

---

[1]Independence is usually used to talk about a lack of relation between two nominal variables. However, if you have studied Chapter 3, it may be helpful to think of independence as roughly the same as the situation of no correlation ($r = 0$).

TABLE 11–4	Contingency Table of Observed (and Expected) Frequencies of Morning and Night People Using Different Types of Transportation (Fictional Data)

Tip for Success

Always ensure that you have the same number of expected frequencies as observed frequencies. For example, with a 2 × 3 contingency table, there will be 6 observed frequencies and 6 corresponding expected frequencies. This time, we have put in the expected frequency (in parentheses) next to each observed frequency.

		Transportation			Total	
		Bus	Carpool	Own Car		
Sleep Tendency	Morning	60 (48)[a]	30 (30)	30 (42)	120	(60%)
	Night	20 (32)	20 (20)	40 (28)	80	(40%)
	Total	80	50	70	200	(100%)

[a]Expected frequencies are in parentheses.

pected frequency in the bus cell for morning people of 60% of 80, which comes out to 48 people. The expected frequency for the bus riders who are night people is 32 (that is, 40% of 80 is 32). The same principle holds for the other columns: The 50 carpool people should have a 60%–40% split, giving an expected frequency of 30 morning people who carpool (that is, 60% of 50 is 30) and 20 night people who carpool (that is, 40% of 50 is 20), and the 70 own-car people should have a 60%–40% split, giving expected frequencies of 42 and 28.

Summarizing what we have said in terms of steps,

❶ **Find each row's percentage of the total.**
❷ **For each cell, multiply its row's percentage times its column's total.**

Applying these steps to the top left cell (morning persons who ride the bus),

Tip for Success

Be sure to check that you are selecting the correct row percentage and column total for each cell. Selecting an incorrect value is a common source of errors in the figuring for chi-square.

❶ **Find each row's percentage of the total.** The 120 in the morning person row is 60% of the overall total of 200 (that is, 120/200 = 60%).
❷ **For each cell, multiply its row's percentage times its column's total.** The column total for the bus riders is 80; 60% of 80 comes out to 48 (that is, .6 × 80 = 48).

These steps can also be stated as a formula,

(11-2)
$$E = \left(\frac{R}{N}\right)(C)$$

A cell's expected frequency is the number in its row divided by the total, multiplied by the number in its column.

In this formula, E is the expected frequency for a particular cell, R is the number of people observed in this cell's row, N is the total number of people, and C is the number of people observed in this cell's column. (If you reverse cells and columns, the expected frequency still comes out the same.)

Applying the formula to the same top left cell,

$$E = \left(\frac{R}{N}\right)(C) = \left(\frac{120}{200}\right)(80) = (.60)(80) = 48$$

Looking at the entire Table 11–4, notice that the expected frequencies add up to the same totals as the observed frequencies. For example, in the first column (bus), the expected frequencies of 32 and 48 add up to 80, just as the observed frequencies in that column of 60 and 20 do. Similarly, in the top row (morning), the expected frequencies of 48, 30, and 42 add up to 120, the same total as for the observed frequencies of 60, 30, and 30.

Tip for Success

As a check on your arithmetic, it is a good idea to make sure that the expected and observed frequencies add up to the same row and column totals.

FIGURING CHI-SQUARE

You figure chi-square the same way as in the chi-square test for goodness of fit, except that you now figure the weighted squared difference for each *cell* and add these up. Here is how it works for our survey example:

$$\chi^2 = \Sigma\, \frac{(O-E)^2}{E} = \frac{(60-48)^2}{48} + \frac{(30-30)^2}{30} +$$

$$\frac{(30-42)^2}{42} + \frac{(20-32)^2}{32} + \frac{(20-20)^2}{20} + \frac{(40-28)^2}{28}$$

$$= 3 + 0 + 3.43 + 4.5 + 0 + 5.14 = 16.07$$

DEGREES OF FREEDOM

A contingency table with many cells may have relatively few degrees of freedom. In our example, there are six cells but only 2 degrees of freedom. Recall that the degrees of freedom are the number of categories free to vary once the totals are known. With a chi-square test for independence, the number of categories is the number of cells; the totals include the row and column totals—and if you know the row and column totals, you have a lot of information.

Consider the sleep tendency and transportation example. Suppose you know the first two cell frequencies across the top, for example, and all the row and column totals. You could then figure all the other cell frequencies just by subtraction. Table 11–5 shows the contingency table for this example with just the row and column totals and these two cell frequencies. Let's start with the Morning, Own Car cell. There is a total of 120 morning people and the other two morning-person cells have 90 in them (60 + 30). Thus, only 30 remain for the Morning, Own-Car cell. Now consider the three night person cells. You know the frequencies for all the morning people cells and the column totals for each type of transportation. Thus, each cell frequency for the night people is its column's total minus the morning people in that column. For example, there are 80 bus riders and 60 are morning people. Thus, the remaining 20 must be night people.

What you can see in all this is that with knowledge of only two of the cells, you could figure out the frequencies in each of the other cells. Thus, although there are six cells, there are only 2 degrees of freedom—only two cells whose frequencies are really free to vary once we have all the row and column totals.

TABLE 11–5 **Contingency Table Showing Marginal and Two Cells' Observed Frequencies to Illustrate Figuring of Degrees of Freedom**

		Transportation			Total
		Bus	Carpool	Own Car	
Sleep Tendency	Morning	60	30	—	120 (60%)
	Night	—	—	—	80 (40%)
	Total	80	50	70	200 (100%)

As a general principle, in a chi-square test for independence, the degrees of freedom is the number of columns minus 1 multiplied by the number of rows minus 1. Put as a formula,

(11-3)
$$df = (N_{Columns} - 1)(N_{Rows} - 1)$$

The degrees of freedom for the chi-square test for independence is the number of columns minus 1 multiplied by the number of rows minus 1.

$N_{Columns}$ is the number of columns and N_{Rows} is the number of rows.

Using this formula for our survey example,

$$df = (N_{Columns} - 1)(N_{Rows} - 1) = (3 - 1)(2 - 1) = (2)(1) = 2.$$

STEPS OF HYPOTHESIS TESTING

With 2 degrees of freedom, Table 11–2 (or Table A–4) shows that the chi-square you need for significance at the .01 level is 9.211. The chi-square of 16.07 for our example is larger than this cutoff. Thus, you can reject the null hypothesis that the two variables are independent in the population.

STEPS OF HYPOTHESIS TESTING

Now let's go through the survey example again, this time following the steps of hypothesis testing.

❶ **Restate the question as a research hypothesis and a null hypothesis about the populations.** There are two populations:

> **Population 1:** People like those surveyed.
>
> **Population 2:** People for whom being a night or a morning person is independent of the kind of transportation they use to commute to work.

The null hypothesis is that the two populations are the same—that, in general the proportions using different types of transportation are the same for morning and night people. The research hypothesis is that the two populations are different, that among people in general the proportions using different types of transportation are different for morning and night people.

Put another way, the null hypothesis is that the two variables are independent (they are unrelated to each other). The research hypothesis is that they are not independent (that they are related to each other).

❷ **Determine the characteristics of the comparison distribution.** The comparison distribution is a chi-square distribution with 2 degrees of freedom. As we have seen, in a 3 × 2 contingency table, if you know the numbers in two cells and the row and column totals, all the others can be determined. Or, using the rule for contingency tables, the number of cells free to vary is the number of columns minus 1 multiplied by the number of rows minus 1.

❸ **Determine the cutoff sample score on the comparison distribution at which the null hypothesis should be rejected.** You use the same table as for any chi-square test. In the example, setting a .01 significance level with 2 degrees of freedom, you need a chi-square of 9.211.

❹ **Determine your sample's score on the comparison distribution.**

❺ **Determine the actual, observed frequencies in each cell.** These are the results of the survey, as given in Table 11–3.

FIGURE 11–3 *For the sleep tendency and transportation example, chi-square distribution (df = 2) showing the cutoff for rejecting the null hypothesis at the .01 level and the sample's chi-square.*

❹ Determine the expected frequencies in each cell. These are shown in Table 11–4. For example, for the bottom right cell (Night Person's Own Car cell),

    ❶ Find each row's percentage of the total. The 80 people in the night person's row are 40% of the overall total of 200 (that is, 80/200 = 40%).

    ❷ For each cell, multiply its row's percentage times its column's total. The column total for those with their own car is 70; 40% of 70 comes out to 28 (that is, .4 × 70 = 28).

    ❸ In each cell, take observed minus expected frequencies. For example, for the Night Person's Own Car cell, this comes out to 12 (that is, 40 − 28 = 12).

    ❹ Square each of these differences. For example, for the Night Person's Own Car cell, this comes out to 144 (that is, $12^2 = 144$).

    ❺ Divide each squared difference by the expected frequency for its cell. For example, for the Night Person's Own Car cell, this comes out to 5.14 (that is, 144/28 = 5.14).

    ❻ Add up the results of step E for all the cells. As we saw, this came out to 16.07.

❺ Decide whether to reject the null hypothesis. The chi-square needed to reject the null hypothesis is 9.211 and the chi-square for our sample is 16.07 (see Figure 11–3). Thus, you can reject the null hypothesis. The research hypothesis that the two variables are not independent in the population is supported. That is, the proportions of type of transportation used to commute to work are different for morning and night people.

A SECOND EXAMPLE

Riehl (1994) studied the college experience of first-year students who were the first generation in their family to attend college. These students were compared to other students who were not the first generation in their family to go to college. (All students in the study were from Indiana University.) One of the variables Riehl measured was whether or not students dropped out during their first semester.

Table 11–6 shows the results along with the expected frequencies (shown in parentheses) based on these percentages. Below the contingency table is the figuring for the chi-square test for independence.

    ❶ Restate the question as a null hypothesis and a research hypothesis about the populations. There are two populations:

    Population 1: Students like those surveyed.

TABLE 11–6   Results and Figuring of the Chi-Square Test for Independence Comparing Whether First-Generation College Students Differ from Others in First Semester Dropouts

	Generation to Go to College		Total
	First	Other	
	ⓐ	ⓑ	
Dropped Out	73 (57.7)	89 (103.9)	162 (7.9%)
Did Not Drop Out	657 (672.3)	1,226 (1,211.1)	1,883 (92.1%)
	730	1,315	2,045

$df = (N_{\text{Columns}} - 1)(N_{\text{Rows}} - 1) = (2 - 1)(2 - 1) = (1)(1) = 1.$ ❷
Chi-square needed, $df = 1$, .01 level: 6.635. ❸

$$\chi^2 = \Sigma\frac{(O - E)^2}{E} = \frac{(73 - 57.7)^2}{57.7} + \frac{(89 - 103.9)^2}{103.9} + \frac{(657 - 672.3)^2}{672.3} + \frac{(1,226 - 1,211.1)^2}{1,211.1}$$

ⓒ
$$= \frac{15.3^2}{57.7} + \frac{-14.9^2}{103.9} + \frac{-15.3^2}{672.3} + \frac{14.9^2}{1,211.1}$$

ⓓ
$$= \frac{234.1}{57.7} + \frac{222}{103.9} + \frac{234.1}{672.3} + \frac{222}{1,211.1}$$

ⓔ
$$= 4.06 + 2.14 + .35 + .18$$
$$= 6.73.$$ ⓕ

Conclusion: Reject the null hypothesis. ❺

Notes. 1. With a 2 × 2 analysis, the differences and squared differences (numerators) are the same for all four cells. In this example, the cells are a little difference due to rounding error. 2. Data from Riehl (1994). The exact chi-square (6.73) is slightly different from that reported in the article (7.2), due to rounding error.

Population 2: Students whose dropping out or staying in college their first semester is independent of whether or not they are the first generation in their family to go to college.

The null hypothesis is that the two populations are the same—that, in general, whether or not students drop out of college is independent of whether or not they are the first generation in their family to go to college. The research hypothesis is that the populations are not the same. In other words, the research hypothesis is that students like those surveyed are unlike the hypothetical population in which dropping out is unrelated to whether or not you are first generation.

❷ **Determine the characteristics of the comparison distribution.** This is a chi-square distribution with 1 degree of freedom.

❸ **Determine the cutoff sample score on the comparison distribution at which the null hypothesis should be rejected.** Using the .01 level and 1 degree of freedom, Table 11–2 and Table A–4 show that you need a chi-square for significance of 6.635. This is illustrated in Figure 11–4.

❹ **Determine your sample's score on the comparison distribution.**

ⓐ **Determine the actual, observed frequencies in each cell.** These are the results of the survey, as given in Table 11–6.

ⓑ **Determine the expected frequencies in each cell.** These are shown in parentheses in Table 11–6. For example, for the top left cell (First Generation's Dropped Out cell),

❶ **Find each row's percentage of the total.** The Dropped Out row's 162 is 7.9% of the overall total of 2,045 (that is, 162/2,045 = 7.9%).

FIGURE 11–4   *For the example from Riehl (1994), chi-square distribution (df = 1) showing the cutoff for rejecting the null hypothesis at the .01 level and the sample's chi square.*

❿ **For each cell, multiply its row's percentage times its column's total.** The column total for the First Generation students is 730; 7.9% of 730 comes out to 57.7 (that is, .079 × 730 = 57.7).

⓫ **In each cell, take observed minus expected frequencies.** These are shown in Table 11–6. For example, for the First Generation Dropped Out's cell, this comes out to 15.3 (that is, 73 − 57.7 = 15.3).

⓬ **Square each of these differences.** These are also shown in Table 11–6. For example, for the First Generation Dropped Out's cell, this comes out to 234.1 (that is, $15.3^2 = 234.1$).

⓭ **Divide each squared difference by the expected frequency for its cell.** Once again, these are shown in Table 11–6. For example, for the First Generation Dropped Out's cell, this comes out to 4.06 (that is, 234.1/57.7 = 4.06).

⓮ **Add up the results of Step E for all the cells.** As shown in Table 11–6, this comes out to 6.73. Its location on the chi-square distribution is shown in Figure 11–4.

❹ **Decide whether to reject the null hypothesis.** Your chi square of 6.73 is larger than the cutoff of 6.635 (see Figure 11–4). Thus, you can reject the null hypothesis. That is, judging from a sample of 2,045 Indiana University students, first-generation students are somewhat more likely to drop out during their first semester than are other students. (Remember, of course, that there could be many reasons for this result.)

HOW ARE YOU DOING?

1. (a) In what situation do you use a chi-square test for independence? (b) How is this different from the situation in which you would use a chi-square test for goodness of fit?
2. (a) List the steps for figuring the expected frequencies in a contingency table. (b) Write the formula for expected frequencies in a contingency table and define each of its symbols.
3. (a) Write the formula for figuring degrees of freedom in a chi-square test for independence and define each of its symbols. (b) Explain the logic behind this formula.
4. Use the steps of hypothesis testing to carry out a chi-square test for independence for the observed scores below (using the .05 significance level).

		Nominal Variable A	
		Category 1	Category 2
Nominal Variable B	Category 1	10	10
	Category 2	50	10

ANSWERS:

1. (a) When you have the number of people in the various combinations of levels of two nominal variables and want to test whether the difference from independence in the sample is sufficiently great to reject the null hypothesis of independence in the population. (b) The focus is on the independence of *two nominal variables;* in a chi-square test for goodness of fit the focus is on the distribution of people over categories of a *single nominal variable.*
2. a. ❶ Find each row's percentage of the total.
   ❷ For each cell, multiply its row's percentage times its column's total.

b. $E = \left(\dfrac{R}{N}\right)(C)$

E is the expected frequency for a particular cell, *R* is the number of people observed in this cell's row, *N* is the total number of people, and *C* is the number of people observed in this cell's column.

3. a. $df = (N_{Columns} - 1)(N_{Rows} - 1)$.

   df are the degrees of freedom, $N_{Columns}$ is the number of columns, and N_{Rows} is the number of rows.

   b. df are the number of cell totals free to vary, given you know the column and row totals. If you know the totals in all the columns but one, you can figure the total in the cells in the remaining column by subtraction. Similarly, if you know the total in all the rows but one, you can figure the total in the cells in the remaining row by subtraction.

4. ❶ **Restate the question as a null hypothesis and a research hypothesis about the populations.** There are two populations:

   Population 1: People like those studied.

   Population 2: People whose being in a particular category of Nominal Variable A is independent of their being in a particular category of Nominal Variable B.

   The null hypothesis is that the two populations are the same; the research hypothesis is that the populations are not the same.

   ❷ **Determine the characteristics of the comparison distribution.** This is a chi-square distribution with 1 degree of freedom. That is, $df = (N_{Columns} - 1)(N_{Rows} - 1) = (2 - 1)(2 - 1) = 1$.

   ❸ **Determine the cutoff sample score on the comparison distribution at which the null hypothesis should be rejected.** From Table A–4, for the .05 significance level and 1 degree of freedom, the needed chi-square is 3.841.

   ❹ **Determine your sample's score on the comparison distribution.**

   ❹ **Determine the actual, observed frequencies in each cell.** These are shown in the contingency table for the problem.

   ❶ **Determine the expected frequencies in each cell.**

   ❶ **Find each row's percentage of the total.** For the top row 20/80 = 25%; for the second row, 60/80 = 75%.

   ❶ **For each cell, multiply its row's percentage times its column's total.** For the top left cell, 25% × 60 = 15; for the top right cell, 25% × 20 = 5; for the bottom left cell, 75% × 60 = 45; for the bottom right cell, 75% × 20 = 15.

   ❹ **In each cell, take observed minus expected frequencies.** For the four cells, 10 − 15 = −5; 10 − 5 = 5; 50 − 45 = 5; 10 − 15 = −5.

   ❶ **Square each of these differences.** This is 25 for each cell (that is, $5^2 = 25$ and $-5^2 = 25$).

   ❶ **Divide each squared difference by the expected frequency for its cell.** These come out to 25/15 = 1.67, 25/5 = 5, 25/45 = .56, and 25/15 = 1.67.

   ❶ **Add up the results of step E for all the cells.** 1.67 + 5 + .56 + 1.67 = 8.9.

   ❺ **Decide whether to reject the null hypothesis.** The sample's chi square of 8.9 is larger than the cutoff of 3.841. Thus, you can reject the null hypothesis: Which category of people are in on Nominal Variable A is not independent of which category they are in on Nominal Variable B.

ASSUMPTIONS FOR THE CHI-SQUARE TESTS

The chi-square tests for goodness of fit and for independence do not require the usual assumptions of normal population variances and such. There is, however, one key assumption: Each score must not have any special relation to any other scores. This means that you can't use these chi-square tests if the scores are based on the same people being tested more than once. Consider a study in which 20 people are tested to see if the distribution of their preferred brand of breakfast cereal changed from before to after a recent nutritional campaign. The results of this study could not be tested with the usual chi-square because the distributions of cereal choice before and after are from the same people.

EFFECT SIZE AND POWER FOR CHI-SQUARE TESTS FOR INDEPENDENCE

EFFECT SIZE

In chi-square tests for independence, you can use your sample's chi-square to figure a number that shows the degree of association of the two nominal variables.

With a 2×2 contingency table, the measure of association is called the **phi coefficient (ϕ)**. Here is the formula,

phi coefficient (ϕ)

> The phi coefficient (effect size for a chi-square test for independence for a 2×2 contingency table) is the square root of the result of dividing the sample's chi-square by the total number of people in the sample.

$$\phi = \sqrt{\frac{\chi^2}{N}} \tag{11-4}$$

The phi coefficient has a minimum of 0 and a maximum of 1 and can be considered similar to a correlation coefficient (see Chapter 3).[2] Cohen's (1988) conventions for the phi coefficient are that .10 is a small effect size, .30 is a medium effect size, and .50 is a large effect size.

For example, in the Riehl (1994) study of first-generation college students, the chi-square we calculated was 6.73 and there were 2,045 people in the study. Applying the formula for the phi coefficient,

$$\phi = \sqrt{\frac{\chi^2}{N}} = \sqrt{\frac{6.73}{2,045}} = \sqrt{.00329} = .06$$

This is a very small effect size. The fact that the chi-square of 6.73 was significant in this study tells you that the greater likelihood of first-generation students dropping out that you saw in the sample is probably not due to the particular people that were randomly recruited to be in this sample. You can thus have some confidence that there is a pattern of this kind in the population. But the small phi coefficient tells you that this true population tendency may not be a very important factor in practice. (See Chapter 7 for a discussion of this kind of situation when a result is statistically significant but has a very small effect size.)

Cramer's phi

You only use the phi when you have a 2×2 situation. **Cramer's phi** is an extension of the ordinary phi coefficient that you can use for contingency tables larger than 2×2. (Cramer's phi is also known as *Cramer's V* and is sometimes written ϕ_C or V_C.) You figure Cramer's phi the same way as the ordinary phi coefficient, except that instead of dividing by N, you divide by N times the degrees of freedom of the smaller side of the table. Stated as a formula,

> Cramer's phi coefficient (effect size for a chi-square test for independence) is the square root of the result of dividing the sample's chi-square by the product of the total number of people in the sample times the degrees of freedom for the smaller side of the table.

$$\text{Cramer's } \phi = \sqrt{\frac{\chi^2}{(N)(df_{Smaller})}} \tag{11-5}$$

In this formula, $df_{Smaller}$ is the degrees of freedom for the smaller side of the contingency table.

---

[2]Phi is actually identical to the correlation coefficient. Suppose you were to take the two variables in a 2×2 contingency table and arbitrarily make one of the values of each equal to 1 and the other equal to 2 (you could use any two numbers). If you then figured a correlation coefficient between the two variables, the result would be exactly the same as the phi coefficient. (Whether it was a positive or negative correlation, however, would depend on which categories in each variable got the 1 and which the 2.)

In the sleep tendency and transportation preference example, the sample's chi-square was 16.07 and the total number of people surveyed was 200. The degrees of freedom for the smaller side of the table (the rows in this example) was 1. Cramer's phi is the square root of what you get when you divide 16.07 by 200 times 1. This comes out to .28. In terms of the formula,

$$\text{Cramer's } \phi = \sqrt{\frac{\chi^2}{(N)(df_{Smaller})}} = \sqrt{\frac{16.07}{(200)(1)}} = \sqrt{.08} = .28$$

Cohen's (1988) conventions for effect size for Cramer's phi depend on the degrees of freedom for the smaller side of the table. Table 11–7 shows Cohen's effect size conventions for Cramer's phi for tables in which the smallest side of the table is 2, 3, and 4. Notice that when the smallest side of the table is 2, the degrees of freedom is 1. Thus, the effect sizes in the table for this situation are the same as for the ordinary phi coefficient.

Based on the table, in the transportation example there is an approximately medium effect size (.28), a medium amount of relationship between type of transportation one uses and whether one is a morning or a night person.

POWER

Table 11–8 shows the approximate power at the .05 significance level for small, medium, and large effect sizes and total sample sizes of 25, 50, 100, and 200. Power is given for tables with 1, 2, 3, and 4 degrees of freedom.[3]

Consider the power of a planned 2×4 study ($df = 3$) of 50 people with an expected medium effect size (Cramer's $\phi = .30$). The researchers will use the .05 level. From Table 11–8 you can find that this study would have a power of .40. That is, if the research hypothesis is true, and there is a true medium effect size, there is about a 40% chance that the study will come out significant.

NEEDED SAMPLE SIZE

Table 11–9 gives the approximate total number of participants needed for 80% power with small, medium, and large effect sizes at the .05 significance level for chi-square tests of independence of 2, 3, 4, and 5 degrees of freedom.[4] Suppose you

| TABLE 11–7 | Cohen's Conventions for Cramer's Phi |

Smallest Side of Contingency Table	Effect Size		
	Small	Medium	Large
2 ($df_{Smaller} = 1$)	.10	.30	.50
3 ($df_{Smaller} = 2$)	.07	.21	.35
4 ($df_{Smaller} = 3$)	.06	.17	.29

[3]Cohen (1988, pp. 228–248) gives more detailed tables. However, Cohen's tables are based on an effect size called w, which is equivalent to phi but not to Cramer's phi. He provides a helpful conversion table of Cramer's phi to w on page 222.

[4]More detailed tables are provided in Cohen (1988, pp. 253–267). When using these tables, see footnote 3. Also, Dunlap and Myers (1997) have shown that with a 2×2 table, the approximate number of participants needed for 80–90% power is $8/\phi^2$.

TABLE 11–8 Approximate Power for the Chi-Square Test for Independence for Testing Hypotheses at the .05 Significance Level

Total df	Total N	Effect Size		
		Small	Medium	Large
1	25	.08	.32	.70
	50	.11	.56	.94
	100	.17	.85	*
	200	.29	.99	*
2	25	.07	.25	.60
	50	.09	.46	.90
	100	.13	.77	*
	200	.23	.97	*
3	25	.07	.21	.54
	50	.08	.40	.86
	100	.12	.71	.99
	200	.19	.96	*
4	25	.06	.19	.50
	50	.08	.36	.82
	100	.11	.66	.99
	200	.17	.94	*

*Nearly 1.

are planning a study with a 3×3 ($df = 4$) contingency table. You expect a large effect size and will use the .05 significance level. According to the table, you would only need 48 participants.

TABLE 11–9 Approximate Total Number of Participants Needed for 80% Power for the Chi-Square Test of Independence for Testing Hypotheses at the .05 Significance Level

Total df	Effect Size		
	Small	Medium	Large
1	785	87	26
2	964	107	39
3	1,090	121	44
4	1,194	133	48

HOW ARE YOU DOING?

1. What are the assumptions for chi-square tests?
2. (a) What is the measure of effect size for a 2×2 chi-square test for independence? (b) Write the formula for this measure of effect size and define each of the symbols. (c) What are Cohen's conventions for small, medium, and large effect sizes? (d) Figure the effect size for a 2×2 chi-square test for independence in which there are a total of 100 participants and the chi-square is 12.
3. (a) What is the measure of effect size for a chi-square test for independence for a contingency table that is larger than 2×2? (b) Write the formula for this measure of effect size

and define each of the symbols. (c) What is Cohen's convention for a small effect size for a 4×6 contingency table? (d) Figure the effect size for a 4×6 chi-square test for independence in which there are a total of 200 participants and the chi-square is 20.

4. What is the power of a planned 3×3 chi-square with 50 participants total and a predicted medium effect size?

5. About how many participants do you need for 80% power in a planned 2×2 study in which you predict a medium effect size and will be using the .05 significance level?

ANSWERS:

1. The only major assumption is that the numbers in each cell or category are from separate persons.

2. a. The phi coefficient.

   b. $\phi = \sqrt{\dfrac{\chi^2}{N}}$

      ϕ is the phi coefficient (effect size for a chi-square test for independence with a 2×2 contingency table); χ^2 is the sample's chi-square; and N is the total number of participants in the study.

   c. .10 is a small effect size, .30 is a medium effect size, and .50 is a large effect size.

   d. = .35.

3. a. Cramer's phi.

   b. Cramer's $\phi = \sqrt{\chi^2 / [(N)(df_{Smaller})]}$

      Cramer's ϕ is Cramer's phi coefficient (effect size for a chi-square test for independence); χ^2 is the sample's chi-square; N is the total number of participants in the study; and $df_{Smaller}$ is the degrees of freedom for the smaller side of the contingency table.

   c. .06.

   d. $\sqrt{20 / [(200)(3)]} = .18$

4. .36.

5. 87.

STRATEGIES FOR HYPOTHESIS TESTING WHEN POPULATION DISTRIBUTIONS ARE NOT NORMAL

This second main part of the chapter examines some strategies researchers use when the variables are quantitative, but the assumption of a normal population distribution is clearly violated. (This assumption underlies most ordinary hypothesis-testing procedures, such as the *t* test and the analysis of variance.) First, we briefly review the role of assumptions in the standard hypothesis-testing procedures. Then we examine two approaches researchers use when the assumptions have not been met: data transformations and rank-order tests.

ASSUMPTIONS IN THE STANDARD HYPOTHESIS-TESTING PROCEDURES

As we saw in Chapters 8 through 10, you have to meet certain conditions (the assumptions) to get accurate results with a *t* test or an analysis of variance. In these hypothesis-testing procedures, you treat the scores from a study as if they came from some larger, though unknown, populations. One assumption you have to make is that the populations involved follow a normal curve. The other main assumption you have to make is that the populations have equal variances.

You also learned in previous chapters that you get fairly accurate results when a study suggests that the populations even very roughly meet the assumptions of following a normal curve and having equal variances. Our concern here, however, is with the situation where it is clear that the populations are nowhere near normal, or nowhere near having equal variances. In such situations, if you use the ordinary t test or analysis of variance, you can get quite incorrect results. For example, you could do all the figuring correctly and decide to reject the null hypothesis based on your results. And yet, if your populations do not meet the standard assumptions, this result could be wrong—wrong in the sense that instead of there actually being only a 5% chance of getting your results if the null hypothesis is true, in fact there might be a 15% or 20% chance!

Remember: Assumptions are about *populations* and not about *samples*. It is quite possible for a sample not to follow a normal curve even though it comes from a population that does. Figure 11–5 shows histograms for several samples, each taken randomly from a population that follows a normal curve. (Notice that the smaller the sample, the harder it is to see that it came from a normal population.) Of course, it is quite possible for non-normal populations to produce any of these samples as well. Unfortunately, the sample is usually all you have when doing a study. One thing researchers do is make a histogram for the sample; if it is not drastically

FIGURE 11–5 *Histograms for several random samples, each taken from a normal population with a mean of 0 and a standard deviation of 1.*

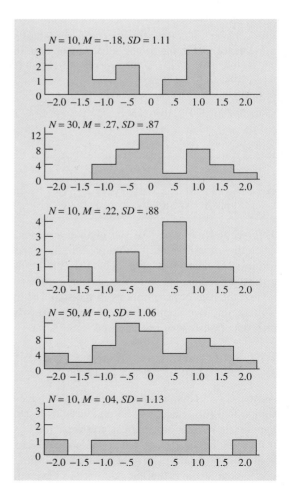

different from normal, the researchers assume that the population it came from is normal. When considering normality, most social and behavioral science researchers consider a distribution innocent until proven guilty.

One common situation where you might doubt the assumption that the population follows a normal distribution is when there is a *ceiling* or *floor effect* (see Chapter 1). Another common situation that raises such doubts is when the sample has outliers, extreme scores at one or both ends of the sample distribution. Figure 11–6 shows some examples of distributions with outliers. Outliers are a big problem in the statistical methods we ordinarily use because these methods rely, ultimately, on squared deviations from the mean. Because it is so far from the mean, an outlier has a huge influence when you square its deviation from the mean. The result is that a single outlier, if it is extreme enough, can cause a statistical test to give a significant result even when all the other scores would not. An outlier can also make a result not significant that would be significant without the outlier.

HOW ARE YOU DOING?

1. What are the two main assumptions for *t* tests and the analysis of variance?
2. (a) How do you check to see if you have met the assumptions? (b) Why is this problematic?
3. (a) What is an outlier? (b) Why are outliers likely to have an especially big distorting effect in most statistical procedures?

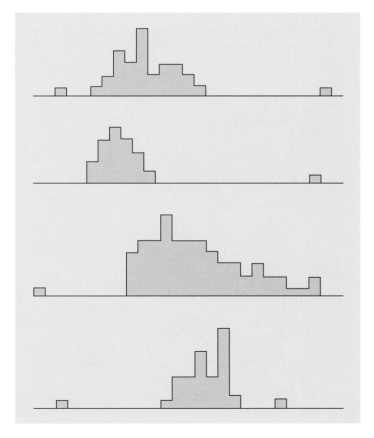

FIGURE 11–6   *Distributions with outliers at one or both ends.*

ANSWERS:

1. The populations are normally distributed and have equal variances.
2. (a) You look at the distributions of the samples. (b) The samples, especially if they are small, can have quite different shapes and variances from the populations.
3. (a) An extreme score. (b) Because most procedures are based on squared deviations from the mean, so that the extremeness of an outlier is greatly multiplied when its deviation from the mean is squared.

DATA TRANSFORMATIONS

data transformation

One widely used procedure when the scores in the sample do not appear to come from a normal population is to change the scores! Not by fudging—although at first it may sound that way, until we explain. The method is that the researcher applies some mathematical procedure to each score, such as taking its square root, to make a non-normal distribution closer to normal. (Sometimes this can also make the variances of two or more groups more similar.) This is called a **data transformation.** Once you have made a data transformation, if the other assumptions are met, you can then go ahead with a usual *t* test or analysis of variance. Data transformation has an important advantage over other procedures of coping with non-normal populations: Once you have made a data transformation, you can use familiar and sophisticated hypothesis-testing procedures.

Consider an example. Measures of reaction time (such as how long it takes a research participant to press a particular key when a light flashes) are usually highly skewed to the right. There are many short (quick) responses, but usually a few quite long (slow) ones. It is unlikely that the reaction times shown in Figure 11–7 come from a population that follows a normal curve. The population of reaction-time scores itself is probably skewed.

FIGURE 11–7   *Skewed distribution of reaction times (fictional data).*

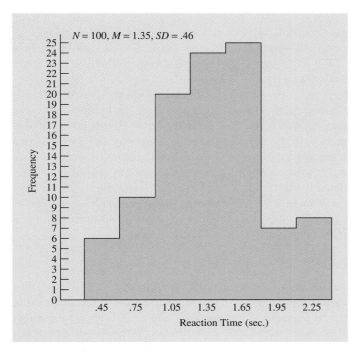

FIGURE 11–8   *Distribution of scores from Figure 11–7 after square-root transformation.*

However, suppose you take the square root of each reaction time. Most reaction times are affected only a little. A reaction time of 1 second stays 1; a reaction time of 1.5 seconds reduces to 1.22. However, very long reaction times, the ones that create the long tail to the right, are much reduced. For example, a reaction time of 9 seconds is reduced to 3, and a reaction time of 16 seconds (the person was really distracted and forgot about the task) reduces to 4. Figure 11–8 shows the result of taking the square root of each score in the skewed distribution shown in Figure 11–7. After a **square-root transformation,** this distribution of scores seems much more likely to have come from a population with a normal distribution (of transformed scores).

square-root transformation

LEGITIMACY OF DATA TRANSFORMATIONS

Do you feel that this is somehow cheating? It would be if you did this only to some scores or in any other way did it to make the result come out more favorable to your predictions. However, in actual research practice, the first step after the data are collected and recorded (and checked for accuracy) is to see if the data suggest that the populations meet assumptions. If the scores in your sample suggest that the populations do not meet assumptions, you do data transformations. Hypothesis testing is done only after this checking and any transformations.

Remember that you must do any transformation for *all* the scores on that variable, not just those in a particular group. Most important, no matter what transformation procedure you use, the order of the scores always stays the same. A person with a raw score that is between the raw scores of two other participating people will still have a transformed score between those same two people's transformed scores.

The procedure may seem somehow to distort reality to fit the statistics. In some cases, this is a legitimate concern. Suppose you are looking at the difference in income between two groups of Americans. You probably do not care about how much the two groups differ in the square root of their income. What you care about is the difference in actual dollars.

On the other hand, consider a survey question in which the person indicates their agreement with the statement "I am satisfied with local law enforcement" on a 7-point rating from 1, strongly disagree, to 7, strongly agree. Higher scores on this scale certainly mean more agreement; lower scores, less agreement. However, each scale-point increase is not necessarily related to an equal amount of increase in an individual's agreement. It is just as likely that the square root of each scale point's increase is directly related to the person's agreement. In many research situations, there may be no strong reason to think that the transformed version is any less accurate a reflection of the reality than the original version. And the transformed version may meet the normality assumption.

KINDS OF DATA TRANSFORMATIONS

There are several types of data transformations. We already have illustrated a square-root transformation: Instead of using each score, you use the square root of each score. We gave an example in Figures 11–7 and 11–8. The general effect is shown in Figure 11–9. As you can see, a distribution skewed to the right becomes less skewed to the right after square-root transformation. To put it numerically, moderate numbers become only slightly lower and high numbers become much lower. The result is that the right side is pulled in toward the middle. (If the distribution is skewed the other way, you may want to *reflect* all the scores—that is, subtract them all from some high number so that they are now all reversed. Then, using the square root will have the correct effect. However, you then have to remember when looking at the final results that you have reversed the direction of scoring.)

There are many other kinds of transformations you will see in social and behavioral science research articles. One common type is called a *log transformation*. (In a log transformation, instead of the square root, the researcher takes the logarithm of each score.) Some other transformations you might see are *inverse transformations* and *arcsine transformations*. We will not go into examples of all these kinds of transformations here. Just learning the square-root transformation will help you get the principle. The main thing to remember about other kinds of transformations is that they all use this same principle of taking each score and applying some arithmetic to it to make the set of scores come out more like a normal curve. Once again, whatever transformation you use, a score that is between two other scores always stays between those two other scores.

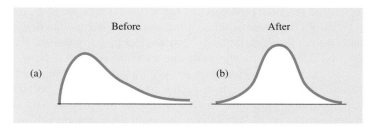

FIGURE 11–9   *Distribution skewed to the right before (a) and after (b) taking the square root of each score.*

AN EXAMPLE OF A DATA TRANSFORMATION

Consider a fictional study in which four children who score high on a test of being "highly sensitive" are compared on the number of books read in the preceding year to four children who score low on the test. (The general idea of being a highly sensitive person is described in Aron [1996, 2002] and Aron & Aron [1997].) Based on theory, the researcher predicts that highly sensitive children will read more books. Table 11–10 shows the results.

Ordinarily, in a study like this, involving a comparison of two independent groups, you would use a t test for independent means. Yet the t test for independent means is like all of the procedures you have learned for hypothesis testing (except chi-square): It requires that the parent populations of scores for each group be normally distributed. In this study, however, the distribution of the sample is strongly skewed to the right—the scores tend to bunch up at the left, leaving a long tail to the right. It thus seems likely that the population of scores of number of books read (for both sensitives and nonsensitives) is also skewed to the right. This shape for the population distribution also seems reasonable in light of what is being measured. A child cannot read fewer than zero books; but once a child starts reading, it is easy to read a lot of books in a year.

Also note that the estimated population variances based on the two samples are dramatically different, 95.58 versus 584. This is another reason you would not want to go ahead with an ordinary t test.

However, suppose you do a square-root transformation on the scores (Table 11–11). Now both samples are much more like a normal curve—both samples have their middle scores bunch up in the middle (for example, for the Yes group, 6.00 and 6.71) and the more extreme (high and low) scores spread out a little from the mean (4.12 and 8.71). Also, the transformation seems reasonable in terms of the meaning of the numbers. Number of books read is meant as a measure of interest in things literary. Thus, the difference between 0 and 1 book is a much greater difference than the difference between 20 and 21 books.

Table 11–12 shows the t test analysis using the transformed scores.

TABLE 11–10	Results of a Study Comparing Highly Sensitive and Not Highly Sensitive Children on the Number of Books Read in the Past Year (Fictional Data)

	Highly Sensitive	
	No	Yes
	0	17
	3	36
	10	45
	22	75
Σ:	35	173
$M =$	8.75	43.25
$S^2 =$	95.58	584.00

TABLE 11–11	Square-Root Transformation of the Scores in Table 11-10

	Highly Sensitive		
	No		Yes	
X	$\sqrt{X}$	X	$\sqrt{X}$
0	0.00	17	4.12
3	1.73	36	6.00
10	3.16	45	6.71
22	4.69	75	8.66

TABLE 11–12	Figuring for a t Test for Independent Means Using Square-Root Transformed Scores for the Study of Books Read by Highly Sensitive Versus Not Highly Sensitive Children (Fictional Data)

t needed for .05 significance level, $df = (4 - 1) + (4 - 1) = 6$, one-tailed $= -1.943$.

	Highly Sensitive	
	No	Yes
	0.00	4.12
	1.73	6.00
	3.16	6.71
	4.69	8.66
Σ:	9.58	25.49
$M =$	9.58/4 = 2.40	25.49/4 = 6.37
$S^2 =$	12.03/3 = 4.01	10.56/3 = 3.52

$$S^2_{Pooled} = 3.77$$

$S^2_M = \qquad 3.77/4 = .94 \qquad\qquad 3.77/4 = .94$

$S^2_{Difference} = .94 + .94 = 1.88$

$S_{Difference} = \sqrt{1.88} = 1.37$

$t = (2.40 - 6.37)/1.37 = -2.90$

Conclusion: Reject the null hypothesis.

1. What is a data transformation?
2. Why is it done?
3. When is this legitimate?
4. Consider the following distribution of scores: 4, 16, 25, 25, 25, 36, 64. (a) Are they roughly normally distributed? (b) Why? (C) Carry out a square-root transformation for these scores (that is, list the square-root transformed scores). (d) Are the square-root transformed scores roughly normally distributed? (e) Why?

ANSWERS:

1. When each score is changed following some rule (such as take the square root or log).
2. In order to make the distribution more like a normal curve (or to make variances closer to equal across groups).
3. It is legitimate when it is done to all the scores, it is not done to make the results come out to fit the researcher's predictions, and the underlying meaning of the distance between scores is arbitrary.
4. (a) No. (b) They are skewed to the right. (c) 2, 4, 5, 5, 5, 6, 8. (d) Yes. (e) The middle scores are bunched in the middle and the extremes spread out evenly on both sides.

RANK-ORDER TESTS

Another way of coping with non-normal distributions is to transform the scores to ranks. Suppose you have a sample with scores 4, 8, 12, and 64. This would be a rather surprising sample if the population was really normal. A **rank-order transformation** would change the scores to 1, 2, 3, and 4, the 1 referring to the lowest number in the group, the 2 to the second lowest, and so forth. (A complication with a rank-order transformation occurs when you have two or more scores that are tied. The usual solution to ties is to give them each the average rank. For example, the scores 12, 81, 81, 107, and 154 would be ranked 1, 2.5, 2.5, 4, and 5.)

rank-order transformation

Changing ordinary scores to ranks is a kind of data transformation. But unlike the square-root transformations we just considered, with a rank-order transformation you aren't trying to get a normal distribution. The distribution you get from a rank-order transformation is rectangular, with equal numbers of scores (one) at each value. Ranks have the effect of spreading the scores out evenly.

There are special hypothesis-testing procedures that make use of rank-ordered data, called **rank-order tests,** that make use of rank-ordered scores. They also have two other common names. You can transform scores from a population with any shaped distribution into ranks. Thus, these tests are sometimes called **distribution-free tests.** Also, the distribution of rank-order scores is known exactly rather than estimated. Thus, rank-order tests do not require estimating any parameters (population values). For example, there is no need to estimate a population variance because you can determine exactly what it will be if you know that ranks are involved. Hence, hypothesis-testing procedures based on ranks are also called **nonparametric tests.**

rank-order tests

distribution-free tests

nonparametric tests

parametric tests

The ordinary hypothesis-testing procedures you have learned (*t* test and analysis of variance) are examples of **parametric tests.** Chi-square, like the rank-order tests, is considered a nonparametric test, but it is distribution-free only in the sense that no assumptions are made about the shape of the population distributions. However, the terms *distribution-free* and *nonparametric* are typically used interchangeably; the subtleties of differences between them are a matter of ongoing debate among statisticians.

TABLE 11–13	Major Rank Order Tests Corresponding to Major Parametric Tests
Ordinary Parametric Test	**Corresponding Rank-Order Test**
t test for dependent means	Wilcoxon signed-rank test
t test for independent means	Wilcoxon rank-sum test or Mann-Whitney *U* test
Analysis of variance	Kruskal-Wallis *H* test

Rank-order tests also have the advantage that they can be used where the actual scores in the study are themselves ranks—for example, a study comparing the class standings of two types of graduates.

OVERVIEW OF RANK-ORDER TESTS

Table 11–13 shows the name of the rank-order test that you would substitute for each of the parametric hypothesis-testing procedures you have learned. (Full procedures for using such tests are given in intermediate statistics texts.) For example, in a situation with three groups, you would normally do a one-way analysis of variance. But if you want to use a rank-order method, you would use the Kruskal-Wallis *H* test.

Next, we will describe how such tests are done in a general way, including an example. However, we do not actually provide all the needed information for you to carry them out in practice. We introduce you to these techniques because you may see them used in articles you read and because their logic is the foundation of an alternative procedure that we do teach you to use (shortly). This alternative procedure does roughly the same thing as these rank-order tests and is closer to what you have already learned.

BASIC LOGIC OF RANK-ORDER TESTS

Consider a study involving an experimental group and a control group. (This is the kind of situation for which you would use a *t* test for independent means if all the assumptions were met.) If you wanted to use a rank-order test, you would first transform all the scores into ranks, ranking all the scores from lowest to highest, regardless of whether a score was in the experimental or the control group. If the two groups were scores randomly taken from a single population, there should be about equal amounts of high ranks and low ranks in each group. (That is, if the null hypothesis is true, the ranks in the two groups should not differ.) Because the distribution of ranks can be worked out exactly, statisticians can figure the exact probability of getting any particular division of ranks into two groups if in fact the two groups were randomly taken from identical distributions.

The way this actually works is that the researcher converts all the scores to ranks, adds up the total of the ranks in the group with the lower scores, and then compares this total to a cutoff from a special table of significance cutoffs for totals of ranks in this kind of situation.

AN EXAMPLE OF A RANK-ORDER TEST

Table 11–14 shows the transformation to ranks and the computation of the Wilcoxon rank-sum test for the kind of situation we have just described, using the books read by highly sensitive versus not highly sensitive children example. The logic is a little different from what you are used to, so be patient until we explain it.

Notice that we first set the significance cutoff, as you would in any hypothesis-testing procedure. (This cutoff is based on a table you don't have but is available in

---

TABLE 11–14 | **Figuring for a Wilcoxon Rank-Sum Test for the Study of Books Read by Highly Sensitive Versus Not Highly Sensitive Children (Fictional Data)**

Cutoff for significance: Maximum sum of ranks in the not highly sensitive group for significance at the .05 level, one-tailed (from a standard table) = 11.

Highly Sensitive

No		Yes	
X	Rank	X	Rank
0	1	17	4
3	2	36	6
10	3	45	7
22	5	75	8
Σ:	11		

Comparison to cutoff: Sum of ranks of group predicted to have lower scores, 11, equals but does not exceed cutoff for significance.

Conclusion: Reject the null hypothesis.

Tip for Success

Remember that when changing ordinary scores to ranks, all of the scores are ranked from highest to lowest, regardless of what group a score is in (for example, experimental versus control).

most intermediate statistics texts.) The next step is to rank all the scores from lowest to highest, then add up the ranks in the group you expect to have the smaller total. You then compare the smaller total to the cutoff. If this smaller total is less than or equal to the cutoff, you reject the null hypothesis. In the example, the total of the ranks for the lower was equal to the cutoff, so the null hypothesis was rejected.

USING PARAMETRIC TESTS WITH RANK-TRANSFORMED DATA

Two statisticians (Conover & Iman, 1981) have shown that instead of using the special procedures for rank-order tests, you get approximately the same results for the *t* test and one-way analysis of variance if you transform the data into ranks and then apply all the usual *t*-test or one-way analysis-of-variance procedures.

The result of using a parametric test with data transformed into ranks will not be quite as accurate as either the ordinary parametric test or the rank-order test. It will not be as accurate as the ordinary parametric test because the assumption of normal distributions is violated. The distribution is, in fact, rectangular when ranks are involved. It will also not be quite as accurate as the rank-order test because the parametric test uses the *t* or *F* distribution instead of the special tables that rank-order tests use, which are based on exact probabilities of getting certain divisions of ranks. However, the approximation seems to be quite close for the *t* test and the analysis of variance.[5]

---

[5]If you want to be very accurate, for a *t* test or one-way analysis of variance, you can convert your result to what is called an *L* statistic and look it up on a chi square table (Puri & Sen, 1985). The *L* statistic for a *t* test is $([N-1]t^2)/(t^2 + [N-2])$ and you use a chi-square distribution with $df = 1$. The *L* statistic for a one-way analysis of variance is $([N-1][df_{Between}]F)/([df_{Between}]F + df_{Within})$, and you use a chi-square distribution with $df = df_{Between}$. The *L* for the significance of a correlation (see Chapter 3 Appendix) is just $(N-1)r^2$ and you use the chi-square table for $df = 1$. It is especially important to use the *L* statistic when using rank-transformed scores for more advanced parametric procedures, such as factorial analysis of variance (Chapter 10), multiple regression (Chapter 3), and those procedures discussed in Chapter 12. Thomas, Nelson, and Thomas (1999) give fully worked-out examples.

TABLE 11–15 Figuring for a *t* Test for Independent Means Using Ranks Instead of Raw Scores for the Study of Books Read by Highly Sensitive Versus Not Highly Sensitive Children (Fictional Data)

t needed for .05 significance level, $df = (4 - 1) + (4 - 1) = 6$, one-tailed $= -1.943$

Highly Sensitive

	No	Yes
	1	4
	2	6
	3	7
	5	8
Σ	11	25
$M =$	$11/4 = 2.75$	$25/4 = 6.25$
$S^2 =$	$8.75/3 = 2.92$	$8.75/3 = 2.92$

$$S^2_{\text{Pooled}} = 2.92$$

$S^2_M =$	$2.92/4 = .73$	$2.92/4 = .73$

$S^2_{\text{Difference}} = .73 + .73 = 1.46$

$S_{\text{Difference}} = \sqrt{1.46} = 1.21$

$t = (2.75 - 6.25)/1.21 = -2.89$

Conclusion: Reject the null hypothesis.

Table 11–15 shows the figuring for an ordinary *t* test for independent means for the fictional sensitive children data, using each child's rank instead of the child's actual number of books read. Again we get a significant result. (In practice, carrying out an ordinary procedure like a *t* test with scores that have been transformed to ranks is least accurate with a very small sample like this. However, we used the small sample to keep the example simple.)

HOW ARE YOU DOING?

1. (a) What is a rank-order transformation? (b) Why is it done? (c) What is a rank-order test?
2. Transform the following scores to ranks: 5, 18, 3, 9, 2.
3. (a) If you wanted to use a standard rank-order test instead of a *t* test for independent means, what procedure would you use? (b) What are the steps of doing such a test?
4. (a) What happens if you change your scores to ranks and then figure an ordinary parametric test using the ranks? (b) Why will this not be quite as accurate even assuming the transformation to ranks is appropriate? (c) Why will this result not be quite as accurate using the standard rank-order test?

ANSWERS:

1. a. Changing each score to its rank (order from lowest to highest) among all the scores.
   b. To make the distribution a standard shape.
   c. A special type of significance testing procedure designed for use with rank-ordered scores.
2. 5 = 3, 18 = 5, 3 = 2, 9 = 4, and 2 = 1.
3. a. Wilcoxon rank-sum test or Mann-Whitney *U* test.
   b. Set the significance cutoff (based on a table) for the maximum sum of ranks for the group predicted to have the lower scores, change all scores to ranks (ignoring what group

they are in), add up the ranks in the group predicted to have the lower scores, compare that total to the cutoff.

4. a. You get fairly similar results to doing the standard parametric test.
    b. Because the population distribution will be rectangular and not normal (an assumption for the t test).
    c. Because the rank-order test is based on knowing for sure the shape of the population distribution and using exact probabilities on that basis.

CHI-SQUARE TESTS, DATA TRANSFORMATIONS, AND RANK-ORDER TESTS IN RESEARCH ARTICLES

CHI-SQUARE TESTS

In research articles, chi-square tests usually include the frequencies in each category or cell, as well as the degrees of freedom, number of participants, the sample's chi-square, and significance level. For example, Harter et al. (1997) reported their finding for the relationship style of the self-focused men as "χ^2 (2, $n = 101$) = 11.89, $p < .005$" (p. 156).

Here is another example of a chi-square test for goodness of fit. Sandra Moriarty and Shu-Ling Everett (1994) did a study of television viewing in which graduate students actually went to 55 different homes and observed people watching television for 45-minute sessions. In one part of their results, they compared the number of people they observed who fell into one of four distinct categories:

> Flipping [very rapid channel changing], the category dominated by the most active type of behavior, occurred most frequently, in 33% of the sessions ($n = 18$). The grazing category [periods of browsing through channels] dominated 24% of the sessions ($n = 13$), and 22% were found to be in each of the continuous and stretch viewing categories ($n = 12$). These differences were not statistically significant ($\chi^2 = 1.79$, $df = 3$, $p > .05$). (p. 349)

Published reports of chi-square tests for independence provide the same basic chi-square information. For example, Durkin and Barber (2002) examined the relationship between playing computer games and positive development (such as being close to one's family, involved in activities, having positive mental health, and low disobedience to parents) among 16-year-old high school students in Michigan. As part of the study, the researchers tested whether male and female students differed in the frequency with which they played computer games. Students indicated how often they played computer games by giving a response on a 7-point scale, from *never* (1) to *daily* (7). Here is how the researchers reported their results:

> The participants were categorized into three groups based on their frequency of play: "None" included participants who did not use computers at all, as well as those who used computers, but never for computer games; "Low" included participants who checked 2, 3, 4, or 5 for frequency of computer use to play computer games; and "High" included participants who checked 6 or 7 for frequency of com-

puter game play. A chi-square test [for independence] indicated that males and females were not evenly distributed across these three categories [$\chi^2(2, N = 1043) = 62.39, p < .001$]. Girls were overrepresented among the nonusers, with a majority never playing computer games (50.6%), compared to 29.4% of boys who never played. Boys were more than twice as likely (23.8%) as girls (9.9%) to be in the high use group. A substantial number of both girls (39.4%) and boys (46.8%) were in the low use group. (p. 381)

You may be interested to read the researchers' conclusions from the overall study: "No evidence was obtained of negative outcomes among game players. On several measures—including . . . [all of the positive development outcomes mentioned earlier]—game players scored more favorably than did peers who never played computer games. It is concluded that computer games can be a positive feature of a healthy adolescence." (Durkin & Barber, 2002, p. 373)

Durkin and Barber (2002) do not give the effect size for their significant result. However, you can figure it out from the chi-square, number of participants, and design of the study (2 × 3 in this example). Using the formula,

$$\phi = \sqrt{\chi^2/[(N)(df_{\text{Smaller}})]} = \sqrt{62.39/[(1043)(1)]} = \sqrt{.060} = .24$$

This suggests that there is something close to a moderate effect size.

DATA TRANSFORMATIONS

Data transformations are usually mentioned in the Results section, just prior to the description of the analysis that uses the data that were transformed. For example, Stake and Malkin (2003) studied students' reports of the quality of their women's and gender studies classes. Prior to presenting the main results, the researchers noted:

> . . . all variables were tested for normality. The following variables were found to be skewed and were logarithmically transformed to normalize the distributions: age, relationship capacity, class expectations, percentage of gender match, percentage of ethnic match, and class experience ratings. All of the above distributions except age were negatively skewed and were therefore reversed [reflected] prior to the log transformation. (p. 178)

RANK-ORDER TESTS

Here is an example of a rank-order test reported in a research study by Rottenstreich and Hsee (2001), focusing on the importance of subjective feeling in making risk-taking decisions. In one of their studies, one group of students was asked how much they would pay for having a 1% chance of winning a $500 coupon toward a European summer vacation. A second group was asked how much they would pay for having a 1% chance of winning a $500 coupon toward their tuition. Here are the results: "Although the two coupons had equivalent redemption value, the median price of the 1% chance of winning the European coupon was $20, whereas the median price of the 1% chance of winning the tuition coupon was only $5 ($p < .05$ by Mann-Whitney test . . .)" (p. 187).

SUMMARY

1. Chi-square tests are used for hypothesis tests with nominal variables. A sample's chi-square statistic (χ^2) shows the amount of mismatch between expected and observed frequencies over several categories. It is figured by finding, for each category or combination of categories, the difference between observed frequency and expected frequency, squaring this difference (eliminating positive and negative signs), and dividing by the expected frequency (making the squared differences more proportionate to the numbers involved). The results are then added up for all the categories or combinations of categories. The distribution of the chi-square statistic is known and the cutoffs can be looked up in standard tables.

2. The chi-square test for goodness of fit is used to test hypotheses about whether a distribution of frequencies over two or more categories of a *single nominal variable* matches an expected distribution. (These expected frequencies are based, for example, on theory or on a distribution in another study or circumstance.) In this test, the expected frequencies are given in advance or are based on some expected percentages (such as equal percentages in all groups). The degrees of freedom are the number of categories minus 1.

3. The chi-square test for independence is used to test hypotheses about the relation between *two nominal variables*—that is, about whether the breakdown over the categories of one variable has the same proportional pattern within each of the categories of the other variable. The frequencies are set up in a contingency table, in which the two variables are crossed and the numbers in each combination are placed in each of the resulting cells. The frequency expected for a cell if the two variables are independent is the percentage of all the people in that cell's row times the total number of people in that cell's column. The degrees of freedom for the test of independence are the number of columns minus 1 times the number of rows minus 1.

4. Chi-square tests make no assumptions about normal distributions of their variables, but they do require that no individual be counted in more than one category or cell.

5. The estimated effect size for a chi-square test for independence (that is, the degree of association) for a 2 × 2 contingency table is the phi coefficient; for larger tables, Cramer's phi. Phi is the square root of the result of dividing your sample's chi-square by the number of persons. Cramer's phi is the square root of the result of dividing your sample's chi-square by the product of the number of persons times the degrees of freedom in the smaller side of the contingency table. These coefficients range from 0 to 1.

6. The *t* test, the analysis of variance, and other standard parametric tests all assume that populations follow a normal curve and have equal variances. When samples suggest that the populations are very far from normal (for example, due to outliers), using the ordinary procedures gives incorrect results.

7. One approach when the populations appear to be non-normal is to transform the scores, such as taking the square root of each score so that the distribution of the transformed scores appears to represent a normally distributed population. The ordinary hypothesis-testing procedures can then be used.

8. Another approach is to rank all of the scores in a study. Special rank-order tests (sometimes called nonparametric or distribution-free tests) use basic principles of probability to determine the chance of the ranks being unevenly distributed across groups. However, in many situations, using the rank-transformed scores in an ordinary parametric test gives a good approximation.

9. Chi-square tests are reported in research articles using a standard format. For example, $\chi^2(3, N = 196) = 9.22, p < .05$. Research articles usually describe data transformations just prior to analyses using them. Rank-order methods are described much like any other kind of hypothesis test.

KEY TERMS

chi-square tests (p. 333)
observed frequency
  (p. 335)
expected frequency
  (p. 335)
chi-square statistic (χ^2)
  (p. 337)
chi-square distribution
  (p. 337)
chi-square table (p. 338)
chi-square test for good-
  ness of fit (p. 338)

chi-square test for inde-
  pendence (p. 341)
contingency table (p. 342)
independence (p. 342)
cell (p. 342)
phi coefficient (ϕ)
  (p. 350)
Cramer's phi (p. 350)
data transformation
  (p. 356)
square-root transforma-
  tion (p. 357)

rank-order transformation
  (p. 360)
rank-order tests (p. 360)
distribution-free tests
  (p. 360)
nonparametric tests
  (p. 360)
parametric tests (p. 360)

EXAMPLE WORKED-OUT PROBLEMS

CHI-SQUARE TEST FOR GOODNESS OF FIT

The expected distribution (from previous years) on an exam roughly follows a normal curve in which the highest scoring 2.5% of the students get A's; the next highest scoring 14%, B's; the next 67%, C's; the next 14%, D's; and the lowest 2.5%, F's. A class takes a test using a new grading system and 10 get A's, 34 get B's, 140 get C's, 10 get D's, and 6 get F's. Use the steps of hypothesis testing to decide whether the new system produces a different distribution of grades (using the .01 level).

ANSWER

Table 11–16 shows the observed and expected frequencies and the figuring for the chi-square test.

❶ **Restate the question as a research hypothesis and a null hypothesis about the populations.** There are two populations:

> **Population 1:** Students graded with the new system.

> **Population 2:** Students graded with the old system.

The research hypothesis is that the populations are different; the null hypothesis is that the populations are the same.

❷ **Determine the characteristics of the comparison distribution.** The comparison distribution is a chi-square distribution with 4 degrees of freedom (5 categories − 1 = 4).

❸ **Determine the cutoff sample score on the comparison distribution at which the null hypothesis should be rejected.** Using the .01 level and $df = 4$, Table A–4 (in the Appendix) shows a needed chi square of 13.277.

❹ **Determine your sample's score on the comparison distribution.** As shown in Table 11–16, this comes out to 18.33.

TABLE 11–16 Figuring for Chi-Square Test for Goodness of Fit Example
                Worked-Out Problem

Grade	Observed ⓐ	Expected ⓑ
A	10	5 (2.5% × 200)
B	34	28 (14.0% × 200)
C	140	134 (67.0% × 200)
D	10	28 (14.0% × 200)
F	6	5 (2.5% × 200)

Degrees of freedom = 5 categories − 1 = 4 ❷

Chi-square needed, df = 4, .01 level: 13.277 ❸

$$\chi^2 = \Sigma\frac{(O-E)^2}{E} = \frac{(10-5)^2}{5} + \frac{(34-28)^2}{28} + \frac{(140-134)^2}{134} + \frac{(10-28)^2}{28} + \frac{(6-5)^2}{5}$$

ⓒ

$$= \frac{5^2}{5} + \frac{6^2}{28} + \frac{6^2}{134} + \frac{-18^2}{28} + \frac{1^2}{5}$$

ⓓ

$$= \frac{25}{5} + \frac{36}{28} + \frac{36}{134} + \frac{324}{28} + \frac{1}{5}$$

ⓔ

$$= 5 + 1.29 + .27 + 11.57 + .20 = 18.33.$$ ⓕ

Conclusion: Reject the null hypothesis. ❺

❺ **Decide whether to reject the null hypothesis.** The sample's chi square of 18.33 is more extreme than the needed chi-square of 13.277. Thus, you can reject the null hypothesis and conclude that the populations are different; the new grading system produces a different distribution of grades than the previous one.

CHI-SQUARE TEST FOR INDEPENDENCE

Steil and Hay (1997) conducted a survey of professionals (lawyers, doctors, bankers, etc.) regarding the people they compare themselves to when they think about their job situation (salary, benefits, responsibility, status, etc.). One question of special interest was how much professionals compare themselves to people of their own sex, the opposite sex, or both. Here are the results:

	Participant Gender	
	Men	Women
Comparison:		
Same sex	29	17
Opposite sex	4	14
Both sexes	26	28

Use the steps of hypothesis testing to decide if the researchers can conclude that the gender of who people compare themselves to is different depending on their own gender (use the .05 level).

ANSWER

Table 11–17 shows the figuring for the chi-square test.

❶ Restate the question as a null hypothesis and a research hypothesis about the populations. There are two populations:

> **Population 1:** Professionals like those surveyed.
>
> **Population 2:** Professionals for whom own sex is independent of the sex of those to whom they compare their job situations.

The null hypothesis is that the two populations are the same, that, in general, professional men and women do not differ in the sex of those to whom they compare their job situations. The research hypothesis is that the populations are not the same, that professionals like those surveyed are unlike the hypothetical population in which men and women do not differ in the sex of those to whom they compare their job situations.

❷ Determine the characteristics of the comparison distribution. This is a chi-square distribution with 2 degrees of freedom.

❸ Determine the cutoff sample score on the comparison distribution at which the null hypothesis should be rejected. Using the .05 level and 2 degrees of freedom, the needed chi-square for significance is 5.992.

❹ Determine your sample's score on the comparison distribution. As shown in Table 11–17, this comes out to 8.78.

❺ Decide whether to reject the null hypothesis. The chi square of 8.78 is larger than the cutoff of 5.992. Thus you can reject the null hypothesis: The gender

---

TABLE 11–17 Figuring for Chi-Square Test for Independence Example Worked-Out Problem

		Response		Total
		Men	*Women*	
Comparisons	*Same sex*	29 (23) Ⓐ	17 (23) Ⓑ	46 (39.0%)
	Opposite sex	4 (9)	14 (9)	18 (15.3%)
	Both sexes	26 (27)	28 (27)	54 (45.8%)
		59	59	118

$df = (N_{\text{Columns}} - 1)(N_{\text{Rows}} - 1) = (2 - 1)(3 - 1) = (1)(2) = 2.$ ❷

Chi-square needed, $df = 2$, .05 level: 5.992. ❸

$$\chi^2 = \Sigma \frac{(O - E)^2}{E} = \frac{(29 - 23)^2}{23} + \frac{(17 - 23)^2}{23} + \frac{(4 - 9)^2}{9} + \frac{(14 - 9)^2}{9} + \frac{(26 - 27)^2}{27} + \frac{(28 - 27)^2}{27}$$

Ⓒ

$$= \frac{6^2}{23} + \frac{-6^2}{23} + \frac{-5^2}{9} + \frac{5^2}{9} + \frac{-1^2}{27} + \frac{1^2}{27}$$

Ⓓ

$$= \frac{36}{23} + \frac{36}{23} + \frac{25}{9} + \frac{25}{9} + \frac{1}{27} + \frac{1}{27}$$

Ⓔ

$$= 1.57 + 1.57 + 2.78 + 2.78 + .04 + .04 = 8.78.$$ Ⓕ

Conclusion: Reject the null hypothesis. ❺

Note. Data from Steil and Hay (1997). The chi-square computed here (8.78) is slightly different from that reported in their article (8.76) due to rounding error.

of the people with whom professionals compare their job situations is likely to be different for men and women.

EFFECT SIZE FOR A 2 × 2 CHI-SQUARE TEST FOR INDEPENDENCE

Figure the effect size for a study with 85 participants and a chi-square of 14.41.

ANSWER

$$\phi = \sqrt{\chi^2/N} = \sqrt{14.41/85} = \sqrt{.170} = .41$$

EFFECT SIZE FOR A CHI-SQUARE TEST FOR INDEPENDENCE WITH A CONTINGENCY TABLE GREATER THAN 2 × 2

Figure the effect size for a 3 × 7 study with 135 participants and the chi-square is 18.32.

ANSWER

$$\text{Cramer's } \phi = \sqrt{\chi^2/[(N)(df_{\text{Smaller}})]} = \sqrt{18.32/[(135)(2)]}$$
$$= \sqrt{18.32/270} = \sqrt{.068} = .26$$

SQUARE-ROOT TRANSFORMATION

Carry out a square-root transformation on the scores below from a study with three groups:

Group A	Group B	Group C
15	21	18
4	16	19
12	49	11
14	17	22

ANSWER

Group A	Group B	Group C
3.88	4.58	4.24
2	4	4.36
3.46	7	3.31
3.74	4.12	4.69

RANK-ORDER TRANSFORMATION

Carry out a rank-order transformation on the same scores you used for the square-root transformation above.

ANSWER

Group A	Group B	Group C
5	10	8
1	6	9
3	12	2
4	7	11

PRACTICE PROBLEMS

These problems involve figuring. Most real-life statistics problems are done on a computer with special statistical software. Even if you have such software, do these problems by hand (with the help of a calculator) to ingrain the method in your mind. Also, in all problems involving figuring, be sure to show your work.

For practice in using a computer to solve statistics problems, refer to the computer section of each chapter of the *Student's Study Guide and Computer Workbook* that accompanies this text. All data are fictional unless an actual citation is given. For answers to Set I problems, see pp. 437–39.

SET I

1. Carry out a chi-square test for goodness of fit for each of the following (use the .05 level for each):

(a)

Category	Expected	Observed
A	20%	19
B	20%	11
C	40%	10
D	10%	5
E	10%	5

(b)

Category	Expected	Observed
I	30%	100
II	50%	100
III	20%	100

(c)

Category	Number in the Past	Observed
1	100	38
2	300	124
3	50	22
4	50	16

2. A director of a social service agency is planning to hire temporary staff to assist with intake. In making plans, the director needs to know whether there is any difference in the use of the agency at different seasons of the year. Last year there were 28 new clients in the winter, 33 in the spring, 16 in the summer, and

51 in the fall. On the basis of last year's data, should the director conclude that season makes a difference? (Use the .05 level.) (a) Carry out the five steps of hypothesis testing. (b) Explain your answer to a person who has never taken a course in statistics. (This problem is like the Harter et al. example from the beginning of this chapter in which you did a chi-square for a single nominal variable. This problem is not a chi-square test for independence and does not involve any contingency tables.)

3. Carry out a chi-square test for independence for each of the following contingency tables (use the .01 level). Also, figure the effect size for each contingency table.

(a)
10	16
16	10

(b)
100	106
106	100

(c)
100	160
160	100

(d)
10	16	10
16	10	10

(e)
10	16	16
16	10	16

(f)
10	16	10
16	10	16

4. A political analyst is interested in whether the community in which a person lives is related to that person's opinion on an upcoming water conservation ballot initiative. The analyst surveys 90 people by phone. The results are shown below. Is opinion related to community at the .05 level? (a) Carry out the five steps of hypothesis testing. (b) Compute Cramer's phi and power. (c) Explain your answers to (a) and (b) to a person who has never taken a course in statistics.

	Community A	Community B	Community C
For	12	6	3
Against	18	3	15
No opinion	12	9	12

5. Figure the effect size for the following studies:

	N	Chi-Square	Design
(a)	100	16	2 × 2
(b)	100	16	2 × 5
(c)	100	16	3 × 3
(d)	100	8	2 × 2
(e)	200	16	2 × 2

6. What is the power of the following planned studies using a chi-square test for independence with $p < .05$?

	Predicted Effect Size	Design	N
(a)	small	2 × 2	25
(b)	medium	2 × 2	25
(c)	small	2 × 2	50
(d)	small	2 × 3	25
(e)	small	3 × 3	25
(f)	small	2 × 5	25

7. About how many participants do you need for 80% power in each of the following planned studies using a chi-square test for independence with $p < .05$?

	Predicted Effect Size	Design
(a)	medium	2×2
(b)	large	2×2
(c)	medium	2×5
(d)	medium	3×3
(e)	large	2×3

8. Lydon, Pierce, and O'Regan (1997) conducted a study that compared long-distance to local dating relationships. The researchers first administered questionnaires to a group of students one month prior to their leaving home to begin their first semester at McGill University (Time 1). Some of these students had dating partners who lived in the McGill area; others had dating partners who lived a long way from McGill. The researchers contacted the participants again late in the fall semester, asking them about the current status of their original dating relationships (Time 2). Here is how they reported their results:

Of the 69 participants . . . 55 were involved in long-distance relationships, and 14 were in local relationships (dating partner living within 200 km of them). Consistent with our predictions, 12 of the 14 local relationships were still intact at Time 2 (86%), whereas only 28 of the 55 long-distance relationships were still intact (51%), $\chi^2(1, N = 69) = 5.55$, $p < .02$. (p. 108)

(a) Figure the chi-square yourself (your results should be the same, within rounding error). (b) Figure effect size. (c) Explain this result to a person who has never had a course in statistics.

9. For each of the distributions below, make a square-root transformation:

   a. 16, 4, 9, 25, 36
   b. 35, 14.3, 13, 12.9, 18

10. A researcher compares the typical family size in 10 cultures, 5 from Language Group A and 5 from Language Group B. The figures for the Group A cultures are 1.2, 2.5, 4.3, 3.8, and 7.2. The figures for the Group B cultures are 2.1, 9.2, 5.7, 6.7, and 4.8. Based on these 10 cultures, does typical family size differ in cultures with different language groups? Use the .05 level. (a) Carry out a t test for independent means using the actual scores. (b) Carry out a square-root transformation (to keep things simple, round off the transformed scores to one decimal place). (c) Carry out a t test for independent means using the transformed scores. (d) Explain what you have done and why to someone who is familiar with the t test for independent means but not with data transformation.

11. A researcher randomly assigns participants to watch one of three kinds of films: one that tends to make people sad, one that tends to make people exuberant, and one that tends to make people angry. The participants are then asked to rate a series of photos of individuals on how honest they appear. The ratings for the sad-film group were 201, 523, and 614; the ratings for the angry-film group were 136, 340, and 301; and the ratings for the exuberant-film group were 838, 911, and 1,007. (a) Carry out an analysis of variance using the actual scores (use $p < .01$). (b) Carry out a square-root transformation of the scores (to keep things simple, round off the transformed scores to one decimal place). (c) Carry out an analysis of variance using the transformed scores. (d) Explain what you

have done and why to someone who is familiar with analysis of variance but not with data transformation.

12. Miller (1997) conducted a study of commitment to a romantic relationship and how much attention a person pays to attractive alternatives. In this study, participants were shown a set of slides of attractive individuals. At the start of the results section, Miller notes, "The self-reports on the Attentiveness to Alternative Index and the time spent actually inspecting the attractive opposite-sex slides . . . were positively skewed, so logarithmic transformations of the data were performed" (p. 760). Explain what is being described here (and why it is being done) to a person who understands ordinary parametric statistics but has never heard of data transformations.

SET II

13. Carry out a chi-square test for goodness of fit for each of the following (use the .01 level for each):

(a)	Category	Expected	Observed
	1	2%	5
	2	14%	15
	3	34%	90
	4	34%	120
	5	14%	50
	6	2%	20

(b)	Category	Proportion Expected	Observed
	A	1/3	10
	B	1/6	10
	C	1/2	10

14. A researcher wants to be sure that the sample in her study is not unrepresentative of the distribution of ethnic groups in her community. Her sample includes 300 whites, 80 African Americans, 100 Latinos, 40 Asians, and 80 others. In her community, according to census records, there are 48% whites, 12% African Americans, 18% Latinos, 9% Asians, and 13% others. Is her sample unrepresentative of the population in her community? (Use the .05 level.) (a) Carry out the steps of hypothesis testing. (b) Explain your answer to a person who has never taken a course in statistics. (Note: This problem is like the Harter et al. example in which you are doing a chi-square for a single nominal variable. This is not a chi-square test for independence and does not involve any contingency tables.)

15. Carry out a chi-square test for independence for each of the following contingency tables (use the .05 level).

a.

0	18
18	0

b.

0	0	18
9	9	0

c.

0	0	9	9
9	9	0	0

d.

20	40
0	40

16. Below are results of a survey of a sample of people buying ballet tickets, laid out according to the type of seat they purchased and how regularly they attend. Is there a significant relation? (Use the .05 level.) (a) Carry out the steps of hypothesis testing. (b) Explain your answer to a person who has never taken a course in statistics.

		Attendance	
		Regular	*Occasional*
	Orchestra	20	80
Seating Category	*Dress circle*	20	20
	Balcony	40	80

17. Figure the effect size for the following studies:

	N	Chi-Square	Design
(a)	40	10	2 × 2
(b)	400	10	2 × 2
(c)	40	10	4 × 4
(d)	400	10	4 × 4
(e)	40	20	2 × 2

18. What is the power of the following planned studies, using a chi-square test for independence with $p < .05$?

	Predicted Effect Size	Design	N
(a)	medium	2 × 2	100
(b)	medium	2 × 3	100
(c)	large	2 × 2	100
(d)	medium	2 × 2	200
(e)	medium	2 × 3	50
(f)	small	3 × 3	25

19. About how many participants do you need for 80% power in each of the following planned studies, using a chi-square test for independence with $p < .05$?

	Predicted Effect Size	Design
(a)	small	2 × 2
(b)	medium	2 × 2
(c)	large	2 × 2
(d)	small	3 × 3
(e)	medium	3 × 3
(f)	large	3 × 3

20. Everett, Price, Bedell, and Telljohann (1997) mailed a survey to a random sample of physicians. Half were offered $1 if they would return the questionnaire (this was the experimental group); the other half served as a control group. The point of the study was to see if even a small incentive would increase the return rate for physician surveys. Everett et al. report their results as follows:

Of the 300 surveys mailed to the experimental group, 39 were undeliverable, 2 were returned uncompleted, and 164 were returned completed. Thus, the response rate for the experimental group was 63% (164/300 − 39 = .63). Of the 300 surveys mailed to the control group, 40 were undeliverable, and 118 were returned completed. Thus, the response rate for the control group was 45% (118/300 − 40) = .45). A chi-square test comparing the response rates for the experimental and control groups found the \$1 incentive had a statistically significantly improved response rate over the control group [$\chi^2(1, N = 521) = 16.0, p < .001$].

(a) Figure the chi-square yourself (your results should be the same, within rounding error). (b) Figure effect size. (c) Explain this result to a person who has never had a course in statistics.

21. For each of the distributions below, make a square-root transformation:

    a. 100, 1, 64, 81, 121
    b. 45, 30, 17.4, 16.8, 47

22. A study compares performance on a novel task for fifth-grade students who do the task either alone, in the presence of a stranger, or in the presence of a friend. The scores for the students in the alone condition are 1, 1, and 0; the scores of the participants in the stranger condition are 2, 6, and 1; and the scores for those in the friend condition are 3, 9, and 10. (a) Carry out an analysis of variance using the actual scores ($p < .05$). (b) Carry out a square-root transformation of the scores (to keep things simple, round off the transformed scores to one decimal place). (c) Carry out an analysis of variance using the transformed difference scores. (d) Explain what you have done and why to someone who is familiar with analysis of variance but not with data transformation.

23. A researcher conducted an experiment organized around a major televised address by the U.S. president. Immediately after the address, three participants were randomly assigned to listen to the commentaries provided by the television network's political commentators. The other three were assigned to spend the same time with the television off, reflecting quietly about the speech. Participants in both groups then completed a questionnaire that assessed how much of the content of the speech they remembered accurately. The group that heard the commentators had scores of 4, 0, and 1. The group that reflected quietly had scores of 9, 3, and 8. Did hearing the commentary affect memory? Use the .05 level, one-tailed, predicting higher scores for the reflected-quietly group. (a) Carry out a t test for independent means using the actual scores. (b) Carry out a square-root transformation (to keep things simple, round off the transformed scores to one decimal place). (c) Carry out a t test for independent means using the transformed scores. (d) Explain what you have done and why to someone who is familiar with the t test for independent means but not with data transformation.

24. June, Curry, and Gear (1990) surveyed black students at a Midwestern university about problems in their use of college services. Surveys were conducted of about 250 students each time at the end of the spring quarter over 5 different years. The researchers ranked the nine main problem areas for each of the years. One of their analyses then proceeded as follows: "A major question of interest was whether the ranking of most serious problems and use of services varied by years. Thus, a Kruskal-Wallis one-way analysis of variance (ANOVA) was performed on the rankings but was not significant" (p. 180). Explain why the researchers used the Kruskal-Wallis test instead of an ordinary analysis of variance and what conclusions can be drawn from this result.

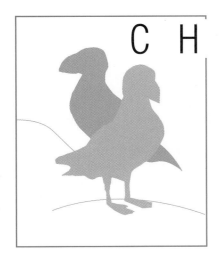

C H A P T E R 12

Making Sense of Advanced Statistical Procedures in Research Articles

Most studies you will read in your social and behavioral science classes use one or more of the statistical procedures you have learned in this book. However, often you will also run into procedures that you will not learn to do yourself until you take more advanced statistics courses. Fortunately, most of these advanced procedures are direct extensions of what you have learned in this book. At the least, after reading this chapter, you should be able to make sense of the general idea of just about any statistical analysis in a research article.

The first part of this chapter considers some widely used advanced statistical techniques that focus on associations among variables. These are essentially elaborations of what you learned in Chapter 3 on correlation and regression. After a brief review of multiple regression as a foundation, we introduce hierarchical and stepwise multiple regression, partial correlation, reliability, factor analysis, and causal modeling. The second part of this chapter considers advanced statistical techniques that focus on differences among groups. These are essentially elaborations of what you learned in Chapter 10 on the analysis of variance. These procedures include the analysis of covariance, multivariate analysis of variance, and multivariate analysis of covariance. We conclude with a discussion of what to do when you read a research article that uses a statistical technique you have never heard of.

Tip for Success

To understand the first part of this chapter, you need a strong grasp of the material in Chapter 3, especially on multiple regression, as well as on the general logic of hypothesis testing from Chapters 4–7. For the second part of this chapter, you need a strong grasp of the material in Chapter 10, including factorial analysis of variance.

BRIEF REVIEW OF MULTIPLE REGRESSION

As you learned in Chapter 3, regression is the prediction aspect of correlation. Multiple regression is about predicting scores on a criterion variable from *two or more* predictor variables. For example, in the sleep and mood study example in Chapter 3, we discussed predicting a person's mood (the criterion variable) from three predictor variables, number of hours slept the night before, how well the person slept, and number of dreams during the night.

A multiple regression prediction rule has a regression coefficient for each predictor variable. If you know a person's scores on the predictor variables, you multiply each predictor variable's score by that variable's regression coefficient. The sum of these multiplications is the person's predicted score on the criterion variable. With Z scores, the regression coefficients are standardized and are called *standardized regression coefficients* or *betas* (βs). For example, with three independent variables, the form of the prediction rule is as follows:

> The predicted Z score for the criterion variable is the standardized regression coefficient for the first predictor variable multiplied by the person's Z score on the first predictor variable, plus the standardized regression coefficient for the second predictor variable multiplied by the person's Z score on the second predictor variable, plus the standardized regression coefficient for the third predictor variable multiplied by the person's Z score on the third predictor variable.

$$\text{Predicted } Z_Y = (\beta_1)(Z_{X_1}) + (\beta_2)(Z_{X_2}) + (\beta_3)(Z_{X_3}) \qquad (12\text{-}1)$$

The overall accuracy of a prediction rule, the amount of variation it accounts for in the criterion variable, is called the proportion of variance accounted for and is abbreviated as R^2. Multiple regression gives you the statistical significance of this overall proportion of variance accounted for, R^2. It also gives you the statistical significance for the regression coefficient for each predictor variable individually.

HIERARCHICAL AND STEPWISE MULTIPLE REGRESSION

HIERARCHICAL MULTIPLE REGRESSION

Sometimes researchers focus on the influence of several predictor variables (or groups of predictor variables) in a sequential way. That is, they want to know how much of the variation in the criterion variable is accounted for by the first predictor variable (or first group of predictor variables), as shown by the value of R^2. Then, how much is added to the overall variance accounted for in the criterion variable (the R^2) by including a second predictor variable (or a second group of predictor variables) on the prediction rule. Then perhaps how much more is added by including a third predictor variable (or a third group of predictor variables). And so on. Thus, when reporting results, a researcher usually describes the amount that each successive predictor variable (or grouping of predictor variables) adds to the overall prediction in terms of an increase in R^2. The procedure is known as **hierarchical multiple regression**.

hierarchical multiple regression

Consider an example. MacDonald, Chamberlain, and Long (1997) studied the relation of various factors to war veterans' symptoms of posttraumatic stress disorder (PTSD). These researchers studied 756 Vietnam War veterans in New Zealand, including 161 Maori individuals (the Maori are the indigenous Polynesian people of New Zealand). Table 12–1 shows the results of their hierarchical regression analysis. The first predictor variable they considered, in Step 1, was combat exposure. This variable by itself had an R^2 of .070; the two asterisks (**) show that this was significant. The second step was to add a group of five predictor variables involving

TABLE 12–1 Regression Coefficients, R^2 and R^2 Change Values for Combat Exposure, Vietnam Experience Variables, and Race Predicting to PTSD

Predictor Variable	Standardized beta		
	Step 1	Step 2	Step 3
Combat exposure	.266[**]	.300[**]	.297[**]
Vietnam military experience			
Length Vietnam service		−.035	−.036
Rank		−.316[**]	−.314[**]
Combat role		.153[*]	.154[*]
Military specialization 1[a]		.015	.017
Military specialization 2[a]		.044	.044
Race[b]			−.024
R^2	.070[***]	.171[**]	.171[**]
R^2 change		.100[*]	.001

[*]$p < .01$, [**]$p < .001$.
[a]Dummy variables: military specialization 1 (infantry/noninfantry); military specialization 2 (artillery/nonartillery).
[b]Dichotomous variable (Maori/non-Maori).
Source: MacDonald, C., Chamberlain, K., & Long, N. (1997). Race, combat, and PTSD in a community sample of New Zealand Vietnam War veterans. *Journal of Traumatic Stress, 10,* 123. Copyright 1997 by the International Society for Traumatic Stress Studies. Reprinted by permission.

Vietnam military experience. The entire group of variables increased the R^2 from .070 to .171, an increase (R^2 change) of .101. (The researchers show the increase as .100 in their table. The discrepancy between .100 and .101 is probably their rounding off the numbers in the table at each stage.) Finally, in Step 3, they added race (Maori or not) as a predictor variable. Adding race increased the R^2 only slightly, and this slight increase was not significant. As shown in the table, the standardized regression coefficient for race (of −.024) was not significant.

These results are especially interesting because the direct ordinary correlation of race with PTSD symptoms was significant. Thus, the hierarchical regression shows that race does not predict PTSD if you have already taken into account combat experience and military situation. In other words, the apparent effect of race was probably due to Maoris having more exposure to combat and different military experience (such as being more likely to be in the infantry).

STEPWISE MULTIPLE REGRESSION

Sometimes, especially in an exploratory study, you measure many variables that are possible predictors of the criterion variable, and you want to pick out which predictor variables make a useful contribution to the overall prediction. This is usually done with a controversial procedure called **stepwise multiple regression** (or *stepwise regression,* for short). The most common form of stepwise multiple regression works as shown in Table 12–2: A computer program goes through a step-by-step procedure, first picking out the single predictor variable that accounts for the most variance in the criterion variable. If this proportion of variance accounted for is not significant, the process stops, since even the best predictor is of no use. However, if the proportion of variance accounted for by this predictor variable is significant, the process goes on to the next step. The next step is to pick out the predictor

stepwise multiple regression

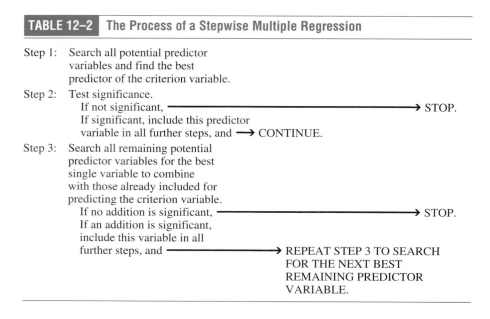

TABLE 12–2 The Process of a Stepwise Multiple Regression

Step 1: Search all potential predictor variables and find the best predictor of the criterion variable.

Step 2: Test significance.
If not significant, ————————————————→ STOP.
If significant, include this predictor variable in all further steps, and ——→ CONTINUE.

Step 3: Search all remaining potential predictor variables for the best single variable to combine with those already included for predicting the criterion variable.
If no addition is significant, ————————————→ STOP.
If an addition is significant, include this variable in all further steps, and ——————————→ REPEAT STEP 3 TO SEARCH FOR THE NEXT BEST REMAINING PREDICTOR VARIABLE.

variable that, in combination with this first one, has the highest R^2. The computer then checks to see whether this combination is a significant improvement over the best single predictor variable alone. If it is not, the process stops. If it is a significant improvement, the computer goes on. The next step is to pick out which of the remaining predictor variables, when combined with these first two, gives the highest R^2. Then, this combination is checked to see if it is a significant improvement in prediction over and above just the first two predictors. The process continues until either all the predictor variables are included or adding any of the remaining ones does not give a significant improvement. This procedure is called "stepwise" because it proceeds one step at a time.

Consider an example. Schwartz and Cohen (2001) studied 223 schizophrenic patients of a Florida community agency, focusing on the variables that might predict suicidality (the tendency to think about suicide, intent to harm oneself, and the seriousness and feasibility of any current suicide plan). Because they had measured a great many variables that might predict suicidality, they used stepwise regression. Here are their results:

> . . . a stepwise regression procedure was used to obtain the most effective overall model for suicidality. Results suggest that depressive symptoms alone accounted for 28% of the variance in ratings of suicidality. When age was added to the prediction model as a second variable, the two-variable combination accounted for 33% of the variance in ratings of suicidality. After traumatic stress was entered into the prediction equation, the three-variable model accounted for 38% of the variance in ratings of suicidality. The addition of other [predictor] variables added only minimally (and insignificantly) to the prediction model. Therefore, although depressive symptoms were found to most strongly associate with ratings of suicidality, the most significant combination of risk factors was the three-variable model including depressive symptoms, age, and recent traumatic stress. (p. 317)

What the authors are telling us is that of the several potential predictors (there were 12), the proportion of variance accounted for by three of these variables was not significantly improved upon by also including any of the remaining variables.

One caution about stepwise regression. We said earlier that stepwise regression is a controversial procedure. The reason it is controversial is that the prediction formula that results from this procedure is the best group of variables for predicting the criterion variable, *based on the sample studied.* However, it often happens that when the same variables are studied with a new sample, a somewhat different combination of variables turns out best. The reason this happens so often is that the variable selected at each step is one that adds the most to the overall prediction. The variable added has to make a significant improvement, but it doesn't have to make a significantly *larger* improvement than the next best variable—it only has to add the most, and the addition has to be significant. The next best variable might also make a significant addition, but just not quite as large an improvement. In a new sample from the same population, a slight difference in one predictor adding more than the other could well be reversed.

COMPARING HIERARCHICAL AND STEPWISE REGRESSION

Hierarchical and stepwise regression are similar in an important way. In both methods, you add variables a step at a time and check whether the addition significantly improves the prediction. However, there is also an important difference. In hierarchical regression, the order of adding the predictor variables is based on some theory or plan, decided in advance by the researcher. In stepwise regression, there is no initial plan. The computer simply figures out the best variables to add until adding more makes no additional contribution.

Thus, hierarchical regression is used in research that is based on theory or some substantial previous knowledge. Stepwise regression is useful in exploratory research where you don't know what to expect. Stepwise regression is also useful in applied research where you are looking for the best prediction formula without caring about its theoretical meaning.

HOW ARE YOU DOING?

1. Write the formula for multiple regression with Z scores for three predictors and define each of the symbols.
2. (a) How does hierarchical regression work? (b) Why is it done?
3. (a) How does stepwise regression work? (b) Why is it done? (c) What is a major limitation of this procedure?
4. How are hierarchical and stepwise regression (a) similar and (b) different?

ANSWERS:

1. Predicted $Z_Y = (\beta_1)(Z_{X_1}) + (\beta_2)(Z_{X_2}) + (\beta_3)(Z_{X_3})$

   Predicted Z_Y is a person's predicted Z score on the criterion variable; β_1, β_2, and β_3 are the standardized regression coefficients (betas) for the first, second, and third predictor variables, respectively; and Z_{X_1}, Z_{X_2}, and Z_{X_3} are the person's Z scores for the first, second, and third predictor variables, respectively.

2. (a) You figure the R^2 for predicting the criterion variable from a predetermined particular predictor variable (or group of predictor variables); then you figure the R^2 for predicting that criterion variable from a prediction rule that includes the original predictor variable (or variables) *plus* a new, additional predictor variable (or variables), and then figure the *difference* (the increase) in R^2 and its significance. You can continue this process for many steps. The focus is on how much each additional predictor or group of predictors adds to those added at the previous step.

   (b) To test a theory about how particular variables predict a criterion variable over and above particular previous ones.

3. (a) You do a series of regressions for each variable predicting the criterion and select the one that gives the highest R^2. If this is not significant, you stop. But if it is, you do another series of regressions, each including the first variable and one of the remaining variables; from these you select the two-variable regression that gives the highest R^2. If this is not a significant *increase* in R^2, you stop the process with one predictor variable. If it is a significant increase, you continue the process, searching for the best three-variable prediction rule that includes the first two plus one of the remaining. This process goes on until adding the best remaining variable does not make a significant increase in R^2.
(b) To sort out, from a large number of possible predictors, the subset that are most useful in predicting the criterion.
(c) The best subset of predictors in this sample might not be the best subset in the population.
4. (a) Both involve systematically adding variables to a multiple regression prediction rule and testing whether the addition at each stage is significant.
(b) In hierarchical regression, you add variables in a planned sequence and continue to the end regardless if additions at earlier stages are significant; stepwise regression is an exploratory procedure that adds a variable at each stage according to which turns out to be the best additional predictor among all remaining variables, and you stop when the addition of the best remaining one is not significant.

PARTIAL CORRELATION

partial correlation

Partial correlation is widely used in the social and behavioral sciences. Partial correlation is the amount of association between two variables, over and above the influence of one or more other variables. Suppose a sociologist wants to know how the stress people experience in married life is related to how long they have been married. However, the researcher realizes that part of what might make marital stress and marriage length go together is whether couples have children. Having children or not could make stress and length go together because those married longer are more likely to have children and having children may create marital stress. Thus, simply figuring the correlation between marital stress and marriage length would be misleading. The researcher wants to know the relation between stress and marriage length that would be found if everyone had the same number of children. Or to put it another way, the researcher wants somehow to subtract out the information provided by number of children from the information provided by marital stress and length.

holding constant

partialing out

controlling for

adjusting for

partial correlation coefficient

In this example, the researcher would figure a partial correlation between marital stress and length of marriage, **holding constant** number of children. Holding a variable constant is also called **partialing out, controlling for,** or **adjusting for** the variable held constant (such as number of children). These terms (holding constant, partialing out, etc.) all mean the same thing and are used interchangeably. The actual statistic for partial correlation is called the **partial correlation coefficient.** Like an ordinary correlation coefficient between two variables, it goes from -1 to $+1$. Just remember that unlike an ordinary correlation coefficient, one or more other variables is being controlled for.

Here is another way to understand partial correlations. In the marriage example, you could figure the ordinary correlation between stress and marriage length using only people who have no children, then figure an ordinary correlation between stress and marriage length for only those with one child, and so on. Each of these correlations, by itself, is not affected by differences in number of children. (This is because the people included within any one of these correlations all have the same number of children.) You could then figure a kind of average of these various correlations, each of which is not affected by number of children. This average of these correlations is the partial correlation. It is literally a correlation that *holds constant* the number of children. (The figuring for a partial correlation is fairly straightforward, and you do not actually have to figure all these individual correlations and average them. However, the result amounts to doing this.)

Researchers often use partial correlation to help sort out alternative explanations for the relations among variables. Suppose the sociologist found an ordinary correlation between marital stress and marriage length. The sociologist might want to use this result to support a theory that the effect of time (marriage length) is to make people feel more stress in their marriage because their partners take them for granted. The sociologist would also be aware that another possible explanation for what is going on is that when people are married longer, they are likely to have more children, and having more children might create stress in the marriage. If the correlation between stress and length holds up, even after controlling for number of children, this alternate explanation about children is made unlikely.

RELIABILITY

In the social and behavioral sciences, most variables are measured with questionnaires or systematic observations of what people do. Measures of these kinds are rarely perfectly consistent or stable over time. The degree of stability or consistency of a measure is called its **reliability.** Roughly speaking, the reliability of a measure is how much you would get the same result if you were to give the same measure again to the same person under the same circumstances. You will often see reliability statistics in research articles.

    reliability

One way to assess a measure's reliability is to use the measure with the same group of people twice. The correlation between the two testings is called **test–retest reliability.** However, this approach often is not practical or appropriate. For example, you can't use this approach if taking a test once would influence the second taking (such as with an intelligence test).

    test–retest reliability

For many measures, such as most questionnaires, you also can assess their reliability by correlating the average of the answers to half the questions with the average of the answers to the other half. For example, you could correlate the average score on all the odd-numbered questions with the average score on all the even-numbered questions. If the person is answering consistently, this should be a high correlation. This is called **split-half reliability.**

    split-half reliability

A problem with the split-half method is deciding which way to split the halves. Using odd-versus-even items makes sense in most situations, but by chance it could give too low or too high a correlation. Fortunately, there is a more general solution. You can divide the measure into halves in all possible ways and figure the correlation using each division, then average all these split-half correlations. A statistic called **Cronbach's alpha (α)** gives you what amounts to this average. Cronbach's alpha is the most widely used measure of reliability. Cronbach's alpha also can be thought of as telling you the overall internal consistency of the test, how much high responses go with highs and lows with lows over all the items in the measure. Thus, Cronbach's alpha is a measure of what is called the **internal consistency reliability** of a measure—the extent to which the items of a measure assess a common characteristic. In general, in the social and behavioral sciences, a good measure should have a Cronbach's alpha of at least .6 or .7 and preferably closer to .9.

    Cronbach's alpha (α)

    internal consistency reliability

Reliabilities are nearly always discussed when a research article is mainly about the creation of a new measure. For example, Valk, Post, Cools, and Shrijvers (2001) developed a measure of disability in elderly nursing home residents. The

TABLE 12–3 Domains: Means, Standard Deviations, Cronbach's Alpha, and Range

Scale	n	Items	Mean	Median	SD	Cronbach's Alpha	Range
Incontinence	112	4	70.1	81.2	32.5	.88	0–8
Mobility	112	3	48.6	40	35.8	.93	0–10
Resistance	111	1	53.1	66.6	41.0	—	0–3
Alertness	111	6	30.8	27.7	22.0	.84	0–18
Cognition	112	7	69.3	72.7	28.9	.78	0–11
ADL	96	3	75.9	87.5	31.4	.90	0–8
Perception	88	2	.30	0	0.65	.54	0–4

Source: Valk, M., Post, M. W. M., Cools, H. J. M., & Shrijvers, G. A. J. P. (2001). Measuring disability in nursing home residents: Validity and reliability of a newly developed instrument. *Journal of Gerontology: Psychological Sciences, 56B,* 187–191. Reprinted by permission of The Gerontological Society of America.

TABLE 12–4 Reproducibility of the Questionnaire: After One Week

Scale	Correlation
Cognition	0.89
Mobility	0.94
ADL	0.90
Alertness	0.85
Incontinence	0.89
Resistance	0.63
Perception	0.76

Note: Spearman correlation coefficients, $p < .001$.
Source: Valk, M., Post, M. W. M., Cools, H. J. M., & Shrijvers, G. A. J. P. (2001). Measuring disability in nursing home residents: Validity and reliability of a newly developed instrument. *Journal of Gerontology: Psychological Sciences, 56B,* 187–191. Reprinted by permission of The Gerontological Society of America.

factor analysis

factor

factor loading

test, which is filled out by staff about residents, initially included 26 items that assessed seven domains of functioning, such as Mobility (sample item, "Is the resident able to walk?") and Alertness (sample item, "Does the resident react if somebody speaks to him/her?"). They tested out their measure with 115 poorly functioning residents of Dutch nursing homes, with an average age of 81.5. All residents were assessed a second time a week later. Here is the reliability discussion from their results section:

> The associations of times with a domain, as measured by means of Cronbach's alpha, were obtained on each of the scales (lowest: Perception, 0.54; highest: Mobility, 0.93). Table [12–3] presents the mean scores, *SD,* median, and Cronbach's alpha of the domains. The test–retest reliability was good to excellent; see Table [12–4]. Correlation coefficients ranged from 0.63 to 0.94. (p. 188)

Looking at the tables, you can see, for example, that Alertness, with six items, has a Cronbach's alpha of .84 and a test–retest reliability (labeled "Reproducibility of the Questionnaire: After One Week") of .85. This is thus a quite adequately reliable scale. (Incidentally, you may have noticed from the note at the bottom of Table 12–4 that test–retest reliability was figured using the Spearman correlation. This is a rank-order correlation method of the kind discussed in Chapter 11. Valk et al. used this kind of correlation because the items used rank-order measurement. Ordinarily, however, these kinds of reliabilities are figured using ordinary correlation coefficients.)

FACTOR ANALYSIS

Suppose you have measured people on a large number of variables. (For example, you might have done a survey with questions about 85 different attitudes.) You use **factor analysis** to tell you which variables tend to clump together—which ones tend to be correlated with each other and not with other variables. Each such clump (group of variables) is called a **factor.** The correlation of an individual variable with a factor is called that variable's **factor loading** on that factor. Variables have loadings on each factor but usually will have high loadings on only one. Factor loadings range from −1, a perfect negative association with the factor, through 0, no relation to the factor, to +1, a perfect positive correlation with the factor. Normally, a variable is considered to contribute meaningfully to a factor only if it has a loading of at least about .3 (or below −.3).

The factor analysis is done using a fairly complex set of formulas that begin with the correlations among all the variables and end up with a set of factor loadings. (It also provides other information, including how much variance each factor accounts for of the total amount of variation among the variables.) There is, however, one subjective part of the process: the name the researcher gives to each factor. When reading about a factor analysis in a research article, think closely about the name the researcher gives to each factor. Do the names really do a good job of describing the variables that make up each factor?

Here is an example of a factor analysis. Koslowsky, Schwarzwald, and Ashuri (2001) gave 232 nurses in Israeli hospitals the following instructions:

> Think about a time when you were being supervised in doing some task. Suppose your supervisor asked you to do your job somewhat differently and, though you were initially reluctant, you did exactly what you were asked.
>
> On the following pages there are a number of reasons why you might have done so. . . . Decide how likely it would be that you complied for this reason. (p. 461)

The nurses responded on a 7-point scale from 1, "definitely not a reason," to 7, "definitely a reason," to items relating to 11 power sources, such as coercion or providing information. As part of their study, the researchers carried out a factor analysis of the 11 power sources. They reported the following results: "The analysis yielded a two-factor solution [see Table 12–5]. The first factor, which explained 41.9 percent of the variance, included seven power sources [see Table 12–5]. The second

TABLE 12–5 Factor Analysis Loadings for the Eleven Power Sources

Power sources by factor	Loadings	
	Factor 1	Factor 2
Harsh power bases		
Impersonal coercion	0.81	−0.17
Impersonal reward	0.80	0.05
Personal reward	0.78	0.31
Legitimate reciprocity	0.71	0.26
Personal coercion	0.66	0.32
Legitimate equity	0.61	0.17
Legitimate position	0.53	0.45
Soft power tactics		
Expertise	0.16	0.78
Information	−0.17	0.76
Reference	0.34	0.70
Legitimate dependence	0.36	0.56
Explained variance (%)	41.9	15.5
Internal consistency (alpha)	0.85	0.79

Source: Koslowsky, M., Schwarzwald, J., & Ashuri, S. (2001). On the relationship between subordinates' compliance to power sources and organisational attitudes. *Applied Psychology: An International Review, 50,* 455–476. Reprinted by permission of Blackwell Publishers Journals.

factor, which explained 15.5 percent of the variance, included four power bases [see Table 12–5]." (pp. 465–66)

For example, Interpersonal Coercion was included in the first factor because it had a high loading (.81) on this factor, but only a small loading (−.17) on the second factor. Information, on the other hand, was included in the second factor because it had a high loading on this factor (.76) but only a small loading (−.17) on the first factor. Notice, however, that some items were not so clearly part of one factor or the other, such as Legitimate Position, which had a loading of .53 on the first factor and .45 on the second. This makes sense, since having a legitimate right to use power is somewhere between the harshness of such things as coercion and the softness of persuading by providing information. Also notice that the names the researchers chose to give to the factors seem reasonable in light of the variables included in them, though it is always possible that other researchers might see the variables within each factor as having a different overall meaning. Finally, notice that at the bottom of the table they also give the internal consistency reliability (alpha), by which they mean Cronbach's alpha for the items in each factor (that is, the ones with high loadings on a factor) if you were to think of them as a scale.

HOW ARE YOU DOING?

1. (a) What is partial correlation? (b) What does it mean if a partial correlation is less than the original correlation? (c) What does it mean if a partial correlation is about the same as the original correlation? (d) How can partial correlation help sort out direction of causality in a correlational study?
2. (a) What is the reliability of a measure? (b) and (c) Not including split-half reliability, list and define two kinds of reliability. (d) How does Cronbach's alpha relate to split-half reliability?
3. In the Valk et al. (2001) example of reliability (see Tables 12–3 and 12–4), indicate which is the most reliable scale and give its reliabilities.
4. (a) When do you use a factor analysis? (b) What information does it give you? (c) What is a factor? (d) What is a factor loading? (e) What is the subjective part of factor analysis?
5. In the Koslowsky et al. (2001) example of factor analysis (see Table 12–5), what are personal reward's loadings on each factor?

ANSWERS:

1. (a) The correlation of two variables controlling for one or more other variables. (b) That the variable, or variables, controlled for account for some of the association between the original two variables. (c) That the variable, or variables, controlled for do not account for the correlation between the original two variables. (d) It helps test whether the correlation might be due to one or more additional variables causing the association between the original two variables.
2. (a) Its consistency and stability. (b) Test–retest reliability, which is how much the measure gives the same results when taken twice by the same people. (c) Internal consistency reliability (measured using Cronbach's alpha), which is the degree to which the items of a measure assess a common characteristic. (d) Cronbach's alpha is like the average of the correlations between all possible pairs of halves of the measure.
3. Mobility; internal consistency reliability (Cronbach's alpha) = .93; test–retest reliability (Spearman's correlation coefficient) = .94.
4. (a) When you have many measures of a group of people. (b) It tells you the groupings of variables that are highly correlated with each other but not very correlated with variables in other groupings. (c) One of these groupings. (d) The correlation of a variable with a factor. (e) Deciding what to name a factor based on the variables with high loadings on it.
5. The personal rewards loadings are .78 on the first factor and .31 on the second factor.

CAUSAL MODELING

As with factor analysis, you use causal modeling when you have measured people on a number of variables. Unlike factor analysis, the goal of causal modeling is to test whether the pattern of correlations among the variables in a sample fits with some specific theory of which variables are causing which.

Causal modeling techniques are widely used in the social and behavioral sciences. We first introduce the older (but still common) method of path analysis. It is also often called *ordinary path analysis* to distinguish it from the newer, more elaborate method of structural equation modeling (which is also in a sense a kind of path analysis) we describe in the next main section.

PATH ANALYSIS

In **path analysis,** you make a diagram with arrows connecting the variables. Each arrow, or **path,** shows what the researcher predicts to be the cause-and-effect connections between variables. Then, based on the correlations of these variables in a sample and the path diagram predicted by the researcher, you can figure path coefficients for each path. The **path coefficient** is like a standardized regression coefficient (a beta, β) in multiple regression. In fact, if the path diagram is a correct description of the causal relationship among the variables, the path coefficient tells you how much of a standard deviation change on the variable at the end of the arrow is produced by a 1 standard deviation change in the predictor variable at the start of the arrow. (Also note that a path coefficient is like a partial correlation, in that it is figured so that it partials out the influence of any other variables that have arrows to the variable at the end of the same arrow.)

path analysis

path

path coefficient

Here is an example. MacKinnon-Lewis, Starnes, Volling, and Johnson (1997) were interested in predictors of social acceptance by peers of 8- to 10-year-old boys. The main predictors they used were the child's rating of parental acceptance and rejection, peers' ratings of acceptance and aggression, and conflict with siblings as observed in a laboratory interaction. They tried several different possible causal models, and concluded that the best was what they called "Model 1."

> The standardized path coefficients of Model 1 are presented in Figure [12–1], which shows that siblings whose mothers were perceived and observed to be more rejecting were observed and reported to be more aggressive with one another than were siblings whose mothers were less rejecting. Moreover, boys who experienced more aggressive sibling interactions were more likely to be nominated by their peers as being aggressive and were less accepted by their peers. Although fathering failed to evince a direct influence on sibling aggression, an indirect effect was evidence as a result of the fact that less accepting fathering was related to more rejecting mothering. (p. 1027)

In this path diagram, the most important paths had significant coefficients (as shown by the asterisks in Figure 12–1) in the predicted directions. Thus, MacKinnon-Lewis et al. considered the results as encouraging support for their theory.

STRUCTURAL EQUATION MODELING

Structural equation modeling is a special elaboration of ordinary path analysis. It also involves a path diagram with arrows between variables and path coefficients for each arrow. However, structural equation modeling has several important advantages over the older path analysis method. One major advantage is that structural equation modeling gives you an overall measure of the fit between the theory (as described by the path diagram) and the correlations among the scores in your

structural equation modeling

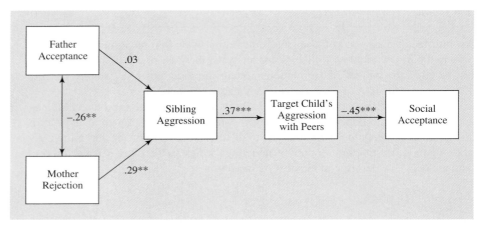

FIGURE 12–1   *Path model of associations among parenting variables, sibling aggres-sion, peer aggression, and social acceptance. Standardized path coefficients are given.* ***p < .01,* ****p < .001.*
Source: MacKinnon-Lewis, C., Starnes, R., Volling, B., & Johnson, S. (1997). Perceptions of parenting as predictors of boys' sibling and peer relations. *Developmental Psychology, 33,* 1024–1031. Copyright © 1997 by the American Psychological Association. Reprinted by permission.

fit index

sample. This measure of overall fit is called a **fit index.** There are several different fit indexes, but for most, a fit of .9 or higher is considered a good fit. (The maximum is usually 1.) Recently, a fit index that works a little differently has become widely used. It is usually referred to by its abbreviation, RMSEA (root mean square error of approximation). The *smaller* the RMSEA, the better the fit. Fits below .05 are considered to be very good, below about .10, good.

In structural equation modeling, you can also do a kind of significance test of this fit. We say a "kind of significance test" because the null hypothesis is that the theory fits. Thus, a significant result tells you that the theory does not fit. In other words, a researcher trying to demonstrate a theory hopes for a nonsignificant result in this significance test!

latent variable

A second major advantage of structural equation modeling over ordinary path analysis is that it uses what are called latent variables. A **latent variable** is not actually measured but stands for a true variable that you would like to measure but can only approximate with real-life measures. For example, a latent variable might be political conservatism, which the researcher tries to approximate with responses on a scale of political conservatism, contributions to the campaigns of politically conservative candidates, and reported voting behavior. No one of these measured variables by itself is a very good stand-in for political conservatism.

In structural equation modeling, the mathematics is set up so that a latent variable is a combination of the measured variables, combined in such a way as to use only what they have in common with each other. What they have in common is the true score, the underlying variable they are all getting at parts of. (A latent variable is actually like a factor in factor analysis, in that the factor is not directly measured itself, but it stands for a combination of several variables that make it up.)

In a structural equation modeling path diagram, the variables that actually are measured are usually shown in boxes. The latent variables are shown in circles or ovals. This is shown in Figure 12–2. Notice in the figure that the arrows from the latent variables (the ones in circles) go to the measured variables (the ones in boxes). The idea is that the latent variable is the underlying cause of the measured

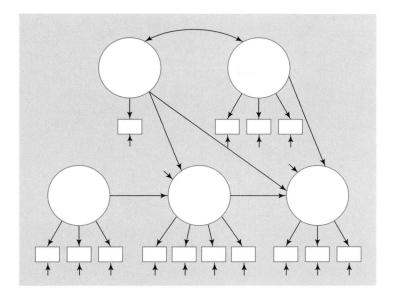

FIGURE 12-2   *A structural equation model path diagram.*

variables, the measured variables being the best we can do to measure the true latent variable.

Also notice that all of the other arrows between variables are between latent variables. Structural equation modeling works in this way: The measured variables are used to make up latent variables, and the main focus of the analysis is on the causal relations (the paths) between the latent variables. (Notice, finally, the short arrows that seem to come from nowhere. These show that there is also error—other unmeasured causes—affecting the variable. These "error" or "disturbance" arrows are sometimes left out in published articles to keep the figure simple.)

Here is an example of structrual equation modeling from a study by Senecal, Vallerand, and Guay (2001). They explain that

> The purpose of the present study was to propose and test a model of work–family conflict. . . . The model posits that positive interpersonal factors both at work (i.e., one's employer) and at home (e.g., one's spouse) influence work and family motivation. Moreover, the model proposes that low levels of self-determined family and work motivation both contributed to family alienation, which in turn influences the experience of work–family conflict. Finally, work–family conflict leads to feelings of emotional exhaustion. (p. 176)

The researchers measured the various variables in this model in a sample of 786 French Canadians who were all working at least part time and were living with a relationship partner and at least one child.

Figure 12–3 shows the diagram of their model and the path coefficients. Notice that each latent variable (shown in ovals) has two to four measured variables associated with it. For example, Feeling Valued by One's Partner has three indicators (labeled V1, V2, and V3). The most important path coefficients are those between the latent variables. For example, Feeling Valued by One's Partner has a substantial path coefficient of .47 leading to Motivation Toward Family Activities. This means that if the path model correctly shows the patterns of causality, a 1 standard deviation increase in Feeling Valued causes .47 of a standard deviation increase in Motivation Toward Family Activities.

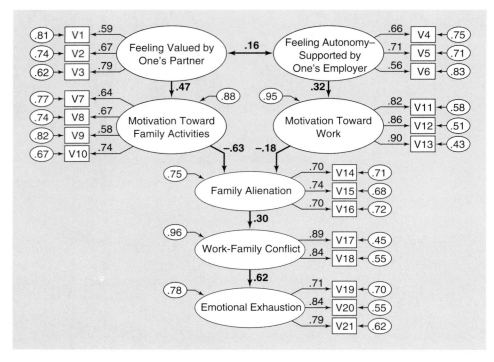

FIGURE 12–3 *Results of the hypothesized model.*
Source: Senecal, C., Vallerand, R. J., & Guay, F. (2001). Antecedents and outcomes of work–family conflict: Toward a motivational model. *Personality and Social Psychology Bulletin, 27,* 176–186. Reprinted by permission of Sage Publications, Inc.

Having laid out the model and figured the path coefficients, the authors then tested the fit of the correlations in their sample to the overall model: "The adequacy of the model was assessed by structural equation modeling . . ." (Senecal et al., 2001, p. 181). In addition to looking at specific path coefficients, Senecal et al. (2001) considered the overall fit of their model, noting that all hypothesized paths had significant coefficients in the predicted direction and "the CFI = .94 and the NNFI = .93 [two fit indexes] were acceptable" (p. 182).

A KEY LIMITATION OF CAUSAL MODELING

It is important to realize how little magic there is behind these wonderful methods. They still rely entirely on a researcher's deep thinking. All the predicted paths in a path analysis diagram can be significant and a structural equation model can have an excellent fit, and yet it is still quite possible that other patterns of causality could work equally well or better.

Alternatives could have arrows that go in the opposite direction or make different connections, or the pattern could include additional variables not in the original diagram. Any kind of causal modeling shows at best that the correlations in the sample are consistent with the theory. The same correlations could also be consistent with quite different theories. Ideally, a researcher tries out plausible alternative theories and finds that the correlations in the sample do not fit them well. Nevertheless, there can always be alternative theories the researcher did not think of to try.

1. What is the purpose of causal modeling?
2. (a) What is a path diagram? (b) What is a path? (c) What is a path coefficient? (d) In an ordinary path analysis, how do you evaluate whether there is a good fit of the model to the correlations in the sample?
3. (a) What is a fit index? (b) What is considered a good fit on most fit indexes? (c) What is considered a very good fit on the RMSEA?
4. (a) What is a latent variable? (b) What is its relation to measured variables? (c) What is the usual direction of causality between a latent variable and its associated measured variables? (d) Why?
5. How is the significance test in structural equation modeling different from an ordinary significance test?
6. What is a major limitation of structural equation modeling?

ANSWERS:

1. To test whether the correlations among the variables in a sample are consistent with a predicted pattern of cause and effect among those variables.
2. (a) A drawing of the predicted causal relationships among variables, showing causality as arrows from cause to effect. (b) A predicted causal relation between two variables, shown as an arrow from the predicted cause to the predicted effect. (c) The size of the causal influence figured based on the correlations among the variables in the sample and assuming the predicted relations in the path diagram are correct. Assuming the pattern of the path diagram is correct, it tells you the fraction of a standard deviation change in the effect variable produced by a 1 standard deviation change in the causal variable. (d) You check whether the path coefficients are all in the predicted direction and significant.
3. (a) A number that tells you how well the predicted pattern of cause and effect in the path diagram is consistent with the correlations in the sample. (b) .90 or higher. (d) below .05.
4. (a) A variable that is not directly measured, but which stands for the true value of the concept the variable is about. (b) It represents what a group of measured variables have in common. (c) From latent variable to measured variables. (d) Because the underlying latent variable is the cause of the observed, measured variables.
5. In structrual equation modeling, a significant result means there is a bad fit.
6. No matter how good the fit, it is possible that some other model would fit equally well.

PROCEDURES THAT COMPARE GROUPS

So far in this chapter, we have looked at statistical procedures about associations among variables, essentially fancy elaborations of correlation and regression. Now we turn to procedures that focus on differences between group means, essentially fancy elaborations of the analysis of variance (Chapter 10).

In such procedures, there are two main kinds of variables. One is the kind that divides the groups from each other, such as experimental versus control group in a *t* test or the different groups in an analysis of variance. A variable of this kind that we used in Chapter 10 was the experimental condition in the criminal record study (which compared participants in the Criminal Record group, the Clean Record group, and the No Information group). A variable like this, especially when which group a person is in is based on the researcher having randomly assigned participants to conditions, is called an **independent variable.** (Even when there are just two groups, such as an experimental and a control group in an experiment, the independent variable is the variable that distinguishes the experimental from the control group.) In a two-way analysis of variance, there are actually two independent variables—for example, mood (sad versus neutral) and stereotype (appropriate versus inappropriate) in the Lambert, Khan, Lickel, and Fricke (1997) study of stereotypes we considered in Chapter 10.

independent variable

dependent variable

The other kind of variable in a study that compares groups is the variable that is measured—in the criminal record example it was ratings of innocence; in the Lambert et al. (1997) study, it was ratings of how likely the participant would be to hire the person. A variable like this, which is measured and represents the effect of the experimental procedure, is called a **dependent variable.** It is *dependent* in the sense that any participant's score on this variable depends on what happens in the experiment.

Note that an independent variable in a *t* test or analysis of variance is like a predictor variable in regression, and a dependent variable in a *t* test or analysis of variance is like the criterion variable in regression. Often, in fact, when discussing regression results, even in formal research articles, researchers use the independent– dependent variable terminology instead of the predictor–criterion variable terminology. But it is rare for researchers doing a *t* test or analysis of variance to use the predictor–criterion variable terminology.

We did not need to introduce these terms (independent and dependent variables) before because the situations we considered were relatively straightforward. However, it would be difficult to understand the remaining procedures covered in this chapter without knowing about the difference between independent and dependent variables.

ANALYSIS OF COVARIANCE (ANCOVA)

analysis of covariance (ANCOVA)

covariate

One of the most widely used of the elaborations on the analysis of variance is the **analysis of covariance (ANCOVA).** In this procedure, you do an ordinary analysis of variance, but one that adjusts the dependent variable for the effect of unwanted additional variables. The analysis of covariance does for the analysis of variance what partial correlation does for ordinary correlation. Each of the variables controlled for (or *partialed out* or *held constant*) is called a **covariate.** The rest of the results are interpreted like any other analysis of variance.

Here is an example. Capaldi and Patterson (1991) compared the adjustment of elementary school boys who had experienced different levels of parental transitions since birth. The different levels of parental transition were no transition, loss of father, new stepfather, and two or more new stepfathers. The authors reported, "An ANOVA showed that there were significant differences among the transition groups, $F(3, 170)$ = 7.53, p < .001." (The pattern of means for the four levels was in the predicted direction of the more parental transitions, the poorer the adjustment of the boy.)

However, Capaldi and Patterson (1991) also wanted to take into account the fact that the boys in the four transition levels came from families of different socioeconomic status (SES) and different income levels. Could these differences, and not the differences in transition level, be the underlying cause of the difference in adjustment?

> Next, we tested the hypothesis that the differences among transition groups were primarily a function of the differences in SES and income. To test this assumption, an ANOVA was run with SES and per capita income as covariates [an ANCOVA]. The difference among the transition groups remained significant, $F(5, 167) = 4.0$, p < .01. (pp. 492–493)

The pattern of means was also the same in this analysis as in the original. Thus, the differences among the transition groups were not caused by differences in socioeconomic status or income.

MULTIVARIATE ANALYSIS OF VARIANCE (MANOVA) AND MULTIVARIATE ANALYSIS OF COVARIANCE (MANCOVA)

In all of the procedures discussed so far in this book, there is only one dependent variable. There may be two or more independent variables, as in the factorial analysis of variance. However, in all the situations we have considered, there has been only one dependent variable.

In this section we introduce **multivariate statistics,** which are procedures used when you have two or more dependent variables. We focus on the two most widely used multivariate procedures. These are multivariate versions of the analysis of variance and the analysis of covariance. That is, these are versions of the analysis of variance and covariance that are able to handle more than one dependent variable.

multivariate statistics

Multivariate analysis of variance (MANOVA) is an analysis of variance in which there is more than one dependent variable. Usually, the dependent variables are different measures of approximately the same thing, such as three different political involvement scales or two different reading ability tests. Suppose you study three groups and measure each participant on four dependent variables. The MANOVA would give an overall F and significance level for the difference among the three groups, in terms of how much they differ on the combination of the four dependent variables.

multivariate analysis of variance (MANOVA)

When you do find an overall significant difference among groups with MANOVA, this says that the groups differ on the combination of dependent variables. You then would want to know whether the groups differ on any or all of the dependent variables considered individually. Thus, you usually follow up a MANOVA with an ordinary analyses of variance for each of the dependent variables. These individual analyses of variance are called *univariate analyses of variance* (as opposed to the overall multivariate analyses), because each has only one dependent variable.

Here is an example of a MANOVA. Frydenberg and colleagues (2003) studied differences in how Australian, Colombian, German, and Palestinian adolescents cope with their problems. The researchers looked at three types of coping: "productive coping," which involves focusing on the problem; "nonproductive coping," which involves avoiding the problem; and "reference to others," in which a person asks other people for help. They described their results as follows:

> To consider the influence of Nationality on coping style, a MANOVA was completed using the 3 coping styles as dependent variables and Nationality as the independent variable. . . . The results show a significant multivariate effect for Nationality (F (9, 1692) = 47.99; $p < .001$). (p. 63)

Having identified an overall difference in coping style among the adolescents from the different countries, the researchers then wanted to sort out effects on specific dependent variables. The results of the follow-up univariate ANOVAs indicated that "All univariate tests were significant" (p. 63). For example, in one analysis, the researchers reported that "Palestinians used this [productive coping] style more than did other students. Australian and Colombian subjects, while not differing in their mean use of this style, used it more than German subjects" (p. 63).

MULTIVARIATE ANALYSIS OF COVARIANCE

An analysis of covariance in which there is more than one dependent variable is called a **multivariate analysis of covariance (MANCOVA).** The difference between it and an ordinary analysis of covariance is just like the difference between a

multivariate analaysis of covariance (MANCOVA)

MANOVA and an ordinary analysis of variance. Also, you can think of a MAN-COVA as a MANOVA with covariates (variables adjusted for).

OVERVIEW OF STATISTICAL TECHNIQUES

Table 12–6 lays out the various procedures considered in this chapter, along with the other parametric procedures covered throughout the book. Just to prove to yourself how much you have learned, cover the right-hand column and play "Name That Statistic."

HOW ARE YOU DOING?

1. In a t test or analysis of variance, (a) what is the independent variable, and (b) what is the dependent variable? (c) How do independent and dependent variables match up with criterion and predictor variables?
2. (a) What is an analysis of covariance? (b) How is it like partial correlation? (c) What is a covariate?
3. How are multivariate statistics unlike all of the procedures covered previously in this book?
4. (a) How does a multivariate analysis of variance differ from an ordinary analysis of variance? (b) After finding a significant effect in a MANOVA, what is the usual next step? (c) How does a multivariate analysis of covariance differ from an ordinary analysis of covariance?
5. What method would you use if you had more than one independent variable, only one dependent variable, and one or more covariates?

ANSWERS:

1. (a) The variable that divides the groups. (b) The variable that is measured. (c) The independent variable is like the predictor variable; the dependent variable is like the criterion variable.

| TABLE 12–6 | Major Statistical Techniques | | | |

Association or Difference	Number of Independent or Predictor Variables	Number of Dependent or Criterion Variables	Any Variables Controlled?	Name of Technique
Association	1	1	No	Bivariate correlation/regression
Association	Any number	1	No	Multiple regression (including hierarchical and stepwise regression)
Association	1	1	Yes	Partial correlation
Association	Many, not differentiated		No	Reliability coefficients, Factor analysis
Association	Many, with specified causal patterns			Path analysis, Structural equation modeling
Difference	1	1	No	One-way ANOVA, t test
Difference	Any number	1	No	Factorial ANOVA
Difference	Any number	1	Yes	ANCOVA
Difference	Any number	Any number	No	MANOVA
Difference	Any number	Any number	Yes	MANCOVA

BOX 12–1   The Golden Age of Statistics: Four Guys around London

In the last chapter of his little book *The Statistical Pioneers,* James Tankard (1984) discusses the interesting fact that the four most common statistical techniques were created by four Englishmen born within 68 years of each other, three of whom worked in the vicinity of London (and the fourth, Gosset, stuck at his brewery in Dublin, nevertheless visited London to study and kept in good touch with all that was happening in that city). What were the reasons?

First, Tankard feels that their closeness and communication were important for creating the "critical mass" of minds sometimes associated with a golden age of discovery or creativity. Second, as is often the case with important discoveries, each man faced difficult practical problems or "anomalies" that pushed him to the solution at which he arrived. (None simply set out to invent a statistical method in itself.)

Tankard also discusses three important social factors specific to this "golden age of statistics." First, there was the role of biometrics, which was attempting to test the theory of evolution mathematically. Biometrics had its influence through Galton's reading of Darwin and Galton's subsequent influence on Pearson. Second, this period saw the beginning of mass hiring by industry and agriculture of university graduates with advanced mathematical training. Third, since the time of Isaac Newton, Cambridge University had been a special, centralized source of brilliant mathematicians for England. They could spread out through British industry and still, through their common alma mater, remain in contact with students and each other and up to date with the most recent breakthroughs.

Today is also an interesting time for statistics. After little change for 30 years, the computer has made possible all kinds of new statistical methods. The fundamentals developed in the Golden Age are mainly what you have learned in this book. They probably will remain the fundamentals for a long time to come. Yet what can be done beyond the fundamentals is changing rapidly. If you go on to take an advanced statistics course, much of what you learn will be procedures developed in the last decade or two. These ideas could well revolutionize the research possibilities open to behavioral and social scientists in the years to come. If we could look back from the future, we would probably say we now live in another Golden Age of Statistics.

---

2. (a) An analysis of variance that controls (or adjusts for or partials out) one or more variables. (b) It finds results after controlling for another variable. (c) The variable that is partialed out (or controlled for or adjusted for).
3. They have more than one dependent variable.
4. (a) A multivariate analysis of variance has more than one dependent variable. (b) Carry out a series of univariate analyses of variance—that is, individual analyses of variance for each dependent variable. (c) A multivariate analysis of covariance has more than one dependent variable.
5. Analysis of covariance.

HOW TO READ RESULTS INVOLVING UNFAMILIAR STATISTICAL TECHNIQUES

Based on this chapter and what you have learned throughout this book, you should be well prepared to read and understand, at least in a general way, the results in most research articles in the social and behavioral sciences. However, you will still now and then come up against new techniques (and sometimes unfamiliar names for old techniques). This happens even to well-seasoned researchers. So what do you do when you run into something you have never heard of before?

First, don't panic. Usually, you can figure out the basic idea. Almost always there will be a *p* level and it should be clear just what pattern of results is being considered significant or not. In addition, there will usually be some indication of the degree of association or the size of the difference.

Suppose you really can't figure out anything about a statistical technique used in a research article. In that situation, you can try to look up the procedure in a statistics book. Intermediate and advanced statistics textbooks are sometimes a good bet, but we have to warn you that trying to make sense of an intermediate or advanced text on your own can be difficult. Many such texts are heavily mathematically oriented. Even a quite accessible textbook will use its own set of symbols. Thus, it can be hard to make sense of a description of a particular method without having read the whole book. Perhaps a better solution in this situation is to ask for help from a professor or graduate student. If you know the basics as you have learned them in this book, you should be able to understand the essentials of their explanations.

If you are often coming upon statistics you don't understand, the best solution is to take more statistics courses. Usually, the next course after this one would be an intermediate statistics course in your particular major. In fact, some people find statistics so fascinating that they choose to make a career of it. You might too!

More generally, new statistical methods are being invented constantly. Social and behavioral scientists all encounter unfamiliar numbers and symbols in the research articles they read. They puzzle them out, and so will you. We say that with confidence because you have arrived, safe and knowledgeable, at the back pages of this book. You have mastered a thorough introduction to a complex topic. That should give you complete confidence that with a little time and attention you can understand anything further in statistics. Congratulations on your accomplishment.

SUMMARY

1. In hierarchical multiple regression, predictor variables are included in the prediction rule in a planned, sequential fashion. This allows you to determine the contribution of each successive variable over and above those already included. Stepwise multiple regression is an exploratory procedure in which potential predictor variables are searched in order to find the best predictor; then the remaining variables are searched for the predictor that, in combination with the first, produces the best prediction. This process continues until adding the best remaining variable does not provide a significant improvement.

2. Partial correlation is the correlation between two variables while holding one or more other variables constant.

3. Reliability coefficients measure how much scores on a test are internally consistent (usually with Cronbach's alpha) or consistent over time (test–retest reliability).

4. Factor analysis identifies groupings of variables, called factors, that correlate maximally with each other and minimally with other variables. A factor loading is the correlation of a variable with a factor.

5. Causal modeling examines whether the correlations among several variables in a sample are consistent with a systematic, hypothesized pattern of causal relationships among them. Path analysis describes these relationships with arrows, each pointing from cause to effect. Each arrow has a path coefficient indicating the influence of the theorized causal variable on the theorized effect variable. Structural equation modeling is an advanced version of path analysis that in-

cludes latent, unmeasured variables (each of which consists of the common elements of several measured variables). It also provides measures of the overall fit of the hypothesized causal pattern to the correlations in the sample.

6. In a *t* test, analysis of variance, and other procedures that compare groups, variables that divide the groups and are considered the cause are called independent variables; variables that are measured and considered the effect are called dependent variables.

7. The analysis of covariance (ANCOVA) is an analysis of variance that controls for one or more variables (called covariates). The multivariate analysis of variance (MANOVA) is an analysis of variance with two or more dependent variables. The multivariate analysis of covariance (MANCOVA) is an analysis of covariance with two or more dependent variables.

8. It is often possible to get the main idea of an unfamiliar statistical procedure by keeping in mind that it probably tells you about association among variables or differences among groups, that *p* values tell you about the significance of that association or difference, and that you will probably be given some numbers from which you can get a sense of the degree of association or amount of difference.

KEY TERMS

hierarchical multiple
  regression (p. 378)
stepwise multiple
  regression (p. 379)
partial correlation (p. 382)
holding constant (p. 382)
partialing out (p. 382)
controlling for (p. 382)
adjusting for (p. 382)
partial correlation
  coefficient (p. 382)
reliability (p. 383)
test–retest reliability
  (p. 383)
split-half reliability
  (p. 383)

Cronbach's alpha (α)
  (p. 383)
internal consistency
  reliability (p. 383)
factor analysis (p. 384)
factor (p. 384)
factor loading (p. 384)
path analysis (p. 387)
path (p. 387)
path coefficient (p. 387)
structural equation
  modeling (p. 387)
fit index (p. 388)
latent variable (p. 388)
independent variable
  (p. 391)

dependent variable
  (p. 392)
analysis of covariance
  (ANCOVA) (p. 392)
covariate (p. 392)
multivariate statistics
  (p. 393)
multivariate analysis of
  variance (MANOVA)
  (p. 393)
multivariate analaysis
  of covariance
  (MANCOVA) (p. 393)

PRACTICE PROBLEMS

For the problems below that ask you to explain results, you need to explain only the general meaning of the results, using only the same level of detail as used when the procedures were described in the chapter. You do not need to describe the logic of the statistical procedures covered here in the way that you have been doing in previous chapters. For answers to Set I problems, see pp. 439–41.

SET I

1. Part of a study conducted by Lindzey, Mize, and Pettit (1997) examined how well mutuality (balance) in father–child interaction predicted social competence in preschool children. In this study, each child and his or her father were observed interacting in a standardized situation. The interactions were rated in

ways that gave measures of who initiates play activities and the mutuality of complying with each other's initiation of play activities.

The researchers also had the children's teachers rate each child's social competence. The researchers found a clear correlation between father–child mutuality and the teacher's social-competence rating for the child. However, the researchers were concerned that the measure of mutuality might be mixed up with the amount that children and fathers each initiated individually.

> We therefore conducted a series of hierarchical regression analyses to examine whether father–child mutual compliance . . . made unique contributions to the prediction of children's social competence after taking account of each individual's behavior. . . . Father initiation rate and child initiation rate were entered first and accounted for 3 percent ($p = .57$) of the variance. Father–child mutual compliance was entered second and accounted for an additional, significant 18 percent ($p = .01$) of the variance in teacher-rated social competence. (pp. 532–533)

Explain this method and result to a person who is familiar in a general way with ordinary multiple regression but who has never heard of hierarchical multiple regression.

2. Mooney, Sherman, and Lo Presto (1991) were interested in what predicts women's adjustment to college. Thus, they studied 82 women who were in the fourth week of their first semester at college. The women in the study were all living away from home. The predictor variables were distance from home (in miles), perceived distance from home (a scale from *just right* to *too far*), a self-esteem scale, and an "academic locus of control" scale that measures how much a person feels in control over being successful at school. One purpose of the study was to find out whether all of these variables made their own unique contributions to predicting college adjustment. And if not all of them, which ones? The authors describe the procedure they used as follows:

> For this analysis, a stepwise procedure was employed. . . . Three predictors were retained: academic locus of control, perceived distance from home, and self-esteem. . . . With these variables in the equation, 59% of the variance in the dependent variable was accounted for ($R = .77$, $R^2 = .59$ . . .). The standardized beta coefficients [of the regression equation including these three predictor variables] indicated that academic locus of control was weighted the most, followed by self-esteem and perceived distance. (p. 447)

Explain this method and result to a person who is familiar in a general way with ordinary multiple regression but is not familiar with stepwise multiple regression.

3. Zimmer-Gembeck, Siebenbruner, and Collins (2001) studied dating practices in a sample of 16-year-olds in Minneapolis. As part of their study they examined the relation of dating involvement, experience, and quality, with various aspects of self-concept and self-worth (that is, how positively the 16-year-olds rated themselves on such things as scholastic competence, social acceptance, etc.). However, the researchers were concerned that the correlations among these variables would be inappropriately influenced by differences in appearance of physical maturity (how old the person looks). Thus, their results, shown in Table 12–7, provide correlations "controlling for appearance of physical maturity" (p. 327). Explain this method and the pattern of a few example results to a person who is familiar with correlation and multiple regression, but is unfamiliar with partial correlation.

4. Boyd and Gullone (1997) studied anxiety and depression in a sample of 783 adolescents attending schools in and around Melbourne, Australia. To measure

TABLE 12–7 Partial Correlations (Controlling for Appearance of Physical Maturity) of Dating and Self-Concept at Age 16

Self-concept/self-worth	Overinvolvement with dating	Level of dating experience	Quality of romantic relationship
Scholastic competence	−0.10	0.08	−0.03
Social acceptance	0.04	0.24**	0.29**
Physical appearance	0.06	0.24**	0.11
Job competence	−0.12	0.12	0.07
Romantic appeal	0.10	0.35***	0.36***
Behavioral conduct	−0.33***	−0.17*	−0.04
Close friendship	0.00	0.09	0.09
Global self-worth	−0.11	0.05	0.18*

N ranged from 125 (when examining quality of romantic relationships) to 166.
*$p < 0.05$, **$p < 0.01$, ***$p < 0.001$
Source: Zimmer-Gembeck, M. J., Siebenbruner, J., & Collins, A. W. (2001). Diverse aspects of dating: Associations with psychosocial functioning from early to middle adolescence. *Journal of Adolescence, 24,* 313–336. Copyright 2001, with permission of Elsevier.

anxiety, they used the Revised Children's Manifest Anxiety Scale (RCMAS). The RCMAS measures a number of different domains of anxiety (such as physiological anxiety and anxiety related to social concerns). In discussing the measure in their methods section, they note the following: "Alpha coefficient reliability estimates of internal consistency for the RCMAS [domains] range from .42 to .87" (p. 192). Explain these results to someone who is familiar with correlation but is unfamiliar with reliability or the statistics associated with it.

5. Fawzi et al. (1997) studied whether the usual way of thinking about posttraumatic stress disorder (PTSD), as described in the fourth edition of the standard *Diagnostic and Statistical Manual of Mental Disorders* (DSM-IV), applies to Vietnamese refugees in the United States. As part of their study, 74 refugees were interviewed (in their native language) regarding various PTSD symptoms and the traumatic events they had experienced, such as torture. As expected, the number of PTSD symptoms correlated with the number of traumatic events. In a further analysis of the pattern of symptoms (which symptoms go together with which), they conducted a factor analysis that resulted in four factors.

In correspondence with the DSM-IV, the first three factors represented dimensions of arousal, avoidance, and reexperiencing, respectively (see Table [12–8]). However, in contrast to the DSM-IV defined subcategories where avoidance represents one dimension of symptomatology, avoidance appeared to be separated into two factors in this sample. The second factor reflected avoidance associated with general withdrawal or numbing of responsiveness, with high factor loadings for "unable to feel emotions" and "less interest in daily activities." The fourth factor reflected avoidance of stimuli related to the traumatic event(s). (p. 104)

Explain these results to a person who is familiar with correlation but is unfamiliar with factor analysis.

6. Williamson, Shaffer, and the Family Relationships in Late Life Project (2001) studied 98 wives and 44 husbands who were caring for an elderly spouse living at home who was impaired in some way, such as with Alzheimer's disease. The research was testing a theory about what causes and what averts potentially harmful

TABLE 12–8	Factor Loadings for Principal Components Analysis [Factor Analysis] of PTSD DSM-IV Symptoms for 74 Vietnamese Refugees

Symptom Dimension	Factor Loading
Arousal	
Recurrent nightmares	.79
Difficulty concentrating	.78
Feeling irritable/outburst of anger	.77
Inability to remember parts of the most traumatic events	.74
Trouble sleeping	.73
Avoiding activities that remind you of traumatic events	.70
Feeling jumpy, easily startled	.67
% Variance explained	44%
Avoidance/withdrawal	
Unable to feel emotions	.79
Less interest in daily activities	.70
Feeling detached or withdrawn	.65
Feeling jumpy, easily startled	.51
Feeling as if you don't have a future	.51
% Variance explained	24%
Reexperiencing	
Recurrent thoughts/memories of most terrifying events	.83
Feeling as though the event is happening again	.83
Sudden emotional or physical reaction when reminded of most traumatic events	.57
% Variance explained	22%
Avoidance of stimuli related to trauma event(s)	
Avoiding thoughts or feelings associated with traumatic events	.71
% Variance explained	11%

Source: Fawzi, M. C. S., Pham, T., Lin, L., Nguyen, T. V., Ngo, D., Murphy, E., & Mollica, R. F. (1997). The validity of posttraumatic stress disorder among Vietnamese refugees. *Journal of Traumatic Stress,* 10, 101–108. Copyright 1997 by the International Society for Traumatic Stress Studies. Reprinted by permission.

behavior by the caregiver toward the partner. Figure 12–4 shows their path analysis diagram of the predicted pattern of cause-and-effect relationships (along with the path coefficients figured from their results) among these different variables. Explain the method they used, illustrating it with some sample results, to a person who is familiar with multiple regression and partial correlation in a general way but not with path analysis.

7. Aron, Aron, and Allen (1998) studied experiences of unreciprocated love, loving someone who does not love you. One of their predictions focused on the intensity of the experience (how much you think about it, how much it disrupts your life). The researchers hypothesized that intensity would be predicted by desirability (how much the lover thought a relationship with the beloved would be wonderful), probability (how much the beloved had led the lover to believe a relationship might develop), and desirability of the state (how much the lover thought it was desirable to be in love, even though it was not reciprocated). Aron et al. carried out a structural equation model analysis testing this model. The results are shown in Figure 12–5.

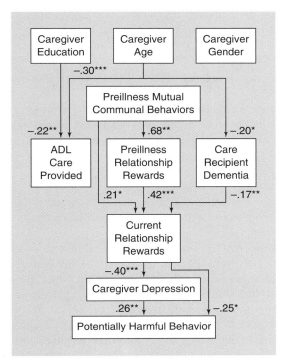

FIGURE 12–4   *Significant pathways emerging in path analyses predicting potentially harmful caregiver behavior. ADL = activities of daily living.* * *p* < .05, ** *p* < .01, *** *p* < .001.
Source: Williamson, G. M., Shaffer, D. R., & The Family Relationships in Late Life Project. (2001). Relationship quality and potentially harmful behaviors by spousal caregivers: How we were then, how we are now. *Psychology and Aging, 16,* 217–226. Copyright © by The American Psychological Association. Reprinted with permission of the authors and The American Psychological Association.

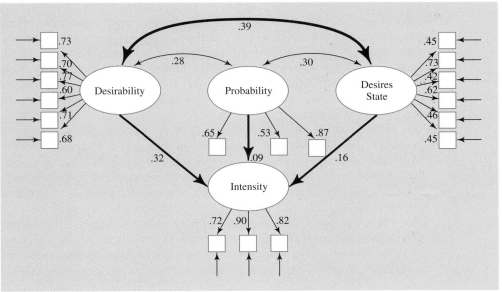

FIGURE 12–5   *Latent variable model based on a three-factor framework of motivation in unreciprocated love that was fitted to data for 743 participants who reported experiencing unreciprocated love. NOTE: Bentler-Bonnett normed fixed index (NFI) = .90; non-normed fit index (NNFI) = .92; average standardized residuals = .04; χ^2 (129) = 430.88; p < .01. All parameter estimates shown were significantly different from 0, at least at the .05 level. The key result is that each of the major causal paths to intensity, from desirability, probability, and desirability of the state, were positive and significant, confirming the hypothesis that each of these variables independently predicts intensity.*
Source: Aron, A., Aron, E. N., & Allen, J. (1998). Motivations for unreciprocated love. *Personality and Social Psychology Bulletin, 24,* 787–796. Reprinted by permission of Sage Publications, Inc.

(a) Explain the pattern of results. (b) Using this diagram as an example, explain the general principles of interpreting a path diagram to a person who understands multiple regression in a general way but who is unfamiliar with path diagrams or structural equation modeling.

8. In each of the following studies, which variable is the independent variable and which is the dependent variable?

   (a) A study examining the number of households that recycle in a neighborhood receiving a recycling awareness campaign compared to the number of households that recycle in a neighborhood that does not receive the campaign.

   (b) A study looking at heart rate change while watching one of three kinds of movies (horror movie, love story, or comedy).

   (c) A study of number of touches between two infants playing in the same room, comparing when their mothers are present versus when their mothers are not present.

9. Roeser, Vander Wolf, and Strobel (2001) conducted a cross-cultural study of self-esteem comparing adolescents from the United States and the Netherlands. In their article they had a section labeled "Covariates" in which they note that "A measure of social desirability was included in each analysis because prior research has shown that self-report measures of mental health often elicit socially desirable response patterns." (p. 120). (That is, social desirability was a kind of nuisance variable they were concerned would disturb their pattern of results.) They then reported a series of analyses of covariance. Here is one of their results: "ANCOVA results for the CBCL [a measure of emotional/behavioral problems] . . . revealed only one significant effect: After covarying out the effect of social desirability . . . , American adolescents reported significantly more externalizing problems than their Dutch peers, $F(1, 136) = 9.80$, $p < .01$" (p. 123). Explain what is being done, using this result as an example, to someone who is familiar with ordinary analysis of variance and with partial correlation, but who is not familiar with the analysis of covariance.

10. Gire (1997) studied the preferred methods of resolving conflicts, comparing people in individualistic versus collectivistic cultures. Participants were 90 Nigerians (Nigeria was considered an example of a relatively collectivist society) and 95 Canadians (Canada was considered an example of a relatively individualistic society). All participants answered questions about how much they preferred each of five methods of resolving conflicts. Half the participants in each country answered the questions regarding an interpersonal conflict (a conflict between two neighbors) and half regarding an intergroup conflict (between two groups of neighbors). This created a two-way factorial design: the two independent variables were culture (Nigeria vs. Canada) and the type of conflict interaction (interpersonal vs. intergroup). The five dependent variables were five measures of conflict resolution preferences.

These data were analyzed by using the multivariate analysis of variance (MANOVA) procedure. The 2-way MANOVA yielded a significant main effect of culture $F(5, 173) = 6.37$, $p < .001$. An examination of the univariate analyses and the means suggests that Nigerians preferred negotiation to a greater extent than Canadians, while the reverse was the case on arbitration, as predicted. . . . The univariate analyses and the means, presented in Table [12–9], reveal that significant differences occurred on three procedures—threats, acceptance of the situation, and arbitration. (p. 41)

TABLE 12–9 Method Preferences as a Function of Culture and Type of Conflict				
	Nigerians		Canadians	
Method	IP	IG	IP	IG
Threats*	2.09	1.50	1.35	1.61
Accept the situation*	2.72	3.16	3.43	2.71
Negotiation	6.07	6.11	5.56	5.64
Mediation	4.70	4.77	4.87	5.13
Arbitration*	3.05	4.90	5.20	5.42

Note: One asterisk (∗) indicates that the means of the culture by type of conflict interaction on a given method was significant at $p < .05$ level. The larger the number, the higher the preference for the method. IP = Interpersonal Conflict; IG = Intergroup Conflict.

Source: Gire, J. T. (1997). The varying effect of individualism–collectivism on reference for methods of conflict resolution. *Canadian Journal of Behavioural Science, 29,* 38–43. Copyright 1997 by the Canadian Psychological Association. Reprinted by permission.

Explain these results to someone who understands factorial analysis of variance but is not familiar with multivariate analysis of variance.

11. For each of the following studies, what would be the most appropriate statistical technique?

(a) A study in which the researcher has a complex theory of the pattern of cause and effect among several variables.

(b) A study of the association between two variables.

(c) A study of whether a questionnaire scale is internally consistent (that is, that the items correlate with each other) and consistent over time in giving the same result.

(d) A two-way factorial design with three dependent measures.

(e) A study in which seven variables have been measured that are thought to predict a particular criterion variable, and the researcher wants to determine which variables contribute significantly to the prediction (but has no theory about which ones might be the most likely).

(f) A study in which a researcher measures 16 variables and wants to explore whether there are any simpler groupings of variables underlying these 16.

(g) A study in which an experimental group and a control group are being compared on a single dependent variable.

(h) A study comparing five groups of individuals on a single dependent variable.

(i) A study of the effect of several predictor variables on a single criterion variable, in which the researcher has a specific theory about their relative importance and wants to check whether each successive additional predictor adds anything to what the preceding variables predict.

SET II

12. Contrada and colleagues (2001) conducted a study of ethnicity-related stress in a sample of 333 undergraduates. Ethnicity-related stress refers to conditions that are perceived as threatening due to a person's membership of an ethnic group. The researchers focused on three types of ethnicity-related stress: *ethnic discrimination,* defined as "unfair treatment attributed to one's ethnicity";

stereotype confirmation concern, defined as chronic concerns about confirming negative stereotypes about one's ethnic group; and *own-group conformity pressure,* defined as "the experience of feeling pressured . . . by expectations from members of one's ethnic group . . . [about] appropriate or inappropriate behavior for that group." Contrada and colleagues studied the relation between these three types of ethnicity-related stress and students' reports of experiencing symptoms of depression (such as being sad, having low energy, and losing interest in activities). (The researchers used a measure of depression that gave a total score of depressive symptoms for each student.) Table 12–10 shows the results of their five-step hierarchical regression analysis. The analysis included measures of the following predictor variables: three types of ethnicity-related stress, general stress, socioeconomic status, three types of ethnic identity, and self-esteem. Explain the pattern of results and the method used to a person who is familiar in a general way with ordinary multiple regression but is unfamiliar with hierarchical multiple regression.

13. Hermann, Blanchard, and Flor (1997) conducted a study of children undergoing biofeedback treatment for migraine headaches. The purpose of the study was to identify variables that predict success of this kind of treatment, so the researchers measured headache activity (HA) at the end of the 8-week treatment program.

TABLE 12–10 Standardized Coefficients for Regression Analysis of Ethnicity-Related Stress and Ethnic Identity With Depressive Symptoms

Independent variables	Regression model				
	1	2	3	4	5
1. Ethnicity-related stress					
PEDQ	$.238^{***}$	$.158^{*}$	$.159^{*}$	$.132^{*}$	$.129^{*}$
SCCS	$.110^{\dagger}$	.090	.094	.095	.040
OGCPS	$.115^{\dagger}$	$.099^{\dagger}$	.092	.084	.059
2. Generic stress					
USQ-R		$.226^{***}$	$.226^{***}$	$.221^{***}$	$.124^{**}$
3. Socioeconomic status					
Parents' education			.034	.023	.014
4. Ethnic identity					
Public				$-.102^{\dagger}$	.020
Identity				.064	.052
Private				$-.001$	.063
5. Self-esteem					
RSS					$-.531^{***}$
R^2	.123	.165	.166	.176	.413
ΔR^2	$.104^{***}$	$.042^{***}$	.001	.010	$.237^{***}$

Note. Main effect terms for gender and ethnicity were included in each model. PEDQ = Perceived Ethnic Discrimination Questionnaire; SCCS = Stereotype Confirmation Concern Scale; OGCPS = Own-Group Conformity Pressure Scale; USQ-R = Undergraduate Stress Questionnaire–Revised; RSS = Rosenberg Self-Esteem Scale.
$^{\dagger}p \le .10, {}^{*}p \le .05, {}^{**}p \le .01, {}^{***}p \le .001.$
Source: Contrada, R. J., et al. (2001). Measures of ethnicity-related stress: Psychometric properties, ethnic group differences, and associations with well-being. *Journal of Applied Social Psychology, 31,* 1775–1820. Reprinted by permission.

Headache activity was a summary variable based on such factors as frequency and intensity of headaches. They also measured a number of predictor variables, including HA at "prebaseline" (before treatment began); behavior problems measured on the Child Behavior Checklist (CBCL), including internalizing and externalizing behavior; psychosomatic distress; age; and family variables as measured by the Family Environment Scale (FES), including the Family Relations Index, organization, and control. They reported their results as follows:

Using hierarchical multiple regression, child characteristics (Model 1) and family environment (Model 2) were evaluated independently as predictors of treatment outcome. To control for baseline differences, HA activity during prebaseline was entered first. The variables reflecting child characteristics and aspects of family functioning, respectively, were entered as a set in Step 2. . . . As summarized in Table [12–11], Model 1 revealed externalizing behavior tendencies, psychosomatic distress, and age as significant predictors accounting for 39% of treatment success. By contrast, the quality of family relationships, control, and organization (Model 2) were not found to exert a significant influence on treatment outcome. There was no evidence for a significant relationship between prebaseline activity and treatment success. (pp. 613–614)

Note that the researchers carried out *two* different hierarchical regressions, one that they called Model 1 and one that they called Model 2. Also, note that the final column in the table (labeled $F\Delta$) shows whether the change in the R^2 value (shown in the $R^2\Delta$ column) is significant.

Explain the pattern of results and the method used to a person who is familiar in a general way with ordinary multiple regression but is unfamiliar with hierarchical multiple regression.

14. In another part of the same study about the predictors of the effectiveness of a biofeedback treatment program for children with migraine headaches, in addition to the hierarchical regressions, Hermann et al. (1997) also conducted a stepwise regression. They report it as follows:

For exploratory purposes, a stepwise regression . . . was computed, allowing all predictor variables, with the exception of prebaseline HA activity, to compete directly with each other. Consistent with Model 1, age ($\beta = 0.38$), and psychosomatic

TABLE 12–11 Prediction of Treatment Outcome Using Hierarchical Multiple Regression

Model and Step	Total R^2	dfs	F	β	$R^2\Delta$	$F\Delta$
Model 1	.39	5, 26	3.3[*]			
Step 1. HA activity prebaseline				−0.04	.02	0.7[*]
Step 2. CBCL: internalizing behavior				−0.27	.37	3.9[*]
CBCL: externalizing behavior				0.57[*]		
Psychosomatic distress				0.37[*]		
Age				−0.43[*]		
Model 2	.03	4, 27	0.2			
Step 1. HA activity prebaseline				−0.18	.02	0.7[*]
Step 2. FES: Family Relationship Index				−0.04	.01	0.06
FES: organization				−0.06		
FES: control				−0.05		

Note: HA = headache; CBCL = Child Behavior Checklist; FES = Family Environment Scale.
[*]$p < .05$.
Source: Hermann, C., Blanchard, E. B., & Flor, H. (1997). Biofeedback treatment for pediatric migraine: Prediction of treatment outcome. *Journal of Consulting and Clinical Psychology, 65,* 611–616. Copyright 1997 by the American Psychological Association. Reprinted by permission.

distress ($\beta = 0.39$) emerged as significant outcome predictors, accounting for 35% of treatment outcome, $F(3, 28) = 4.9, p < .01$. (p. 614)

Explain the results and the method used to a person who is familiar in a general way with ordinary multiple regression but is not familiar with stepwise regression.

15. Frank, Poorman, Van Egeren, and Field (1997) studied adolescents' depressive concerns and their relation with their parents. These researchers focused on two aspects of depressive concerns: a self-critical preoccupation and an interpersonal preoccupation. They also focused on two aspects of what they called "separation–individuation conflict" with parents, how much the adolescents perceived their parents as constraining them (exerting strong control over their behaviors), and how insecure the adolescents felt about their parents. Frank et al. reported their analysis and results as follows:

We then correlated the mother and father versions of the Perceived Constraint and Insecurity scales with scores for self-critical and interpersonal concerns. Bivariate and partial correlational analyses are summarized in Table [12–12]. Partial analyses controlled for one aspect of separation–individuation conflict . . . and each type of depressive concern.

Explain this method and illustrate your answer by focusing on some example results to a person who is familiar with correlation and, in a general way, with ordinary multiple regression but is unfamiliar with partial correlation.

16. Schmader, Major, and Gramzow (2001), as part of a study of students' beliefs about ethnic injustice in a university setting, describe one of their key measures as follows: "Beliefs about systemic ethnic injustice were assessed with four items ($\alpha = .69$)" (p. 101). (Here is an example item: "Differences in status between ethnic groups are the result of injustice" p. 101.) Explain the meaning of "$\alpha = .69$" to someone familiar with correlation but not with reliability or Cronbach's alpha.

TABLE 12–12 **Bivariate and Partial Correlations Showing Relations between the Constraint and Insecurity Scales and Self-Critical and Interpersonal Preoccupations**

Scale	Bivariate r		Partial r	
	Interpersonal	Self-Critical	Interpersonal	Self-critical
Constraint				
Fathers	.12	.23***	.00	.18**
Mothers	.08	.23***	−.12*	.14**
Insecurity				
Fathers	.24***	.13	.20**	.02
Mothers	.33***	.12*	.29***	−.07

Note: Partial correlation analyses assessing relations between constraint (or insecurity) and depressive concerns control for insecurity (or constraint) as well as adolescent depression.
*$p < .05$, **$p < .01$, ***$p < .001$.
Source: Frank, S. J., Poorman, M. O., Van Egeren, L. A. & Fields, D. T. (1997). Perceived relationships with parents among adolescent inpatients with depressive preoccupations and depressed mood. *Journal of Clinical Child Psychology, 26,* 205–215. Copyright © 1997 by Lawrence Erlbaum Associates, Inc. Reprinted by permission.

17. Crick, Casas, and Mosher (1997) developed a teachers' rating measure of "relational aggression" in preschoolers. Ordinary, overt aggression harms others directly, but "relational aggression harms others through damage to their peer relationships (e.g., using social exclusion or rumor spreading as a form of retaliation)" (p. 579). As part of this study, they first administered a 23-item teacher rating scale of preschoolers' social behavior. They described the key analysis of this measure as follows:

A . . . factor analysis . . . was first conducted to assess whether . . . relational aggression would emerge as a separate factor independent of overt aggression. The analysis yielded the four predicted factors, relational aggression, overt aggression, prosocial behavior, and depressed affect. (p. 582)

Table 12–13 shows the factor loadings. Explain their results to a person who is familiar with correlation but is unfamiliar with factor analysis.

18. Kwan, Bond, and Singelis (1997) predicted that the relation of self-esteem and social harmony to life satisfaction would be different in different cultures. In more communal cultures, such as many Asian cultures, social harmony would matter more. However, in more individualistic cultures, such as most North

TABLE 12–13	Factor Loadings for the Teacher Measure of Social Behavior (PSBS–T)			
Item	Relational Aggression	Overt Aggression	Prosocial Behavior	Depressed Affect
Tells a peer that he or she won't play with that peer or be that peer's friend unless he or she does what this child asks	.84			
Tells others not to play with or be a peer's friend	.83			
When mad at a peer, this child keeps that peer from being in the play group	.81			
Tells a peer that they won't be invited to their birthday party unless he or she does what the child wants	.88			
Tries to get others to dislike a peer	.89			
Verbally threatens to keep a peer out of the play group if the peer doesn't do what the child asks	.85			
Kicks or hits others		.81		
Verbally threatens to hit or beat up other children		.75		
Ruins other peer's things when he or she is upset		.82		
Pushes or shoves other children		.72		
Hurts other children by pinching them		.83		
Verbally threatens to physically harm a peer in order to get what they want		.81		
Is good at sharing and taking turns			.76	
Is helpful to peers			.83	
Is kind to peers			.62	
Says or does nice things for other kids			.75	
Doesn't have much fun				.90
Looks sad				.87
Doesn't smile much				.82

Note: All cross-loadings were less than .40. PSBS–T = Preschool Social Behavior Scale—Teacher Form.
Source: Data from Crick, N. R., Casas, J. F., & Mosher, M. (1997). Relational and overt aggression in preschool. *Developmental Psychology, 33,* 579–588. Copyright 1997 by the American Psychological Association. Reprinted by permission.

American and European cultures, self-esteem would matter more. As part of the focus on cultural differences, the researchers also measured independent self-construal (how much a person emphasizes personal development and achievement) and interdependent self-construal (how much a person emphasizes getting along and fitting in with others). The participants in the study were 389 college students from the United States and Hong Kong. Figure 12–6 shows their basic results. Note that Kwan et al. give two path coefficients for each path—the ones not in parentheses are for the Hong Kong sample; those in parentheses are for the U.S. sample.

(a) Explain the pattern of results. (b) Using this diagram as an example, explain the general principles of interpreting a path diagram (including any limitations) to a person who understands multiple regression in a general way but is unfamiliar with path diagrams or structural equation modeling.

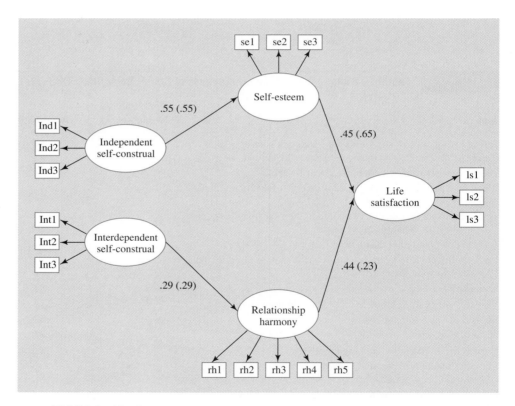

FIGURE 12–6   *The final Self-Construal Scale model. N = 194 for the Hong Kong sample; N = 184 for the U.S. sample. Ellipses (ovals) represent latent constructs, boxes represent indicators, arrows pointing from latent constructs to indicators depict factor loadings, and arrows relating latent constructs represent path coefficients. Standardized path coefficients are shown; factor loadings and measurement errors are omitted for clarity. Numbers inside parentheses are coefficients for the U.S. sample; numbers outside parentheses are coefficients for the Hong Kong sample. All these coefficients were significant at p < .05 or less. Source: Kwan, V. S., Bond, M. H., & Singelis, T. M. (1997). Pancultural explanations for life satisfaction: Adding relationship harmony to self-esteem. Journal of Personality and Social Psychology, 73, 1038–1051. Copyright 1997 by the American Psychological Association. Reprinted by permission.*

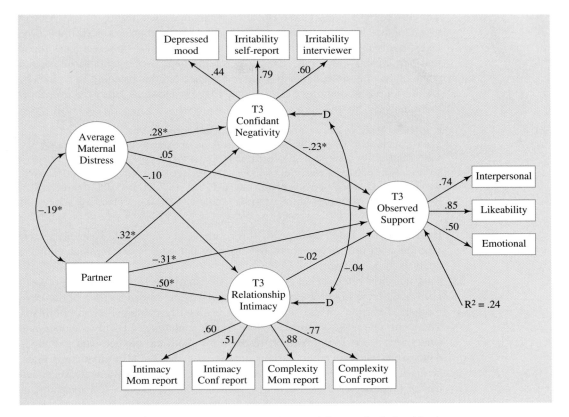

FIGURE 12–7   *Support process model with mother, confidant, and relationship characteristics, controlling for repartnering with a man and for change in maternal distress. T3 =
Time 3; Conf = Confidant. χ²(67, N = 138 = 84.82, p = .07; comparative fit index = .963: *p <
.05.*
Source: DeGarmo, D. S., & Forgatch, M. S. (1997). Determinants of observed confidant support for divorced mothers. *Journal of Personality and Social Psychology, 72,* 336–345. Copyright 1997 by the American Psychological Association. Reprinted by permission.

19. DeGarmo and Forgatch (1997) studied the social support divorced mothers re-
    ceived from their closest confidant. The researchers measured a number of
    variables and then examined the predicted relationships among the variables
    using structural equation modeling. Figure 12–7 shows the results.
    (a) Explain the pattern of results. (b) Using this diagram as an example, ex-
    plain the general principles of interpreting a path diagram (including any
    limitations) to a person who understands multiple regression in a general
    way but is unfamiliar with path diagrams or structural equation modeling.

20. In each of the following studies, indicate which variable is the independent
    variable and which is the dependent variable:
    (a) A study of speed of performance on a complex task, in which one
        group does the task at night and the other in the morning.
    (b) A study comparing women in the United States versus women in
        Denmark on their attitudes toward preschool education.
    (c) A study of voting preferences of people from three different regions
        of Canada.

21. Thompson, Schellenberg, and Husain (2001) conducted a study of the "Mozart effect"—that listening to music written by Mozart improves performance on tasks involving spatial abilities. In their initial analysis, the researchers found that participants did better on a paper folding task after listening to a Mozart sonata than after an equivalent period of silence or after listening to a piece by another classical composer (an Albioni adagio). However, they then repeated their analyses, but this time

> a series of analyses of covariance . . . tested whether the Mozart effect would remain in evidence when individual differences in enjoyment, arousal, and mood were statistically controlled. For each analysis . . . the covariate represented the scores on one of [these] measures. Although the Mozart effect remained significant when . . . mood scores were partialed out, $F(1, 10) = 12.93$, $p < .05$, it was no longer reliable when enjoyment ratings, . . . arousal scores, or subjective mood-arousal ratings were held constant. (p. 250)

Explain what is being done, using this result as an example, to someone who is familiar with ordinary analysis of variance, but who is not familiar with the analysis of covariance.

22. This question refers to another part of the study by DeGarmo and Forgatch (1997), described in problem 19. These researchers studied a group of divorced mothers, focusing on the support they received from their closest confidant. That confidant was sometimes a close friend, sometimes a family member, and sometimes a cohabiting partner. In the study, both the mothers and the confidants were interviewed on various measures; they were also videotaped interacting in a special laboratory task, and the interaction was systematically coded by the researchers. These various approaches created quite a few measures of the relationship between the mother and her closest confidant, including three measures of confidant support, four measures of confidant negativity, and four measures of the intimacy of their relationship.

One aspect of the study focused on how the relationship with the confidant differed for confidants who were friends, family members, or cohabiting partners. DeGarmo and Forgatch (1997) described the analysis as follows:

> Multivariate and univariate analyses of variance were conducted on the indicators of support, negativity, and intimacy for close friends, family members, and cohabiting partners. The mean values, tests of differences, and significant contrasts are displayed in Table [12–14].

> Significant differences were found among relationship types in the multivariate analysis of variance (MANOVA) on the indicators, $F(20, 254) = 4.10$, $p < .001$. (p. 340)

> Degarmo and Forgatch then discussed the results of the univariate analyses of variance. For example, they noted that the "analysis of variance showed a pattern in which partners were observed to provide less support" (p. 340).

Explain these results to a person familiar with analysis of variance but not with MANOVA.

23. In a recent issue of a journal in an area of behavioral and social sciences that especially interests you, find an article that uses one of the statistical procedures described in this chapter. Write a brief summary of the study, referring specifically to the statistics. With your answer, include a photocopy or printout of the article, marking clearly the part that reports the statistics you describe.

TABLE 12–14 Means and Standard Deviations for Construct Indicators by Confidant Relationship Types

Construct Indicator	Friend (1)		Family (2)		Partner (3)		$F(2, 135)$	Significant contrasts
	M	SD	M	SD	M	SD		
Observed confidant support								
Interpersonal	3.34	.67	3.35	.63	2.92	.65	5.93**	1, 2 > 3
Likeability	3.39	.86	3.24	.94	2.68	1.21	6.58**	1, 2 > 3
Emotional	1.04	.36	.96	.37	.69	.35	12.17***	1, 2 > 3
Confidant negativity								
Self-report, irritability	1.91	.84	1.70	.70	2.25	.65	5.27**	3 > 2
Intimacy-report irritability	1.36	.50	1.33	.35	1.48	.40	1.65	
Depressed mood	1.06	.32	.93	.36	.95	.34	2.02	
Relationship intimacy								
Mother-report intimacy	3.18	.73	3.19	.75	3.65	.58	5.94**	3 > 1, 2
Confidant-report intimacy	3.05	.78	3.29	.69	3.48	.64	4.62**	3 > 1
Mother-report complexity	1.91	.84	2.29	.74	2.87	.33	22.52***	3 > 1, 2
Confidant-report complexity	2.01	.74	2.19	.75	2.73	.55	13.36***	3 > 1, 2

Note: ns = 65, 33, and 40 for the friend, family, and partner relationship types, respectively.
**$p < .01$, ***$p < .001$.
Source: DeGarmo, D. S., & Forgatch, M. S. (1997). Determinants of observed confidant support for divorced mothers. *Journal of Personality and Social Psychology, 72,* 336–345. Copyright 1997 by the American Psychological Association. Reprinted by permission.

24. In a recent issue of a journal in an area of behavioral and social sciences that especially interests you, find an article that uses a statistical procedure *not* covered anywhere in this book. Write a brief summary of the study you found, referring specifically to the statistics. With your answer, include a photocopy or printout of the article, marking clearly the part that reports the statistics you describe.

A P P E N D I X

Tables

TABLE A–1	Normal Curve Areas: Percentage of the Normal Curve between the Mean and the Z Scores Shown				
Z	% Mean to Z	Z	% Mean to Z	Z	% Mean to Z
.00	.00	.24	9.48	.48	18.44
.01	.40	.25	9.87	.49	18.79
.02	.80	.26	10.26	.50	19.15
.03	1.20	.27	10.64	.51	19.50
.04	1.60	.28	11.03	.52	19.85
.05	1.99	.29	11.41	.53	20.19
.06	2.39	.30	11.79	.54	20.54
.07	2.79	.31	12.17	.55	20.88
.08	3.19	.32	12.55	.56	21.23
.09	3.59	.33	12.93	.57	21.57
.10	3.98	.34	13.31	.58	21.90
.11	4.38	.35	13.68	.59	22.24
.12	4.78	.36	14.06	.60	22.57
.13	5.17	.37	14.43	.61	22.91
.14	5.57	.38	14.80	.62	23.24
.15	5.96	.39	15.17	.63	23.57
.16	6.36	.40	15.54	.64	23.89
.17	6.75	.41	15.91	.65	24.22
.18	7.14	.42	16.28	.66	24.54
.19	7.53	.43	16.64	.67	24.86
.20	7.93	.44	17.00	.68	25.17
.21	8.32	.45	17.36	.69	25.49
.22	8.71	.46	17.72	.70	25.80
.23	9.10	.47	18.08	.71	26.11

TABLE A–1 (cont.)

Z	% Mean to Z	Z	% Mean to Z	Z	% Mean to Z
.72	26.42	1.19	38.30	1.66	45.15
.73	26.73	1.20	38.49	1.67	45.25
.74	27.04	1.21	38.69	1.68	45.35
.75	27.34	1.22	38.88	1.69	45.45
.76	27.64	1.23	39.07	1.70	45.54
.77	27.94	1.24	39.25	1.71	45.64
.78	28.23	1.25	39.44	1.72	45.73
.79	28.52	1.26	39.62	1.73	45.82
.80	28.81	1.27	39.80	1.74	45.91
.81	29.10	1.28	39.97	1.75	45.99
.82	29.39	1.29	40.15	1.76	46.08
.83	29.67	1.30	40.32	1.77	46.16
.84	29.95	1.31	40.49	1.78	46.25
.85	30.23	1.32	40.66	1.79	46.33
.86	30.51	1.33	40.82	1.80	46.41
.87	30.78	1.34	40.99	1.81	46.49
.88	31.06	1.35	41.15	1.82	46.56
.89	31.33	1.36	41.31	1.83	46.64
.90	31.59	1.37	41.47	1.84	46.71
.91	31.86	1.38	41.62	1.85	46.78
.92	32.12	1.39	41.77	1.86	46.86
.93	32.38	1.40	41.92	1.87	46.93
.94	32.64	1.41	42.07	1.88	46.99
.95	32.89	1.42	42.22	1.89	47.06
.96	33.15	1.43	42.36	1.90	47.13
.97	33.40	1.44	42.51	1.91	47.19
.98	33.65	1.45	42.65	1.92	47.26
.99	33.89	1.46	42.79	1.93	47.32
1.00	34.13	1.47	42.92	1.94	47.38
1.01	34.38	1.48	43.06	1.95	47.44
1.02	34.61	1.49	43.19	1.96	47.50
1.03	34.85	1.50	43.32	1.97	47.56
1.04	35.08	1.51	43.45	1.98	47.61
1.05	35.31	1.52	43.57	1.99	47.67
1.06	35.54	1.53	43.70	2.00	47.72
1.07	35.77	1.54	43.82	2.01	47.78
1.08	35.99	1.55	43.94	2.02	47.83
1.09	36.21	1.56	44.06	2.03	47.88
1.10	36.43	1.57	44.18	2.04	47.93
1.11	36.65	1.58	44.29	2.05	47.98
1.12	36.86	1.59	44.41	2.06	48.03
1.13	37.08	1.60	44.52	2.07	48.08
1.14	37.29	1.61	44.63	2.08	48.12
1.15	37.49	1.62	44.74	2.09	48.17
1.16	37.70	1.63	44.84	2.10	48.21
1.17	37.90	1.64	44.95	2.11	48.26
1.18	38.10	1.65	45.05	2.12	48.30

TABLE A–1 (cont.)

Z	% Mean to Z	Z	% Mean to Z	Z	% Mean to Z
2.13	48.34	2.44	49.27	2.75	49.70
2.14	48.38	2.45	49.29	2.76	49.71
2.15	48.42	2.46	49.31	2.77	49.72
2.16	48.46	2.47	49.32	2.78	49.73
2.17	48.50	2.48	49.34	2.79	49.74
2.18	48.54	2.49	49.36	2.80	49.74
2.19	48.57	2.50	49.38	2.81	49.75
2.20	48.61	2.51	49.40	2.82	49.76
2.21	48.64	2.52	49.41	2.83	49.77
2.22	48.68	2.53	49.43	2.84	49.77
2.23	48.71	2.54	49.45	2.85	49.78
2.24	48.75	2.55	49.46	2.86	49.79
2.25	48.78	2.56	49.48	2.87	49.79
2.26	48.81	2.57	49.49	2.88	49.80
2.27	48.84	2.58	49.51	2.89	49.81
2.28	48.87	2.59	49.52	2.90	49.81
2.29	48.90	2.60	49.53	2.91	49.82
2.30	48.93	2.61	49.55	2.92	49.82
2.31	48.96	2.62	49.56	2.93	49.83
2.32	48.98	2.63	49.57	2.94	49.84
2.33	49.01	2.64	49.59	2.95	49.84
2.34	49.04	2.65	49.60	2.96	49.85
2.35	49.06	2.66	49.61	2.97	49.85
2.36	49.09	2.67	49.62	2.98	49.86
2.37	49.11	2.68	49.63	2.99	49.86
2.38	49.13	2.69	49.64	3.00	49.87
2.39	49.16	2.70	49.65	3.50	49.98
2.40	49.18	2.71	49.66	4.00	50.00
2.41	49.20	2.72	49.67	4.50	50.00
2.42	49.22	2.73	49.68		
2.43	49.25	2.74	49.69		

TABLE A–2   Cutoff Scores for the *t* Distribution

	One-Tailed Tests			Two-Tailed Tests		
df	*.10*	*.05*	*.01*	*.10*	*.05*	*.01*
1	3.078	6.314	31.821	6.314	12.706	63.657
2	1.886	2.920	6.965	2.920	4.303	9.925
3	1.638	2.353	4.541	2.353	3.182	5.841
4	1.533	2.132	3.747	2.132	2.776	4.604
5	1.476	2.015	3.365	2.015	2.571	4.032
6	1.440	1.943	3.143	1.943	2.447	3.708
7	1.415	1.895	2.998	1.895	2.365	3.500
8	1.397	1.860	2.897	1.860	2.306	3.356
9	1.383	1.833	2.822	1.833	2.262	3.250
10	1.372	1.813	2.764	1.813	2.228	3.170
11	1.364	1.796	2.718	1.796	2.201	3.106
12	1.356	1.783	2.681	1.783	2.179	3.055
13	1.350	1.771	2.651	1.771	2.161	3.013
14	1.345	1.762	2.625	1.762	2.145	2.977
15	1.341	1.753	2.603	1.753	2.132	2.947
16	1.337	1.746	2.584	1.746	2.120	2.921
17	1.334	1.740	2.567	1.740	2.110	2.898
18	1.331	1.734	2.553	1.734	2.101	2.879
19	1.328	1.729	2.540	1.729	2.093	2.861
20	1.326	1.725	2.528	1.725	2.086	2.846
21	1.323	1.721	2.518	1.721	2.080	2.832
22	1.321	1.717	2.509	1.717	2.074	2.819
23	1.320	1.714	2.500	1.714	2.069	2.808
24	1.318	1.711	2.492	1.711	2.064	2.797
25	1.317	1.708	2.485	1.708	2.060	2.788
26	1.315	1.706	2.479	1.706	2.056	2.779
27	1.314	1.704	2.473	1.704	2.052	2.771
28	1.313	1.701	2.467	1.701	2.049	2.764
29	1.312	1.699	2.462	1.699	2.045	2.757
30	1.311	1.698	2.458	1.698	2.043	2.750
35	1.306	1.690	2.438	1.690	2.030	2.724
40	1.303	1.684	2.424	1.684	2.021	2.705
45	1.301	1.680	2.412	1.680	2.014	2.690
50	1.299	1.676	2.404	1.676	2.009	2.678
55	1.297	1.673	2.396	1.673	2.004	2.668
60	1.296	1.671	2.390	1.671	2.001	2.661
65	1.295	1.669	2.385	1.669	1.997	2.654
70	1.294	1.667	2.381	1.667	1.995	2.648
75	1.293	1.666	2.377	1.666	1.992	2.643
80	1.292	1.664	2.374	1.664	1.990	2.639
85	1.292	1.663	2.371	1.663	1.989	2.635
90	1.291	1.662	2.369	1.662	1.987	2.632
95	1.291	1.661	2.366	1.661	1.986	2.629
100	1.290	1.660	2.364	1.660	1.984	2.626
∞	1.282	1.645	2.327	1.645	1.960	2.576

TABLE A–3 Cutoff Scores for the *F* Distribution

Denom-inator df	Signi-ficance Level	Numerator Degrees of Freedom					
		1	2	3	4	5	6
1	.01	4,052	5,000	5,404	5,625	5,764	5,859
	.05	162	200	216	225	230	234
	.10	39.9	49.5	53.6	55.8	57.2	58.2
2	.01	98.50	99.00	99.17	99.25	99.30	99.33
	.05	18.51	19.00	19.17	19.25	19.30	19.33
	.10	8.53	9.00	9.16	9.24	9.29	9.33
3	.01	34.12	30.82	29.46	28.71	28.24	27.91
	.05	10.13	9.55	9.28	9.12	9.01	8.94
	.10	5.54	5.46	5.39	5.34	5.31	5.28
4	.01	21.20	18.00	16.70	15.98	15.52	15.21
	.05	7.71	6.95	6.59	6.39	6.26	6.16
	.10	4.55	4.33	4.19	4.11	4.05	4.01
5	.01	16.26	13.27	12.06	11.39	10.97	10.67
	.05	6.61	5.79	5.41	5.19	5.05	4.95
	.10	4.06	3.78	3.62	3.52	3.45	3.41
6	.01	13.75	10.93	9.78	9.15	8.75	8.47
	.05	5.99	5.14	4.76	4.53	4.39	4.28
	.10	3.78	3.46	3.29	3.18	3.11	3.06
7	.01	12.25	9.55	8.45	7.85	7.46	7.19
	.05	5.59	4.74	4.35	4.12	3.97	3.87
	.10	3.59	3.26	3.08	2.96	2.88	2.83
8	.01	11.26	8.65	7.59	7.01	6.63	6.37
	.05	5.32	4.46	4.07	3.84	3.69	3.58
	.10	3.46	3.11	2.92	2.81	2.73	2.67
9	.01	10.56	8.02	6.99	6.42	6.06	5.80
	.05	5.12	4.26	3.86	3.63	3.48	3.37
	.10	3.36	3.01	2.81	2.69	2.61	2.55
10	.01	10.05	7.56	6.55	6.00	5.64	5.39
	.05	4.97	4.10	3.71	3.48	3.33	3.22
	.10	3.29	2.93	2.73	2.61	2.52	2.46
11	.01	9.65	7.21	6.22	5.67	5.32	5.07
	.05	4.85	3.98	3.59	3.36	3.20	3.10
	.10	3.23	2.86	2.66	2.54	2.45	2.39
12	.01	9.33	6.93	5.95	5.41	5.07	4.82
	.05	4.75	3.89	3.49	3.26	3.11	3.00
	.10	3.18	2.81	2.61	2.48	2.40	2.33
13	.01	9.07	6.70	5.74	5.21	4.86	4.62
	.05	4.67	3.81	3.41	3.18	3.03	2.92
	.10	3.14	2.76	2.56	2.43	2.35	2.28
14	.01	8.86	6.52	5.56	5.04	4.70	4.46
	.05	4.60	3.74	3.34	3.11	2.96	2.85
	.10	3.10	2.73	2.52	2.40	2.31	2.24
15	.01	8.68	6.36	5.42	4.89	4.56	4.32
	.05	4.54	3.68	3.29	3.06	2.90	2.79
	.10	3.07	2.70	2.49	2.36	2.27	2.21

TABLE A-3 (cont.)

Denom-inator df	Signi-ficance Level	Numerator Degrees of Freedom					
		1	2	3	4	5	6
16	.01	8.53	6.23	5.29	4.77	4.44	4.20
	.05	4.49	3.63	3.24	3.01	2.85	2.74
	.10	3.05	2.67	2.46	2.33	2.24	2.18
17	.01	8.40	6.11	5.19	4.67	4.34	4.10
	.05	4.45	3.59	3.20	2.97	2.81	2.70
	.10	3.03	2.65	2.44	2.31	2.22	2.15
18	.01	8.29	6.01	5.09	4.58	4.25	4.02
	.05	4.41	3.56	3.16	2.93	2.77	2.66
	.10	3.01	2.62	2.42	2.29	2.20	2.13
19	.01	8.19	5.93	5.01	4.50	4.17	3.94
	.05	4.38	3.52	3.13	2.90	2.74	2.63
	.10	2.99	2.61	2.40	2.27	2.18	2.11
20	.01	8.10	5.85	4.94	4.43	4.10	3.87
	.05	4.35	3.49	3.10	2.87	2.71	2.60
	.10	2.98	2.59	2.38	2.25	2.16	2.09
21	.01	8.02	5.78	4.88	4.37	4.04	3.81
	.05	4.33	3.47	3.07	2.84	2.69	2.57
	.10	2.96	2.58	2.37	2.23	2.14	2.08
22	.01	7.95	5.72	4.82	4.31	3.99	3.76
	.05	4.30	3.44	3.05	2.82	2.66	2.55
	.10	2.95	2.56	2.35	2.22	2.13	2.06
23	.01	7.88	5.66	4.77	4.26	3.94	3.71
	.05	4.28	3.42	3.03	2.80	2.64	2.53
	.10	2.94	2.55	2.34	2.21	2.12	2.05
24	.01	7.82	5.61	4.72	4.22	3.90	3.67
	.05	4.26	3.40	3.01	2.78	2.62	2.51
	.10	2.93	2.54	2.33	2.20	2.10	2.04
25	.01	7.77	5.57	4.68	4.18	3.86	3.63
	.05	4.24	3.39	2.99	2.76	2.60	2.49
	.10	2.92	2.53	2.32	2.19	2.09	2.03
26	.01	7.72	5.53	4.64	4.14	3.82	3.59
	.05	4.23	3.37	2.98	2.74	2.59	2.48
	.10	2.91	2.52	2.31	2.18	2.08	2.01
27	.01	7.68	5.49	4.60	4.11	3.79	3.56
	.05	4.21	3.36	2.96	2.73	2.57	2.46
	.10	2.90	2.51	2.30	2.17	2.07	2.01
28	.01	7.64	5.45	4.57	4.08	3.75	3.53
	.05	4.20	3.34	2.95	2.72	2.56	2.45
	.10	2.89	2.50	2.29	2.16	2.07	2.00
29	.01	7.60	5.42	4.54	4.05	3.73	3.50
	.05	4.18	3.33	2.94	2.70	2.55	2.43
	.10	2.89	2.50	2.28	2.15	2.06	1.99
30	.01	7.56	5.39	4.51	4.02	3.70	3.47
	.05	4.17	3.32	2.92	2.69	2.53	2.42
	.10	2.88	2.49	2.28	2.14	2.05	1.98

TABLE A-3 (cont.)

Denom- inator df	Signi- ficance Level	Numerator Degrees of Freedom					
		1	2	3	4	5	6
35	.01	7.42	5.27	4.40	3.91	3.59	3.37
	.05	4.12	3.27	2.88	2.64	2.49	2.37
	.10	2.86	2.46	2.25	2.11	2.02	1.95
40	.01	7.32	5.18	4.31	3.83	3.51	3.29
	.05	4.09	3.23	2.84	2.61	2.45	2.34
	.10	2.84	2.44	2.23	2.09	2.00	1.93
45	.01	7.23	5.11	4.25	3.77	3.46	3.23
	.05	4.06	3.21	2.81	2.58	2.42	2.31
	.10	2.82	2.43	2.21	2.08	1.98	1.91
50	.01	7.17	5.06	4.20	3.72	3.41	3.19
	.05	4.04	3.18	2.79	2.56	2.40	2.29
	.10	2.81	2.41	2.20	2.06	1.97	1.90
55	.01	7.12	5.01	4.16	3.68	3.37	3.15
	.05	4.02	3.17	2.77	2.54	2.38	2.27
	.10	2.80	2.40	2.19	2.05	1.96	1.89
60	.01	7.08	4.98	4.13	3.65	3.34	3.12
	.05	4.00	3.15	2.76	2.53	2.37	2.26
	.10	2.79	2.39	2.18	2.04	1.95	1.88
65	.01	7.04	4.95	4.10	3.62	3.31	3.09
	.05	3.99	3.14	2.75	2.51	2.36	2.24
	.10	2.79	2.39	2.17	2.03	1.94	1.87
70	.01	7.01	4.92	4.08	3.60	3.29	3.07
	.05	3.98	3.13	2.74	2.50	2.35	2.23
	.10	2.78	2.38	2.16	2.03	1.93	1.86
75	.01	6.99	4.90	4.06	3.58	3.27	3.05
	.05	3.97	3.12	2.73	2.49	2.34	2.22
	.10	2.77	2.38	2.16	2.02	1.93	1.86
80	.01	6.96	4.88	4.04	3.56	3.26	3.04
	.05	3.96	3.11	2.72	2.49	2.33	2.22
	.10	2.77	2.37	2.15	2.02	1.92	1.85
85	.01	6.94	4.86	4.02	3.55	3.24	3.02
	.05	3.95	3.10	2.71	2.48	2.32	2.21
	.10	2.77	2.37	2.15	2.01	1.92	1.85
90	.01	6.93	4.85	4.01	3.54	3.23	3.01
	.05	3.95	3.10	2.71	2.47	2.32	2.20
	.10	2.76	2.36	2.15	2.01	1.91	1.84
95	.01	6.91	4.84	4.00	3.52	3.22	3.00
	.05	3.94	3.09	2.70	2.47	2.31	2.20
	.10	2.76	2.36	2.14	2.01	1.91	1.84
100	.01	6.90	4.82	3.98	3.51	3.21	2.99
	.05	3.94	3.09	2.70	2.46	2.31	2.19
	.10	2.76	2.36	2.14	2.00	1.91	1.83
∞	.01	6.64	4.61	3.78	3.32	3.02	2.80
	.05	3.84	3.00	2.61	2.37	2.22	2.10
	.10	2.71	2.30	2.08	1.95	1.85	1.78

TABLE A–4 Cutoff Scores for the Chi-Square Distribution

	Significance Level		
df	.10	.05	.01
1	2.706	3.841	6.635
2	4.605	5.992	9.211
3	6.252	7.815	11.345
4	7.780	9.488	13.277
5	9.237	11.071	15.087
6	10.645	12.592	16.812
7	12.017	14.067	18.475
8	13.362	15.507	20.090
9	14.684	16.919	21.666
10	15.987	18.307	23.209

TABLE A–5 Index to Power Tables and Tables Giving Number of Participants Needed for 80% Power

Hypothesis-Testing Procedure	Chapter	Power Table	Number of Participants Table
Correlation coefficient (r)	3	p. 105	p. 106
t test for dependent means	8	p. 241	p. 242
t test for independent means	9	p. 273	p. 275
One-way analysis of variance	10	p. 310	p. 311
Chi-square test for independence	11	p. 352	p. 352

Answers to Set I Practice Problems

Chapter 1

1. (a) Satisfaction with the vocational counselor; (b) 1, 2, 3, or 4; (c) the particular rating the client makes.
2. (a) Likelihood of voting; (b) 1, 2, 3, 4, or 5; (c) 5
3. (a) Nominal (or categorical); (b) numeric (or quantitative) —more precisely, equal interval; (c) numeric (or quantitative)—more precisely, rank order (or ordinal).
4. (a) Frequency table

Number of Children	Frequency	Percent
6	1	5
5	0	0
4	1	5
3	2	10
2	7	35
1	5	25
0	4	20

(b) Histogram

(c) Frequency polygon

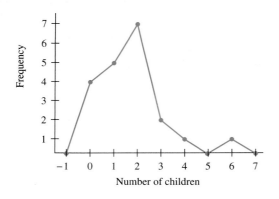

Number of children

(d) Unimodal, skewed to the right.

5. (a) Frequency table

Hours	Frequency	Percent	Hours	Frequency	Percent
18	1	2	8	5	10
17	0	0	7	11	22
16	0	0	6	4	8
15	1	2	5	2	4
14	0	0	4	3	6
13	2	4	3	4	8
12	1	2	2	2	4
11	3	6	1	1	2
10	5	10	0	1	2
9	4	8			

(b) and (c) are based on frequency table above. See answer to question 4 for examples.
(d) Approximately unimodal, slightly skewed to the right.

6. (a) Frequency table

Speed	Frequency	Percent	Speed	Frequency	Percent
52	2	5	33	2	5
51	0	0	32	3	8
50	0	0	31	3	8
49	0	0	30	3	8
48	0	0	29	0	0
47	0	0	28	1	3
46	1	3	27	1	3
45	1	3	26	0	0
44	0	0	25	0	0
43	0	0	24	1	3
42	1	3	23	1	3
41	0	0	22	0	0
40	3	8	21	0	0
39	0	0	20	1	3
38	1	3	19	0	0
37	2	5	18	0	0
36	6	15	17	0	0
35	2	5	16	0	0
34	4	10	15	1	3

(b) and (c) are based on frequency table above. See answer to question 4 for examples.
(d) Unimodal, approximately symmetrical.

7. (a) Frequency table

Score	Frequency	Percent	Score	Frequency	Percent
96	1	4	72	0	0
95	0	0	71	1	4
94	0	0	70	1	4
93	0	0	69	1	4
92	1	4	68	2	8
91	1	4	67	1	4
90	0	0	66	0	0
89	0	0	65	0	0
88	0	0	64	2	8
87	1	4	63	0	0
86	0	0	62	0	0
85	1	4	61	0	0
84	0	0	60	0	0
83	2	8	59	1	4
82	0	0	58	0	0
81	1	4	57	0	0
80	1	4	56	0	0
79	0	0	55	0	0
78	0	0	54	0	0
77	0	0	53	0	0
76	2	8	52	0	0
75	2	8	51	0	0
74	1	4	50	1	4
73	1	4			

(b) Based on frequency table above. See answer to question 4b for an example.
(c) Grouped frequency table

Interval	Frequency	Percent
90–99	3	12
80–89	6	24
70–79	8	32
60–69	6	24
50–59	2	8

(d) Based on frequency table in (c) above. See answer to question 4b for an example.
(e) Unimodal, approximately symmetrical (slightly negatively skewed).

8. (a) Similar to 7a above.
(b) Based on frequency table in (a); see answer to question 4c for an example.
(c) Grouped frequency table

Interval	Frequency	Percent
80–89	10	29.4
70–79	0	0
60–69	5	14.7
50–59	0	0
40–49	5	14.7
30–39	7	20.6
20–29	7	20.6

(d) Histogram

(e) Roughly rectangular.
9. (a) Bimodal; (b) approximately normal (or unimodal or symmetrical); (c) multimodal.
10. (a) A distribution is the way a group of numbers is spread out over the possible values the numbers can have. You can describe such a distribution with a graph, called a histogram—a kind of bar graph with one bar for each possible value with one unit of height for each time its particular value occurs. In a histogram, a symmetrical distribution has a symmetrical shape (the right and left halves are mirror images). A unimodal distribution is one in which this graph has a single high point, with the other values gradually decreasing around it. (b) A negatively skewed unimodal distribution has a single high point, is not symmetrical, and its tail—the long, low side—extends to the left (where the negative scores go on the graph).
11. A ceiling effect describes the situation when many scores pile up at the high end of a distribution because it is not possible to have a higher score. This usually causes the distribution to be negatively skewed (skewed to the left).
12. (a) This is called a frequency table because it lays out how frequently (how many times) each category occurs for nine different categories. A frequency table makes the pattern of numbers easy to see. For example, of the 90 college students

in the study, 19 gave bad news about Relationship with family (the first category). The table also gives the percentages. For example, 19 students is 19/90 of the total, or 21.1 percent. (b) The most bad news is given in four of the nine categories: Relationship with family, Relationship with actual/potential girlfriend/boyfriend, Relationship with friends, and Health of family member/friend. All of these categories had to do with family members or friends and most with relationships and there were few cases in the other categories (which had little directly to do with family or friends).

Chapter 2

1. (a) $M = \Sigma X/N = 261/9 = 29$; (b) 28; (c) $\Sigma(X - M)^2 = (32 - 29)^2 + (28 - 29)^2 + (24 - 29)^2 + (28 - 29)^2 + (28 - 29)^2 + (31 - 29)^2 + (35 - 29)^2 + (29 - 29)^2 + (26 - 29)^2 = 86$; (d) $SD^2 = \Sigma(X - M)^2/N = 86/9 = 9.56$; (e) $SD = \sqrt{SD^2} = \sqrt{9.56} = 3.09$.
2. (a) 4; (b) 4; (c) 26; (d) 3.25; (e) 1.80.
3. The average temperature, in the sense of adding up the 10 readings and dividing by 10, was −7 degrees Celsius. This is the *mean*. However, if you line up the temperatures from lowest to highest, the middle two numbers are both −5 degrees. The middle number is the *median*. The specific temperature that came up most often is the *mode*—there are two modes, −1 and −5.

As for the variation, one approach is the *variance*—the average of each temperature's squared deviation from the mean temperature, which is 46.8. You get a more direct sense of how much a group of numbers vary among themselves if you take the square root of the variance, which gives the standard deviation—the square root of 46.8 is 6.84. This means, roughly, that on an average day the temperature differs by 6.84 degrees from the average of −7 degrees.
4. (a) .4; (b) .14; (c) similar to 3 above.
5. (a) $Z = (X - M)/SD = (91 - 79)/12 = 1$; (b) −.92; (c) 2.
6. (a) $Z = (X - M)/SD = (-13.12 + 11.46)/2.28 = -.73$; (b) 1.84; (c) .10.
7. (a) $X = (Z)(SD) + M = (0)(19) + 145 = 145$; (b) 172.17; (c) 96.74.
8. Wife: $Z = (X - M)/SD = (63 - 60)/6 = .5$. Husband: $Z = (59 - 55)/4 = 1$. The husband has adjusted better in relation to other divorced men than the wife has adjusted in relation to other divorced women.

For wives, a score of 63 is 3 points better than the average of 60 for divorced women in general. (The "mean" in the problem is the ordinary average—the sum of the scores divided by the number of scores.) There is, of course, some variation in scores among divorced women. The approximate average amount that women's scores differ from the average is 6 points—this is the SD (standard deviation) referred to in the problem. (SD is only approximately the average amount scores differ from the mean. To be precise, SD is the square root of the average of the square of the difference of each score from the mean.) Thus, the wife's score is only half as far as above the mean of wives' scores. This gives her what is called a Z score of +.5, which gives her location on a scale that compares her score to that of divorced women in general. Using the same logic, the husband's divorce adjustment is as much above the mean as the average amount that men differ from the mean; that is, he has a Z score of +1. What this all means is that both have adjusted better than average for their gender, but the husband had adjusted better in relation to other divorced men than the wife has adjusted in relation to other divorced women.

9. The "mean" is the ordinary arithmetic average—add up the total number of nights of too little sleep and divide by the number of students. The total number of nights of too little sleep over the 4-week period was 6.84. The *SD* (standard deviation), roughly speaking, is the average amount that the number of nights of too little sleep are spread out from their average—in this case, by 3.18 nights. This is quite a lot of spread. To be more precise, you figure the standard deviation by taking each person's number of nights of too little sleep and subtracting 6.84 from it and squaring this difference; the standard deviation is the square root of the average of these differences.

10. Like the answer to 9 above, focusing on means of 5.02, 5.11, 32.27, and 31.36 and on standard deviations of 2.16, 2.08, 20.36, and 21.08.

Chapter 3

1. (a) Curvilinear; (b) linear, positive, strong; (c) linear, negative, strong; (d) linear, positive, strong; (e) linear, positive, small to moderate; (f) no correlation.
2. Set A:

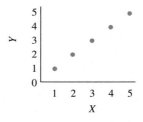

X		Y		Cross-Product of Z Scores
Raw	Z	Raw	Z	
1	−1.41	1	−1.41	2.0
2	−.71	2	−.71	.5
3	.00	3	.00	0
4	.71	4	.71	.5
5	1.41	5	1.41	2.0
$M = 3$; $SD = 1.41$				5.0
				$r = 5.0/5 = 1.00$.

Set B: $r = 4.5/5 = .90$; Set C: $r = -3.0/5 = -.60$; Set D: $r = 3.0/5 = .60$.

3. Possibility A:

Take Drug		Get Cold		Cross-Product of Z Scores
Raw	Z	Raw	Z	
0	−1	1	1	−1
0	−1	1	1	−1
0	−1	1	1	−1
0	−1	1	1	−1
1	1	0	−1	−1
1	1	0	−1	−1
1	1	0	−1	−1
1	1	0	−1	−1
				−8
				$r = -8/8 = -1.00$

Possibility B: $r = -4/8 = -.50$; Possibility C: $r = 0/8 = .00$; Possibility D: $r = -6.2/8 = -.78$.

4. (a) See answer to 2 above for an example; (b) linear, negative, moderate.
(c)

Approximate Age (Years)		Number of People Stopping to Look		Cross-Product of Z Scores
X	Z_X	Y	Z_Y	$Z_X Z_Y$
465	1.39	68	−.69	−.96
515	1.71	71	−.59	−1.01
240	−.09	123	1.19	−.11
107	−.96	112	.82	−.79
376	.80	48	−1.38	−1.10
355	.67	84	−.14	−.09
140	−.75	66	−.76	.57
115	−.91	148	2.05	−1.87
122	−.86	71	−.59	.51
99	−1.01	91	.10	−.10
				−4.95

$r = -4.95/10 = -.50$

5. (a) See answer to 2 above for an example; (b) linear, no correlation (or very small positive correlation).
(c)

Neatness Rating		Achievement Test		Cross-Product of Z Scores
X	Z_X	Y	Z_Y	$Z_X Z_Y$
18	−.52	60	−.66	.34
24	1.43	58	−1.09	−1.56
14	−1.82	70	1.47	−2.68
19	−.20	58	−1.09	.22
20	.13	66	.62	.08

23	1.11	68	1.04	1.15
20	.13	65	.40	.05
22	.78	68	1.04	.81
15	−1.50	56	−1.51	2.27
21	.46	62	−.23	−.11
				.57

$$r = .57/10 = .06$$

6. (a) See answer to 2 above for an example; (b) linear, positive, strong.
(c)

Hours of Violent TV per Week		Number of Violent or Aggressive Acts		Cross-Product of Z Scores
X	Z_X	Y	Z_Y	$Z_X Z_Y$
14	1.27	9	.97	1.23
8	−.63	6	.00	.00
6	−1.27	1	−1.62	2.06
12	.63	8	.65	.41
Σ = 40		Σ = 24		3.70
M = 10		M = 6		
SD = 3.16		SD = 3.08		r = 3.70/4 = .93

(d) The first thing I did was make a graph, called a scatter diagram, putting one variable on each axis, then putting a dot where each person's pair of scores goes on that graph. This gives a picture of the pattern of relationship between the two variables. In this example, high scores generally go with high scores and lows with lows. The scores going together in a systematic pattern makes this a *correlation;* that highs go with highs and lows with lows makes this correlation *positive;* that dots fall roughly near a straight line makes this positive correlation *linear.*

Next, I figured the *correlation coefficient,* a number describing the degree of linear correlation (in a positive correlation, how consistently highs go with highs and lows with lows). To do this, I changed all the scores to Z scores because Z scores tell you how much a score is low or high relative to the other scores in its distribution. You figure the correlation coefficient by multiplying each person's two Z scores by each other, totaling up these products, and then averaging this total over the number of people. This will be a high number if highs go with highs and lows with lows, because with Z scores, highs are always positive and positive times positive is positive, and with Z scores, lows are always negative and negative times negative becomes positive too. Following this procedure, the highest number you can get, if the scores for the two variables are perfectly correlated, is +1. If there were no linear correlation between the two variables, the results would be 0 (because highs would sometimes be multiplied by highs and sometimes by lows, giving a mixture of positive and negative products that would cancel out).

In this example, the products of the Z scores add up to 3.70, which when divided by the number of children is .93.

This is called a *Pearson correlation coefficient (r)* of .93 and indicates a strong, positive linear correlation between the hours of violent TV watched each week and the number of violent or aggressive acts toward playmates.
(e) Three logically possible directions of causality: (i) Watching violent TV makes children act more aggressively toward playmates; (ii) being aggressive makes children more interested in watching violent TV; (iii) a third factor—such as living in a violent family environment—makes children more interested in watching violent TV and also makes them act aggressively toward playmates.
(f) Formulas: Predicted $Z_Y = (\beta)(Z_X)$; Predicted $Y = (SD_Y)(\text{Predicted } Z_Y) + M_Y$
$Z_X = -2$: Predicted $Z_Y = (.93)(-2) = -1.86$; Predicted $Y = (3.08)(-1.86) + 6 = .27$.
$Z_X = -1$: Predicted $Z_Y = (.93)(-1) = -.93$; Predicted $Y = (3.08)(-.93) + 6 = 3.14$.
$Z_X = 0$: Predicted $Z_Y = (.93)(0) = 0$; Predicted $Y = (3.08)(0) + 6 = 6.00$.
$Z_X = +1$: Predicted $Z_Y = (.93)(1) = .93$; Predicted $Y = (3.08)(.93) + 6 = 8.86$.
$Z_X = +2$: Predicted $Z_Y = (.93)(2) = 1.86$; Predicted $Y = (3.08)(1.86) + 6 = 11.73$.
(g) $r^2 = .93^2 = .86$.

7. (a) See answer to 2 above for an example; (b) linear, positive, strong.
(c)

Number of Town-Hall Meetings		Percentage of People Who Can Name Candidate		Cross-Product of Z Scores
X	Z_X	Y	Z_Y	$Z_X Z_Y$
4	.63	70	.36	.23
5	1.26	94	1.45	1.83
2	−.63	36	−1.17	.74
1	−1.26	48	−.63	.79
Σ = 12		Σ = 248		3.59
M = 3		M = 62		
SD = 1.58		SD = 22.14		r = 3.59/4 = .90

(d) See 6d above.
(e) Three logically possible directions of causality: (i) If a candidate has more town-hall meetings, this makes more people become aware of the candidate; (ii) If a candidate is well-known, this causes the candidate to have more town-hall meetings; (iii) A third factor—such as the amount of campaign money the candidate has—means the candidate can afford to hold more town-hall meetings and also causes more people to be aware of the candidate (perhaps because the candidate has been able to afford a large advertising campaign).
(f) Formulas: Predicted $Z_Y = (\beta)(Z_X)$; Predicted $Y = (SD_Y)(\text{Predicted } Z_Y) + M_Y$
$Z_X = -2$: Predicted $Z_Y = (.90)(-2) = -1.80$; Predicted $Y = (22.14)(-1.80) + 62 = 22.15$.
$Z_X = -1$: Predicted $Z_Y = (.90)(-1) = -.90$; Predicted $Y = (22.14)(-.90) + 62 = 42.07$.
$Z_X = 0$: Predicted $Z_Y = (.90)(0) = 0$; Predicted $Y = (22.14)(0) + 62 = 62.00$.

$Z_X = +1$: Predicted $Z_Y = (.90)(1) = .90$; Predicted $Y = (22.14)(.90) + 62 = 81.93$.
$Z_X = +2$: Predicted $Z_Y = (.90)(2) = 1.80$; Predicted $Y = (22.14)(1.80) + 62 = 101.85$.
(g) $r^2 = .90^2 = .81$.

8. (a) This table shows the degree of association among scores on several measures given to pregnant women and their partners. (Here continue with an explanation of the correlation coefficient like that in 6d above; except in this problem you also need to explain the mean, standard deviation, and Z scores—which you do in the same way as in answering the problems in Chapter 2.) For example, the correlation of .17 between women's reports of stress and men's reports of stress indicates that the association between these two measures is quite weak. That is, how much stress a women is under is not highly related to how much stress her partner believes she is under. On the other hand, the correlation of .50 (near the middle of the first column of correlations) tells you that there is a much stronger association between a woman's report of stress and her depressed mood in the second interview. That is, women who report being under stress are also likely to report being depressed, those reporting being under not much stress are likely to report not being very depressed. (b) In general, the correlations shown in this table are strongest among the stress, support, and mood items; correlations of these variables with demographics (age, ethnicity, etc.) were fairly weak. Partner support seemed to be strongly correlated with stress and mood, and depressed mood at the second testing was particularly related to the other variables. (c) Just because two variables are correlated, even strongly correlated, does not mean that you can know the particular direction of causality that creates that association. For example, there is a strong negative correlation between partner support at time 1 and depressed mood at time 2. There are three logically possible directions of causality here: Support can be causing lower depression, lower depression can be causing support, or some third factor can be causing both. You can rule out the second possibility, since something in the future (low depression) can't cause the past (initial support). However, the other two possibilities remain. It is certainly plausible that having her partner's support helps reduce depression. But it is also possible that a third factor is causing both. For example, consider level of income. Perhaps when a couple has more income, the partner has more time and energy to provide support and the greater comfort of living keeps depression down.

9. (a) Score on knowledge of fitness training principles; (b) number of injuries over subsequent year; (c) .4; (d) Predicted $Z_{Injuries} = (.4)(Z_{Score})$; (e) $(.4)(-2) = -.8$; (f) $-.4$; (g) 0; (h) .4; (i) .8.

10. This study used a statistical procedure called multiple regression. This procedure produces a formula for predicting a person's score on a criterion variable (in this example, third graders' reading comprehension) from his or her scores on a set of predictor variables (in this example, the three specific measures of reading ability). The formula is of the form that you multiply the person's score on each of the predictor variables by some particular number, called a regression coefficient or beta, and then add up the products. The procedure produces the most accurate prediction rule of this kind.

In this example, the prediction rule for the Z score for Reading Comprehension is $-.227$ times the Z score for Let-

ter-Word Identification, plus .299 times the Z score for Word Attack, plus .671 times the Z score for Oral Reading Fluency. (These are the numbers in the table next to each predictor variable in the Beta column.)

These regression coefficients suggest that reading comprehension is most strongly related to Oral Reading Fluency. Reading comprehension is also somewhat positively related to Word Attack. However, in the context of this prediction equation, reading comprehension is somewhat negatively related to Letter-Word Identification. This means that for any given level of Oral Reading Fluency and Word Attack, the better the child is at Letter-Word Identification, the child will be somewhat *worse* at reading comprehension!

It is important to note, however, that the regression coefficients for each of these predictors reflect what the scores on each predictor contribute to the prediction, over and above what the others contribute. If we were to consider ordinary correlations between each of the predictor variables with the criterion variable, their relative importance could be quite different. (Those correlations, however, were not provided.)

Another important piece of information in this table is R^2. This number tells you the proportion of variance accounted for in the criterion variable by the three predictor variables taken together. That is, 53.4% of the variation in the third graders' reading comprehension is accounted for by these three measures of specific reading abilities. This is equivalent to a correlation between reading comprehension and these three predictor variables of .73 (the square root of .534).

11. (a) Predicted $Z_{Comprehension} = (-.227)(Z_{Identification}) + (.299)(Z_{Attack}) + (.671)(Z_{Fluency})$ (b) A: Predicted $Z_{Comprehension} = (-.227)(1) + (.299)(1) + (.671)(1) = .743$; B: Predicted $Z_{Comprehension} = 0$; C: Predicted $Z_{Comprehension} = -.743$; D: Predicted $Z_{Comprehension} = -.227$; E: Predicted $Z_{Comprehension} = .299$; F: Predicted $Z_{Comprehension} = .671$; G: Predicted $Z_{Comprehension} = .289$; H: Predicted $Z_{Comprehension} = 1.341$; I: Predicted $Z_{Comprehension} = 1.631$.

Chapter 4

1. (a) 50%; (b) 16%; (c) 98%; (d) 84%; (e) 50%; (f) 84%; (g) 2%; (h) 16%.
2. (a) 50; (b) 45; (c) 40; (d) 35; (e) 30.
3. (a) From the normal curve table, 43% (.43) have Z scores between the mean and 1.5. By definition, 50% have Z scores below the mean. Thus, the total percentage below 1.5 is 50% + 43% = 93%; (b) 7%; (c) 7%; (d) 93%; (e) 2%; (f) 98%; (g) 33%; (h) 4%; (i) 5%.
4. (a) $Z = (16 - 15)/5 = .2$; from the normal curve table, percent between mean and .2 = 7.93; with 50% above the mean, the percent above .2 is 50% $- 7.93% = 42.07%$; (b) 34.46%; (c) 27.43%; (d) 72.57%; (e) 42.07%.
5. (a) Top 40% means 10% between the mean and this score; the nearest Z score from the normal curve table for 10% is .25; a Z score of .25 equals a raw score of $(.25)(5) + 15 = 16.25$; (b) 17.6; (c) 19.2.
6. (a) 21.90%; (b) 22.24%; (c) 42.79%; (d) 44.06%; (e) 21.90%.
7. (a) The bottom 30% means 20% between the mean and this score; the nearest Z score from the normal curve table for 20% is $-.52$; (b) -1.88.

8. (a) The top 10% means 90% are below. Of this 90%, 50% are below the mean. Thus, the top 10% is the point where 40% of scores are between it and the mean. Looking this up in the normal curve table, 40.00 (the closest actual value is 39.97) is a Z score of 1.28; (b) 2.33.

9. (a) Needed $Z = 1.64$; this corresponds to a raw score of $(1.64)(10) + 50 = 66.4$; (b) The scores for many things you measure, in nature and the behavioral and social sciences, tend approximately to follow the particular pattern shown below, called a normal curve. In a normal curve, most of the scores are near the middle, with fewer numbers of scores at each extreme. Because the normal curve is mathematically defined, the precise proportion of scores in any particular section of it can be calculated, and these have been listed in special tables. (Then explain mean, standard deviation, and Z scores as in answers to Chapter 2 problems.) The normal curve table tells the percentage of score in the normal curve between the mean and any particular Z score.

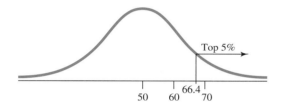

The coordination test scores are known to follow a normal curve. Thus, you can look up in the table the Z score for the point on the normal curve at which 45% of the scores are between it and the mean. The normal curve is completely symmetrical. Thus, 50% of the scores fall above the mean, leaving 5% above 45%. This is a Z score of 1.64 (actually, there is not an exact point on the table for 45%, so I could have used either 1.64 or 1.65). With a standard deviation of 10, a Z score of 1.64 is 16.4 points above the mean. Adding that to the mean of 50 makes the score needed to be in the top 5% 66.4.

10. (a) 10/50: $p = 10/50 = .2$; (b) .4; (c) $(10 + 20)/50 = .6$; (d) .6; (e) 1.
(f) The probability of a particular thing happening is usually defined as the number of possible ways the thing could happen (the number of *possible successful outcomes*) divided by the number of possible ways things like this could happen (the number of *all possible outcomes*). For part (a) there are 10 different drug/alcohol people you might pick out of a total of 50 people. Thus, the probability is 10/50 = .2.

11. A *sample* is a group of people studied that represents the entire group to which the results are intended to apply, called the *population*. (In this example, the population is all Australian high school students.) You study a sample because it would be impractical or impossible to test the entire population. One way of ensuring that the sample is not systematically unrepresentative is to select the sample randomly. This does not mean haphazardly. For example, just taking the students who are easily available to test would be haphazard sampling. But this would not be a good method because whatever factors make them easily available—such as living in a nearby town—might make them unrepresentative of the population as a whole. An example of a truly random method would be to acquire a list of all the high school students in Australia, number each student, and then use a table of random numbers to pick as many as are to be surveyed.

12. Similar to 11 above.

Chapter 5

1. (a) The logical, statistical procedure for determining the likelihood of your study having gotten a particular pattern of results if the null hypothesis is true. (b) The situation in hypothesis testing in which you decide to reject the null hypothesis because the probability of getting your particular results if the null hypothesis were true is less than 5%. (c) A procedure used in hypothesis testing when the research hypothesis does not specify a particular direction of difference—it tests for extreme results that are either higher or lower than would be expected by chance.

2. It is possible that the research hypothesis is correct but the result in the particular sample was not extreme enough to be able to reject the null hypothesis.

3. (i) (a) Population 1: Canadian children of librarians; Population 2: All Canadian children. (b) Population 1 children have a higher average reading ability than Population 2 children. (c) Population 1's average reading ability is not higher than Population 2's. (d) One-tailed, because the question is whether they "score higher," so only one direction of difference is of interest.
(ii) (a) Population 1: People who live in a particular city; Population 2: All people who live in the region. (b) Populations 1 and 2 have different mean incomes. (c) Populations 1 and 2 have the same mean income. (d) Two-tailed, because the question is whether the income of the people in the city is "different" from those in the region as a whole, so a difference in either direction would be of interest.
(iii) (a) Population 1: People who have experienced an earthquake; Population 2: People in general. (b) Populations 1 and 2 have different mean levels of self-confidence. (c) Populations 1 and 2 have the same mean level of self-confidence. (d) Two-tailed, because the question specifies "more or less," so a difference in either direction would be of interest.

4.

Study	Cutoff	Z Score on Comparison Distribution	Decision
A	+ 1.64	2	Reject null hypothesis
B	± 1.96	2	Reject null hypothesis
C	+ 2.33	2	Inconclusive
D	± 2.57	2	Inconclusive
E	+ 1.64	1	Inconclusive

5.

Study	Cutoff	Z Score on the Comparison Distribution	Decision
A	+ 1.64	1	Inconclusive
B	± 2.57	4	Reject null hypothesis
C	± 2.57	3	Reject null hypothesis
D	± 2.57	3.5	Reject null hypothesis
E	+ 1.64	−1	Inconclusive

6. ❶ **Restate the question as a research hypothesis and a null hypothesis about the populations.** There are two populations of interest:

Population 1: Students who are prevented from using their sense of smell.
Population 2: Students in general.

The research hypothesis is that students prevented from using their sense of smell (Population 1) will do worse on the taste task than students in general (Population 2). The null hypothesis is that students prevented from using their sense of smell (Population 1) will not do worse on the taste task than students in general (Population 2).
❷ **Determine the characteristics of the comparison distribution.** The comparison distribution will be the same as Population 2. As stated in the problem, Population $M = 14$ and Population $SD = 4$. We assume it follows a normal curve.
❸ **Determine the cutoff sample score on the comparison distribution at which the null hypothesis should be rejected.** For a one-tailed test at the .05 level, the cutoff is −1.64. (The cutoff is a *negative value,* because the research hypothesis is that Population 1 will *do worse* on the task than Population 2—that is, Population 1 will have a *lower score* on the task than Population 2.)
❹ **Determine your sample's score on the comparison distribution.** The sample's score was 5. $Z = (5 - 14)/4 = -2.25$.
❺ **Decide whether to reject the null hypothesis.** A Z score of −2.25 is more extreme than the cutoff of −1.64. Thus, you can reject the null hypothesis. The research hypothesis is supported—not having a sense of smell makes for fewer correct identifications.

Explanation: In brief, you solve this problem by considering the likelihood that being without a sense of smell makes no difference. If the sense of smell made no difference, the probability of the student studied getting any particular number correct is simply the probability of students in general getting any particular number correct. We know the distribution of the number correct that students get in general. Thus, you can figure that probability. It turns out that it would be fairly unlikely to get only 5 correct—so the researcher concludes that not having the sense of smell does make a difference.

To go into the details a bit, the key issue is determining these probabilities. We assumed that the number correct for the students in general follows a normal curve—a specific bell-shaped mathematical pattern in which most of the scores are in the middle and there are fewer scores as the number correct gets higher or lower. There are tables showing exactly what proportions are between the middle and any particular Z score on the normal curve.

When considering what to conclude from a study, researchers often use a convention that if a result could have happened by chance less than 5% of the time under a particular scenario, that scenario will be considered unlikely. The normal curve tables show that the top 5% of the normal curve begins with a Z score of 1.64. The normal curve is completely symmetrical; thus, the bottom 5% includes all Z scores below −1.64. Therefore, the researcher would probably set the following rule: The scenario in which being without the sense of smell makes no difference will be rejected as unlikely if the number correct (converted to a Z score using the mean and standard deviation for students in general) is less than −1.64.

The actual number correct for the student who could not use the sense of smell was 5. The normal curve for students in general had a mean of 14 and a standard deviation of 4. Getting 5 correct is 9 below the mean of 14; in terms of standard deviations of 4 each, it is 9/4 below the mean. A Z score of −2.25 is more extreme than −1.64. Thus, the researcher concludes that the scenario in which being without smell has no effect is unlikely. This is illustrated below:

7. Cutoff (.01 level, one-tailed) = −2.33; Z score on comparison distribution for patient studied = 1.2; the experiment is inconclusive. Hypothesis testing steps, explanation, and sketch similar to 6 above.

8. The two Ms (5.7 and 4.8) and the $p < .05$ are crucial. M stands for *mean*, the average of the scores in a particular group. The average number of times per day the high-narcissism participants looked in the mirror was 5.7, while the average for the low-narcissism participants was only 4.8. The $p < .05$ tells us that this difference is statistically significant at the .05 level. This means that if a person's level of narcissism made no difference in how often the person looked in the mirror, the chances of getting two groups of participants who were this different on looking in the mirror just by chance would be 5%. Hence, you can reject that possibility as unlikely and conclude that the level of narcissism does make a difference in how often people look in the mirror.

9. Similar to 8 above.

Chapter 6

1. There is less variation among means of samples of more than one score than there are among individual scores. This

is because the likelihood of two extreme scores in the same direction randomly ending up in the same sample is less than the probability of each of those extreme scores being chosen individually.

2. (a) Population $SD^2 = 10^2 = 100$; Population $SD_M^2 =$ Population $SD^2/N = 100/2 = 50$; Population $SD_M = \sqrt{\text{Population } SD_M^2} = \sqrt{50} = 7.07$; (b) 5.77; (c) 5; (d) 3.33.

3. (a) Population $SD^2 = 20^2 = 400$; Population $SD_M^2 =$ Population $SD^2/N = 400/2 = 200$; Population $SD_M = \sqrt{\text{Population } SD_M^2} = \sqrt{200} = 14.14$; (b) 11.55; (c) 10; (d) 6.67.

4. (a) The best estimate of the population mean is the sample mean of 100. From question 2a, the standard deviation of the distribution of means (Population SD_M) is 7.07. For the 95% confidence limits, the Z scores you want are -1.96 and $+1.96$. Lower limit $= (-1.96)(7.07) + 100 = 86.14$. Upper limit $= (1.96)(7.07) + 100 = 113.86$; (b) 88.69, 111.31; (c) 90.2, 109.8; (d) 93.47, 106.53.

5. (a) The best estimate of the population mean is the sample mean of 10. From question 3a, the standard deviation of the distribution of means (Population SD_M) is 14.14. For the 99% confidence limits, the Z scores you want are -2.57 and $+2.57$. Lower limit $= (-2.57)(14.14) + 10 = -26.34$; upper limit $= (2.57)(14.14) + 10 = 46.34$; (b) -19.68, 39.68; (c) -15.7, 35.7; (d) -7.14, 27.14.

6. (a)

❶ Restate the question as a research hypothesis and a null hypothesis about the populations. There are two populations of interest:

Population 1: People given the experimental treatment.
Population 2: People in general (who do not get the experimental treatment).

The research hypothesis is that the population given the experimental treatment (Population 1) has a different mean score than people in general (Population 2). The null hypothesis is that Population 1's mean is the same as Population 2's.

❷ Determine the characteristics of the comparison distribution. Comparison distribution is a distribution of means of samples of 10 taken from the distribution of Population 2. Population M_M = Population M = 40; Population SD_M^2 = Population $SD^2/N = 6^2/10 = 3.6$; Population $SD_M = \sqrt{\text{Population } SD_M^2} = \sqrt{3.6} = 1.90$. Because the population is normal, the distribution of means is normal.

❸ Determine the cutoff sample score on the comparison distribution at which the null hypothesis should be rejected. For a two-tailed test at the .05 level, the cutoffs are -1.96 and 1.96.

❹ Determine your sample's score on the comparison distribution. $Z = (44 - 40)/1.90 = 2.11$.

❺ Decide whether to reject the null hypothesis. 2.11 is more extreme than 1.96. Thus, you can reject the null hypothesis. The research hypothesis is supported; those who receive the experimental treatment score differently from the general population. The distributions involved are shown at the top of the next column.

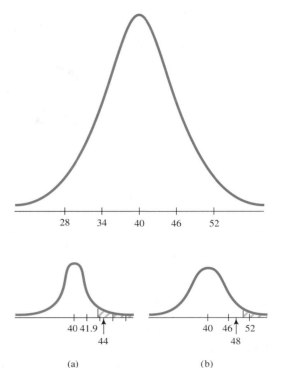

(a)   (b)

95% confidence interval: Lower limit $= (-1.96)(1.9) + 44 = 40.28$; Upper limit $= (1.96)(1.9) + 44 = 47.72$.
(b) Hypothesis-testing steps similar to (a) above. Population $SD_M = 6$; $Z = (48 - 40)/6 = 1.33$; do not reject null hypothesis; study is inconclusive as to whether those who receive the experimental treatment are different from those in the general population. 95% confidence interval: 36.24 to 59.76.

7. Hypothesis-testing steps and drawing similar to 6 above.
(a) Population $SD_M = .8$; $Z = (82 - 81)/.8 = 1.25$; do not reject null hypothesis; 99% confidence interval: 79.94 to 84.06. (b) Population $SD_M = 2.53$; $Z = (84 - 81)/2.53 = 1.19$; do not reject null hypothesis; 99% confidence interval: 77.5 to 90.5.

8. (a) and (b) Hypothesis-testing steps and drawing similar to 6 above. Population $SD_M = .1$; $Z = (1.5 - 1.8)/.1 = -3$; reject the null hypothesis. (c) 99% confidence interval: 1.24 to 1.76.
(d) This is a standard hypothesis-testing problem, with one exception. You can't compare directly the reaction times for the group of 25 women tested to a distribution of reaction times for individual women. The probability of a group of scores having an extreme mean just by chance is much less than the probability of any one individual having an extreme score just by chance. (When taking a group of scores at random, any extreme individual scores are likely to be balanced out by less extreme or oppositely extreme scores.) Thus, you need to compare the mean of the group of 25 reaction times to a distribution of what would happen if you were to take many random groups of 25 reaction time scores and find the mean of each group of 25 scores.

Such a distribution of many means of samples has the same mean as the original distribution of individual scores (there is no reason for it to be otherwise). However, it is a narrower curve. This is because the chances of extremes are less. In fact, its variance will be exactly the variance of the original distribution of individuals divided by the number of scores in each sample. In this example, this makes a distribution of means with a mean of 1.8 and a standard deviation of .1 (that is, the square root of the result of $.5^2$ divided by 25). This will be a normal distribution because a distribution of many means from a normally distributed population is also normal.

The cutoff for significance, using the .01 level and a one-tailed test, is -2.33. The mean reaction time of the group of 25 women who received the special program, 1.5, was 3 standard deviations below the mean of the distribution of means, making it clearly more extreme than the cutoff. Thus, you can reject the null hypothesis and conclude that the results support the hypothesis that elderly women who take part in the special program have lower reaction times.

The confidence interval is an estimate (based on your sample's mean and the standard deviation of the distribution of means) of the range of values that is likely to include the true population mean for the group studied (Population 1: in this example, women who receive the special reaction-time program). A 99% confidence interval is the range of values you are 99% confident include the true population mean. The lower limit of this interval is the mean of the lowest distribution of means that would have a 99% chance of including this sample mean; its upper limit is the mean of the highest distribution of means that would have a 99% chance of including this sample mean.

To figure the confidence interval, you first consider that the best single point estimate of the mean of Population 1 is the sample's mean (in this case, 1.5). You then assume that the standard deviation of the distribution of means for this population is the same as for the known population (which we figured earlier to be .1). Based on this information, if the true population mean was 1.5, 99% of the time, sample means would fall between a Z score of -2.57 (the point on the normal curve that includes 49.5% of the scores below the mean) and $+2.57$. In our example, these Z scores correspond to raw scores of 1.24 and 1.76.

It turns out that the values figured in this way are the limits of the confidence interval. Why? Suppose the true population mean was 1.24. In this case, there would be a .5% chance of getting a mean as large as or larger than 1.5. (That is, with a mean of 1.24 and a standard deviation of .1, 1.5 is exactly 2.57 standard deviations above the mean, which is the point that corresponds to the cutoff for the top .5% of this curve.) Similarly, if the true population mean was 1.76, there would only be a .5% chance of getting a mean lower than 1.5.

9. (a) and (b) Hypothesis-testing steps and drawing similar to 6 above. Population $SD_M = .2$; $Z = (5.9 - 5.5)/.2 = 2$; reject the null hypothesis. (c) 95% confidence interval; 5.51 to 6.29. (d) Similar to 8d above, plus an explanation of material from previous chapter on hypothesis testing, normal curve, means, and standard deviations.

10. The error bars are the lines that go above and below the top of each bar. The error bars show, for each particular group, the standard deviation of the distribution of means for people like those in this group. (Then explain a distribution of means as in 8d above.)

11. Similar to confidence interval part of 8d above.

Chapter 7

1. (a)

Conclusion from Hypothesis Testing	Real Situation	
	Null Hypothesis True	Research Hypothesis True
Research Hypothesis Supported (Reject null)	*Type I Error* Decide more recess time improves behavior but it really doesn't	*Correct Decision* Decide more recess time improves behavior and it really does
Study Inconclusive (Do no reject null)	*Correct Decision* Decide effect of recess time on behavior is not shown in this study; actually more recess time doesn't improve behavior	*Type II Error* Decide effect of recess time on behavior is not shown in this study; actually more recess time improves behavior

(b) and (c) are similar to 1a above.

2. (a) You can never know for certain if you have made a Type I error. (b) You can never know for certain if you have made a Type II error.

3. (a) Effect size = (Population 1 M − Population 2 M)/Population SD = $(19 − 25)/12 = −.5$, medium; (b) $−.25$, small; (c) 0, no effect; (d) .42, medium; (e) .83, large.

4. (a) Effect size = (Population 1 M − Population 2 M)/Population SD = $(50 − 50)/5 = 0$, no effect; (b) .4, medium; (c) .8, large; (d) 1.2, large; (e) $−.6$, medium.

5. (a) Predicted effect size = (Population 1 M − Population 2 M)/Population SD = $(91 − 90)/4 = .25$; (b) .5; (c) 1; (d) $−1$.

6. (a) Not affected; (b) Possibly of small importance; (c) Regarding situation (a), the significance tells you the probability of getting your results if the null hypothesis is true; sample size is already taken into account in figuring the significance. Regarding situation (b), it is possible to get a significant result with a large sample even when the actual practical effect is slight—such as when the mean of your sample (and this, your best estimate of the mean of the population that gets the experimental treatment) is only slightly higher than the mean of the known population. This is possible because significance is based on the difference between the mean of your sample and the known population mean divided by the standard deviation of the distribution of means. If the sample size is very large, then the standard deviation of the distribution of means is very small (because it is figured by taking the square root of the result of dividing the population variance by the sample size). Thus, even a small difference between the means when divided by a very small denominator can give a large overall result, making the study significant.

7. Power is the chance of rejecting the null hypothesis if the research hypothesis is true. In other words, the power of a study represents the likelihood that you will get a statistically significant result in your study, if in fact the research hypothesis is true. Ideally, a study should have power of 80% or more. If a study has low power and does not get a statistically significant result, the result of the study is entirely inconclusive. This is because it is not clear whether the nonsignificant result is due to the low power of the study or because the research hypothesis is in fact false.

Effect size can be thought of as the degree to which populations do not overlap. The larger the effect size, the larger the power. As noted by Aron et al., their study had a high level of power (about 90%) for detecting both large and medium-sized effects. Given this high level of power, the researchers were able to conclude that the most likely reason for the nonsignificant study results is that the research hypothesis is in fact false. As the researchers noted, with such a high level of power, it is very unlikely that the results of the study would be nonsignificant if there were in fact a medium-sized or large effect in the population. Since smaller effect sizes are associated with lower power, the researchers were careful not to rule out the possibility that there is in fact a small effect in the population (which may not have been detected in the study due to the lower power for identifying a small effect size).

8. (a) Increases power; (b) decreases power; (c) increases power; (d) decreases power; (e) decreases power.

9. (i) When planning an experiment, to permit changes of various kinds (or even abandon the project) if power is too low. (Or possibly make the study less costly, for example, by reducing the number of participants, if power is higher than reasonably needed.) (ii) After a study is done that had nonsignificant results, to evaluate whether the result should be attributed to the null hypothesis being false (in the high-power situation) or to inadequate power so that it is still reasonable to think that future research might have a chance of being significant. (Also, in the case of a significant result with a large sample, if power is very high, this suggests that a low effect size is possible, so that although the result is significant, it may not be very important.)

Chapter 8

1. (a) t needed ($df = 63$, $p <.05$, one-tailed) $= −1.671$; $S_M^2 = S^2/N = 9/64 = .141$. $S_M = \sqrt{S_M^2} = \sqrt{.141} = .38$; $t = (M − \text{Population } M)/S_M = (11 − 12.40)/.38 = −3.68$; reject null hypothesis. (b) t needed $= −2.690, 2.690$; $S_M = 2.55$; $t = 1.32$; do not reject null hypothesis. (c) t needed $= 2.364$; $S_M = .13$; $t = 3.15$; reject null hypothesis.

2. (a)

❶ **Restate the question as a research hypothesis and a null hypothesis about the populations.** There are two populations of interest:

Population 1: Response times under the new sheriff.
Population 2: Response times under the old sheriff.

The research hypothesis is that the two populations are different. The null hypothesis is that the two populations are the same.

❷ **Determine the characteristics of the comparison distribution.** Population 2: shape = assumed normal; Population $M = 30$; The estimated population variance is $S^2 = \Sigma(X − M)^2/df = (124)/(10 − 1) = 13.78$. Distribution of means: shape = t ($df = 9$); mean of the distribution of means $= 30$; variance of the distribution of means is $S_M^2 = S^2/N = 13.78/10 = 1.378$; standard deviation of the distribution of means is $S_M = \sqrt{S_M^2} = \sqrt{1.378} = 1.17$.

❸ **Determine the cutoff sample score on the comparison distribution at which the null hypothesis should be rejected.** t needed ($df = 9$, $p <.05$, one-tailed) $= −1.833$.

❹ **Determine your sample's score on the comparison distribution.** $M = \Sigma X/N = 280/10 = 28$; $t = (M − \text{Population } M)/S_M = (28 − 30)/1.17 = −1.71$.

❺ **Decide whether to reject the null hypothesis.** $−1.71$ is not more extreme than $−1.833$; do not reject the null hypothesis.

(b)

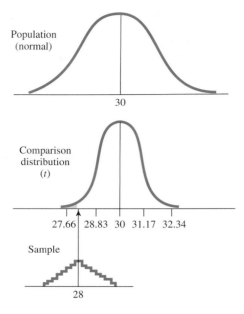

(c) Similar to 5c below, except instead of difference scores, actual scores are used here, and the expected population mean is the 30 minutes that the sheriff had promised to do better than the current sheriff.

3. (a) and (b) Hypothesis-testing steps and sketch similar to 2a and 2b above; t needed $= -2.776, 2.776$; $t = (M -$ Population $M)/S_M = (46 - 40)/2.3 = 2.61$; do not reject the null hypothesis. (c) Similar to 5c below, except instead of difference scores, actual scores are used here, and the expected population mean is the 40 questions that people usually get correct.

4. (a) t needed $(df = 19, p <.05, \text{one-tailed}) = 1.729$; $S_M^2 = S^2/N = 8.29/20 = .415$; $S_M = \sqrt{S_M^2} = \sqrt{.415} = .64$; $t = (M -$ Population $M)/S_M = (1.7 - 0)/.64 = 2.66$; reject null hypothesis.

(b) t needed $= -1.984, 1.984$; $S_M^2 = S^2/N = 414.53/164 = 2.53$; $S_M = \sqrt{S_M^2} = \sqrt{2.53} = 1.59$; $t = (2.3 - 0)/1.59 = 1.45$; do not reject null hypothesis.

(c) t needed $= -2.625$; $S_M^2 = S^2/N = 4/15 = .27$; $S_M = \sqrt{S_M^2} = \sqrt{.27} = .52$; $t = -4.23$; reject null hypothesis.

5. (a)
❶ **Restate the question as a research hypothesis and a null hypothesis about the populations.** There are two populations of interest:

Population 1: Cities like those who participated in the anti-littering program.
Population 2: Cities that do not change in the amount of litter over a 1-year period.

The research hypothesis is that Population 1 has a greater mean decrease in litter than Population 2. The null hypothesis is that Population 1 doesn't have a greater mean decrease in litter than Population 2.
❷ **Determine the characteristics of the comparison distribution.** Population 2: shape = assumed normal; Popu-

lation $M = 0$; The estimated population variance is $S^2 = \Sigma(X - M)^2/df = (50)/(4 - 1) = 16.67$. Distribution of means: shape $= t$ $(df = 3)$; mean of the distribution of means of difference scores $= 0$; variance of the distribution of means of difference scores is $S_M^2 = S^2/N = 16.67/4 = 4.17$; standard deviation of the distribution of means of difference scores is $S_M = \sqrt{S_M^2} = \sqrt{4.17} = 2.04$.
❸ **Determine the cutoff sample score on the comparison distribution at which the null hypothesis should be rejected.** t needed $(df = 3, p <.01, \text{one-tailed}) = 4.541$.
❹ **Determine your sample's score on the comparison distribution.** Change scores $= 7, 6, -1, 8$; $M = 20/4 = 5$; $t = (M -$ Population $M)/S_M = (5 - 0)/2.04 = 2.45$.
❺ **Decide whether to reject the null hypothesis.** 2.45 (from Step 4) is not more extreme than the cutoff of 4.541 (from Step 3); do not reject the null hypothesis.
(b)
(c) The first thing I did was to simplify things by converting the numbers to difference scores—preprogram (2003) litter

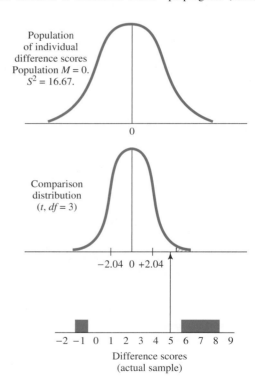

minus postprogram (2004) litter for each city. Then I found the mean of these difference scores, which was 5. That is, there is an average decrease of 5 pounds of litter per block per day.

The next step was to see whether this result, found in these four cities, indicates some real difference, more generally due to being in this program. The alternative is the possibility that this much change could have happened in four randomly selected cities just by chance even if in general the program has no real effect. That is, we imagine that the average change for cities in general is actually 0, and maybe this study just happened to pick four cities that would have decreased this much anyway.

I then considered just how much a group of four cities would have to change before I could conclude that they have changed too much to chalk it up to chance. This required figuring out the characteristics of this imagined population of cities in which, on the average, there is no change. An average of no change is the same as saying it has a mean of 0 change. Since I didn't know the variance of this hypothetical distribution of cities that don't change, I estimated it from the information in the sample of four cities. If the sample cities were drawn at chance from the hypothetical distribution of no change, the variance of these cities should reflect the variance of this distribution (which would be the distribution they come from). However, the variance figured from a particular group (sample) from a larger population will in general be slightly smaller than the true population's variance. Thus, I had to modify the variance formula to take this into account: Instead of dividing the sum of the squared deviations by the number of scores, I divided it instead by the "degrees of freedom," which is the number of scores minus 1—in this case, 3. (This adjustment exactly accounts for the tendency of the variance in the sample to underestimate the true population variance.) As shown in the calculations in the steps of hypothesis testing, this gave an estimated population variance (S^2) of 16.67.

I was interested not in individual cities but in a group of four. Thus, what I really needed to know was the characteristics of a distribution of means of samples of four taken from this hypothetical population of individual city difference scores. Such a distribution of means will have the same mean of 0 (since there is no reason to expect the means of such groups of four drawn randomly to be systematically higher or lower than 0). However, such a distribution will have a much smaller variance (because the average of a group of four scores is a lot less likely to be extreme than any individual score). Fortunately, it is known (and can be proved mathematically) that the variance of a distribution of means is the variance of the distribution of individuals divided by the number of individuals in each sample. In our example, this works out to 16.67 divided by 4, which is 4.17. The standard deviation of this distribution is thus the square root of 4.17, or 2.04.

It also turns out that if we assume that the hypothetical population of individual cities' difference scores is normally distributed (and we have no reason to think otherwise), the distribution of means of samples from that distribution can be thought of as having a precise known shape, called a t distribution (which has slightly thicker tails than a normal curve). Thus, I looked in a table for a t distribution for the situation in which there are 3 degrees of freedom used to estimate the population variance. The table shows that there is less than a 1% chance of getting a score that is 4.541 standard deviations from the mean of this distribution.

The mean difference score for the sample of four cities was 5, which is 2.45 (that is, 5/2.04) standard deviations above the mean of 0 change on this distribution of means of difference scores. This is not as extreme as 4.541. Thus, there is more than a 1% chance that these results could have come from a hypothetical distribution with no change. Therefore, the researcher would not rule out that possibility, and the experiment would be considered inconclusive.

6. (a), (b), and (c). Hypothesis-testing steps, sketch, and explanation similar to 5 above. t needed $= -2.776, 2.776$; $t = (M - \text{Population } M)/S_M = (.014 - 0)/.005 = 2.8$; reject the null hypothesis. (Note: This result is very close to the cutoff

level; if you round off slightly, your result might not be significant. This is one of those rare situations in which different ways of rounding can produce different results.)

7. (a) Estimated effect size $= M/S = 20/32 = .63$, medium effect size; (b) .5, medium; (c) .25, small; (d) .2, small.

8. From Table 8–8: (a) .22; (b) .71; (c) .86; (d) .77; (e) .99.

9. From Table 8–9: (a) 33; (b) 12; (c) 156.

10. Similar to 5c above except focusing on this study and the simpler situation involving just a single sample and also does not need to explain the basic logic of hypothesis testing (only what is added when you have an unknown population variance).

11. Similar to 5b and 5c above, except the explanation should focus on this study and material on mean, standard deviation, and variance should be added, as in the answers to Chapter 2 problems.

Chapter 9

1. (a) Independent; (b) dependent; (c) dependent.

2. (a) $S^2_{\text{Pooled}} = (df_1/df_{\text{Total}})(S^2_1) + (df_2/df_{\text{Total}})(S^2_2) = (19/38)(1) + (19/38)(2) = 1.5$; $S^2_{M_1} = S^2_{\text{Pooled}}/N_1 = 1.5/20 = .075$; $S^2_{M_2} = .075$; $S^2_{\text{Difference}} = S^2_{M_1} + S^2_{M_2} = .075 + .075 = .15$; $S_{\text{Difference}} = .39$.

(b) .35; (c) .32; (d) .27; (e) .35.

3. (a) t needed ($df = 58$, $p < .05$, two-tailed) $= -2.004, 2.004$; $S^2_{\text{Pooled}} = (df_1/df_{\text{Total}})(S^2_1) + (df_2/df_{\text{Total}})(S^2_2) = (29/58)(2.4) + (29/58)(2.8) = 2.6$; $S^2_{M_1} = S^2_{\text{Pooled}}/N_1 = 2.6/30 = .087$; $S^2_{M_2} = .087$; $S^2_{\text{Difference}} = S^2_{M_1} + S^2_{M_2} = .087 + .087 = .174$. $S_{\text{Difference}} = .417$; $t = (M_1 - M_2)/S_{\text{Difference}} = (12 - 11.1)/.417 = 2.16$. Conclusion: Reject the null hypothesis. The difference is significant. (b) $S^2_{\text{Pooled}} = 2.67$; $S_{\text{Difference}} = .45$; $t = 2.00$; do not reject the null hypothesis. (c) $S^2_{\text{Pooled}} = 2.6$; $S_{\text{Difference}} = .416$; $t = 2.16$; reject the null hypothesis.

4. (a)

❶ **Restate the question as a research hypothesis and a null hypothesis about the populations.** There are two populations of interest:

Population 1: People who get their news from TV.
Population 2: People who get their news from radio.

The research hypothesis is that the two populations have different means. The null hypothesis is that the two populations have the same mean.

❷ **Determine the characteristics of the comparison distribution.** $S^2_{\text{Pooled}} = (60/80)(4) + (20/80)(6) = 4.5$; comparison distribution (distribution of differences between means): $M = 0$; $S_{\text{Difference}} = .54$; shape $= t$ ($df = 80$).

❸ **Determine the cutoff sample score on the comparison distribution at which the null hypothesis should be rejected.** t needed ($df = 80$, $p < .01$, two-tailed) $= -2.639, 2.639$.

❹ **Determine your sample's score on the comparison distribution.** $t = (24 - 26)/.54 = -3.70$.

❺ **Decide whether to reject the null hypothesis.** -3.70 is more extreme than -2.639; reject the null hypothesis; the prediction is supported by the experiment.

(b)

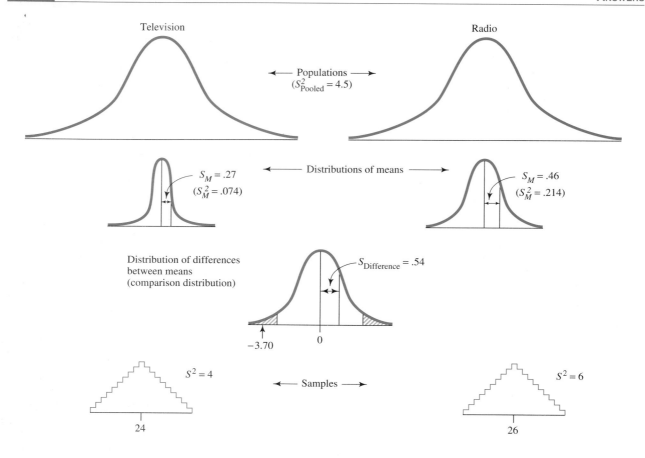

(c) In this situation, I am testing whether the two samples come from identical populations. I have two estimates of those identical populations, one from each sample. Thus, to get the most accurate overall estimate of the population variance, I can average the two estimates of the population variance. In order to give more weight to the estimate based on the larger degrees of freedom, I figure a weighted average, multiplying each estimate by its proportion of the total degrees of freedom and adding up the results. This pooled estimate of the population variance comes out to 4.5.

    Because I was interested not in individual scores but in the difference between the mean of a group of 61 and the mean of another group of 21, I needed to figure out what would be the characteristics of a distribution of differences between means of groups of 61 and 21 that are randomly taken from the two identical populations whose variance I just estimated. This required two steps. First, I figured the characteristics of the distribution of means in the usual way for the population associated with each sample, but using my pooled estimate for the variance of each population of individuals. This came out to .074 for the TV group and .214 for the radio group. The second step is directly about the distribution of differences between means. It is like a distribution you would get if you took a mean from the distribution of means for the TV group and took one from the distribution of means for the radio group and figured their difference. After doing this many times, the distribution of these differ-

ences would make up a new distribution, called a distribution of differences between means. Because we are assuming (if radio versus TV made no difference) that the two original populations have the same means, on average, the difference between a mean taken from the TV group and a mean taken from the radio group should come out to 0 (because sometimes one will be bigger and sometimes the other, but in the long run these random fluctuations should balance out). The variance of this distribution of differences between means is affected by the variation in both distributions of means—in fact, it is just the sum of the two. Thus, its variance is .074 plus .214, or .288. Its square root, the standard deviation of the distribution of differences between means, is .54.

    Because this whole process is based on estimated variances, the distribution of means is a t distribution with degrees of freedom equal to the total number of degrees of freedom that went into the two estimates—thus $df = 80$. Looking this up on the t table for .01 two-tailed gives a cutoff needed of -2.639 and 2.639. The t for my sample is the difference between the two groups divided by the standard deviation of the distribution of differences between means: $(24 - 26)/.54 = -3.70$. This is more extreme than the cutoff, so I can reject the null hypothesis.

5. (a), (b), and (c). Hypothesis-testing steps, sketch, and explanation similar to 4 above (except c also needs to include basic material as in answers to previous chapters' problems). t needed $= -2.262, 2.262$; $S^2_{\text{Pooled}} = (5/9)(5.6) +$

$(4/9)(19.3) = 11.69$; $S_{\text{Difference}}^2 = 1.95 + 2.34 = 4.29$; $S_{\text{Difference}} = 2.07$; $t = (6 - 9.6)/2.07 = -1.74$. Do not reject the null hypothesis; the experiment is inconclusive as to whether including the child's name makes a difference. (Note: The scores in this problem seem to violate the assumption of equal population variances. However, because the result was not significant even using the ordinary procedure, it would probably not be significant using a modified procedure.)

6. (a), (b), and (c). Hypothesis-testing steps, sketch, and explanation similar to 4 above. t needed = 1.943; $S_{\text{Pooled}}^2 = (4/6)(6.7) + (2/6)(12.33) = 8.58$; $S_{\text{Difference}}^2 = 2.86 + 1.72 = 4.58$; $S_{\text{Difference}} = 2.14$; $t = (5.33 - 5.2)/2.14 = .06$. Do not reject the null hypothesis; the experiment is inconclusive as to whether older children do better.

7. (a) Estimated effect size = $(M_1 - M_2)/S_{\text{Pooled}} = (24 - 26)/\sqrt{4.5} = -.94$; (b) -1.05; (c) .04. (d) Effect size represents the degree to which two populations do not overlap. The less that two populations overlap, the larger the effect size. In the behavioral and social sciences, we often want to know not just if a result is significant, but how big the effect is—effect size provides a measure of how big the effect is. Effect size for the t test for independent means is the difference between the population means divided by the standard deviation of the population of individuals. However, you do not know the population means, so you estimate them using the sample means. You also do not know the standard deviation of the population of individuals, so you estimate it by using the pooled estimate of the population standard deviation. So, in part (a), the effect size was the difference between the sample means (24 minus 26, which gives -2), divided by the pooled estimate of the population standard deviation (which was the square root of 4.5, or 2.12). This gave an estimated effect size of $-.94$, which is a large effect size according to Cohen's effect size conventions for the t test for independent means.

8. (a) Harmonic mean = $2(N_1)(N_2)/(N_1 + N_2) = (2)(3)(57)/(3 + 57) = 5.7$; from Table 9–4 approximate power = .11; (b) harmonic mean = 16.7, power = .15; (c) harmonic mean = 26.7, power = .19; (d) power = .19.

9. (a) Estimated effect size = $(M_1 - M_2)/S_{\text{Pooled}} = (107 - 149)/84 = -.50$, medium effect size; needed N (from Table 9–5) = 50 per group, 100 total. (b) Estimated effect size = .20; needed N = 393 per group, 786 total. (c) Estimated effect size = .80; needed N = 20 per group, 40 total. (d) Estimated effect size = $-.80$; needed N = 26 per group, 52 total.

10. [Along with the following, include a full explanation of all terms and concepts as in 4c and answers to previous chapters' explanation problems.] This study shows that using a conventional .05 significance level, German children who receive low levels of support—whether from their mother, father, or classmates—showed lower levels of self-worth. Furthermore, the effect sizes were fairly large (.78 and .69) with regard to support from mother or father; however, the effect size was only small to moderate (.35) with regard to support from classmates. This would seem to imply that support from parents is more important than support from classmates in terms of a child's feeling of self-worth. The power of the study for a large effect size is .98. (This assumes there were about equal numbers of children in the high and low support groups, that the test is two-tailed, and uses the figure for 50 in each group.) The power for a

medium effect size is .70. Because we already know that the results are significant and we know the effect sizes, the power calculations are not very important.

11. Similar to 4c above, focusing on the results of this study.

Chapter 10

1. (a) F needed ($df = 2, 27$; $p < .05$) = 3.36; $S_M^2 = \Sigma(M - GM)^2/df_{\text{Between}} = [(7.4 - 7)^2 + (6.8 - 7)^2 + (6.8 - 7)^2]/2 = .12$; $S_{\text{Between}}^2 = (S_M^2)(n) = (.12)(10) = 1.2$; $S_{\text{Within}}^2 = (S_1^2 + S_2^2 + \cdots + S_{\text{Last}}^2)/N_{\text{Groups}} = (.82 + .90 + .82 + .90 + 80)/3 = .84$; $F = 1.2/.84 = 1.43$; do not reject the null hypothesis; Estimated effect size = $\sqrt{F}/\sqrt{n} = \sqrt{1.43}/\sqrt{10} = .38$; from Table 10–8, approximate power = .45. (b) F needed ($df = 3, 96$; $p < .05$) = 2.70 (actually using $df = 3, 95$); $S_M^2 = 164.67$; $S_{\text{Between}}^2 = (164.67)(25) = 4116.75$; $S_{\text{Within}}^2 = 736.5$; $F = 5.59$; reject the null hypothesis; estimated effect size = .47; approximate power = between .85 and .96. (c) F needed ($df = 4, 120$; $p < .05$) = 2.46 (actually using $df = 4, 100$); $S_M^2 = 123.5$; $S_{\text{Between}}^2 = (123.5)(25) = 3087.5$; $S_{\text{Within}}^2 = 735$; $F = 4.20$; reject the null hypothesis; estimated effect size = .41; approximate power = between .90 and .98.

2. (a) F needed ($df = 2, 9$; $p < .01$) = 8.02; Group 1: $M = 8$, $S^2 = .67$; Group 2: $M = 6$, $S^2 = .67$; Group 3: $M = 4$, $S^2 = .67$; $S_{\text{Between}}^2 = (4)(4) = 16$; $S_{\text{Within}}^2 = .67$; $F = 16/.67 = 23.88$; reject the null hypothesis; Estimated effect size = $\sqrt{F}/\sqrt{n} = \sqrt{23.88}/\sqrt{4} = 2.44$. (b) F needed ($df = 2, 9$; $p < .01$) = 8.02; Group 1: $M = 8$, $S^2 = 21.33$; Group 2: $M = 6$, $S^2 = 21.33$; Group 3: $M = 4$, $S^2 = 21.33$; $S_{\text{Between}}^2 = (4)(4) = 16$; $S_{\text{Within}}^2 = 21.33$; $F = 16/21.33 = .75$; do not reject the null hypothesis; estimated effect size = .43.

3. (a)

❶ **Restate the question as a research hypothesis and a null hypothesis about the populations.** There are three populations of interest:

Population 1: Patients with affective disorders.
Population 2: Patients with cognitive disorders.
Population 3: Patients with drug-related conditions.

The research hypothesis is that the three population means differ. The null hypothesis is that the three populations have the same mean.
❷ **Determine the characteristics of the comparison distribution.** F distribution with 2 and 9 degrees of freedom.
❸ **Determine the cutoff sample score on the comparison distribution at which the null hypothesis should be rejected.** 5% level, $F(2, 9)$ needed = 4.26.
❹ **Determine your sample's score on the comparison distribution.** $S_{\text{Between}}^2 = (5.33)(4) = 21.32$; $S_{\text{Within}}^2 = (.67 + 3.33 + 2.67)/3 = 2.22$; $F = 21.32/2.22 = 9.60$.
❺ **Decide whether to reject the null hypothesis.** F from step 4 (9.60) is more extreme than cutoff F from step 3 (4.26); reject the null hypothesis.

(b) Estimated effect size = $\sqrt{F}/\sqrt{n} = \sqrt{9.60}/\sqrt{4} = 1.55$.
(c) The null hypothesis is that the three groups are from populations of length-of-stay scores with equal means (and, as

with a *t* test, we must be able to assume that they have equal variances). If this null hypothesis is true, then you can estimate the variance of these equal populations in two ways:

(i) You can estimate from the variation within each of the three groups and then average them. (This is just what you would do in a *t* test for independent means, except now you are averaging three instead of just two. Also in a *t* test you would weight these variances according to the degrees of freedom they contribute to the overall estimate. However, because all three groups have equal numbers, you can simply average them—in effect weighting them equally.) In this example, the three variance estimates were .67, 3.33, and 2.67, which gave a pooled estimate of 2.22. This is called the within-groups estimate of the population variance.

(ii) You can estimate the variance using the three means. If we assume the null hypothesis is true, the means of the three groups are based on samples taken from identical populations. Each of these identical populations will have an identical distribution of means of samples taken from that population. The means of our three samples are all from identical populations, which is the same as if they were all from the same population. Thus, the amount of variation among our three means should reflect the variation in the distribution of means that they can be thought of as coming from. As a result, I can use these three means (6, 10, and 10) to estimate the variance in this distribution of means. Using the usual formula for estimating a population variance, I get 5.33.

However, what we want is the variance of a distribution of individuals. So the question is, what would be the distribution of individuals that would produce a distribution of means (of four scores each) with a variance of 5.33? To find the distribution of means from a distribution of individuals, you divide the variance of the distribution of individuals by the size of the samples. In this case, you want to do the reverse. Thus, you multiply the variance of the distribution of means by the size of the samples to get the variance of the distribution of individuals. This comes out to 5.33 times 4, or 21.32. This is called the between-groups estimate of the population variance.

If the null hypothesis is true, the within-groups and between-groups estimates of the population variance should be about the same because they are estimates of essentially the same population. Thus, the ratio of the between-groups estimate divided by the within-groups estimate should be about 1.

However, suppose the null hypothesis is false and the three populations from which these groups come have different means. In that situation, the estimate based on the variation among the group means will be bigger than the one based on the variation within the groups. The reason it will be bigger is as follows. If the null hypothesis is true, the only reason that the means of our groups vary is because of the variance inside of each of the three identical distributions of means. But if the null hypothesis is false, each of those distributions of means also has a different mean. Thus, the variation in our means is due to *both* the variation inside of each of these now *not* identical distributions of means, and also to the differences in the means of these distributions of means. Thus, there is an additional source of variation in the means of our groups. If you estimate the variance

of the population using these three means, it will be larger than if the null hypothesis were true. On the other hand, the within-groups variance is not affected by whether the three groups have different means, because it considers variation only within each of the groups. The within-groups variance thus does not get any bigger if the null hypothesis is false. Therefore, when the null hypothesis is false, the ratio of the between-groups variance to the within-groups variance will be more than 1.

The ratio of the between-groups estimate to the within-groups estimate is called an *F* ratio. In this example, our *F* ratio is 21.32 to 2.22: 21.32/2.22 = 9.60.

Statisticians have made tables of what happens when you figure *F* ratios based on the situation in which you randomly take a group of four scores from each of three identical populations. This is the situation in which the null hypothesis is true. Looking at these tables, it turns out that there is less than a 5% chance of getting an *F* ratio larger than 4.26. Because our actual *F* ratio is bigger than this, we can reject the null hypothesis.

4. (a), (b), and (c). Hypothesis-testing steps, estimated effect size, and explanation similar to 3 above (except c needs to include material similar to explanations from earlier chapters' practice problems). *F* needed ($df = 2, 147; p < .05$) = 3.09 (actually using $df = 2, 100$); $S^2_{\text{Between}} = (.09)(50) = 4.5$; $S^2_{\text{Within}} = (5.2 + 5.8 + 4.8)/3 = 5.27$; $F = .85$; do not reject the null hypothesis. Estimated effect size = .13.

5. (a) and (b). Hypothesis-testing steps and explanation similar to 3 above (except b needs to include material similar to explanations from earlier chapters' practice problems). *F* needed ($df = 3, 28; p < .01$) = 4.57; $S^2_{\text{Between}} = (155)(8) = 1240$; $S^2_{\text{Within}} = (3.5^2 + 4.6^2 + 3.8^2 + 4.9^2)/4 = 17.97$; $F = 69.0$; reject the null hypothesis.

6. From Table 10–8: (a) .09; (b) .12; (c) .10; (d) .38.
7. From Table 10–9: (a) 322; (b) 21; (c) 274; (d) 52.
8. (i) (a) and (b)

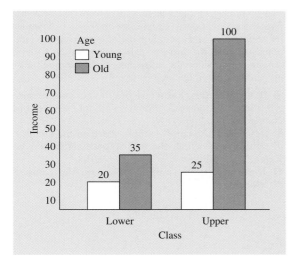

(c) Main effects model for class and age, interaction effect; (d) income is greater in general for upper-class and for older individuals, but the combination of older and upper class has a higher income than would be expected just from the effects of either variable alone.

(ii) (a) and (b) Graphs of the same kind as in (i) (a) and (b) above; (c) no main effects, interaction effect; (d) neither type of college nor type of major, by itself, predicts grades, but there is a clear pattern if one considers the combinations: Grades are highest for community college arts majors and for liberal arts college science majors.

(iii) (a) and (b) Graphs of the same kind as in (i) (a) and (b) above; (c) both main effects significant; no interaction; (d) females miss fewer days per month than males; those who exercise miss fewer days per month than controls. Each combination misses the number of days you would expect knowing their level of each variable separately.

9. (i) (a) and (b) Graphs of the same kind as in 8 (i) (a) and (b) above; (c) main effect for relationship and an interaction; (d) conversations are longer with friends; but the difference is much greater for personal than for nonpersonal topics.

(ii) (a) and (b) Graphs of the same kind as in 8 (i) (a) and (b) above; (c) main effect for city and cost, plus an interaction; (d) restaurant quality if different in different cities, with New York highest and Chicago lowest. Restaurant quality is different in different price ranges, with expensive the best and inexpensive the least. The two factors do not simply combine, however, as price makes more difference in New York than in other cities.

(iii) (a) and (b) Graphs of the same kind as in 8 (i) (a) and (b) above; (c) main effects for brand and type and an interaction; (d) flavor is rated on the average more positively for regular than decaf and brands Z and X are rated more favorably than Y. However, there is an interaction in which there is no difference between regular and decaf for brand Z, but for brands Z and Y, regular is rated 2 points higher.

10. Similar to 3c (and also including material from Chapter 9) but focusing on this study's results.

11. Similar to 3c (and also including material from previous chapters) but focusing on this study's results.

Chapter 11

1. (a) χ^2 needed ($df = 5 - 1 = 4$, .05 level) = 9.488.

Category	O	Expected	O − E	(O − E)²	(O − E)²/E
A	19	(.2)(50) = 10	9	81	8.10
B	11	(.2)(50) = 10	1	1	.10
C	10	(.4)(50) = 20	−10	100	5.00
D	5	(.1)(50) = 5	0	0	0.00
E	5	(.1)(50) = 5	0	0	0.00
Total	50	50	0		χ^2 = 13.20

Conclusion: Reject the null hypothesis

(b) χ^2 needed = 9.488; χ^2 = 44.45, reject the null hypothesis; (c) χ^2 needed = 7.815; χ^2 = 1.23, do not reject the null hypothesis.

2. (a)

❶ **Restate the question as a research hypothesis and a null hypothesis about the populations.** There are two populations of interest:

Population 1: Clients like those of this social service agency.
Population 2: Clients for whom season makes no difference in when they use the social service agency.

The research hypothesis is that the distribution over seasons of when clients use the social service agency is different between the two populations. The null hypothesis is that the distributions over seasons of when clients use the social service agency is not different between the populations.

❷ **Determine the characteristics of the comparison distribution.** Chi-square distribution with 3 degrees of freedom ($df = 4$ categories − 1 = 3).

❸ **Determine the cutoff sample score on the comparison distribution at which the null hypothesis should be rejected.** .05 level, $df = 3$: χ^2 needed = 7.815.

❹ **Determine your sample's score on the comparison distribution.**

Season	O	Expected	O − E	(O − E)²	(O − E)²/E
Winter	28	(1/4)(128) = 32	−4	16	.50
Spring	33	(1/4)(128) = 32	1	1	.03
Summer	16	(1/4)(128) = 32	−16	256	8.00
Fall	51	(1/4)(128) = 32	19	361	11.28
Total	128	128	0		χ^2 = 19.81

❺ **Decide whether to reject the null hypothesis.** 19.81 is larger than 7.815; reject the null hypothesis; the research hypothesis is supported.

(b) If the season makes no difference, you would expect about 25% of clients to use the social service agency each season (for last year, 25% of 128 is 32). Are last year's actual numbers in each season so discrepant from these expectations that you should conclude that in general the numbers of new clients are not equally distributed over the seasons? The chi-square statistic reflects the discrepancy between observed and expected results. For each category (such as the four seasons), you figure that discrepancy, square it, and divide by the expected number; then you add up the results. In the winter, 28 less than 32 is −4, squared is 16, divided by 32 is .5. Doing the same for the other three seasons and adding up the four gives a total chi-square of 19.81. (Chi-square uses squared discrepancies so that the result is not affected by the directions of the differences. You divide by the expected number to reduce the impact of the raw number of cases on the result.)

Statisticians have determined mathematically what would happen if you took an infinite number of samples from a population with a fixed proportion of cases in each category and figured chi-square for each sample. This distribution depends only on how many categories are free to take on different expected values. (The total number expected is the total number of cases; thus, if you know the expected for any three categories, you can just subtract to get the number expected for the fourth.) A table of the chi-square distribution when three categories are free to vary shows that there is only a 5% chance of getting a chi-square of 7.815 or greater. Because our chi-square is larger than this, the observed result differs from the expected more than you would reasonably expect by chance—the number of new clients, in the long run, is probably not equal over the four seasons.

3. For (a), (b), and (c): $df = (N_{\text{Columns}} - 1)(N_{\text{Rows}} - 1) = (2 - 1)(2 - 1) = 1$; χ^2 needed = 6.635.

(a)

10	(13)	16	(13)	26	(50%)
16	(13)	10	(13)	26	(50%)
26		26		52	

$\chi^2 = (10 - 13)^2/13 + (16 - 13)^2/13 + (16 - 13)^2/13 + (10 - 13)^2/13 = 2.77$. Do not reject the null hypothesis. Effect size, $\phi = \sqrt{\chi^2/N} = \sqrt{2.77/52} = \sqrt{.053} = .23$.
(b) $\chi^2 = .36$, do not reject the null hypothesis; Effect size, $\phi = .03$. (c) $\chi^2 = 27.68$, reject the null hypothesis. Effect size, $\phi = .23$.
For (d), (e), and (f): $df = (N_{\text{Columns}} - 1)(N_{\text{Rows}} - 1) = (3 - 1)(2 - 1) = 2$; χ^2 needed = 9.211.
(d) $\chi^2 = 2.76$, do not reject the null hypothesis; Effect size, Cramer's $\phi = \sqrt{\chi^2/[(N)(df_{\text{Smaller}})]} = \sqrt{2.76/[(72)(1)]} = \sqrt{.0383} = .20$. (e) $\chi^2 = 2.76$, do not reject the null hypothesis; Effect size, Cramer's $\phi = .18$. (f) $\chi^2 = 3.71$, do not reject the null hypothesis. Effect size, Cramer's $\phi = .22$.

4. (a)
❶ **Restate the question as a research hypothesis and a null hypothesis about the populations.** There are two populations of interest:

Population 1: People like those surveyed.
Population 2: People for whom the community they live in is independent of their opinion on the upcoming ballot initiative.

The research hypothesis is that the two populations are different (the community people live in is not independent of their opinion on the upcoming ballot initiative.) The null hypothesis is that the two populations are the same (the community people live in is independent of their opinion on the upcoming ballot imitative).

❷ **Determine the characteristics of the comparison distribution.** Chi-square distribution with four degrees of freedom. $df = (N_{\text{Columns}} - 1)(N_{\text{Rows}} - 1) = (3 - 1)(3 - 1) = 4$.
❸ **Determine the cutoff sample score on the comparison distribution at which the null hypothesis should be rejected.** .05 level, $df = 4$: χ^2 needed = 9.488.
❹ **Determine your sample's score on the comparison distribution.**

	Community			
	A	B	C	Total
For	12 (9.8)	6 (4.2)	3 (7)	21 (23.33%)
Against	18 (16.8)	3 (7.2)	15 (12)	36 (40.00%)
No opinion	12 (15.4)	9 (6.6)	12 (11)	33 (36.67%)
Total	42	18	30	90

$\chi^2 = (12 - 9.8)^2/9.8 + (6 - 4.2)^2/4.2 + (3 - 7)^2/7 + (18 - 16.8)^2/16.8 + (3 - 7.2)^2/7.2 + (15 - 12)^2/12 + (12 - 15.4)^2/15.4 + (9 - 6.6)^2/6.6 + (12 - 11)^2/11 = .49 + .77 + 2.29 + .09 + 2.45 + .75 + .75 + .87 + .09 = 8.55$.

❺ **Decide whether to reject the null hypothesis.** χ^2 in Step 4 (8.55) is less extreme than Step 3 cutoff (9.488). Therefore, do not reject the null hypothesis; the study is inconclusive.

(b) Cramer's $\phi = \sqrt{[8.55/(90)(2)]} = \sqrt{[8.55/180]} = \sqrt{.05} = .22$. From Table 11–8, approximate power for a medium effect size and total $N = 100$ (the closest to the $N = 90$ in the study) is .66.
(c) In this example, 23.33% of all survey respondents were for the ballot initiative. Thus, if community is not related to opinion, 23.33% of the people in each community should be for the initiative. For example, you'd expect 9.8 of the 42 people surveyed in Community C to be for the initiative. Are the survey results so discrepant from these expectations that we should conclude that the community people live in is related to their opinion on the upcoming ballot initiative?

Chi-square is a measure of the degree of difference between observed and expected results. For each combination of the 3 × 3 arrangement, you figure that discrepancy between observed and expected, square it, and divide by the expected number; then you add up the results. In the For-Community-A combination, 12 minus 9.8 is 2.2, squared is 4.84, divided by 9.8 is .49 (rounded off). Doing the same for the other eight combinations and adding them all up gives 8.55.

Chi-square uses squared discrepancies so that the result is not affected by the directions of the differences. It is divided by the expected number to adjust for the relatively different numbers expected in the combinations.

Statisticians have determined mathematically what would happen if you took an infinite number of samples from a population with a fixed proportion of people in each of several groupings and figured the chi-square for each such sample. The distribution of such chi-squares depends only on the number of groupings free to take on different expected values. We always presume you know the row and column totals. Thus, for each community, if you know the numbers For and Against, you can figure out how many have no opinion. Furthermore, you need to know only two of the communities—say A and B for any particular opinion, and you can figure out the third by subtracting these from the total of that row. So only four combinations—say For and Against for Communities A and B—are "free to vary."

A table of the chi-square distribution when four groupings are free to vary shows that there is only a 5% chance of getting a chi-square of 9.488 or greater if the null hypothesis is true. Because our chi-square is smaller than this, the observed numbers in each category differ from the expected numbers less than they would need to before we would be willing to reject the idea that a person's opinion is unrelated to his or her community. The survey is inconclusive.

We can, however, estimate the actual degree of linkage in this group surveyed between community and opinion. The procedure is called "Cramer's phi," figured by dividing your chi-square by the number of people included in the analysis times the sample side at the table less one, then taking the square root of the results. In this example, this comes out to .22.

This statistic ranges from 0 (no relationship) to 1 (a perfect relationship—knowing a person's status on one of the dimensions, such as what community they are from, would let you perfectly predict their status on the other dimension, such as their opinion). Thus, .22 is a fairly low figure, although given the amount of other things that affect any relationship, by the standards of social and behavorial science research, a Cramer's phi of .22 would be considered a medium-sized relation. (To be exact, a Cramer's phi of .21 is the number given for a medium effect size.)

Looking at this another way, we can ask, if there really is a moderate relationship between opinion and community in the population, what is the chance that this whole process would have led to a positive conclusion? Statisticians have provided tables that give this probability. In this situation, it turns out that there would be about a 66% chance. If there were truly a large effect in the population (which would be a Cramer's phi of about .35), there is a 99% chance we would have come to a positive conclusion. Thus, given the result of this study, if any relationship exists, it is almost surely not a large one.

5. (a) $\phi = \sqrt{\chi^2/N} = \sqrt{16/100} = .40$;

   (b) Cramer's $\phi = \sqrt{\chi^2/[(N)(df_{Smaller})]} = \sqrt{16/[(100)(1)]} = .40$; (c) Cramer's $\phi = .28$; (d) $\phi = .28$; (e) $\phi = .28$.

6. From Table 11–8: (a) .08; (b) .32; (c) .11; (d) .07; (e) .06; (f) .06.

7. From Table 11–9: (a) 87; (b) 26; (c) 133; (d) 133; (e) 39.

8. (a) You should get the same results within rounding error.

   (b) $\phi = \sqrt{\chi^2/N} = \sqrt{5.55/69} = .28$; (c) Similar to 4c but focusing on this study's results.

9. (a) 4, 2, 3, 5, 6; (b) 5.92; 3.78, 3.61, 3.59, 4.24.

10. (a) t needed ($df = 8$, $p < .05$, two-tailed) $= -2.306$, 2.306; Group A: $M = 3.8$, $S^2 = 5.06$; Group B: $M = 5.7$, $S^2 = 6.76$; $S^2_{Pooled} = 5.91$; $S_{Difference} = 1.54$; $t = -1.23$; do not

reject the null hypothesis. (b) Group A: 1.1, 1.6, 2.1, 1.9, 2.7; Group B: 1.4, 3.0, 2.4, 2.6, 2.2. (c) t needed $= -2.306$, 2.306; Group A: $M = 1.88$, $S^2 = .35$; Group B: $M = 2.32$, $S^2 = .35$; $S^2_{Pooled} = .35$; $S_{Difference} = .37$; $t = -1.19$; do not reject the null hypothesis. (d) It would not have been correct to carry out a t test on the numbers as they were (without transforming them). This is because the distributions of the samples were very skewed for both language groups. Thus, it seemed likely that the population distributions were also seriously skewed. That would clearly violate the assumption for a t test that the underlying population distributions are normal. Thus, I took the square root of each score. This had the advantage of making the sample distributions much closer to normal. This suggests that the population distributions of square roots of family sizes are probably nearly normally distributed. I realize that taking the square root of each family size distorts its straightforward meaning, but the impact for the individuals in the family of each additional child is probably not equal. That is, going from no children to 1 child has a huge impact. Going from 1 to 2 has less, and going from 7 to 8 probably makes much less difference for the family.

In any case, having taken the square root of each score, I then carried out an ordinary t test for independent means using these transformed scores. As with the original t test, the result was inconclusive (the null hypothesis could not be rejected)—but at least I could be confident that I had done the analysis correctly.

11. (a) F needed ($df = 2$, 6; $p < .01$) $= 10.93$; Sad: $M = 446$, $S^2 = 47,089$; Angry: $M = 259$, $S^2 = 11,727$; Exuberant: $M = 918.67$, $S^2 = 7,184$; $S^2_{Between} = 346,775.22$; $S^2_{Within} = 22,000$; $F = 15.76$; reject the null hypothesis. (b) 14.2, 22.9, 24.8; 11.7, 18.4, 17.3; 28.9, 30.2, 31.7. (c) $M = 20.63$, $S^2 = 31.94$; $M = 15.8$, $S^2 = 12.91$; $M = 30.27$, $S^2 = 1.96$; $S^2_{Between} = 162.82$; $S^2_{Within} = 15.60$; $F = 10.44$; do not reject the null hypothesis. (d) Similar to 10d above, except note that the square root transformation does *not* solve the problem of skew and that it also creates distributions very likely to violate the assumption of equal population variances.

12. Miller wanted to examine the relationships among the variables he was studying, probably including various parametric hypothesis-testing techniques such as the t test or an analysis of variance. Such procedures are based on the assumption that the distributions of the variables in the population follow a normal curve. However, Miller first checked the distributions of the variables he was studying and found that the scores on two key measures were skewed, suggesting that the population distributions for these variables probably violated the normal distribution assumption. (Rest of your answer similar to 10d above.)

Chapter 12

1. Hierarchical regression is a variation of ordinary multiple regression in which you add the predictor variables in predetermined stages and figure the additional contribution of each. The order the predictor variables are entered is decided by the researcher in advance. In the Lindzey et al. study, the criterion variable was children's social competence. The first

two predictor variables considered were father- and child-initiation rates, which accounted for only 3% of the variance in the dependent variable. That is, the R^2 was .03. (This R^2 was not significant—they note that the significance level was far from below .05—it was a huge .57.) So far, this is like an ordinary multiple regression situation with two predictor variables and one dependent variable.

Then, however, the researchers added an additional predictor variable—father–child mutual compliance. Lindzey et al. report that the overall variance accounted for increased by 18%. This means that the R^2 had to have gone from .03 to .21 (that is, 3% + 18% = 21%). Furthermore, they note that this increase of 18% was significant.

What this tells us is that father- and child-initiation rate is not very important in predicting children's competence. Most important, it tells us that even taking those two variables into account, mutual compliance makes an important contribution to predicting social competence.

2. Stepwise regression is a variation of ordinary multiple regression you use when you have a lot of predictor variables and you want to pick out the best ones. You first figure a regression of each predictor by itself and select the one that accounts for the most variance in the criterion variable. If this proportion of variance accounted for is not significant, you stop. If the proportion of variance accounted for is significant, you figure a regression of each remaining predictor in combination with the first and pick out the variable that gives the highest proportion of variance accounted for in combination with the best single predictor. If this proportion of variance is not significantly greater than the proportion of variance for the best single variable alone, the process stops. If it is a significant improvement, you continue in the same way until you either run out of predictors or adding any remaining predictor variables does not give a significant improvement in the proportion of variance accounted for. In the Mooney et al. study, this procedure led to their keeping three of their four original predictors.

3. "Controlling for" refers to partial correlation, a procedure based on multiple regression in which you figure the correlation between two variables, subtracting out the influence of one or more other variables (the variables that are controlled for). It amounts to figuring the correlation between your variables at each level of the controlled-for variable and then averaging these correlations.

For example, in this study, the moderately strong correlation between romantic appeal and level of dating experience can't be explained as both being due somehow to appearance of physical maturity, because appearance of physical maturity is controlled for.

4. Boyd and Gullone are describing the reliability of the study's measures. Reliability is how much a test measures something consistently. One method of assessing reliability is by looking at how one half of the test correlates with the other half of the test, the idea being that the same person is taking two tests (the two halves of the test) at the same time under the same circumstances. A more general way to assess the reliability of a measure is to divide the measure into halves in all possible ways and figure the correlation between halves using each division—averaging all of these correlations gives a statistic called Cronbach's alpha (which

Boyd and Gullone refer to as an alpha coefficient). Cronbach's alpha is a measure of the internal consistency reliability of a measure, which is the extent to which the items of a measure assess a common characteristic. An alpha of .60 or .70 is usually considered a minimum adequate level of reliability—that some of Boyd and Gullone's measures had lower alphas means that some of the variables studied may not be giving very precise information and may not be doing a good job of assessing a common characteristic.

5. You use a factor analysis to uncover the underlying pattern among a large number of variables—to find out which variables group together in the sense of correlating with each other but not with other variables in other groupings. Fawzi et al.'s results suggest that the best underlying pattern among the 16 PTSD symptom ratings has four groupings or factors (called "dimensions" in their table). The table shows the correlation, called "Factor Loadings," of each individual variable with the grouping. (In this table, the researchers listed only each symptom's factor loading on the factor on which it had the highest loading. Each variable has a loading on each factor, but ordinarily has a high loading on only one factor, and it is thought of as being part of that factor.) The researchers note that the first three factors correspond to the three key aspects of PTSD as it is usually understood. Their fourth factor (which has only one item), however, suggested that there is an additional and somewhat separate aspect of avoidance that has not been considered in previous work as being a separate aspect.

6. The procedure described here is path analysis, an elaboration of ordinary multiple regression in which you make specific predictions about the pattern of causality among your variables (your casual model), usually including making a diagram showing the causality as arrows between boxes, as in Williamson et al.'s figure. You then figure the regression coefficients (called "path coefficients"). Based on the correlations among the variables in their sample of caregivers, the path coefficients show the direction and degree of the predicted effects. The asterisks (*, **, and ***) show the level of significance for a path. As an example, the diagram tells you that Caregiver Age is predicted to affect ADL (activities of daily living) Care Provided, which in turn is not predicted to affect any other variables in the model. However, Caregiver Age is also predicted to affect the degree of Care Recipient Dementia, which is one of the predicted causes of Current Relationship Rewards, which in turn is predicted to affect Potentially Harmful Behavior in two ways: indirectly through Caregiver Depression (high levels of rewards leading to less depression, which then reduces the likelihood of Potentially Harmful Behavior) and directly, with high levels of rewards directly reducing the likelihood of Potentially Harmful Behavior.

7. (a) In the context of the proposed model, the key result is that all three hypothesized paths to intensity were significant. However, you can also see that the path from desirability to intensity was strongest and the path from probability to intensity, though significant, was not very strong. This means that how intensely one feels unrequited love is very strongly predicted by how desirable one finds the beloved, moderately by how much one finds the state of being in love desirable, but only slightly by one's belief that the other will eventually reciprocate.

(b) Structural equation modeling is a statistical technique in which you specify a pattern of causal links among variables, diagramed with arrows connecting each cause to its effects. You can also specify that some variables measured in the study may actually be indicators of an underlying unmeasured "latent" variable. In this example, the researcher has specified paths from the three motivational factors to intensity. Furthermore, each of the motivational factors and intensity (shown in ovals) are actually latent variables that are seen as the underlying causes of several measured variables (shown here as boxes—if there were not a shortage of space, each of these boxes would have a name for the specific questionnaire items it stands for).

A key statistical aspect of structural equation modeling involves using the correlations among variables to compute a "path coefficient" for each arrow. This tells the degree to which changes on the variable at the tail of the arrow are associated with changes in the variable at the head of the arrow (under conditions in which all other causes for that effect variable are held constant). That is, the path coefficient is a standardized regression coefficient (a "beta") for the causal variable in a prediction model in which the effect variable is the criterion variable and all of the causal variables are predictor variables. For example, the path of .32 from desirability to intensity means that holding constant probability and desires state, for each standard deviation of change in desirability, there would be .32 of a standard deviation of change in intensity.

8. (a) Independent: whether or not a neighborhood receives a recycling awareness campaign; dependent: number of households that recycle. (b) Independent: kind of movie; dependent: heart rate change. (c) Independent: whether or not mother is present; dependent: number of touches between the two infants.

9. ANCOVA, or analysis of covariance, is analysis of variance in which one or more variables have been controlled for—ANCOVA is to ordinary ANOVA as a partial correlation is to ordinary correlation. In this example, Roeser et al. are making the point that the country main effect in their factorial ANOVA holds up even after social desirability is controlled for.

10. MANOVA, or multivariate analysis of variance, is ordinary analysis of variance, except that it looks at the overall effect on more than one dependent variable. In this example, there were five measures of conflict resolution preference. The significant "main effect of culture" means that the two cultures differed significantly when considering the entire set of dependent variables at once. Similarly, the significant "culture by type of conflict interaction" means that the effect of culture on the set of dependent variables varies according to the type of conflict. To understand which of the several conflict resolution variables were accounting for these overall effects, the researchers carried out univariate analyses, ordinary analyses of variance on one dependent variable at a time. The pattern of results was quite different according to the specific dependent variable considered.

11. (a) Causal modeling (path analysis or structural equation modeling); (b) bivariate correlation and regression; (c) reliability statistics, such as Cronbach's alpha and test–retest reliability; (d) multivariate analysis of variance, probably followed up by univariate analyses of variance; (e) stepwise regression; (f) factor analysis; (g) t test for independent means; (h) one-way analysis of variance; (i) hierarchical multiple regression.

Glossary

Numbers in parentheses refer to chapters in which the term is introduced or substantially discussed.

Adjusting for. Same as *partialing out.* (12)

Alpha (α). Short for *Cronbach's alpha.* (12) Also, probability of a Type I error; same as *significance level.* (7)

Analysis of covariance (ANCOVA). Analysis of variance that controls for the effect of one or more unwanted additional variables. (12)

Analysis of variance (ANOVA). Hypothesis-testing procedure for studies with three or more groups. (10)

Assumption. A condition, such as a population's having a normal distribution, required for carrying out a particular hypothesis-testing procedure; a part of the mathematical foundation for the accuracy of the tables used in determining cutoff values. (8–11)

Beta (β). Same as *standardized regression coefficient.* (3, 12)

Between-groups degrees of freedom (df_{Between})**.** Same as *numerator degrees of freedom.* (10)

Between-groups estimate of the population variance (S^2_{Between})**.** In an analysis of variance, estimate of the variance of the population of individuals based on the variation among the means of the groups studied. (10)

Biased estimate. Estimate of a population parameter that is likely systematically to overestimate or underestimate the true population value. For example, SD^2 would be a biased estimate of the population variance (it would systematically underestimate it). (8)

Bimodal distribution. Frequency distribution with two approximately equal frequencies, each clearly larger than any of the others. (1)

Categorical variable. Same as *nominal variable.* (1, 11)

Causal analysis. Procedure, such as path analysis or structural equation modeling, that analyzes correlations among a group of variables in terms of a predicted pattern of causal relations among them. (12)

Ceiling effect. Situation in which many scores pile up at the high end of a distribution (creating skewness) because it is not possible to have a higher score. (1, 11)

Cell. In a factorial design, a particular combination of levels of the variables that divide the groups. (10) In chi-square, the particular combination of categories for two variables in a contingency table. (11)

Cell mean. Mean of a particular combination of levels of the variables that divide the groups in a factorial design. (10)

Central limit theorem. Mathematical principle that the distribution of the sums (or means) of scores taken at random from any distribution of individuals will tend to form a normal curve. (4, 6)

Central tendency. Typical or most representative value of a group of scores. (2)

Change score. After score minus before score. A kind of *difference score*. (8)

Chi-square distribution. Mathematically defined curve used as the comparison distribution in chi-square tests; the distribution of the chi-square statistic. (11)

Chi-square statistic (χ^2). Statistic that reflects the overall lack of fit between the expected and observed frequencies; the sum, over all the categories or cells, of the squared difference between observed and expected frequencies divided by the expected frequency. (11)

Chi-square table. Table of cutoff scores on the chi-square distribution for various degrees of freedom and significance levels. (11)

Chi-square test. Hypothesis-testing procedure that uses the chi-square distribution as the comparison distribution. (11)

Chi-square test for goodness of fit. Hypothesis-testing procedure that examines how well an observed frequency distribution of a nominal variable fits some expected pattern of frequencies. (11)

Chi-square test for independence. Hypothesis-testing procedure that examines whether the distribution of frequencies over the categories of one nominal variable are unrelated to the distribution of frequencies over the categories of another nominal variable. (11)

Comparison distribution. Distribution used in hypothesis testing. It represents the population situation if the null hypothesis is true. It is the distribution to which you compare the score based on your sample's results and is made up of the same kinds of numbers as those of the sample's results (such as a sample mean, a difference between sample means, *F* ratios, or chi-squares). (5)

Computational formula. Equation mathematically equivalent to the definitional formula; it is easier to use for hand computation but does not directly show the meaning of the procedure. (2)

Confidence interval. Roughly speaking, the region of scores (that is, the scores between an upper and lower value) that is likely to include the true population mean; more precisely, the region of possible population means for which it is not highly unlikely that one could have obtained one's sample. (6)

Confidence limit. Upper or lower value of a confidence interval. (6)

Contingency table. Two-dimensional chart showing frequencies in each combination of categories of two nominal variables. (11)

Controlling for. Same as *partialing out*. (12)

Conventional levels of significance ($p < .05, p < .01$). The levels of significance widely used in the social and behavioral sciences. (5, 7)

Correlation. Association between scores on two or more variables. (3)

Correlation coefficient (*r*). Measure of the degree of linear correlation between two variables, ranging from −1 (a perfect negative linear correlation) through 0 (no correlation) to +1 (a perfect

positive linear correlation); average of the cross-products of *Z* scores of two variables; square root of the proportion of variance accounted for. (3)

Correlation matrix. Common way of reporting the correlation coefficients among several variables in a research article; table in which the variables are named on the top and along the side and the correlations among them are all shown (only half of the resulting square, above or below the diagonal, is usually filled in, the other half being redundant). (3)

Covariate. A variable controlled for in an analysis of covariance. (12)

Cramer's phi. Measure of association between two nominal variables; effect-size measure for a chi-square test of independence with a contingency table that is larger than 2×2; square root of result of dividing chi-square by number of participants times the degrees of freedom of the smaller side of the contingency table; also known as *Cramer's V* and sometimes written as ϕ_C or V_c. (11)

Criterion variable (usually *Y*). In regression, a variable that is predicted. (3)

Cronbach's alpha (α). Widely used measure of a test's reliability that reflects the average of the split-half correlations from all possible splits into halves of the items on the test. (12)

Cross-product of *Z* scores. The result of multiplying a person's *Z* score on one variable times the person's *Z* score on another variable; for a group of individuals, the average of the cross-products of *Z* scores between two variables is the correlation coefficient for those two variables. (3)

Curvilinear correlation. Relation between two variables that shows up on a scatter diagram as dots following a systematic pattern that is not a straight line; any association between two variables other than a linear correlation. (3)

Cutoff sample score. In hypothesis testing, point on the comparison distribution at which, if reached or exceeded by the sample score, you reject the null hypothesis. (5)

Data transformation. Mathematical procedure (such as taking the square root) applied to each score in a sample, usually done to make the sample distribution closer to normal. (11)

Decision error. Incorrect conclusion in hypothesis testing in relation to the real (but unknown) situation, such as deciding the null hypothesis is false when it is really true. (7)

Definitional formula. Equation for a statistical procedure directly showing the meaning of the procedure. (2)

Degrees of freedom (*df*). Number of scores free to vary when estimating a population parameter; usually part of a formula for making that estimate—for example, in the formula for estimating the population variance from a single sample, the degrees of freedom is the number of scores minus 1. (8–11)

Denominator degrees of freedom (df_{Within}). Degrees of freedom used in the within-groups estimate of the population variance in an analysis of variance; denominator of the *F* ratio; number of scores free to vary (number of scores in each group minus 1, summed over all the groups) in figuring the within-group population variance estimate; *within-groups degrees of freedom*. (10)

Dependent variable. Variable considered to be an effect; usually a measured variable. (12)

Descriptive statistics. Procedures for summarizing a group of scores or otherwise making them more comprehensible. (1)

Deviation score. Score minus the mean. (2)

Difference score. Difference between a person's score on one testing and the same person's score on another testing; often an after score minus a before score, in which case it is also called a *change score.* (8)

Dimension. In a factorial design, one of the variables that divides the groups that is crossed with another variable that divides the groups; in a contingency table, one of the nominal variables. (10, 11)

Direction of causality. Path of causal effect; if X is thought to cause Y, then the direction of causality is from X to Y. (3)

Directional hypothesis. Research hypothesis predicting a particular direction of difference between populations—for example, a prediction that one population has a higher mean than the other). (5)

Distribution-free test. Hypothesis-testing procedure making no assumptions about the shape of the populations; approximately the same as a *nonparametric test.* (11)

Distribution of differences between means. Distribution of differences between means of pairs of samples such that for each pair of means, one is from one population and the other is from a second population; the comparison distribution in a t test for independent means. (9)

Distribution of means. Distribution of means of samples of a given size from a particular population (also called a sampling distribution of the mean); comparison distribution when testing hypotheses involving a single sample of more than one individual. (6–10)

Effect size. Standardized measure of difference (lack of overlap) between populations. Effect size increases with greater differences between means and decreases with greater standard deviations in the populations, but it is not affected by sample size. (7)

Effect size conventions. Standard rules about what to consider a small, medium, and large effect size, based on what is typical in social and behavioral science research; also known as Cohen's conventions. (7)

Effect size for the analysis of variance. Standard deviation of the means of the groups divided by the standard deviation of the individual scores. (10)

Expected frequency (E). In a chi-square test, number of people in a category or cell expected if the null hypothesis were true. (11)

Expected relative frequency. Number of successful outcomes divided by the number of total outcomes you would expect to get if you repeated an experiment a large number of times. (4)

F distribution. Mathematically defined curve that is the comparison distribution used in an analysis of variance; distribution of F ratios when the null hypothesis is true. (10)

F ratio. In analysis of variance, ratio of the between-groups population variance estimate to the within-groups population variance estimate; score on the comparison distribution (an F distribution) in an analysis of variance; also referred to simply as F. (10)

F table. Table of cutoff scores on the F distribution for various degrees of freedom and significance levels. (10)

Factor. In factor analysis, a group of variables that correlate maximally with each other and minimally with variables not in the group. (12)

Factor analysis. Statistical procedure applied in situations where many variables are measured and that identifies groups of variables correlating maximally with each other and minimally with other variables. (12)

Factor loading. In factor analysis, correlation of a variable with a factor. (12)

Factorial analysis of variance. Analysis of variance for a factorial research design. (10)

Factorial research design. Way of organizing a study in which the influence of two or more variables is studied at once by setting up the situation so that a group of people are tested for every combination of the levels of the variables; for example, in a 2×2 factorial research design there would be four groups, those high on variable 1 and high on variable 2, those high on variable 1 but low on variable 2, those high on variable 2 but low on variable 1, and those low on variable 1 and low on variable 2. (10)

Fit index. In structural equation modeling, measure of how well the pattern of correlations in a sample corresponds to the correlations that would be expected based on the hypothesized pattern of causes and effects among those variables; usually ranges from 0 to 1, with 1 being a perfect fit. (12)

Floor effect. Situation in which many scores pile up at the low end of a distribution (creating skewness) because it is not possible to have any lower score. (1)

Frequency distribution. Pattern of frequencies over the various values; what a frequency table, histogram, or frequency polygon describes. (1)

Frequency polygon. Line graph of a distribution in which the values are plotted along the horizontal axis and the height of each point is the frequency of that value; the line begins and ends at the horizontal axis, and the graph resembles a mountainous skyline. (1)

Frequency table. Listing of the number of individuals having each of the different values for a particular variable. (1)

Grand mean (GM). In analysis of variance, overall mean of all the scores, regardless of what group they are in; when group sizes are equal, mean of the group means. (10)

Grouped frequency table. Frequency table in which the number of individuals is given for each interval of values. (1)

Haphazard selection. Procedure of selecting a sample of individuals to study by taking whoever is available or happens to be first on a list; should not be confused with true random selection. (4)

Harmonic mean. Special average influenced more by smaller numbers; in a t test for independent means when the number of scores in the two groups differ, the harmonic mean is used as the equivalent of each group's sample size when determining power. (9)

Heavy-tailed distribution. Distribution that differs from a normal curve by being too spread out so that a histogram of the distribution would have too many scores at each of the two extremes ("tails"). (1)

Hierarchical multiple regression. Method of multiple regression in which predictor variables are added, one or a few at a time, in a planned sequential fashion, allowing you to figure the contribution to the prediction of each successive variable over and above those already included. (12)

Histogram. Barlike graph of a frequency distribution in which the values are plotted along the horizontal axis and the height of each bar is the frequency of that value; the bars are usually placed next to each other without spaces, giving the appearance of a city skyline. (1)

Holding constant. Same as *partialing out.* (12)

Hypothesis testing. Procedure for deciding whether the outcome of a study (results for a sample) support a particular theory or practical innovation (which is thought to apply to a population). (5)

Independence. Situation of no relationship between two variables; term usually used regarding two nominal variables in the chi-square test for independence. (11)

Independent variable (usually *X*). Variable considered to be a cause, such as what group a person is in in a *t* test or analysis of variance. (12)

Inferential statistics. Procedures for drawing conclusions based on the scores collected in a research study (sample scores) but going beyond them (to conclusions about a population). (1, 4)

Interaction effect. Situation in the factorial analysis of variance in which the combination of variables has an effect that could not be predicted from the effects of the two variables individually. (10)

Interval. In a grouped frequency table, range of values that are grouped together. (For example, if the interval size was 10, one of the intervals might be from 10.00 to 19.99.) (1)

Interval estimate. Region of scores (that is, the scores between some specified lower and upper value) estimated to include a population parameter such as the population mean; this is in contrast to a *point estimate; a confidence interval* is an example of an interval estimate. (6)

Interval size. In a grouped frequency table, difference between the start of one interval and the start of the next. (1)

Inverse transformation. Data transformation using the inverse (1 divided by the number) of each score. (11)

Latent variable. In structural equation modeling, unmeasured variable assumed to be the underlying cause of several variables actually measured in the study. (12)

Level of significance. Same as *significance level.* (7)

Light-tailed distribution. Distribution that differs from a normal curve by being too peaked or pinched so that a histogram of the distribution would have too few scores at each of the two extremes ("tails"). (1)

Linear correlation. Relation between two variables that shows up on a scatter diagram as the dots roughly following a straight line; a correlation of *r* unequal to 0. (3)

Log transformation. Data transformation using the logarithm of each score. (11)

Long-run relative-frequency interpretation of probability. Understanding of probability as the proportion of a particular outcome that you would get if the experiment were repeated many times. (4)

Main effect. Difference between groups on one variable in a factorial design; result for a variable that divides the groups, averaging across the levels of the other variable that divides the groups (sometimes used only for significant differences). (10)

Marginal frequency. In chi-square, frequency (number of people) in a row or column of a contingency table. (11)

Marginal mean. In a factorial design, mean score for all the participants at a particular level of one of the variables; often shortened to *marginal.* (10)

Mean (*M*). Arithmetic average of a group of scores; sum of the scores divided by the number of scores. (2)

Median. Middle score when all the scores in a distribution are arranged from highest to lowest. (2)

Meta-analysis. Statistical method for combining effect sizes from different studies. (7)

Mode. Value with the greatest frequency in a distribution. (2)

Multimodal distribution. Frequency distribution with two or more high frequencies separated by a lower frequency; a bimodal distribution is the special case of two high frequencies. (1)

Multiple comparisons. Hypothesis-testing procedures for testing the differences among particular means in the context of an overall analysis of variance. (10)

Multiple correlation. Correlation of a criterion variable with two or more predictor variables. (3)

Multiple correlation coefficient (*R*). Measure of degree of multiple correlation; positive square root of the proportion of variance accounted for in a multiple regression analysis. (3)

Multiple regression. Procedure for predicting scores on a criterion variable from scores on two or more predictor variables. (3, 12)

Multivariate analysis of covariance (MANCOVA). Analysis of covariance with more than one dependent variable. (12)

Multivariate analysis of variance (MANOVA). Analysis of variance with more than one dependent variable. (12)

Multivariate statistics. Statistical procedures involving more than one dependent variable. (12)

Negative correlation. Relation between two variables in which high scores on one go with low scores on the other, mediums with mediums, and lows with highs; on a scatter diagram, the dots roughly follow a straight line sloping down and to the right; a correlation of *r* less than 0. (3)

95% confidence interval. Confidence interval in which, roughly speaking, there is a 95% chance that the population mean falls within this interval. (6)

99% confidence interval. Confidence interval in which, roughly speaking, there is a 99% chance that the population mean falls within this interval. (6)

No correlation. No systematic relation between two variables. (3)

Nominal variable. Variable with values that are categories (that is, they are names rather than numbers); same as *categorical variable.* (1, 11)

Nondirectional hypothesis. Research hypothesis that does not predict a particular direction of difference between populations. (5)

Nonparametric test. Hypothesis-testing procedure making no assumptions about population parameters; approximately the same as *distribution-free test*. (11)

Normal curve. Specific, mathematically defined, bell-shaped frequency distribution that is symmetrical and unimodal; distributions observed in nature and in research commonly approximate it. (1, 4)

Normal curve table. Table showing percentages of scores between the mean of a normal distribution and various numbers of standard deviations above the mean. (4)

Normal distribution. Frequency distribution following a normal curve. (4)

Null hypothesis. Statement about a relation between populations that is the opposite of the research hypothesis; a statement that in the population there is no difference (or a difference opposite to that predicted) between populations; a contrived statement set up to examine whether it can be rejected as part of hypothesis testing. (5)

Numerator degrees of freedom (df_{Between}). Degrees of freedom used in the between-groups estimate of the population variance in an analysis of variance (the numerator of the F ratio); number of scores free to vary (number of means minus 1) in figuring the between-groups estimate of the population variance; same as *between-groups degrees of freedom*. (10)

Numeric variable. Variable whose values are numbers (as opposed to a nominal variable). (1)

Observed frequency (O). In a chi-square test, number of individuals actually found in the study to be in a category or cell. (11)

One-tailed test. Hypothesis-testing procedure for a directional hypothesis; situation in which the region of the comparison distribution in which the null hypothesis would be rejected is all on one side (tail) of the distribution. (5)

One-way analysis of variance. Analysis of variance in which there is only one independent variable (as distinguished from a factorial analysis of variance). (10)

Ordinal variable. Same as *rank-order variable*. (1, 11)

Outcome. Term used in discussing probability for the result of an experiment (or almost any event, such as a coin coming up heads or it raining tomorrow). (4)

Outlier. Score with an extreme (very high or very low) value in relation to the other scores in the distribution. (2, 11)

Parametric test. Ordinary hypothesis-testing procedure, such as a t test or an analysis of variance, that requires assumptions about the shape or other parameters (such as the variance) of the populations. (11)

Partial correlation coefficient. Measure of degree of correlation between two variables, over and above the influence of one or more other variables. (12)

Partialing out. In multiple regression, partial correlation, or analysis of covariance, removing the influence of a variable from the association among the other variables; same as *holding constant, controlling for, and adjusting for*. (12)

Path analysis. Method of analyzing the correlations among a group of variables in terms of a predicted pattern of causal relations; usually the predicted pattern is diagramed as a pattern of arrows from causes to effects. (12)

Path coefficient. Degree of relation associated with an arrow in a path analysis (including structural equation modeling); same as a regression coefficient from a multiple regression prediction rule in which the variable at the end of the arrow is the criterion variable and the variable at the start of the arrow is the predictor, along with all the other variables that have arrows leading to that criterion variable. (12)

Perfect correlation. Relation between two variables that shows up on a scatter diagram as the dots exactly following a straight line; correlation of $r = 1$ or $r = -1$; situation in which each person's Z score on one variable is exactly the same as that person's Z score on the other variable. (3)

Phi coefficient (ϕ). Measure of association between two dichotomous nominal variables; square root of division of chi-square statistic by N; equivalent to correlation of the two variables if they were each given numerical values (for example, of 1 and 0 for the two categories); effect-size measure for a chi-square test of independence with a 2×2 contingency table. (11)

Point estimate. Estimate from a sample of the most likely single value of a population parameter. (6)

Pooled estimate of the population variance (S^2_{Pooled}) In a t test for independent means, weighted average of the estimates of the population variance from two samples (each estimate weighted by the proportion of the degrees of freedom for its sample divided by the total degrees of freedom for both samples). (9)

Population. Entire group of people to which a researcher intends the results of a study to apply; the larger group to which inferences are made on the basis of the particular set of people (sample) studied. (4)

Population mean. Mean of the population (usually not known). (4)

Population parameter. Actual value of the mean, standard deviation, and so on, for the population (usually population parameters are not known, though sometimes they are estimated). (4)

Population standard deviation. Standard deviation of the population (usually not known). (4)

Population variance. Variance of the population (usually not known). (4)

Positive correlation. Relation between two variables in which high scores on one go with high scores on the other, mediums with mediums, and lows with lows; on a scatter diagram, the dots roughly follow a straight line sloping up and to the right; a correlation of r greater than 0. (3)

Power. Same as *statistical power*. (7)

Power table. Table for a hypothesis-testing procedure showing the statistical power of a study for various effect sizes and sample sizes. (7–11)

Prediction model. Formula for making predictions; that is, formula for predicting a person's score on a criterion variable based on the person's score on one or more predictor variables. (3)

Predictor variable (usually *X*). In regression, variable that is used to predict scores of individuals on another variable. (3)

Probability (*p*). Expected relative frequency of a particular outcome; the proportion of successful outcomes to all outcomes. (4)

Proportion of variance accounted for (r^2 or R^2). Measure of association between variables used when comparing associations found in different studies or with different variables; correlation coefficient squared or multiple correlation coefficient squared; variance of the predicted criterion variable scores (based on a regression formula) divided by the variance of the actual scores. (3, 12)

Protected *t* tests. In analysis of variance, *t* tests among pairs of means after finding that the *F* for the overall difference among the means is significant. (10).

Quantitative variable. Same as *numeric variable*. (1)

Random selection. Method for selecting a sample that uses truly random procedures (usually meaning that each person in the population has an equal chance of being selected); one procedure is for the researcher to begin with a complete list of all the people in the population and select a group of them to study using a table of random numbers; should not be confused with haphazard selection. (4)

Rank-order test. Hypothesis-testing procedure that makes use of rank-ordered data. (11)

Rank-order transformation. Changing a set of scores to ranks, so that the highest score is rank 1, the next highest rank 2, and so forth. (11)

Rank-order variable. Numeric variable in which the values are ranks, such as class standing or place finished in a race; also called *ordinal variable*. (1, 11)

Raw score. Ordinary measurement (or any other number in a distribution before it has been made into a *Z* score or otherwise transformed). (2)

Rectangular distribution. Frequency distribution in which all values have approximately the same frequency. (1)

Regression coefficient. Number multiplied by a person's score on the predictor variable as part of a prediction model. (3)

Regression line. Line on a graph such as a scatter diagram showing the predicted value of the criterion variable for each value of the predictor variable. (3)

Reliability. Degree of consistency of a measure; the extent to which, if you were to give the same measure again to the same person under the same circumstances, you would obtain the same result. (12)

Repeated-measures analysis of variance. Analysis of variance in which each individual is tested more than once so that the levels of the independent variable(s) are different times or types of testing for the same people. (10)

Repeated-measures design. Research strategy in which each person is tested more than once; same as *within-subject design*. (8, 10)

Research hypothesis. In hypothesis testing, statement about the predicted relation between populations (usually a prediction of difference between population means). (5)

Sample. Scores of the particular group of people studied; usually considered to be representative of the scores in some larger population. (4)

Sample statistic. Descriptive statistic, such as the mean or standard deviation, figured from the scores in a particular group of people studied. (4)

Scatter diagram. Graph showing the relationship between two variables: the values of one variable (often the predictor variable) are along the horizontal axis; the values of the other variable (often the criterion variable) are along the vertical axis, with each score shown as a dot in this two-dimensional space; also called *scatter plot*. (3)

Scatter plot. Same as *scatter diagram*. (3)

Score. Particular person's value on a variable. (1)

Shape of a distribution of means. Contour of a histogram of a distribution of means, such as whether it follows a normal curve or is skewed; in general, a distribution of means will tend to be unimodal and symmetrical and is often normal. (6)

Significance level. Probability of getting statistical significance if the null hypothesis is actually true; probability of a Type I error. (7)

Skewed distribution. Distribution in which the scores pile up on one side of the middle and are spread out on the other side; distribution that is not symmetrical. (1, 11)

Skewness. Extent to which a frequency distribution has more scores on one side of the middle as opposed to being perfectly symmetrical. (1)

Split-half reliability. One index of a measure's reliability, based on a correlation of the scores of items from the two halves of the test. (12)

Square-root transformation. Data transformation using the square root of each score. (11)

Squared deviation score. Square of the difference between a score and the mean. (2)

Standard deviation (*SD*). Square root of the average of the squared deviations from the mean; the most common descriptive statistic for variation; approximately the average amount that scores in a distribution vary from the mean. (2)

Standard deviation of a distribution of differences between means ($S_{\text{Difference}}$). In a *t* test for independent means, square root of the variance of the distribution of differences between means. (9)

Standard deviation of a distribution of means (Population SD_M, S_M). Square root of the variance of the distribution of means; same as *standard error (SE)*. (6)

Standard error (*SE*). Same as *standard deviation of a distribution of means;* also called *standard error of the mean.* (6)

Standard score. *Z* score in a distribution that follows a normal curve; sometimes refers to any *Z* score. (2)

Standardized regression coefficient (beta, β). Regression coefficient in a prediction model using *Z* scores; also called a *beta weight.* (3)

Statistical power. Probability that the study will give a significant result if the research hypothesis is true. (7)

Statistically significant. Conclusion that the results of a study would be unlikely if in fact there were no difference in the populations the samples represent; an outcome of hypothesis testing in which the null hypothesis is rejected. (3, 5)

Statistics. A branch of mathematics that focuses on the organization, analysis, and interpretation of a group of numbers. (1)

Stepwise multiple regression. Exploratory procedure in which all the potential predictor variables that have been measured are tried in order to find the predictor variable that produces the best prediction; then each of the remaining variables is tried to find the predictor variable, which in combination with the first produces the best prediction; this process continues until adding the best remaining variable does not provide a significant improvement. (12)

Structural equation modeling. Sophisticated version of path analysis that includes paths with latent, unmeasured, theoretical variables and that also permits a kind of significance test and provides measures of the overall fit of the data to the hypothesized causal pattern. (12)

Sum of squared deviations. Total over all the scores of each score's squared difference from the mean. (2)

Symmetrical distribution. Distribution in which the pattern of frequencies on the left and right side are mirror images of each other. (1)

t distribution. Mathematically defined curve that is the comparison distribution used in a t test. (8)

t score. On a t distribution, number of standard deviations from the mean (like a Z score, but on a t distribution). (8)

t table. Table of cutoff scores on the t distribution for various degrees of freedom, significance levels, and one- and two-tailed tests. (8)

t test. Hypothesis-testing procedure in which the population variance is unknown; it compares t scores from a sample to a comparison distribution called a t distribution. (8, 9, 11)

t test for a single sample. Hypothesis-testing procedure in which a sample mean is being compared to a known population mean and the population variance is unknown. (8)

t test for dependent means. Hypothesis-testing procedure in which there are two scores for each person and the population variance is not known; it determines the significance of a hypothesis that is being tested using difference or change scores from a single group of people. (8)

t test for independent means. Hypothesis-testing procedure in which there are two separate groups of people tested and in which the population variance is not known. (9)

Test–retest reliability. One index of a measure's reliability, obtained by giving the test to a group of people twice; the correlation between scores from the two testings. (12)

Two-tailed test. Hypothesis-testing procedure for a nondirectional hypothesis; the situation in which the region of the comparison distribution in which the null hypothesis would be rejected is divided between the two sides (tails) of the distribution. (5)

Two-way analysis of variance. Analysis of variance for a two-way factorial research design. (10)

Two-way factorial research design. Factorial design with two variables that each divide the groups. (10)

Type I error. Rejecting the null hypothesis when in fact it is true; getting a statistically significant result when in fact the research hypothesis is not true. (7)

Type II error. Failing to reject the null hypothesis when in fact it is false; failing to get a statistically significant result when in fact the research hypothesis is true. (7)

Unbiased estimate of the population variance (S^2). Estimate of the population variance, based on sample scores, which has been corrected (by dividing the sum of squared deviations by the sample size minus 1 instead of the usual procedure of dividing by the sample size directly) so that it is equally likely to overestimate or underestimate the true population variance. (2, 8)

Unimodal distribution. Frequency distribution with one value clearly having a larger frequency than any other. (1)

Value. Number or category that a score can have. (1)

Variable. Characteristic that can have different values. (1)

Variance (SD^2). Measure of how spread out a set of scores are; average of the squared deviations from the mean; standard deviation squared. (2)

Variance of a distribution of differences between means ($S^2_{Difference}$). One of the numbers figured as part of a t test for independent means; it equals the sum of the variances of the distributions of means for each of the two samples. (9)

Variance of a distribution of means (Population SD^2_M, S^2_M). Variance of the population divided by the number of scores in each sample. (6)

Weighted average. Average in which the scores being averaged do not have equal influence on the total, as in figuring the pooled variance estimate in a t test for independent means. (9)

Within-groups degrees of freedom (df_{Within}). Same as *denominator degrees of freedom*. (10)

Within-groups estimate of the population variance (S^2_{Within}). In analysis of variance, estimate of the variance of the distribution of the population of individuals based on the variation among the scores within each of the actual groups studied. (10)

Within-subject design. Same as *repeated-measures design*. (8)

Z score. Number of standard deviations a score is above (or below, if it is negative) the mean of its distribution; ordinary score transformed so that it better describes that score's location in a distribution. (2)

Z test. Hypothesis-testing procedure in which there is a single sample and the population variance is known. (6)

Glossary of Symbols

α Significance level; probability of a Type I error. Also Cronbach's alpha, a measure of reliability. (12)

β Standardized regression coefficient. (3, 12)

Σ Sum of; add up all the scores following. (2)

ϕ Phi coefficient; effect size in a chi-square test for independence with a 2×2 contingency table. (11)

ϕ_c Cramer's phi, effect size in chi-square test for independence with a contingency table larger than 2×2. (11)

χ^2 Chi-square statistic. (11)

df Degrees of freedom. (8–11).

$df_1, df_2,$ and so on. Degrees of freedom for the first group, second group, and so on. (9, 10)

df_{Between} Numerator (between-groups) degrees of freedom in analysis of variance. (10)

df_{Smaller} Degrees of freedom for the nominal variable (the row or column in the contingency table) with the smaller number of categories in a chi-square test of independence. (11)

df_{Total} Total degrees of freedom over all groups. (9, 10)

df_{Within} Denominator (within-groups) degrees of freedom in analysis of variance. (10)

F ratio Ratio of the between-groups population variance estimate to the within-groups population variance estimate in analysis of variance. (10)

GM Grand mean; mean of all scores in the analysis of variance. (10)

M Mean. (2)

$M_1, M_2,$ and so on. Mean of the first group, second group, and so on. (9, 10)

n In analysis of variance, number of scores within each group. (10)

N Number of scores. (2)

$N_1, N_2,$ and so on. Number of scores in the first group, second group, and so on. (9, 10)

N_{Columns} Number of columns in a contingency table. (11)

N_{Groups} Number of groups in an analysis of variance. (11)

N_{Rows} Number of rows in a contingency table. (11)

p Probability. (4)

r Correlation coefficient. (3)

r^2 Proportion of variance accounted for. (3)

R Multiple correlation coefficient. (3, 12)

R^2 Proportion of variance accounted for in multiple regression. (3, 12)

S Unbiased estimate of the population standard deviation. (2, 8)

S^2 Unbiased estimate of the population variance. (2, 8)

S_1^2, S_2^2, *and so on.* Unbiased estimate of the population variance based on scores in the first sample, second sample, and so on. (9, 10)

$S_{Between}^2$ Between-groups population variance estimate. (10)

$S_{Difference}$ Standard deviation of the distribution of differences between means. (9)

$S_{Difference}^2$ Variance of the distribution of differences between means. (9)

SE Standard error (standard deviation of the distribution of means). (6)

S_M Standard deviation of the distribution of means based on an estimated population variance. (8)

S_M^2 Variance of a distribution of means based on an estimated population variance in a t test or as estimated from the variation among means of groups in the analysis of variance. (8, 10)

$S_{M_1}^2, S_{M_2}^2$, *and so on.* Variance of the distribution of means based on a pooled population variance estimate, corresponding to the first sample, second sample, and so on. (9)

S_{Pooled} Pooled estimate of the population standard deviation. (9)

S_{Pooled}^2 Pooled estimate of the population variance. (9)

S_{Within}^2 Within-groups population variance estimate. (10)

SD Standard deviation. (2)

SD^2 Variance. (2)

t **score** Number of standard deviations from the mean on a t distribution. (8)

X Score on a particular variable; in regression X is usually the predictor variable. (1–3)

X_1, X_2, *and so on.* First predictor variable, second predictor variable, and so on. (3)

$\overline{X}$ Mean of variable designated X. (2)

Y Score on a particular variable, usually the criterion variable in regression. (3)

Z Number of standard deviations from the mean. (2)

Z_X Z score for variable X. (3)

Z_Y Z score for variable Y. (3)

References

ALTMAN, D. G., LEVINE, D. W., HOWARD, G., & HAMILTON, H. (1997). Tobacco farming and public health: Attitudes of the general public and farmers. *Journal of Social Issues, 53,* 113–128.

ARON, A., ARON, E. N., & ALLEN, J. (1998). Motivations for unreciprocated love. *Personality and Social Psychology Bulletin, 24,* 787–796.

ARON, A., MELINAT, E., ARON, E. N., VALLONE, R., & BATOR, R. (1997). The experimental generation of interpersonal closeness: A procedure and some preliminary findings. *Personality and Social Psychology Bulletin, 23,* 363–377.

ARON, A., NORMAN, C. C., ARON, E. N., MCKENNA, C., & HEYMAN, R. E. (2000). Couples' shared participation in novel and arousing activities and experienced relationship quality. *Journal of Personality and Social Psychology, 78,* 273–284.

ARON, A., PARIS, M., & ARON, E. N. (1995). Falling in love: Prospective studies of self-concept change. *Journal of Personality and Social Psychology, 69,* 1102–1112.

ARON, E. N. (2002). *The highly sensitive child.* New York: Broadway Books.

ARON, E. N. (1996). *The highly sensitive person.* New York: Birch/Lane.

ARON, E. N., & ARON, A. (1997). Sensory processing sensitivity and its relation to introversion and emotionality. *Journal of Personality and Social Psychology, 73,* 345–368.

BLOCK, N. (1995). How heritability misleads about race. *Cognition, 56,* 99–128.

BOYD, C. P., & GULLONE, E. (1997). An investigation of negative affectivity in Australian adolescents. *Journal of Clinical Child Psychology, 26,* 190–197.

BUBOLTZ, W. C., JR., JOHNSON, P., & WOLLER, K. M. P. (2003). Psychological reactance in college students: Family-of-origin predictors. *Journal of Counseling and Development, 81,* 311–317.

BUSHMAN, B. J., & ANDERSON, C. A. (2001). Media violence and the American public: Scientific facts versus media misinformation. *American Psychologist, 56,* 477–489.

CAPALDI, D. M., & PATTERSON, G. R. (1991). Relation of parental transitions to boys' adjustment problems: I. A linear hypothesis; II. Mothers at risk for transitions and unskilled parenting. *Developmental Psychology, 27,* 489–504.

CASPI, A., BEGG, D., DICKSON, N., HARRINGTON, H., LANGLEY, J., MOFFITT, T. E., & SILVA, P. A. (1997). Personality differences predict health-risk behaviors in young adulthood: Evidence from a longitudinal study. *Journal of Personality and Social Psychology, 73,* 1052–1063.

CHAPMAN, H. A., HOBFOLL, S. E., & RITTER, C. (1997). Partners' stress underestimations lead to women's distress: A study of pregnant inner-city women. *Journal of Personality and Social Psychology, 73,* 418–425.

CHIU, C., HONG, Y., & DWECK, C. S. (1997). Lay dispositionism and implicit theories of personality. *Journal of Personality and Social Psychology, 73,* 19–30.

COHEN, D. D., MASON, K., BEDIMO, A., SCRIBNER, R., BASOLO, V., & FARLEY, T. A. (2003). Neighborhood physical conditions and health. *American Journal of Public Health, 93,* 467–471.

COHEN, J. (1992). A power primer. *Psychological Bulletin, 112,* 155–159.

COHEN, J. (1988). *Statistical power analysis for the behavioral sciences.* Hillsdale, NJ: Erlbaum.

CONOVER, W., & IMAN, R. L. (1981). Rank transformations as a bridge between parametric and nonparametric statistics. *American Statistician, 35,* 124–129.

CONTRADA, R. J., ASHMORE, R. D., GARY, M. L., COUPS, E. J., EGETH, J. D., SEWELL, A., EWELL, K., GOYAL, T. M., & CHASSE, V. (2001). Measures of ethnicity-related stress: Psychometric properties, ethnic group differences, and associations with well-being. *Journal of Applied Social Psychology, 31,* 1775–1820.

COOPER, S. E., & ROBINSON, D. A. G. (1989). The influence of gender and anxiety on mathematics performance. *Journal of College Student Development, 30,* 459–461.

CRICK, N. R., CASAS, J. F., & MOSHER, M. (1997). Relational and overt aggression in preschool. *Developmental Psychology, 33,* 579–588.

DANE, F. C., & WRIGHTSMAN, L. S. (1982). Effects of defendants' and victims' characteristics on jurors' verdicts. In N. L. Kerr & R. M. Bray (Eds.), *The psychology of the courtroom* (pp. 83–115). Orlando, FL: Academic Press.

DECARLO, L. T. (1997). On the meaning and use of kurtosis. *Psychological Methods, 2,* 292–307.

DEGARMO, D. S., & FORGATCH, M. S. (1997). Determinants of observed confidant support for divorced mothers. *Journal of Personality and Social Psychology, 72,* 336–345.

DENENBERG, V. H. (1999). A critique of Mody, Studdert-Kennedy, and Brady's "Speech perception deficits in poor readers: Auditory processing or phonological coding?" *Journal of Learning Disabilities, 32,* 379–383.

DESART, J. A., & HOLBROOK, T. M. (2003). Statewide trial-heat polls and the 2000 presidential election: A forecast model. *Social Science Quarterly, 84,* 561–573.

DUNLAP, W. P., & MYERS, L. (1997). Approximating power for significance tests with one degree of freedom. *Psychological Methods, 2,* 186–191.

DURKIN, K., & BARBER, B. (2003). Not so doomed: Computer game play and positive adolescent development. *Applied Developmental Psychology, 23,* 373–392.

DWINELL, P. E., & HIGBEE, J. L. (1991). Affective variables related to mathematics achievement among high-risk college freshmen. *Psychological Reports, 69,* 399–403

EPPLEY, K. R., ABRAMS, A. I., & SHEAR, J. (1989). Differential effects of relaxation techniques on trait anxiety: A meta-analysis. *Journal of Clinical Psychology, 45,* 957–974.

ESCUDERO, V., ROGERS, L. E., & GUTIERREZ, E. (1997). Patterns of relational control and nonverbal affect in clinic and non-clinic couples. *Journal of Social and Personal Relationships, 14,* 5–29.

EVANS, R. (1976). *The making of psychology.* New York: Knopf.

EVERETT, S. A., PRICE, J. H., BEDELL, A. W., & TELLJOHANN, S. K. (1997). The effect of a monetary incentive in increasing the return rate of a survey to family physicians. *Evaluation and the Health Professions, 20,* 207–214.

EYSENCK, H. J. (1981). *A model for personality.* Berlin: Springer-Verlag.

FAWZI, M. C. S., PHAM, T., LIN, L., NGUYEN, T. V., NGO, D., MURPHY, E., & MOLLICA, R. F. (1997). The validity of posttraumatic stress disorder among Vietnamese refugees. *Journal of Traumatic Stress, 10,* 101–108.

FISKE, S. T. (1998). Stereotyping, prejudice, and discrimination. In D. T. Gilbert, S. T. Fiske, & G. Lindzey (Eds.) *The handbook of social psychology* (4th ed., pp. 357–411). New York: McGraw-Hill.

FRANK, S. J., POORMAN, M. O., VAN EGEREN, L. A., & FIELD, D. T. (1997). Perceived relationships with parents among adolescent inpatients with depressive preoccupations and depressed mood. *Journal of Clinical Child Psychology, 26,* 205–215.

FRICK, R. W. (1995). Accepting the null hypothesis. *Memory and Cognition, 23,* 132–138.

FRISCH, A. S., SHAMSUDDIN, K., & KURTZ, M. (1995). Family factors and knowledge: Attitudes and efforts concerning exposure to environmental tobacco among Malaysian medical students. *Journal of Asian and African Studies, 30,* 68–79.

FRYDENBERG, E., LEWIS, R., KENNEDY, G., ARDILA, R., FRINDTE, W., & HANNOUN, R. (2003). Coping with concerns: An exploratory comparison of Australian, Colombian, German, and Palestinian adolescents. *Journal of Youth and Adolescence, 32,* 59–66.

GABLE, S., & LUTZ, S. (2000). Household, parent, and child contributions to childhood obesity. *Family Relations, 49,* 293–300.

GALLAGHER-THOMPSON, D., DAL CANTO, P. G., JACOB, T., & THOMPSON, L. W. (2001). A comparison of marital interaction patterns between couples in which the husband does or does not have Alzheimer's disease. *The Journals of Gerontology Series B: Psychological Sciences and Social Sciences, 56,* S140–S150.

GALLUP, D. G. H. (1972). *The Gallup poll: Public opinion, 1935–1971.* New York: Random House.

GIRE, J. T. (1997). The varying effect of individualism-collectivism on preference for methods of conflict resolution. *Canadian Journal of Behavioural Science, 29,* 38–43.

GOIDEL, H. K., & LANGLEY, R. E. (1995). Media coverage of the economy and aggregate economic evaluations: Uncovering evidence of indirect media effects. *Political Research Quarterly, 48,* 313–328.

GONZAGA, G. C., KELTNER, D., LONDAHL, E. A., & SMITH, M. D. (2001). Love and the commitment problem in romantic relations and friendship. *Journal of Personality and Social Psychology, 81,* 247–262.

GRAHAM, S., WEINER, B., & ZUCKER, G. S. (1997). An attributional analysis of punishment goals and public reactions to O. J. Simpson. *Personality and Social Psychology Bulletin, 23,* 331–346.

GREENWALD, A. G. (1975). Consequences of prejudice against the null hypothesis. *Psychological Bulletin, 82,* 1–19.

GRILO, C. M., WALKER, M. L., BECKER, D. F., EDELL, W. S., & MCGLASHAN, T. H. (1997). Personality disorders in adolescents with major depression, substance use disorders, and co-existing major depression and substance use disorders. *Journal of Consulting and Clinical Psychology, 65,* 328–332.

GUNN, B., BIGLAN, A., SMOLKOWSKI, K, & ARY, D. (2000). The efficacy of supplemental instruction in decoding skills for Hispanic and non-Hispanic students in early elementary school. *Journal of Special Education, 34,* 90–103.

HARTER, S., WATERS, P. L., PETTITT, L. M., WHITESELL, N., KOFKIN, J., & JORDAN, J. (1997). Autonomy and connectedness as dimensions of relationship styles in men and women. *Journal of Social and Personal Relationships, 14,* 147–164.

HAZAN, C., & SHAVER, P. (1987). Romantic love conceptualized as an attachment process. *Journal of Personality and Social Psychology, 52,* 511–524.

HERMANN, C., BLANCHARD, E. B., & FLOR, H. (1997). Biofeedback treatment for pediatric migraine: Prediction of treatment outcome. *Journal of Consulting and Clinical Psychology, 65,* 611–616.

HINDLEY, C., FILLIOZAT, A., KLACKENBERG, G., NICOLET-MEISTER, D., & SAND, E. (1966). Differences in age of walking in five European longitudinal samples. *Human Biology, 38,* 364–379.

HOLDEN, G. W., THOMPSON, E. E., ZAMBARANO, R. J., & MARSHALL, L. A. (1997). Child effects as a source of change in maternal attitudes. *Journal of Social and Personal Relationships, 14,* 481–490.

HOSP, J. L., & RESCHLY, D. J. (2003). Referral rates for intervention or assessment: A meta-analysis of racial differences. *Journal of Special Education, 37,* 67–80.

HU, F. B., LI, T. Y., COLDITZ, G. A., WILLETT, W. C., & MANSON, J. E. (2003). Television watching and other sedentary behaviors in relation to risk of obesity and type 2 diabetes mellitus in women. *Journal of the American Medical Association, 289,* 1785–1791.

HUSSERL, E. (1970). *The crisis of European sciences and transcendental phenomenology: An introduction to phenomeno-logical philosophy* (D. C. Carr, Trans.). Evanston, IL: Northwestern University Press.

JACKSON, L. A., ERVIN, K. S., GARDNER, P. D., & SCHMITT, N. (2001). Gender and the Internet: Women communicating and men searching. *Sex Roles, 44,* 363–379.

JUNE, L. N., CURRY, B. P., & GEAR, C. L. (1990). An 11-year analysis of black students' experience of problems and use of services: Implications for counseling professionals. *Journal of Counseling Psychology, 37,* 178–184.

KAGAN, J. (1994). *Galen's prophecy: Temperament in human nature.* New York: Basic Books.

KARNEY, B. R., & BRADBURY, T. N. (1997). Neuroticism, marital interaction, and the trajectory of marital satisfaction. *Journal of Personality and Social Psychology, 72,* 1075–1092.

KOSLOWSKY, M., SCHWARZWALD, J., & ASHURI, S. (2001). On the relationship between subordinates' compliance to power sources and organisational attitudes. *Applied Psychology: An International Review, 50,* 455–476.

KRAEMER, H. C., & THIEMANN, S. (1987). *How many subjects? Statistical power analysis in research.* Newbury Park, CA: Sage.

KWAN, V. S. Y., BOND, M. H., & SINGELIS, T. M. (1997). Pancultural explanations for life satisfaction: Adding relationship harmony to self-esteem. *Journal of Personality and Social Psychology, 73,* 1038–1051.

LAMBERT, A. J., KHAN, S. R., LICKEL, B. A., & FRICKE, K. (1997). Mood and the correction of positive versus negative stereotypes. *Journal of Personality and Social Psychology, 72,* 1002–1016.

LARSON, R., DWORKIN, J., & VERMA, S. (2001). Men's work and family lives in India: The daily organization of time and emotions. *Journal of Family Psychology, 15,* 206–224.

LEE, K., BYATT, G., & RHODES, G. (2000). Caricature effects, distinctiveness, and identification: Testing the face-space framework. *Psychological Science, 11,* 379–385.

LI, K. Z. H., LINDERBERGER, U., FREUND, A. M., & BALTES, P. B. (2001). Walking while memorizing: Age-related differences in compensatory behavior. *Psychological Science, 12,* 230–237.

LINDZEY, E. W., MIZE, J., & PETTIT, G. S. (1997). Mutuality in parent-child play: Consequences for children's peer competence. *Journal of Social and Personal Relationships, 14,* 523–538.

LYDON, J., PIERCE, T., & O'REGAN, S. (1997). Coping with moral commitment to long-distance dating relationships. *Journal of Personality and Social Psychology, 73,* 104–113.

MARKMAN, H. J., RENICK, M. J., FLOYD, F. J., STANLEY, S. M., & CLEMENTS, M. (1993). Preventing marital distress through communication and conflict management training: A 4- and 5-year follow-up. *Journal of Consulting and Clinical Psychology, 61,* 70–77.

MACKINNON-LEWIS, C., STARNES, R., VOLLING, B., & JOHNSON, S. (1997). Perceptions of parenting as predictors of boys' sibling and peer relations. *Developmental Psychology, 33,* 1024–1031.

MacDonald, C., Chamberlain, K., & Long, N. (1997). Race, combat, and PTSD in a community sample of New Zealand Vietnam War veterans. *Journal of Traumatic Stress, 10,* 117–124.

McCracken, G. (1988). *The long interview.* London: Sage.

McKee, T. L. E., & Ptacek, J. T. (2001). I'm afraid I have something bad to tell you: Breaking bad news from the perspective of the giver. *Journal of Applied Social Psychology, 31,* 246–273.

McLaughlin-Volpe, T., Aron, A, & Reis, H. T. (2001, February). *Closeness during interethnic social interactions and prejudice: A diary study.* Paper presented at the annual meeting of the Society for Personality and Social Psychology, San Antonio, TX.

McLeod, D. M., Eveland, W. P., & Signorelli, N. (1994). Conflict and public opinion: Rallying effects of the Persian Gulf War. *Journalism Quarterly, 71,* 20–31.

Mickelson, K. D., Kessler, R. C., & Shaver, P. R. (1997). Adult attachment in a nationally representative sample. *Journal of Personality and Social Psychology, 73,* 1092–1106.

Miller, R. S. (1997). Inattentive and contented: Relationship commitment and attention to alternatives. *Journal of Personality and Social Psychology, 73,* 758–766.

Mirvis, P., & Lawler, E. (1977). Measuring the financial impact of employee attitudes. *Journal of Applied Psychology, 62,* 1–8.

Mody, M., Studdert-Kennedy, M., & Brady, S. (1997). Speech perception deficits in poor readers: Auditory processing or phonological coding? *Journal of Experimental Child Psychology, 64,* 1–33.

Mooney, S. P., Sherman, M. F., & Lo Presto, C. T. (1991). Academic locus of control, self-esteem, and perceived distance from home as predictors of college adjustment. *Journal of Counseling and Development, 69,* 445–448.

Moorehouse, E., & Tobler, N. S. (2000). Preventing and reducing substance use among institutionalized adolescents. *Adolescence, 35,* 1–28.

Moorehouse, M. J., & Sanders, P. E. (1992). Children's feelings of school competence and perceptions of parents' work in four sociocultural contexts. *Social Development, 1,* 185–200.

Moriarty, S. E., & Everett, S-L. (1994). Commercial breaks: A viewing behavior study. *Journalism Quarterly, 71,* 346–355.

Mouradian, V. E. (2001). Applying schema theory to intimate aggression: Individual and gender differences in representation of contexts and goals. *Journal of Applied Social Psychology, 31,* 376–408.

Norcross, J. C., Hanych, J. M., & Terranova, R. D. (1996). Graduate study in psychology: 1992–1993. *American Psychologist, 51,* 631–643.

Nownes, A. J. (2000). Policy conflict and the structure of interest communities: A comparative state analysis. *American Politics Quarterly, 28,* 309–327.

Olthoff, R. K. (1989). *The effectiveness of premarital communication training.* Unpublished doctoral dissertation, California Graduate School of Family Psychology, San Francisco.

Pecukonis, E. V. (1990). A cognitive/affective empathy training program as a function of ego development in aggressive adolescent females. *Adolescence, 25,* 59–76.

Perna, F. M., Antoni, M. H., Baum, A., Gordon, P., & Schneiderman, N. (2003). Cognitive behavioral stress management effects on injury and illness among competitive athletes: A randomized clinical trial. *Annals of Behavioral Medicine, 25,* 66–73.

Peters, W. S. (1987). *Counting for something: Statistical principles and personalities.* New York: Springer-Verlag.

Pettigrew, T. F., & Meertens, R. W. (1995). Subtle and blatant prejudice in western Europe. *European Journal of Social Psychology, 25,* 57–75.

Prenda, K. M., & Lachman, M. E. (2001). Planning for the future: A life management strategy for increasing control and life satisfaction in adulthood. *Psychology and Aging, 16,* 206–216.

Puri, M. L., & Sen, P. K. (1985). *Nonparametric methods in general linear models.* New York: Wiley.

Reber, P. J., & Kotovsky, K. (1997). Implicit learning in problem solving: The role of working memory capacity. *Journal of Experimental Psychology: General, 126,* 178–203.

Riehl, R. J. (1994). Academic preparation, aspirations, and first-year performance of first-generation students. *College and University, 70,* 14–19.

Robins, R. W., & John, O. P. (1997). Effects of visual perspective and narcissism on self-perception: Is seeing believing? *Psychological Science, 8,* 37–42.

Roeser, R. W, van der Wolf, K., & Strobel, K. R. (2001). On the relation between social-emotional and school functioning during early adolescence: Preliminary findings from Dutch and American samples. *Journal of School Psychology, 39,* 111–139.

Rottenstreich, Y., & Hsee, C. K. (2001). Money, kisses, and electric shocks: On the affective psychology of risk. *Psychological Science, 12,* 185–190.

Russell, D., Peplau, L. A., & Cutrona, C. E. (1980) The revised UCLA Loneliness Scale: Concurrent and discriminant validity evidence. *Journal of Personality and Social Psychology, 39,* 472–480.

Salsburg, D. (2001). *The lady tasting tea: How statistics revolutionized science in the twentieth century.* New York: Freeman.

Schimel, J., Greenberg, J., & Martens, A. (2003). Evidence that projection of a feared trait can serve a defensive function. *Personality and Social Psychology Bulletin, 29,* 969–979.

Schmader, T., Major, B., & Gramzow, R. H. (2001). Coping with ethnic stereotypes in the academic domain: Perceived injustice and psychological disengagement. *Journal of Social Issues, 57,* 93–111.

SCHRAM, C. M. (1996). A meta-analysis of gender differences in applied statistics achievement. *Journal of Educational and Behavioral Statistics, 21,* 55–70.

SCHUSTER, M. A., STEIN, B. D., JAYCOX, L. H., COLLINS, R. L., MARSHALL, G. N., ELLIOTT, M. N., ZHOU, A. J., KANOUSE, D. E., MORRISON, J. L., & BERRY, S. H. (2001). A national survey of stress reactions after the September 11, 2001, terrorist attacks. *New England Journal of Medicine, 345,* 1507–1512.

SCHWARTZ, R. C., & COHEN, B. N. (2001). Risk factors for suicidality among clients with schizophrenia. *Journal of Counseling and Development, 79,* 314–319.

SENECAL, C., VALLERAND, R. J., & GUAY, F. (2001). Antecedents and outcomes of work-family conflict: Toward a motivational model. *Personality and Social Psychology Bulletin, 27,* 176–186.

SIEGEL, M., & BIENER, L. (1997). Evaluating the impact of statewide anti-tobacco campaigns: The Massachusetts and California Tobacco Control Programs. *Journal of Social Issues, 53,* 147–168.

SINCLAIR, L., & KUNDA, Z. (2000). Motivated stereotyping of women: She's fine if she praised me but incompetent if she criticized me. *Personality and Social Psychology Bulletin, 26,* 1329–1342.

SKINNER, B. F. (1956). A case history in scientific method. *American Psychologist, 11,* 221–233.

SPEED, A., & GANGSTEAD, S. W. (1997). Romantic popularity and mate preferences: A peer-nomination study. *Personality and Social Psychology Bulletin, 23,* 928–937.

SPENCER, S. J., STEELE, C. M., & QUINN, D. M. (1999). Stereotype threat and women's math performance. *Journal of Experimental Social Psychology, 35,* 4–28.

STAKE, J. E., & MALKIN, C. (2003). Students' quality of experience and perceptions of intolerance and bias in the women's and gender studies classroom. *Psychology of Women Quarterly, 27,* 174–185.

STEELE, C. M. (1997). A threat in the air: How stereotypes shape intellectual identity and performance. *American Psychologist, 52,* 613–629.

STEEN, L. A. (1987). Foreword. In S. Tobias, *Succeed with math: Every student's guide to conquering math anxiety* (pp. xvii–xviii). New York: College Entrance Examination Board.

STEIL, J. M., & HAY, J. L. (1997). Social comparison in the work place: A study of 60 dual-career couples. *Personality and Social Psychology Bulletin, 23,* 427–438.

STIGLER, S. M. (1986). *The history of statistics.* Cambridge, MA: Belknap Press.

TABACHNICK, B. G., & FIDELL, L. S. (2001). *Using multivariate statistics* (4th ed.). New York: HarperCollins.

TANKARD, J., JR. (1984). *The statistical pioneers.* Cambridge, MA: Schenkman.

THOMAS, J. R., NELSON, J. K., & THOMAS, K. T. (1999). A generalized rank-order method for nonparametric analysis of data from exercise science: A tutorial. *Research Quarterly for Exercise and Sport, 70,* 11–27.

THOMPSON, W. F., SCHELLENBERG, E. G., & HUSAIN, G. (2001). Arousal, mood, and the Mozart effect. *Psychological Science, 12,* 248–251.

TOBIAS, S. (1982, January). Sexist equations. *Psychology Today,* pp. 14–17.

TOBIAS, S. (1995). *Overcoming math anxiety.* New York: W. W. Norton.

VALK, M., POST, M. W. M., COOLS, H. J. M., & SHRIJVERS, G. A. J. P. (2001). Measuring disability in nursing home residents: Validity and reliability of a newly developed instrument. *Journal of Gerontology: Psychological Sciences, 56,* 187–191.

VAN AKEN, M. A. G., & ASENDORPF, J. B. (1997). Support by parents, classmates, friends, and siblings in preadolescence: Covariation and compensation across relationships. *Journal of Social and Personal Relationships, 14,* 79–93.

VON FRANZ, M. L. (1979). *The problem of puer aeternus.* New York: Springer-Verlag.

WELLER, A., & WELLER, L. (1997). Menstrual synchrony under optimal conditions: Bedouin families. *Journal of Comparative Psychology, 111,* 143–151.

WILLIAMSON, G. M., SHAFFER, D. R., & THE FAMILY RELATIONSHIPS IN LATE LIFE PROJECT. (2001). Relationship quality and potentially harmful behaviors by spousal caregivers: How we were then, how we are now. *Psychology and Aging, 16,* 217–226.

WISEMAN, H. (1997). Interpersonal relatedness and self-definition in the experience of loneliness during the transition to university. *Personal Relationships, 4,* 285–299.

ZEIDNER, M. (1991). Statistics and mathematics anxiety in social science students: Some interesting parallels. *British Journal of Education, 61,* 319–329.

ZIMMER-GEMBECK, M. J., SIEBENBRUNER, J., & COLLINS, A. W. (2001). Diverse aspects of dating: Associations with psychosocial functioning from early to middle adolescence. *Journal of Adolescence, 24,* 313–336.

Index

Steps of Hypothesis Testing for Major Procedures

	Z test for a single sample (Ch. 6)	t test for a single sample (Ch. 8)	t test for dependent means (Ch. 8)	t test for independent means (Ch. 9)
❶	**Restate the question as a research hypothesis and a null hypothesis about the populations.**	**Restate the question as a research hypothesis and a null hypothesis about the populations.**	**Restate the question as a research hypothesis and a null hypothesis about the populations.**	**Restate the question as a research hypothesis and a null hypothesis about the populations.**
❷	**Determine the characteristics of the comparison distribution.** Population M_M = Population M; Population SD_M^2 = Population SD^2/N; Population SD_M = $\sqrt{\text{Population } SD_M^2}$; approximately normal if population normal or $N > 30$.	**Determine the characteristics of the comparison distribution.** (a) The mean of the distribution of means is the same as the population mean. (b) Figure its standard deviation: ❶ $S^2 = \Sigma(X - M)^2/(df)$ ❷ $S_M^2 = S^2/N$ ❸ $S_M = \sqrt{S_M^2}$ (c) t distribution, $df = N - 1$.	**Determine the characteristics of the comparison distribution.** (a) All based on difference scores. (b) Figure mean of the difference scores. (c) Mean of distribution of means of difference scores = 0. (d) Figure its standard deviation: ❶ $S^2 = \Sigma(X - M)^2/(df)$ ❷ $S_M^2 = S^2/N$ ❸ $S_M = \sqrt{S_M^2}$ (c) t distribution, $df = N - 1$.	**Determine the characteristics of the comparison distribution.** (a) Its mean will be 0. (b) Figure its standard deviation: ❶ For each population, $S^2 = \Sigma(X - M)^2/(N - 1)$ ❷ $S_{\text{Pooled}}^2 = (df_1/df_{\text{Total}})(S_1^2) + (df_2/df_{\text{Total}})(S_2^2); df_1 = N_1 - 1$ and $df_2 = N_2 - 1; df_{\text{Total}} = df_1 + df_2$. ❸ $S_{M_1}^2 = S_{\text{Pooled}}^2/N_1; S_{M_2}^2 = S_{\text{Pooled}}^2/N_2$ ❹ $S_{\text{Difference}}^2 = S_{M_1}^2 + S_{M_2}^2$ ❺ $S_{\text{Difference}} = \sqrt{S_{\text{Difference}}^2}$ (c) t distribution, degrees of freedom = df_{Total}
❸	**Determine the cutoff sample score on the comparison distribution at which the null hypothesis should be rejected.** Use normal curve table.	**Determine the cutoff sample score on the comparison distribution at which the null hypothesis should be rejected.** Use t table.	**Determine the cutoff sample score on the comparison distribution at which the null hypothesis should be rejected.** Use t table.	**Determine the cutoff sample score on the comparison distribution at which the null hypothesis should be rejected.** Use t table.
❹	**Determine your sample's score on the comparison distribution.** $Z = (M - \text{Population } M_M)/\text{Population } SD_M$	**Determine your sample's score on the comparison distribution.** $t = (M - \text{Population } M)/S_M$	**Determine your sample's score on the comparison distribution.** $t = (M - \text{Population } M)/S_M$	**Determine your sample's score on the comparison distribution.** $t = (M_1 - M_2)/S_{\text{Difference}}$
❺	**Decide whether to reject the null hypothesis.** Compare scores from Steps 3 and 4.	**Decide whether to reject the null hypothesis.** Compare scores from Steps 3 and 4.	**Decide whether to reject the null hypothesis.** Compare scores from Steps 3 and 4.	**Decide whether to reject the null hypothesis.** Compare scores from Steps 3 and 4.